Families, Professionals, and Exceptionality

Collaborating for Empowerment

Fourth Edition

Ann P. Turnbull

H. Rutherford Turnbull, III

Beach Center on Families and Disability,
The University of Kansas

Merrill
Prentice Hall

Upper Saddle River, New Jersey
Columbus, Ohio

Library of Congress Cataloging in Publication Data

Turnbull, Ann P.
    Families, professionals, and exceptionality : collaborating for
empowerment / Ann P. Turnbull, H. Rutherford Turnbull III. — 4th ed.
      p. cm.
    Includes bibliographical references and index.
    ISBN 0-13-016303-1
    1. Parents of exceptional children—United States. 2. Exceptional children—United
States—Family relationships. 3. Counselor and client—United States. I. Turnbull, H.
Rutherford. II. Title

HQ759.913 T87 2001
649'.15—dc21
                                        00-035140

Vice President and Publisher: Jeffery W. Johnston
Executive Editor: Ann Castel Davis
Editorial Assistant: Pat Grogg
Production Editor: Sheryl Glicker Langner
Production Management: Amy Gehl, Carlisle Publishers Services
Design Coordinator: Diane C. Lorenzo
Cover Designer: Louis Weldon
Illustrator: Steve Botts
Production Manager: Laura Messerly
Director of Marketing: Kevin Flanagan
Marketing Manager: Amy June
Marketing Services Manager: Krista Groshong

This book was set in Optima by Carlisle Communications, Ltd. It was printed and bound by
Von Hoffmann Press, Inc. The cover was printed by Von Hoffmann Press, Inc.

10 9 8 7 6 5 4 3 2 1
ISBN 0-13-016303-1

Dedication

To Ursula Arceneaux Markey and D. J. Markey, parents of Duane Jr., who died unexpectedly on December 16, 1998

and

To Tricia Baccus-Luker and Calvin Luker, parents of Jessica, who died unexpectedly on September 10, 1999

Here are four parents and two children whose lives are—and have been—of inestimable worth. They have informed, inspired, and lifted up all families with whom they have made contact. They have ceaselessly advocated for their children and for all others who have disabilities. They have given generously—of their wisdom, their grace, their compassion, and their love—to us and others. They have humbled us and have made us mindful of the many blessings that we enjoy. And they have made the world a better place. No words are adequate to convey our love and respect for them and for their children, taken untimely and unexpectedly from them and from us all. Yet, Duane and Jessica live on in their parents. For that, we must all be boundlessly grateful.

and

We also dedicate this book to Harrie R. Chamberlin, M.D., of The University of North Carolina at Chapel Hill. Dr. Chamberlin was professor of pediatrics, the founder and long-time director of the University Affiliated Program at UNC, our son's specialist-physician, and our colleague and mentor.

Harrie played two critical roles in our lives. He hired Ann; he asked Rud to be a consultant; and the result of those two decisions was that we met each other and soon thereafter married each other. Harrie and his wife Bets attended our wedding and reception and during the next six years celebrated with us not only our work but also the birth and early years of our two daughters, Amy and Kate. He and Bets were, in many ways, adopted uncle and aunt to us, great uncle and great aunt to our girls.

More than that, Harrie was a model of parent-professional collaboration, an expert in child development and developmental disabilities who always—yes, always—had the eagerness to hear and the ability to heed the concerns of the many family members who brought their children to him. Like so many other parents, we came to Harrie for guidance about our son Jay, and, like so many others, we left with more than we sought. We left with confidence that Harrie would devote the full resources of the university to our son and that, despite whatever diagnoses we might receive about Jay, there was and always would be hope. Harrie's unabashed optimism buoyed us, as it buoyed other parents; more, it taught us, early in our careers, how we should respond to other parents. Harrie died in 1998, but his lessons live on in our work and his and Bets' joy in living still happily infuses itself into our own lives.

Rud and Ann Turnbull

Lawrence, Kansas

Preface

Welcome to *Families, Professionals, and Exceptionality: Collaborating for Empowerment.* This, our fourth edition, retains the features of the third—the family systems perspective, an emphasis on empowerment through parent/family and professional collaboration, and a multicultural approach.

In addition, this edition highlights ten of the same families who appeared in the third edition: the Smith family (chapter 1), the Cooper family (chapter 3), the Rocco family (chapter 4), the Cofresi family (chapter 5), the Benito family (chapter 6), the Battles family (chapter 7), the Baccus-Luker family (chapter 8), the Manos family (chapter 9), the Hoyt family (chapter 14), and the Roach family (chapter 15).

This edition, however, adds five new families: the Wade family (chapter 2), the Markey family (chapter 10), the Lee family (chapter 11), the Motley family (chapter 12), and the Gonzalez family (chapter 13).

Text Organization

This text is organized into three parts. Part 1, "Understanding Empowerment," describes the concept of empowerment historically and currently. Part 2, "Understanding Families," describes families as interactive systems, enabling you to understand them from a systems perspective. Part 3, "Collaborating for Empowerment," explains how you can empower families, professionals, and yourself by using seven opportunities for partnerships and by committing to eight obligations to develop reliable alliances. We not only present the theory of empowerment, but we also suggest techniques for advancing empowerment through collaboration. And we synthesize the literature on empowerment, relying on the concepts and research dates reported in several disciplines. Through our synthesis, we create a framework that transforms this complex theory and implements techniques into an approach that is easy to understand and apply.

Throughout the text we emphasize mutual empowerment, believing that whatever empowers one person should and can empower another. As one person in a collaborative partnership becomes more empowered, so will all of them. Empowerment, after all, is a value that families, professionals, and you as an individual can pursue and obtain through collective action.

Text Features

We bring together theory, research, and the best practices related to family-professional partnership from both general and special education. The effort to merge these two bodies of knowledge is, we believe, a "first." With this merger comes the opportunity for families of all students to participate in tomorrow's schools in a more empowered and effective way.

In each chapter, we feature "family voices," portraying a family in the opening and closing vignette and relying on the family's experience and voice throughout the chapter. The vignette and the "My Voice" feature are not ornamental. Rather, they are instrumental, linking the concepts and content of the chapter to real families, real professionals, and real schools. Through these voices, you will acquire a richer, real-life understanding of the family systems approach.

These families and professionals speak with many dialects and accents; represent a broad spectrum of American life; and show how people of every economic and social stratum, of every color, race, and ethnic origin, in every part of this country empower themselves, their family members, and their colleagues in schools and communities. To repeat: Empowerment is for everyone, and these voices show exactly how everyone can become more empowered through collaboration.

The chapters are strong theoretically and empirically in terms of their research base. Just as important (because we want this book to make a difference for you and others, personally and professionally), each chapter is highly applied, setting out techniques for you and others to use in collaborating for empowerment. The "Together We Can" and "Tips" features exemplify the applied nature of each chapter.

Acknowledgments

We have been privileged to have an "empowerment team" to assist us in preparing and writing this book. Lois Weldon has been our mainstay in the production phase, preparing draft after draft after draft and never once failing to produce work of the highest quality and with the maximum "smile factor." We could not do our work without her. Two new colleagues have helped us in other production aspects: Mary Woodward and Anette Lundsgaarde have been liaison to the families we feature in the vignettes. Anette was particularly helpful early on but, because she was so important in other aspects of work at the Beach Center on Families Disability, she was obligated not to complete that which she had begun. Mary has applied her sharp editorial eyes to our work, assuring that it represents the families fairly and that it is clear and engaging in its presentation. She also has pursued, Sherlock Holmes-like, all of our permissions and references, a task for which only the most assiduous person is qualified. Both have been upbeat when other mortals might have been downcast because of the tedious nature of some of our work. Erin Jones has assisted with the arduous and painstaking task of making certain that our scholarship is fully and accurately referenced—a task she completed with good cheer and reliability.

Of course, this book builds on the previous edition, to which Opal Folks, Ben Furnish, and Richard Viloria, all from the Beach Center, made important contributions.

And, talking about contributions, let us acknowledge the willingness—indeed, the eagerness—of the families whom we feature in the vignettes to be part of our team. Each of them is, indeed, a "professor"—a person who professes a certain perspective or base of knowledge. They profess—they teach—that families are indispensable partners with professionals in providing a free, appropriate, and inclusive education to their children who have disabilities. They not only profess that message, but they also live it. And they do so in trying circumstances but with optimism, determination, and faith. They help us realize, once again, how very blessed we are to have them as friends and colleagues; how much we learn from their experiences; how much we value them and their contributions to "the cause" (the parent/family-professional partnership cause); and how fortunate we are to be, like them, parents of a person with a disability—J. T. (Jay Turnbull), who has so enriched and transformed our lives.

It is fashionable nowadays to be "post-modern"—by which is meant that the "voices" of "ordinary people" are "validated." That sometimes amuses us, for we were, we believe, "post-modern" before the term entered the common language. We say that because in 1978 we co-edited a book, *Parents Speak Out,* that contained the life stories of professionals who were also parents of children with disabilities. That book provided a forum for those "voices," and in this book, we simply carry forward the commitment we have had for the last 21 years to be a modest vehicle for those voices to be heard nationally. When *Parents Speak Out* was first published, the publisher was—you guessed it—the same publisher that is responsible for this book. Our hats are off, then, to Merrill/Prentice-Hall.

Specifically, we thank those at Merrill/Prentice-Hall who have helped so much with this book: Ann Davis, our executive editor; Pat Grogg, liaison between Ann on the one hand and ourselves on the other; and Sheryl Langner, our production editor; and Steve Botts, our artist and illustrator.

Each of them has been an effective collaborator and reliable ally; their respective expertise and conscientiousness have significantly improved the quality of our work. We gratefully acknowledge their individual and collective contributions.

We would also like to acknowledge the following individuals who reviewed the manuscript and offered suggestions for improvement: Greg Conderman, University of Wisconsin at Eau Claire; Louise Fulton, California State University at San Bernardino; Robert W. Ortiz, California State University at Fullerton; Alec F. Peck, Boston College; and Ellen Williams, Bowling Green State University.

Finally, we are grateful to Amy Gehl at Carlisle Communications, Ltd., for her skillful and patient work in the "go-to-press" stages of this book.

Rud and Ann Turnbull
Lawrence, Kansas

DISCOVER THE COMPANION WEBSITE
ACCOMPANYING THIS BOOK

The Prentice Hall Companion Website: A Virtual Learning Environment

Technology is a constantly growing and changing aspect of our field that is creating a need for content and resources. To address this emerging need, Prentice Hall has developed an online learning environment for students and professors alike–Companion Websites–to support our textbooks.

In creating a Companion Website, our goal is to build on and enhance what the textbook already offers. For this reason, the content for each user-friendly website is organized by chapter and provides the professor and student with a variety of meaningful resources. Common features of a Companion Website include:

For the Professor—

Every Companion Website integrates **Syllabus Manager™,** an online syllabus creation and management utility.

- **Syllabus Manager™** provides you, the instructor, with an easy, step-by-step process to create and revise syllabi, with direct links into Companion Website and other online content without having to learn HTML.
- Students may logon to your syllabus during any study session. All they need to know is the web address for the Companion Website and the password you've assigned to your syllabus.
- After you have created a syllabus using **Syllabus Manager™,** students may enter the syllabus for their course section from any point in the Companion Website.
- Class dates are highlighted in white and assignment due dates appear in blue. Clicking on a date, the student is shown the list of activities for the assignment. The activities for each assignment are linked directly to actual content, saving time for students.
- Adding assignments consists of clicking on the desired due date, then filling in the details of the assignment—name of the assignment, instructions, and whether or not it is a one-time or repeating assignment.

- In addition, links to other activities can be created easily. If the activity is online, a URL can be entered in the space provided, and it will be linked automatically in the final syllabus.
- Your completed syllabus is hosted on our servers, allowing convenient updates from any computer on the Internet. Changes you make to your syllabus are immediately available to your students at their next logon.

For the Student—

- **Chapter Objectives**—outline key concepts from the text
- **Interactive Self-quizzes**—complete with hints and automatic grading that provide immediate feedback for students

  After students submit their answers for the interactive self-quizzes, the Companion Website **Results Reporter** computes a percentage grade, provides a graphic representation of how many questions were answered correctly and incorrectly, and gives a question by question analysis of the quiz. Students are given the option to send their quiz to up to four e-mail addresses (professor, teaching assistant, study partner, etc.).
- **Message Board**—serves as a virtual bulletin board to post—or respond to—questions or comments to/from a national audience
- **Net Searches**—offer links by key terms from each chapter to related Internet content
- **Web Destinations**—links to www sites that relate to chapter content

To take advantage of these and other resources, please visit the *Families, Professionals, and Exceptionalities: Collaborating for Empowerment* Companion Website at

www.prenhall.com/turnbull

Contents

Part One

Understanding Empowerment

Part 1 introduces you to our central theme—empowerment. In chapter 1, we trace the history of family-professional relationships, showing how parents' roles and professionals' views of parents' roles have evolved. As the philosopher George Santayana has cautioned us, we will surely repeat our histories unless we understand them. Repeating some of the family-professional history is not desirable, but moving from that history into different kinds of futures is.

Just as family-professional relationships have changed, so, too, have the schools—the places where the relationships are played out. In chapter 2, we describe the recent changes in special and general education, paying particular attention to efforts to reform both types of education and to make schools more effective and inclusive for children with disabilities and gifts/talents. Because schools are the contexts where history is reflected and the future shaped and where professionals, families, and students are expected to collaborate to achieve various outcomes, they are particularly important to understand.

Having laid a foundation, we address our main theme in chapter 3—empowerment of families, professionals, and students. Here, we state for the first time our simple, straightforward message: You can be a better professional if you seek to empower families and students, your professional colleagues, and yourself. Having said as much, we introduce the conceptual framework for empowerment and link it to the context of the schools.

In chapter 4, we describe eight obligations that professionals such as yourself have for establishing reliable alliances with families. These obligations focus on the affective or attitudinal qualities and skills that you bring to your work and that are at the heart of empowering partnerships.

At the end of part 1, you should be able to trace the history of family-professional relationships, describe the schools as the contemporary context for empowerment, define empowerment and its components, and explain the eight obligations of reliable alliances.

Chapter One

Historical and Current Roles of Families and Parents

It's a long way from Omaha, Nebraska, to Washington, D.C., and a longer way from being the mother of a newborn with a disability to being the executive director of a national network of parent-directed organizations that advocate for children with disabilities. But Patricia McGill Smith is quite a traveler, and in more ways than one. Patty and her daughter Jane, who has autism, are more than just zip-code travelers. They are travelers across the historical and current roles of families, having assumed many roles in the nearly 30 years that Jane has been alive.

When Jane was born, Patty searched and searched for reasons to explain why her daughter had a disability. Was it because Patty had had a stressful pregnancy, during which her mother was extremely ill and her father died? That seemed not to be the case, and "blaming it on God didn't seem to work, either," says Patty.

"I was assisted by another parent within 24 hours of Jane's diagnosis. That led to calls and assistance from the founders of the Pilot Parents, the original parent-to-parent program in the United States. These parent leaders were the beginning of a new idea—intervene with parents—on day one if possible. Pilot Parents was founded by a parent and professional who understood the need for parents and professionals working together.

This assistance led Patty to go to the University of Nebraska Medical Center's Meyer Children's Rehabilitation Institute for the help that put her on the road to a personal parent/professional relationship. This was the experience that led her to the knowledge of "how it could work." Those helpers, both Pilot Parents and later staff from the university, provided Patty, Jane and eventually their whole family, with the help and early intervention that transformed all their lives.

Lacking an explanation, however, did not mean that Patty lacked an ability to help herself and then others. Three years after Jane was born, Patty became a paid staffer of the Pilot Parent Program at the Greater Omaha Association for Retarded Children. There, she helped to connect parents of newborns to parents of older children with disabilities for information and emotional support and thus created new services for parents and children.

Nonetheless, Patty still faced convoluted issues about how to support Jane without overlooking the needs of her six other children. It was a few years after Jane was born before Patty could talk with her other children about Jane's disability. Until then, those brothers and sisters were "left to swim in the morass that I was in, only I didn't know it. I was just so completely caught up with my own emotions and my own fears and my own sadness that it didn't dawn on me to think in terms of the brothers and sisters and the support they needed.

"My first recognition of the overlooked needs of the younger children was when I had Jane's two older sisters take dance lessons. They were four- and five-years-old then."

"It was six or seven years before I ever really, really sat down and talked to the older boys, to really ask, 'How do you deal with this fact? What are your feelings? How did it impact your life?'"

What triggered those heart-to-heart conversations was Patty's realization that she was spending "so much of my time and energy, every waking hour, just on Jane." Sadly, she recalls, her efforts on Jane's behalf were so intense that she could not remember watching her daughter Marianne growing up. More than anything else, that lack of memory was the source of Patty's courage when she told one of Jane's teachers that, despite the teacher's insistence, she would not attend one of Jane's extracurricular presentations but was going to watch her son Matt pitch his first Little League game. Fortunately for Patty, another professional told her, several years later, that she was right to split her time among all her children: None of them was Jane's mother and none should have to assume so much responsibility. Indeed, Patty's best advice to her children was simply the truth: "You need to know that Jane takes more time, more energy, more resources, more of everything we've got, and I don't regret giving it to her, but you need to know that our family is imbalanced. This is the way it is, and we must all work together."

"My five years at GOARC (Greater Omaha Association for Retarded Citizens)—at Pilot Parents—set a stage. I had traveled to at least 20 states and five countries spreading the word on the effectiveness of parents helping parents. I directed a Pilot Parent grant for a four-state effort of national significance. Later I was awarded the Dybwad award for International Travel."

Patty's growth into a national advocate continued when she was hired as the parent consultant at Meyer Children's Rehabilitation Institute at the University of Nebraska Hospital in Omaha. "I moved from the kitchen table to a paid staff position, as a parent. I probably was the first parent in the country to be paid for giving a parent perspective on the health care of children with disabilities. For me, that was a dramatic turn of events in parent-professional relationships. NICHCY (National Information Center for Handicapped Children and Youth brought me to Washington." Later, Patty became the deputy assistant secretary of special education, U.S. Department of Education, working with assistant secretary Madeleine Will (herself the mother of a young man with mental retardation); and still later she became executive director of the National Parent Network on Disabilities.

Not every parent will become an advocate, and Patty's advice to parents is simple: "You can learn so much and you can do so much, but you don't have to become an 'outside advocate.' Take care of yourself so you can take care of your family. Whatever age or stage you

Jane Smith, with her mother, Patti, on her graduation day. (1995)

are in your life, do what's the right thing for you. The steps for being an advocate will unfold if that is to be."

Collaboration with professionals, Patty is quick to point out, is one way of being an effective parent. Collaboration comes from creating the "trust bond" between parents and professionals.

The trust bond is established when professionals listen to and are sensitive to the myriad of feelings parents go through. At the same time, the professional conveys the most positive and helpful information to the parents. At this time, the professional has to go the extra mile in patience, perseverance, gentleness, and understanding.

"The beginning of the trust bond occurred for me at Meyer Children's Rehabilitation Institute when Dr. Rene Simionison listened and listened to my grief and dismay.

He listened to my concerns. Never put me down. Always gave positive feedback and good, solid suggestions. Jane was only 14, 15 months old then . . . what a gift!"

The trust bond grows when parents and professionals open up to each other—first when professionals listen to parents and later when professionals tell parents why and how they became professionals, who has had the greatest influence on them, and what they like about their jobs. These three simple conversation topics, Patty says, let professionals enter into a personal dialogue with families, potentially creating the trust bond that lets families and professionals collaborate. This collaboration benefits professionals in a special way: "They get personal satisfaction, they experience the growth and the development that the parent's experiencing because both are walking together through this same developmental stage."

Why is it important for you to know about the history of family and parent roles in the care and education of children and youth with exceptionalities? First, history helps us understand contemporary issues and approaches, many of which are legacies from the past. Second, many of the challenges that families and professionals now face can be overcome if we heed history's lessons. Third, history teaches us that today's approaches may seem as improbable to the next generation of families and professionals as earlier approaches seem to us now. And fourth, families and parents have had eight major roles over time: (1) the source of their child's disability, (2) organization members, (3) service developers, (4) recipients of professionals' decisions, (5) teachers, (6) political advocates, (7) educational decision makers, and (8) collaborators. These roles do not represent discrete eras, each with a clear beginning and end. Rather, the roles overlap. There is, however, a general and approximate chronological order to them.

Parents as the Source of Their Child's Disability

The eugenics movement (1880–1930) pointed to parents as the source or cause of their child's disability (Barr, 1913). To eliminate or reduce the number of "unfit" parents, the eugenicists argued, would improve the human race through selective breeding. The eugenics movement was based on (1) genealogical investigations such

as Goddard's (1912) study of the Kallikak family, (2) Mendel's laws of heredity, and (3) studies by MacMurphy (1916) and Terman (1916) indicating that delinquent behaviors were strongly associated with "feeble-mindedness" (Scheerenberger, 1983).

The eugenics movement resulted in laws that restricted marriage by persons with intellectual disabilities and required them to be sterilized and institutionalized (Ferguson, 1994). Upholding a compulsory-sterilization law, U.S. Supreme Court Justice Oliver Wendell Holmes, Jr., wrote: "Three generations of imbeciles are enough" (*Buck v. Bell,* 1927). By the same token, only 9,334 persons with mental retardation were institutionalized in 1900, but 68,035 were in institutions in 1930 (Scheerenberger, 1983).

The parents-as-cause perspective extended beyond mental retardation to autism (Bettelheim, 1950, 1967); asthma (Gallagher & Gallagher, 1985); learning disabilities (Oliver, Cole, & Hollingsworth 1991; Orton, 1930; Thomas, 1905); and emotional disorders (Caplan & Hall-McCorquodale, 1985). Nowhere has professional blaming behavior been more evident than with respect to autism. It was typical in the 1940s and 1950s for professionals to describe parents of children and youth who had autism as rigid, perfectionist, emotionally impoverished, and depressed (Kanner, 1949; Marcus, 1977). Indeed, a leading professional, Bruno Bettelheim (1950, 1967), contended that a child who had autism—characterized by severe withdrawal—was simply responding to the stress created by the parents' "extreme and explosive" hatred of the child. Bettelheim even advocated a "parentectomy"—namely, institutionalizing the child and thereby replacing natural parents with institutional staff and professionals allegedly more competent and caring.

By contrast, the current definition of autism states that "no known factors in the psychological environment of a child have been shown to cause autism" (National Society for Autistic Children, 1977). This definition is the one accepted by professionals, families, and Congress (in the federal special education law). In box 1–1, Frank Warren (1985), the father of a young man with autism and a national advocate, totally rejects the Bettelheim position. He comments on Bettelheim's position in light of the new definition.

Congenital malformations occur in approximately 3 percent of all births. Only 25 percent of those malformations have genetic causes. Another 10 percent have environmental causes, and 65 percent have causes that are currently unknown (Beckman & Brent, 1986; Buyse, 1990). Of course, some disabilities in children may be traced to the parents. For example, some conditions (such as cystic fibrosis) are clearly genetic in nature. Excessive use of alcohol or drugs by pregnant women may cause children to have disabling conditions such as fetal alcohol syndrome or cocaine addiction (Batshaw & Conlon, 1997; Poulsen, 1994). Likewise, pregnant women who use intravenous drugs put their children at risk for human immunodeficiency virus (HIV), the cause of acquired immunodeficiency syndrome (AIDS). In fact, more than 90 percent of children with pediatric AIDS acquired HIV from their mothers during gestation, birth, or postnatally (Rutstein, Conlon, & Batshaw, 1997). Malnutrition during pregnancy or in the child's early life may lead to mild mental retardation or motor impairment (Baumeister, Kupstas, & Woodley-Zanthos, 1993; Coulter, 1987). Nonetheless, some children who are exposed to extremely detrimental environments early in life develop relatively unscathed by their experiences, whereas other children who are subjected to less stressful environments may fail to thrive and experience developmental delays (Flach, 1988; Werner & Smith, 1992).

Our best advice to you is this: Avoid blaming parents! If you need to know the cause of a disability, investigate it. If you learn that the parents may have been a cause, use that information to design supports and services that can be particularly helpful to the family and find ways to identify and affirm their strengths and positive contributions to their child. As you do so, you may be able to contribute to preventing disabilities in their other children and avoid exacerbating their child's existing disability. But do not blame. Blaming can create a barrier to collaboration between you and the family; and without collaboration you will be less effective in supporting the family, and the family will derive less benefit from you. In short: Blame is a barrier, but empathy and a strengths perspective (Allen & Petr, 1996) are conducive to collaboration.

Parents as Organization Members

Parents and other family members began to organize on a local level in the 1930s and on the national level in the late 1940s and 1950s (see box 1–2). Many parents and families believed that public and professional responses to their children's educational and other needs were inadequate; additionally, many sought emotional support from others who were facing similar challenges. They were the predecessors of people such as Patty Smith whom you learned about in the opening vignette.

The United Cerebral Palsy Associations (UCPA) was founded in 1949 largely through the efforts of

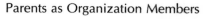

Leonard H. Goldenson, the father of a child with cerebral palsy. Here is what he says about UCPA's beginnings:

One day, realizing the cost of driving our child into New York City from Westchester, my wife said to me, "Leonard, I know we can afford to do this but what about the poor people? How can they afford to do it?" And she added, "Why don't we look into the possibility of trying to help others in this field?"

It was on that basis that I started to investigate the whole field of cerebral palsy.

Upon investigation, I found there were probably only twenty-some-odd doctors in the entire United States who knew anything about cerebral palsy. I found there were only a few local parents groups in

the country that were trying to do something about it. But the parents were so involved with their own children and had to take so much time with them, they could not get out to raise money and inform the public about the subject. (Goldenson, 1965, pp. 1–2)

Other parent groups include the National Society for Autistic Children, founded in 1961 and now called Autism Society of America; the National Association for Down Syndrome, founded in 1961; the Association for Children with Learning Disabilities, founded in 1964; and the Federation of Families for Children's Mental Health, founded in December 1988. The federation's mission statement appears in figure 1–1.

Federation of Families for Children's Mental Health Mission Statement

- To ensure the rights to full citizenship, support and access to community-based services for all children and youth with emotional, behavioral, or mental disorders and their families.
- To address the unique needs of children and youth with emotional, behavioral, or mental disorders from birth through the transition to adulthood.
- To provide information and engage in advocacy regarding research, prevention, early intervention, family support, education, transition services, and other services needed by these children, youth, and their families.
- To provide leadership in the field of children's mental health and develop necessary human and financial resources to meet its goal.

Source: Steering Committee for the Federation of Families for Children's Mental Health. (1989, March). *Mission statement.* Alexandria, VA: Author. Reprinted by permission.

Despite their impact on service delivery and political advocacy, parent organizations cannot be all things to all parents. The late Elizabeth Boggs, one of the founding members of The Arc, wrote the following concerning her role as a parent advocate:

> I am proud to be the only person who has been continuously active in some volunteer capacity with the National Association for Retarded Citizens [now called The Arc] since I participated in its founding in 1950. . . . The cause has taken me to 44 states, plus Puerto Rico and 10 foreign countries. It is hard to put a job title on the role I've played. One could say that I've been a social synergist with a predisposition toward communication and collaboration rather than confrontation. (Boggs, 1985, pp. 39–40)

By contrast, Janet Bennett, also a parent, sees organizational membership in a much different light.

> My first phone call to my local unit produced a pleasant enough response from the office secretary and a promise of some information to be mailed. This material consisted of a short summary of the unit's pro-

grams and services and a long questionnaire on which I could indicate areas in which I would be delighted to volunteer. . . . The message was clear: a parent in my circumstances, trying to cope with a trauma of uncertain dimensions, should marshal her forces, muster her energies, and get out and work for the cause. . . .

> If I had had an unretarded baby, I'd never in a million years have thought of volunteering for anything during that period. Now that I had Kathryn, why in the world would I be expected to do anything of the kind? Yet in the face of minimal help from the organization, it was telling me I should help it. And numb from shock and diminished self-confidence, I did my best to comply. (Bennett, 1985, pp. 163, 164)

Moreover, many parent organizations tend to consist primarily of white, middle-class parents. Parents from culturally diverse backgrounds have not joined many parent organizations. The Arc's last membership survey on this topic revealed that 95 percent of the respondents were white and only one-fourth of all members had yearly incomes under $20,000 (Haller & Millman, 1987). An exception is the Federation of Families for Children's Mental Health. At their annual conferences held each fall, approximately half of the participants are from culturally diverse backgrounds. Furthermore, the federation has demonstrated cultural sensitivity by providing a strand of sessions in Spanish, having conference materials available in English and Spanish, having a strand of programs particularly targeted for Native American families, and having a broad array of entertainment and social opportunities that build on the traditions and priorities of various cultures. Such accommodations enable families from culturally and linguistically diverse backgrounds to experience authentic participation. Then if they are interested in organizational affiliation, they have that option—they are not blocked by cultural barriers.

Here is the simple point for you to remember: Some parents, but not others, are helped by and participate in parent organizations. This fact means that you, as a collaborating professional, should share information with parents about appropriate local, state, and national organizations and encourage them to determine the level and type of their own participation. One caution: Despite the increased emphasis on noncategorical services in schools and special education, most parent organizations are based on disability categories. If you teach in schools that do not categorize children by type of disability, parents may need information about the type of disability so they can get support from the appropriate parent organizations.

Parents as Service Developers

Parents have played a major role in developing services for children at all stages in the lifespan. During the 1950s and 1960s, they and the organizations they created focused on establishing education programs for children who were excluded from public schools solely because of their disabilities. These parents organized classes in community buildings and church basements, solicited financial support from charitable organizations, and did the job the schools should have been doing. During those two decades and especially since then, parents and their organizations have spearheaded recreation, residential options, and employment services. In all of these endeavors, parents have had four jobs: They have created public awareness, raised money, operated services, and advocated for others to assume responsibility for service operations.

Samuel Kirk (1984), a distinguished special education pioneer, describes the profound impact of parent organizations in developing special education services:

> I found a satisfaction in associating with many intelligent and knowledgeable parents in these organizations. I found that through association with other parents they learned what the best programs were for their children. If I were to give credit to one group in this country for the advancements that have been made in the education of exceptional children, I would place the parent organizations and parent movement in the forefront as the leading force. (p. 41)

Although some family members prefer to be service developers and providers, professionals should not expect them to start and maintain services that are the professionals' responsibility. For example, you should not expect parents to start a supported employment program for secondary students with disabilities; after all, parents of children without disabilities are not expected to start and maintain a college-preparatory curriculum in their local high school. Of course, families should have full opportunities to collaborate with professionals in creating educational, vocational, and recreational programs; but they should not have to assume the full responsibility for starting and operating any program. There is one very good reason for this: Many parents simply do not have the time to develop and operate services. They often already devote extraordinary time just to meeting their own needs and satisfying the demands of their for-pay jobs (Knoll, 1992). In other words, parents should be supported to be parents, first and foremost. That is one of the points Patty Smith makes in the vignette. For parents, service development should be an option and often is, not an expectation.

Parents as Recipients of Professionals' Decisions

Even as recently as the 1970s, and certainly long before then, professionals generally expected parents to comply passively and gratefully with their decisions about the programs in which their children should participate and how those programs should operate. As Kolstoe (1970), an author of an early leading textbook on the methods of educating students with disabilities, wrote in 1970:

> Should it be judged that special class placement will probably be of most benefit to the child, then placement should be made without delay. Both the child and his parents should be told that the child is being transferred into the special class because the class is special. . . . The entire program should be explained so the parents will understand what lies ahead for the child and so they can support the efforts of the teachers with the child. (Kolstoe, 1970, p. 42)

This was not a novel perspective for students who were regarded as gifted, as a typical 1960s text shows:

> Some "guts" to speak straight from the shoulder would be helpful to the educators in this situation. Then the lay groups probably would realize they must delegate some of their authority to the educators to make necessary decisions for improving the education of students. For example, an overwhelming majority of parents do not have the sophistication in educational matters to decide whether or not their youngster would be better off educationally if placed in a differential program for the gifted. . . . Parents could better spend their time: a) supporting parent organizations for raising funds and influencing state and federal legislation, and b) learning techniques to aid their own youngsters toward high achievement. (Lucito, 1963, pp. 227–228)

Some professionals still believe that they and the school systems know what is best for a student, so they still expect families to assume a totally deferential role, especially regarding the student's evaluation, individualized program, and educational placement. Professionals with this expectation create a psychological barrier to effective family-professional collaboration; for example, parents may feel intimidated and angered by the professionals' authoritarian approach (Turbiville, Turnbull, Garland, & Lee, 1996). This barrier can be particularly problematic for all families but especially those families from culturally diverse backgrounds when there are clashes in cultural values between the professionals and families (Harry, Kalyanpur, & Day, 1999; Kalyanpur & Harry, 1999). Try to be an equal partner with families when making decisions, and do not lead them to expect to be—or expect all of them to be—the passive recipients of your decisions. Cultivate the approach that Patty Smith advocates, creating a trust bond and joint decisions. Throughout this book, we will be providing you with information about how you can collaborate as reliable allies in various decision-making situations. Understanding these principles will give you the ability to assist parents in a profound way.

Parents as Teachers

The role of parents as teachers emerged during the late 1960s, peaked during the 1970s, and was moderated during the mid to late 1980s. At the root of the parent-as-teacher role was evidence that family environment influences children's intelligence (Hunt, 1972). The data showed that families from economically deprived backgrounds had problems associated with their home lives, and these problems created child-rearing environments that lacked the opportunities typically available in middle- and upper-class homes (Zigler & Muenchow, 1992). Thus, President Kennedy's New Frontier and President Johnson's Great Society programs (for example, Head Start) included training parents to teach their children; in turn, the children would make more progress, a theory largely credited to researcher Urie Bronfenbrenner.

> Bronfenbrenner's notion of parent involvement and the ecological model of child development emerged from two sources—his own childhood and his cross-cultural research. Born in Moscow, he emigrated to the United States in 1923. His father, a physician, took a job as director of an institution for the "feeble-minded" in Letchworth Village, New York.
>
> From time to time, Bronfenbrenner's father would anguish over the commitment to the institution of a person who was not retarded. Sadly, after a few weeks there, these people of normal intelligence would begin to mimic the mannerisms of the rest of the residents. When one of these patients came to work in the Bronfenbrenners' household, however, she gradually resumed a "normal" life. To young Urie, it was an important lesson in how family and community expectations influence human behavior.
>
> After such an upbringing, Bronfenbrenner decided to become a psychologist. During the course of cross-cultural studies in western and eastern Europe, he was struck by the observation that Russian parents, both fathers and mothers, seemed to spend more time with their children than did American parents. When he was asked to present his findings at a National Institute for Child Health and Human Development meeting in

1964, a woman named Florence Mahoney commented, "Why, the president ought to hear about this."

> A few weeks later the White House called, and Bronfenbrenner and his wife were soon presenting their observations on Russian childrearing complete with slides to Lady Bird and her daughters. The Johnsons were impressed, especially by the pictures of Russian preschools. One of the Johnson daughters asked, "Why couldn't we do something like this?" (Zigler & Muenchow, 1992, pp. 16–17)

Bronfenbrenner's approach—called *ecological* because it linked family environment to human development—was the basis on which professionals prepared parents for increasing their children's progress and achievement. The 1970s brought an emphasis on parents' learning behavioral principles and child development so they could teach their children how to develop. Enthusiasm for this approach was sparked by encouraging research results that parents can be effective teachers of their children (Bricker & Bricker, 1976; Shearer & Shearer, 1977). Professionals, more than many parents, endorsed the parent-as-learner-and-teacher role. Because parents *could* be effective teachers, many professionals believed that parents *should* be teachers. They also believed that "good" parents were those who frequently served as teachers, not "just" parents, for their children.

The use of the term *parent* is actually a misnomer in this context. It is more correct to substitute "mothers" for "parents" because literature of this period contains almost no reference to the role that fathers might play in their children's development (Turbiville, Turnbull, & Turnbull, 1995).

Given the optimism that the research data justified (Baker, 1989), it was only natural for early childhood education programs to insist that parents should be effective teachers of their own children (Shearer & Shearer, 1977). And just what should parents be taught? During the height of the parent-training era, Karnes and Teska (1980) identified the competencies that parents need to acquire to fulfill their "teacher" role:

> The parental competencies required for direct teaching of the handicapped child at home involve interacting with the child in ways that promote positive behavior; reinforcing desired behavior; establishing an environment that is conducive to learning; setting up and maintaining a routine for direct teaching; using procedures appropriate for teaching concepts and skills; adapting lesson plans to the child's interests and needs; determining whether the child has mastered knowledge and skills; keeping meaningful records, including notes on child progress;

participating in a staffing of the child; communicating effectively with others; and assessing the child's stage of development. (p. 99)

Surprisingly, these are fewer than half the skills the authors regarded as essential to the parent-as-teacher role. Now, compare these skills to the ones you have to master through your own professional training program and ask yourself whether it is realistic to expect parents to develop so many didactic skills.

Some parents find teaching to be very satisfying. Others say it produces unintended consequences such as guilt and stress if they are not constantly working with their son or daughter with a disability (Robbins, Dunlap, & Plienis, 1991). Another unintended consequence is the impact that didactic instruction from parents, provided even within the context of *typical routines,* can have on the self-esteem of children and youth with disabilities. Diamond (1981) describes her experiences with her parents as she grew up as a child with a physical disability:

> Something happens in a parent when relating to his disabled child; he forgets that they're a kid first. I used to think about that a lot when I was a kid. I would be off in a euphoric state, drawing or coloring or cutting out paper dolls, and as often as not the activity would be turned into an occupational therapy session. "You're not holding the scissors right," "Sit up straight so your curvature doesn't get worse." That era was ended when I finally let loose a long and exhaustive tirade. "I'm just a kid! You can't therapize me all the time! I get enough therapy in school every day! I don't think about my handicap all the time like you do!" (Diamond, 1981, p. 30)

Indeed, many of today's parents of children and youth with disabilities, unlike parents during the 1970s and early 1980s, seem to place less importance on their roles as teachers. Instead, many families want more information (not necessarily formal training sessions) on various topics (Cooper & Allred, 1992). That is why many families today welcome information on topics such as advocacy, homework, and future planning. Consider information exchanges (a more collaborative term than parent training) and find out from not only mothers—but also fathers, brothers and sisters, and extended family members—their preferences for gaining relevant and helpful information.

In the parent-as-teacher role, collaboration (joint planning of parent education programs) will do everyone more good than a professional-knows-best approach. Many educational programs are best provided by a parent-professional instructional team with families and professionals as colearners (Roberts, Rule, & Innocenti, 1998; Winton & DiVenere, 1995).

Parents as Political Advocates

Parents have been tremendously successful as advocates in the political process, but they have had to work for many years at the federal, state, and local levels and in legislatures, courts, and executive agencies. It was because educational services for most students with disabilities were woefully inadequate throughout 1950–1970 that parents took on a new role—as political advocates. In the early 1970s, parents of students with mental retardation and the Pennsylvania Association for Retarded Children won a lawsuit against the state to obtain a free, appropriate education for children with mental retardation (*Pennsylvania Association for Retarded Citizens (PARC) v. Commonwealth of Pennsylvania,* 1971, 1972). Thereafter, parents and the organizations to which they belonged brought right-to-education suits in almost every state, usually successfully. Buoyed by their success in court, parents sought federal legislation to implement the courts' decisions (Turnbull & Turnbull, 2000). Parent organizations representing all areas of exceptionality, particularly The Arc, joined forces with professionals, particularly the Council for Exceptional Children, and successfully advocated for comprehensive federal legislation requiring the states to provide all students with disabilities a free, appropriate public education. A review of highlights from the disability rights movement is included in Turnbull and Turnbull (1996).

The parent groups were immensely successful as political advocates, convincing Congress to pass the Education for All Handicapped Children Act (P.L. 94-142) in 1975 and five major amendments since then (1978, 1983, 1986, 1990, and 1997). (We discuss this legislation, now referred to as the Individuals with Disabilities Education Act, in chapter 2.) It is a tribute to parent advocacy—always greatly aided by and sometimes led by professional organizations—that Congress passed these laws, that the parent organizations were able to form coalitions with each other and professional groups, and that all of this has been accomplished over such an extended period of time in a continuous and consistent manner. In box 1–3, Tom Gilhool, the attorney representing parents in the *Pennsylvania Association for Retarded Citizens (PARC) v.*

Tom Gilhool Speaks Out
On Significant Accomplishments
of Parents As Political Advocates

The parents and families on whose shoulders we stand reversed in this century, and most particularly in the past three decades, the weight and the pattern of the historical legacy that the start of the century left for us. It is entirely correct, and a gentle understatement, to say that the parent movement has nearly eliminated segregation of disabled people into large, separate, horrific public institutions. . . .

Indeed, in 1970, just prior to the PARC decision and the decisions in the other 37 court cases which led to the passage of The Education for All Handicapped Children Act of 1975 [also known as P.L. 94-142], some 12,000 children of school age had been committed to institutions in that year. That was the annual rate of admission. In 1981, three years after the effective date of P.L. 94-142, fewer than 1,200 were admitted. . . . The parent movement has reversed the course of history in this century by insisting that these segregated institutions cannot stand and must go.

Second, the opening of the schools and the requirement that schools provide to every child, including every child with a disability, a strong, effective education are the work of the parent movement. Seymour Sarason regards P.L. 94-142 as one of just two significant changes in all of public education in the last 75 years and the only one to come in an Act of Congress. The change he refers to, of course, is the empowerment of parents, putting parents and families in charge of the education of their children. This change was birthed by The Education for All Handicapped Children Act and, so far, remains a keystone of IDEA. (The other significant change referred to by Sarason was collective bargaining.) Both of those accomplishments are signal, resonant achievements in the name of the American commitment to equality. They have advanced, and promise to advance still further, equality for very, very many American citizens. Thus far, they have been sustained even while the American politic in the last two decades has moved so strongly away from equality, even against it.

Source: Gilhool, T. (1997, Spring). Tom Gilhool speaks out on significant accomplishments of parents as political advocates. In *The Parent Movement: Reflections and Directions. Coalition Quarterly, 14*(1).

Commonwealth of Pennsylvania court case and leading national advocate for individuals with disabilities, describes his perspectives on these significant accomplishments of parents as political advocates.

Lowell Weicker (1985), a former United States senator from Connecticut and the father of a son with Down syndrome, played an important role in the advocacy movement. In the mid 1980s, he described the impact of political advocacy on attempts by President Reagan's administration to deemphasize the federal role in special education, attempts that he and the parent advocacy movement thwarted:

> The administration did not gets its way. Why? Because the disabled people in this country and their advocates repudiated a long-held cliché that they were not a political constituency, or at least not a coherent one. It was assumed that in the rough and tumble world of politics they would not hold their own as a voting block or as advocates for their cause. But that assumption was blown to smithereens in the budget and policy deliberations of 1981, 1982, and again in 1983. In fact, I would be hard-pressed to name another group within the human service spectrum that has not only survived the policies of this administration but has also defeated them as consistently and as convincingly as the disabled community has. Indeed, it has set an example for others, who were believed to be better organized. (p. 284)

As the federal role in disability services changes and as state and local governments and even the private-sector providers play more significant roles in implementing disability policy and funding disability services, parents once again will be obliged to be advocates. Just as with every other parental role, not all parents have the time, interest, or resources to be political advocates. (Chapter 15 provides much more detail for you in discussing your own role as a political advocate and how you can support parents who choose this role to be successful in their efforts.)

Parents as Educational Decision Makers

The role of parents as educational decision makers grows directly out of the 1975 Education of All Handicapped Children Act (P.L. 94-142), now called Individuals with Disabilities Education Act (IDEA). This law was revolutionary when enacted in 1985 because it grants active decision-making rights to parents of children and youth with disabilities. But the law is also very traditional because it recognizes the critical role that families play in their children's development and the necessity of subjecting schools to parental oversight. Although children who are gifted are not included in the federal laws for children with disabilities, approximately two-thirds of the states have mandates, accompanied by some level of funding, for gifted education (Coleman, Gallagher, & Foster, 1994).

In granting these decision-making and accountability rights to parents, Congress adopted the basic premise that families of children and youth with disabilities could make no assumptions that the public schools would allow parents to enroll their children, much less that schools would educate the children appropriately (Turnbull, Turnbull, & Wheat, 1982). Thus, Congress viewed parents as persons who should or could ensure that professionals provide an appropriate education; this view reflected a major reversal in expectations about parents' roles. No longer were parents to be passive recipients of professionals' decisions concerning services to their children. Now they were to be educational decision makers and monitors of professionals' decisions, doing what Patty Smith has been doing for all of Jane's life.

Parents' relationships with professionals may have indeed become more equal than a couple of decades ago; however, the majority of parents participate in educational decision making in a passive rather than an active style, as we will discuss, particularly in chapters 2 and 12.

Sometimes parents do not have the motivation (such as energy or hope) to be educational decision makers; at other times they have the motivation but do not have the knowledge and skills (such as information or problem-solving skills); and even those parents who have motivation, knowledge, and skills face an educational context that disempowers (inhibits) rather than

empowers (facilitates) them to be partners. This is particularly so for culturally diverse parents (Harry & Kalyanpur, 1999; Kalyanpur & Harry, 1999). But the roles of parents as educational decision makers—particularly moving from a passive role to one of educational decision maker—are changing. The current emphasis is on collaboration.

Families as Collaborators

In their current role, families are regarded as collaborators. An important word in that sentence is *families*. Until the early 1990s, all roles typically focused on parents. This is the first time that we have used *family* to describe a role. The reason for the change is that there has been increasing recognition that partnerships do not need to be limited—and should not be limited—to parents only (especially to mothers only). Partnerships can and should involve relationships between professionals and other family members, such as grandparents, brothers and sisters, and even close family friends, who are vital resources in supporting and enhancing educational outcomes for students with exceptionalities. Just consider Patty and Jane Smith; the entire Smith family should have the opportunity to be collaborators with Jane's professional providers.

As Patty said in the opening vignette, brothers and sisters were generally left out of the process of professional support. Patty appreciated affirmation from a professional that it was appropriate for her to divide her time among all of her children rather than to focus exclusively on Jane. This approach has paid huge dividends as Jane's brothers and sisters have moved into roles of teacher, advocate, friend and role model for her. As you will learn in chapter 7, increasingly today there are support programs for brothers and sisters to address their unique questions, preferences, and needs.

Although families from different cultures define themselves in many and varied ways, we have chosen to define *family* as "two or more people who regard themselves as a family and who perform some of the functions that families typically perform. These people may or may not be related by blood or marriage and may or may not usually live together" (Turnbull, Turnbull, Shank, & Leal, 1995, pp. 24–25). Thus, four generations of women who are living together might call themselves a family unit; another family might describe a broad network of parents, grandparents, aunts and uncles, cousins, and a host of others who are part of close-knit family relationships.

Beginning in the mid 1980s, both professionals and parents began to emphasize that successful family life requires that the needs of all family members should be identified, addressed, and balanced (Friesen & Koroloff, 1990; Morgan, 1988; Patterson, 1991; Turnbull & Summers, 1987). This premise is consistent with family systems theory. That theory views the family as a social system with unique characteristics and needs. It asserts that the individual members of a family are so interrelated that any experience affecting one member will affect all (Carter & McGoldrick, 1989; Goldenberg & Goldenberg, 1980; Minuchin, 1974). Certainly Patty Smith, when discussing Jane's siblings, makes that fact clear. It has helped us, and we hope it will help you, to combine family systems theory with research on the impact of children and youth on families (Benson & Turnbull, 1986; Turnbull, Summers, & Brotherson, 1984; Turnbull, Brotherson, & Summers, 1985). In chapters 5 through 8, we will introduce you to family systems theory and its implication for families.

Why is family systems theory important to you? Briefly, it will help you know families; and when you know families in an individual and personalized way, you can be attuned to their strengths, high expectations, priorities, and needs. In turn, the family systems approach can help you work more effectively and collaboratively with the family members who are most able to promote students' positive educational outcomes.

Now that you have learned the definition and composition of *family* and have been introduced to a family systems perspective, we need to clarify what we mean by collaboration. (We will refer to this definition throughout this book, particularly in chapter 3 when we talk about collaboration for empowerment.) *Collaboration* refers to the dynamic process of families and professionals equally sharing their resources (that is, motivation and knowledge/skills) in order to make decisions jointly. When collaboration is carried out successfully, all participants can become more empowered.

The role of parents as collaborators differs from the role of parents as decision makers and certainly from that of parents as recipients of professionals' judgments. The role of parents as collaborators presumes that families will be equal and full partners with educators and school systems and that this collaboration will benefit the student and the entire school system as well (Cheney & Osher, 1997; Erwin & Rainforth, 1996; Roberts, Rule, & Innocenti, 1998). Sometimes family views will prevail; at other times they will not. Always families, in alliance with educators, will grapple with the difficult task of providing a free, appropriate public education to each student.

State-of-the-art collaboration involves a wide range of stakeholders in promoting the most successful educational experiences for students. Those stakeholders include families, students with exceptionalities, class-

mates, teachers, administrators, paraprofessionals, and related service providers. This kind of collaboration benefits not only family members but also educators, who derive support and assistance from professional colleagues and families. For example, a general classroom teacher who has primary responsibility for educating a student with autism is not left alone to generate solutions to all challenges but instead has a dynamic team of supporters, helpers, and friends who provide assistance to find the most successful solutions to those challenges.

Students with exceptionalities are key collaborators; their participation is referred to as self-determination. *Self-determination* means choosing how to live one's life consistent with one's own values, preferences, strengths, and needs (Turnbull, Blue-Banning et al., 1996; Turnbull & Turnbull, in press). For too many years, it has been assumed that either professionals or parents or both know what is in a student's best interest and that they should represent a student's interest when it comes to educational decision making. Indeed, many secondary school programs have developed curricula and model opportunities for students to be involved in their own educational planning and decision making (Agran & Wehmeyer, 1999; Field, Martin, Miller, Ward, & Wehmeyer, 1998; Wehmeyer & Sands, 1998). As we will point out in chapters 5, 8, and 12, however, self-determination is also culturally rooted in a value system that emphasizes individual achievement and autonomy. For that reason, some families may reject self-determination as a culturally inappropriate goal (Kalyanpur & Harry, 1999).

What are the benefits of collaboration when we take into account (a) a broader definition of family, (b) self-determination, and (c) prospects of a much larger number of collaborators? Collaboration has two important benefits. First, it benefits the student by bringing to bear on the student's behalf the multiple perspectives and resources of the collaborators to improve educational outcomes. Second, it benefits the collaborators by making available to each the resources (that is, motivation and knowledge/skills) of the others and thereby increasing their own resources through the process of being supported by others and learning from others. A fundamental premise of this book is that collaboration is mutually beneficial; it is the most effective way of being a professional (Audette & Algozzine, 1997; Cheney & Osher, 1997; Erwin & Rainforth, 1996; Hudson & Glomb, 1997; Roberts, Rule, & Innocenti, 1998; Turnbull, Turnbull, Shank, & Leal, 1999).

Because collaboration occurs in a school context, we turn next (in chapter 2) to that context, which is general and special education in today's schools and the family-professional partnership approaches associated with each.

Summary

Parents and families have had many roles, some of them unwelcome or unjustified, some born out of necessity, and some of them eagerly embraced. These roles were the sources of their child's problems, organization members, service organizers, recipients of professionals' decisions, learners and teachers, political advocates, educational decision makers, and collaborators.

No one role can fully and perfectly characterize all parents, and some parents have played all or most roles. Families vary in the roles they assume, and professionals vary in the roles they consider appropriate and in turn recommend to and expect from families. This much is clear, however: The pendulum of role playing has swung back and forth along several dimensions:

- From viewing parents as part of the child's problem to viewing them as collaborators in addressing the challenges of exceptionality
- From insisting on passive roles for parents to expecting active and collaborating roles for families
- From viewing families as a mother-child dyad to recognizing the preferences and needs of all members of a family
- From responding to family needs in a general way to individualizing for the family as a whole and for each member of the family

Families and professionals alike may feel caught up in time-zone changes, much like world travelers. Dorothy "Tot" Avis (1985), a parent who is also a professional in the disability field, describes the concept of "deinstitutionalization jet lag," referring to parents who were told years ago that the state institution was best for their child and who now are told that the community is preferable. Families and professionals alike experience "family-role jet lag." Expectations and philosophies have drastically changed since the eugenics movement and the formation of parent organizations. Understanding the distance that families have traveled paves the way for the journey into mutually beneficial family-professional collaboration. This journey starts by considering a major theme that runs throughout this book—collaboration.

What does it mean to have time-traveled and role-traveled, as Patty and many other parents and professionals have? It means understanding the roles that families have assumed and continue to assume and seeing that they—and the professionals who work with them—will, together, have different roles in the future.

Very little about family-professional partnerships is static; very much is dynamic. Among the most dynamic aspects of the partnerships are those that rely on collaboration, not professional dominance or parent dominance within the relationships.

As Patty has said, "My experience has been that having professionals work with, around, above, behind, anywhere with me, has been the most absolutely wonderful thing that has happened to me. I have never thought that I, as a parent and a parent leader, ever could do it on my own, and I never did. My greatest successes have been in collaboration with other parents and with professionals, too. Those collaborations have made all the difference."

Chapter Two

Schools as Systems:
The Context for Family-Professional Collaboration

*S*ally Wade wears two hats, each one comfortably but not uncritically. On the one hand, she is the mother of two children who have disabilities: Rachel, 20, who has learning disabilities; and Wakefield, 15, who is mathematically gifted but also has learning disabilities, visual disabilities, and attention-deficit disorder. As a parent, she also was the first president of the combined Parent Training and Information Center and the statewide Parent to Parent program (see chapter 10 for descriptions of those programs). On the other, she has been a teacher in general education and in special education. She is a member of the staff at the University of South Florida, where she works in a regional diagnostic and learning center; and she is about to assume the directorship of a federally funded center that provides information to low socioeconomic families and families of at-risk children. As a parent and parent-advocate and as a professional, she has been active at the state policy-making level, often testifying before the Florida legislature and securing from the state board of education a requirement that all teachers be competent in teacher-parent collaboration. If anyone is in a good position to appreciate the effect of school reform and system change on families and their children, Sally is. She cannot give school reform and teacher-parent relationships unstinting praise; hers is a balanced judgment.

As a parent, and for any parent, it is good (as Sally says) to have the law "standing behind you," and it is good that the reauthorized federal special education law, Individuals with Disabilities Education Act (reauthorized in 1997), em-phasizes parent partnerships to a greater degree than it did before. But there are still two big barriers to change: ignorance and attitude. Sally says, "Teachers don't know what to do with families, and families don't know what to do with educators. They don't know how to interact with each other." Why? Because the teachers learned, and still believe, that they are "here for the children." They are "trying to do what's best for them" and "don't have to think in terms of family." As a teacher, "You never know what to do with these parents when they come to you. So, mostly educators seem afraid of them, to talk with them, afraid parents are going to sue them or that they are going to get into trouble. They're just afraid of parents," Sally notes.

She adds parents carry their own baggage, too. "We have one bad experience, then we kind of view educators just that way . . . we have been beaten up by the system so much that by the time we get somebody to talk to us, we already have this chip on our shoulder."

The consequence: "There's not much trust on either side." The solution: That's the hard part. Hard because the policies that drive schools nowadays do not always fit nicely together, especially when they affect children like Rachel and Wakefield.

On the one hand, the national and state policies seek improved outcomes from general and special education. One way those policies are played out is through "high stakes" assessments. In Florida, as in many states, if a child does not pass a state competency test, the student does not move ahead in grades or is denied a diploma. Unless the state finds some way to accommodate in the

giving of the test or adjust the grade for students like Wakefield, they can get into college but have no chance to get a high school diploma: no pass, no diploma. But, as Sally makes it clear, "There's no way I'm going to accept a special education diploma for my son." The solution that some families find—enrolling their child in a private school or sending them out of state for their senior year—simply is not acceptable to Sally and her husband Rodney. They have already seen the social consequences of separate schooling: Rachel and Wakefield both were bused across town to a special class and were, as a result, unable to make any social connections with peers who went to the neighborhood school; and the cost of private schooling is not inconsequential.

Laid alongside the "performance-based" general education policies are those of special education. They include an appropriate education—one that benefits the student; placement in the neighborhood schools and access to the general curriculum; and education that leads to jobs and college (among other things). And here lies the irony: To get an appropriate education for Rachel and Wakefield, Sally and Rodney had to accept their children's placement in separate school programs—schools and programs just for students with learning disabilities. That was the only way the children would be able to learn; they needed the intensive instruction so that they would be able to read and not go through life illiterate.

"They would drown in the mainstream," says Sally. Yet, in accepting that benefit, they incurred high costs: separation from peers in the neighborhood and, thus, few social relationships over the weekends and holidays; myths about why the kids were in separate schools ("Wakefield hit a teacher"); placement with other students who, on the whole, were less likely to graduate and more likely to be involved with the juvenile justice system than other children; and distance from school activities ("why sell chocolates to raise cash for school activities when my kid can't even read the word 'chocolate' when he's in the 6th grade?").

Talking about spelling, if you ask Sally how to spell school reform, she will use eight letters to answer: "politics." The politics are, of course, motivated by political posturing; but they are also motivated by an earnest desire to produce better outcomes for students and to encourage parent-professional collaboration. Sally does not deny that, but she recognizes, "We haven't sorted it all

The Wade children, Rachel and her brother, Wakefield. (1999)

out yet." School reform and educational systems in which parents and professionals are expected to collaborate are, in a very real sense, "in process."

In chapter 1, you learned about the eight roles that parents have played in the education of children and youth with exceptionalities and that the most contemporary role is viewing families as collaborators. To prepare you for collaboration, we will describe in this chapter the context of general and special education—how it has changed over the last two decades and how today it requires general and special education professionals to collaborate with each other and with families, students, and community representatives. We will focus on the general education reform movement, the special education reform movement, and contemporary school-restructuring efforts.

General Education Reform Movement

General education school reform has been on the agenda since the early 1980s and has occurred in three phases (Turnbull, Turnbull, Shank, & Leal, 1999):

- *Enhancing the curriculum:* improving education by increasing academic excellence across basic subjects
- *Restructuring school governance:* creating local flexibility and innovation
- *Reshaping service delivery:* integrating educational, social services, mental health, public health, and other services into one delivery system

These three phases are illustrated in figure 2–1.

Enhancing the Curriculum and Student Outcomes

The major purpose of enhancing the curriculum was to ensure excellence. This impetus was supported by a national commission report, *A Nation at Risk* (National Commission on Excellence in Education, 1983), that emphasized the United States' loss of economic competitiveness with countries such as Japan and Germany because U.S. students were scoring lower than their peers from these and other countries. *A Nation at Risk,* as well as other national reports, recommended curriculum reform (for example, requiring more math and science) and called upon school staff to increase their effectiveness in educating students. Enhancing the curriculum was a top-down strategy in which federal leaders recommended curriculum guidelines for state and local educators.

The curriculum enhancement movement—in Florida, where Sally lives, it is known as the *high stakes assessment movement*—undoubtedly encourages educators, families, and community leaders to recognize that schools' and students' educational performance may not be up to par. In Florida, for example, each school receives a grade (on a scale of A to F) that reflects how well its students do on the statewide assessment examinations, and the grades are published for all to know. Although the schools were the first source of reform, many people have expected parents to assume more responsibility for extending learning to the home.

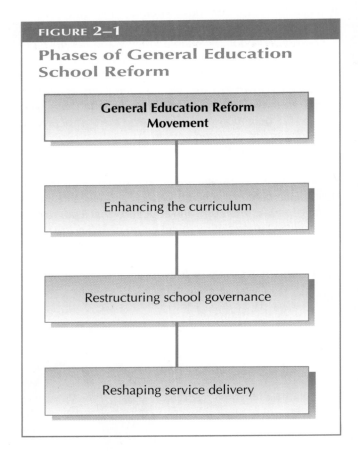

FIGURE 2–1

Phases of General Education School Reform

General Education Reform Movement

↓

Enhancing the curriculum

↓

Restructuring school governance

↓

Reshaping service delivery

Restructuring School Governance

A different change strategy is a bottom-up approach that seeks to reform school policies, improve school organizations, and allocate governance authority to local schools and away from district, state, and federal education agencies. Restructuring means that state and local boards of education, not bureaucrats in Washington, D.C., would say what schools would do and how they would do it.

Restructuring school governance gave significantly more opportunities to parents to advocate for systems change as members of site-based management teams. But simply having opportunities for decision making that are closer to the local level does not guarantee an authentic family voice (Wade, 1994). School power structures typically give the greatest decision-making authority to administrators and teachers. As we will discuss later in this chapter, school organization typically has reflected hierarchical authority, formalized procedures, regulated paperwork reporting, and centralized power (Skrtic, 1995; Ware, 1994). Even schools that set out to develop decision-making structures characterized by parity among educators and families often encounter unanticipated challenges (Gruber & Trivette, 1987). And, as Sally Wade points out, statewide assessments and federal and state monitoring of special education decision making encourage schools to be "compliant." To her, "It seems that compliance is the goal . . . We're spending a lot of time on IEP forms and revising those . . . Money is going into compliance rather than on relationships with people" and on "providing the best education possible for children." In her view, "People are worried about lawsuits; they're missing the point that really the purpose of the IEP is not the paper but the process and the outcome."

A promising model for restructuring has come from Yale University professor James Comer. In his model, school planning and management teams are comprised of parents, teachers, administrators, related service providers, and nonprofessional support staff (for example, custodians and clerks). The teams are responsible for (1) developing and implementing a comprehensive plan to improve school morale and the academic program, (2) organizing and delivering staff development consistent with the schools goals, and (3) identifying and remedying problems as they arise (Comer, 1986; Comer & Haynes, 1991).

A key to the Comer bottom-up strategy is using a no-fault problem-solving approach, consensus decision making based on child development principles, and collaborative management that does not paralyze the school principal (Comer & Haynes, 1991, p. 273). As an educator, Sally Wade concurs: "I could have gotten more academic achievement (in my students) if I had had a relationship that involved the families in their education." This phase of general education school reform led to islands of excellence within restructured school governance, with parents having a strong role in advocating for systems change. Box 2–1 describes how one educator used the Comer model to restructure his school and invite parents to volunteer in his school.

Reshaping Service Delivery

Throughout the 1990s, another technique of school reform has focused on using the schools as the "one-stop shopping" site where children and youth and their families who face multiple challenges and risks can have all their service needs met (Dryfoos, 1997; Gerry, in press; Koren et al., 1997; Lawson & Briar-Lawson, 1997; Skrtic & Sailor, 1996). To educate multiply challenged students, reformers advocate providing school-linked comprehensive services—an integrated and comprehensive linkage of social, mental health, and public health services offered within the schools. The reformers assert that a single point of service delivery and coordination will be more cost- and time-efficient and more effective for children and families. Reform focuses on meeting families' basic needs (see chapter 10).

In the school-linked comprehensive services model, community service councils represent all human service agencies within the community, services and supports are available and coordinated through a single point of entry, and paperwork hassles for families are minimized. In chapter 13, we will discuss how you can collaborate with families through school-linked comprehensive services.

Nature of Family-Professional Collaboration Model within General Education

While the three phases of general education school reform were developing, another and equally important change was underway. It focused on home-school partnerships and has become particularly relevant because it addresses an issue that cuts across all three phases of school reform. This issue is collaboration—partnerships—between the student's family and the student's teachers. As you are about to learn, the home-school partnership approach is especially relevant to family-professional collaboration for empowerment and the education of children with educational exceptionalities.

Drawing a Circle of Collaborators

Practicing "Comer schooling" came easily for Dwight Fleming. He was born, grew up, and now works as school principal in the northeast quadrant of Hartford, Connecticut, a deprived urban area where the greatest majority of the families are African-American. It's a place characterized by single parenthood, poverty, homelessness, housing developments, incarceration, and hard work for low wages (when work is available).

Dwight's work focuses on, among other things, how to connect parents, their children, and the school.

"Each parent is a potential service provider or connector. My job is to help them become part of the education team, a team that consists of the school, the student, and the parents. I want them to see school as a positive experience for their children and the children to see it as a safe place to learn and grow."

To help a parent become part of the team, Dwight allows the family to define itself and to share itself:

"I don't care who's taking care of the kid at home . . . a mother, aunt, grandparent, father, sister, whoever. I find a way to get them to spend time at King School, and then to feel good about being there and then share their talents. You know, everyone has talents."

How does Dwight "find a way" to get the parents to come to school?

"I smile at parents, pay attention to what they say, invite them to come here, tell them we'd like to have them involved here, walk them around, show them what other parents have done, give them some ideas about what we need to have done, and let their imaginations go to work. I make them feel like somebody. Everybody is somebody special. I work one-to-one."

Thinking of his work as a collaborator, Dwight says:

"I begin to draw a circle, starting with the student and then extending to family and friends and neighbors. In each of these contacts, I offer hope, not pity."

And he tells them, "My job, the King School's job, is to give the student the best education we can and to protect that child's development and future."

In a word, parent participation is a one-to-one business based on inclusion, hope, and assurances. Does it work? Comer's data say so, and Dwight Fleming's experiences say so, too.

"It does kids good to see neighborhood people in school and then after school. They know they're being supported and watched. And with neighbors looking in during school and after school, I can find out a lot about students that I couldn't learn just by the student being here and by talking with the family."

Sources: Comer, J. P. (1986). Parent participation in the schools. *Phi Delta Kappan, 67*(6), 442–446; Turnbull, A. P., Turnbull, H. R., Shank, M., & Leal, D. (1995). *Exceptional lives: Special education in today's schools.* Englewood Cliffs, NJ: Merrill/Prentice Hall.

Joyce Epstein's research and demonstration models are widely recognized and useful bases for new approaches to developing school, family, and community partnerships (Epstein, in press; Epstein, 1995; Epstein & Sanders, in press; Sanders & Epstein, 1998a; 1998b). She uses the term *partnership* to emphasize the equal role that all stakeholders have in working together for students' benefit. Figure 2–2 illustrates the partnership through overlapping spheres of influence (Epstein, 1987, 1992).

Epstein describes this model as follows:

The spheres can, by design, be pushed together to overlap to create an area for partnership activities or pushed apart to separate the family and school based on forces that operate in each environment. The external model of the spheres of influence shows that the extent of overlap is effected by forces of (a) time, to account for changes in age and grade levels of students and the influence of historic changes, and (b) efforts in behavior to account for the backgrounds, philosophies and practices that occur in each environment. The *external model* recognizes pictorially that there are some practices that schools and families (and other spheres) conduct separately and some practices that they conduct jointly in order to influence children's learning and development. (Epstein, 1994, p. 40)

Epstein's model targets students as the beneficiary of the overlapping spheres of influence.

School and family partnerships do not "produce" successful students. Rather, the partnership activities that include teachers, parents, and students engage,

FIGURE 2–2

Overlapping Spheres of Influence of Family, School, and Community on Children's Learning

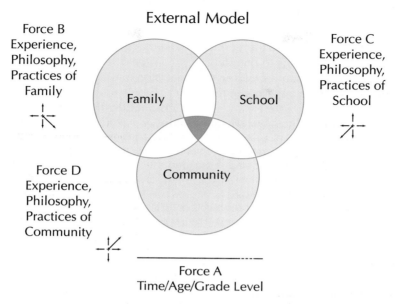

External Model

Force B
Experience,
Philosophy,
Practices of
Family

Force C
Experience,
Philosophy,
Practices of
School

Force D
Experience,
Philosophy,
Practices of
Community

Family

School

Community

Force A
Time/Age/Grade Level

Source: Epstein, J. L. (1994). Theory to practice: School and family partnerships lead to school improvement and student access. In C. L. Fegnano & B. Z. Werber (Eds.), *School, family, and community interaction: A view from the firing lines* (p. 41). Boulder, CO: Westview.

guide, energize, and motivate students so that they produce their own success. The model assumes that student learning, development, and success, broadly defined—not just achievement test scores—are the main reasons for school and family partnerships. Further, productive connections of schools, families, and communities, and pertinent individual interactions of teachers, parents, and students are conducted in order to help students increase their academic skills, self-esteem, positive attitudes toward learning, independence, other achievements, talents, accomplishments, and other desired behaviors that are characteristic of successful students. (Epstein, 1994, p. 42)

Epstein describes six types of partnerships that can promote outcomes associated with successful students (see figure 2–3). She and others have conducted extensive research and implemented comprehensive systemic models at all school levels—elementary, middle, and secondary—mostly in urban schools, but not entirely so (Epstein, 1995, 1996; Epstein & Sanders, in press; Sanders & Epstein, in press). As comprehensive as their work is in so many aspects, issues related to parent-professional partnership opportunities that have been

most prevalent in special education (such as joint parent and educator involvement in IEP conferences) are noticeably absent from the research and literature describing the Epstein model.

How does Epstein's framework of school, family, and community partnerships interact with the three phases of general education reform? Throughout all of the partnership types, but particularly in parenting (type 1), communicating (type 2), and extending learning in home (type 4), there is a strong emphasis on supporting students to master the curriculum and attain higher standards of academic achievement; this emphasis is consistent with enhancing the curriculum. Likewise, decision making (type 5) strongly encourages collaboration among families, educators, students, and community representatives to formulate and implement policy at the school-building level; this emphasis is consistent with restructuring school governance. Finally, parenting (type 1), where the major emphasis is on supporting families to meet their basic obligations, is consistent with reshaping service delivery.

In connection with family-professional collaboration within special education, it is interesting to note

Epstein Model for Partnerships

K now

Type 1: Parenting—Assisting families with basic obligations of parenting skills and setting home conditions for learning at each age and grade level

Type 2: Communicating—Increasing the effectiveness of the school's basic obligations to communicate clearly about school programs and children's progress through school-to-home and home-to-school communications

Type 3: Volunteering—Improving the organization, work, and schedules of volunteers and audiences to involve families at the school or in other locations to support the school and students

Type 4: Extending Learning in Home—Involving families with their children in learning activities at home, including homework and other curricular-linked activities and decisions

Type 5: Decision Making—Including families in decision making, governance, and advocacy

Type 6: Collaborating with Community—Coordinating the work and resources of community businesses, agencies, colleges or universities, and other groups to strengthen school programs

Source: Epstein, J., & Connors, L. J. (1994). *Trust fund: School, family, and community partnerships in high school* (Report No. 24) (p. 5). Boston: Boston University, Center on Families, Communities, Schools, and Children's Learning.

teachers' attitudes toward parents, as well as the general public's attitude toward the support provided by teachers and parents. A recent national poll of teachers' attitudes toward the public schools (Langdon, 1997) revealed that in 1984, 1989, and 1996, teachers identified the lack of interest and support of parents as the biggest problem with which the schools in their communities were facing. Teachers indicated that they are less likely to believe that parents will support them if they tell parents that their child has a discipline problem than if they tell parents that their child is not working hard at school. A comparison of the reports of teachers and parents further revealed that teachers' expectations of the extent of support they will get from parents is much lower than what parents themselves said that they would do to support teachers. Overall, teachers graded parents lower than they graded administrators or their local school board. And approximately one-fourth of the teachers said they would award parents the grade of A or B on how they were bringing up their children; by contrast, approximately three-fourths of the teachers would give parents the grade of C, D, or F.

As contrasted to the perspectives of teachers, the 30th Annual Phi Delta Kappa/Gallup Poll of the Public's Attitudes Toward the Public Schools (Rose & Gallup, 1998) reported that 87 percent of public school parents give the school that their oldest child attends a passing grade. A majority of the parents awarded their child's school a grade of A or B. Interestingly, parents tend to assign higher grades when their children are experiencing more success

in school. For example, 69 percent of parents indicating that their child is above average in achievement assigned the grade of A or B, but the percentages dropped to 53 percent for parents who reported that their child's achievement is average or below average.

Special Education Reform Movement

Significantly and sadly, there has been a distinct separation between general education and special education reform. But, as we point out later in this chapter, general and special education reform activities are just beginning to converge, and we believe that such a convergence can be beneficial for all students. The history of special education, however, has played itself out on a separate reform track. The major special education reform phases include (1) reshaping the provision of a free, appropriate public education and (2) restructuring student placement. Figure 2–4 highlights the phases of the special education reform movement.

Reshaping the Provision of Free, Appropriate Public Education

As you learned in chapter 1, 1975 was a landmark year in special education, for it was the year that Congress enacted the Education for All Handicapped Children Act, P.L. 94-142. That law was renamed in 1990—Individuals

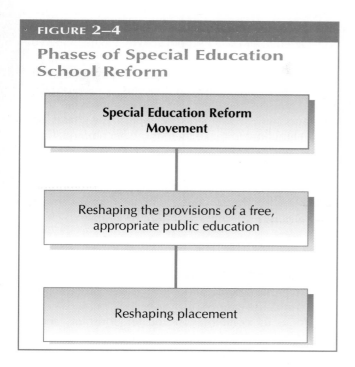

FIGURE 2–4

Phases of Special Education School Reform

Special Education Reform Movement

Reshaping the provisions of a free, appropriate public education

Reshaping placement

with Disabilities Education Act (IDEA)—and was reauthorized (reenacted with significant amendments) in 1997. IDEA's cornerstone is the provision of a free, appropriate public education, and upon that cornerstone many school reforms have been built.

Before IDEA was passed, special and general education were even more separate than they have been during the last decade. Many students with disabilities were educated in separate classes and separate schools; indeed, it was relatively common for students, particularly those with more severe disabilities, to be completely excluded from public schools. Many schools simply had no policy to educate students with the most severe disabilities. It was within this context (as you learned in chapter 1) that parents and professionals joined forces to make their voices heard as advocates for the enactment of IDEA.

IDEA provides a federal mandate and federal money to state and local education agencies to assist them in educating students from birth to age 21. Like almost all laws, IDEA has many different provisions, so it is divided into many discrete parts. Part B provides for the education of students ages 3 through 21, and Part C provides for the education of infants and toddlers, birth to age 3. Part B and Part C are alike in many ways, but we will indicate their relevant differences as we explain their basic provisions.

In order to qualify for the federal funding, states must adhere to six principles of educating students with disabilities (Turnbull & Turnbull, 2000). We will briefly

highlight the requirements of the six IDEA principles (each of which creates rights for Wakefield and Rachel, the two children who are the focus of Sally and Rodney Wade's parenting), and we will emphasize their implications for family-professional collaboration.

Zero Reject Zero reject is a principle against the exclusion from school of any student ages 3 through 21 who has a disability. In other words, it is a principle for the inclusion in school of every student ages 3 through 21 without regard to the type or extent of the student's disability. Part B has an explicit zero-reject rule, but Part C (birth to age 3) allows, or gives discretion to, states to educate some or all infants and toddlers; Part C, unlike Part B, does not have a zero-reject provision. For collaboration purposes, the zero-reject principle means that professionals and families can collaborate to secure education services.

Nondiscriminatory Evaluation Nondiscriminatory evaluation is a principle in favor of a fair, unbiased evaluation of the student's educational needs and strengths (see chapter 11). It assures that an evaluation team (including the student's parents) will assess the student's needs and strengths across all relevant domains and subjects. The team must use more than one assessment instrument to determine the student's functioning in and outside of school. Furthermore, parents have the right to submit and require the evaluation team to consider evaluation and other information that parents themselves initiate or provide. With respect to each evaluation, schools must first obtain parents' consent to have the evaluation administered. For collaboration purposes, these provisions create opportunities for professionals and families to:

- Secure a full understanding of the student's needs and strengths
- Take into account the observations of parents and others (including educators) as they develop that understanding
- Ensure that the evaluation is useful to and used by the student's teachers and other involved professionals and by the family as they work together to provide a free, appropriate public education

Appropriate Education Appropriate education is a principle in favor of a beneficial education (see chapter 12). The principle requires professionals to comply with important processes in providing an appropriate education. These processes include relying on the evaluation and, through it, developing an individualized family service plan (IFSP) for infants and toddlers (birth to age 3) or an individualized education program (IEP) for all other students. IFSPs and IEPs must state what related services (such as physical, speech, and occupational therapy) will be provided to the student in order to make the other special education services effective. The 1997 IDEA reauthorization provides that parents are members of the IFSP and IEP teams: they have a right to be invited to attend, to attend, and to "vote" or otherwise participate in all decision making at the team meetings. These teams must meet at times and places and in ways that are accessible to parents. If parents refuse to attend or cannot attend, the school-based team members may proceed without the parents or make arrangements for the parents to participate (for example, through telephone conference calls).

For collaboration purposes, the appropriate education principle creates opportunities for professionals and parents to develop the individualized approaches (that is, set annual goals and short-term objectives, specify evaluation measures, determine what related services will be provided, and set forth the student's placement). Certainly, the IFSP/IEP process is viewed as the key to the student's education, and the process for developing that plan is expected to afford professionals and parents a significant collaboration opportunity.

Least Restrictive Environment
After students have been enrolled in school (zero-reject principle), fairly evaluated (nondiscriminatory evaluation principle), and provided with an IFSP or IEP (appropriate education principle), IDEA requires them to be educated in the least restrictive environment to the maximum extent appropriate for each student (least restrictive environment principle). This principle creates a presumption in favor of educating students with a disability with their peers who do not have disabilities. IDEA further requires that the school may not remove a student with a disability from the general education curriculum unless he or she cannot be educated there successfully even after the school provides supplementary aids and support services for the student. (Remember that Sally's children were placed into separate special education classes because they otherwise could not learn to read, but also bear in mind that Rachel participated in the general curriculum for other subjects and was in the gifted/advanced classes in English and science.)

IDEA also requires schools to offer a continuum of placements, from less to more restrictive, and within that continuum students must be placed in the setting that is as least restrictive as possible and that also provides an appropriate education. Furthermore, schools must ensure that students with disabilities may participate in extracurricular and in other general education activities (such as recess, athletics, counseling, special interest groups, and

meals). Again, schools must include students in these nonacademic and other school activities to the maximum extent appropriate for the student and must provide supplementary aids and support services in these activities.

This principle creates an opportunity for professionals and families to collaborate to determine what school programs and environments are appropriate (that is, beneficial) and how to make them more accommodating to and beneficial for the student.

Due Process
Two other principles—procedural due process and parent participation—assure that the schools and parents are accountable to each other; they are checks and balances. The due process principle gives professionals and parents the opportunity to challenge each other's decisions about zero-reject, nondiscriminatory evaluation, individualized plans, and least restrictive placement. Although the due process provisions can cause schools to "cover their behinds" rather than focus on collaboration and relationships, and although the due process provisions can also create an adversarial process (a quasi-judicial hearing before an independent hearing officer or a lawsuit in federal or state court), they also afford schools and parents an opportunity to submit their disagreements to mediation. The 1997 IDEA amendments strongly encourage parents and school professionals to engage in mediation before going to a due process hearing. This is so because, if parents make the decision to forego mediation, IDEA requires schools to enter into agreements with parent support groups and to refer to these groups parents who do not want to enter into mediation; the groups in turn must explain to the parents the benefits of mediation. (No similar refusal is required if the schools refuse to enter mediation but the parents want to.) If either parents or schools are not satisfied with the results of a due process hearing at the school (local) level, they may appeal to the state-level due process hearing and, from it, to a state or federal court (Turnbull & Turnbull 2000). Regarding opportunities for collaboration, due process requirements encourage professionals and families to hold each other accountable and, as each sees what the other is doing to educate the student, to challenge the other.

Parent Participation
The parent participation principle grants the student's parents the right to have access to school records concerning the student and to control access to those records by others, to be eligible to participate on state or local special education advisory committees, and to use the other principles for the student's benefit. In the broadest of ways, it legalizes and legitimizes the role of parents as education decision makers

(see chapter 1) and thus permits parents and professionals to become collaborators with each other.

Themes of IDEA Reform

These six principles were bound to have significant effects on students, their families, school systems, professionals, and indeed every community in America. There is no doubt that the effects have been positive. Likewise there is no doubt that, as Congress said when it reauthorized IDEA in 1997, IDEA's promises have been only partially fulfilled. One promise was of a life (during schooling and after schooling has concluded) characterized by independence, productivity, and inclusion; that promise has been only partially kept (Blackorby & Wagner, 1996; Coker, Menz, Johnson, & McAlees, 1997; Kortering & Braziel, 1999; Koyanagi & Gaines, 1993; Levine & Nourse, 1998; Lovitt, Plavins, & Cushing, 1999; U.S. Department of Education, 1998).

A second promise was of a partnership between families and educators, one in which (as you learned in chapter 1) parents would be educational decision makers and partners in shared decision making. That, too, is an only partially kept promise, as we will discuss throughout this chapter and as Sally Wade has pointed out.

Indeed, routinized family participation became the norm; whether the new parent-participation provisions of the reauthorized IDEA will change that result is open to question. Clearly, however, authentic collaboration of the type we hope you will practice has been the exception to the norm. You can take action to change the routinized norm, as we suggest later in the chapter and as we demonstrate throughout this book.

Restructuring Placement

The second phase of special education reform was less concerned with providing free, appropriate public education to students than with assuring more inclusive placements for them, that is, greater and more meaningful access to the general curriculum (academic, extracurricular, and other school activities). There have been two major efforts aimed at restructuring placement of students with disabilities: the Regular Education Initiative and the current emphasis on inclusion. Both efforts rest on IDEA's least restrictive environment principle and are motivated by educators and parents who have been dissatisfied with the slow implementation of that principle.

The Regular Education Initiative (REI) was led by Madeleine Will, then assistant secretary of education and director of the U.S. Office of Special Education and Rehabilitative Services. Her son has a cognitive disability. She and the educators and families who supported her position believed that the linchpin for improving the educational outcomes for students with disabilities was to merge special and general education into a unified system and dismantle their separateness.

Although this effort was referred to as the Regular Education Initiative, it really was a special education initiative. Many special educators joined Will in seeking to merge much of regular and general education (Jenkins, Pious, & Peterson, 1988; Pugach & Lilly, 1984; Wang, Reynolds, & Wahlberg, 1986). But many other special educators—particularly those primarily associated with learning disabilities, emotional disabilities, and hearing impairment—raised serious concerns about it, as did many general educators (Hallahan, Keller, McKinney, Lloyd, & Bryan, 1988; Kauffman, Gerber, & Semmel, 1988; Schumaker & Deshler, 1987).

Throughout the REI debate, the major emphasis was on creating instructional flexibility and adaptation within general education classrooms for students with mild disabilities. This reform effort was professionally dominated. There was limited concerted effort to form family-professional partnerships to advance the REI, and family-professional collaboration took a back seat to the REI debate over placement. Indeed, while attention was directed to the REI, routinized implementation of IDEA's principles for nondiscriminatory evaluation and appropriate education persisted, and paperwork compliance was the norm. Remember what Sally has said about paperwork. That it is evidence that the schools are compliance-bound but primarily in the sense of being concerned that they will not be sued, not in the sense that their compliance will assure an appropriate education. Not all schools and educators can be criticized for that kind of compliance, but some surely can be.

Undergirding the REI was a concern about outcomes for special education students. This concern escalated when, in 1991, the National Longitudinal Study reported the following (Wagner et al., 1991):

- Approximately one-third of all special education students (from a sample of 6,000 students with disabilities ranging in age from 13 to 21) were failing one or more classes.

- Of the students who were failing, approximately one-fifth were failing in six or more classes.

- Less than one-half of the special education graduates were fully employed after leaving high school.

- Approximately one-fifth of youth with serious emotional disorders were arrested.

Additional bleak news about student outcomes focused particularly on students with emotional and behavioral disorders. Approximately one-third of all students with disabilities were receiving failing grades, but 44 percent of students with serious emotional disorders were receiving failing grades. Additionally, compared to a 71 percent graduation rate for students without disabilities and a 54 percent graduation rate for students with disabilities, students with emotional and behavioral disorders have a 36 percent graduation rate (Koyanagi & Gaines, 1993).

This report gave credence to the post-REI reformers—inclusion advocates—who had become impatient with the REI, especially as it related to students with severe disabilities. Many professionals working within the area of severe disability long have had a strong philosophical orientation toward placement in least restrictive settings. They focused on changing classroom instruction for the benefit of all students and on comprehensive school restructuring of all policies and procedures. They also emphasized creating a dialogue with general education. The inclusion movement, started in the early 1990s, incorporated the following principles (Sailor, 1991; Turnbull, Turnbull, Shank, & Leal, 1999):

- All students receive education in the school they would attend if they had no disability.
- A natural proportion (that is, representative of the school district at large) of students with disabilities occurs at each school site.
- A zero-reject philosophy exists so that typically no student will be excluded on the basis of type or extent of disability.
- School placements are age- and grade-appropriate so that no self-contained special education classes will exist.
- Special education supports exist within the general education class and in other integrated environments.

Recently, reformers have emphasized creating an inclusive culture that builds on the strengths and supports the needs of all students (Sailor, in press). Figure 2–5 describes the expectations for a merger of school reform and inclusion as articulated by Pugach (1995), a leading advocate of this two-pronged approach.

Although parents may have strong opinions about inclusion (both pro and con, as we will discuss in chapter 8), the inclusion reform effort has focused more on two-way special and general education collaboration than on creating three-way general education/special education/family collaboration. Because of the overwhelming task of merging separate educational systems while also making accommodations for appropriate (beneficial) placements in inclusive settings, family-professional collaboration again has not been a high priority in special education reform. That is not to say, however, that it has been ignored or that three-way

collaboration cannot occur among general education, special education, and families—as we will show you throughout this book.

Nature of Family-Professional Collaboration with Special Education

Within the special education field, family-professional collaboration has had different models at the early intervention/early childhood stage and at the elementary and secondary school stage.

Early Intervention and Early Childhood Stage

Using the Epstein model of the six types of parent participation, family-professional collaboration within early intervention/early childhood special education closely parallels all six partnership types as described in figure 2–3. There is extensive literature favoring family-centered practices during the early years. This family-centered emphasis represents a philosophical shift:

> The term *parent involvement* sums up the current perspective. It means we want parents involved with us. It means the service delivery system we helped create is at the center of the universe, and families are revolving around it. It brings to mind an analogy about the old Polemic view of the universe with the earth at the center. . . . Copernicus came along and made a startling reversal—he put the sun in the center of the universe rather than the Earth. His declaration caused profound shock. The earth was not the epitome of creation; it was a planet like all other planets. The successful challenge to the entire system of ancient authority required a complete change in philosophical conception of the universe. This is rightly termed the "Copernican Revolution." Let's pause to consider what would happen if we had a Copernican Revolution in the field of disability. Visualize the concept: The family is the center of the universe and the service delivery system is one of the many planets revolving around it. Now visualize the service delivery system at the center and the family in orbit around it. Do you see the difference? Do you recognize the revolutionary change in perspective? We would move from an emphasis on parent involvement (i.e., parents participating in the program) to family support (i.e., programs providing a range of support services to families). This is not a semantic exercise—such a revolution leads us to a new set of assumptions and a new vista of options for service. (Turnbull & Summers, 1987, pp. 295–296)

According to the extensive literature on family-centered practices, four major characteristics tend to define practices as family-centered (Allen & Petr, 1996; Bailey,

FIGURE 2–5

Expectation for a Merger of Inclusion and School Reform

Expectation 1: School-wide reform includes inclusion. "A school would not have an inclusion program alone as evidence of reform. The move toward inclusion would be part of a dynamic effort to rethink what it means to educate all children, an effort rich with coordinated curriculum and instructional and social reform. Our observers 10 years hence would need to look how the full context for reform supports inclusion."

Expectation 2: Teacher renewal is an acknowledged and prominent goal of the partnerships formed between special and general education teachers. "Through collaborative action research projects, special and general education teachers could work together as equal partners toward implementing curricular and instructional change (Pugach & Johnson, 1990). . . . A coordinated agenda would drive the partnership with students *and* teacher growth both as focal points of their work. More than anything, such teachers would be interested in new frameworks for teaching and learning, so that when promising approaches they cannot yet imagine are developed, they are eager to try them out. At the same time, they would be wary of each successive bandwagon, measuring new approaches against their philosophical orientation to teaching."

Expectation 3: Intensive student needs are important. "But in the next generation of inclusive classrooms, a flexible approach to grouping that enables teachers to meet with students who need remediation as well as those who need enrichment needs to be in place (Pugach & Wesson, 1995). . . . Group membership would depend upon the project assignment or task, and as part of their regular planning, teachers would reflect on whether they are flexible in the expectations they hold for their students. . . . By monitoring their own attitudes, teachers can push the limits of what they expect from their students."

Expectation 4: What counts as "special" may not always stand out. These classrooms offer something special, then, because "they provide a context in which students are given a real opportunity to discard their labels of disability and teachers are given the opportunity to create classrooms where such labels do not drive practice. They exemplify new sets of beliefs about who does and does not belong and incorporate sound methodologies to enact those beliefs."

Source: Pugach, M. C. (1995). On the failure of imagination in inclusive schools. *Journal of Special Education, 29,* 219–229. Copyright 1995 by Pro-Ed. Reprinted with permission.

Buysse, Edmondson, & Smith, 1992; Beckman, Robinson, Rosenberg, & Filer, 1994; Dunst, Johnson, Trivette, & Hamby, 1991; Roberts, Rule, & Innocenti, 1998; Shelton, Jeppson, & Johnson, 1989). These practices generally:

> (a) include families in decision making, planning, assessment, and service delivery at family, agency, and system levels; (b) develop services for the whole family and not just the child; (c) are guided by families' priorities for goals and services; and (d) offer and respect families' choices regarding the level of their participation. (Murphy, Lee, Turnbull, & Turbiville, 1995, p. 25)

A family-centered approach was incorporated into 1986 amendments to IDEA and is still part of IDEA. IDEA requires professionals who serve children with disabilities from birth to age 3 to collaborate with the child's family to develop an IFSP that assures services for the family and the child alike. One of the requirements for the IFSP is to document the family's resources, priorities, and concerns related to the child's development, and to provide the family with services, consistent with members' preferences, so the family can increase its capacity to meet the child's special needs.

When a student becomes 3 years old, the early intervention services end and two new types of services begin. During the ages of 3, 4, and 5, the student receives early childhood special education. During the ages of 6 through 21, the student receives special education.

Similarly, the name and nature of the student's individualized plan change when the student achieves certain ages. During the ages of birth through 2, the student and family have an IFSP. During the ages of 3 through 21, the student, but not the family, has an IEP. (In recognition of the fact that families and young children benefit from a family-centered approach, IDEA now provides that the child's IFSP—modified as appropriate—will become the IEP if the school and family agree; the IFSP may serve as the child's IEP until the child becomes 6 years old.)

Under the IFSP and in model early intervention programs, both the student and the family receive services. By contrast, under the IEP and in typical special education services (ages 3 through 21), the student is the primary focus of services; the family may receive only some related services such as parent counseling and training (to help the parents understand their child's special needs), school social work services (group or individual counseling), school psychology services, or school health services (psychological counseling for the parents and child).

So the name of the individualized plan differs (IFSP or IEP), and the services under each (family and student jointly, or student primarily and family secondarily) change with the student's age and transition from early intervention to early childhood special education.

With these two changes, there also is a challenge for families. So many families become accustomed to having family-centered services to a greater degree during early intervention programs that they experience a form of education culture shock when their children enter early childhood special education or elementary school.

This is because the services in those programs focus on the student, not the family. More than that, the professionals in first-class early intervention/IFSP programs typically have received more training in family-centered service delivery, are more able to work with the family, and are indeed acculturated to doing just that (Romer & Umbreit, 1998). By contrast, the professionals in early childhood education (ages 3 to 5) and beyond (ages 6 through 21) often lack the training, the skills, and the professional acculturation to work with families as effectively or willingly as early intervention specialists (Kalyanpur & Harry, 1999; Lovitt & Cushing, 1999).

Despite IDEA's provisions and many promising practices for family-centered services, research continues to underscore professional dominance in decision making and child rather than family orientation. Staff often use a standard format for communicating with families in IFSP and IEP meetings and assume that they know parents'

needs and preferences and do not need to communicate with them directly (Minke, 1991). This may be the case because, although many professionals report that they understand the importance of a family-centered approach and the legal requirements for serving families, they regard their services as primarily child-oriented (Hammond, 1999; Katz & Scarpati, 1995; McBride, Brotherson, Joanning, Whiddon, & Demmit, 1993). That certainly is the point that Sally Wade makes in the vignette.

Elementary, Middle, and Secondary School Stage What partnership types are most prevalent in elementary, middle, and secondary schools? How does family-professional collaboration in special education at the elementary, middle, and secondary school levels compare and contrast with the Epstein partnership model?

Families helped to answer these questions by testifying before the National Council on Disability, an independent federal advisory agency, as it conducted hearings in 10 regions throughout the United States during the fall of 1994. The overwhelming testimony from families was that IDEA should be fine-tuned and its implementation improved (National Council on Disability, 1995). Based on our synthesis of the professional literature and our work with families locally and nationally, we believe that a useful way to think about family perspectives (albeit overly simplistic) is to regard families as falling on a continuum, as illustrated in figure 2–6.

At one end of this continuum are families who have a high participation rate. These families are assertive, knowledgeable, and empowered. They invest tremendous time and energy in attempting to get an appropriate education for their son or daughter. Typically, they are frustrated with the school system and believe that the provision of a free, appropriate public education requires them to be eternally vigilant.

In the middle range are families who generally participate by passively taking advantage of IDEA's benefits for their child and themselves (nondiscriminatory evalu-

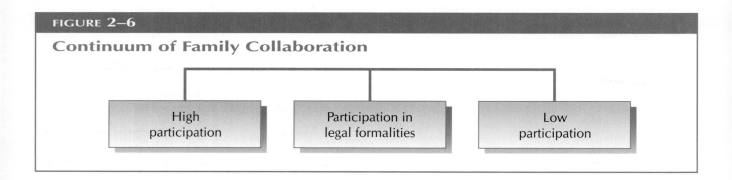

FIGURE 2–6

Continuum of Family Collaboration

| High participation | Participation in legal formalities | Low participation |

ation and IFSP/IEP development) but who do not have a lot of knowledge about the nature of their child's program and the outcomes that their child is achieving. Typically, these families are satisfied with their child's program.

At the other end of the continuum are families whose participation is at a low level. Typically, these families feel disenfranchised by the system and rarely participate in any meaningful way. Often they feel intimidated, angry, and devalued and perceive that their child is receiving an inferior education. (Just as family participation falls on a continuum, so does the participation of professionals. Additionally, remember that the same family and professional can move back and forth on the continuum at different times and under different circumstances, depending on the issues that are being addressed and the willingness of individuals in the context to encourage collaboration.)

The following testimony at the National Council on Disability hearings was most likely provided by families on the high-participation end of the continuum:

> I have come to call myself Bonnie, the bitch, because of what I've had to become to fight the system for the handicapped child, and yet I have contacted multiple state offices. I have followed through with every lead that anybody has ever given me. I have talked with the Governor's office here in the state. I've gone so far as to call the White House. . . . I guess my feeling at this point is, "Is there anybody out there who really cares?" I don't know what more to do. I, as a parent, have pursued every option. (testimony by Bonnie Weninger, in National Council on Disability, 1995, p. 123)

> Special education is sometimes perceived as being a kind of white middle class issue. I just want to point out and underscore what a number of parents here said tonight. The kind of resources it takes for a family to get appropriate programs and services is so totally overwhelming in terms of time, energy, money, and skills, that it's really not surprising that the people who tend to be the most visible are the parents with the most resources. (testimony by Diane Lipton, in National Council on Disability, 1995, pp. 34–35)

> We really need to put the responsibility again on the educators and not make all the parents professionals, because parents also have jobs, and the amount of time, energy, emotions that every parent . . . has put into the education of our children's special needs [is] just tremendous. It shouldn't be that way. We really need to distribute that kind of energy more evenly. It's very frustrating. (testimony by Birgit Schweingruber, in National Council on Disability, 1995, p. 108)

There are, of course, parents and other family members who are in the middle of the continuum (Bennett,

Lee, & Lueke, 1998; Hilton & Henderson, 1993; Lovitt & Cushing, 1999). A study of 21 parents of elementary students reported a rather high level of satisfaction with special education (Green & Shinn, 1994). Each of the students in this study had been identified as having a learning disability and received services in a resource room for less than half the school day.

- Parents rated their satisfaction with special education, giving a mean rating of 4.8 on a scale of 5.0.
- The majority of parents emphasized that getting extra help and attention was the primary benefit of special education.
- A majority also endorsed the positive characteristics of special education teachers, such as "warm, caring person" and "immense patience" (Green & Shinn, 1994, p. 274).
- Ninety percent of the parents reported that they had seen positive changes in their child since receiving resource room services, with 75 percent of the comments emphasizing changes related to self-esteem or an improved school attitude; for example, "she looks forward to school now and thinks more of herself" and "he feels good about himself" (Green & Shinn, 1994, p. 275).
- Only two parents made reference to their child's improved academic skills.

The researchers concluded that the parents' perceptions of progress and satisfaction were not necessarily related to the students' academic performance or gain. Parents did report that they would appreciate having more objective information about their child's performance and about their child's standing as compared to other students in the general education program. Almost three-quarters of the parents indicated that school personnel had not discussed ultimate goals or exit criteria with them when the child was initially placed in special education. The authors concluded:

> This outcome is the proverbial "good news-bad news" situation. . . . "good news" for local schools and the special education community is that parents report liking what special educators do and what they think they do. . . . The "bad news" is that parental satisfaction with the services provided to their children may not be related to their children's academic performance. Simply stated, improved achieved outcomes were not the basis for parent satisfaction in this sample. (Green & Shinn, 1994, p. 278)

A third group of parents, representing the right side of the continuum, apparently feels disenfranchised by the school system; consequently, their participation is low. The seminal work of Beth Harry, Maya Kalyanpur, and their colleagues speaks poignantly and with disturbing candor about the conflicts that exist for many parents who perceive their disenfranchisement from the special education system, particularly those from culturally diverse backgrounds (Harry, Kalyanpur, & Day, 1999; Kalyanpur & Harry, 1999). A Puerto Rican mother said:

> It is only their opinions that matter. If I do not want the child in a special class or if I want her in a different school, they will still do what they want. Because that is what I tried to do, and Vera [the social worker] talked with them too and tried to help me, but—no! Our opinions are not valued. Many parents do not want their child in a special class or in a school so far away, but they keep quiet. It is very hard to struggle with these Americans. In America, the schools are for Americans. (Harry, 1992b, p. 486)

The paperwork associated with special education can be overwhelming for many of these same parents:

> So many papers! I have a lot of work to do—in the mornings I do my work and then in the afternoon I take care of my mother and do her groceries and wash her clothes. I have a lot of boxes with a lot of papers and I told my husband I would throw them away and he said, "No, no!" So I took them to the LAA [Latin American Association] and gave them to them. I can't stand having so many papers! (Harry, 1992b, p. 482)

Harry describes the factors contributing to the disenfranchisement of parents from culturally and linguistically diverse backgrounds:

> The combination of the "direct," informal manner of American professionals, with their assumptions of the validity of detached, scientific information (Wright et al., 1983), can be alienating rather than reassuring for people accustomed to a slower pace, more personal yet more generalized approach. . . . The bureaucratic structure of schools, and, certainly of the special education system, with its formal procedures and systems, presents people from such cultures with a formidable challenge. When these systems are implemented without regard for the need for personalized information, and, as has been emphasized earlier, without opportunity for dialogue, the result is often confusion and alienation on the part of parents and increasing impatience on the part of professionals. When they are implemented in a vein of compliance rather than communication the results can be disastrous (Harry, 1992b). (Harry & Kalyanpur, 1994, p. 160)

If we relate the testimony and research data to the Epstein model, we learn that the special education em-

phasis has been on type 2 (communicating) and type 5 (decision making). One difference with respect to decision making, as Epstein describes it for general education, is that special education decision making has primarily concentrated on advocacy for the student, not on advocacy at the systems level (participation in school-based councils, PTAs, and other school-improvement efforts). Indeed, as Sally Wade has noted, she and Rodney were singularly uninvolved in their neighborhood school because their children were placed in a different school—a place where there was a critical mass of students with similar disabilities and, thus, a more cost-efficient place to benefit them. The trade-off between, on the one hand, having their children enrolled in the neighborhood school's mainstream and thereby having a social life with their peers and, on the other, of being given intensive education and learning to read was an uncomfortable decision for Sally and Rodney to make. "I think (Rachel) missed a lot in our community . . . you get to know people who live in your area by going to school with them. (Rachel and Wakefield) missed that part of things. Once (she) went to junior high school and was with her peers and caught the bus with the neighborhood and all that, I became aware of the social cost of not walking down to that bus with your friends, you know, with the neighborhood kids. Not having that and how important that is." There was another cost, too: Sally's and Rodney's uninvolvement in, and indeed their not caring about, the parent-teacher activities in the neighborhood school.

The two additional types of partnerships that have primarily dominated the time and energy of parents whose children are in special education are evaluating for special education (chapter 11) and individualizing for appropriate education and placement (chapter 12). These two types of partnerships are not included in the Epstein model for general education. They represent the most unique aspects of special education family-professional partnerships, as contrasted to general education partnerships.

Unified Systems Reform

Having reviewed the general and special education reform phases and observed that they have operated independently of each other, let's now consider a reform that is powerfully affecting today's schools. It seeks school restructuring and deliberately brings general and special education together. McLaughlin (1998), a leader within this contemporary school reform movement, refers to it as *unified systems reform*. She states:

> A unified system centers around the core set of student outcomes or standards which define the goals for the system. There is also a means for assessing student progress toward those outcomes. The curriculum and instruction are aligned with the standards and outcomes and the entire core supported by a system of policies and programs which guide professional preparation and development and the allocation of resources. Over the entire system is public accountability for each student's learning.
>
> A unified system accommodates and supports diverse learners without unnecessary categorization of students or program resources. The system values flexibility and collaboration at all levels in order to promote student attainment of the goals. (McLaughlin, 1998, p. 21)

This reform movement goes by a number of other names, including *standards-based reform* and *results-based accountability* (Erickson, 1998; Kleinhammer-Tramill & Gallagher, in press). In Florida, as Sally tells us, it is also called *high stakes assessment*.

The separate reform movements in general education and in special education converged in 1994 when Congress enacted Goals 2000: Educate America Act (Kleinhammer-Tramill & Gallagher, in press; Riley, 1995; Smith & Scoll, 1995). The Goals 2000 legislation seeks simultaneously to incorporate top-down and bottom-up education reform to accomplish eight national education goals, which are described in figure 2–7.

Notable aspects of this school restructuring effort are its emphasis on (1) improving and assessing student outcomes and (2) encouraging site-based management as a strategy of restructuring school governance. In figure 2–8, we show how the phases of the general education reform movement (the left-hand column) and the phases of the special education reform movement (the right-hand column) have merged into the unified systems reform phase (bottom).

Improving Student Outcomes

Goals 2000 calls for states to establish standards for all students and to assess students' progress toward meeting those standards (Erickson, 1998; McLaughlin, 1998). Florida responded with its high stakes assessments of students and schools; for Rachel, Wakefield, and Josh Wade and for their schools, the issue is now, very clearly, outcomes. Unlike previous general education reform efforts, which excluded from consideration students with exceptionalities, Goals 2000 specifically includes all students. The Senate committee that recommended Goals 2000 noted, "In far too many districts around the country, two separate educational systems have developed with little or no coordination—one system for regular or general education and one separate and distinct system for special education." Accordingly, Goals 2000 should serve as a vehicle for making the promise of IDEA a reality for students with disabilities, and those students, therefore, must be an integral part of all aspects of education reform and entitled to the same high expectations, treatment, and leadership offered to their nondisabled peers (Sen. Report 103-85, 103rd Congress, 1st Session).

Tom Hehir (1994), the former head of the federal Office of Special Education Programs, the U.S. Department of Education, emphasized the importance of setting higher expectations for students with exceptionalities, providing them with access to the general education curriculum consistent with the content standards, and ensuring reasonable accommodations are in place for them to participate in local and state assessments. A special

---

FIGURE 2–7

The National Educational Goals

By the year 2000:

- All children ready to learn
- 90 percent graduation rate
- All children competent in core subjects
- First in the world in math and science

- Every adult literate and able to compete in the workforce
- Safe, disciplined, drug-free schools
- Professional development for educators
- Increased parental involvement in learning

FIGURE 2–8

Phases of General and Special Education School Reform

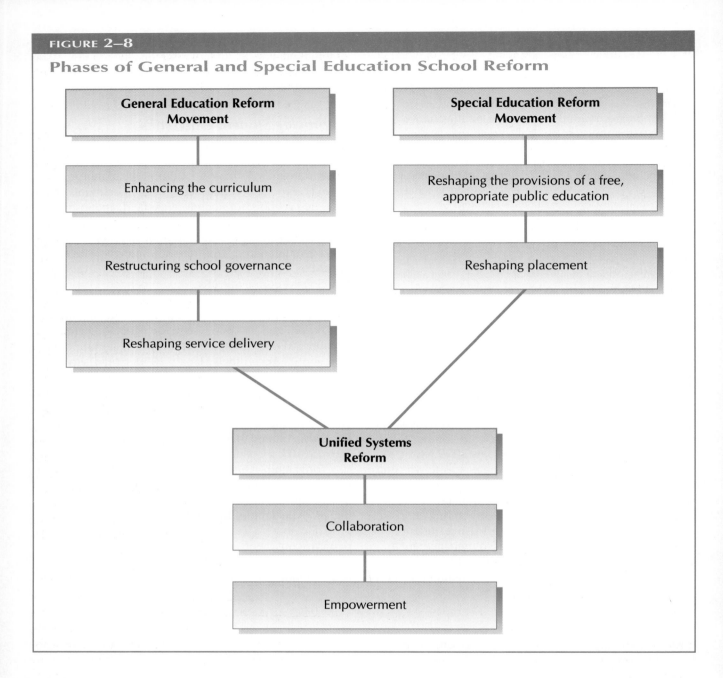

committee of the National Academy of Sciences studied the impact of standards-based reform on the education of students with disabilities and made recommendations based on the following two principles:

- All students should have access to challenging standards.
- Policymakers and educators should be held publicly accountable for every student's performance (McDonnell et al., 1999, p. 9).

In Florida, access to the general curriculum is problematic, and accountability has posed problems, at least for the Wade children. Rachel had very little access to the general curriculum, and Wakefield has very little, too. For the schools, it was "cost effective" to cluster students like Rachel and Wakefield into separate self-contained, non-neighborhood programs; and with that clustering came not only isolation from neighborhood peers but also isolation within the schools that they did attend. For example, despite the fact that Rachel has a magnificent voice, she was never invited to compete for the school choir; indeed, *none* of her peers in the "LD" program were invited to compete. The music faculty just considered them "special . . . needing help, needy" and incapable of singing well. It is as though they were "invisible." And outcomes are just as problematic. To graduate, the student must be able to read on a high-school level. That poses a challenge for Wakefield. To date, Florida has not decided what accommodations it will make for students like him; and Sally and Rodney simply will not accept a special education diploma for their boy. They see college in the future, and colleges do not accept students with special education diplomas.

Encouraging Site-Based Management

A second major characteristic of the current school restructuring movement is site-based management (McLaughlin, 1998; Sailor, in press). This management approach gives increasing autonomy and flexibility to schools so they may use local problem solving and innovation and thus involve all stakeholders—families, students, educators, and community citizens. Site-based management allows state and local educational agencies a great deal of flexibility in how they choose to meet those standards. Indeed, Congress enacted the Education Flexibility Partnership Act of 1999 (P.L. 106-25) to allow states (with approval of the U.S. secretary of education) to waive (not be bound by) some provisions of other federal education laws. Significantly, the "ed-flex" law does not exempt states from any of the requirements under IDEA. The Government Accounting Office (1994) reported that site-based management has led to more innovation and school practices; alternatively, other research has pointed out that site-based management has basically maintained the status quo (Wholstetter & Odden, 1992).

As we will discuss more in chapter 15, research conducted by Sally Wade (1994) pointed to the fact that the site-based management teams were not making important decisions and that the needs of students with disabilities were not a major concern of the team. Advocacy for students with disabilities appears to be a continuing need as the general and special education school reform movements seek to converge (McLaughlin, 1998; Wade, 1994).

Convergence of General and Special Education Model of Family-Professional Collaboration

Instead of "your family in general education/my family in special education," a unified conceptualization—

"our students/our families, typical and exceptional"— emerges in unified school reform. Do you remember what Sally has said about her children's and her alienation from the social life of school, especially the neighborhood school? If so, you understand the meaning of "our."

For all of these changes to happen, educators need to combine the empirical knowledge base and experiential lessons of general education with the special education family-professional collaboration models. Our suggestion of the most appropriate convergence is set out in figure 2–9.

The figure includes seven opportunities for family-professional partnerships and eight obligations for reliable alliances. Let us explain why we used the terms *opportunities* and *obligations*. On the left-hand side of figure 2–9, we list the most frequent ways in which parents and educators can collaborate with each other. These ways of collaborating represent what we are calling *opportunities for partnerships*—opportunities are *what* educators and families do that enhances the likelihood of positive outcomes. As you have learned in this chapter, three of those ways arise directly from IDEA: (a) referring and evaluating for special education (the principle of nondiscriminatory evaluation), (b) individualizing for appropriate education (the principle of appropriate education), and (c) advocating for systems improvements (the principles of due process and parent participation). As we have pointed out, the other ways reflect good professional practices that have been occurring in general education. If these are the ways in which parents and educators typically can collaborate with each other, we think they are "opportunities" for partnerships.

On the right-hand side of figure 2–9, we list the relationship aspects of partnerships—we call these relationship aspects *obligations for reliable alliances*. Rather than focusing on *what* families and professionals do together, as reflected in the opportunities for partnerships, the obligations for reliable alliances emphasize *how* the relationship is carried out. Some of these obligations are explicitly referred to by IDEA, including "knowing families" (within the IFSP process), honoring their cultural diversity (within the nondiscriminatory evaluation process and within the IFSP and IEP development process), and affirming family strengths and promoting family choices (within the IFSP, IEP, and parent participation principles and processes). Others reflect the essence of human relationships that seem to make those relationships flourish. That is why we refer to them as *obligations*— requirements that can create reliable alliances among professionals and families.

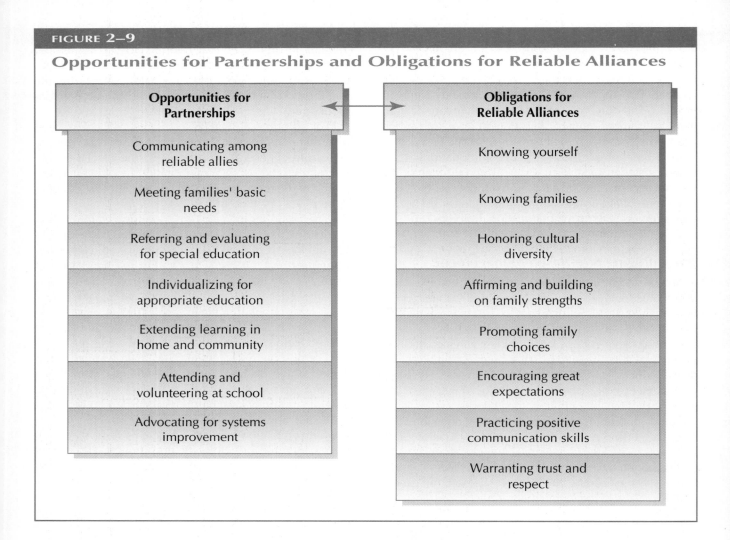

FIGURE 2—9

Opportunities for Partnerships and Obligations for Reliable Alliances

Opportunities for Partnerships

- Communicating among reliable allies
- Meeting families' basic needs
- Referring and evaluating for special education
- Individualizing for appropriate education
- Extending learning in home and community
- Attending and volunteering at school
- Advocating for systems improvement

Obligations for Reliable Alliances

- Knowing yourself
- Knowing families
- Honoring cultural diversity
- Affirming and building on family strengths
- Promoting family choices
- Encouraging great expectations
- Practicing positive communication skills
- Warranting trust and respect

In identifying these seven opportunities for partnerships (depicted in the left-hand column), we relied on five of the partnership types specified by Epstein (see figure 2–3) and merged her final type—collaborating with community—into all other opportunities; it is not a separate opportunity in our framework. Thus, instead of the six types from the Epstein model, there are five. These five are then combined with two additional opportunities that are unique to special education—evaluating for special education and individualizing for appropriate education—for a total of seven partnership opportunities.

If any of these opportunities is missing in the programs you develop for family collaboration, you should consider adding them and bringing all of these opportu-

nities together into a comprehensive program in which the whole is likely to be greater than the sum of the parts. If you do this, you probably will see increased benefit for all stakeholders because you will be offering a broad array of family-professional collaborative opportunities.

Depicted in the right-hand column of figure 2–9 are the components of a reliable alliance. Research and experience over the last 20 years in special education show that professionals and families need to create reliable alliances rather than hierarchical relationships as they carry out all seven opportunities to be partners with families. That certainly is the import of the testimony given to National Council on Disability (1995). And it is consistent with the findings of fact that Congress set out in the reauthorized IDEA: education of children with disabilities "can be made more effective by strengthening the role of parents and ensuring that families of such children have meaningful opportunities to participate in the education of their children at school and at home" (IDEA, 1997, 20 U.S.C. Sec. 1400 (c)(5)(A)). Yet transforming the hierarchical imbalance is essential—it becomes an obligation—if students, families, and professionals are to collaborate and consequently experience greater empowerment.

An alternative to professional hierarchies is becoming a reliable ally of families. What is a reliable alliance? What does it mean to be a reliable ally? Consider the people in your life on whom you depend for nonjudgmental, unconditional, and ever-available support. You know that you can turn to them in good times and bad to get the support that you need. They probably make you feel better about yourself, provide support and information to you within the context of a personal relationship, and therefore strengthen your belief in yourself. This is the essence of a reliable ally for all people.

A survey of families and professionals, not limited to those in special education, underscored what professionals think that parents want from them and what parents actually want:

> In a classic example of misunderstood cues, the reported preferences of parents are not what school personnel think they are. School personnel passionately believe that a professional, businesslike manner will win the respect and support of parents. The response of parents to questions about their contacts with the school revealed that they view "professionalism" on the part of teachers, school psychologists, guidance counselors, or principals as undesirable. Parents mention their dissatisfaction with school people who are too businesslike, patronizing, or who talk down to us. . . . Parents reported a "personal touch" as the most enhancing factor in school relations. (Lindle, 1989, p. 13)

A parent whose child was receiving home-based early intervention services described the personal touch:

> At first, I was tense with a professional coming to my home. But it was a nice little conversation. The professional's mannerism and the way she asked questions was like we were sitting down for a cup of coffee. She got a lot of information without asking. (Summers et al., 1990, p. 87)

Standards-based reform now more than ever before creates an obligation for educators and families to become reliable allies for each other. We believe that, as a professional, you have certain obligations to build reliable alliances with families across all seven opportunities for partnerships. We will discuss those obligations in detail in chapter 4, but for now just note that they are incorporated into the right-hand column of figure 2–9.

For you to make this shift from hierarchical interactions to reliable alliances in your partnerships with families, you should be insightful about the use and misuse of power. There are many forms of power, and as you read about them, you should ask yourself which of these might enhance or impede your teaching of students and your collaborating with families. Zipperlen and O'Brien (1994), list the types of power:

- *Power-over* other people arises from the ability and willingness to make decisions for others and to enforce their compliance by authoritative control of rewards and punishments.

- *Power-with* other people arises from people's ability and willingness to listen to and be influenced by another's perceptions and suggestions and to offer their perceptions and suggestions in turn. Power-with requires the kind of respect that grows with the willingness to be personally involved with one another and to share by choice in a common project that will shape and shift patterns of relationships among people. Differences provide information and the occasion to clarify and strengthen relationships by negotiating creatively. Because power-with depends on and reinforces cooperation, its exercise depends on people's mutual restraint and willingness to learn from their experience together.

- *Power-from-within* arises from a person's willingness and ability to discover and creatively express the abilities and concerns that they find spiritually meaningful. . . . Power-from-within gives a person courage to act when important values are threatened, even if the short-term prospects for success are poor. . . . People acting on the basis of power-from-within need to exercise personal discipline to sharpen their discernment of what ultimately matters to them and to strengthen their abilities to creatively express what matters to them in everyday life with other people.

One of the major goals of site-based management is to abandon power-over roles and to develop collaborative relationships among all stakeholders, including families and professionals. These relationships will be characterized by power-with, so that the end result for all participants in the relationships will be a power-from-within approach. Because moving from a power-over approach to a power-with and a power-from-within one requires a major system-wide shift in how many schools operate and, indeed, in the perspectives that educators and families hold of each other (remember Sally Wade's words: "It's not much trust on each side"), we need to identify a major barrier to new collaborations.

For you to be successful in developing a reliable alliance with families—establishing power-with and power-from-within relationships—you have to confront a hard fact: Traditional school organization has entrenched power-over structures and procedures. These power-over approaches are characterized by standard routines, which are often highly superficial, for meeting the IDEA mandates. (For example, one of the reasons Rachel Wade's school gave for not allowing her greater access to the general curriculum was that it would disrupt the class scheduling that it had developed for her. We have already given some examples, and we will continue to do so throughout the book.) Your ability to provide families with a range of opportunities for partnerships and your obligations to form reliable alliances (see figure 2–9) will be influenced by the willingness of the school district to participate in school restructuring. In doing so, the school will move away from the traditional bureaucratic compartmentalization of each professional's role and adopt a dynamic and flexible organization for bringing teams together to address mutual problems and devise creative solutions (Berres, Ferguson, Knoblock, & Woods, 1996; Sailor, in press; Skrtic, 1995).

As you interview for jobs and select the school system where you will work, or as your present school system employer considers restructuring, explore the extent to which the system provides the seven opportunities for family-professional partnerships and undertakes the eight obligations of reliable alliances. The more you have the opportunity to work in an empowering organization characterized by flexibility, fluidity, and decentralized management, the more you will have your own reliable allies to support you in your quests to establish reliable alliances with families. When you find yourself working in bureaucratic (power-over) organizations, you can and should commit yourself to working collaboratively, to the extent possible, with administrators, teachers, families, and others. After all, finding and creating those reliable alliances, while difficult in power-over structures, is a necessary step in transforming those structures. More than a necessary step in contemporary school restructuring, it is a necessary step in empowerment, which we define and demonstrate in chapter 3.

Summary

Parents play a new role in today's schools—as collaborators with professionals. That role has emerged from and, indeed, furthers the reforms that general and special education have experienced.

In general education, the reforms consist of enhancing the curriculum, restructuring school governance, and reshaping service delivery systems. In special education, the reforms consist of assuring that each student with a disability has access to a free, appropriate education (access is guaranteed by their legal rights based on six principles of the Individuals with Disabilities Education Act) and restructuring the placement through the Regular Education Initiative and the inclusion initiative.

Collaboration between families and professionals is a powerful technique for carrying out the general and special education reforms. Collaboration can and should occur at all stages of a student's school career and is consistent with contemporary school-restructuring activities.

Those restructuring activities are based on eight national educational goals agreed on by the governors in 1989 and enacted by Congress as the heart of its 1994 Goals 2000 law.

As restructuring has occurred, general and special educators have been provided a chance to collaborate with parents of children in all school programs—general and special alike. Indeed, there are seven opportunities for family-professional partnerships—seven normally occurring activities within which collaboration can and should be the norm. Additionally, there are eight obligations for reliable alliances that can be infused into every partnership opportunity.

The bottom line for educators in today's schools is simply this: to move from relationships with families in which professionals have power over families to relationships with families in which professionals and families have power with each other and in which power from within the relationships is naturally occurring and beneficial to professionals and families alike.

Every teacher and every parent has "horror stories" to tell—stories about how "bad" some parents and some teachers have been. That's Sally Wade's assessment. But, for every horror story she hears, she can "top it" with one of her own. And for her, horror stories are utterly profitless; they don't take us forward. What does? "Lack of blaming each other." That's a negative, albeit a valuable one. What about some positive steps? Here are the words and phrases that come easily to Sally: "Communicate. Forgive. Be honest. Be un-derstanding. Be open. Don't question my high aspirations for my children. Don't expect me to have lower expecta-tions for them. Stop spelling 'school reform' with eight let-ters: politics. Recognize that parents and schools have to make hard trade-offs. Try to reduce the number of trade-offs they have made by changing school financing, assess-ment methods, and philosophies." OK, she didn't use the term "reliable allies." But that's what she's getting at. That, and a different way of administering our schools.

Chapter Three

Empowerment

In south-central Los Angeles there is a woman who lives the "African American experience," but with a difference. Theresa Cooper is the mother of Eric, an 11-year-old boy who has a disability, a serious auditory processing problem. Theresa also is the director of Loving Your Disabled Child (LYDC), a successful nonprofit family support group that itself is 11 years old.

LYDC is housed on the first floor of a modest church in the center of one of Los Angeles' "ghettos." It is a community center where parents can get support, training, and information; and it is funded with federal and state money. Its location tells a great deal about LYDC and about Theresa, and its funding reveals a lot, too. LYDC straddles several worlds—one that is grounded in a religious ministry, another that is based in the secular world, and a third that is family and disability related.

How do these worlds merge, and what differences do the mergers make? Theresa says that being Eric's parent gives her "such a compassion and such a will to help other families beat the system and make it." In a word, Theresa "connects"; in a different way of looking at it, she is empowered and is empowering.

That connecting skill is a product of Theresa's youth. When her mother died, Theresa was only 10. For a while, she lived with her father, a workaholic who, out of frustration and stress, physically abused both Theresa and her 4 siblings. When one day her baby sister was taken away from school in a police car because her teacher had discovered that she had been physi-

cally abused, Theresa learned how to get out of the house: provide evidence of her own abuse. More than that, she learned how to convert a bad situation into a good one. So when she was 12 and had suffered an especially bad beating, she turned to child protective services and soon was placed with her relatives, who then raised her.

When Eric was born, Theresa volunteered for LYDC. In a short while, she became its director. And it is in that role that she—the one who knows how to get what she wants, even in the face of daunting odds—is the empowering person.

At LYDC, Theresa gives parents more than information about disabilities and "beating the system"; she also gives them hope. To give parents hope, she likes making connections with people, finding out "what's in them that I can help enhance or bring out, identifying their strength and playing on that, building that up so that they can do what they need to do."

Theresa sees LYDC and her work as a ministry of hope, sharing, and caring: "We have to minister to a person's hurt." She does that by being an example, just as her sister was an example to her (of how to escape from a bad situation). Theresa exemplifies—she ministers—by being a Christian. "We are to be Christlike." So it does not surprise her that people "see the Godliness in us. It's all about denying ourselves and helping someone else."

Paradoxically, being "about someone else" empowers Theresa even as it simultaneously empowers those who come to LYDC and some of the professionals with whom she deals. True, Theresa doesn't have "a lot of alphabets after (her) name. I don't have a degree, except the BA—Born Again." Or, the Ex.D.—Doctor of Experience. But she is an advisor to the National Institute for Urban School Improvement; she has successfully completed federal, state, and private-sector grants; she operates an effective nonprofit agency; she collaborates comfortably with academics and with her peers in the minority-population community; and she makes a difference in her community. LYDC's "all the buzz . . . people just come by to talk." They come to talk with Theresa; that is to say, they come to an empowered person to become an empowered person. Her mission and her experience make a difference to her: "I don't feel 'less than.' I can hold my head up high." Because I know I'm making a difference in the lives of others."

"AT LYDC, we are living the African American experience." There, Theresa and her staff know the families' needs and how to respond, whether it is to bring food to the family when a child has died or to provide bus fare so the family can come to LYDC and also not go hungry.

Part of the African American experience is experiencing prejudice. White teachers or consultants will come to LYDC but only during the day; their African American counterparts, on the other hand, will come at night, when the families can come to LYDC.

Coming to LYDC . . . what does that mean? It means coming to Theresa, to see and learn from an empowered person. But it signifies more than that. It entails encountering a ministry that is characterized by empowerment of self and others and that is based on collaboration, on being "real." Being yourself, not being or thinking you are better than others, is the basis for collaboration.

The recurring theme in this book, exemplified by Theresa, is empowerment through collaboration. This theme will permeate your partnerships with families. The more you understand empowerment—its implications for yourself, your professional colleagues, and families—and how to collaborate for empowerment of families, yourself, and other professionals, the more effective you are likely to be.

Theresa Cooper and her son, Eric. (1999)

Professional literature, popular media, and everyday conversations are replete with the word empowerment. What does the word really mean? For starters, we encourage you to first define empowerment. One way to do this is to think of the people whom you consider to be most empowered and the people whom you regard as most disempowered. Try to limit your thinking to families and professionals. What are their respective characteristics? Would you describe yourself as being more or less empowered than your professional peers, your own family members, families whom you respect, and others whom you know? What are Theresa's characteristics? Now what do you know about the meaning of empowerment?

Definition and Rationale

Empowered people strive to have control over their lives; they try to take action to get what they want and need (Akey, Marquis, & Ross, in press; Bennett, DeLuca, & Allen, 1996; Cochran, 1992; Dempsey, 1996; Dunst, Trivette, & LaPoint, 1992; Gutiérrez & Nurius, 1994; Koren, DeChillo, & Friesen, 1992; Man, 1999; Pinderhughes, 1994; Rappaport, 1981; Turnbull, Turbiville, & Turnbull, 2000; Valentine, 1998). Often they succeed magnificently; sometimes they succeed only partially; sometimes they fail. Why do they have these different experiences with empowerment?

The answer is that empowerment—the ability to get what one wants and needs—depends on the context in which one finds oneself. Empowerment takes different forms in different contexts (Kieffer, 1984; Man, 1999; Singh et al., 1997; Thompson et al., 1997. When Theresa was a preteenager and lived with her father, her behavior took one form—report and flee. Her behavior in another context, such as the "community work group" of the National Institute for Urban School Improvement, takes another form—looking at what she has accomplished and not feeling or acting "less than" all the "high-falutin'" people with many degrees. Moreover, what one does or experiences in one context (such as the family home or a neighborhood) may not be the same as what one does or experiences in another context (such as institute or school-board meetings). Empowerment also differs among individuals in the same context; some individuals may be more empowered than others in the same context. And empowerment may change over time for the same individual; an individual may become more and more empowered over time because becoming empowered is a developmental process (Kieffer, 1984; Zimmerman, 1995).

Think about the most empowered and most disempowered people you know. The highly empowered people probably take frequent action to satisfy their preferences and needs and to build on their strengths. They have the means, knowledge, or opportunity to act; they know what they want and take action to get it. As a professional, you can and should be a person who provides families with some of the means they need to become more empowered. Is there any doubt in your mind that Theresa is a person who empowers others? What a role model she can be for you!

By contrast, the most disempowered people probably often feel stuck, knowing that they face problems but feeling very unclear about what to do and sometimes being unable to take any action at all. Some parents may be mired in hopelessness until they come to LYDC. After all, it's "the buzz" in south-central Los Angeles.

How does empowerment apply to special education or, for that matter, to any human service system? If a father of a daughter who is gifted wants information on summer enrichment programs, being empowered means taking the necessary steps to make sure that, consistent with his daughter's preferences and family resources, he has access to that information, reviews it, and selects a summer program. For the foster parent of a child with a severe disability, empowerment may mean finding help to obtain and pay for necessary medical care for the child, obtaining the help, determining whether her needs have been met, and taking further action if necessary. The professionals collaborating with these and other families can and should provide the information or refer families to an appropriate source and then provide support according to their preferences. This support should ensure that their needs are satisfactorily addressed, just as Theresa meets the needs of the families involved in LYDC, whether those needs are for the basics of life (such as food and clothing) or for disability-related services.

Empowerment is important not just for families who have a member with an exceptionality but also for you, for other professionals, and for students in special education. Collective empowerment—empowerment of yourself and others—should be your goal in all of your roles and responsibilities. In this book, we primarily focus on the role that professionals such as yourself play in supporting families to be empowered. Yet we also want you to know that all of the empowerment techniques you will learn in this book apply not just to your work with families but also to your work on your own behalf, your work with other professionals, and your work with students.

For example, special or general education teachers are empowered when they know how to secure the related services their students need and to collaborate with related service providers, which enables the teachers to be successful with their students. Similarly, school administrators, school faculty, community employers, and related service providers who work in agencies other than the school (such as local rehabilitation agencies) are empowered to secure programs for students in transition from special education to jobs and inclusive adult education programs. Here, too, they secure the result they all want—namely, satisfying careers for students.

Likewise, students with exceptionalities are empowered when, during conferences to develop or review their IEP, they clearly and succinctly share their preferences, great expectations, strengths, and needs and suggest ways to address them. Student participation in IEP conferences can benefit teachers, administrators, families, and students, as we describe in chapter 12.

Most of the special education literature about family-professional partnerships emphasizes how important it is for professionals to enable families to be empowered (Dunst, Trivette, & Deal, 1988; Garlow, Turnbull, & Schnase, 1991; Knoll et al., 1990; Turnbull, Garlow, & Barber, 1991; Weiss, 1989). We repeat, however, that professional empowerment—your own and your colleagues' empowerment—is just as important (Turnbull, Turbiville, & Turnbull, 2000). So as we describe how professionals can collaborate with families or other professionals to empower families, bear in mind that the concepts we present and the techniques we suggest are just as useful to you as an individual and a professional as they are to families. Because the concepts and techniques can help families and you, they also can help other professionals.

We encourage you to set a goal during this course—indeed, throughout the rest of your life—to become more empowered and to support others to be empowered. You will be most successful in enabling families, students, and others to achieve greater empowerment if you yourself are empowered. As you will read throughout this book, this type of win-win situation, where there is collective empowerment, enables everyone to benefit from and contribute to each other. One of the truly remarkable aspects of LYDC is that its one professional staffer (Theresa), and the other parents involved all contribute to each other. Not surprisingly, this reciprocity enables them to get something

they want—whether it is emotional support and the motivation to press on or information and new skills.

Having said this, let us now return to our single narrow purpose: teaching you how to foster families' empowerment.

Empowerment Framework

Overview

In a nutshell, empowerment—increasing control over one's life and taking action to get what one wants—occurs when there is a transaction between one or more individuals and the context in which they are taking action. In Theresa's case, the transaction involved herself, her father, her sister, and professionals (in school and in child-protective service agencies). For our purposes, the individuals are the family members, professionals, or a combination of both. Also for our purposes, the context is special education (but it also can be general education or other service-delivery systems). The transaction in this case is collaboration. When families and professionals are connected through collaboration, then empowerment—action to get what one wants—is probable.

In figure 3–1, you will see an illustration of how we conceptualize empowerment. Let's look at the four major parts of this figure.

- On the far left is a boxed column that we call *family resources.* These consist of two elements—motivation and knowledge/skills. Thus, we begin by acknowledging that the family's resources (its motivation and knowledge/skills) are one part of empowerment.

- On the far right is another boxed column that we call *professional resources.* As you see, these generally consist of the identical elements as the family resources, namely, motivation and knowledge/skills. Thus, we also acknowledge that the professionals (and their motivation and knowledge/skills) are part of empowerment.

- At the very bottom of figure 3–1 is a foundation that we call *collaborating for empowerment.* This foundation signifies that when families and professionals collaborate with each other, they become more empowered.

- Superimposed on top of the family resources and professional resources and on top of the foundation called collaborating for empowerment is a box that we call *education context resources.* This box consists of the two elements that we briefly discussed in chapter 2: (1) opportunities for partnerships and (2) obligations for reliable alliances.

FIGURE 3–1

Empowerment Framework: Collaborating for Empowerment

Education Context Resources

Professional Resources

Knowledge/Skills

Information: Being knowledgeable

Problem solving: Knowing how to bust the barriers

Life management skills: Knowing how to handle what happens to us

Communication skills: Being on the sending and receiving ends of expressed needs and wants

Motivation

Self-efficacy: Believing in our capabilities

Perceived control: Believing we can apply our capabilities to affect what happens to us

Great expectations: Believing our visions will come true

Energy: Lighting the fire and keeping it burning

Persistence: Putting forth a sustained effort

Obligations for Reliable Alliances

Reliable Alliances Consist Of . . .

Knowing yourself

Knowing families

Honoring cultural diversity

Affirming family strengths

Promoting family choices

Envisioning great expectations

Communicating positively

Warranting trust and respect

Opportunities for Partnerships

Opportunities Arise At . . .

Communicating among reliable allies

Meetings families' basic needs

Evaluating for special education

Individualizing for appropriate education and placement

Extending learning into home and community

Attending and volunteering at school

Advocating for systems improvement

Family Resources

Knowledge/Skills

Information: Being knowledgeable

Problem solving: Knowing how to bust the barriers

Life management skills: Knowing how to handle what happens to us

Communication skills: Being on the sending and receiving ends of expressed needs and wants

Motivation

Self-efficacy: Believing in our capabilities

Perceived control: Believing we can apply our capabilities to affect what happens to us

Great expectations: Believing our visions will come true

Energy: Lighting the fire and keeping it burning

Persistence: Putting forth a sustained effort

Collaborating for Empowerment

Figure 3–1 is a "model"—a design—that illustrates our concept about empowerment. It signifies that the education context is the setting within which families and professionals collaborate. That context consists of (1) the school in which a family has enrolled the child with an exceptionality and in which professionals provide that child with a free, appropriate public education and (2) the state, regional, or local school system of which the student's particular school is part. More than that, however, the model shown in figure 3–1 signifies that the education context not only influences but also is influenced by the ways in which families and professionals collaborate. The context, we believe, influences families and professionals by encouraging or discouraging collaboration. And the context also is influenced by how and how much families and professional collaborate with each other (Turnbull, Turbiville, & Turnbull, 2000).

As we point out later in this chapter, there is an interaction among family resources, professional resources, collaboration, and education context resources. That is why each of these is connected to each of the others. There is not just simple interaction of one component with another but there also is a system of complex interactions of all of the components.

Now, we grant you that figure 3–1 requires you to study it hard and to think carefully about the challenging concept of empowerment. That is why, in the following sections of this chapter, we break figure 3–1 apart and discuss each part of it separately: the family resources, then the professional resources, and then the collaboration component. Finally, after we have discussed each part, we reassemble the model. In this way, you will learn, bit by bit, building on what you have just learned, until you have a full grasp of empowerment.

Family and Professional Resources

The first part of the empowerment model consists of the potential resources that are identical and common to families and professionals alike. We call these the *family resources* and *professional resources*. There are two general categories of resources: (1) motivation and (2) knowledge/skills. Do you remember what motivated Theresa when she was a child? Can you guess what motivated her to come to LYDC after Eric was born? It was her search for knowledge about disability and how to get services. Motivation consists of five resources, and knowledge consists of four. These resources are identical for families and professionals alike. When families and professionals are *motivated* to take action and when they have the *knowledge/skills* to act, then empowerment is much more likely to occur.

Motivation There are five components of motivational resources: (1) self-efficacy, (2) perceived control, (3) great expectations, (4) energy, and (5) persistence in pursuing goals. We briefly introduce each here and discuss the components throughout the rest of this book.

Self-efficacy refers to the belief in one's own capabilities (Bandura, 1997; Zimmerman, 1995; Zimmerman & Rappaport, 1988). Feelings of self-efficacy clearly influence behavior (Bandura, 1997; Bandura, Barbaranelli, Caprara, & Pastorelli, 1996); people tend to avoid activities and situations when they believe they cannot succeed, but they undertake activities when they think they can be effective. How does self-efficacy relate to families and professionals? Families' self-efficacy refers to their beliefs about their own ability to care for their children and to enhance their children's quality of life, including positive school outcomes. That is why LYDC is so dedicated to supporting families to feel good about themselves. Teachers' self-efficacy refers to their beliefs concerning the degree to which they can make a difference in enhancing student learning (Ashton & Webb, 1986; DiBella-McCarthy, McDaniel, & Miller, 1995).

Research on parent and teacher self-efficacy shows that there is a positive relationship among families, teachers, student development, and home-school interaction (Hoover-Dempsey, Bassler, & Brissie, 1992):

1. Higher levels of parents' self-efficacy are related to increased parent involvement in volunteering at school, participating in educational activities, and communicating with teachers on the telephone.
2. Teachers with higher self-efficacy reported higher levels of parent participation, suggesting that higher efficacy teachers may encourage more active parent collaboration.
3. Teachers with higher self-efficacy characterized parents as also having higher efficacy.

Teachers with higher self-efficacy encourage parents to believe more in their capabilities (that is, to augment their self-efficacy). The augmented self-efficacy that parents have, in turn, reciprocally encourages teachers to be even more efficacious. Simply put, if you believe in your own effectiveness, you probably will act; and actions you take will probably encourage others to be more effective. It is this mutuality between families and teachers—between families on the one hand and yourself and your colleagues on the other—that makes empowerment (or, at least, beliefs in self-efficacy) a reciprocal matter. It is also what LYDC exemplifies: an empowered director (Theresa) and staff who, in turn, empower others. "It's all about someone else, it's not about yourself."

In a comprehensive review of why parents become involved in their children's education, self-efficacy emerged as a key factor (Hoover-Dempsey & Sandler, 1997):

> . . . a stronger sense of efficacy . . . seems essential to a positive parental decision about involvement. This is because a sense of efficacy for helping children succeed in school fundamentally predisposes a parent to choose (or not choose, in the case of low efficacy) an active involvement role in the child's education. The predisposition is grounded in the parent's belief that their personal actions related to their child's schooling will be effective in improving school outcomes. Rooted in this belief about the likely outcomes of personal involvement, parents who hold the positive sense of efficacy for helping children succeed in school are likely to choose involvement. This is particularly true . . . if parents also hold a role construction of affirming the importance and appropriateness of involvement in children's schooling and if they perceive general opportunities and demands for involvement from both the child and the child's school. (Hoover-Dempsey & Sandler, 1997, p. 27)

What does self-efficacy mean for your role? As a teacher, can your own self-efficacy be a catalyst for your own empowerment and the empowerment of others? Imagine the collective self-efficacy that is generated through the teaching of Donna McNear, a special education itinerant teacher in seven rural school districts in Minnesota. In box 3–1, Donna describes her role.

Perceived control, believing you can apply your capabilities to affect what happens to you, is a second element of motivation. Research underscores the importance of families' having choices about issues concerning their child (Allen & Petr, 1996; Donahue-Kilburg, 1992;

Dunst, Trivette, Gordon, & Starnes, 1993; Scorgie, Wilgosh, & McDonald, 1999). A parent of a child with cerebral palsy describes the role of choice this way:

> Choice is really important. Parents need to know there are choices and be able to make decisions. Choice is having the freedom to decide what you need for your family and to be able to ask for it. Making choices on everyday things are building blocks for empowerment. (Jones, Garlow, Turnbull, & Barber, 1996, p. 101)

As you learned in chapter 1, many professionals traditionally have expected families to defer to professional direction and advice. This approach, however, can be disempowering if families are deferential to professionals, if they simply and always acquiesce to the professionals. A more empowering approach is for all stakeholders in educational decision making to share their expertise and resources for the collective benefit of all (Allen & Petr, 1996; Jones et al., 1996; Turbiville, Turnbull, Garland, & Lee, 1996; Turnbull, Turbiville, & Turnbull, 2000). This is the essence of a power-with and power-from-within approach rather than a power-over approach. It is the sort of approach that Theresa practices when she describes the process she uses: "We lay out the options, tell them our views, and say, 'It's up to you,' because it really is up to the person who has the problem. . . ."

Families can make a broad range of choices related to educational decisions. Some of the types of choices include the following (Petr, 1998):

- The definition of their family in terms of who was involved in decisions
- The individuals within the family who actually make decisions

MY VOICE BOX 3–1

Donna McNear Speaks Out on Her Role as a Teacher

I do many things in a day for children, but what I realized about teaching and my students is what my life is all about. I realize that I am a mirror, a window, and a doorway for my students: A mirror to reflect positively who they are and their capabilities, talents, and dreams; a window to show them their opportunities, possibilities, choices, and other ways of being; and, finally, a doorway for their future.

I have also realized my own mission in my work life: I see the meaning in my labor (beyond the reward of a check); I've seen my abilities recognized and valued; I view myself as a crafts person, creating something of beauty and value; I have a job that is large enough for my spirit; and I feel I am leaving the world better than when I found it. (Turnbull, Turnbull, Shank, & Leal, 1999, p. 700)

- The extent to which services focus on the child as well as other family members
- The nature of the family-professional relationship
- The people who should have access to information about the child
- The identification of strengths, needs, goals, and instructional strategies

Great expectations, believing that our vision will come true, is the fourth element of motivation. To begin to appreciate fully the importance of great expectations as an aspect of motivation, you should start by being skeptical about special educators' and other professionals' traditional concerns for "being realistic." From her perspective as a social psychologist, Taylor (1989) developed a theory of "positive illusions." This theory helps to explain how people adapt to threatening situations. She believes that a person's perception is marked by positive, self-enhancing illusions about one's own self, the world, and the future, rather than by accuracy. Instead of seeing such positive illusions (or as we call them, *great expectations*) as representing denial or repression, she suggests that positive illusions are adaptive and promote rather than undermine good mental health.

> Overall, the research evidence indicates that self-enhancement, exaggerated beliefs and control, and unrealistic optimism typically lead to higher motivation, greater persistence at tasks, more effective performance, and, ultimately greater success. A chief value of these illusions may be that they help to create self-fulfilling prophecies. They may lead people to try harder in situations that are objectively difficult. Although some failures are certainly inevitable, ultimately the illusions will lead to success more often than will lack of persistence. (Taylor, 1989, p. 64)

The late Norman Cousins (1989), a distinguished editor in his time, reflected on his own treatment for cancer and deplored the fact that many professionals were worried about giving "false hope" to people facing threatening situations. But these same professionals never realized how frequently they gave "false despair" and how "false despair" can dissuade people from creating any kind of desirable future (Cousins, 1989, p. 100). In describing individuals with AIDS who tended to be empowered rather than disempowered in pursuing their recovery, Cousins stated: "Perhaps the most important of these characteristics is the refusal to accept the verdict of a grim inevitability. . . . What it means is that any progress in coping . . . involves not denial but a vigorous determination to get the most and the best out of whatever is now possible" (Cousins, 1989 p. 76, 78).

What does all of this mean to the enhancement of motivation? In today's state-of-the-art services, special educators, social psychologists, and mental health professionals are emphasizing great expectations and positive outcomes for people with exceptionalities (Epstein, Kutash, & Duchnowski, 1998; Schwartz, 1997; Seligman, 1990; Snyder, 1994; Turnbull & Turnbull, 1996). So are parents of children and adults with disabilities, such as Janet Vohs:

> Families of children with disabilities are not allowed—or at least not encouraged—to have a dream or a vision for their children's future. What the past has given as possible outcomes for people with disabilities is far less than inspiring. If all we have to look forward to is an extension of the past, I should think we would want to avoid the pain of that future as long as possible. But I have a motto: Vision over visibility. Having a vision is not just planning for a future we already know how to get to. It is daring to dream about what is possible. (Vohs, 1993, pp. 62–63)

The notion of great expectations is consistent with the unified systems reform that we discussed in chapter 2—remember that the current emphasis in general and special education is on having high expectations for students and holding students and educators accountable in achieving those higher standards.

Do you recall the discussion about synergy in chapter 2? As powerful as one's own sense of great expectations can be, even more powerful is a collective and mutually developed vision of great expectations. Senge (1990) underscores the importance of collaborative envisioning:

> A shared vision is not an idea. . . . It is rather a force in people's hearts, a force of impressive power. It may be inspired by an idea, but once it goes further—if it is compelling enough to acquire the support of more than one person—then it is no longer an abstraction. It is palpable. People begin to see it as if it is this. Few, if any, forces in human affairs are as powerful as shared vision. (Senge, 1990, p. 206)

For many families and professionals, it can be a developmental process to move from being disempowered or focusing on negative outcomes to having collective vision. One of the first steps is to move in the direction of being hopeful and having positive thinking. When some people encounter events they think they cannot affect, they may experience learned helplessness, a psychological state in which people expect events in their life to be externally controlled and anticipate that they will likely fail rather than succeed in what they try to do (Seligman, 1990). The opposite of learned helplessness is learned hopefulness, a psychological state in which people perceive that, through affecting what happens to them, they will achieve positive outcomes (Zimmerman,

1990). Families and professionals frequently report how important positive thinking becomes as they face the challenges of exceptionality. One parent described the importance of positive thinking this way (Scorgie, Wilgosh, & McDonald, 1999; Seligman, 1990):

> I was involved in a abusive relationship. I lost me in all that negative stuff. I got out of that . . . and I'm free and I'm me. I'm loving myself again, and my eyes are open, and I see, you understand? So I'm back at that point where I'm happy, and things are just flowing smoothly. When something negative happens, I just turn the other way. Because you're surrounded by negative and positive things, but it's how you look at it. Even everyday at work, people, people can be negative, but I just turn the other way. Or I smile, you know, "How was your day? Oh, mine's great, well yours can be great too." You know, I turn the other way. (Beach Center, unpublished transcript, 1999)

Your own positive thinking can be a catalyst for families' positive thinking; and positive thinking can be the springboard for great expectations.

Energy is the fourth element of motivation—lighting the fire and keeping it burning. Energy has two components: (1) what it takes initially to light the fire and (2) what it takes to keep it burning. In terms of lighting the fire, taking the first steps of action to get what one needs or wants, research has pointed to the importance of a "mobilizing episode" (Kieffer, 1984, p. 19).

A mobilizing episode for families might be the initial diagnosis of a disability, having their child excluded from the neighborhood school, or being told that their child is not "college material." Immobilizing episodes for professionals might be having a student in their class who they find especially challenging to teach, being told by their colleagues that what they want to do "will never work," or not being able to find the community resources that a child and family need. These episodes can provoke strong reactions of injustice or outrage that impel people away from a "business as usual" approach and lead them to take action. Mobilizing episodes can also be positive; for example, a child may get a new power wheelchair, parents may attend a conference and be especially inspired and informed by a speaker about what is possible in supported employment, or teachers may have an opportunity to serve as a consulting teacher for others. Whatever the mobilizing episode, the point is that action takes energy, and energy is necessary for people to become mobilized.

The initial burst of energy is necessary but not sufficient. There must be energy to carry out actions one after another, each building toward the ultimate goal. Because empowerment is time and labor intensive, initial and subsequent bursts of energy are necessary. One way to encourage empowerment is to encourage a wellness approach to everyday living. Covey (1990) includes the habit called *sharpening the saw* as one of his seven habits of highly effective people. Physical renewal—exercise, nutrition, and stress management—is an essential element of sharpening the saw.

The final element of motivation is *persistence*—putting forth sustained effort over time. Persistence is closely related to energy for keeping the fires burning, but persistence requires tenacity—a never-say-die, bulldog attitude. It entails refusing to give up when one's initial efforts do not immediately produce the desired results (Scorgie, Wilgosh, & McDonald, 1999). Sometimes certain goals, such as finding the best medication regimen for a child with diabetes or working through challenging behavior for a youngster with an emotional disorder, are especially elusive. Families and professionals will go through periods of trial and error before obtaining a successful solution. Persistence is required to work through these kinds of seemingly insoluble challenges as well as to solve discrete, time-limited, or relatively short-term challenges.

Persistence is also needed in working toward long-term goals. One of those goals is an appropriate education for students. This goal begins when students are in early intervention programs and continues through their transition from high school into adulthood. Parents have described the importance of persistence in asking questions—even the same questions—until they get answers that are understandable and relevant for the educational decisions they need to make (Scorgie, Wilgosh, & McDonald, 1999). Many parents will be advocates throughout their child's adult years and need to be persistent to run the marathon of long-term disability challenges (Turnbull, 1988). Likewise, many professionals are effective advocates for decades—not just years—as we will discuss in chapter 15. The capacity for sustained effort is a critical element of an individual's motivation.

In summary, the five elements of motivation are self-efficacy, perceived control, great expectations, energy, and persistence. Think about the people who, in your experience, exemplify each of these five elements. What jump-starts and then continues to propel their motivation? What are the catalysts for their motivational strength? Could it be that they are connected to others who enhance these five resources? Could it be—shouldn't it be—that families and professionals connect and collaborate for empowerment?

Knowledge and Skills Motivation is only one of the individual resources of empowerment. The second resource is *knowledge/skills* (Jones, Garlow, Turnbull, & Barber, 1996; Man, 1999; Turnbull, Turbiville, & Turnbull,

2000). Many families and professionals who are highly motivated also have knowledge/skill strengths. It is possible, however, to have strong motivation but to be slightly or significantly lacking in knowledge/skills. Empowered families and professionals have sufficient knowledge/skills to get what they want and need. Figure 3–1 identifies the four elements of knowledge and skills resources: (1) information, (2) problem solving, (3) life management skills, and (4) communication skills.

There is no doubt about this one fact: Families want and need *information* (Bailey, Blasco, & Simeonsson, 1992; Bailey et al., 1999; Hadadian & Merbler, 1995; Scorgie, Wilgosh, & McDonald, 1999). Families say that their greatest needs for information relate to (1) future services, (2) present services, (3) how to teach their child, (4) the nature of their child's disability, (5) experiences of other parents who have a child with similar needs, (6) handling the emotional and time demands of parenthood, (7) community resources, and (8) legal rights (Cooper & Allred, 1992; Gowen, Christy, & Sparling, 1993). Families and professionals alike need state-of-the-art information that is accessible, relevant, and time efficient. They need to be "in the know." One of Theresa's goals is to put families in the know by offering training or other information sessions and by making other consultants or experts available to families. When asked what professionals should do to empower families, Theresa answers, "Don't be stingy with information. Give it out to everyone. Don't feel bad if they don't use it right away. Leave that choice to them. But give them the information." And, she adds, you must acquire information for yourself. Theresa takes advantage of many workshops, new books, and other learning opportunities to make sure that she stays current in information so she, in turn, can pass along that information to families. Ironically, one of the greatest barriers to empowerment is the large gap between research and the accessibility and affordability of this information for families and professionals (Ruef, Turnbull, Turnbull, & Poston, 1999; Turnbull, Friesen & Ramirez, 1998). We encourage you to acquire, use, and exchange state-of-the-art information with families and professionals. Everyone wants and needs to be in the know.

Problem solving consists of the ability to establish and implement a plan to get what you want in spite of problems standing in the way (Cochran, 1992; Cornell Empowerment Group, 1989; Heller, 1990; Jones, Garlow, Turnbull, & Barber, 1996; Knackendoffel, Robinson, Deshler, & Schumaker, 1992). Problem solving is a way of busting the barriers that stand between what is (the present) and what is ideal (the future). As parents might say, "Our son with spina bifida wants to be a disc jockey. The fact that he's in a wheelchair shouldn't stop

him. Let's see what it will take for him to volunteer at the local radio station after school and during the summer."

As we point out in chapter 4, problem solving consists of (1) developing a vision; (2) agreeing on a specific goal; (3) brainstorming options for addressing the goal; (4) evaluating benefits and drawbacks of each option; (5) selecting the most appropriate option; (6) specifying an implementation plan, including next steps, person responsible, resources needed, and time lines; (7) implementing the plan; (8) evaluating how closely the results of action match the goals; and (9) modifying the plan and continuing to make progress. This is a lot of work. Indeed, it is so much work that families and professionals can and should collaborate to refine their problem-solving skills (Hudson & Glomb, 1997; Shank & Turnbull, 1993).

The third element of the knowledge/skills factor is *life management* skills—knowing how to handle what happens to you (Scorgie, Wilgosh, & McDonald, 1999). Olson and associates (1983) have categorized these skills into five types. We briefly define them here, including citations to literature related to families who have a member with an exceptionality. Do you see how these life management strategies apply to professionals as well?

1. *Passive appraisal:* setting aside worries about a problem

   When things really get bad I go and soak in the bath for an hour. My husband was told I was on the verge of a nervous breakdown but I haven't had it yet! (Lonsdale, 1978, p. 108)

2. *Reframing:* changing the way one thinks about a situation in order to emphasize positive rather than negative aspects (Blue-Banning, Santelli, Guy, & Wallace, 1994; Hayden & Heller, 1997; Sandler & Mistretta, 1998; Scorgie, Wilgosh, & McDonald, 1999; Summers, Behr, & Turnbull, 1988; Turnbull et al., 1993)

   My only daughter is profoundly retarded. She's loved and in return she's lovely. She's not able to walk or talk, but she can smile and laugh. She is loved. (Turnbull, Blue-Banning, Behr, & Kerns, 1986, p. 130)

3. *Spiritual support:* deriving comfort and guidance from one's spiritual beliefs (Bennett, DeLuca, & Allen, 1996; Fewell, 1986; Hughes, 1999; Scorgie, Wilgosh, & McDonald, 1999; Weisner, Belzer, & Stolze, 1991)

   I have faith in God, and word of God's faith. He'll never forsake you, or leave you, so whatever you're going through, he's going through with you. And you'll never get more than you can handle. So, having the faith draws things into focus, the peace, the joy, the happiness. (Beach Center, unpublished transcripts, 1999)

4. *Social support:* receiving practical and emotional assistance from friends and family (Bennett, DeLuca, & Allen, 1996; Crinc & Stormshak, 1997; Hayden & Heller, 1997; Man, 1999; Sarason, Sarason, & Pierce, 1990)

> At a critical time, one of my good friends said, "Don't give up, don't lose faith." It was real energizing to know that others believed in my daughter, too. (Turnbull & Ruef, 1996, p. 287)

5. *Professional support:* receiving assistance from professionals and agencies (Bennett, DeLuca, & Allen, 1996; Clatterbuck, & Turnbull, 1996; Elliott, Koroloff, Koren, & Friesen, 1998; Kairys, 1996; Karp, 1996; Schoenwald, Borduin, & Henggeler, 1998; Wehmeyer, Morningstar, & Husted, 1999)

> It was the first day of summer vacation and my son was off the wall, because he really needed structure. I was freaking out, and I couldn't deal with it. I called the teacher and told her I didn't know what to do. She came across town and took him to her house and said, "Do something fun for two hours." (Turnbull & Ruef, 1997, p. 219)

We encourage you to reflect on the life management strategies that Theresa uses, especially her reliance on her spiritual support and social support, and to think about your own coping skills and challenging situations that you have faced. Families and other members of collaboration teams vary in their life management capabilities, in the number of different life management strategies that they use, and in the quality or effectiveness of each strategy. Moreover, the strategies that people choose change from time to time depending on the issues they face and the contexts in which they face them. Throughout this book, we discuss these life management strategies.

We want to add a caveat, however, about the term *life management.* Typically in professional literature, the term *coping strategies* has been used rather than life management strategies; however, families often do not use the term *coping* as readily as do professionals. Also the term *coping* typically refers to dealing with a crisis situation, whereas many of the challenges of families of children with exceptionalities relates to the daily and weekly strategies that they use to enhance their quality of life (Scorgie, Wilgosh, & McDonald, 1999). Additionally, for some families coping has a negative connotation (Vohs, 1997). For example, a parent described her view of coping as follows:

> For the first 33 years of my life I wasn't once accused of coping, not even well. I just got on with, actually enjoyed it, and did many things with varying degrees of success. Then my daughter with Down syndrome was born and ever since I've been coping well. Mind you, that's not how it felt. After the initial vacuum of shock I thought I just went on getting on with life with the usual success-failure rate. But I must have been coping well because everybody kept telling me I was. . . . Why do I feel so offended by the praising people who tell me I'm coping well? I guess because I see it as an attempt to reduce me to a unidimensional figure—the mother of a child with Down syndrome who copes. . . . Cope comes from an Old French word meaning to strike (a blow) and I still feel like coping the next well-meaning person who says it to me. (Boyce, 1992, p. 37)

Professional terminology can create barriers in professional-family relationships. So we encourage you to communicate with families by using terms that are meaningful to them.

The last knowledge/skills element is *communication skills.* Communication skills—being on the sending and receiving ends of the needs and wants that you, families, and other professionals express—are at the heart of empowerment and substantially contribute to the collaborative process. In chapter 4, we describe in detail nonverbal communication skills, verbal communication skills, influencing skills, and group communication skills. We also point out how and why cultural values and traditions strongly influence preferred communication skills and require both speakers and listeners to make accommodations.

In summary, knowledge/skills consists of four elements—information, problem solving, life management skills, and communication skills. For families and professionals to be empowered, it is necessary for them to have sufficient knowledge/skills. When motivation and knowledge/skills are present simultaneously, families and professionals will be far more likely to experience empowerment.

Education Context Resources

So far in this chapter we have been discussing only two of the three resources involved in empowerment—family resources and professional resources. Figure 3–1 displays the third resource—the education context resources. Families may indeed possess a great deal of motivation and knowledge/skills; but if the education context is constraining, families' motivation and knowledge/skills may be overwhelmed by that context (Maton & Salem, 1995; Turnbull, Turbiville, & Turnbull, 2000). Likewise, professionals may be highly empowered on an individual level but run into numerous barriers as they work within the educational context of their school building and school district. By contrast, if a context is empowering, then the families, and even their children, become agents of each others' empowerment. That is the way it is at LYDC: Theresa models or exemplifies her own power and thereby supports and enables other family members to act powerfully. By the same token, when a school system or a family support program is empowering, it can turn professionals who work within or with it into empowered individuals (Jones, Garlow, Turnbull, & Barber, 1996; Turnbull, Turbiville, & Turnbull, in press). A circle or chain of empowerment can begin with just one person. Or it can begin with a system.

In chapter 2, we introduced and discussed the context factors of seven opportunities for partnerships and eight obligations for reliable alliances (illustrated in figure 3–1). We define these seven opportunities for partnerships in figure 3–2. At the end of each definition, we refer to the chapter that focuses exclusively on that type of partnership and describe how you can create an empowering context for each partnership.

In chapter 2, we also introduced the eight obligations for a reliable alliance, briefly defined in figure 3–3. To create an empowering context, you need to infuse these eight obligations into all seven opportunities for partnerships—that is, into all of your interactions with families. The more you incorporate the eight obligations of a reliable alliance into your interactions with families, the more empowering you will make the context and the more you will empower families.

Let's review what you have been reading. What kind of professional do we want you to be? We want you to be an empowered professional who enables families to be empowered within the context that is today's

---

FIGURE 3–3

Obligations for a Reliable Alliance

1. *Knowing yourself:* involves having accurate self-knowledge—knowing and appreciating your own perspectives, opinions, strengths, and needs

2. *Knowing families:* involves being able to identify the unique aspects of each family's characteristics, interactions, functions, and life cycle and to respond in ways that are personalized and individually tailored to respect families' uniqueness

3. *Honoring cultural diversity:* means relating to others in personalized, respectful, and responsive ways in light of values associated with factors such as ethnicity, race, religion, income status, gender, sexual orientation, disability status, occupation, and geographical location

4. *Affirming and building on family strengths:* means identifying, appreciating, and capitalizing upon families' strengths

5. *Promoting family choices:* involves selecting the family members to be involved in collaborative decision making, deciding which educational issues should take priority over others, choosing the extent to which family members are involved in decision making for each educational issue, and selecting appropriate goals and services for the student

6. *Envisioning great expectations:* means recognizing that one can have an exceptionality and also have an enviable life

7. *Practicing positive communication skills:* means using nonverbal skills (such as physical attending and listening), verbal communication skills (such as furthering responses, paraphrasing, and summarizing), and influencing skills (such as providing information, providing support, and offering assistance) in ways that most sensitively and respectfully connect with families

8. *Warranting trust and respect:* means having confidence that everyone is pulling in the same direction in a supportive, nonjudgmental, and caring way

educational system. Consider how you can transform yourself to be more empowered, how you can encourage and support families to be more empowered, and how you can transform policies, procedures, and programs in the school context to be more empowering. Let's put that in a different but still familiar way: Consider how you and the school system can move from power-over approaches to power-with and power-within approaches.

Now, how can you carry out this goal? You can do it by enhancing your own motivation and knowledge/skills related to the seven opportunities for partnerships and the eight obligations for reliable alliances. Those constitute the education context factors. If you understand and then act upon the opportunities that the education context provides you for partnerships, and if you take it upon yourself to meet your obligations for reliable alliances, and if you do so by knowing about the family resources and the identical professional resources, then you will be collaborating for empowerment—building the foundation for empowerment.

Think about it: You are laying the foundation for you to become a more empowered person and more empowered professional. True, you do not have the sufficient information you need about family resources and professional resources, but you will obtain this information in the chapters that follow. And you will get an introduction to the process of collaborating for empowerment in the next section.

Collaboration

Overview

We remind you of the definition of collaboration that we included in chapter 1 so you will see how it ties to the empowerment framework illustrated in figure 3–1. As we said in chapter 1, *collaboration* refers to the dynamic process of families and professionals equally sharing their resources (motivation and knowledge/skills) in order to make decisions jointly. When collaboration incorporates families' and professionals' resources (moti-

BOX 3–2

TOGETHER WE CAN

Collaborating for Empowerment

To ask Hortense Walker about the family and context factors and collaboration as a connector, it is best to ask about the characteristics of the most and least effective professionals she and her family have worked with.

Their best experiences came with Eric's teacher in an early intervention program. Before Eric entered the program at age 18 months, Marlene (the teacher) visited the Walker home and quickly became encouraging so that she and Hortense easily bonded.

How was she encouraging? By not being a "hammer" and insisting that Eric should be in the program but by explaining how the program would help Eric and the whole family and then letting the family decide whether to enter it. She gave them a reason to enroll Eric (motivation) and information on which to make a decision. She acknowledged to them that they have the power within themselves to be empowerful to make decisions.

How was she able to create a bond? She was considerate of the family, keeping her appointments and gently prompting Hortense and her husband Michael to ask questions they were afraid to ask, questions about Eric and his impact on the family.

"We came to see Marlene as a person whose first objective was to meet the needs of our family as a whole. She emphasized the positives of the program for us and for Eric. We just ate up her time and her knowledge. She felt appreciated by us, and she was. That made the difference."

In a very real sense, Marlene became the context: She offered herself as a resource, and in doing so she created opportunities for partnerships. Clearly, by her offer and especially the manner in which she made the offer, she displayed her sense of obligation to be a reliable ally.

By contrast, the least effective professional, a social worker at the regional service center, never asked Hortense and Michael what they needed. "Eric was very young, throwing up everything he ate, very skinny, and never asleep. I'd work all day and then sleep just an hour a night," recalled Hortense. But the social worker visited only once and never asked if Hortense needed respite.

"She was rationing the respite to families whose children were more severely involved than Eric."

Yet in Hortense's mind. Eric was indeed a child with a severe disability, and Hortense herself was fast approaching the end of her rope.

The result of that interaction with the social worker? "I grew up in a home that respected professionals. I was raised by my grandmother and oldest sister; my mother died at childbirth, and I was the last of nine children. My oldest sister is 20 years older than I. They taught me to respect doctors and teachers and to do as they say."

The social worker taught Hortense just the opposite. Now, Hortense questions everyone closely and doesn't let anyone take her or her family lightly.

Well, almost everyone. With Marlene, it's not necessary to question closely. After all, Marlene acknowledges Hortense's and her family's power. In doing so, she creates a different kind of life for them, one in which they are invited by her to be collaborators and in which they gladly accept her invitation.

---

vation and knowledge/skills) with responsive education context factors (opportunities for partnerships and obligations for reliable alliances), empowerment results: Families and professionals can take action to get what they want and need.

In figure 3–1 the foundation (a crossbar at the bottom) represents the combination of family and professional factors in the educational context factors. When professionals and families collaborate within a genuine and authentic relationship, we call that relationship a *reliable alliance*. This is just the kind of collaborative relationship Hortense Walker, a consumer and volunteer at LYDC, has had with one of the professionals in the life of her own son, also named Eric, . . . but not with another, as box 3–2 describes.

Theresa thinks collaboration results from "connecting" with families, and she offers some good tips on how to connect. These are set out in figure 3–4.

Throughout this book, we discuss collaboration in its many different forms. When you collaborate with a single family and have the outcome of empowerment for the family and for yourself, you will begin to enhance your own motivation and knowledge/skills. You will realize that you are competent to make a significant

FIGURE 3—4

"Tips: Theresa's Suggestions for Connecting with Parents

1. Don't be "prissy and high-falutin.'" Don't be snobbish and condescending. Don't look down on parents.

2. Show that you really want to help and that you are asking questions so you can help, not just to be nosy or to use the answers against the parents.

3. Guide the parents with questions that allow themselves to open up and express themselves to you. Meet them where they are; don't start out where you think they should be.

4. Be real. Go to where they live. Go to the ghetto, because that's where they live.

5. Don't distance yourself from them. Don't think of them as "those people over there." After all, you are getting paid to work with them.

---

difference in the lives of students and families; when you realize that, you will acquire a genuine feeling of satisfaction about being an effective individual and teacher.

Collective Empowerment

As one collaboration occurs, and then another, and then still another, you may experience the height of collaboration, which is collective empowerment. You and the families will experience success in your relationships with each other because all of you are getting what you want and need. You will experience collective empowerment; and as you attain this stage, you may experience a qualitative change in yourself and your relationship with families. Three outcomes have been associated with collective empowerment: (1) synergy, (2) creation of renewable resources, and (c) increased participant satisfaction.

Synergy Synergy involves combined actions. By definition, *synergy* occurs only when at least two people act in concert with each other in mutually compatible ways and for mutually compatible purposes. When synergy does exist, the "whole is greater than the sum of the parts." In this type of situation (ideally, a responsive educational context), each person's efforts (both families'

and professionals' efforts) significantly and exponentially advance individual and group goals (Bond & Keys, 1993; Craig & Craig, 1974; Senge, 1990).

Synergy results when the collaboration between families and professionals moves their mutual goals ahead in the same direction and usually in the same way. By contrast, when individuals are empowered without collaboration, they may proceed with a different agenda and in a different direction. So when people are highly empowered and collaborative, individual efforts are united and the collective whole becomes more powerful and effective than any nonunited effort. Thus, one outcome of synergy is a more potent action system, which we call *collective empowerment.*

Susan Rocco, whom you will meet in the opening vignette of chapter 4, describes her perspectives on synergy:

> As the parent of a teenager with both medical and education challenges, I had experienced most points on the power continuum. The unequal power relationship with Jason's teachers and therapists generally put the burden on me to wheedle, cajole, threaten, flatter—in essence, work harder at the relationship than anyone else—to get the desired outcome. The few times I have experienced true synergy, when we partners are working from our strengths and shared values, the burden has fallen away. The beauty of the synergistic model is that there is no more "them" and "us." "We" pool our resources and our creative juices, and "we" all celebrate in the success. (Turnbull, Turbiville, & Turnbull, in press)

Creation of New and Renewable Resources A second outcome of collective empowerment is the creation of new and renewable resources. Many people believe that resources are generally scarce and unavailable; therefore, they have to be very careful to preserve—even hoard—them (Katz, 1984). An alternative perspective is that when there is collective empowerment, everyone participating in a collaborative effort has *increased* motivation and knowledge/skills to contribute to the effort. Let us give you an example of new resources. In late 1999, LYDC was funded through a large grant from the U.S. Department of Education to substantially expand LYDC's capability to provide resources to more families. Theresa and LYDC were able to compete successfully for this grant because they collaborated with other people who were all working together toward a common goal, as Theresa describes in box 3–3.

Now, you might ask, what keeps the ideal from being the reality? At least part of the answer is that sometimes people fear that if others around them are more empowered, then they, by necessity, will have less power. In such a win-lose game, what one group gains, another group loses; there is no "win-win" possibility. In this scenario, a context cannot respond to and empower all of its members.

For example, some people may erroneously assume that, in an IEP team meeting consisting of a parent, a student with an exceptionality, a teacher, and a school psychologist, the professionals and student will lose power if the parent gains power to exercise choices and exert some control. This assumption rests on the notion that there is only a fixed amount of power: If one person has a bigger piece of the power pie, others will have to be satisfied with smaller pieces. This is a prevailing perspective in Western cultures. A cultural strength of some non-Western thinking, however, is that resources are regarded as abundant rather than limited (Katz, 1984).

One of the characteristics of collective empowerment (families, professional, and education systems), then, is that empowerment can be an expanding and renewable resource distributed equitably among those who are working toward a common goal (Katz, 1984; Swift & Levin, 1987; Turnbull, Turbiville, & Turnbull, in press). Let's return to box 3–2 and recall the two professionals whom Hortense described. As Marlene provided choices to Hortense in decision making, Hortense became more empowered and so did Marlene: Both got what they wanted and needed. On the other hand, the social worker who attempted to hold on to her power cut herself off completely from a reliable alliance with Hortense. In effect, she was unable to take action to help get what either she or Hortense wanted or needed. The lesson of box 3–2 is very straightforward: Collective empowerment creates win-win situations.

Increased Satisfaction The third outcome of collective empowerment is increased satisfaction for all participants. It stands to reason that people who feel that they are part of the greater whole and that they have new and renewable resources would also have an increase in satisfaction. This is because, generally, individuals who experience collective empowerment have a sense that their needs are being met at present, they are capable of ensuring that their needs will also be met in the future, and they have a group of reliable allies on whom they can depend in making their dreams come true (Craig & Craig, 1974; Swick, 1988; Turnbull, Turbiville, & Turnbull, 2000).

Empowerment as a Developmental Process

Do individual empowerment and especially collective empowerment occur rapidly? No, particularly because (as we pointed out in chapter 1) professionals and families have had longstanding relationships that too often denigrate, or disempower, families but elevate professionals. History is a powerful teacher; it teaches that new collaborations, different relationships, and radically changed thinking are desirable but difficult to achieve.

Indeed, empowerment is a developmental process. Empowerment—empowering individually and collectively—takes time; it does not happen automatically just because one wishes for it to occur. In fact, an in-depth study of highly empowered community leaders concluded that their journeys toward empowerment took three to four years (Kieffer, 1984).

How can you, a single professional, orchestrate your own empowerment, enable families do the same for themselves, and thereby spark a collective empowerment that expands a context's responsiveness? The answer is the one we have already given and restate now: When families and professionals collaborate in sharing their motivation and knowledge/skills within a respon-sive educational context in order to make decisions collectively, they can enhance their own individual empowerment and, ultimately, the environment (schools) within which all collaborators find themselves. Achieving collective empowerment, where each and every person increases the likelihood of getting what he or she wants and needs, comes from win-win approaches.

You have a key role in creating an empowering context in which families, you, and other professionals can be collectively empowerful. To get to that result, we suggest that you put into place the seven opportunities for family-professional partnerships (chapters 9 through 15) and try to infuse each of those partnerships with the eight obligations of a reliable alliance (chapter 4 and all others).

Summary

Professionals who work effectively with families not only understand the roles that families have played over the years (chapter 1) and the contexts in which they work with families (chapter 2) but also accept new responsibilities. These responsibilities are (1) to enable families to enhance their motivation and knowledge/skills and to do the same for themselves and other professionals and (2) to create an empowering context, one in which opportunities for partnerships and obligations for reliable alliances coexist. To achieve this result, professionals need to collaborate with families, students, other professionals, and other interested individuals. Professionals, through their role as collaborators, have opportunities and obligations to create collective empowerment.

Empowerment consists of identifying one's most important needs and preferences and then taking steps to satisfy them. Empowerment occurs within a three-part framework. One part consists of family resources—families are motivated and have knowledge/skills. A second part consists of professional resources—professionals are motivated and have knowledge/skills. The third part of empowerment consists of education context factors—schools and professionals that take advantage of opportunities for partnerships and undertake obligations for reliable alliances. Of course, the foundation connecting family factors, professional factors, and education context factors is collaboration. Empowerment can occur when professionals and families collaborate by enhancing motivation, expanding knowledge and skills, taking advantage of opportunities for partnerships, undertaking obligations to create reliable alliances, and taking action to get what they want and need.

There are two kinds of knowledge: that which derives from research, which we call head or book knowledge, and that which derives from living, which we call heart or street knowledge. At Loving Your Disabled Child (LYDC), both kinds of knowledge combine. They do so in a way that empowers everyone and that is collaborative.

Theresa Cooper and her staff practice heart knowledge, but they also reflect the book knowledge that we have described in this chapter. They practice collective empowerment, demonstrating and thus inculcating into others the attitudes and skills that facilitate empowerment, enabling action by others, and creating a context within LYDC that responds to what its families want and need.

They collaborate with LYDC's families, sometimes in unexpected ways. There is an implicit promise of collaboration in this relatively atypical message that Theresa shares with the parents: Parents need to know that they can love their child who has a disability and that their love can grow. . . . Your marriage can stay together, your children can love their brother or sister, there can be just an overabundance of love, and the family can be stable and together.

The promise is that Theresa and other LYDC families will help each other be loving and strong. Doesn't collaboration begin when two or more people have expectations of the kind about which Theresa speaks? Isn't it established when they find ways to solve their problems and then celebrate their successes?

Theresa and the LYDC families think so, and that's why they do not find it unusual that LYDC parents talk and laugh when they come together. They may not have solved all of their problems, not by any means; but their empowering attitudes, their abilities to reinforce each other's strengths, their skills in sharing information and referring each other to services, and their celebrations—all of these are hallmarks of empowerment and collaboration.

Chapter Four

Building Reliable Alliances

When it comes to creating empowering relationships and building reliable alliances, Susan Rocco has more than a few lessons to teach other parents and professionals. Some of those lessons were hard to come by, but not all.

For example, when she wanted her son Jason to be removed from his self-contained elementary school and included in a general education program in Honolulu, Susan had to know a great deal about herself and about the culture of her adopted state.

After all, at age 10, Jason was a bit of a challenge: As handsome as he was, he nevertheless had a serious, pervasive developmental delay, severe mental retardation, mild cerebral palsy, and epilepsy. Although he usually expressed his strong preferences in what Susan calls "prosocial" ways, he sometimes was fairly stubborn and challenging, especially as he began to feel the effects of hormone changes and adolescence.

What Susan knew was that "you get more flies with honey than vinegar." Abandoning the mainland confrontational style, she adopted the nonassertive, nonconfrontational mores of Hawaii. "Being able to just play the game by those social rules and genuinely trying to connect with people and get them to know Jason" was a key to Jason's admission to an inclusive setting in a new school.

She also had to trust professionals in order to secure their trust in her. She knew she had created a powerful alliance with his teachers in his "sending" school. All those teachers knew Jason and encouraged Susan to pursue in-clusion because they would back her up. They did just that, meeting with his teachers in his new school and persuading them to give Jason a reception before spring semester ended and before he showed up for school in the fall.

That strategy was necessary to create partnerships with the "receiving" school and its staff, a partnership similar to the one Susan had created with one of Jason's sending teachers, Cindy.

To create partners, Susan found that she had to validate the teachers' efforts, writing compliments to them and sending copies to their administrators.

"I had come to an understanding that the teachers had a really hard job and that the more I could have them thinking positively about Jason and me, the better we would be."

Being an inclusion pioneer did not come naturally to Susan. Inspired by experiences of other parents in Hawaii and elsewhere and by the research and demonstration efforts of a few special education professors, Susan finally just bit the bullet. "I just really had my doubts . . . yet I thought, why not go for it? Let's try it."

That sense of great expectations paid off as Jason's peers "took ownership" of him and his education and began to regard him as a capable young man. Their attitude was infectious, and his new teacher, Mrs. Ching, began to develop a friendly relationship with Jason. Her relationship made it possible for Susan and Mrs. Ching to deal directly and candidly with each other.

But that sense of great expectations also has its downside, no matter how many reliable alliances Susan builds.

With Jason now 18 and having only two years of school eligibility left, Susan has begun to have doubts—not about whether she was right to pursue inclusion but about whether she might have done more to have Jason's schools offer him an inclusive experience throughout high school. It is not as if Jason is wholly separate from his typically developing peers. He is enrolled in the English-as-a-second language class; his peers without disabilities like him; various clubs take him on as a "project"; and once Jason graduates, Susan hopes he will be allowed to return as a neighborhood volunteer, watering the lawns or doing similarly useful acts, not because the school staff feels sorry for him but because he contributes—there is mutual benefit.

Despite all these relationships, however, Jason is not sufficiently included in most of the normal activities of the school.

"Inclusion is so difficult to keep going. I ask myself: Are we settling for less or are we just learning the limitations of the system? It's very emotional at the tail end of the educational system, when we know the system can't provide all we want. Was I too idealistic in trying to create a life for him that simply couldn't be? Our household is lovely, but, in school, Jason has a poor social life and no buddies." There is no doubt about the barriers to inclusion, what Susan calls "Contextual factors" that relate to how schools do what they do. "Still," admits Susan, "it is hard not to take on the blame, as a parent, for not moving those mountains. Perhaps because I am so keenly aware of what Jason is missing; the loss of that inclusion dream is far more painful to me than to him."

The root causes for this result include Jason's own disabilities and a health problem he had: until he was given a pacemaker in the fall of 1998, his biological rhythms were so erratic that he was undoubtedly a challenge to his teachers. Now, he's "Mr. Perky." Whether perky or not, and whether the school can or will do all that Susan wants for Jason, Jason's future depends so much on how Susan deals with those responsible for his education. Her strategy, through thick and thin, is to support those who help Jason to have choices and to be happy. "Relationships are still the key. One of Jason's teachers has put him on his 'loyalty list' even though Jason can be a pain in the butt. That relationship makes Jason feel appreciated. Instead of

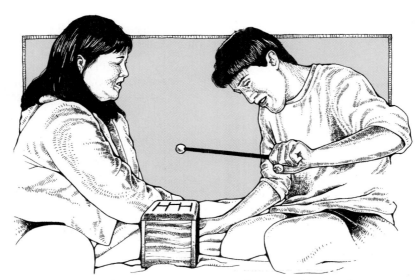

Caregiver Gina Ebato encourages Jason Rocco as he practices playing a musical instrument. (1999)

being a disciplinarian and power freak, this teacher, and others, deal with Jason and me in a different way. And that changes our behavior. Jason is so sensitive; he's a love-magnet. He reminds me—and others—to be kind and sensitive to others.

That's how people grow. Love is the only power on earth to move anyone. If we operate out of love and compassion and empathy, all will be well."

But, Susan is quick to add, "We also have to learn to love eccentricity."

As you learned in chapter 3, individual and collective empowerment occurs when families and professionals share equally the factors that constitute their resources (that is, motivation and knowledge/skills) in order to make decisions jointly. We described the education context factors as opportunities for partnerships and obligations for reliable alliances. This chapter focuses on the obligations for reliable alliances. In this chapter we describe the eight obligations for reliable alliances. Then throughout all remaining chapters in this book, especially chapters 9–15, we will describe many different ways for you to carry out these obligations in your relationships with families.

The eight obligations of reliable alliances include the following:

- Knowing yourself
- Knowing families
- Honoring cultural diversity
- Affirming and building on family strengths
- Promoting family choices
- Affirming great expectations
- Communicating positively
- Warranting trust and respect

Knowing Yourself

The first obligation for a reliable alliance is self-knowledge—knowing yourself. The more you know yourself, the better you can understand and appreciate the personalities and behaviors of others. What you need at the outset is a willingness to understand your own perceptions and to reflect on how they may be affecting your relationships with families (Kroth & Edge, 1997).

What does it mean to understand your own perceptions? The way in which people view the world varies widely and depends on a complex interaction of internal (such as mood, energy, and optimistic or pessimistic orientation) and external (such as environmental expectations and adequacy of resources) forces. The complexity

of this interaction prevents any two people from perceiving the world in exactly the same way. Why and how is this so?

First, we perceive the world through our sensory receptors. Although this fact accounts for much consistency in perception among people, it is possible that differences exist even at this basic level. Those differences are obvious when we interact with persons who experience deafness or blindness.

Through our sensory receptors, we filter and edit information to understand what we hear, feel, see, and smell. This part of perception, called *interpretation*, characteristically takes the form of impressions, conclusions, assumptions, expectations, or prejudices.

Interpretations differ from observations: Two people may observe the same event but interpret it differently. For example, some of the characteristic behaviors of autism are rocking, hand flapping, jumping up and down, and repeating words (Turnbull, Turnbull, Shank, & Leal, 1999). These behaviors are generally considered to be inappropriate. An alternative interpretation of these behaviors was described by an African American family who consistently focused on their son's similarities with others rather than his differences:

> On one occasion, as the family sat watching a high-speed chase scene on television, Chas jumped up and began to make a loud humming noise. He flapped his hands rapidly and paced back and forth. His mother looked at him calmly after it was over and said, "You really got excited at that Chas, didn't you?" He was not told to stop flapping his arms; rather his mother responded naturally, seeing what might be interpreted as "autistic behavior" as a characteristic related to his likes and dislikes. (O'Connor, 1995, pp. 74–75)

When we acknowledge our tendency to interpret sensory data, we realize that our interpretations may not always be accurate and may not be the same as families' interpretations.

As Susan Rocco learned after moving to Hawaii from the mainland, cultural differences can be a major factor contributing to alternative perceptions. For example, the principle of normalization emphasizes that individuals with disabilities should have the same opportunities in life as do similar-aged citizens who do not have disabilities (Wolfensberger, 1972). Under a normalization, it is generally assumed that as individuals with disabilities mature, they will pursue employment and move from their parents' home to their own home. A research study of seven families from culturally and linguistically diverse backgrounds reported that only one family (who was American-born and having upper-middle income) adhered to this normalization priority. Alternatively, the other six families all expected their child to continue to live at home with one of the spouses; a couple of the families also suggested that a group home might be appropriate (Harry, Rueda, & Kalyanpur, 1999). Because normalization is such a pervasive principle and is Euro-American in its values, it is likely that these families will encounter at least one special educator who holds that out-of-home living is an expected outcome from special education.

Many individuals in the dominant culture group have a difficult time gaining a clear understanding of their own cultural values because they assume that the cultural values that they hold are the right way to do things rather than only one cultural interpretation (out of many different cultural interpretations) of what seems right (Harry, Kalyanpur, & Day, 1999). One reason for this is that the dominant culture is as enfolded in their own cultural values as they are in the air that they breathe. That is why it is particularly important for all people—whether they are most or least represented in the American culture—to devote substantial time in being aware of their cultural values. A first step can be to learn more about one's own roots as a way of becoming grounded in one's cultural heritage. Figure 4-1 includes some cultural self-awareness questions that might guide you in your own reflections. The first section (Step 1) is particularly helpful in examining one's roots and heritage (Lynch, 1998). With this new insight of cultural origins, we encourage you to examine some of your own beliefs, biases, and behaviors that are reflected in Step 2 of figure 4–1. As you enhance your own cultural self-awareness, you will likely make strides in knowing yourself, which is the foundation of the other reliable alliance obligations.

To develop reliable alliances with others, you need to be willing to admit that your perceptions may be inaccurate, or at least incomplete, as well as different from theirs. By understanding your own perceptions and recognizing that differences in perceptions are natural results of different human experiences, you may be able to alter your approach when these differences exist. When in Hawaii (or Rome), do as the Hawaiians (or Romans) do; or at least know how you and they differ. Instead of viewing differences as problems or as "parents being wrong," regard differences as opportunities for families and you to broaden your respective understandings of one another and for you to try to "walk in the family's shoes," sand and all. Consider the family with empathy, remembering that *empathy* means an intuitive and sensitive understanding of the feelings and perspectives of another person. Bear in mind what the principal in Jason's high school did. He admitted Jason even though Jason and Susan had moved out of his district. His reason: It would have been too hard for Jason to change schools—hard because, above all else, Jason is sensitive to how others relate to him. To comprehend another's feelings, thoughts, and motives, you first need to understand yourself; then, empathetically understanding another will likely come more easily. And it will produce a reliable ally, such as Susan Rocco is to the principal of Jason's school.

Knowing Families

Just as it is important to know and understand yourself in order to establish reliable alliances, you also need to understand families. By their nature, families are complex. There are literally hundreds of ways that families can vary, so your challenge is to avoid simplistic general understandings of families and instead appreciate each family in terms of the unique dimensions of its own life.

You have already been briefly introduced to the family systems approach; we first brought it to your attention in chapter 1. A family systems approach enables you to be attuned to a family's:

- characteristics (such as cultural background, size and form, special challenges),
- interactions (within and between marital, parental, sibling, and extended-family relationships),
- functions (tasks or responsibilities that the family carries out such as affection, socialization, economics, and daily care), and
- life cycle issues (developmental stages and transitions that the family experiences).

The family systems approach in turn will enable you to develop a comprehensive and relevant appreciation of families' individuality and thereby to work more effectively and collaboratively with everyone in the family. You will have an opportunity to learn about family characteristics, interactions, functions, and life cycle in chapters 5 through 8. For right now, you might consider how the Smith, Cooper, Walker, and Rocco families vary in terms of some

FIGURE 4–1

A Cultural Self-Awareness Journey

Step 1: Your Cultural Roots and Heritage

1. When you think about your roots, what country(ies) other than the United States do you identify as a place of origin for you or your family?

2. Have you ever heard any stories about how your family or your ancestors came to the United States? Briefly, what was the story?

3. Are there any foods that you or someone else prepares that are traditional for your country(ies) of origin? What are they?

4. Are there any celebrations, ceremonies, rituals, holidays that your family continues to celebrate that reflect your country(ies) of origin? What are they? How are they celebrated?

5. Do you or anyone in your family speak a language other than English because of your origins? If so, what language?

6. Can you think of one piece of advice that has been handed through your family that reflects the values held by your ancestors in the country(ies) of origin? What was it?

Step 2: Your Cultural Values, Biases, and Behaviors

1. Have you ever heard anyone make a negative comment about your country(ies) of origin? If so, what was it?

2. As you were growing up, do you remember discovering that your family did anything differently from other families to which you were exposed because of your culture, religion, or ethnicity? Name something that you remember that was different.

3. Have you ever been with someone in a work situation who did something because of his or her culture, religion, or ethnicity that seemed unusual to you? What was it? Why did it seem unusual?

4. Have you ever felt shocked, upset, or appalled by something that you saw when you were traveling in another part of the world? If so, what was it? How did it make you feel? Pick some descriptive words to explain your feelings. In retrospect, how do you wish you would have reacted?

5. Have you ever done anything that you think was culturally inappropriate when you have been in another country or with someone from a different culture? In other words, have you ever done something that you think might have been upsetting or embarrassing to another person? What was it? What did you do to try to improve the situation?

6. If you could be from another culture or ethnic group, what culture would it be? Why?

7. What is one value from that culture or ethnic group that attracts you to it?

8. Is there anything about that culture or ethnic group that concerns or frightens you? What is it?

9. Name one concrete way in which you think your life would be different if you were from that culture or ethnic group.

Source: Adapted from Lynch, E. W. (1998). Developing cross-cultural competence. In E. W. Lynch & M. J. Hanson (Eds.). *Developing cross-cultural competence: A guide for working with young children and their families* (2nd ed.) (pp. 87–89). Baltimore: Brookes. Paul H. Brookes Publishing Co., P.O. Box 10624, Baltimore, MD 21285-0624. Reprinted by permission.

of their family characteristics, functions, and life cycle. Each of these four families is unique, and our goal is to prepare you to be responsive to the particular constellation of experiences, priorities, strengths, and needs of each of these families in addition to every family with whom you have an opportunity to develop a reliable alliance.

Honoring Cultural Diversity

To honor cultural diversity, your first step is to try to "stand in the shoes" (sand and all) of the families with whom you work, to the greatest extent possible. In the following situation, imagine you are an Inuk mother of a toddler with profound deafness. A communication specialist is giving you guidance about child development.

> This Inuk boy lived in an isolated northern village [in Alaska] and had not developed any spoken language. The mother had just reluctantly attempted to follow the therapist's model of working on sound-object association using an airplane, a car, and a boat. The therapist offered the following suggestion:
>
> Therapist: "See—look! He's really interested in letting the cars zoom down the ramp. What you could do would be to talk about just what he's interested in doing—whatever he's looking at or playing with. Like, "Whee! Up, up, up, up. Wait! One, two, three—GO! Whee! That's fun! Let's do it again!"
>
> [The therapist demonstrated the kind of interactive play that she used with the families with whom she worked, talking and pausing for the child's responses.]
>
> Inuk mother: "I just can't talk to my son in that way. It doesn't feel right." (Crago & Eriks-Brophy, 1993, pp. 123–124)

What are the fundamental elements that do not "feel right" to the mother? What does it really mean to "feel right" within relationships? Feeling right is one of the major outcomes of reliable alliances that honor cultural diversity. And as we show throughout this chapter and the entire book, reliable alliances are the essential ingredients of empowering contexts.

The matter of feeling right is by no means a trivial one when families from culturally diverse backgrounds are involved. Here is what a Native American professional says about trying to encourage members of her own tribe to enroll their children with disabilities in an early intervention program:

> I felt that the families were a little bit reluctant. [Even though] I'm a member of their own tribe, that they still considered me an intruder of some type, because a lot of other times when programs came in, they felt that there were too many people hounding them or hovering over them and wanting them to do this and do that, but as I explained to them, I'm also the parent of a child with disabilities, and that made it a little bit easier. I share their culture and beliefs, and I encourage them to use traditional medicines, never doubting that, and that always comes first, but at the same time, getting them to believe that in reality, too, there is something different. And that's how I've gained a lot of the parents' trust. (testimony by Norberta Sarracino, in National Council on Disability, 1995, p. 38)

Definition and Rationale

Culture refers to many different elements that influence one's sense of "we-ness." A sense of "we-ness"

group identity, includes race, ethnicity, religion, geographical location, income status, gender, sexual orientation, disability status, and occupation (Kalyanpur & Harry, 1999; Lynch & Hanson, 1998; Hernandez & Isaacs, 1998). As we said in discussing self-awareness, it is the framework within which individuals, families, or groups perceive and interpret their experiences. Additionally, culture is the springboard for developing visions that shape life choices. Often the term *culture* is used synonymously with the words *race* and *ethnicity*. That kind of terminology seems too limiting; culture is a much broader concept than only race and ethnicity.

There are many other factors that shape one's sense of culture or group identity (Banks & McGee-Banks, 1999). A White religious fundamentalist from the Midwestern Bible Belt who is the father of a child with a learning disability may very well have world views and ways of collaborating (or not) with professionals that are different from, say, those of an African American Muslim from the inner city of a large Eastern metropolis whose child is deaf. Further, the African American Muslim may have world views different from those of newly immigrated intact Vietnamese family members who were highly paid professionals and leaders in their Roman Catholic church and whose child has extraordinary mathematical or scientific talents.

In each of these three families, there are different cultural (not just racial or ethnic) attributes. These attributes may change over the family's lifespan. One family may change its religion or choose atheism, another's economic status may improve or decline precipitously, and still another's may be influenced by racial or religious intermarriage. Disability status also can strongly influence one's cultural affiliations, such as with the strong group identity known as *deaf culture* (Dolnick, 1993; Lane, Hoffmeister, & Bahan, 1996; Parasnis, 1996; Tucker, 1997).

Honoring cultural diversity is a means for establishing reliable alliances with people from different cultural backgrounds, ensuring that those alliances are characterized by nonstereotypical, respectful, and comfortable exchanges of communication, supports, and services, and creating empowering contexts (Boutte & DeFlorimonte, 1998). These alliances take into consideration the values, decision-making styles, family roles, language, background knowledge, and influences of significant others. How can you honor cultural diversity so that families with whom you interact will "feel right"—feel that your approach has responded to and affirmed their values and priorities?

Framework to Enhance Cultural Competence

To begin with, you will want to enhance your own cultural competence. Figure 4–2 describes a five-step process for doing just that.

Enhancing Self-Awareness We have already discussed the necessity of becoming more culturally self-aware (figure 4–1). As you reflect on your cultural roots and your own values, biases, and behaviors, you might complete the profile in figure 4–3 to identify how you believe that each of these different elements of your culture impacts you in your personal life and in your professional life (Banks & McGee-Banks, 1999; Harry, Kalyanpur, & Day, 1999).

The important thing, of course, is for you to be keenly aware of who you are and what factors shape your own cultural views and to understand that your cultural beliefs and traditions may work very well for you but not necessarily for others. The most dangerous trap for culturally unaware people is assuming that their way is the only right way. Susan Rocco knew that she would have to change her "mainland" approaches when she came to Hawaii; to Jason's benefit, she was culturally aware and adaptable.

Enhancing Culture-Specific Awareness One way to enhance your awareness about others' cultures is to learn more about individuals whose personal and professional profiles of cultural characteristics vary substantially from your own. A survey of American Indian parents revealed that approximately two-thirds stress the need for educators to learn more about American Indian cultures (Robinson-Zañartu & Majel-Dixon, 1996). You might consider opportunities in your community to follow this advice. Plus, you might explore a wide range of diversity in areas such as income and religion. For example, if your income level is at the middle-income range, you might explore what life is like for people who are substantially more limited in financial resources than you are. If your religion is Protestant, you might particularly want to seek out experiences of how religious values differ in the Hindu or Buddhist religions. If you are Euro-American, you might want to start participating in activities in your community that are attended by large groups of people from other ethnic/racial groups as a way to establish personal relationships and become acquainted with diverse traditions, music, crafts, and food. As you enhance your culture-specific awareness, you might reflect on how people new to your social network from these diverse groups might answer the questions in figure 4–1 and might respond to the profile in figure 4–3.

As you become more aware of traditions, customs, and values of various cultural groups, we caution you against stereotyping. For example, is it possible to characterize "the Hispanic family" or "the Asian family" accurately and fully? Absolutely not. For one thing, the group called *Hispanics* represents over 20 separate nationalities, each with differing degrees of acculturation, educational status, income, geographic location, and occupation (Zuniga, 1998). Similarly, Asian Americans originate from three major geographic areas and at least 15 different countries (Chan, 1998):

- East Asia: China, Japan, and Korea
- Southeast Asia: Burma, Cambodia, Laos, Vietnam, Malaysia, Singapore, Indonesia, the Philippines, Thailand
- South Asia: India, Pakistan, Sri Lanka, Bangladesh, Bhutan, and Nepal

---

FIGURE 4–2

Steps in Process to Enhance Cultural Competence

Enhancing self-awareness

↓

Enhancing culture-specific awareness

↓

Enhancing culture-generic awareness

↓

Enhancing culture-specific and culture-generic awareness related to exceptionality and family issues

↓

Establishing relationships that "feel right" with families from culturally diverse backgrounds

---

FIGURE 4–3

Personal Identity Web

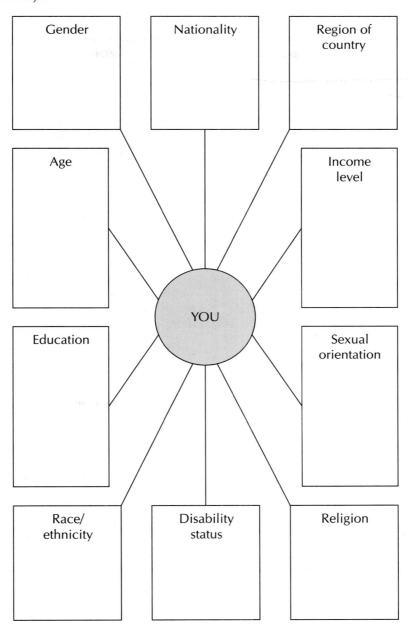

Gender | Nationality | Region of country

Age | Income level

YOU

Education | Sexual orientation

Race/ethnicity | Disability status | Religion

Source: Adapted from Banks, J. A., & McGee-Banks, C. A. (Eds.). (1999). *Multicultural education: Issues and perspectives* (3rd ed., p. 15). Needham Heights, MA: Allyn & Bacon; adapted by permission.

These three regions and 18 countries represent 60 different ethnic groups and three major religious orientations—Confucianism, Taoism, and Buddhism—and countless other diversities. That is why it is unwise to assume that there is any such thing as a stereotypical Asian American family. The best you can do, in a broad way, is to become familiar with general traditions, customs, and values of the families characterized by cultural diversity in your community. It is important to recognize, however, that there are tremendous family variations within cultural groups that do not let your general culture awareness lead you into overgeneralizations.

Enhancing Culture-Generic Awareness

Once you understand your own and others' cultures, your next step is to recognize crosscutting or generic traits of a number of groups who share cultural characteristics. For example, in chapter 5 you will learn about perspectives pertaining to individualism versus collectivism, system-centered versus relationship-centered orientation, a taking-charge perspective toward change versus an acceptance perspective toward tradition, and other perspectives that influence how families and professionals regard key elements of special education decision making. These perspectives are parts of the world views of individuals who sometimes share cultural affiliation; again, there are variations within and across groups (Kalyanpur & Harry, 1999).

Once you have characteristics such as these in mind, you can begin to understand the dimensions along which people representing different cultural characteristics can vary. For one thing, some individuals from a particular culturally or linguistically diverse background continue to hold traditional values of their particular cultural group; others become bicultural; and still others adopt values and traditions of the dominant culture (Hanson, 1998; Pewewardy, 1998). This is particularly important for the large number of children who are either immigrants or the American-born children of immigrants (Holman, 1997). The largest study ever of children of immigrants recently reported that this group of children grew to 13.7 million in 1997 (a 58 percent increase since 1990), making them the fastest-growing segment of Americans under the age of 18. In fact, one in five American children are either immigrants or the children of recent immigrants (Rumbaut, 1998).

Culturally generic issues do not relate to exceptionality specifically or to family issues associated with exceptionality. Rather, a generic cultural awareness serves as a guide to alliances that feel right to others and that can become reliable because they do indeed feel right.

Enhancing Cultural-Specific and Culture-Generic Awareness Related to Exceptionality and Family Issues

As your own cultural competence increases, so will your understanding of how you can foster reliable alliances with families from cultures other than your own. In chapter 11 you will learn that families from culturally diverse backgrounds interpret the definition and meaning of exceptionality in alternative ways. You will need this information as you collaborate with families when conducting evaluations, sharing evaluation results, and planning individualized programs. For example, you will understand how to collaborate with this grandmother, whose daughter and granddaughter spent many years in special education programs. The grandmother commented:

> [Special educators] say that word "handicap" means a lot of things, it doesn't just mean that a person is crazy. But for us, Puerto Ricans, we still understand this word as "crazy." For me, a person who is handicapped is a person who is not of sound mind or has problems in speech or some problems of the hands or legs. But my children have nothing like that, thanks to God and the Virgin! (Harry, 1992c, p. 31)

As this example shows, culture influences the definition and meaning of exceptionality. As you will learn later, it also influences respective professional and family roles, communication patterns, expectations for independence and achievement, discipline, and anticipated outcomes of education. As you gain more culture-specific and culture-generic awareness related to exceptionality and family issues, consider the cultural characteristics that can affect a family's responses to collaboration and to the educational services you provide. Box 4–1 includes tips for enhancing your own cultural competence with families.

Establishing Feel-Right Alliances with Families from Culturally Diverse Backgrounds

The more you honor cultural diversity, the more you will be able to establish feel-right alliances. Returning to the illustration about the Inuk mother at the beginning of this section, how could the speech therapist have done a better job of creating a feel-right alliance? Unfortunately, much of the professional literature in the field assumes that what feels right to middle- and upper-middle-class White mothers feels right to all family members representing the broad range of cultural diversity.

The research on families of children with exceptionalities has concentrated on middle- and upper-middle-class White mothers. For example, a review of all articles published in four journals (*Journal of Early Intervention*,

Enhancing Your Own Cultural Competence with Families: Being More Culturally Competent

- Learn about the families in the community served. What cultural groups are represented? Where are they from? When did they arrive? How closely knit is the community? What language(s) is spoken? What are the cultural practices associated with child rearing? What cultural beliefs surround health and healing, disability, and causation? Who are the community leaders and/or spiritual leaders, and what are their roles in advising and counseling families?

- Work with cultural mediators or guides from the families' cultures to learn more about the extent of cultural identification within the community at large and the situational aspects of this identification and regional variations.

- Learn and use words and forms of greeting in the families' languages if families are English-language learners; ensure that trained interpreters are present for assessments and meetings with family members.

- Allow additional time to work with interpreters to determine families' concerns, priorities, and recourses, and to determine the next steps in the process. Remember that rapport building may take considerable time but that it is critical to effective intervention.

- Recognize that some families may be surprised by the extent of parent-professional collaboration that is expected in intervention programs in the United States. Do not expect every family to be comfortable with such a high degree of involvement. However, never assume that they do not want involvement and are not involved from their own perspective. Likewise, do not assume that they will become involved or will feel comfortable doing so.

- Use as few written forms as possible with families who are English-language learners or non-English speaking. If forms are used, be sure that they are available in the family's language. Rely on the interpreter, your observations, and your own instincts and knowledge to know when to proceed and when to wait for the family to signal the readiness to move to the next step.

- Recognize the power differentials that many families experience between agency representatives and themselves; be aware of the larger sociopolitical climate that is influencing families' decision making.

Source: Lynch, E. W., & Hanson, M. J. (1998). Steps in the right direction: Implications for interventionists. In E. W. Lynch & M. J. Hanson (Eds.), *Developing cross-cultural competence: A guide for working with young children and their families* (pp. 491–512). Baltimore: Brookes. Paul H. Brookes Publishing Co., P.O. Box 10624, Baltimore, MD 21285-0624. Reprinted by permission.

Topics in Early Childhood Special Education, Infant-Toddler Intervention, and *Infants and Young Children*) that had one or more of the words *parent, family, mother, father,* or *primary caregiver* in the title and were published during a 12-month period (1998) showed that the sample populations in the research studies included a 16-to-1 ratio in favor of mothers to fathers. During this time, no studies had the word *father* in the title. Hispanics, Asians, and Native Americans were especially underrepresented in the research samples. There has been a clear tendency to conduct research on Euro-American mothers and to apply the results to all family members of all races (Turnbull, Turbiville, Turnbull, & Gabbard, 1993). Generalizing the results of this research to all families from culturally diverse backgrounds is unwarranted.

Furthermore, over the last decades the research on culturally diverse families has often ignored families' strengths and has confused the effects of race with the effects of socioeconomic factors. Often the research has not been done by researchers from culturally diverse backgrounds, who may well have the keener cultural understanding that seems necessary for interpreting data in a nondiscriminatory way (Marion, 1979; Ruiz & Padilla, 1977; Harry, 1992a). Beth Harry and Maya Kalyanpur (Harry & Anderson, 1999; Harry, Rueda, & Kalyanpur, 1999; Harry & Kalyanpur, 1999; Kalyanpur & Harry, 1999; Kalyanpur, Harry, & Skrtic, in press; Kalyanpur, 1999; Kalyanpur, 1998), as well as Eleanor Lynch and Marci Hanson (Lynch & Hanson, 1998), have made major strides in conducting research and promoting best practices related to cultural responsiveness.

Moreover, the vast number of special education textbook writers, federal and state policy leaders, school-board members, state and local educational agency administrators, and teachers and related service providers have been and still are from the Euro-American, middle-class culture (Wald, 1996). For example, approximately 86 percent of special education teachers are White, 10 percent are Black, 2 percent are Hispanic, and 2 percent are from other racial groups (Cook & Boe, 1995). Likewise, similar statistics have been found at the state and local levels of vocational rehabilitation agencies (National Council on Disability, 1999). Quite naturally, these people, often lacking cultural competence, frequently have assumed that "good parents" are ones who fit the Euro-American mold and behave in Euro-American ways (Kalyanpur & Harry, 1999).

In order to establish feel-right alliances, it is necessary for you to get beyond the overt (for example, language and dress) and covert (for example, communication style and mannerisms) levels to the more subtle (for example, values and embedded beliefs) nuances that shape the thinking of individuals from culturally and linguistically diverse backgrounds (Harry & Kalyanpur, 1999; Kalyanpur & Harry, 1999). One way to establish meaningful dialogue is to follow the posture of cultural reciprocity. This approach involves steps of sharing perspectives between families and educators in an effort to "get on each other's wavelength" (Harry & Kalyanpur, 1999; Kalyanpur & Harry, 1999). Box 4–2 includes an adaptation of the posture of cultural reciprocity to fit it within the suggestions that we provide for you (especially in chapter 9) on getting to know each family's unique situation and seeking the perspectives *prior to* making your own interpretations and recommendations about what is appropriate in a given situation.

Kalyanpur and Harry (1999) describe the purpose of using this posture of reciprocity as follows:

> Awareness of cultural differences provides merely the scaffolding for building collaborative relationships. Knowledge of the underlying belief and value that brings about the difference in perspective provides the reinforcing strength to the relationship. Toward this end, we have developed an approach that we call "a posture of cultural reciprocity." We suggest that professionals adopt this approach whereby they engage in explicit discussions with families regarding differential cultural values and practices, bringing to the interactions an openness of mind, the ability to be reflective in their practice, and the ability to listen to the other perspectives. Furthermore, they must respect the new body of knowledge that emerges from these discussions and make allowances for differences in perspective when responding to the family's need. (Kalyanpur & Harry, 1999, p. 118)

TIPS

BOX 4–2

Adapted Posture of Cultural Reciprocity

1. Learn about the family's strengths, needs, and expectations that evolve from the "family story." Also find out the priorities and preferences for their child's educational program—IEP, placement, related services, extracurricular activities, and so on. Seek to understand and honor the cultural values and priorities as you establish a reliable alliance with them.

2. Converse with the family about the assumptions that underlie the cultural values and priorities. Seek to find out about their rationales.

3. As you reflect on their priorities and preferences, identify any disagreements or alternative perspectives that you or other professionals have, as compared to those of the family, associated with providing educational supports and services to the student and/or family. Identify the cultural values that are embedded in *your* underlying interpretation or in the interpretation of other professionals. Identify how the family's views differ from your own.

4. Acknowledge and give explicit respect to any cultural differences identified, and fully explain the cultural basis of your professional assumptions or the assumptions of other professionals.

5. For discussion and collaboration, determine the most effective way of adapting your professional interpretations to the family's value system.

Affirming and Building on Family Strengths

As you read in chapter 1, many professionals have tended to focus on families' deficiencies rather than their strengths. Yet highlighting and appreciating families' strengths is one of the key aspects of supporting families to enhance their own self-efficacy (Cowger, 1994; Goldstein, 1990; Powell, Batsche, Ferro, Fox, & Dunlap, 1997; Saleebey, 1996; Summers, Templeton-McMann, & Fuger, 1997). Remember that self-efficacy is an element of motivation in chapter 3's empowerment framework. Building reliable alliances depends on your respecting families' inherent strengths and building upon them through the collaborative process. Figure 4–4 provides a comparison of a pathology and strengths approach. As a professional, which approach is more empowering for you to provide? As a family member, which approach is more empowering for you to receive?

All families have strengths. For children who are gifted, family strengths have been identified as spending time in out-of-school activities with adult interaction, having stimulating adult conversation around the dinner table, creating opportunities for full development of the child's abilities and talents, and modeling engagement in intellectual and artistic activities (Alsop, 1997; Bloom, 1985; Friedman, 1994; Schlosser & Yewchuk, 1998). Even families who face major challenges, such as substance abuse or child or spousal maltreatment, can have strengths in other areas of their lives. Figure 4–5 includes a list of strengths that you might consider as you interact with families. If you regard the family as having only challenges or needs—not strengths—you may have difficulty becoming a reliable ally. If, on the other hand, you recognize and affirm its strengths, you will likely become a more reliable ally.

Reflect on those relationships with people you regard as your reliable allies. Do they believe in your strengths or focus on your weaknesses? Your own preferences are probably like the preferences of almost everyone else: We all tend to be more comfortable with and effective around people who value our strengths and do not "put us down." That was the way Jason Rocco's teachers responded to him and Susan; and, remember, Susan made a point of emphasizing the teachers' strengths.

FIGURE 4–4

Comparison of Pathology and Strengths

Pathology

Person is defined as a "case"; symptoms add up to a diagnosis.

Therapy is problem focused.

Personal accounts aid in the evocation of a diagnosis through reinterpretation by an expert.

Practitioner is skeptical of personal stories, rationalizations.

Childhood trauma is the precursor or predictor of adult pathology.

Centerpiece of therapeutic work is the treatment plan devised by practitioner.

Practitioner is the expert on clients' lives.

Possibilities for choice, control, commitment, and personal development are limited by pathology.

Resources for work are the knowledge and skills of the professional.

Help is centered on reducing the effects of symptoms and the negative personal and social consequences of actions, emotions, thoughts, or relationships.

Strengths

Person is defined as unique; traits, talents, resources add up to strengths.

Therapy is possibility focused.

Personal accounts are the essential route to knowing and appreciating the person.

Practitioner knows the person from the inside out.

Childhood trauma is not predictive; it may weaken or strengthen the individual.

Centerpiece of work is the aspirations of family, individual, or community.

Individuals, family, or community are the experts.

Possibilities for choice, control, commitment, and personal development are open.

Resources for work are the strengths, capacities, and adaptive skills of the individual, family, or community.

Help is centered on getting on with one's life, affirming and developing values and commitments, and making and finding membership in or as a community.

Source: National Association of Social Workers, Inc. (1996). *Social Work, 41,* 296–305.

FIGURE 4–5

Samples of Families' Strengths

- Lots of caring, extended families ✓
- Being very optimistic
- Being very knowledgeable
- Making the child feel loved and accepted
- Maintaining an orderly, well-organized, and safe home
- Having a yard or park for playing
- Encouraging the child to notice, hear, and smell different interesting things around the house
- Encouraging wellness and health in all family members through exercise, balanced diet, and healthy habits
- Seeking out support from friends or counseling as needed
- Finding unique ways to use informal teachable moments as part of a typical home life
- Communicating thoughts and feelings to family members in a supportive and authentic way
- Having a sense of humor
- Being persistent in seeking help and support from others
- Having a strong religious faith
- Having interesting hobbies to share with children

Source: Adapted from Turbiville, V.., Lee, I., Turnbull, A., & Murphy, D. (1993). *Handbook for the development of a family friendly individualized service plan (IFSP).* Lawrence, KS: University of Kansas, Beach Center on Families and Disability.

Promoting Family Choices

Because perceived control is a critical factor contributing to the motivation of individuals and families to take action in their lives (review chapter 3), it is necessary in building reliable alliances and creating empowering contexts to increase families' opportunities to express their choices and have those choices heard and heeded by professionals such as yourself (Petr, 1998; Singer, Powers, & Olson, 1996; Turnbull, Turbiville, & Turnbull, 2000). There are many different areas in which family choice can be exercised, including the following (Petr, 1998):

1. Selecting the family members to be involved in collaborative decision making

2. Choosing the extent of choice that family members will exercise pertaining to decision making for each priority issue
3. Determining the family members who will be involved in the service-delivery process
4. Deciding the nature of the family-professional relationship (such as the times and places for meetings)
5. Determining information that the family feels comfortable disclosing to professionals
6. Identifying the priority needs, goals, and nature of support that will be provided

Promoting family choices requires planning and delivering educational services in a way that maximizes flexibility for the family. When nearly 100 families were asked what they need to make their days easier, what would contribute to the well-being of their families and children, and how the public sector could best support them (Knoll, 1992), they did not respond by listing a series of "whats," such as specific services or resources that they would like to have. Instead, they described the "hows" and the process through which professionals and agencies furnish resources. The process they mentioned most frequently was flexibility in all aspects of services. Flexibility connotes that professionals and agencies recognize that each family is different—each has its own characteristics, patterns of interaction, priorities for different family functions, and issues associated with life cycle stages and transitions. Families want the flexibility directed to support the choices that are highest priority for them.

Reliable alliances are like a kaleidoscope. Just as every turn of the kaleidoscope creates a different pattern, so does every family, consistent with its choices, call forth a different pattern of communication, services, and supports. A change in one aspect of the family's characteristics, interactions, functions, or life cycle might require professionals and agencies to change accordingly.

This means that flexible professionals and organizations do not have a rigid set of rules for every situation, and they do not act on the basis that "we've always provided services this way, and there's no need for us to change now." Rather, they are creative and follow the family's lead (Jones, Garlow, Turnbull, & Barber, 1996; Schorr, 1997). This is basically the way in which the staff in Jason Rocco's "sending" school followed Susan's lead as she sought his inclusion. And it is how the principal in his present high school behaved, admitting Jason despite the fact that Jason now lived outside that school's district. In schools (as you learned in chapter 2), following families' leads involves moving away from bureaucracy and embracing "adhocracy"—emphasizing collaborative partnerships that respond to specific school-based, student-focused priorities and needs (Skrtic, 1995).

Affirming Great Expectations

You learned about the importance of great expectations in chapter 3. In addition to great expectations being one of the elements of motivation resources in chapter 3, it is also one of the eight obligations of a reliable alliance. Several studies have indicated that parental expectations for students with disabilities are more similar than different to parental expectations for students without disabilities. In a national study of eighth-grade students carried out to investigate the effects of the child's disability on parental educational expectations, results indicated the following:

- Parents of students with disabilities had slightly higher expectations than parents of students without disabilities.
- Parents of students with visual impairments had the highest expectations as compared to parents of children with other types of disabilities.
- The parents were more likely to have the expectation that their children would attend college if their child was doing well academically or if the parents themselves had attended college.
- Expectations were higher for families who were White and Asian as contrasted to families who were African American, Hispanic, and Native American (Masino & Hodapp, 1996).

The second study found that mothers of children with disabilities and children who attended vocational education were influenced by similar factors in terms of setting expectations for their adolescents' futures (Lehmann & Roberto, 1996). Again, mothers of youth with disabilities expressed more positive expectations than did mothers of students in vocational education, suggesting that it was the limitations of adult services, not the limitations of their children, that was a barrier.

A study that particularly focused on the impact of parental expectations on the achievement of adolescents with and without learning disabilities found that parental expectations for both groups of students have a significant impact on their academic achievement and on their future career choices (Patrikakou, 1996). In addition to student expectations, this research also underscored the critical importance of the students' own expectations for their academic achievement.

An important area for ensuring great expectations is in the education of students from culturally and linguistically diverse backgrounds (Obiakor, 1999). Students from diverse backgrounds can be at particular risks for prejudicial decision making on the part of educators and the educators' failure to use the posture of cultural reciprocity (see box 4–2) in truly understanding students' and families' perspectives and collaborating with them to affirm great expectations. A Native American father shared his letter to his son's teacher regarding expectations that he hoped the teacher would hold for his son:

> My son, Wind-Wolf, is not an empty glass coming into your class to be filled. He is a full basket coming into a different environment and society with something special to share. Please let him share his knowledge, heritage, and culture with you and his peers. (Lake, 1990, p. 53)

Terms such as *great expectations* and *visions* are not ones that you will typically hear from parents; you are much more likely to hear them talk about hope. Parents typically want professionals to have and express hope about their child's future and their own future—a sense of great expectation, a vision that good things are possible in the future. That is why you should cherish and nurture families' hope and great expectations; as you value and enhance their hope and great expectations, you also become a more empowering professional and a more reliable ally. But also remember that some parents, such as Susan Rocco, may legitimately question whether their great expectations were too high. If they do, you may want to consider this: Is the outcome for their children—the one that causes them to be disappointed—the result of their child's limitations, or is it the result of the limitations of a school or other service-delivery system? Or is it the result of both?

One of the best ways to enhance families' great expectations is to share with them the success of other individuals with disabilities whose characteristics are similar to those of their son or daughter. One book that we think is particularly helpful for parents of children and youth with learning disabilities focuses on 71 adults with learning disabilities who have been especially successful in their employment (Reiff, Gerber, & Ginsberg, 1997). In this book, *Exceeding Expectations,* individuals with learning disabilities tell how they developed their own sense of self-efficacy and how that sense enabled them to be strengthened, not defeated, by what they characterized as the "chronic torture" of their educational experiences. Similarly, children, youth, and adults with disabilities who have successfully overcome some of the particular problems associated with their challenging behaviors are described in a book by

Lucyshyn, Dunlap, and Albin (in press). You might share these and similar resources with families, or you might introduce families to other families in your own community who will share their own success stories. (We will discuss more about parent matching—which is referred to as the parent-to-parent model—in chapter 10.)

Communicating Positively

Positive communication skills are especially important for educators and families. The more accurately and constructively you and families communicate thoughts and feelings, the more successful your alliances with them will be, the more you will create an empowering context, and the more the families will be able to experience empowerment. Some individuals, such as Susan Rocco, seem to have a natural ability to communicate well, but most of us must work consciously to develop this ability. Fortunately, professionals and families can learn and apply communication skills to one-on-one and group discussions (Edwards, 1986; Hackney & Cormier, 1996; Hirsch & Altman, 1986; Ivey, Ivey, & Simek-Morgan, 1993; Ivey, 1994; Kohl, Parrish, Neef, Driessen, & Hallinan, 1988; Kroth & Edge, 1997; Lombana, 1983).

Although many communication skills can be taught, some theorists contend that effective communication is an art, not a science. Indeed, there is an art in communication skills that relies heavily on the user's attitudes and personal qualities. We encourage you to master both the art and the science of communication skills and to incorporate these techniques and qualities into your personal style so that they become natural and spontaneous. That requires systematic practice and use of the skills. It also requires cultural and disability sensitivity.

Refining nonverbal communication skills is challenging enough when done within a uni-cultural context, but it is even more so when you have partnerships with families from cultures different than your own. For example, looking the speaker directly in the eye is typically considered being attentive and polite within a Euro-American culture (Lynch, 1998). But eye-to-eye contact with members of the opposite sex, people in authority, or elders can be considered disrespectful within an Asian culture (Sileo & Prater, 1998).

Moreover, disabilities sometimes interfere with communication skills, so accommodations are necessary. For example, a parent who is deaf and communicates through signs will need an interpreter or professional collaborators who themselves can sign.

In this section, you will learn about nonverbal communication skills, verbal communication skills, influ-encing skills, group communication skills, communication skills for difficult situations, and techniques for improving your communication. Figure 4–6 highlights the communication skills we will discuss.

Nonverbal Communication Skills

Nonverbal communication includes all communication other than the spoken or written word. When most of us communicate verbally, we also communicate nonverbally through the use of gestures, facial expressions, voice volume and intonations, physical proximity to others, and posture. Often, we are unconscious of the many nonverbal cues that any of us transmit to others. So, if you wish to improve the nature of your interactions with families, you will need to use nonverbal communication skills such as physical attending and listening.

Physical Attending Physical attending consists of contact, facial expressions, and gestures. The contact component involves both eye contact and the degree of physical contact, or closeness, between people who are communicating with one another. Because your eyes are a primary vehicle for communicating, maintaining culturally appropriate eye contact is a way of showing your respect for and interest in another person. It is estimated that White middle-class people look away from the listener approximately 50 percent of the time when speaking but make eye contact with the speaker about 80 percent of the time when listening. On the contrary, a trend for Black Americans is to make greater eye contact when speaking and less eye contact when listening. Navajos are described as using more peripheral vision, believing that direct stares are a way to express hostility and to discipline children when they are being reprimanded (Sue, 1981).

In a similar way, adjusting the physical space between yourself and family members with whom you are communicating may also convey a particular level of interest. Again, cultural considerations come into play.

Hall (1966) has identified four interpersonal distance zones characteristic of Anglo culture: intimate, from contact to 18 inches; personal, from 1 1/2 feet to 4 feet; social, from 4 to 12 feet; and public (lectures and speeches), greater than 12 feet . . . However, different cultures dictate different distances in personal space. For Latin Americans, Africans, Black Americans, Arabs, South Americans, French, and Indonesians, conversing with a person dictates a much closer stance than normally comfortable for Anglos (Jensen, 1985). A Latin American client may cause the counselor to back away because of the closeness taken. The client may interpret the counselor's behavior as indicative of aloofness, coldness, or desire not to

> ### FIGURE 4–6
>
> ## Interpersonal Communication Skills
>
> - Nonverbal communication skills
>   - Physical attending
>   - Listening
> - Verbal communication skills
>   - Furthering responses
>   - Paraphrasing
>   - Response to affect
>   - Questions
>   - Summarization
> - Influencing skills
>   - Providing information
>   - Focusing support attention
>   - Offering assistance
> - Group communication
> - Using communication skills in difficult situations

communicate. In some cross-cultural encounters, it may even be perceived as a sign of haughtiness and superiority. On the other hand, the counselor may misinterpret the client's behavior as an attempt to become inappropriately intimate, a sign of pushiness or aggressiveness. Both the counselor and the culturally different client may benefit from understanding that their reactions and behaviors are a chance to create the spatial dimension to which they are culturally conditioned. (Sue & Sue, 1990, p. 53)

As you become more culturally aware of the specific traditions of families with whom you interact, observe their interactions with each other and with others and get recommendations from professionals who have worked successfully with them in the past so that you will be able to determine the personal space that is culturally comfortable.

A second component of physical attending is facial expressions. Typically, desirable facial expressions are described as being appropriately varied and animated, occasionally smiling, and reflecting warmth and empathy. Again, cultural groups vary in the emphasis and frequency of smiling. For example, many people from southeast Asia tend to smile regardless of being happy or sad or even when they are being reprimanded (Sileo & Prater, 1998).

As contrasted to smiling, having a stiff facial expression, smiling slightly, or pursing the lips is often considered undesirable within the typical physical attending expecta-

tions of a Euro-American culture. Despite these general rules regarding facial expressions, you should recognize that some people have facial differences that necessitate accommodations by them and appropriate interpretation of these accommodations by others. Some have no ability to smile, frown, or otherwise express their feelings through their face or eyes. In an earlier edition of this book, we included a checklist that stated "desirable" and "undesirable" characteristics of physical attending. One of the readers of the book, Sandy Goodwick from California, took issue with how we presented the information because we did not adequately account for the facial differences that she and others experience. Sandy wrote us a very helpful letter in enabling us to become more informed about and sensitive to facial differences. We share an excerpt from Sandy's letter with you in box 4–3, because her perspectives are particularly enlightening.

Gestures are a third component of physical attending. Not surprisingly, the meaning of gestures can vary across cultural groups. Some hand gestures mean one thing for one cultural group but a different thing for a different group; some groups may regard "thumbs up" or "V for victory" as vulgar signs, whereas other groups may regard them as entirely positive.

Listening Listening is the "language of acceptance" and is one of the most essential ingredients of a reliable alliance. One of the seven habits of highly effective people as described by Steven Covey, is to "Seek first to understand, then to be understood" (Covey, 1990, p. 237). When we truly seek to understand the other person before stating our own perspectives, we will find ourselves in a listening mode.

Unfortunately, true listening rarely occurs naturally or spontaneously. To listen with genuine, undivided attention requires both diligence and practice and your awareness of different types of listening (Covey, 1990):

- *Ignoring:* not paying attention at all to the person who is talking
- *Pretending:* giving the outward appearance that we are listening but actually thinking about something entirely different or thinking about what we are going to say in response
- *Selective listening:* listening to only parts of what someone is saying based on our own energy, time, interests, or emotions
- *Attentive passive listening:* listening to what the other person is saying but not using nonverbal attending skills, using silence or minimal encouragement for them to continue, or not communicating any acceptance of what they are saying

My Face

I was born with absolutely no facial expression—smile, frown, wink, etc. Due to the "wonders" of microscopic surgery, I now can "smile," albeit artificially. . . . It is because of my unique disability, and the seemingly "unknown" difficulties inherent in such a condition that I am writing this letter to you. . . .

"Warmth and concern reflected in facial expression, appropriately varied and animated facial expressions," ". . . . occasional smiles" are all [regarded] as "desirable" traits while "Frozen or rigid facial expressions" is listed as "undesirable." While these characteristics may imply that the practitioner is caring or uncaring, they by themselves are only indicative of facial animation—perhaps a "window" into the mindset or personality of the "practitioner." I, and the others affected by facial "difference," have individually fought a life-long battle of ignorance and stigma—while I ulti-

mately can accept the fact that families may lack the professional knowledge and skills necessary to "understand" what it is like to have a facial difference. I cannot condone what I perceive as "ignorance" by the "helping profession" any longer. . . . I *resent* having a physical disability categorized as "undesirable."

I have been an elementary school teacher for 20 years. The road to a successful career was not easy— as a sophomore in college, I was called in to the Dean of Students' office. It was suggested that I not go into teaching "because of . . . uh . . . your 'problem,' Sandy." (Which one?—my absolute ignorance in knowing even the *name* of this condition . . . or the accumulation of emotional "garbage" inherent in single-handedly coping with a facial difference). I had, years ago, decided to become a teacher, because I wanted to undo the horrendous experience I had encountered

while in elementary school, via becoming, "the world's best teacher." One and a half years later I began student teaching—I went from "excellent" to "barely passing," when I perceived the students were teasing me because I could not smile. . . .

Contrary to the Dean of Students' wishes, I went into teaching (despite the horrific student teaching experience!) and became a well-respected educator. I am completely convinced that neither my students nor their parents or other teachers say my "frozen or rigid facial expression" as indicative of a frozen personality. While I had not yet fully addressed my myriad of internal emotional baggage related to having a facial difference, I *knew* my lack of facial expression was not, by itself, an insurmountable obstacle in becoming a warm, caring and effective teacher.

Sandy Goodwick
September 1993

- *Active listening:* assuming a much more involved and direct role by being animated, making comments, asking questions, and even sharing personal experiences to foster a dialogue
- *Empathetic listening:* standing in the shoes of the person who is talking and seeing the world and their situation as they see it and feel it

Although none of us likes to admit it, we all have ignored, pretended, and selected what we have heard. In addition, we have all used passive and active listening. But empathetic listening will help build reliable alliances. In his description of highly effective people, Covey (1990) describes empathetic listening:

When I say empathetic listening I mean listening with intent to understand. I mean seeking first to under-

stand, to really understand. It's an entirely different paradigm. . . . Empathetic listening involves much more than registering, reflecting, or even understanding the words that are said. . . . In empathetic listening, you listen with your ears, but you also, and more importantly, listen with your eyes and with your heart. You listen for feeling, for meaning. You listen for behavior. You use your right brain as well as your left. You sense, you intuit, you feel. (Covey, 1990, pp. 240–241)[1]

Empathy requires you to set aside your own internal frames of reference so that you can understand and experience the world from the other person's point of view, nonjudgmentally and nonevaluatively. When you listen empathetically, you do not agree or disagree but simply understand what it means to be "in the other person's

---

[1]©Fireside/Simon & Schuster, *The seven habits of highly effective people: Restoring the character ethic,* Stephen R. Covey. All rights reserved. Used with permission of Covey Leadership Center, Inc. 1-800-331-7716.

shoes." You convey genuine interest, understanding, and acceptance of the family's feelings and experiences (Perl, 1995). This does not mean that you will necessarily approve of or agree with the family's point of view but that you will try to understand the family's situation from the family's point of view—not your own. Remember what Susan Rocco said: "I had come to the understanding that the teachers had a really hard job." That understanding came because Susan cared enough to listen empathetically. "Your best shot," she says, "is to make friends with somebody." After all, "Relationships are the key"—not only to Jason's being in a school that ordinarily he would not attend but also in having a chance to return there, "where he is known and liked," as a community volunteer. What good advice for professionals and families alike!

Verbal Communication Skills

Although the nonverbal communication skills of physical attending and empathetic listening are effective and essential means for communicating with families, verbal responses are also essential in facilitating communication. Examples of verbal responses include (1) furthering responses, (2) paraphrasing, (3) response to affect, (4) questioning, and (5) summarization.

Furthering Responses Furthering responses indicate attentive listening and encourage people to continue to speak and examine their thoughts and feelings. There are two types of furthering responses:

1. Minimal encouragers, sometimes referred to as the "grunts and groans" of communication, usually include short but encouraging responses such as "Oh?" "Then?" "Mm-hm," "I see," or "And then?" Minimal encouragers can also be nonverbal and take the form of head nods, facial expressions, and gestures that communicate listening and understanding.
2. Verbal following involves restating the main points or emphasizing a word or phrase contained in what the family member has said, using the language system of the family. Verbal following not only encourages the family member to go on speaking but also provides the professional with a means of checking listening accuracy, as in the following example:

   Family member: I've had a really rough day.
   Professional: Oh? [a minimal encourager]
   Family member: Stanley woke up with wet sheets and cried all through breakfast. To

   top it off, the bus came early, and I had to send him to school without any lunch.
   Professional: You've had a really rough day. [a verbal follow]

Paraphrasing Paraphrasing involves using your own words to restate the family's message in a clear manner. Paraphrasing emphasizes your restating the cognitive aspects of the message (such as ideas or objects) but not necessarily the affective state of the speaker. Use language as similar to the family's as possible. Paraphrasing responds to both the implicit and explicit meanings of what is said, and its goal is to check for accuracy and make sure that there is a clear understanding of the issues before moving ahead to engage in collaborative problem solving, as in this example:

   Family member: Everything seems to be a burden these days, doing the housework, taking care of the kids, paying the bills. I just don't know how much longer I can keep up the pace.

   Professional: All your responsibilities really cause a drain on your time and energy.

In this example, you try empathetically to comprehend the situation from the person's perspective and to sense how challenging it is to be spread across so many different tasks and responsibilities. Again, it is not just the words but the frustration, fatigue, and overload that is communicated. In paraphrasing, the task is not just to feed back mechanically a rephrased statement but, through the verbal statement and the nonverbal communication, to let this person know that you empathize with the tremendous drain on time and energy.

Paraphrasing is an extremely useful technique in clarifying content, tying a number of comments together, highlighting issues by stating them more concisely, checking one's empathetic understanding, and—most important—communicating interest in and understanding of what the family member is saying.

Response to Affect Response to affect involves the ability to (1) perceive accurately and sensitively the other person's apparent and underlying feelings and (2) communicate understanding of those feelings in language that is attuned to the other person's experience at that moment. You pay attention not only to what is said but also to how it is said. When you use this technique, try to verbalize the family member's feelings and attitudes and use responses that are accurate and match the intensity of the family member's affect. Developing a vocabulary of affective words and phrases can be helpful. The following is an example of response to affect:

> *Family member:* Ever since Elliot was born, my family and friends have put a wall up between me and them. I guess they don't want to do the wrong thing, but what they don't realize is that the worst thing of all is doing nothing and staying away. I have no one to turn to and feel my "resentment gauge" going up by the day. It really hurts me and makes me angry when I've always tried to be there for them, and now when I need them most, they just seem to back away.
>
> *Professional:* You're feeling very let down by family who you thought would always be there for you.

The purpose of responding to affect is to provide a mirror in which family members can see their feelings and attitudes. This reflection, in turn, helps them move toward greater self-understanding and problem solving (Covey, 1990). Finally, response to affect can enable you to check the accuracy of your own perceptions of the family member's feelings.

Questioning Questions generally fall into two categories: closed-ended and open-ended questions. Closed-ended questions are used mostly to ask for specific factual information. Skillful communicators keep their use of closed-ended questions to a minimum because this type of question limits responses to a few words or a simple yes or no. Moreover, overuse of closed-ended questions also can make an interaction seem like an interrogation. While closed-ended questions can restrict conversation and often yield limited information, they are appropriate when used sparingly and propitiously. Here are some examples of closed-ended questions that are usually appropriate:

- "When did Carlos first start having seizures?"
- "How old is Betty Sue?"
- "Would a ten o'clock meeting be O.K. for you?"

Unlike closed-ended questions, open-ended questions invite family members to share and talk more. Some open-ended questions are unstructured and open the door for family members to talk about whatever is on their mind (for example, "What things seem to be going best for you right now?" or "How can I be of assistance?"). Other open-ended questions are more structured and impose boundaries on possible responses by focusing the topic (for example, "What are some of the specific methods you've tried to help Matthew behave more appropriately?").

Open-ended questions can be formulated in three general ways:

1. *Asking a question.* "How is Miko getting along with her new wheelchair?"

2. *Giving a polite request.* "Would you please elaborate on your feelings about the new bus route?"

3. *Using an embedded question.* "I'm interested in finding out more about Ansel's toileting training at home."

Open-ended questions generally involve using the words *what* and *how.* We encourage you to be cautious about why questions. The word *why* can connote disapproval, displeasure, blame, or condemnation (for example, "Why don't you listen to me?" or "Why are you late?") and evoke a negative or defensive response from the person with whom you are speaking.

We want to express cautions about questioning. The first caution relates to the tendency of educators to phrase questions in a way that focuses on problems, deficits, and concerns:

> We often start our initial contact with phrases like "How can I help you? What are your needs as a family? What kinds of problems are you having with your child? What are your child's most immediate problems?" These words immediately focus attention on what is going wrong and on a relationship based on the professional being in a position of expertise and power. (Winton, 1992, p. 1)

In contrast to this problem-finding approach, we encourage you to use open-ended and problem solving questions such as the following:

- "What are some of the things that have pleased you most about your child's progress over the last year?"
- "What is one of the best experiences that you have had with a professional? What can we learn from that experience about how we might best work together?"
- "What would an ideal day be like in the life of your family?"
- "Who are some of the people whom you would most like to involve in supporting you and your family?"
- "What is a great expectation that you have for your child's future that we might all share and work toward?"

The second caution is to guard against being intrusive. Families vary in their comfort about having any questions asked at all. Some families believe that most or all questions challenge their competency, invade their privacy, or both. One African American parent said that she was raised by her parents and she has raised her own children with the firm belief that "what happens in this house stays in this house." She indicated that it was totally foreign to her to go into a conference with educators and be asked questions about what happens in her house and how she raises her children. Our advice: Individualize your communication by respecting family boundaries about what is private and what is public information.

Summarization Summarization is a recapitulation of what the family member has said, with an emphasis upon the most salient thoughts and feelings. While similar to paraphrasing, summarization is different in one important respect: Summaries are substantially longer. Summarization is particularly useful in recalling the highlights of a previous meeting; tying together confusing, lengthy, or rambling topics; and acknowledging the point at which a topic has become exhausted (Walker & Singer, 1993).

Influencing Skills

The third major category of interpersonal communication skills is influencing skills. *Influencing* refers to communication aimed at participating in a conversation between a parent and professional or among the members of a collaborative team. There are four types of influencing skills: (1) providing information, (2) providing support, (3) focusing attention, and (4) offering assistance (Walker & Singer, 1993).

Providing Information You learned in chapter 3 about the importance of information as one of the family factors related to empowerment. When families prioritize their needs, they frequently say their greatest need is for relevant information (Bailey, Blasco, & Simeonsson, 1992; Turnbull & Ruef, 1997), particularly about (1) future services, (2) present services, (3) how to teach their child, (4) the nature of their child's disability, and (5) experiences of other parents who have a child with similar needs (Cooper & Allred, 1992). State-of-the-art information enables decisions to be fully informed by capitalizing on the best knowledge available. Families emphasize the importance of information being free of technical language, provided by a credible source (preferably another parent who has experienced some of the same challenges), hopeful about positive outcomes for their child, presented in their native language, and concisely focused on their priority questions or concerns (Ruef, Turnbull, Turnbull, & Poston, 1999). Some parents have expressed that they believe that professionals sometimes use jargon as a way of "reminding them who is in charge" (Stonestreet, Johnston, & Acton, 1991, p. 40). In enhancing empowerment, present information in a way that does not result in families' feeling that information

is being used to persuade or push them into making a decision that they are not ready to make.

> A new, rather officious medical social worker on an Indian reservation attempted to convince the women that their children should receive polio vaccine. In spite of her well-prepared presentation, which included statements like "You don't want them to get polio, do you?", the women did not bring their children to the clinic. They listened politely and sometimes giggled among themselves. Two years later, the social worker learned through another professional that the women had named her "Woman Who Can't Stop Talking." (Yates, 1987, p. 322)

In this situation, the social worker not only barraged the families with information but did not take into account their cultural values of being in harmony with nature and viewing disease, death, and disability as milestones in the natural progression of life. Thus, her attempt to provide information, although well intended, was not delivered in a way that resulted in creating a reliable alliance.

Providing Support There are many different ways to provide support to families. The two that we will highlight here are providing social support and providing affirming support.

In chapter 3 we discussed social support as a coping strategy (part of the knowledge/skills component of the empowerment framework). People who perceive that they have social support experience less stress and better mental health and feelings of self-efficacy (Barrera, 1986; Cohen & Wills, 1985; Crnic & Stormshak, 1997; Dunst, Trivette, & Jodry, 1997). A key component of social support is expressing empathy. A mother of three children with muscular dystrophy, two of whom also have mental retardation, writes:

> When we are injured, we need nurturance—whatever age we are. I think one of the dilemmas for the professional . . . is that they have to try to help parents, who may also acutely need nurturance themselves, to give extra care and nurturance to the child. Some of the professionals who worked with us let us know that they understood our pain, and that was often all the care we needed. But sometimes the concern for the child became the total focus, and I felt drained and discouraged. (Weyhing, 1983, p. 127)

One study compared the impact on parental satisfaction when professionals used reassurance, encouragement, and empathy as part of their communication with parents. Empathetic communication was found to lead to the most satisfied response on the part of parents. The study concluded that empathetic support from professionals makes a positive difference in how parents react to professionals (Wasserman, Inui, Barriatua, Carter, & Lippincott, 1984).

The second type of support is affirming support. Affirming support ties to the overall communication principle of affirming and building on family strengths. Providing support through verbal comments gives you an opportunity to express genuine compliments, point out areas of appreciation, and underscore the valuable contribution that families are making to their children. Box 4–4 includes examples of these statements. As you read them, keep in mind that supportive comments should be specific and authentic as well as delivered in a way that expresses respect and appreciation. You might also reflect on the people with whom you interact who are most likely to make supportive statements to you. What do you particularly appreciate, and how can you incorporate those same communication skills in your relationships with families?

Anyone can provide support, but often empowered professionals who feel confident about themselves find the most creative and natural ways to affirm others. We encourage you to take every opportunity to let others know what you particularly appreciate about their contributions.

Focusing Attention Focusing attention has two aspects: (1) making comments to underscore a comment that a family member or another team member has made that may have been overlooked or not adequately addressed in the flow of conversation and (2) making a statement that directs attention to a particular priority issue. For example, if a father expresses several concerns and some of them are addressed and others are not, it can be especially important to pick up on the unaddressed issues to make sure that they do not get pushed to the side. You can support families by specifically acknowledging their comments in meetings.

Can you recall meetings in which you said something and then the next speaker made a totally unrelated comment, as if your contribution were irrelevant? How did lack of acknowledgment of your comment make you feel? Often when this happens, people assume that their contributions are not useful and may stop making them. You can focus attention on the helpfulness of family comments by acknowledging, affirming, and expanding upon what you have said with comments such as the following:

- "What a helpful insight for all of us. What you say about Yolanda's hesitancy to read puts a different light on what she may be communicating to us by that behavior."
- "Your comment underscores why it is so important for us to work together. I hadn't considered that point of view. Thank you for that clarification."

Offering Assistance When you offer assistance to families, try to do so by presenting options rather than directives. In reflecting on people with whom you regularly communicate, are there some people who routinely

TOGETHER WE CAN BOX 4–4

Affirming Families

- "You're so insightful about Danny's moods and can read him like a book. Your insights help us get on his wavelength."

- "It's such a thrill to me to see the way that you and Ramona get such a kick out of eating lunch together. You are always welcome here. Your energy brings a boost to all of us."

- "I look forward to seeing Lucy every day for lots of reasons, but one of them is just to see what new outfit you have sewed for her. What a talent you have! And Lucy feels like a queen in the dresses that you make."

- "The treats that you sent last week for Jason's birthday were the biggest hit that I have ever seen. How can something be healthy and also taste that great? Any chance you might share the recipe with me?"

- "Because you have been spending many hours on the restructuring committee, it probably has created lots of challenges in balancing everything you do. I just want to let you know how very much I and other teachers here appreciate your commitment to creating a better school for all students and for all teachers as well. The next time you are at one of those long, drawn-out meetings, I just hope that you will remember how much we appreciate your contributions."

provide directives, making statements such as "you should," "you ought to," or "you're really making a mistake if you don't"? When these statements are made to you, how do you feel about them, and how does that feeling translate to the person who says them to you? Families, like everyone, often resist relationships that are carried out in an authoritarian style. You might reflect on Theresa Cooper's wise words about providing choices in the opening vignette to chapter 3. To increase the likelihood that families will accept your offers, try using the comments in box 4–5.

Group Communication

All of the communication skills that we have discussed can occur not only in a two-way relationship between yourself and a family member but also in group discussions that characterize team meetings (Lambie, 2000). Whether it is a school-based management council meeting or an IEP conference, skills such as empathetic listening, paraphrasing, providing information, and summarizing can facilitate positive communication and ultimately the relationships between and among participants.

In addition to nonverbal communication skills, verbal communication skills, and influencing skills, another communication option for you is to refine your skills in both facilitating and participating in group problem solving. It is unfortunate that so much time is typically spent in team meetings by having different individuals give re-

ports developed before the meetings instead of incorporating a dynamic and creative problem-solving process (Mehan, 1993). Although the steps of problem solving can be described in a number of ways, they typically involve those listed in figure 4–7.

Box 4–6 illustrates how group problem solving can be used to resolve a situation associated with truancy. The

---

FIGURE 4–7

Steps of Group Problem Solving

- Developing a vision
- Agreeing on a specific goal
- Brainstorming options for addressing the goal
- Evaluating benefits and drawbacks of each option
- Selecting the most appropriate option
- Specifying an implementation plan, including person responsible, resources needed, and time line
- Implementing the plan
- Evaluating how closely the results of action matched the goals
- Modifying the plan and continuing to make progress

TOGETHER WE CAN   BOX 4–5

Offering Assistance to Families

- "It sounds as if those evening homework sessions are really painful for everyone. If it would be helpful, I'd certainly be happy to do some brainstorming about some ideas that could possibly result in things going more smoothly."

- "You are really feeling worried about where Rahul will work after graduation. I remember several parents who expressed that same concern when their sons or daugh-

ters were in high school, and now several years after graduation things are working out very well for them. If it sounds like something that might be helpful, I would be happy to invite them to our next meeting. We could get their ideas about what some of our next steps might be."

- "I share your concern that Denise seems to feel so isolated. I'd be happy to give more attention to what we can do here at school to

help her connect more with classmates. Maybe those connections could lead to some friendships. Is that an area that you would like to explore together?"

- "If we put our heads together and commit to some hard work on figuring out this assistive technology need, I'll bet we could come up with something that would be useful. I'm willing to give it my best effort if this is a priority for you."

Solving Problems and Creating Action Plans

Problem-Solving Situation

When Lekia came to the conference, she was frustrated and tired. James had been steadily going down hill since the beginning of the school year. It was early October and James had been in trouble for skipping classes and was not academically successful. After each time he skipped, the school had held a conference. Behavior plans were written, his schedule was changed, and his teachers were switched. Lekia really felt that the school was trying to help her help James, but nothing was working.

Lekia had received a phone call at 10:00 A.M. from the school saying that James had been picked up by a local police officer while eating at a fast-food restaurant. James knew the officer and didn't resist going back to school, but he had to be reported as truant. This was the fourth report filed. He has had 10 days of suspension, and Lekia knows that this isn't the answer for James's problems. She hopes that today's conference will lead toward a vision for her son that is acceptable to everyone here.

Next Steps

In order to reach our goal and to work toward our visions. . .

	Person Responsible	Resources Needed
Starting tomorrow (date: _____), we will		
A. Find an adult "buddy" with whom James can spend time before or after school.	Teacher of record	
B. Have established a safe place where James can go when he feels too much pressure at school. Document each time it's used.	Teacher of record	Safe place
C. Call his mom at work each day before he goes home and calls here when he gets home. This must be documented.	TOR/Admi/James/Mom	Phone, private place at school
In one month, we will:		
A. Formally check in with James' buddy and rotate successes and failures. Have James there for the discussion.	Buddy, James, TOR	
B. Review how many time James has used his safe place versus skipping school. Begin to lessen the times the safe place is used.		Safe place
C. Review documentation on phone calls and revise system if necessary.	James/Mom/TOR	Documents, phone
In three months, we will:		
A. Sit with James and his buddy. James has made more "buddies." If not, encourage this.	TOR, James, Buddy	
B. Wean James from his safe place almost entirely. It should be available but not consistently used.	TOR	Safe place
C. Have James talk to Lekia about how he feels things have gone and whether or not he needs more supports.	James, mom	Time to meet

implementation planning form provides a structured framework for documenting next steps, the person responsible, resources needed, and time lines. The problem-solving process can be helpful in dealing with minor or major issues, but it is often especially beneficial in times of crisis. Because crisis situations often involve heightened risk, danger, or emotional turmoil for the key players, a comprehensive action plan can help everyone move together in a comprehensive, collaborative, and supportive manner.

Using Communication Skills in Difficult Situations

Your knowledge and application of communication skills will provide you with a whole range of options for relating to families. Each interaction will be unique and will require its own blend of skills. As a skilled communicator, you will need to choose the communication skills that seem most appropriate for each family in its current situation (Lambie, 2000).

While communication skills are vitally important at any time to build reliable alliances, they are particularly important during times of crisis. This is because families, when in crisis, may respond to you with anger, hostility, fear, or resistance, making meaningful communication between you more difficult to initiate or maintain.

During difficult interactions with families, you may need to use the whole spectrum of communication skills. You may especially need to use empathetic communication so that you can stay in touch with families, know how to respond to their sometimes volatile emotions, and gauge the effectiveness of your use of empathetic communication by observing the family's response immediately following your interaction.

Family responses that suggest that your use of empathetic communication is beneficial to the family include the following:

- Exploring a problem or staying on the topic
- Expressing pent-up emotions
- Looking within themselves
- Sharing more personally relevant material
- Affirming verbally or nonverbally the validity of your response

On the other hand, if your use of empathetic communication is not particularly helpful to the family, you may see the family engaging in some or all of the following responses:

- Rejecting, either verbally or nonverbally, your response
- Changing the subject
- Ignoring the message
- Becoming more emotionally detached
- Continuing to express anger rather than looking at the relevance of the feelings involved

Your sensitive observations of the family's responses will help you determine the effectiveness of your interactions with the family.

When you are dealing with families in crisis, you may find that other communication skills are helpful, including assertiveness, conflict resolution, negotiation, and ways to diffuse anger. Box 4–7 contains some valuable tips for how to deal with anger.

We also encourage you to remember that crises offer unique opportunities to strengthen empowering relationships. Because of heightened vulnerability and the urgency for collaboration, families and professionals can come through a crisis in such a way that their relationship truly bonds. Rather than bemoan a crisis, you can embrace it as a unique opportunity for relationship enhancement. Susan and Jason Rocco are headed for a major transition two years from now. Jason will be 21 and no longer eligible to attend school. Rather than have his ineligibility be a cause for crisis, the staff at his school and Susan can turn it into an opportunity—namely, a chance for him to return to his alma mater, a place where he knows people and where he knows others like him ("Jason needs a place to go where he will feel comfortable"), and a place to contribute his lawn-watering and gardening talents. For Susan, what frustrates her so much is that "the world doesn't appreciate Jason the way I do. . . . We want a source of unconditional love, and no one yet has been able to provide that except a parent." Or, perhaps, except for a school itself.

Another consideration is to realize the positive aspects of anger in motivating people to take action. In chapter 3 you learned about transforming events as a catalyst for energy in the motivation component of the empowerment framework (Kieffer, 1984). Often it is anger that leads to transforming events, as outrage is channeled into positive action. Given the critical importance of motivation in the empowerment equation, we encourage you to view each crisis as an opportunity to get things moving in a positive direction, sometimes with a sense of urgency that is hard to establish when all is going well.

Dealing with Anger

Do

- Listen.
- Write down what family members say.
- When the person slows down, ask what else is bothering him or her.
- Exhaust the person's list of complaints.
- Ask the person to clarify any specific complaints that are too general.
- Show the person the list and ask if it is complete.
- Ask the person for suggestions about solving for any of the problems listed.
- Write down the suggestions.
- As much as possible, mirror the person's body posture.
- As the person speaks louder, speak softer.

Don't

- Argue.
- Defend or become defensive.
- Promise things you can't produce.
- Own problems that belong to others.
- Raise your voice.
- Belittle or minimize the problem.

Developed at the Parent Center, Albuquerque, NM.

Improving Communication Skills

One method to improve your own or someone else's communication abilities is to use audiotapes or videotapes. Although audiotapes are ideal for practicing and evaluating verbal communication skills, videotapes offer the additional advantage of feedback on both verbal and nonverbal behaviors. Ask a friend or colleague to spend 10 to 20 minutes talking over an issue or problem with you. Tape your conversation. As you talk, practice using at least one or two of the skills we have described. Then review the tape critically, taking note of the positive and not-so-positive contributions you made. Set personal goals for improvement. Ask your friend to provide you with feedback on your performance. As you begin to feel confident about the skills you have practiced, try adding more skills to your repertoire. Over time, and with enough practice, these skills can become a natural and spontaneous part of your communication style.

We also hope that you will practice these skills throughout all of your class discussions, conversations with families, and even communication throughout your personal relationships that do not have anything to do with special education issues. Improving communication requires a personal and professional commitment of time, effort, and attention and a genuine desire on your part to be the most empowering communicator you can possibly be.

Warranting Trust and Respect

All of the components that we have discussed for building reliable alliances and creating empowering contexts are really prerequisites to the most important element of all—warranting trust and respect. When you have trusting and respectful relationships with families, you can practically ensure that collaboration and empowerment will be enhanced. By the same token, when families trust professionals (and professionals earn families' trust), they create opportunities for all sorts of otherwise unattainable results. It was precisely because Susan Rocco trusted the teachers in Jason's sending school that she was willing to go for his inclusion in a new school with a new teacher.

When you do not have trusting and respectful relationships, no matter how hard you try or how good your instructional ideas are, problems will permeate almost all that you do with families. The bottom line is that trust and respect are absolutely essential aspects of the reliable alliances that can lead to the empowerment of all team members.

An essential element of a trusting relationship is for all family information to be kept confidential. A parent commented:

> I was horrified when I ran into a friend downtown and she told me that she had heard through the grapevine what my son's teacher had been saying about his behavior. As problematic as his behavior has been, the teacher had even exaggerated to make it sound worse. That's just what happens when people start gossiping. I was so crushed. I went home and vowed to never tell that teacher one more personal thing about my son, myself, or my family. It was all over from that point on.

As you have already learned in chapter 2, the organization of school systems and the strong emphasis on legal compliance sometimes, paradoxically, work against trust and respect rather than in their favor. So what are the ingredients that most enhance trust and respect?

One of them is that trust and respect evolve from establishing power-with and power-from-within rather than power-over relationships with families. As one parent said, professionals need to "come down from their high status and walk with us rather than direct us." That is particularly so for professionals who work with families from culturally and linguistically diverse backgrounds. In discussing their passive participation, Harry (1992b) commented:

> When such parents' traditional trust in school authorities is undermined, parents who do not believe that they can challenge school authorities are likely to withdraw from participation. Out of a traditional respect for authority, however, they may continue to defer to professionals, yet fail to cooperate with professional recommendations or even to respond to invitations to participate.
>
> Parents' behavior may then be interpreted by the professional as a sign of disinterest or apathy. In the light of these observations, it is evident that increasing parental participation is not simply a matter of giving adequate information or providing parents with logistical supports or even being respectful to parents to make them feel more comfortable. The challenge to professionals is to earn the reasoned trust of cultural minority parents through the creation of participation structures that ensure their inclusion rather than their exclusion from the decision-making process. (Harry, 1992b, p. 475)

A study of low-income African American mothers reveals the factors that facilitate or inhibit professionals in moving away from hierarchies and emphasizing partnerships (Kalyanpur & Rao, 1991). The facilitating factors include the following:

- Responding to needs (for example, providing emotional support; providing specific services)
- Establishing rapport (for example, being conversational, interpreting, sharing, and accepting)

The inhibiting factors include the following:

- Being disrespectful
- Focusing on deficits
- Discounting differences

The authors describe the essence of a trusting, respectful relationship and how such a relationship contributes to empowerment:

> Empowerment signifies changing the role of a service provider from that of an expert to that of an ally or friend who enables families to articulate what they need. . . . While the expertise of professionals is an integral aspect of the interaction between parents and professionals, the manner in which the expertise is communicated determines the nature of the relationship. It involves caring, which builds supportive relationships; respect, which builds reciprocity; and the acceptance of differences, which builds trust. . . . Such empathy involves the acceptance and open acknowledgement of the parents' competence, the willingness to interact with them on equal terms, and the adoption of a nonjudgmental stance. (Kalyanpur & Rao, 1991, p. 531)

To empower families, students with educational exceptionalities, and professionals alike is a daunting task; but it is quite possible—indeed, quite probable—when reliable alliances exist. After all, reliable alliances are the ingredients of an empowering context; and an empowering context is the foundation within which collaboration can flourish.

Summary

Building reliable alliances consists of seven elements. Effective professionals—and effective family members like Susan Rocco—understand and apply these elements as they take advantage of the opportunities to be partners with each other:

- They know about families.
- They honor families' cultural diversity and mores.
- They affirm and build on families' strengths.
- They promote families' choices.
- They create great expectations for themselves and students.

- They practice positive interpersonal communication techniques.
- And, as a result of doing all of this, they warrant the trust and respect of one another.

To create a reliable alliance requires a great deal of empathy—the ability to understand each other's feelings, thoughts, and motives. Practicing the seven techniques helps families such as Susan Rocco's and professionals such as Jason's teachers develop empathy for each other and become each other's reliable allies.

When Jason entered high school a few years ago, Susan resolved to "just develop a relationship with Jason's teachers and give them a sense that I am going to be totally supportive and that we are going to work on these goals together and this is going to be so nice for Jason. I really think I'm going to get that cooperation and that support, but I might not if I was just insistent about this, that, or the other thing. I'll have opportunities to invite people to lunch and to talk about people we know in common and just kind of find those common grounds in our lives that are of course going to have some connection to Jason but that are not totally focused around him and his needs. I want them to see me as a regular person and not just a special education parent."

She has been exceptionally effective. Witness the accommodation the school principal made. Witness the teacher who, ignoring Jason's sometimes challenging behavior, put Jason on his "loyalty list."

And at the same time that Jason headed into high school, Susan had reached a conclusion about the quality of his life.

"I've learned what Jason's life is all about. It's not whether he learns to wipe tables. It's whether or not he has friends. . . . I really believe that if we don't make it pleasurable—you know, the old exchange theory—then

Jason's peers will drop him like a hot potato. You know, it's just unrealistic to think folks are going to do it either because they are told to or because it's morally right."

"There has to be a payback. We're having fun; we're getting something out of it; we're having this sense of accomplishment; we're feeling valued. That's what it's all about."

That and finding the answers to some hard questions: Was it too idealistic to try to create an inclusion-based life for him, one where he can have buddies who do not have disabilities? And why do hard things happen, if not for a loving reason? And what is that reason?

These are the questions that Susan asks now that Jason has only two more years of high school. They are existential; they go to the very core of her and Jason's existence. If they are to be answered in any satisfactory way, it will be because Susan and Jason have friends. The relationships they cultivate—the reliable alliances they make—will give them the answer: Things happen so that you can discover who your friends are and that friendship counts. If we learn together to love Jason's eccentricity, we learn together how to grow, how to make all things well. Relationships, Susan knows, are the key. And they come because of, and through, Jason.

Part Two

Understanding Families

Because this book is about collective empowerment of and collaboration with families, we describe in part 2 a useful way for understanding families. Knowing families is one of the eight obligations of a reliable alliance, and we enable you to know families through a family systems perspective. When you regard families as systems, you recognize their interactive and dynamic qualities.

We characterize the family as a system by focusing on family characteristics (chapter 5), the way that family members interact within the family and with people outside the family (chapter 6), the way that a family functions (chapter 7), and the way that a family changes over time (chapter 8).

At the end of part 2, you should be able to describe the family systems perspective through the four components of characteristics, interaction, functions, and life cycle.

Chapter Five

Family Characteristics

Marta Cofresi hasn't had it easy. Raising four children is no piece of cake in any circumstances. But being a monolingual immigrant (Spanish only); having twin girls (Roxela and Roxana), each of whom has cerebral palsy; and being a single parent ever since the twins' father abandoned the family just after they were born could get even a lesser person down. But Marta is not a lesser person, and certainly her children aren't either.

Marta and the twins have close friends in school, church, and the community, and they have great expectations for the future all because when Roxela and Roxana were born, Marta declared, "I accept you and I will focus on what you can do. Because of that, people will accept you and focus on what you can do, too."

The first people she helped to accept the twins were their two older siblings, Juan Carlos and Louisa. "The first task was to make them feel no shame because of their sisters," so Marta required Juan Carlos and Louisa to take their sisters out for walks and encouraged the older siblings' friends to visit the twins. And she spent hard-earned money on the twins' clothes because appearance is important. "That is how I introduced the girls to the community."

But Roxela and Roxana had to do their parts, too. A lesson she taught the girls was to "treat others as you like to be treated" and to "accept others as they are." So when one of their peers looks at them or asks why they use crutches or a voice synthesizer, the twins must "tell all the story and be honest."

Moreover, Marta told them, "You can do it, so you can go for it" (the it being whatever Roxela and Roxana wanted). Constant rewards and encouragement coupled with Marta's deep faith sustained the family. "I had to find the answer in God, because God made them that way, so how God would think of them and treat them is how I wanted to be."

Marta has not been alone in her efforts to have Roxela and Roxana lead typical but assisted lives. One of Roxana's 10th-grade teachers, Mr. Arias, played a big role, too. As the only girl placed in his vocational tech class, Roxana wanted to drop the course. As she tells it, Mr. Arias made the class "real fun" and "kept insisting, 'stay in my class, stay in my class.' " He became her friend, and she stayed there for two years and received an award from him as the student of the year. In her first year in class, she was elected and then reelected president of the local chapter of Vocational Opportunities Clubs of Texas. The Riverside High School chapter has excelled, winning citywide competitions and placing second in a statewide contest.

Because the twins have a "believe-in-them" network, they believe in themselves. They participate regularly in their IEP conferences. They turn the other cheek when someone makes fun of them; they are friendly and open. They expect to date, to be married, and to have many children. First, however, Roxela and Roxana want to go to the University of Texas at El Paso and study computer science.

Most of all, they want to be role models for their nieces and nephew and their community. As Roxana says, "We want to show them that just because I'm on

crutches and their aunt Roxela is in a wheelchair doesn't mean they can't go to us with a problem and tell us, because we'll help."

What more do they need? Roxana answers, "We need more people that believe in us." That is one reason Roxana wants Roxela to be included in general educa-tion: She believes that Roxela will create her own reliable allies in school and the community.

There is no doubt that Marta Cofresi and Mr. Arias believe that, too. And so do Roxela's and Roxana's sib-lings and many friends. And why shouldn't they? After all, the twins give everyone reason to believe in them.[1]

[1]We have written about the Cofresi family and Mr. Arias in a couple of other publications. We encourage you to read those to find out more about this highly empowered team. You can learn more about how Ms. Cofresi encouraged friendships for Roxela and Roxana in an article in the *Journal of the Association for Persons with Severe Handicaps* by Turnbull, Pereira, & Blue-Banning (1999). You can learn more about how Mr. Arias supported Roxela in an article in *Teaching Exceptional Children* by Turnbull, Pereira, & Blue-Banning (in press). The full citations are in the reference list.

Marta Cofresi and her children, Roxela, Roxanna, Juan Carlos, and Louisa. (1995)

Traditionally, the word *family* brings to mind the nostalgic picture of a mother, father, and two or three children living together at home. The father works during the week and spends evenings and weekends repairing household goods and fixtures, mowing the yard, and playing with the children. The mother keeps house and nourishes her family's body and soul with home-cooked meals and plenty of love. Grandparents are nearby, ready to take the kids fishing, bake cookies, and dispense wise counsel. On national or religious holidays, all the aunts, uncles, cousins, and grandparents gather for a day of family solidarity and joyous feasting.

The truth is that few American families today fit this nostalgic picture (Popenoe, 1988). Indeed, it is doubtful that a typical American family ever existed (Hareven, 1982; Zinn & Eitzen, 1993). Like the Cofresi family, many have only one parent. This chapter focuses on how families differ and how those differences affect and are affected by the child or youth who has an exceptionality—children such as the Cofresi twins.

Families vary in a multitude of ways, as you learned in chapter 4. We have developed a visual illustration of the systems nature of families—the *inputs* into the system, the *process* or *interaction* within the system, and the *outputs* of the system—and show how all of these components are dynamic and *change* throughout time (see figure 5–1). Each of the next four chapters will focus on one of the components of this framework. This chapter focuses on the first component—the *inputs* into the family system, which are called the family characteristics. As you will note in figure 5–1, family characteristics consist of three dimensions: (1) characteristics of the family, (2) personal characteristics, and (3) special challenges. Characteristics of the family refer to dimensions such as family culture, socioeconomic level, and geographic location. In addition to all of these variations in family life, each individual family member also varies in personal characteristics—characteristics related to exceptionality, health status, and coping styles. Finally, many families face special challenges such as poverty, substance abuse, and abuse or neglect of children. Every family is such a mixture of characteristics that it is probably safe to say that every family is idiosyncratic.

Yet the nostalgic image of the traditional family continues to cloud professional-family relationships to such an extent that, even today, many home-school programs for families with children with exceptionalities often are best suited for nuclear two-parent, one-worker, middle-class families—a minority today. To individualize for Marta Cofresi and her daughters and for other families, you need to understand how they differ from other families and the three factors that create these diversities:

characteristics of the entire family, the individual characteristics of each family member, and the family's special challenges. The family characteristics section of the family systems framework highlights these three diversity factors, each of which we will discuss.

Whatever a family's characteristics, they do not preclude the family from being motivated or from having or developing skills to be empowered; just consider the Cofresi family and how Marta, Roxela, and Roxana have been motivated to "go for it" and have acquired the skills they need to achieve their goals.

Characteristics of the Family

The term *family characteristics* refers to the characteristics of the family as a whole: its size and form, cultural background, socioeconomic status, and geographic location. Each of these characteristics shapes the family's responses to a member's exceptionality, and each is a potential resource for collaboration and empowerment.

Family Size and Form

Family size and form refers to the number of children, the number of parents, the presence and number of stepparents, the extensiveness of the extended family, and live-in family members who are unrelated by blood or marriage. Tremendous variation exists in how people define family membership. Figure 5–2 illustrates the diversity that exists in family size and form by describing two families, each of which may have a child with an exceptionality with very similar characteristics. The impact of that child on each of these families is influenced by many factors, including the family's size and form.

Perhaps in large families more people are available to help with the chores and any special adaptations the child needs. A larger number of siblings may absorb parents' expectations for achievement, expectations that otherwise might fall on the shoulders of the only child without an exceptionality (Powell & Gallagher, 1993; Stoneman & Berman, 1993). Finally, other children may give their parents a frame of reference that reminds them that their child with an exceptionality is more like than unlike his or her brothers and sisters and that all children have various combinations of strengths and needs.

For example, a father of an adolescent daughter with Williams syndrome noted that the problems of his daughter with a disability are often no greater and perhaps even

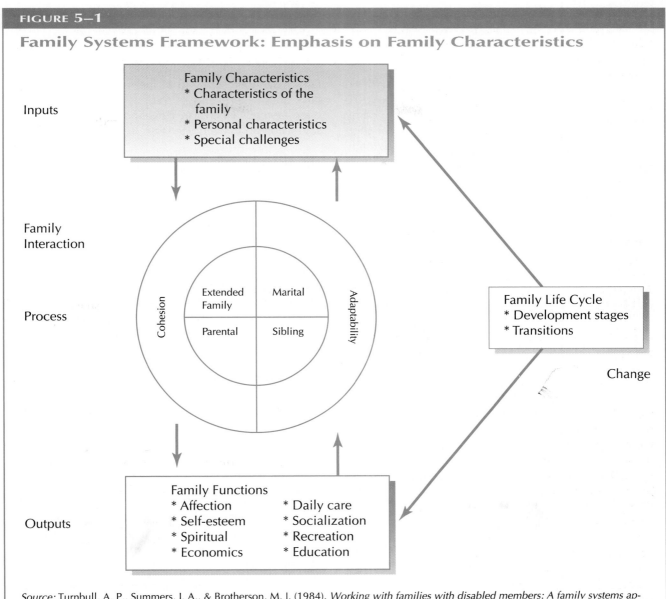

FIGURE 5–1

Family Systems Framework: Emphasis on Family Characteristics

Inputs

Family
Interaction

Process

Outputs

Family Characteristics
* Characteristics of the
  family
* Personal characteristics
* Special challenges

Cohesion

Extended Family | Marital

Parental | Sibling

Adaptability

Family Life Cycle
* Development stages
* Transitions

Change

Family Functions
* Affection
* Self-esteem
* Spiritual
* Economics
* Daily care
* Socialization
* Recreation
* Education

Source: Turnbull, A. P., Summers, J. A., & Brotherson, M. J. (1984). *Working with families with disabled members: A family systems approach* (p. 60). Lawrence: University of Kansas, Kansas Affiliated Facility. Adapted by permission.

less difficult than the problems his other children experienced during adolescence.

> Adeliza had been, in many respects, the easiest of our six children. As she was the fourth daughter with two younger brothers, we as parents were "old pros" at raising teenage daughters by the time Adeliza turned 13. She doesn't date and is not as rebellious as our other three daughters. Instead of being another stressful situation, her teenage years have, in general, been a very positive experience for our entire family.

Similarly, the number of parents (single parent or two parents) may influence a family's reaction to the exceptionality. A supportive husband—even one who does not participate in child care—seems to be an important predictor of a mother's sense of well-being (Crnic & Booth, 1991; Nagy & Ungerer, 1990). In addition, a family usually adapts more positively to a child's exceptionality if it is a two-parent family (Trute & Hauch, 1988). It stands to reason that in a two-parent family, there is the potential of a coalition of parents who share

FIGURE 5—2

Tale of Two Families

The Angelino Family

The Angelino family has five children and a sixth on the way. The children are aged 14 (girl), 12 (boy), 10 (girl), 7 (boy), and 6 (girl). They all attend a nearby parochial school. Mr. Angelino owns a butcher shop that had been his father's and that was originally opened by his grandfather, who immigrated from Italy in 1904. Although at one time the butcher shop had living quarters upstairs for the family, approximately ten years ago they moved into a large, Victorian-style house about a block away.

Both Mr. and Mrs. Angelino come from large families; most of their brothers and sisters still live in the "little Italy" section of this large Eastern city. The grandparents are all dead with the exception of Mrs. Angelino's mother (Mama). She lives in the home with them and is very frail. One of Mrs. Angelino's brothers or sisters is sure to stop by nearly every day bringing children, flowers, and/or food, for a "visit with Mama." They often take Mama for drives or to their homes for short visits—depending on her health—and help with her basic care.

Life with the Angelinos can be described as a kind of happy chaos. Kids are always running in and out of the butcher shop, where the older brothers and male cousins are often assigned small tasks in return for a piece of salami or some other treat. The old house is always full of children—siblings and cousins—from teenagers to toddlers. Though young children are pretty much indulged, by the time they reach nine or ten years of age, they are expected to begin taking responsibility, which is divided strictly along traditional sex-role lines. Child care, cooking, and cleaning are accomplished by the women: older sisters or cousins, aunts or mothers. Evening meals are a social event. There is virtually always at least one extended family member or friend at the table, and everyone talks about the events of the day—sometimes all at once—except when Mr. Angelino has something to say, whereupon everyone stops to listen.

The McNeil Family

Mr. and Mrs. McNeil have been married for two years; she is expecting their first child. Mr. McNeil is the youngest partner in a prestigious law firm in this Midwestern city. Everybody considers him upwardly mobile and thinks it is phenomenal that he should achieve a partnership only three years out of law school. Mrs. McNeil has a degree in interior design and worked full time for a while for a decorating firm in another city. After their marriage, the McNeils moved to this city, and she has a part-time, "on call" job with an exclusive architectural firm. She has ambitions of opening her own shop.

Mr. McNeil is an only child. His parents live on the East Coast. They are both successful in business; he is a banker, and she is a real estate broker. They have always demanded perfection from their son, and he seems to have lived up to their expectations. Mrs. McNeil has one younger sister; her parents live on the West Coast. They are both professional persons; he is a college professor, and she is a social worker. Mrs. McNeil's family has always been very close. She calls her parents about once a week, and the family occasionally has joint conference calls between parents and the two siblings to decide some important issue or to relay some big news. Mrs. McNeil's parents place no demands on her except that she be true to herself. They often tell her how proud they are of her accomplishments.

responsibilities and support each other emotionally during the "ups and downs" of childrearing (Scorgie, Wilgosh, & McDonald, 1998). Their coalition does not have to be based on a formal marriage; rather, adult companionship and support may be the key factor in enabling family members to be more resourceful in supporting their child with an exceptionality (Fagan & Schor, 1993).

You are certain to encounter single-parent families (such as the Cofresi family). The U.S. Department of Education (1992) reports that approximately 37 percent of high school students with disabilities live in single-parent families, as contrasted to approximately 30 percent of high school students in general education. A majority of single parents with custody of children are women, but about 15 percent of all children are being raised by single fathers because of divorce, death of spouse/mother of child, or adoption (Seligmann, 1992).

An extensive inquiry into family demographics has shown that the poverty rate among families headed by a single, female householder is almost 40 percent when a child in the family has a disability (Fujiura & Yanaki, 1997). Of the 3.2 million single, female households in poverty, approximately 1 in 5 has a member with a disability. Thus, two characteristics that are strongly associated with increasing the likelihood that families will experience poverty are single-parent, female-headed households and the presence of children (particularly more than one child) who have a disability.

Given these demographics and accompanying pressures on families, some single parents may have neither the time nor the emotional energy to be heavily involved in their child's education; however, other single parents (like Marta Cofresi) are very active partners of their children's teachers (Cigno & Burke, 1997).

A study of single mothers of children with learning disabilities revealed that the lack of in-home, partner support is a major factor to be taken into consideration in how single parents carry out their roles and responsibilities (Cigno & Burke, 1997). Single parents ranked contact with the school and the need to connect with families who face similar circumstances as even more important when they did not have a partner at home with whom to share parenting roles. These parents also had major needs for assistance with transportation and with planning for the future.

A single parent describes some of the challenges of her situation:

> Tired. Lonely. Isolated. This is how it was as a single parent, raising three children, one of whom was disabled. I fell asleep crying, many nights, because I did not have a partner to share the daily responsibilities and problems of raising Katherine. . . I was both father and mother, trying to meet the emotional needs of all three children, working a forty-hour week, dealing with emergencies, Katherine's therapy schedule, and after-school homework and activities of her brother and sister. (Barnes, 1986, p. 47)

But benefits for single parents include "relief from marital conflict, increased self-esteem derived from one's competency in managing work and family matters, greater autonomy and independence, opportunities for increased self-growth, and closer relationships with children" (Reid, 1985, p. 263).

A different pattern of family size and form—more than two parents—exists when one or both parents in the original family have remarried. Approximately three out of four divorced women and five out of six divorced men remarry, with approximately one-half of all of the remarriages occurring within three years after the divorce. Approximately 40 percent of all of the second marriages involve stepchildren (Zinn & Eitzen, 1993).

A wide array of family variations and emotional situations exists in remarried families (Hetherington & Arasteh, 1988). The new blended family may include children from two or more marriages. Boys typically experience more emotional trauma from the divorce of their parents than do girls (Zinn & Eitzen, 1993). Children may regard their acceptance of a stepparent as a sign of disloyalty to their biological parent. They may have to adopt rules and lifestyles in two different households or give up adult roles that they may have assumed while the custodial parent was single. Stepparents may be uncertain about their authority over their spouses' children; or with a ready-made family from the first day of marriage, parents may not have the privacy or time to establish their new relationship. Finally, negotiations among all of the adults—both former and current spouses—may be required to resolve conflicts concerning the children, including visitation schedules, discipline, lifestyle, and so on (Zinn & Eitzen, 1993). The positive side of a remarried family is that a wide circle of interested family members may be able and willing to support both each other and the person with the exceptionality.

You would do well to be sensitive to various roles in single-parent or remarried families when parents who are divorced and remarried spouses are involved in educational decision making. For example, an IEP conference may range from being an amiable discussion about the child's best interests to a family power struggle where professionals are thrust in the middle (Turnbull & Turnbull, in press). You may want to consult with the school social worker or school counselor for suggestions of how you can be most supportive in situations that you find especially challenging.

In your partnerships with families, we encourage you to avoid regarding a family who has experienced divorce—or for that matter, any family—as "broken," whether it is divorced, remarried, adoptive, or foster. As the Cofresi family shows, there are simply too many characteristics that affect a family to justify your picking any one characteristic or type of family as the basis for any negative judgment. How wrong it would have been to characterize the Cofresi family as broken solely because Marta is a single parent. Strive instead to see the strengths of every family. Every family has them, as Marta and her daughters and son demonstrate. That attitude will help you collaborate with the family and will reinforce the family's motivation and knowledge/skills for empowerment.

Cultural Background

We encourage you to reflect on what you learned in chapter 4 about honoring cultural diversity. We emphasize the fact the culture is an extremely broad concept and includes many factors in addition to race/ethnicity—factors such as geographic location, religion, socioeconomic status, sexual orientation, and disability status. All of these cultural factors influence the family's characteristics; those characteristics, in turn, shape family interaction.

Figure 5–3 sets out the percentages of students in special education according to different racial/ethnic groups and differing categories of exceptionality. We encourage you to compare and contrast the information in this table and detect trends related to the disproportionate representation of students—particularly African American students—in special education.

As you will see from the data, African American students are twice as likely to be enrolled in programs for students with mental retardation and only half as likely to be enrolled in programs for students who are gifted and talented. White students are consistently overrepresented in the categories of giftedness (similar to Asian American students) and in the category of learning disabilities. An analysis of trends related to the disproportionality of African American students in special education pointed to issues related to the socioeconomic status of the student (as poverty increased, more African American students were identified as having mental retardation) and demographic factors related to the community (as wealth of the community increased, there was more tendency to

identify African American students as having emotional disorders). Thus, the complex interaction of culture, socioeconomic status, and geographic location underscore the fact that these family systems characteristics are not discrete from each other but are highly interrelated and overlapping (Oswald, Coutinho, Best, & Singh, 1999).

The U.S. Department of Education provides further data on the racial/ethnic distribution of youth with disabilities. Within the group of students from diverse racial/ethnic backgrounds, numbers of students with limited English proficiency are growing rapidly. The U.S. Department of Education estimates that in 1990 there were approximately 1.9 million students with limited English proficiency in grades kindergarten through 12 (U.S. Department of Education, 1991). Slightly more than three-fourths of these students speak Spanish; but 7 percent speak other European languages, 6 percent speak Southeastern Asian languages, 3 percent speak East Asian languages, and 8 percent speak other languages (U.S. Department of Education, 1993). The number of students with limited English proficiency who have been identified as having disabilities is between one-quarter of 1 million to 1 million (Baca & Cervantes, 1989, cited in U.S. Department of Education, 1993). These students have been identified as being particularly at risk for special education placement (U.S. Department of Education, 1993).

FIGURE 5–3

Representation of Students in Special Education As Opposed to Representation in the Total School Population

	Native American (%)	Asian (%)	Hispanic (%)	African American (%)	Caucasian (%)
Representation in total population	1	3	12	16	68
Percent labeled gifted and talented	1	6	6	8	79
Percent labeled educable mentally retarded	1	1	8	35	56
Percent labeled trainable mentally retarded	1	2	20	32	46
Percent labeled seriously emotionally disturbed	1	1	6	22	71
Percent labeled specific learning disability	1	1	11	17	70

Note: From 1990 Elementary and Secondary School Civil Rights Survey Adjusted National Estimated Data (February 1993) by U.S. Department of Education, Office for Civil Rights, Washington, DC: U.S. Department of Education. (numbers rounded)

Likewise, many families of children with disabilities have limited English proficiency. In a study of many characteristics associated with 200 Latino parents, the characteristic that most influenced the needs and supports of the families was their English-language proficiency (Bailey et al., 1999). Research with Korean families has revealed a similar pattern of emphasis on the challenges that are associated with limited English proficiency, as we will describe in more detail in chapter 9 (Park, 1998). To provide an empowering context for family-professional collaboration, some special education professionals will need to be multilingual or have access to interpreters (Lynch, 1998); and all professionals will need to honor cultural diversity and develop cultural competence.

Chapter 4 introduced cultural aspects of families and suggested a five-step process for increasing your own cultural competence in family-professional collaboration. In this section, concentrate on step 4 in the five-step process depicted in figure 4–2. That step can help you enlarge your cultural-specific and cultural-generic awareness related to exceptionality and family issues by analyzing cultural perspectives on three family factors: (1) individualism versus collectivism, (2) system-centered versus relationship-centered approaches, and (3) a take-charge perspective toward change versus an acceptance perspective toward tradition.

Individualism versus Collectivism

The most dominant racial/ethnic culture in the United States is Euro-American, which typically values individualism, self-reliance, early achievement of developmental milestones, and competition with others (Hanson, 1998; Kalyanpur & Harry, 1999).

> For example, politicians today still strive to point to humble roots and their climb to a higher status, much like heroes such as Abraham Lincoln. As Althen (1988) related, Americans revere those who do things the biggest, the best, or first; hence, the fascination with sports legends such as Jesse Owens, Jackie Robinson, and Babe Ruth; aviator heroes such as Charles Lindbergh, Amelia Earhart; and astronauts such as Neil Armstrong and Sally Ride. (Hanson, 1998, p. 104)

The individualistic perspective is a fundamental premise of the field of special education and pervades IDEA (Kalyanpur & Harry, 1999). Instruction in special education focuses on individual outcomes. Students with disabilities have *individualized* education programs that target their *individual* levels of performance and then specify *individual* goals and objectives to be achieved. Furthermore, priorities such as self-determination that foster autonomy and individual decision making are

strongly emphasized (Field, Martin, Miller, Ward, & Wehmeyer, 1998; Wehmeyer, 1999; Wehmeyer, Agran, & Hughes, 1998). Similarly, students who are gifted are rewarded in highly individualistic ways by winning contests (for example, national essay contests), achieving National Merit status on the college board examination, and earning admission to prestigious colleges and universities. These educational practices strongly influence families' expectations for their children and their own child-raising practices; achievement is the coin of the educational realm.

By contrast, some cultures emphasize collectivism, which values the group more strongly than the individual (Greenfield, 1994; Kalyanpur & Harry, 1999; Kim & Choi, 1994). In Marta Cofresi's family, her children without disabilities played important roles in creating friendship networks for their sisters with disabilities; a collective approach to the twins' inclusion came naturally to the Cofresis. Within the African American culture, a group orientation seems to be valued over private gain (Logan, 1996; Willis, 1998). Similarly, in Asian cultures individuals are viewed "as the product of all generations of the family from the beginning of time." Individual behaviors therefore reflect upon one's ancestors as well as the entire "race" (Chan, 1998, p. 293). Thus, honoring the family's cultural traditions receives utmost importance. The Middle Eastern belief that "children are like canes in the hands of old parents" expresses quite well the collective obligation that family members have to each other (Sharifzadeh, 1998, p. 454).

What is the relevance of individualism and collectivism for collaborating with families? There are two implications—one affecting process and the other affecting curriculum and outcomes. With respect to process, some families from some diverse cultures may regard individualized education programs as contradictory to their orientation of collective, cooperative, and mutually reciprocal priorities. With respect to curriculum, some families may not be interested in their child's accomplishing developmental milestones or specific academic tasks if the accomplishment singles out their child for special attention, acclaim, and/or recognition. Similarly, some families may be far more interested in their sons' and daughters' learning to take care of the home and elderly family members rather than acquiring job skills in a competitive industry.

System-Centered versus Relationship-Centered Approaches

Members of the dominant racial/ethnic group—Euro-Americans—typically expect solutions for disability-related problems to be system based; that is, they expect for solutions to be guided by federal (IDEA) and state law and policy and implemented through bureaucratic procedures. This viewpoint emphasizes two contrasting theories of normalcy—the pathological model from medicine and the statistical model from psychology. The pathological model seeks to identify the "pathology" within the child and to "fix" it through technological and knowledge-based solutions. The statistical model seeks to identify an individual's deviations from those projected on the normal curve and to provide remediation to the individual to make up for the deviation (Kalyanpur & Harry, 1999). It should not be surprising that this value is reflected in the legal underpinnings of special education and that the vast majority of families who participate in policy-reform advocacy are White, middle-class, and upper-middle-class families (Turnbull & Turnbull, 1996; Zirpoli, Wieck, Hancox, & Skarnulis, 1994).

By contrast, members of many diverse racial/ethnic groups regard personal relationships, not policies and procedures, as the bases of decision making (Harry, Kalyanpur, & Day, 1999; Kalyanpur & Harry, 1999; Lynch & Hanson, 1998).

> It is this personalism that makes it difficult for the Puerto Rican to adjust easily to what Americans call efficiency. For Puerto Ricans, life is a network of personal relationships. They trust people; they rely on people. . . . They do not have that same trust for a system or an organization. Americans, on the other hand, expect the system to work; they have confidence in the organization. . . . Americans become impatient and uneasy when systems do not work. . . . The Latins become uneasy and impatient if the system works too well, if they feel themselves in a situation where they must rely on impersonal function rather than personal relationships. (Fitzpatrick, 1987, p. 79)

Similarly, the native Hawaiian culture emphasizes not only relationships with other people but also relationships with the community at large, the land, and the spiritual world (Mokuau & Tauili'ili, 1998). And Native American cultures strongly prize relationships with nature, especially those that promote a sense of harmony with nature (Joe & Malach, 1998).

What does this mean for you and your interactions with families? For one thing, bear in mind that the legal and bureaucratic process of referring, evaluating, and individualizing the delivery of special education services (chapters 11 and 12) and advocacy for systems improvement (chapter 15) may be culturally disharmonious for families who approach their child's education from a relationship orientation. You may need to spend significant time establishing genuine relationships in which you and families get to know each other before you and the family start making educational decisions. This has

major implications for your time—a rare commodity for many professionals—and your willingness to establish personal familiarity as the basis for trust. Whereas many Euro-American professionals and families may be eager "to get to the bottom line" in a meeting, many families from culturally diverse backgrounds may prefer to spend much more time, especially up-front time, on building relationships.

In addition, people with whom the family already has a reliable alliance can be part of their circle of support in collaborating with you and other professionals. As you have learned, not all encounters need to be two-way (between an educator and a parent); rather, the family's other trusted reliable allies—the members of the family's own cultural communities and tribes—can make valuable contributions to professional-family collaboration.

Taking-Charge Perspective toward Change versus Acceptance Perspective toward Tradition

Hanson (1998, p. 105) comments on some Euro-American perspectives: "Change, newness, and progress are all highly valued. Americans believe that individuals, as well as people working together, can 'make a difference' and that change is positive. Related to these notions is the assumption that social and physical environments are under human control or domination." This belief translates into a highly "valued action orientation" and frequently results in empowerment's being interpreted as a "taking charge" orientation. Because empowerment can mean many different things in different cultures, you should be cautious about adopting and about asking some families to adopt Euro-American interpretations of empowerment. We say this while also acknowledging that we have defined empowerment as getting what a person wants and needs (chapter 3) and that we have highlighted the Cofresi family, as well as Theresa from chapter 3, as people whose motivation and ability to acquire and apply new skills make them good examples of empowerment. Empowerment for some families from culturally diverse backgrounds may be quite a different concept; you will want to learn what meaning a family gives it and then support the family to act on that meaning.

For example, cultural traditions lead some families to accept the status quo or preserve traditions that have always been part of their cultural heritage. Indeed, some cultures believe that families should persevere without complaint and suffer in silence, and these cultures adopt a fatalistic orientation in which life is presumed to be essentially unalterable and unpredictable. Accepting external conditions and events over which one presumably has little or no control is a way of life for some families (Chan, 1998). But this is not so for all, as the Cofresi family shows.

Reliance on traditionalism has its benefits. For example, vocational rehabilitation provided through tribal services for American Indians is more holistic than the vocational rehabilitation typically provided by agencies in the majority culture (Marshall & Largo, 1999). The holistic vocational rehabilitation focuses on the individual issues from a vocational, physical, psychological, and spiritual perspective. Native healing arts were kept alive as an asset of this holistic approach. In Arizona, Blue Cross/Blue Shield allows coverage for a Medicine Man Benefit; this coverage involves reimbursement at 50 percent up to $500 per person per calendar year.

The value of traditionalism is poignantly expressed from a Native American perspective by Allen Kuetone of the Kiowa tribe:

> Within each of our tribes, there are certain people who are traditionalists. These are the people who hold on to and perpetuate our customs and traditions. They provide those of us who are on the outside, who are in the Bureau of Indian Affairs and other places across the country, with an opportunity to come back and participate. In other words, any time I want to charge my battery, I can go back and enjoy many of these Indian ways; I can participate in them; I can regain a feeling for our traditional values; and I might say that it is the greatest feeling there is. (Morey & Gilliam, 1974, p. 183)

In contrast to an acceptance perspective, what difference might a taking-charge perspective have on your collaboration with families? Just consider what special educators value: individual developmental gain and outcomes of independence, productivity, and inclusion, always at the maximum accelerated rate. These emphases, however, may be viewed very differently by people who have a traditionalist view. Furthermore, concepts such as supported employment, supported living, and self-determination are all rooted in creating new and innovative opportunities for people with disabilities to experience as much independence as possible; creating those opportunities often requires major family, community, and systems change. People who tend to accept their fates may not want to take risks of participating in, much less creating, innovative programs.

We have discussed three ways that cultures may differ, but other variations occur across cultures and even within the same culture. Figure 5–4 identifies other variations that exist across cultures and fundamental beliefs that can very much influence family life and special education decision making (Kalyanpur & Harry, 1999; Kalyanpur, Harry, & Skrtic, in press; Lynch & Hanson, 1998). We encourage you to read more about these cultural variations to supplement the information that we include here (Kalyanpur & Harry, 1999; Kalyanpur, Harry, & Skrtic, in press; Lynch & Hanson, 1998; McGoldrick, Giordano, & Pearce, 1996).

To appreciate within-group cultural variation, reflect on the similarities and differences that you experience with your brothers or sisters, cousins, or other family members. Are you sometimes surprised that people who are members of the same culture and who even share family experiences can have remarkably different values?

Because honoring cultural diversity is essential in all aspects of family-professional collaborations, we will discuss throughout this book how you can collaborate with families who have different cultural traditions. Bear in mind that, whatever a family's stereotypical cultural characteristics may be (that is, whatever they "should" be if they meet all or most of the characteristics of families from the same cultural group), some families such as the Cofresi family will defy the stereotype. They will display cultural traits from their own cultural traditions as

---

FIGURE 5—4

Continua of Cultural Beliefs

Individuals should have equal rights and responsibilities	Individuals have differentiated rights and responsibilities
Respect for ancestors and tradition	Respect for youths and the future
Emphasis on harmony	Emphasis on achievement
Nurturance of young children	Independence of young children
Choice and roles in responsibilities	Ascribed roles and responsibilities
People have equal status	People have unequal status

well as personal traits not strongly associated with their cultural traditions. We caution you against pigeonholing a family solely on the basis of certain cultural aspects; that is too simplified an approach, as Marta Cofresi and her twin daughters demonstrate.

Socioeconomic Status

A family's socioeconomic status (SES) includes its income, the level of family members' education, and the social status associated with the occupations of its wage earners. Here, disability and SES factors interact with each other quite dramatically. More than two-thirds of high school students with disabilities live in families with yearly household incomes below $25,000, as compared to 55 percent of high school students in general education. Also, 23 percent of the household heads of secondary students with disabilities have completed at least some college course work, compared to 35 percent of heads of household of high school students in general education (U.S. Department of Education, 1992).

Although a number of research studies have investigated the impact of SES status on family well-being, the results are mixed (Scorgie, Wilgosh, & McDonald, 1998; Shapiro, Blacher, & Lopez, 1998). Some studies point to SES not being influential regarding family adjustment (Flynt & Wood, 1989; Gallimore, Weisner, Bernheimer, Guthrie, & Nihira, 1993); but other studies suggest that families with higher incomes have higher satisfaction (Barakat & Linney, 1992; Willoughby & Glidden, 1995) and a more comprehensive support network (Barakat & Linney, 1992).

The data suggest that families of children in special education are more likely to have lower socioeconomic levels as contrasted to families of children in general education. Furthermore, families with a higher socioeconomic status have more resources available to address exceptionality issues than families who have a lower socioeconomic status. Indeed, the ability to pay for services and a higher level of education (remember, knowledge/skills is a component of the family empowerment factor) are definite resources. But the equation is not that simple; higher SES does not guarantee increased collaboration with professionals or family empowerment. Obviously, families such as the Cofresi family with fewer socioeconomic resources may also have major resources such as close families and extensive informal support networks that are positive forces for collaboration and empowerment. We encourage you to reflect on the "Tale of Two Families" in figure 5–2. The Angelino and McNeil families differ significantly in their socioeconomic resources. How do these differences influence each family's strengths and potential needs?

Because families with higher SES resources are often more achievement oriented, they may consider their child's disability to be a severe disappointment and a significant impediment to their child's independence and other types of success. This is what Farber and Ryckman (1965) called the tragic crisis for these families: the fundamental dashing of their hopes and aspirations. Families from lower socioeconomic backgrounds, on the other hand, are thought to regard achievement as being less important than values such as family solidarity or happiness (Lee, 1982; Logan, 1996). To them, a disability arguably represents less of a tragic crisis than a challenge of how to care for the child: a role organization crisis (Farber & Ryckman, 1965). These perspectives are the common or conventional wisdom; as such, they are generalizations, they do not apply to all families in the same SES groups, and they are fraught with the stereotypes—even the stigma—that necessarily accompany them. Some families, such as the Cofresi family, will be the exception to these generalizations.

Another difference between families characterized by higher and lower SES is that families with a higher SES status apparently want and believe that they have a good deal of control of their immediate lives and their futures (Kalyanpur, Harry, & Skrtic, in press). Consider the reaction of one father, a professional, to his son's diagnosis of Down syndrome:

> In those first days, my initial reaction was to control. I wanted to understand. I wanted to control the situation by the intellectual process with which I was familiar. But what I learned was not very helpful. . . . While every child's future is uncertain, my son's future seemed hopeless. I could not imagine for him a life so very different from my own. (Isbell, 1983, p. 22)

By contrast, some family researchers theorize that many families who have limited SES resources may be well justified in believing that they have little control over their environment (Kaplan & Girard, 1994; Sidel, 1996), so very few will plan for any child's future, let alone for the future of a child with an exceptionality. According to this theory, while families with higher SES resources may be more stressed by an event such as an exceptionality that contradicts their belief that they are in control of their lives, families with lower SES resources may have difficulty considering future options for their child and might be caught unprepared when it is time for their child to enter new programs (for example, finding a long waiting list at a child care program). Furthermore, their theory holds that families with lower SES resources may believe that it is useless to try to control a situation or to plan ahead and, accordingly, are relatively passive or inactive participants in educational decision making and transition planning.

In research on the beliefs of parents who have children without disabilities and who are from working-class and upper-middle-class backgrounds, Lareau (1987, 1989) has described differences in their views of home-school partnerships. Working-class families tended to have a "separated" view of home and school and deferred decision-making responsibility to educators. Alternatively, upper-middle-class parents had an "interconnected" view and believed it was important to be informed of their children's progress and to be involved in educational decision making. A key difference in these orientations is the perceived control that the families anticipated having. We encourage you to remember that perceived control is one of the elements of empowerment.

A study of former Head Start children who had particularly high academic competence revealed that their parents were more responsive to them and more frequently communicated to them the importance of their school work as compared to the parents of Head Start children who were not as high achieving (Robinson, Weinberg, Redden, Ramey, & Ramey, 1998). The families of the students who were more highly achieving still had a low SES level (the majority having monthly incomes of less than $1,000), but these mothers reflected values that are typically more associated with families at higher SES levels.

The theory that families at lower SES levels may perceive less control and be less interested in educational partnerships may hold true for some families. But for others such as the Cofresi family and still others you will read about in this book, the theory simply does not apply—nor should it. In our experience, a family's SES is not a wholly reliable indicator of its motivation or knowledge/skills, that is, of its empowerment quotient.

To develop professional-family collaboration, you will need to encourage predictable, nonjudgmental, and supportive reliable alliances that convey to all families regardless of their SES that you respect them and recognize their strengths, whatever their characteristics may be. That is your supportive role, a function valued by all families. You will learn more in chapter 10 about ways to collaborate with families in enabling them to meet their basic needs, including having greater access to financial resources.

*G*eographic Location

As a result of electronic media and increased mobility in most segments of society, regional differences in family values and forms are becoming less apparent. Yet regional patterns remain; Southern hospitality, Yankee stoicism, Midwestern conformity, and Western independence are still attributed to families by family therapists and sociologists (McGill & Pearce, 1996). Rural and urban factors also significantly influence service delivery and family life (Kozol, 1995; U.S. Department of Education, 1995, 1996).

The U.S. Department of Education (1995) reports that approximately 475,000 students with disabilities receive special education services in rural school districts. As compared to urban areas, students in rural areas tend to experience more poverty over a longer period of time. Some of the particular challenges in providing special education in rural areas include population fluctuation caused by the inadequacy of local industry, providing services in the least restrictive environment when students are spread so far apart and it is difficult to provide a high number of options, recruiting and retaining qualified personnel, maintaining active family collaboration when distances are great between home and school, and having sufficient post-secondary options that are tied to students' strengths and preferences. Strengths in rural areas can be social support from informal networks such as neighbors, churches, and civic/social organizations (Thurston, 1996).

Challenges are also great in urban areas (U.S. Department of Education, 1996). Schools in urban areas enroll almost twice as many African American and Hispanic students as do nonurban areas (U.S. Department of Commerce, 1992) and have a much larger percentage of students of limited English proficiency than other schools (Valdés, Williamson, & Wagner, 1990). Factors associated with the provision of special education to students with disabilities in urban areas include difficulty with nondiscriminatory assessment given the complicated effects of poverty, race/ethnicity, and limited English proficiency; recruiting and retaining qualified personnel; maintaining active family collaboration given all of the complications of living in urban environments that require extensive time and energy; and upkeep and adequacy of school property. As stated by Kozol (1995):

> So long as the most vulnerable people in our population are consigned to places that the rest of us will shun and flee and view with fear, I'm afraid that educational denial, medical and economic devastation, and aesthetic degradation will be virtually inevitable . . . so long as there are ghetto neighborhoods and ghetto hospitals and ghetto schools, I'm convinced there will be ghetto desperation, ghetto violence, and ghetto fear because a ghetto is itself an evil and unnatural construction. (p. 162)

You can gain perspectives on the viewpoints of families of children from diverse cultural and linguistic backgrounds in urban areas through a number of valuable resources (Dash, 1996; Harry, Allen, & McLaughlin, 1995; Kozol, 1995; Winters, 1993).

Geographic location is not a fixed characteristic of families, and indeed some families move in order to find services. A mother of two children with hearing impairments remarked:

> We lived in a small town where they had almost nothing . . . in the schools. We decided that if our children were to get an education, we would have to move; so we started looking at programs all over the country. . . Finally we settled on Starr King because it had a first-rate oral program. My husband had to quit a good job; we moved to [another town and], he had to search for another job and take a cut in pay. But it was worth it! (Spradley & Spradley, 1978, pp. 214–215)

Military families, migrant farm workers, construction workers, corporate executives, and others whose jobs require frequent relocations face this challenge repeatedly. You would do well to be aware of the anxiety that often accompanies a family's relocation. How can you minimize the anxiety? Communicate with and secure records from the student's previous school. Avoid routine family and medical history questions except when information is missing or when families appear to appreciate the opportunity to retell their story to new professionals. Offer to provide relocated families with tours of facilities, descriptions of programs, and introductions to staff and other families in the program. Try to make their process of settling in a new child and themselves as painless and smooth as possible.

In this description of family characteristics, we have emphasized some of the many ways in which families can vary and relevant issues for your consideration. Factors such as different family sizes and forms, different cultural backgrounds, and different geographic locations (or relocations) each present unique sets of challenges. Yet the underlying common themes of a good collaborative approach are: (1) respect for diverse values, (2) an understanding of some of the many other issues—in addition to their child's exceptionality—the family may be facing, and (3) a creative willingness to capitalize on families' unique strengths and resources.

Personal Characteristics

Diversity resulting from variations in family characteristics multiplies as individual family members present their own idiosyncrasies. For example, the characteristics of a member's exceptionality, each family member's state of mental and physical health, and individual coping styles are all examples of personal characteristics. These personal characteristics of individual family members can be either strengths or limitations for the family as a whole, and each of them and all of them in the aggregate affect the family's reaction to an exceptionality and the extent of the family's empowerment. Thus, a family's overall well-being is greatly influenced by the individual well-being of each of its members and then the aggregate well-being of each individual as the individuals are viewed as a family unit.

Characteristics of a Member's Exceptionality

The characteristics of a member's exceptionality will influence a family's reaction to the exceptionality. Characteristics include (1) the nature of the exceptionality (for example, is the student considered gifted?) and (2) the extent or degree of the exceptionality (for example, is the student's disability considered mild or severe?). Each of these areas raises special issues in regard to a family's reaction.

Nature of the Exceptionality The nature of the exceptionality influences the family's response to it. For example, when children have medically complex needs, their families often make many adaptations in family routines in order to provide ongoing care and often have special needs for illness-specific information, special equipment, and financial assistance (Bernbaum & Batshaw, 1997; Jones, Clatterbuck, Barber, Marquis, & Turnbull, 1995; National Commission on Childhood Disability, 1995). The need to learn how to foster the independence of children who are blind as well as to assist them in learning orientation, mobility, and communication skills can be especially challenging for families (Harrison & Crow, 1993). The threat of unpredictable seizures can increase worry and protectiveness in parents of children with epilepsy (Pianta & Lothman, 1994; Vining, 1989). Likewise, the primary concerns of parents of children with emotional disorders, attention deficit/hyperactivity disorder, head injury, and autism often relate to behavioral issues and the family's responses to behavioral challenges (Blum & Mercugliano, 1997; Conoley & Sheridan, 1996; Guralnick, 1994; Singer & Nixon, 1996; Turnbull & Ruef, 1996, 1997; Wodrich, 1999).

By the same token, a child with a hearing impairment needs communication accommodations resources (that is, interpreters) or equipment (that is, special telephones and captioned television) for others to understand what the child wants and to make sure the child understands the rest of the family (Morgan-Redshaw, Wilgosh, & Bibby, 1990; Turnbull, Turnbull, Shank, & Leal, 1999).

Families who have a child who is gifted may be concerned about their child's being publicly recognized as different, their own capability to support their child's gifts and talents, strategies for promoting positive peer and sibling relationships, and techniques for alleviating family stress associated with students who do not fulfill the educational potential that their giftedness indicates (Alsop, 1997; Carandang, 1992; Friedman & Gallagher, 1991; Rimm & Lowe, 1988).

Different exceptionalities can and usually do bring different kinds of challenges for families (Seltzer, Greenberg, Wyngaarden-Krauss, Gordon, & Judge, 1997). There is no clear-cut evidence that the particular nature of the disability alone can predict how parents, siblings, or extended family will respond and adapt to the disability (Shapiro, Blacher, & Lopez, 1998). Each exceptionality poses its own special needs, including needs to connect and collaborate with specialists and with other families whose members experience the same kind of exceptionality.

In understanding the impact of the nature of the exceptionality on families, it is extremely important to recognize that exceptionalities bring benefits to families as well as special concerns. Research has clearly docu-mented that children and youth with exceptionalities make their own positive contributions to their families (Behr & Murphy, 1993; Sandler & Mistretta, 1998; Scorgie, Wilgosh, & McDonald, 1998; Summers, Behr, & Turnbull, 1989). In box 5–1 you will learn how Mr. Arias, Roxana's teacher, identified and then built on her positive contributions. Indeed, what Mr. Arias did was a two-pronged collaboration. He recognized and affirmed that Roxana had what it takes to be a school leader, and then he collaborated with her and Marta Cofresi in achieving those goals. He knew that empowerment is a matter of the family's motivation and skills, coupled with a context that he helped to create. As you read box 5–1, think of the Cofresi family and Mr. Arias having empowerment within themselves and of the programs he sponsored as the empowering context.

Marta Cofresi and Mr. Arias are not the only parents and professionals who see the positive contributions of children with disabilities. Indeed, more than 1,200 birth parents, foster and adopted parents, and legal guardians of children with disabilities have affirmed that their children with disabilities are sources of happiness and fulfillment, strength and family closeness, and opportunities to learn through experiences associated with disabilities

MY VOICE
BOX 5–1

The Natural Leader and a Teacher's Response

Fernando Arias understands special education and students' positive contributions from a unique perspective. For three years he himself was in special education, classified as mentally retarded because he could not read or speak English but was monolingual in Spanish.

Perhaps because of that experience and certainly because of his association with the twins, he knows how to highlight their strengths and positive contributions. "Right away upon meeting Roxana, I could tell she was a natural born leader, and she is, she's a leader. She took charge—what needed to be done she took charge."

Taking charge is a benefit to Mr. Arias. When he has to speak in public, for example, he often becomes nervous; so he asks Roxana to speak for him. "She's able to communicate well with others," he says.

Having seen how influential Marta Cofresi is in including her twins in the family and community, Mr. Arias follows her example, taking the twins on overnight hiking trips, often accompanied by Mrs. Cofresi as a chaperone for them and the other female students, or to state vocational education competitions.

As a result of emphasizing what the twins can do and involving them and Marta, Mr. Arias feels a strong bond with Marta and the twins. "We just developed a close bond between all us . . . really, a small family." Whatever Mr. Arias and the twins or the family are doing, especially when they are with their peers, "I try to make that bond stronger amongst each other, because I feel that's very important. Just bonding and becoming good friends, I think that helps anybody out."

Source: Arias, F., Turnbull, A. P., Blue-Banning, M. J., & Pereira, L. (1995, Spring). Personal communication.

(Behr & Murphy, 1993). Moreover, they reported stress and well-being levels similar to those of adults in the general population.

Children with disabilities are often viewed by their families as contributing in a positive way to the family's overall quality of life, as expressed by this mother:

> I've had by-pass surgery, three husbands, a son who left for the army and never came back, a pile of bills that never got paid and Colin, who was born with microcephaly. I've had lots of troubles in my life but Colin sure hasn't been one of them. Troubles with doctors, neighbors, late SSI payments, wheelchairs that won't move, and funny questions I never felt like answering. But never had any trouble with Colin. Churches that never came through, relatives that never came by, one grandbaby I've yet to meet, and heartburn must be since the day I was born. And Colin, he was my sweet-boy. Light my day with that funny smile, and how he'd make up to me when I came to get him in the morning. Why, if it weren't for Colin, I'd have thought life had pulled a dirty trick. (Josetta, mother of Colin, quoted in Blue-Banning, Santelli, Guy, & Wallace, 1994, p. 69)

Extent and Age of Onset of the Exceptionality

The extent or degree of an exceptionality also influences families. You may be tempted to assume that a severe exceptionality has a greater impact, but that assumption is not always valid (Barakat & Linney, 1992; Scorgie, Wilgosh, & McDonald, 1998; Shapiro, Blacher, & Lopez, 1998).

For example, if a child has a severe disability, it may be apparent at birth, causing the parents to deal immediately with the shock. When a disability such as an emotional disorder or a learning disability appears later, the parents may feel not so much shock as a sense of relief that their concerns about their child's special needs have been resolved. These families may have to cope with a complex set of mixed emotions. With a learning disability, for example, some may experience confusion and frustration at the discovery that their child, who appears capable in so many ways, indeed has a disability (Dyson, 1996; Stoddard, Valcante, Roemer, & O'Shea, 1994). Others may be relieved to learn that there are reasons for the problems they have observed and yet feel guilty that they did not identify the disability earlier (Walther-Thomas, Hazel, Schumaker, Vernon, & Deshler, 1991).

Alternatively, when a disability has a sudden onset, such as a head injury resulting from an adolescent's diving accident, the family is thrust into the world of trauma and rehabilitation units, typically with highly ambiguous prognoses (Conoley & Sheridan, 1996; Wade, Taylor, Drotar, Stancin, & Yeates, 1996). Families often have to make a series of ongoing readjustments as their child's characteristics fluctuate and permanently change.

In addition, severe exceptionalities are often more apparent than milder disabilities. On the one hand, the obvious disability may enable people to readily accommodate a child's inappropriate public behavior; on the other hand, it may cause the family more social stigma and rejection. By contrast, milder exceptionalities may be invisible, leading siblings to worry whether something is wrong with them, too (Powell & Gallagher, 1993). With a severe disability, the family may be able to develop a more definitive understanding of the child's support needs. But with a milder disability, the family may find itself on a roller coaster of expectations, with hopes for the future alternately raised and dashed as the child makes progress or falls back.

Now, consider just how that student's exceptionality can affect professionals' collaboration with the family. Instructional objectives that could help the student and family (such as improved communication, expanded social relationships, or positive behavioral support) probably should be given high priority. For some students and families, learning more about how best to support their son or daughter in being successful with homework or in acquiring more appropriate behavior would be helpful (see chapter 13). Other families might welcome information about services in the community such as child care or personal care attendant services (see chapter 10). To repeat, the nature and extent or degree of each student's exceptionality have special implications for the family and for how you as a professional can best collaborate with the family. No doubt, the Cofresi twins' disability affects their family, but it also affects how a professional such as Mr. Arias collaborates with them: He saw Marta's and the twins' motivation and knowledge/skills and committed himself to augmenting those traits.

Family Health

People who do not feel well have more difficulty coping with stressful situations. For example, a mother's health status contributes to the parenting stress in families where there is a child with AD/HD (Anastopoulos, Guevremont, Shelton, & DuPaul, 1992). Conversely, stress produces physiological responses that can make people ill. Some research has found that parents of children with exceptionalities have a higher level of stress than parents who do not have such children and that their stress is associated with additional caregiving responsibilities (Beckman, 1991; Kazak & Marvin, 1984; Roach, Orsmond, & Barratt, 1999; Shapiro, Blacher, & Lopez, 1998; Solis & Abidin, 1991); other research, however, has not shown that these parents have higher stress levels (Behr & Murphy, 1993; Frey, Greenberg, & Fewell, 1989; Harris & McHale, 1989; Scott, Atkinson, Minton, & Bowman, 1997; Seltzer, Krauss, & Janicki, 1994).

Not all family stress is purely disability-related. Some is socially created. Thus, some families of children with exceptionalities experience a wide range of stresses and worries associated with issues such as poverty and racism (Harry, Kalyanpur, & Day, 1999).

Whether a parent's or a family's stress or health problems are caused by worry about the child's exceptionality or whether their sources lie elsewhere, the result is the same: The parent or family faces greater challenges in taking action to get what the family wants and needs. As we discussed in chapter 4, you can support the family by being flexible in all aspects of providing services and by being responsive to their preferences, strengths, and needs.

Coping Styles

As we pointed out in chapter 3, Olson and associates (Olson et al., 1983) developed the following categories of coping styles: passive appraisal, reframing, spiritual support, social support, and professional support. Coping within the Cofresi family consists of the following:

Reframing: looking at the twins' positive contributions instead of their disabilities

Spiritual support: in Marta's words, "I had to find the answer in God, because God made them that way, so how God would think of them and treat them is how I wanted to be"

Social support: support by their friends

Professional support: support from Mr. Arias

Family members vary in their coping capability in both the number of different coping strategies they use and the quality or effectiveness of each strategy (Bailey et al., 1999; Bennett, DeLuca, & Allen, 1996; Sandler & Mistretta, 1998; Scorgie, Wilgosh, & McDonald, 1998; Turnbull et al., 1993). Within the same family, some members may have strong coping capabilities and others may need much more support because their own capabilities have not yet been developed fully. Think of individual coping metaphorically: "The end of the rope is the end of the rope, regardless of how long the rope is" (Avis, 1985, p. 197). Individual family members have ropes of differing lengths.

Avoid judging one family member in relation to another and wondering why one individual but not another is having such a challenging time coping with what may appear to be a similar situation. Rather than making comparative judgments, remember that the length of everyone's rope varies and depends on all of the situations that they are handling in their life at a given time or that they have faced over time. As a collaborator, regard yourself as a "rope lengthener," supporting everyone involved (families, professionals, friends, and community citizens) to lengthen their ropes so that they will be more empowered (more motivated and connected to sources of knowledge/skills) rather than being at the end of their rope.

Special Challenges

Families face challenges over and above a child's disability or extraordinary gifts and talents. Examples of special challenges include teenage pregnancy (Coley, 1998; Corcoran, 1998; Dunifon, 1999; Rhein et al., 1999; Roth, Hendrickson, & Stowell, 1998); exposure to violence and other fearful experiences (Carta, 1997; Groves, 1997; Houle, 1996; Ramirez, Nguyen, & Kratochwill, 1998; Vig, 1996); having a family member who is incarcerated (National Resource Center for Family Support Programs, 1993); and having HIV/AIDS (Cohen, Grosz, Ayoob, & Schoen, 1997; Rutstein, Conlon, & Batshaw, 1997). Other special challenges that we will address in this section include living in poverty, engaging in substance abuse, and living in a family in which a parent has a disability.

Families in Poverty

Current U.S. poverty profiles are depressing and reveal the vast extent of poverty in a very wealthy country:

- Over 10 million young children live in poverty or near poverty.
- Black and Hispanic young children are much more likely to be poor than are White young children, with the poverty rate increasing the fastest among Hispanics. Given the population of the United States, Whites are the largest ethnic group of young children in poverty.
- The majority of young children living with unmarried mothers are poor. These young children are particularly at risk for poverty.
- One parent's full-time employment is no guarantee against poverty (National Center for Children in Poverty, 1998).

Rudimentary and harsh survival problems face families who live in poverty (Sidel, 1996). Poverty impacts the lives of 14.5 million children in the United States—more than one in every five (Sherman, 1997). Children who live in poverty are

- two times more likely to repeat a grade
- 3.4 times more likely to be expelled
- 1.5 to 3 times more likely to die in childhood
- two times more likely to have a serious physical or mental disability
- one-third less likely to attend a 2- or 4-year college
- one-half as likely to graduate from college (Sherman, 1997)

Reasons for these problems include the families' inability to provide adequate nutrition, health care, housing, and child care. Other risk factors include increased lead poisoning, limited learning opportunities at home, and multiple challenges that their families face continuously and simultaneously (Betson & Michael, 1997; Corcoran & Chaudry, 1997; Sherman, 1997).

Earlier in this chapter we wrote that poverty is more closely associated with lives of students in special education than with those in general education (U.S. Department of Education, 1992) and with single-female head of families than with those with two-parent families (LaPlante, Carlson, Kaye, & Bradsher, 1996).

Homeless families, generally headed by women, are a subgroup of families in poverty (Butera & Maughan, 1998; Dubus & Buckner, 1998; Riley, Fryar, & Thornton, 1998). A study of homeless families in New York City produced a typical demographic profile:

> Almost 100 percent of all families were headed by single women. The majority of these single mothers were younger than 25 years of age with an average of 22. Most of these families have never had a traditional family structure with almost 90 percent reporting never having been married. African-American constituted the largest ethnic group among the families; two-thirds were African-American, roughly one-fourth were Hispanic, and less than seven percent were White or from other ethnic groups. (Homes for the Homeless, 1992, p. 3)

In his book, *Rachel and Her Children: Homeless Families in America*, Kozol (1988) tells about the lives of homeless people he has interviewed. One child describes the room in which she lives with her mother and three other children.

> Ever since August we been livin' here. The room is either very hot or freezin' cold. When it be hot outside it's hot in here. When it be cold outside we have no heat. We used to live with my aunt but then it got too crowded there so we moved out. We went to welfare and they sent us to the shelter. Then they shipped us to Manhattan. I'm scared of the elevators. 'Fraid they be stuck. I take the stairs. (Kozol, 1988, p. 62)

Homelessness has devastating effects on children, including an increase in problems of health, peer interactions, transitions, academics, and school attendance (Cauce et al., 1998; Heflin & Rudy, 1991; Stronge & Tenhouse, 1990).

Nonetheless, many families from low socioeconomic backgrounds are vitally interested in special education issues (Harry, 1992a, 1992b). In an in-depth study of 12 Puerto Rican parents from low-income backgrounds, Harry reported the parents' cogent insights about labeling, curriculum and bilingual issues, efficacy of special versus general education placement, and methods for teaching reading. Harry concluded:

> This study shows that the power of parents may be seriously undermined by culturally different ways of understanding. Yet it also shows that poor parents, with little formal education, and a different language and culture, may, through their own analysis of their children's difficulties, have a significant contribution to make to current debates in the field of special education. (Harry, 1992b, p. 38)

In every relationship with families, including those from low-income backgrounds, we encourage you to demonstrate respect, be nonjudgmental, and recognize their unique strengths and their important contributions to their child and family. That is the point that an inner-city mother of an infant makes as she describes the importance of a home visitor's informality and nonintrusive questions:

> She [the previous early intervention specialist] came out to the house when [the child] was 8 months [old], and she said, "He has problems," and I said, "No, he don't, he's just a baby". . . . She asks me all kinds of stuff like if I have a crib, how many people live here, and she writes it down. She was a nosy lady nosy, nosy! I kept hiding from her, and finally I moved so they wouldn't bug me. . . . When she [the current specialist] came out, I thought, "Oh, gee, here we go again." So I asked her, "What's wrong?" and she just says, "Nothing, I just want to know if you need anything." (Summers et al., 1990, p. 87)

As you become more of a reliable ally with families, you will become less like the previous early intervention specialist that this mother described and more like the current specialist who seeks to find a relevant connection with her. In chapter 9, you will learn more about communicating with families, *including those* from diverse cultural backgrounds; and in chapter 10 you will find ways to provide concrete assistance by helping families connect with community agencies that can assist them to meet their basic needs.

Families with Substance Abuse

In 1996 the National Institute on Drug Abuse reported that the illicit use of drugs by women during their pregnancy was 5.5 percent, or approximately 221,000 women (National Institute on Drug Abuse, 1996). Within a group of women who experienced poverty and received Aid to Families with Dependent Children assistance, the prevalence for alcoholism and drug abuse was reported to be between 16 and 21 percent (Sisco & Pearson, 1994). Drug and alcohol abuse are particularly problematic for American Indian and Alaska Native youth (Abel, 1995; Streissguth, 1994).

While substance abuse involves the use of many different drugs, we will particularly focus on alcohol and cocaine. Children who are exposed to alcohol in utero are at risk for fetal alcohol syndrome. Approximately one to two children per 1,000 are affected annually by this syndrome (Poulsen, 1994; U.S. Department of Health and Human Services, 1993). These children typically have decreased growth, a particular pattern of facial and physical anomalies, some central nervous system problems, and lower IQ scores than children who have not been exposed to alcohol (D'Apolito, 1998; Olson & Burgess, 1997; Phelps & Grabowski, 1992; Shriver & Piersel, 1994).

Family size and SES coupled with how a family adjusts to exceptionality and how it interacts with alcohol exposure determine, at least partially, a child's development and long-term outcomes (Carta et al., 1997). For example, children who have been exposed to alcohol who come from smaller families or have fathers with higher levels of education have higher intellectual and achievement scores than peers from larger families or lower SES families (Sampson, Streissguth, Barr, & Bookstein, 1989). To understand the family, consider not only a family's separate characteristics (family size and SES) but also how the characteristics interact (family size, SES, and special challenges). The book, *Fetal Alcohol Syndrome: A Guide for Communities and Families*, by Ann Streissguth, is a helpful guide for family and community support related to families affected by fetal alcohol syndrome (1997).

Cocaine is the most frequently used and strongly addictive drug associated with such increased risk factors as prematurity and neurobehavioral impairment (Batshaw & Conlon, 1997). Infants who have been exposed to cocaine may be at risk for an atypical behavior pattern particularly related to temperament (Olson & Burgess, 1997; Patterson, Reid, & Dishion, 1992). They are drowsier and sleep more than infants who have not had drug exposure; their mothers are more passive during play interactions (Batshaw & Conlon, 1997).

In what way should families who experience substance abuse be supported by educational professionals? The Children's Defense Fund studied 50 successful programs that provide support to families who face multiple challenges including substance abuse (Allen & Larson, 1999). These programs, which go by the name of Family Care, provide comprehensive, coordinated, and family-centered support to parents and children who face multiple challenges. They provide a triple-pronged emphasis on a woman's needs (dealing with substance abuse, addressing issues of sexual abuse), needs as a mother (teaching parenting skills, providing counseling), and needs as a community member (providing opportunities for job training and adult education). Family care is unique in that the parents and children are placed in the home of a host family whose members are trained to provide support and mentorship to the parents and their children as they move from a disempowerment to an empowerment orientation. The length of stay varies—for women who experience substance abuse, the average is between 3 months and 18 months. Training, respite care, and usually compensation is provided to the mentor families. Box 5–2 describes how one mother and her son, Sonja and Michael, were provided family care.

The bottom line is that highly comprehensive and family-centered services need to be available starting during the neonatal period. When comprehensive and appropriate programs are not available, educators will need to collaborate with public health nurses and substance abuse professionals to develop an array of services and supports that can assist parents in getting necessary intervention and that can enhance their child's development. From an empowerment perspective, every dimension of motivation and knowledge/skill factors needs to be addressed, and the context needs to be as empowering as possible. This is equally true when there are other kinds of child abuse and neglect, as we point out in more detail in chapter 10.

Parents with Disabilities

As people with disabilities begin to lead more typical lives, the likelihood increases that they will become parents. When a parent has a physical disability, the

Project BASTA—All Under One Roof

Just before giving premature birth to Michael, who weighed one and one-half pounds, Sonja entered Project BASTA in Boston. Sonja was not a drug user, but her mother had died when Sonja was very young, her father suffered from mental illness and alcoholism, and she had witnessed a tremendous amount of violence as a child. When her stepmother became physically abusive toward her, 20-year-old Sonja sought emergency shelter at Casa Myrna Vasquez, which has been serving battered women and their children in the Boston area for more than two decades.

After three months, staff there referred Sonja to Project BASTA, a residential program that Casa Myrna Vasquez created in 1992 to offer adolescent victims of domestic violence and their children comprehensive services, including substance abuse prevention, treatment, and recovery services. . . . Project BASTA serves 16 mothers (eight of whom are teenagers) and their children, during average stays of about 14 months. Staff say their first concern when a young woman such as Sonja enters the program is to help her feel safe, so that the healing process can begin. On entry, the teens are given both mental health and legal assessments and are referred to prenatal and other health care services immediately. Then, through daily structured activities, the young mothers gain the tools they need to change their lives and give their children the healthy upbringing they never had.

Project BASTA staff say that from the beginning, Sonja partici-

pated fully in the program. She responded well to her work with a staff therapist and attended all the required meetings and groups, including a clinical support group, psychoeducational workshops on domestic violence, house meetings, and substance abuse prevention workshops. All of the young women attend substance abuse prevention workshops because their circumstances put them at high risk for future use. . . .

Sonja . . . found that during her first months in the program she had to focus much of her attention on Michael, who spent his first month of life in a neonatal intensive care unit. Sonja's case manager at Project BASTA realized that he would likely be eligible for Supplemental Security Income (SSI) disability benefits and helped Sonja apply right away. Staff also helped Sonja find an early childhood intervention program in the community, and the family soon began receiving weekly visits from a specialist there who taught Sonja how to care for such a small and medically fragile baby. . . .

Staff members acknowledge that serving teenagers with such traumatic backgrounds is not easy. "The developmental issues of the teens make it very difficult for them to abide by the rules," says the director. Yet Project BASTA manages to make a positive difference in the lives of the young women it serves. The program reports that 95 percent of its participants who made it to graduation either reduced their use of alcohol, maintained sobriety, or did not begin to drink; 100 percent reported a reduction or elimination of physical abuse; and 94 percent

received postpartum health care. At a two-year follow-up, 88 percent of the young women continued to report a reduction in physical abuse.

About eight months after entering the program, Sonja was informed that her application for subsidized housing had been accepted, and she began looking for an apartment. She also started filling out applications for nursing school.

It took two months, but Sonja finally moved into her own apartment, furnished with donations from local charities. Project BASTA staff put her in touch with an early intervention program in her new neighborhood so that Michael could continue to progress. Sonja also checked in regularly with Project BASTA staff and attended weekly support groups. After two years, she is in the same apartment, has completed a one-year nursing program, and is looking for a full-time job. She has a nonabusive boyfriend and has had no abusive relationships. Michael is in child care and is developing well.

Sonja says that Project BASTA helped her learn how to be strong, how to say no, and how to choose the right kind of friends. The most important part of the program for her, she says, was her relationships with the staff.

Although not all of Project BASTA's participants are able to take control of their lives as quickly and completely as Sonja, the staff work tirelessly to help them succeed, step-by-step. "Embracing the whole [of the young women's experiences]," says the director, "that's our strength and greatest challenge."

Source: Allen, M., & Larson, J. (1999). Healing the whole family: A look at family care programs. Washington, DC: Children's Defense Fund.

effects on your relationship with them primarily involve logistics (for example, providing accessible meeting rooms or perhaps communicating through the most accessible and convenient means, such as the telephone).

Parents with visual or hearing impairments rely on their children in many situations. For example, parents with visual impairments may ask their children to read prices in grocery stores and otherwise guide them through daily transactions. They may depend on an older child to provide care for younger siblings, expecting the older child to take on parental roles (a member of the parental subsystem [see chapter 6]). Whether this is detrimental depends, of course, on the individual family and whether parents can also enable the children on whom they depend to have the time to be "just kids."

The child's role in assisting a parent may require the child to forego some school extracurricular activities or may create conflict with a parent. For example, during the following description of a parent-teacher conference with a mother who has a hearing impairment, the child plays a critical but problematic role:

> We didn't have anybody who had sign language because our district's deaf education teacher was strictly from the oral school. So I asked Jeannie to interpret at our conference, since I knew she was very good at sign language. Unfortunately, what I needed to tell Jeannie's mother was that I had some concerns about her behavior in class. . . . The mother just nodded and smiled. I didn't understand her reaction. . . . It was only later that I discovered that Jeannie had not, to say the least, translated accurately what I was saying!

It is critically important to recognize the strengths of parents with disabilities. Often the disability itself does not interfere with how the family functions. There are also instances when the disability may actually enhance the parent's understanding of the child as, for example, when deaf parents raise deaf children.

> Deaf mothers, accustomed to dealing with their own hearing loss, are well aware of and skilled in the use of the visual strategies that facilitate effective communication among deaf children. They are, therefore, unlikely to encounter the sense of powerlessness that overwhelms many hearing parents when confronted with the diagnosis of their child's hearing loss. (Jamieson, 1995, p. 112)

Special issues arise in the family when mothers (Nicholson, Sweeney, & Geller, 1998a; Nicholson, Sweeney, & Geller, 1998b; Oyserman, Mowbray, & Zemencuk, 1994) or fathers (Nicholson, Nason, Calabresi, & Yando, 1999) have mental illness. Particular challenges can include the stigma from mental illness, struggles with day-to-day parenting, difficulty with the effects on other family members of the parent's medication and hospitalization, the threat of the children being placed in foster or adoptive care, and difficulty maintaining family cohesion and adaptability.

What happens when adults with mental retardation have children? Feldman (1997) synthesizes research related to parents with mental retardation. Some of his conclusions are as follows:

- Children of parents with mental retardation typically have lower IQ scores than would be expected from a random sample of the general population, with approximately 40 percent of the children having IQs less than 70.
- Children of parents with mental retardation are at high risk for behavioral and psychiatric disorders.
- The basis for the cognitive, behavioral, and psychiatric disorders appears to be limitations in parenting skills rather than the poverty that is associated with the parents' living conditions.
- Affective supports and services, involving intensive parent training, can substantially improve the parenting skills of parents with mental retardation.
- The performance of children of parents of mental retardation improved after parent training.
- Highly intensive early intervention for children can substantially offset a reduction in the IQ that is sometimes seen in children of parents with mental retardation.

An extremely helpful resource for supporting parents who have disabilities is Through the Looking Glass—an organization in San Francisco that produces extremely helpful materials for supporting parents who have a broad range of disabilities. One of their publications, *Adaptive Parenting Equipment: Idea Book One* (DeMoss et al., 1995), describes and illustrates adaptive parenting equipment for parents who have physical disabilities in terms of caring for their babies. Adaptive equipment covers bathing, diapering, feeding, dressing, and play. We encourage you to review their website (http://www.lookingglass.org).

Summary

So many families, so many differences! Yes, that's true, but there are ways you can simplify your work with the Cofresi family and others whose children have disabilities, unusual gifts, or, in the case of Roxela and Roxana Cofresi, both disability and special talents.

What affects families? Clearly, the family's own characteristics—size and form, cultural background, socioeconomic status, and geographic location.

Of course, the personal characteristics of each family member come into play. The nature and severity of the child's exceptionality play important roles but not always in predictable ways. The family's need for support is also influenced by the type and extent of the exceptionality. And the family members' health and coping styles influence family well-being.

Some families face special challenges, and so do the professionals who work with these multiply challenged families. Poverty, substance abuse, and disability all create unusual parenting circumstances.

Whatever a family's characteristics might be, nearly every family is motivated to support its members, and most families have or can develop skills that help them get what they want. In your work with families, you should regard yourself as a collaborator who, like Mr. Arias, creates or assures that they will have a context in which their motivation and knowledge/skills will be welcomed.

If you were bold enough to be a fortune teller, what fortune would you tell for Marta Cofresi, Roxela, and Roxana? If you did not know them except as a statistic (single parent, monolingual, twins with disabilities, father left family when twins were born, older siblings, immigrants, not well off financially), you might describe a scenario quite different from the one that Marta and the twins describe.

What could account for that discrepancy? The answer lies in the family's characteristics. Of course, the nature and severity of the twins' disabilities make a difference, but even more influential are the characteristics of the Cofresi family.

These characteristics are much more than the sum of statistical profiles about the family. At their core, the characteristics have more to do with character than attributes, with courage and attitudes rather than quantifiable facts related to their ethnicity, socioeconomic status, and geographical location.

There is much to learn from Marta Cofresi's early acceptance of her twins' disabilities, the way she molded Juan Carlos, Louisa, and the twins into a single unit of caring, and the way the older siblings and, in time, Roxela and Roxana themselves decided to meet and beat the odds (to use the phrase that Theresa Cooper employs in chapter 3).

One last fact is worth noting: Remember Mr. Arias, who was Roxana's vocational education teacher? He was the professional who insisted that Roxana remain in his class, who developed the trust bond with her that Patty Smith spoke about in chapter 1. He had great expectations for her fixed firmly in his mind, and he collaborated with her and her classmates so she would be a success in school and a person with ambition for higher education. Like Mr. Arias, you can make similar contributions to students and families!

Chapter Six

Family Interaction

*V*incent and Joseph Benito, ages 9 and 8, are lucky little guys. Sure, they've both got autism. But they've also got what it takes to combat it: a big—a really big—family.

For starters, there's Nila, their mother, and Joe, their dad. And then there's grandmother, also named Nila and aunt Nancy. And even though he died long before the boys were born, there's granddad Bill, whose teachings ("kill them with kindness," "think the problem through," and "don't be emotional") guide Nila even now. Finally, there are Nila's friends, her colleagues at the University of South Florida's Florida Department of Child and Family Studies, Florida's Children's Medical Services, and the staff at the boys' school in Tampa, Florida.

So when any school administrator or teacher works with the boys, they also work with the whole Benito family, blood and chosen. That doesn't mean that each member of the family duplicates another. Far from it.

Nila describes herself as the planner and organizer; she writes down what she wants to say at the meetings with the educators, she runs it by Joe (who is away on business a couple of weeks each month), she checks off with grandmother Nila, she asks her sister Nancy for input, she tells her friends what she wants to do, and she consults her late father's wisdom. In a way, says Nila, she's like legendary football coach Vince Lombardi: "It's like I'm coaching and setting up all the plays and teaching all the players."

And then there's the team that executes those plays, guided by the quarterback. There's Joe, grandmother Nila, aunt Nancy, great-grandmother Francesca, and the extended family. All of them have been to individual program conferences, all have collaborated with each other, all share Nila's and Joe's concerns and great expectations, all share the pain of persistent problems, and all share the celebrations of the boys' and the family's successes.

That family collaboration helps Vincent and little Joe, but it also "makes us feel stronger" as a family. Feeling that way helps because family members don't always see eye to eye about the boys. They also have some differences in style. "I tend to focus more on the big picture, he [Joe] more on smaller things, so we really complement each other when we meet with professionals," Nila says. Nila is oriented toward the future, always thinking five years ahead: what will the boys need then, and how can she work today to make sure their future is secure? Joe is grounded in the present; he's the "muscle" in the family team, a man who sometimes attends meetings to hold people accountable for what should happen here and now. But as for their vision of the big picture, they are in agreement: "We have high expectations, we're cautiously optimistic, and we look at our life just as a family in general."

It wasn't that way when Nila decided to go for inclusion after Vincent was subjected to aversive interventions

in a preschool he attended before Head Start. She had to persuade Joe, her sister Nancy, and her mother Nila to buy into her vision.

What brought them around? They attended a personal-futures planning meeting that the staff from the University of South Florida's Individualized Support Program hosted for the Benito family, they acquired information about inclusion from the university staff and Nila, they met the staff at the Head Start program where inclusion was the norm, and they were exposed to great expectations for inclusion.

So the professionals have to deal with the Benito family as a united family. It's a family that tries to collaborate with the professionals. When the boys were in preschool, it was common for Nancy and grandmother Nila to attend almost all of the program planning conferences. Now, however, they tend to not attend as regularly. Instead, they attend the "big three" conferences and they support Nila emotionally in her role as the "quarterback."

The boys have benefited from three different types of conferences. The first, held at Nila's home, focused on their education; the second, also held at the boys' home, focused on their lives within the family; and the third, likewise at the boys' home, focused on their lives in the community. In attendance at each were Nila, Joe, family members, and a large number of the educators involved with the boys. The process calls for everyone to say what their priorities are for the boys—the priorities at school, at home, and in the community.

With so many people and so many different perspectives, it is common for disagreements to exist—along with consensus. To reach consensus on priorities, every person attending has the right to vote on priorities. For example, at the school-focused meeting, eleven priorities emerged. That was far too many. So each person there was given six votes. The "voter" could cast them in any way the person wanted—say, three votes for one priority, and one for each of three others.

This democratic system of "weighted voting" narrowed the priorities to six and reflected a consensus. More than that, it gave everyone a sense of control, removed Nila from a role of seeming to dominate the meeting, and resulted in agreed-upon strategies and action plans that each person agreed to carry out.

Especially for Nila, this process has its benefits—collaboration in thinking about the boys and the family, about the present and the future, about priorities and action plans; and collaboration in acting on the plans. "It's okay to give up control," Nila says, "so long as everyone follows through and stays with us."

Following through—there lies the rub. When the boys' behavior gets really difficult (usually at holiday times, when school is out and routines change), Nila becomes the one who is the designated "fixer." What she hears is, "You've got all the answers, Nila, you fix this up."

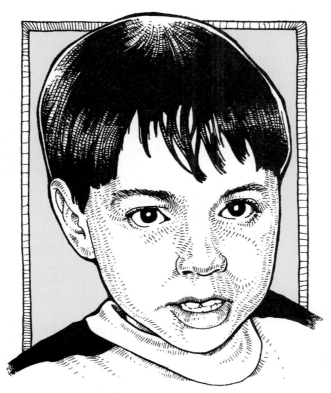

Joseph Benito, age 8. (1999)

107

Not so, says Nila: "All I have is ideas. When everyone looks to me, I feel incompetent. And when I can't fix things up, I fear that people will give up on my boys, even those who love them dearly. So, I draw away from my support, and then they draw away from me and the boys. It's a self-fulfilling prophecy. The family system can become really confusing at times."

But it doesn't stay that way, and it doesn't have to be that way, either. Nila knows one solution: "I need people to work with me every day, and I could use a person from outside the family who can facilitate the family's communication and support." And Nila knows another solution, too: returning to the base of support she has at work and in the boys' school.

In chapter 1, we defined family as two or more people who regard themselves as a family and perform some of the functions that families typically perform. This chapter is about the "two or more people who regard themselves as a family." In other words, it is about family members and their *interactions* within the family and among its members, about their relationships to each other. As the family systems framework shows (the circle within figure 6–1), there are four basic types of interactions or relationships—marital, parental, sibling, and extended family. We display the types of relationships in the inner quadrants of the framework and their qualities, which are described as *cohesion* and *adaptability,* in the outer ring.

Assumptions of Family Systems Theory

One of the most significant recent changes within special education, particularly in early childhood special education, has been the shift from focusing primarily on the child or on the parental subsystem (especially the mother and child subsystem) to focusing more broadly on the whole family (Allen & Petr, 1996; Turnbull, Turbiville, & Turnbull, 2000). This emphasis on the whole family and on the systemic (systemwide), reverberating impact of input/output through the entire family system brings to mind a mobile:

> In a mobile all the pieces, no matter what size or shape, can be grouped together and balanced by shortening or lengthening the strings attached or rearranging the distance between the pieces. So it is with a family. None of the family members is identical to any other; they are all different and at different levels of growth. As in a mobile, you can't arrange one without thinking of the other.[1] (Satir, 1972, pp. 119–120)

A single mother of several children, one of whom is an elementary-age son with attention deficit/hyperactivity disorder (AD/HD), described how a family's interactions reverberate across all family members:

> Quality of life for me is being happy and that means doing what makes me feel happy, because if I'm happy, then it comes across and falls into my children's lives. If I'm not happy, then it creates a whole lot of chaos, and a negative environment. So I've learned to let go of things, and concentrate on what makes me happy, so in turn, my kids will be happy. And it's working. (Unpublished Beach Center transcript, 1999)

The family systems theory approach provides a framework for understanding what a family is and how it functions (chapters 5 through 8) and shows professionals how to collaborate with families (chapters 9 through 15). Three of the most relevant assumptions of systems theory in general and of family systems theory in particular are (1) the input/output configuration of systems, (2) the concepts of wholeness and subsystems, and (3) the role of boundaries in defining systems (Whitechurch & Constantine, 1993).

Input/Output

The first assumption is that certain characteristics provide input into the system. The system then interacts with these inputs, and the interaction produces output. Systems theory focuses primarily on "what happens to the *input* as it is processed by the system on its way to becoming an *output*" (Broderick & Smith, 1979, p. 114; our emphasis). As you examine the family systems framework (figure 6–1), you will see that the family characteristics you read about in chapter 5 are the inputs into family interaction. The family interaction occurs as families perform roles and interact with each other. The output of

---

[1]Copyright © 1972. Reprinted by permission, Science and Behavior Books.

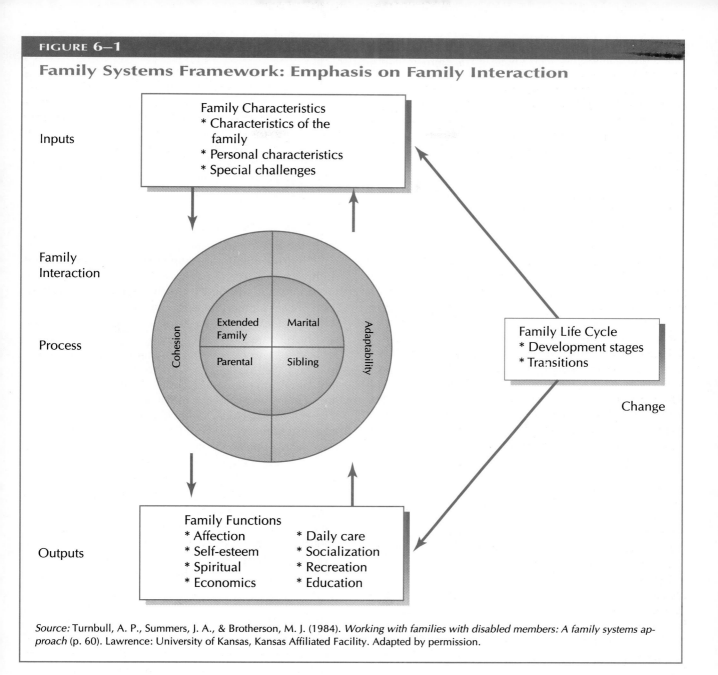

FIGURE 6–1

Family Systems Framework: Emphasis on Family Interaction

Inputs

Family Characteristics
* Characteristics of the family
* Personal characteristics
* Special challenges

Family Interaction

Process

Cohesion

Extended Family | Marital

Parental | Sibling

Adaptability

Family Life Cycle
* Development stages
* Transitions

Change

Outputs

Family Functions
* Affection
* Self-esteem
* Spiritual
* Economics
* Daily care
* Socialization
* Recreation
* Education

Source: Turnbull, A. P., Summers, J. A., & Brotherson, M. J. (1984). *Working with families with disabled members: A family systems approach* (p. 60). Lawrence: University of Kansas, Kansas Affiliated Facility. Adapted by permission.

these roles and interactions is related to family functions that we discuss in chapter 7. Think of the Benito family and its inputs. They consist of the family's characteristics (for example, a large united family), their members' personal characteristics (such as the boys' autism and each member's coping styles), and special challenges (two sons with disabilities). In this chapter, you will learn how those characteristics influence or shape how the Benitos interact within and outside the family.

Wholeness and Subsystems

The second assumption is that the system must be understood as a whole and cannot be understood by examining only its component parts—that is, just one or more of its members (Whitechurch & Constantine, 1993). While simply understanding the child does not mean that you will understand the family, understanding the family is necessary to understanding the child. Moreover, many professionals mistakenly assume that they can understand and collaborate with the family if they know only the mother's or the student's perspective.

This is a mistaken assumption because the family consists of the sum of its members' mutual and reciprocal interactions. The aggregation, or the combination of interactions, is the sum—the whole family. There are interacting component parts or subsystems: marital, parental, sibling, and extended family relationships. Those are the subsystems in the inner quadrant of figure 6–1. Think of the task that professionals face as they establish a reliable alliance with the Benito family: to understand the boys, Vincent and Joe, and then understand and collaborate with all of the highly involved family members. It is safe to say that when a school gets one of the Benito boys, it gets a whole family and needs to partner with each member.

*B*oundaries

The third and last assumption is that family subsystems are separated by boundaries and that these boundaries are created by the interaction of family members with each other and by the family unit in its interactions with outside influences. For example, there are boundaries between parents and children and between the children themselves. Likewise, the boundary between the family and the educators with whom they are collaborating may be a different boundary than the one that exists between the family and friends, clergy, other professionals, or tradespeople.

Families vary in the degree to which their boundaries are open or closed to educators or any other nonmember. The openness or closedness of the boundaries affects the degree to which the family will collaborate with educators or others. In the Benitos' case, the boundaries between the professionals and themselves are fairly open, and opportunities for various kinds of partnerships are abundant.

By the same token, the boundaries within a family, for example, help to define its members' roles with respect to each other as parental and extended family subsystems. In some families, extended family members take on parents' roles because the boundary between the two subsystems (extended family and parental) is open. In other families, there might be great resentment if one of the grandparents tries to make suggestions about child rearing. In those families, the boundary between parental and extended family subsystems is closed. In the Benito family, there are open, issue-specific boundaries among Nila, Joe, and Nila's sister and mother.

In this chapter, we describe the four family subsystems and the "operating boundary rules" of family systems and subsystems—cohesion and adaptability.

*F*amily Subsystems

Within the traditional nuclear family, there are four major subsystems (see figure 6–1):

1. Marital subsystem: marital partner interactions
2. Parental subsystem: parent and child interactions
3. Sibling subsystem: child and child interactions
4. Extended-family subsystem: interactions of nuclear family relatives and others who are regarded as relatives

Interactions differ according to the subsystems within each family and according to the membership within each subsystem. For example, a family with only one child has no sibling subsystem. Similarly, single parents do not have a formal marital subsystem that influences the family, but they may have the equivalent if they have a significant partner. Because you may not know exactly who each family considers to be part of the family system, simply ask parents to tell you about "their family" and listen carefully to the people they mention. These people may very well be able to help create broadly based collaborations. In the Benito family, the extended members are so many and so active that it would have been a mistake not to ask Nila whom she considers to be family. Likewise, it probably would be wise to develop partnerships with all the involved family members, not just Nila, and to infuse the eight obligations of a reliable alliance into each of the partnerships. After all, what happens to one of the Benitos surely will affect all of them.

*M*arital Partner Interactions (The Marital Subsystem)

The marital subsystem consists of interactions between marital partners or significant others who function as marital partners. The presence of a child or youth with an exceptionality can influence marital relationships and interactions.

Impacts: Negative, Positive, and Mixed How are marital relationships influenced by the presence of a child with an exceptionality? Are marriages on the whole hurt, unaffected, or improved by the presence of the child? As confusing as it may be, research responds affirmatively to each of those questions about marital effects.

Some studies indicate that a child or youth with an exceptionality has a negative impact on the parents' marriage. The role of divorce, marital disharmony, and desertions by husbands have been reported to be disproportionately high in marriages where there is a child or youth with an exceptionality (Gath, 1977; Hodapp & Krasner, 1995; Murphy, 1982). One group of researchers assessed marital harmony in 59 couples soon after the birth of a child with spina bifida and again nearly a decade later (Tew, Payne, & Lawrence, 1974). The researchers maintained contact with these couples as well as with 58 comparison couples (those who did not have a child with spina bifida). The couples who had a child with spina bifida had lower marital harmony and twice the divorce rate as the control group couples. Thus, it appeared that the birth of a child with spina bifida presented a serious challenge to marital stability and caused many marital needs and activities to be subordinated to the child's needs. As Helen Featherstone (1980), herself the parent of a child with a disability, has noted: "A child's handicap attacks the fabric of a marriage in four ways. It excites powerful emotions in both parents. It acts as a dispiriting symbol of shared failure. It reshapes the organization of the family. It creates fertile ground for conflict" (p. 91).

On the contrary, however, the majority of studies have indicated that the divorce rate is not higher when a family has a child with an exceptionality (Benson & Gross, 1989). Indeed, some husbands and wives report higher levels of marital adjustment, partially because of their shared commitment for their child (Raghavan, Weis-ner, & Patel, 1999; Sandler & Mistretta, 1998; Scorgie, Wilgosh, & McDonald, 1998). Elsie Helsel (1985) reflected this perspective (see box 6–1) when she wrote about her marriage and the contribution to it made by her son, Robin, who has cerebral palsy.

Researchers have validated what Elsie Helsel asserted. Kazak and Marvin (1984) compared marital stress in 56 couples with children with spina bifida and in 53 couples with children without an exceptionality. Their results revealed no significant difference between the groups in terms of total marital satisfaction. In fact, they found that the couples with children with spina bifida actually experienced somewhat higher levels of marital satisfaction. These findings are in direct contrast to the study (Tew et al., 1974) that we discussed previously. According to Kazak and Marvin (1984), their results support the idea that the presence of a child with an exceptionality in some cases may strengthen marital relationships.

Finally, other research has found no difference between families with and without a child with an exceptionality: The child essentially does not affect marriage positively or negatively. Comparing a matched sample of 60 families with and without children with disabilities, Abbott and Meredith (1986) found no significant differences between the two groups on measures of marital

MY VOICE   BOX 6–1

Robin's Positive Contributions

Professionals are constantly probing and asking questions concerning how Robin's constant presence and problems affect our marriage. Once again, there are pluses and minuses. I really don't believe any one factor in a marriage can be pinpointed as a strengthener or strainer. There are too many variables affecting a marriage for such a simplistic explanation. The temperament of the individuals; the physical, emotional, and financial strengths; the problem-solving and coping skills; the commitment people bring—all have some bearing on the strain a handicapped child places on a marriage. From my point of view, Robin has added more strength than strain. At least my husband and I are still living together after thirty-seven years of marriage! For one thing, at those points in a marriage when you are contemplating divorce (intellectually, emotionally, or actually), the presence of a child such as Robin is a major deterrent. The focus quickly changes from your own needs, wishes, and desires to our responsibilities, commitment, and the needs of the child. Somehow this helps you work through a problem, and you find another way. I have never bought the argument that the presence of an adult person in a family, handicapped or not, is a disruptive factor. I feel society has lost a mooring with the breakdown of the extended family. Romantic twosomes are great for novels and certain periods of our lives. I do not see such a pattern as essential for a successful marriage. My husband and I will not have a footloose, carefree, romantic retirement lifestyle, but we will have something else—the opportunity to feel needed.

Source: Helsel Family. (1985). The Helsels' story of Robin. In H. R. Turnbull & A. P. Turnbull (Eds.) *Parents speak out: Then and now* (2nd ed.) (pp. 85–86). Englewood Cliffs, NJ: Merrill/Prentice Hall.

strength, family strength, or personality characteristics. Young and Roopnarine (1994) reported similar findings in their research on families who have preschool children with and without a disability.

Furthermore, research suggests that issues associated with the exceptionality can *simultaneously* strengthen and impair a couple's relationship (Singer & Nixon, 1996). We also remind you of the importance of considering the full range of family characteristics as inputs into the marital relationship. One of those that we have particularly emphasized is cultural values. Cross-culturally there is tremendous variation in how marriages are formed, lived out, and disrupted (McGoldrick, Giordano, & Pearce, 1996). For example, some trends that have been noted among Middle Eastern marriages (that is, Arab, Iranian, Lebanese, and Armenian), include having the parents of a partner pick the marriage partner for their son or daughter, marrying within the same lineage (cousins) to assure economic and blood kinship, allowing men to have up to four wives, and strongly discouraging divorce (Abudabbeh, 1996; Dagirmanjian, 1996; Jalali, 1996; Simon, 1996). You might consider how these trends are similar to and different from the marital trends of Euro-Americans within the United States. As you consider what you have already learned in chapter 5 about all of the different ways that family characteristics can vary, it should be obvious that many characteristics within families, not just the child with an exceptionality, influence marital stability.

Marital Satisfaction Despite the inconsistency in research results related to the positive, negative, neutral, or compound impact of children with an exceptionality on marriage, one consistent finding is that higher levels of marital satisfaction are generally associated with overall family adjustment to a child with an exceptionality (Bristol, Gallagher, & Schopler, 1988; Lichtenstein, 1993; Scorgie,

Wilgosh, & McDonald, 1998; Willoughby & Glidden, 1995). Furthermore, marital harmony is associated with higher levels of self-esteem in brothers and sisters (Rodrigue, Geffkin, & Morgan, 1993). Thus, it appears that a strong marriage can make a difference in overall family well-being. At the same time, a strong marriage is not a prerequisite for positive family outcomes; many single parents of children with an exceptionality also experience strong family well-being, such as Patty Smith and Marta Cofresi, about whom you read in the opening vignettes of chapters 1 and 5. As partners in marriage, spouses have specific needs for themselves and specific roles to fulfill for their partners (such as affection, socialization, and self-esteem). Thus, it makes good sense for programs and supports for children and youth with exceptionalities to respect the importance of the marital relationship. Box 6–2 suggests ways you might enhance marital interactions as you form partnerships with families.

There are situations in which couples can benefit from marital counseling or other therapy provided by professionals such as psychiatrists, psychologists, and social workers (Lichtenstein, 1993). If you believe that families with whom you are working might benefit from marital counseling or therapy, discuss your perspectives with the school social worker or counselor, asking for advice on how best to approach the family about the availability of counseling or therapy. In some cases, the social worker or counselor might take the lead and have an initial conversation with a family. One way to help a family is to determine which issues are appropriately handled by teachers and which ones by professionals who specialize in family counseling or therapy and then to make an appropriate referral. Remember that providing families with information and referring them to appropriate services are components of reliable alliances and empowering contexts.

TIPS

BOX 6–2

Enhancing Marital Interactions

- Encourage parents to consider activities they may wish to engage in separately from their child or children.
- Make information available to couples on child care and companionship services.
- Consider the time and energy implications of homework and home-based teaching on the needs of the parents to spend quality time together as a couple.
- Seek ways to offer flexible scheduling or alternatives if a planned school activity conflicts with a couple's plans.

Parent and Child Interactions
(The Parental Subsystem)

The parental subsystem consists of interactions between parents and their child or children. Couples experience parenthood in many different ways. Couples can be biological, step, adoptive, and/or foster parents. Some stay married to each other; some divorce. Some remarry; others do not (see chapter 5). Some families are comprised of lesbian, gay, and bisexual members who often must contend with the type of homophobic discrimination that Bonnie Tinker describes in box 6–3. Bonnie laments that educators have blamed her daughter's emotional disorder on Bonnie's sexual orientation and have refused to listen to her and her daughter as they state their perspectives about the reasons for her daughter's emotional challenges. We encourage you to be supportive of all parents in the relationships that they have chosen for their own preferred lifestyle. In the situation of lesbian, gay, and bisexual families, we encourage you to pursue information and learning opportunities that will enable you to develop reliable alliances with parents who may be similar to or different from your own sexual orientation (Hare, 1994; Martin, 1993; Patterson, 1992; Raymond, 1997; Strickland, 1995).

In this section, we will discuss (1) foster and adoptive families, (2) issues associated with fatherhood, and (3) issues associated with motherhood.

Foster and Adoptive Parents. Congress enacted the Adoption and Safe Families Act of 1997 to address two problems: (1) the prolonged period between children's removal from their biological family and their permanent placement in terms of being reunited with their families or being adopted and (2) the tendency for social service agencies to too quickly return children to their biological families and put them at risk for maltreatment (H.R. Rept. No. 105-77, 1997). This Act affects approximately one-half million children who are in out-of-home placements (Craig & Herbert, 1997).

Some of the frequent indicators of children's out-of-home placement are parental substance abuse, abuse and neglect of children, juvenile delinquency, and lack of economic options (Barbell, 1996; Tatara, 1993; U.S. General Accounting Office, 1994).

Alarmingly, infants and young children who have physical, cognitive, and health-related disabilities comprise the fastest-growing population of children in need of foster care (Benton Foundation, 1998). Approximately one-fifth of children in out-of-home placements have developmental disabilities (Kocinski, 1998), and one-third to two-thirds have mental health disorders (Schor, 1988). The U.S. Government Accounting Office (1995) surveyed a large number of files of foster children in three large cities. They reported that 12 percent of the children received no routine health care; approximately one-third received no immunization; approximately one-third had identified health needs that were not being addressed; and while

MY VOICE
BOX 6–3

Speaking Out on Gay and Lesbian Families

My son spent every day all day long last summer with his friend, a girl whom he has known from infancy. And now her father, a young man who grew up down the street from us and was a "friend" of my spouse's son, has decided that his daughter cannot play at our house. After all of these years of knowing we were gay, he decided to cleanse his family of our imagined sinfulness. And finally, in a burst of anger at me, he told my

son that he was not welcome in their house, either. It is like a death for all of us, but there are no support groups for mourning this loss.

Of course, my spouse and I know we were taking a risk when we dared to create our family. We knew we would not be understood nor welcomed by much of the world. We have agonized over the pain homophobia has caused our children. But, we reasoned, life may be hard, but it

would be no easier if we lived in violation of the truth of our own reality. In the midst of life's many uncertainties, we knew that we loved each other; and we could not respect ourselves nor abide our lives if we turned away from that fact. We believe it is important to teach our children that life must be lived with integrity, even if this brings hardship.

Bonnie Tinker
Love Makes a Family, Inc.

about three-fourths of the children were at high risk for HIV infection, only 9 percent had been tested for it. Similarly, another study reported that children entering long-term foster care typically have psychosocial problems; however, 85 percent have not received adequate mental health treatment five years after entry (Tuma, 1989).

There are many challenges related to providing adequate support for foster parents. Typically they are either left out of the educational decision-making process or included at only a superficial level (Altshuler, 1997). As children move from one placement to another, it can be more likely that schools will lose track of children in foster care and the delivery of their special education programs will be interrupted (Goerge, VanVoorhis, Grant, Casey, & Robinson, 1992).

Children of non-European ethnic descent typically make up approximately two-thirds of the foster care population (Barbell, 1996); stated alternatively, this is three times more than the proportion of children of non-European ethnic descent represented in the United States population (Benton Foundation, 1998). Given what you have already learned about the disproportionate representation of particularly African American students in special education, there is a higher likelihood that this group of students will have disruptive special education placements because of their foster care services.

What does this mean as you develop reliable alliances with foster parents as well as the biological parents of children who are in foster care? As appropriate to the out-of-home placement arrangements of each child, we encourage you to work very closely with your school social worker and/or school counselor in establishing partnerships with biological and foster parents and in providing information that is vital to both families. Also, we encourage you to recognize the strengths of foster and biological families alike. An informative and timely resource guide on foster care for infants and young children is provided by Silver, Amster, & Haecker (1999).

In box 6–4 you will read about the differences that foster families can make. The individual who wrote this was identified in elementary school as having a serious emotional disorder; several years later she also was identified as gifted. We hope you will seek to stand in her shoes and to view her two families from her perspective.

MY VOICE BOX 6–4

My Two Families

Coping Styles

My Biological Family
In general, the higher the level of stress in the family, the more externally active the family members became. My father devoted himself to his work, my mother to luncheons and shopping, my sister to school and social activities.

My Foster Family
My foster family's primary coping style was a reliance on sharing experiences with friends and family, a strong belief that ultimately experiences work out for the good, and a willingness to ask for and accept help in time of need and to provide help and assistance when needed. . . . A strong spiritual belief system helped to provide strength in meeting difficulties, as did a sense of family unity.

Socialization Needs

My Biological Family
My parents participated in many social activities involving my father's professional organizations and at the country club in which they had membership.

My Foster Family
Many social activities took place within the framework of church activities in which we participated fully. There were often visitors of all ages in the house and these people were incorporated into the ongoing activities on a regular basis. It was always possible to find someone to play with, talk to, or interact with.

Affection Needs

My Biological Family
Overt physical or emotional displays of affection were not highly valued in my biological family. Achievement was rewarded with a special dinner at times or perhaps an allowance bonus. My parents believed that their relationship should be kept private—I do not remember them touching or hugging. Because of the cycle of abuse, physical contact was something that was very difficult for me, and I fought or ran away more often than not.

My Foster Family
My foster family engaged in frequent displays of affection, with individual and family hugs abounding. We cuddled each other as well as dogs, cats, and others, strayed or in need, who came into the home. Not many people can remember hearing "I love you" for the first time, but I can remember when my mom said it to me.

Adoptive families also can enhance the quality of life of children with exceptionalities (Fishman, 1992; Lightburn & Pine, 1996; Marcenko & Smith, 1991; Rosenthal, Groze, & Aguilar, 1991). Research with mothers who have adopted children with mental retardation shows that adopted families typically experience a high level of well-being (Glidden, 1989; Glidden, Kiphart, Willoughby, & Bush, 1993; Todis & Singer, 1991). In one of the most recently reported studies, families who had adopted children with development disabilities were followed for 12 years (Glidden & Johnson, 1999). The mothers reported being generally positive about the outcomes for themselves and their children and indicated good adjustment for their adoptive children. The mothers reported that the strongest benefits were giving and receiving love, positive child characteristics, pride in the child's achievement, and happiness. The major problems were negative child characteristics; worry, anxiety, or guilt; and developmental delay. Benefits were consistently rated as higher in importance than problems. Interestingly, 50 percent of the families had adopted at least one additional child since the initial adoption of their child with developmental disabilities.

There is a higher incidence of disabilities among children who are adopted. For example, approximately 10–15 percent of children in residential treatment facilities for emotional disorders are adopted as contrasted to about 2 percent of adopted children under 18 in the general population (Brodzinsky, 1993). Cross-culturally, adopted children are referred for psychological treatment two to five times more frequently than their peers who are not adopted (Grotevant & McRoy, 1990; McRoy, Grotevant, & Zurcher, 1988).

A number of factors influence the high incidence of mental health issues, including: (1) adoptive parents are more accustomed to seeking help from social service agencies, (2) adoptive parents typically are more economically advantaged and may be able to access services easier, (3) the social stigma associated with adoption in some places may create distress for the child and family, and (4) the child and family may feel especially vulnerable in their relationship with each other since they are not biologically related (McRoy & Grotevant, 1996; Warren, 1992; Wilson, 1985).

In addition to special issues that can arise because of the nature of the child's disability, some children with disabilities may also be involved with a transracial adoption (Neal, 1996) and/or intercountry adoption (Cox, 1996). In these situations, there may be special issues to take into account as you form partnerships with the adoptive parents.

In box 6–5 a parent who adopted a son with emotional disorders describes some of the special issues that arose in raising her son and in trying to get appropriate services and supports. As you read box 6–5, we hope you will consider what you might have done if you had had the opportunity to develop a reliable alliance with Stephanie and Dennis. What difference might you have made in the enhancement of the empowerment of each one of them as well as yourself?

Fathers Have you ever wondered if in raising children with disabilities it is typical for fathers to experience more stress than mothers, mothers to experience more stress than fathers, or for mothers and fathers to experience about the same amount of stress? As on a number of other topics, the research is mixed. An early study (Cummings, 1976) reported more stress by fathers; other studies have reported that fathers experience less parental stress than mothers (Kazak & Marvin, 1984; Tavormina, Boll, Dunn, Luscomb, & Taylor, 1981); some studies have reported that mothers and fathers have both experienced stress but that the sources of their stress come from different sources (Roach, Orsmond, & Barratt, 1999); and finally more recent studies have indicated no differences between stress levels of fathers and mothers (Ainge, Covin, & Baker, 1998; Dyson, 1997; Hagborg, 1989; Spaulding & Morgan, 1986). We encourage you to read some of the first-person accounts written by fathers in which their perspectives are poignantly shared (Greenwald, 1997; MacDonald & Oden, 1978; Meyer, 1995; Naseef, 1997; Stallings & Cook, 1997). Box 6–6 is a first-person author's perspective—Rud Turnbull's thoughts on some of the existential issues of his own fatherhood. What is the nature of relationship between fathers and their children—especially when the child has an exceptionality?

The father-child relationship influences a child's cognitive, personal-social, and sex-role–identification development (Lamb, 1983; Pruett & Litzenberger, 1992; Turbiville, Turnbull, & Turnbull, 1995). Although little information is available about the father's influence when the child has an exceptionality, one study found that children advanced in daily living skills and social competence more successfully when their fathers had positive, not neutral or negative, perceptions of them (Frey, Fewell, & Vadasy, 1989).

A study of the fathers of children who were in kindergarten through third grade reported that fathers of children with and without disabilities spend a comparable amount of time in child care and that fathers of both groups of children assess their level of competence as a parent in a similar way (Turbiville, 1994). Interestingly, fathers of both groups of children reported spending similar amounts of time in school-related activities, but they indicated that they often do not complete the activities that teachers send

Speaking Out on Adoption

I met Dennis when he was nearly five years old and in the legal custody of my state's Department of Health and Welfare. Dennis is Native American. He is the youngest of six brothers and sisters. I was a professor of social work, single and had always loved and worked with children as a teacher, as a therapist and as a parent. Not one of these experiences had prepared me for how much I longed to be the mother of this little boy.

I was told that Dennis was "normal." Despite chronic neglect and some abuse in his birth home, he had adapted well to foster placement. The worker said that Dennis was "delightful and engaging" and that if I didn't want him somebody else would "snap him up" quickly. I didn't need to be told that twice.

Dennis' problems began right away. He had bedtime fears. He screamed and cried for hours, hid food under the mattress and prowled through the house in the middle of the night. . . . He had tantrums that lasted for hours. He secretly drove knives into furniture. One time Dennis hid in the ceiling of his bedroom; another time he hid within the frame of his bed. . . . I now know that Dennis lived in terror throughout the first few years of our lives together as a family. . . .

I was frequently asked about what had I done in Dennis' early years to give him these problems.

I had been given no history of Dennis' family. . . . I had no way of knowing about his family history of chronic mental illness and chemical dependency. I didn't know about the family's history of sexual abuse. And I certainly didn't know that at least one of the foster families had physically and emotionally abused Dennis.

I did know that one of the foster families had told Dennis that he had to be white to go to heaven. I learned about that when I found Dennis—a handsome Chippewa-Cree boy—washing himself in bleach when he bathed trying to become white.

. . . I had come to realize that I had two full-time jobs; social worker/therapist and parent/therapist. The enormity of it hit me. . . .

I naively thought that I would tell people what had happened, and that they would help me find services to correct his problems. State officials said that they had no help to give. I had adopted Dennis and—as a parent—I had full responsibility for his care and well-being.

We have found a private case manager to help us identify whatever services may be available. The state vocational rehabilitation agency is involved. . . . A dedicated adult educator tutors Dennis on a weekly basis.

Dennis is slowly accumulating the necessitates to move toward independent living (supported housing) within the next year or so. Things are certainly not perfect, nor do I expect them to ever be perfect. I no longer feel isolated. I am blessed to be able to attend a support group for families of chronically mentally ill young people and to count these families among my friends. I am beginning to be active in the Alliance for the Mentally Ill.

There is actually a bittersweet quality to life now. My life has been explicably changed by being family with Dennis. I am honored to have been trusted by a child who had absolutely no earthly reason to trust anyone. I am pleased to have come to love and trust Dennis as an honorable and compassionate young man. I know we are real family and I know we are not alone.

Source: Ward, S. (1996). My family: Formed by adoption. In *Focal Point, 10*(1), 30–32.

---

home. Perhaps the activities suggested by teachers are not consistent with fathers' preferences. The activity these fathers most often shared with their children was watching television; thus, a likely avenue for enhancing father-child interaction may be supporting fathers to be more actively engaged with their children around television shows.

What special considerations need to be taken into account in terms of fathers from culturally and linguistically diverse backgrounds? There has been a great deal written about the concept of *machismo* (Garcia-Preto, 1996; Zuniga, 1998). This concept holds that in Latino families there is a traditional gender boundary between the roles of women as nurturers and men as authority figures and breadwinners. This boundary seems to have a diminishing influence given that more females are working and there is greater equality of male and female roles within many Latino families (Zuniga, 1998). A Latino mother of a child with a disability believes there is an erroneous negative stereotype associated with machismo that anticipates that Latino women are passive. She explains:

> My Mom would always say, "Never let your husband think that you are the key person. Let him know that he's got the forefront, but you're the one that's going to make the difference." That's a culture that I see pre-

Our Children, Our Darkness and Light

As a young boy, I'd heard my father, my uncle, and my favorite aunt speak about my uncle Mark in hushed tones and oblique conversation: "Mark is doing fine; your uncle John sends him money, and your aunt Ellen visits him."

Mark was the invisible uncle: as a child, a member of the intact family of seven children; but as an adult, a patient/resident of one of Maryland's state institutions/hospitals for "the mentally retarded"; as an old man, a resident of a group home; and now, dead, buried with his brother, who was my father, with one of his sisters, and with my mother.

They share a small plot and common headstone in a very old cemetery, a plot that is beside the graves of Mark's mother and father and of their mothers and fathers. There they lie: three generations crowded together in death, with inclusion in death if not in life symbolized by the all-encompassing headstone.

They are portents for my life as the father of a young man with both mental retardation and autism. They are portents because disability is a common, intergenerational theme; because "family matters!" is, too;

and because, at least in death, Mark "belonged" to the family in a far more intimate and physical way than he did while he lived. Mark was unlike my son, Jay, in that "placement" respect: Jay belongs intimately and physically to our family and our community. That's the difference between Mark and Jay: when a person belongs has changed across the span of two generations.

Mark and the headstone are, respectively, portents and symbols in yet another way: There is a terribly dark aspect of disability. To me and many, Mark was as invisible during his life as he is in death. The darkness of disability is itself an invisible yet palpable phenomenon—a universal, often unspoken of, often repressed, and yet very real aspect of the lives of men affected by disability, men who write in this extraordinary book.

Who does not yearn for his son—his first-born, and, in my case, only son—to "carry on" a legacy that, at least in my family, has been consistent across the male generations. What father does not, as one author writes, struggle with "letting go of the ghost" of the son he expected but did not have? What father, looking at his

unexpected son, does not, as another writes, see him to be "the perfect representation of his forefather"? What father does not feel, as I do, the dead hand of primogeniture?

And yet, what father does not also see in his daughter and in the impact on his own life the positive contributions that she makes—her instrumental value to father, to family, to community? And what father does not see beyond instrumental utilitarianism to inherent worthiness: My child is inherently worthy. Less able does not mean less worthy.

The Turnbull Family headstone—the portent of my own life—has its own final and very particular meaning, for on the day when I last visited it, a butterfly, the symbol of the resurrected spirit, flew overhead, lighted on the headstone, and flew away—all that on the very day when another beloved father in our family died.

Our children are our darkness and our light, and, in the end, they are our butterflies, emblematic of our own spirits, often crushed, but never dead. They will hover around our lives and our graves, incandescent, generative and generational, ultimately reassuring.

Source: From Turnbull, R. (1996). *Journal of The Association for Persons with Severe Handicaps, 22*(2). Adapted with permission.

---

vails. . . . I see the character in the Latino woman is to respect other's roles. . . . The Anglo culture misunderstands that and sees the woman as, perhaps, passive when she's not being passive at all. She's just giving him his respect. (Turnbull, 1994)

Because fathers have tended to be the "less apparent parent" (Turbiville, 1994), we believe it is all the more important for professionals working with them to make an extra effort to establish partnerships (Flynn & Wilson, 1998; Levine, Murphy, & Wilson, 1993; Levine & Pitt,

1995). We also encourage you to remember that there can be a number of significant men in the lives of children that do not have a formal father role—grandfathers and non-paternal males such as male partners of mothers, teachers, men from the religious community, Big Brothers, and neighbors—who can all have the potential of bringing an important male presence into the lives of children (Pruett, 1997). If a context empowers only one of the parents (or only one of several family members), it will probably fall short of the goal of empowering the entire family unit.

Mothers Although there is a trend toward more role sharing between fathers and mothers, the fact remains that mothers typically assume the largest part of the responsibility of tending to family needs (Osmond & Thorne, 1993; Renwick, Brown, & Raphael, 1998; Stoller, 1994; Traustadottir, 1991; Traustadottir, 1995; Wickham-Searl, 1992). Indeed, an in-depth study of 14 mothers shows that mothers who provide care for children with severe disabilities organize their lives around their caring role and provide that care in three ways (Traustadottir, 1991):

1. *Caring for:* taking care of the child—in particular, acquiring the specialized knowledge and management procedures that are necessary for the child's development
2. *Caring about:* loving the child as a way of caring
3. *Extended caring:* performing collaborative advocacy roles that address the broader community and societal concerns related to issues of exceptionality

The majority of the mothers were full-time housewives and mothers. The one exception was a mother who combined parenting responsibilities with a professional career in medicine at a large research university. She commented on the pressures that she felt were pushing her to abandon her career and become a full-time caretaker:

> The agency; the care giver; the doctor; the physical, occupational, and speech therapists with whom I came in contact, and with whom I continue to come in contact, assume that I, not my husband, am responsible for this child. But if anything has to be done in order to take care of her, I am the one who is responsible for that. It was assumed by almost everyone that I would give up my career. (Traustadottir, 1991, p. 223)

The mothers also commented on what they perceived to be appropriate father roles: (1) providing financial support, (2) being supportive of the mother's caretaking of the child and family as well as her extended caring role, and (3) discussing with the mother what she learns from investigating services and programs and contributing to joint decision making. Interestingly, in the families where the fathers helped in these roles, the mothers tended to describe the marriage as being good; but when fathers did not support these roles, mothers frequently expressed disappointment and frustration with the extent of fathers' involvement and support. Other research has also documented the importance of fathers' helping with child care; indeed, fathers' greater child-care participation is related to higher marital satisfaction for both parents (Willoughby & Glidden, 1995). As you will recall, we discussed single mothers in chapter 5 and pointed out the potential drawbacks and benefits of attending to family responsibilities without a marital partner.

Teenage parents warrant special considerations (Coley & Chase-Lansdale, 1998; Corcoran, 1998; Rhein et al., 1997; Roth, Hendrickson, Schilling, & Stowell, 1998). Annually more than 1 million American teenagers become parents (Alan Guttmacher Institute, 1996). Some of the consequences of adolescent childbearing have been documented as follows:

- Adolescent mothers tend to have lower educational achievement and lower graduation rates (Maynard, 1996).
- Adolescent parenthood is typically associated with low levels of employment and with jobs characterized by lower skills and lower pay (Furstenberg, Brooks-Gunn, & Morgan, 1987).
- Adolescent parents are at higher risk for single-parent status and have higher rates of divorce (Furstenberg et al., 1987; McAnarney & Hendee, 1989).
- Adolescent mothers tend to have more health problems, and their children experience more health challenges as well (McAnarney & Hendee, 1989; Stevens-Simon & Beach, 1992).
- Adolescent parents tend to have more limited communication with their infants as compared to adult parents (Brookes-Gunn & Furstenberg, 1986).

It becomes obvious that teenage parents benefit from an empowerment approach in which you seek to establish a reliable alliance with them and support them in achieving their goals for themselves and their children.

Similar to our suggestion related to fathers, we encourage you to read first-person accounts written by mothers. There are many excellent sources for getting mothers' perspectives, including Gill (1997), Leff & Walizer (1992), Miller (1994), and Rose (1998).

In summary, the parental subsystem is complex rather than simple. This is because there are different types of parental units, because each unit is influenced by cultural considerations, and because each member of the parental unit has different needs. As you adopt various strategies to become a reliable ally for each of the people in the parental subsystem, you create an empowering context for the entire family.

*B*rother and Sister Interactions
(The Sibling Subsystem)

The sibling subsystem consists of the interactions between brothers and sisters. Siblings can be thought of as socialization agents who provide the first and perhaps the most intense peer relationships that children experience (Powell & Gallagher, 1993; Zukow, 1999). By providing a context for socialization, these relationships give children the opportunity to experience sharing, companionship, loyalty, rivalry, and a wide host of other feelings. As with all family relationships, it is especially important to recognize that the nature of the sibling bond and roles are culturally rooted, with different cultures having some very different expectations for siblings, often in light of age, birth order, and gender (Nuckolls, 1993; Harry, Day, & Quist, 1998).

Although siblings are socialization agents during their younger years, they often are increasingly responsible for providing care and service coordination as their parents age. In fact, research on families whose members with an exceptionality have lived with their parents well into their early and middle adulthood shows that elderly parents have consistently identified brothers and sisters as the ones whom they expect to take over the parental role once they themselves are no longer able to do so (Krauss, Seltzer, Gordon, & Friedman, 1996).

Just as children with exceptionalities have multiple impacts on their parents' marriage, so do brothers or sisters with an exceptionality have various impacts on their siblings (Atkins, 1991; Riebschleger, 1991; Seltzer, Greenberg, Wyngaarden-Krauss, Gordon, & Judge, 1997; Stoneman & Waldman-Berman, 1993; Stoneman, 1998). Some siblings benefit from the relationship, others experience negative impacts, and others regard it as a neutral experience. Again, because of all of the different ways that family life varies, there is no single definitive impact.

Some studies have found that brothers and sisters have a higher incidence of emotional/behavioral problems (Cornell & Grossberg, 1987; Lobato, Barbour, Hall, & Miller, 1987; McHale & Gamble, 1989; Orsillo, McCaffrey, & Fisher, 1993). Other research has not found significantly greater behavioral problems (Gath & Gumley, 1987; Hannah & Midlarsky, 1999; Renzulli & McGreevey, 1986). Indeed, some studies have found these siblings to have fewer behavioral problems than the siblings of children who do not have disabilities (Carr, 1988). In addition, a number of studies have found that brothers and sisters of children with exceptionalities have greater responsibilities for household chores (Stoneman, Brophy, Davis, & Crapps, 1987; Wilson, Blacher, & Baker, 1989); but other research contradicts this finding (Cuskelly & Gunn, 1993; Damiani, 1999; Gath & Gumley, 1987).

Finally, some research indicates that children who have siblings with exceptionalities experience lower self-esteem as compared to children who do not have a sibling with an exceptionality (McHale & Gamble, 1989). Other research, however, indicates no difference in self-esteem or self-concept (self-esteem/self-concept is highly related to self-efficacy, which you will remember

to be an element of motivation for families and professionals) between children with and without a sibling with an exceptionality (Dyson, Edgar, & Crnic, 1989; Dyson & Fewell, 1989; Hannah & Midlarsky, 1999; Lobato et al., 1987). Research also points to a significantly higher level of internal locus of control (perceived control, also an element of motivation) in children who have a sibling with an exceptionality (Burton & Parks, 1994).

Although most research on siblings has focused on the impact of a brother or sister with a disability, sibling effects also occur when one of the children in the family is identified as gifted or talented. Some researchers report that the other siblings feel more jealousy and competition with each other when one is gifted and the other is not or when both are gifted (Grenier, 1985; Pfouts, 1980). Birth order appears to be an important factor given the finding that labeling one child as gifted can create greater sibling problems when the second-born sibling is identified as gifted and fewer problems when the labeled child is first born (Tuttle & Cornell, 1993).

In a study of parents' perceptions of siblings' interactions with their brothers and sisters who are deaf-blind, the parents described the relationships primarily as helping rather than as playing (Heller, Gallagher, & Fredrick, 1999). Approximately one-fourth of the parents reported that the siblings without disabilities can best be described as "does very little" with their brother or sister. They indicated that the siblings rarely made adaptations in activities to compensate for the vision or hearing impairment or had successful ways to adequately communicate with their brother or sister. Interestingly, the majority of parents reported that their children without disabilities wanted to learn additional ways to communicate, play games, and interact with their brother or sister with deaf-blindness. Whether the exceptionality is deaf-blindness or other types, the implication here is that you and other educational professionals can have valuable information to share with siblings and parents about how to connect in a way so that relationships are reciprocally beneficial.

The impact of children with exceptionalities on siblings varies and depends upon a large number of individual and family characteristics (remember what you read in chapter 5). These include the size of the family, birth order, gender, nature of the exceptionality, coping styles, and other special challenges occurring within the family. Potential negative sibling impacts include overidentification; embarrassment; guilt; isolation, loneliness, and loss; resentment; increased responsibility; and pressure to achieve. On the other hand, opportunities and positive contributions can accrue. These include enhanced maturity, self-concept, social competence, insight, tolerance, pride, vocational opportunities, advocacy, and loyalty.

A number of these positive contributions are incorporated in the following perspective of our own daughter, Amy, when she was a teenager. She is commenting on the impact that her brother, J.T., has had on our family—especially on herself.

> Because my brother has presented my family so many challenges, we all have had to learn how to seek out help for him and ourselves. I have learned to be an initiator, not a reactor. I have had to be active, not passive; a challenge-seeker, not fearful. I've seen my family in action and, being part of that action, even though we may not have chosen these challenges, I have learned that I can influence my own destiny. Moreover, I learned the satisfaction of taking charge of my own life. (Turnbull, 1993, pp. 1–2)

As parents, it is extremely gratifying to us that both of our daughters, Amy and Kate, resonate with the incredible positive influence that J.T. has been on their own development and on the joy they derive from their social connections with him.

Don Meyer, a national leader in creating support programs for siblings of children with exceptionalities, has created a model known as "sibshops." "Sibshops" are workshops that provide information and emotional support for brothers and sisters (Meyer & Vadasy, 1994). If your community does not sponsor sibshops, you might collaborate with families, educators, people with disabilities, and other community citizens to start one using the excellent resource material provided by Don Meyer (Meyer & Vadasy,

1994). An evaluation of a program (operated along the lines of sibshops) for school-aged siblings found that siblings reported that they had learned how to improve their relationships with their brother or sister with a disability and had become more aware of special needs (Dyson, 1998).

Siblings can be valuable collaborators with educators in supporting their brother's or sister's inclusion or, indeed, the inclusion of other students with exceptionalities. Box 6–7 describes the "kid power" potential of sibling collaboration.

Because brothers and sisters of almost any age carry out important roles within a family, it behooves professionals to include them in family partnerships. Reflect on the roles that siblings have played in some of the families about whom you have read, including Patty and Jane Smith (chapter 1), Marta Cofresi and her children (chapter 5), and Nila Benito and her sons (this chapter). To be an empowering professional, we encourage you to create a context that can empower all family members. Reading first-person siblings's perspectives will help you gain insight (Gans, 1997; Meyer, 1997; Meyer & Vadasy, 1994).

*E*xtended-Family Interactions (*The Extended-Family Subsystem*)

Whom do you consider to be part of your extended family? Think of each person, and then add up how many people are in your extended family. Reflect on the role that they have had in your life, beginning when you were

---

TOGETHER WE CAN
BOX 6–7

Kid Power

As a fourth grader required to conduct a scientific experiment, Amy Turnbull, the sister of an adolescent brother who has mental retardation and autism, taught a lesson to second graders about mental retardation. She encouraged those students to have positive attitudes about people with mental retardation (Turnbull & Bronicki, 1986). She collected information from students whom she taught and from students whom she did not teach, in an effort to learn what differences (if any) her instruction made. When her results showed a significant increase in positive attitudes in the class that she taught but no change in her comparison group, she made the following

four conclusions about "kid power" as a collaborative resource:

(a) I'm a kid and I understand the words I used. . . . Sometimes when adults try to teach kids they use words that are too big, or they use too many words and the kids get all mixed up;

(b) They paid attention because they know me and like me; kids in the second grade respect those in higher grades, they listen to the things they say to them;

(c) I worked hard to present an interesting lesson using a film, book, and discussion;

(d) I was able to tell them about my brother.

Source: Turnbull, A., & Bronicki, G. J. (1986). Changing second graders' attitudes toward people with mental retardation: Using kid power. *Mental Retardation, 24*(1), 44–45.

a young child until the present time. What factors have either increased or decreased their availability and support?

The answers to these questions may depend upon your particular cultural background, because cultures tend to define the composition of extended family and the frequency of contact between the nuclear and extended families (Lynch & Hanson, 1998; McGoldrick, Giordano, & Pearce, 1996). Consider the following three examples:

> Elderly persons of Cuban origin are, in comparison with the rest of the Spanish-origin population (and with the total population), more likely to live with their children, probably in a three-generation household. (Perez, 1986, p. 14)
>
> In many Indian families, the child-rearing activities may rest with other family members. In many instances, the grandparents are responsible for the children. Aunts and uncles are also likely to be involved, especially if the family resides on the reservation and not in an urban area. Indian families who live in the city tend to have nuclear households, whereas families on the reservation tend to include extended family members. In fact, in some tribes, the uncles instead of the parents may provide most of the discipline, while grandparents provide most of the spiritual guidance and teaching. (Joe & Malach, 1998, p. 144)
>
> The concept of *family* in the Anglo-European American United States typically refers to immediate family members such as the mother, father, and children. Other extended family members may or may not live close by and may or may not participate actively in the "nuclear family." Other members are usually termed *relatives* as opposed to *family*. (Hanson, 1998, pp. 107–108)

From the outset, then, ask the parents to define which family members they want to involve with you and other professionals. Only after they identify these extended family members should you try to identify culturally sensitive ways for creating a reliable alliance. Who are the members of the Benito extended family? To determine who they are and how they participate in the lives of young Vincent and Joe, you first have to ask one or both of their parents.

There has not been as much research on extended-family members as on siblings. There is little current research about disability issues and extended-family members. A survey of mothers and fathers of infants and young children in early childhood special education programs reported that the most frequent family supports offered by grandparents include babysitting and financial assistance, particularly buying clothes at birthday or other holiday times (Sandler, Warren, & Raver, 1995). When investigating the relationship between paternal and maternal adjustment and grandparent support, results showed that, when compared to mothers, fathers

appeared to have higher levels of adjustment when grandparents offered greater levels of support.

Researchers who collected information from 42 mothers of children with varying disabilities reported that mothers indicated that their own mothers were more supportive of their child with a disability as contrasted to their spouses' mothers (Seligman, Goodwin, Paschal, Applegate, & Lehman, 1997). The study also found that grandmothers were generally found to be more supportives than grandfathers and that grandparents provided more emotional support than instrumental support (help with daily care tasks). In comparing single and married mothers, there was no difference in the amount of grandparent support received.

New Zealand researchers conducted in-depth interviews with 12 parent-grandparent pairs in order to describe the experiences and relationships of grandparents who have a grandchild with a disability (Mirfin-Veitch, Bray, & Watson, 1996, 1997). The grandparents reported providing two types of assistance: (1) practical involving tasks such as babysitting, household chores, and respite care, and (2) emotional support involving listening, acceptance, and affirmation of parents' coping ability. The authors pointed out that what seemed to distinguish the parents who were characterized as more rather than less involved was the relationship history in the family. Families tended to state, "We are that sort of family" (Mirfin-Veitch, Bray, & Watson, 1997, p. 306), meaning that this would be the way that the family would handle any particular challenge or problem that came along. The authors pointed out that often people assume that it is the characteristics of the child such as the nature of the disability that most determines relationships with other family members, but they suggest that many families have natural strengths on which to build (remember the important reliable alliance obligation of affirming family strengths). For families who do not have a relationship history that involves pitching in when special challenges come along, they may need more in-depth support in order to see the possibilities that exist for forming a reliable alliance *within* the family.

Grandparents of children with exceptionalities as well as other extended-family members need information and support to enable them to deal with their own feelings and to know how to provide care for the rest of the family (George, 1988; Meyer & Vadasy, 1986; Nicholson, Sweeney, & Geller, 1998; Urwin, 1988). Grandparents' or extended-family members' ideas about people with disabilities may have been formed when they were growing up and may be more traditional than parental views (Meyer & Vadasy, 1986). For example, a Latino mother of a young child with a disability described how her own mother agreed to make a mandos (bargain) related to her grandchild with a disability. She made a promise to the Virgin of

Guadalupe that she would visit the basilica and wear the colors of the Virgin every day if the Virgin would heal her grandchild. Although the mother did not have this belief in spiritual healing, the child's grandmother clearly did.

Some families have reported that members of the extended family are extremely supportive, understanding, and helpful with a wide range of everyday tasks (Able-Boone, Sandall, Stevens, & Frederick, 1992). This is true for the Benito family: grandmother Nila and aunt Nancy provide emotional support—a sort of cheerleader and sounding board contribution all in one. Not all families are as fortunate as the Benitos. In describing their experiences with their child's traumatic brain injury, one of the parents commented:

> You have your extended family who is there grieving also, and sometimes I think you want to say, "What are you feeling sorry for yourself about? I'm the one in this situation." You have to deal with their grief when you aren't even through dealing with your own grief, so sometimes it's even more hard to have them around depending on the relationship. (Singer & Nixon, 1996, p. 27)

Grandparents play a critical role in providing family support to teenage mothers and their children (Christmon, 1996; Denby, 1996; Edwards, 1998; Flaherty, Facteau, & Garner, 1994; Hinest & Boyd-Franklin, 1996). In one study, the grandmothers' average age was early 40s. Although these grandmothers provided extensive support to their teenage daughters and grandchildren, they reported a high level of stress because they were also trying to deal with the roles and responsibilities of middle age and many had young children of their own (Brookes-Gunn & Chase-Lansdale, 1991). These researchers concluded that service programs need to target grandmother supports as a much higher priority.

An estimated one-half million grandparents are the primary caregivers for their grandchildren, with African American grandparents represented nearly twice as often as Euro-Americans (Turner, 1995). Box 6–8 describes how "Grandma's Hand" was what was needed in raising five grandchildren whose mother (her daughter) became addicted to drugs. When you read this story, you will note that Ms. Mason, the Grandma who came to the rescue of her daughter and grandchildren, is being supported by Theresa Cooper at Loving Your Disabled Child in South Central Los Angeles—the program you learned about in chapter 3's vignette. This is another example of how an empowering program can serve as the foundation for empowering not only parents but grandparents as well in carrying out their family roles.

Although there is a strong reliance on extended-family support in some diverse cultures, we encourage you to not overgeneralize and assume that every family characterized by cultural and linguistic diversity gains its greatest support from extended-family members (Bailey et al., 1999). For example, despite what some literature reports about the collective orientation of extended-family support for Latino families (Zuniga, 1998), some Latino families report just the opposite situation.

> I've got brothers and a half-sister. If I go ask for help, they'll say why do you need help? You've got money, you go hire somebody or go get somebody or a specialist or whatever. Why do you come to me? What can I help you with? . . . That's the way they are. That's the way I feel with my family. If I had a choice between a brother and a pastor or a president or anything, a stranger, I think I would prefer to go to a stranger than my brother. (Blue-Banning, 1995, p. 11)

Few programs have been developed to support extended-family members. Research on a support-group program for grandparents found that about half the grandparents surveyed had never visited a medical professional (52 percent) or an educational professional (48 percent) regarding their grandchild's exceptionality or specific needs (Vadasy, Fewell, & Meyer, 1986). Fifty-seven percent reported they had doubts that they were doing the right things for their grandchild. Sixty-seven percent understood some of their grandchild's needs, but they wanted many questions answered.

Many extended-family members can provide support for the child and the family when some of their needs for knowledge, experience, and skills have been met (Burton, 1988; Gervasio, 1993; Mirfin-Veitch, Bray, & Watson, 1997). Box 6–9 includes some suggestions about how to provide extended-family members the information and skills that can enable them to support the child and family. Remember that a family's empowerment includes the acquisition of knowledge/skills. So the more you add to members' storehouse of knowledge/skills, the more you augment their empowerment and demonstrate that you are a reliable ally, a person committed to creating an empowering context.

Cohesion and Adaptability

We have just described the subsystems—the people who interact in the family. Now it is time to consider how they interact; that is, we must consider the quality of their

Grandma's Hand

There are many grandparents of all cultures and creeds across the nation who are helping to raise their grandchildren to be church-going, educated, civic-minded, family-oriented people. For many families, grandparents continue to set the standards and rules for values and behavior for their children's children.

Ms. Evelyn Mason is a grandmother who lives in South Central Los Angeles. A quiet, unassuming individual, not many people are aware of her history as an opera singer with the Pepperdine University Opera Company, the University of Southern California Opera, and the Chicago Conservatory, among other companies. Ms. Mason was known as "Eva-Lyn" in the world of opera from 1952 through 1979 when a tragedy set her on another path.

Ms. Mason's life was touched by tragedy when her oldest daughter became addicted to drugs. She understood immediately that she would have to provide parental guidance and supervision to her adult daughter and to her daughter's five children.

This grandmother, despite her own adverse medical conditions, opted to take custody of her five grandchildren rather than let the State of California assign them to foster homes. Ms. Mason knew all of her daughter's children had special needs. She says she knew she would be able to take care of them through her faith in God and her confidence in her ability to help her grandchildren and other children with disabilities.

Ms. Mason participates in the activities of Loving Your Disabled Child (LYDC), a community-based program for parents of children with special needs in South Central Los Angeles. She says she has found useful information in helping her get appropriate special education programs for her grandchildren. She says she has also found comfort and support from the other parents she has met at LYDC.

This family was kept together by "Grandma's hand," an expression sometimes used in the African American community to indicate the strong presence of a grandmother in raising the children of a family.

Ms. Mason believes families should never be separated. She still laments the lost ancestral ties that resulted from the forced separation of family members during slavery. She thinks of family as a sacred, God ordained bond between people.

"Nothing is as important as the bond of family," Grandmother Mason says.

From Cooper, T. (Spring, 1997). *Tapestry, 1*(3), Grassroots Consortium on Disabilities.

Enhancing Extended-Family Interactions

- Provide parents with information to help them better understand the needs and reactions of extended-family members.
- Provide information about exceptionality, the needs of children, and the needs of families that parents can give to extended-family members.
- Encourage the development of grandparent or extended-family–member support groups. Those groups might be facilitated by school social workers, psychologists, PTA volunteers who are grandparents, or extended-family members of students with an exceptionality.
- Encourage extended-family participation in IEP conferences, classroom visits, school events, and family support programs.
- Provide library materials and resources for extended-family members.

relationships. We will start by explaining two elements of interaction—cohesion and adaptability. The degrees of cohesion and adaptability in a family describe the ways that subsystems interact and the nature of boundaries among family subsystems and among family members and nonmembers (Olson, Russell, & Sprenkle, 1980). After describing these two elements, we will discuss the implications for your partnerships with families.

We want to issue a significant caution from the outset. The rules governing family interaction are rooted in one's culture (for example, individualism or collectivism), as you have already learned in chapter 5. There is likely to be tremendous variation in what the families of your students consider appropriate in terms of cohesion and adaptability and what works for them (Lynch & Hanson, 1998; McGoldrick, Giordano, & Pearce, 1996).

Moreover, theory and research about family systems has been conducted mostly by Euro-American researchers with Euro-American research participants (Scott-Jones, 1993). Unfortunately, some professionals fall into the trap of thinking that the level of cohesion and adaptability that is generally appropriate for and acceptable to Euro-American families is the level to which all families should adhere. Cohesion and adaptability can be interpreted only in light of a family's culture and the other characteristics that you learned about in chapter 5. As you have already learned, an empowering context is one that honors a family's culture.

Cohesion

You have already learned that one of the basic tenets of family systems theory is that certain boundaries serve as lines of demarcation between people who are inside and outside a subsystem. Often these boundaries are defined by the roles that the subsystem's members play (Minuchin & Fishman, 1981). For example, the two adult members in a traditional nuclear family may interact with each other in the roles of husband and wife and with their children as father and mother. Boundaries may be open or closed; that is, they may or may not be accessible to interaction with people outside the subsystem. From a Euro-American perspective, subsystems are typically open enough to allow individual autonomy and closed enough to provide support for each family member (Summers, 1987).

These boundaries also help define families' bonding relationships. Thus, family members typically feel closer to each other than to those outside the family or its subsystem relationships. This element of family bonding relates to cohesion (Olson, Sprenkle, & Russell, 1979).

Family cohesion refers to family members' close emotional bonding with each other as well as the level of independence they feel within the family system (Olson et al., 1980; Olson, 1988). Cohesion exists across a continuum, with high disengagement on one end and high enmeshment on the other. One author uses the physical metaphor of "the touching of hands" to describe cohesion in the family:

> The dilemma is how to be close yet separate. When the fingers are intertwined, it at first feels secure and warm. Yet when one partner (or family member) tries to move, it is difficult at best. The squeezing pressure may even be painful. . . . The paradox of every relationship is how to touch and yet not hold on. (Carnes, 1981, pp. 70–71)

Some families may perceive themselves or be perceived by others as not touching enough or as being highly intertwined. Most families, however, operate in the wide swath in the center of the cohesion continuum.

Range of Cohesion When families are highly cohesive, the boundaries among their subsystems are blurred or weak (Minuchin & Fishman, 1981). Take, for example, a family in which a mother with many physical-care demands for a child who is deaf and blind delegates many of the responsibilities to an older daughter. The daughter may have fewer parent-child and other-sibling interactions because she has been drawn into the parental subsystem; her own needs as a child and a sibling may be overlooked or subordinated.

In some families, siblings (especially sisters) frequently do assume additional caretaking roles (Damiani, 1999; Stoneman et al., 1987; Wilson et al., 1989). Often this fact is interpreted as problematic for the siblings. Although Euro-American families do distinguish more clearly between parental and sibling roles, that is not necessarily so for families from Asian cultures:

> As the child matures and acquires younger siblings, he or she must further assume selected childrearing responsibilities that augment those of his or her parents. Older siblings are routinely delegated the responsibility of caring for younger siblings and are expected to model adult-like behaviors, thereby setting good examples. The eldest son, in particular, is entrusted with the greatest responsibility as the leader among his siblings who must provide them with guidance and support. Like the parent, the older sibling also is periodically expected to sacrifice personal needs in favor of younger siblings. (Chan, 1998, p. 300)

Your challenge is to interpret the appropriate extent of cohesion and protectiveness according to families' cultural beliefs. What may appear to be overprotection in one culture may be appropriate protection, nurturance, and affection in another. For example, Latino families may find it acceptable for preteens or even adolescents to sit on their mother's lap or for preschoolers to drink from a baby bottle long after Euro-American parents would consider those actions inappropriate (Zuniga, 1998). When you honor families' cultures, you infuse into your partnerships with them a necessary component of the reliable alliances. You thereby create an empowering context by honoring their customs.

What happens when families have low degrees of cohesion, even to the point that children with an exceptionality are isolated from the emotional support and friendship of other family members? Limited interaction leaves children without the support, closeness, and assistance needed to develop independence. Disengaged family interactions often are characterized by underinvolvement, few shared interests or friends, excessive privacy, and a great deal of time apart. Few decisions require family input and involvement. For all family members, particularly the member with an exceptionality, such a family situation can be both lonely and difficult.

Disengaged relationships can take place within and between subsystems. For example, disengagement within a subsystem exists when a father denies the fact of the child's exceptionality and withdraws both from parental and marital interactions. Disengagement between subsystems may be found when the members of the extended-family subsystem are unable to accept the child, leading to the sharing of increasingly fewer family celebrations.

Again, it is important to view disengagement within a cultural frame. For example, research shows that children of the Ojibwa tribe who have partially acculturated families are more passive and less responsive than children in either highly traditional or more acculturated families (Boggs, 1965):

> The parents of somewhat acculturated children interacted less in the home and appeared less involved with the children. This may be an early symptom of an important component of acculturative stress: Intergenerational conflict. Young people acculturate more rapidly as they attend school and have greater contact with the majority culture. Because of their age, young people may be more open to change than are their parents. Parents feel abandoned and denied in response to their children's greater acculturation. (Yates, 1987, pp. 319–320)

Obviously, you will want to understand the reasons for certain relationships as you work at creating an empowering context, one that is comfortable and personalized for each family because it respects the family's cultural traditions.

An extreme example of a disengaged relationship occurs when adolescents have separated from their parents by leaving home early (Cauce et al., 1998). More than half of young homeless youths have been identified as having an emotional or behavior disorder, including conduct disorders and depression (Feitel, Margetson, Chamas, & Lipman, 1992). An Australian study indicated that the youths reported that their family life lacked sufficient opportunities for autonomy as well as sufficient care and support. The reaction of the youths was to rebel against the autonomy limitations by leaving the family and thereby separating from family relationships (Schweitzer, Hier, & Terry, 1994). (This information was gathered from the adolescents alone. If information had been gathered from their parents, siblings, or extended family, it may have offered different views on the family interactions. It is difficult to get a clear understanding of family dynamics by getting the viewpoints of only one member.)

The point is that when family situations may be at an extreme level of cohesion or disengagement, some family members may make an effort to counteract or counterbalance the one extreme by taking an extreme action toward the opposite direction.

Implications of Cohesion. A number of studies have pointed to the positive outcomes that accrue for families when family cohesion is at a balanced level (Dyson, 1993; Krauss, 1993). For example, cohesion has been found to be an early predictor of children's growth and communication, social skills, and skills of daily living (Hauser-Cram et al., 1999). In addition, low family cohesion has been found to be a key predictor of greater parenting and child-related stress at important transition points such as leaving early intervention programs and entering kindergarten (Warfield, Krauss, Hauser-Cram, Upshur, & Shonkoff, 1999). Interestingly, low family cohesion was a much stronger predictor of parenting and child stress than such child characteristics as the child's age or the level of cognitive impairment. Alternatively, a study of the adjustment of families of adult children with mental retardation did not find a significant relationship between family adjustment and cohesion (Lusig & Akey, 1999).

In studies of the positive contributions that individuals with disabilities make to their families, parents have reported that they have especially valued the increased family unity and closeness (Behr & Murhpy,

1993; Stainton & Hilde, 1998; Summers, Behr, & Turnbull, 1989; Turnbull, Guess, & Turnbull, 1988).

Given these implications, there are two important reasons for you to support families in establishing the cohesion that is comfortable for them. First, by recognizing the levels of cohesion both among and within subsystems, you can create a context that supports the family as a whole to meet its needs as well as the child's—that is, to get what it wants and needs.

In the Benito family, for example, there is a great deal of cohesion both among and within subsystems. As Nila herself has noted, the members play different roles, but they play as members of the same team—the Benito family team. Nonetheless, the team's boundaries are quite open to outsiders (people not related by blood or marriage) such as Nila's colleagues at the University of South Florida's Florida Department of Child and Family Studies and the local Head Start program. Indeed, staff at the Institute and the Head Start program are collaborators with the family and serve an empowering role for the Benitos as they seek an inclusive education for the two youngsters. The staff creates a context for motivation and knowledge/skills, thus complementing the family's individual and collective empowerment.

Second, by considering the degree of cohesion that exists in a family, you can determine what services and supports may be appropriate, and you can provide or refer the family to those services (Taanila, Järvelin, & Kokkonen, 1999). For example, you will know to ask whether a particular program encourages a culturally appropriate level of cohesion, or you will be competent to make appropriate early education recommendations. Mothers highly involved in early childhood programs are sometimes unintentionally reinforced for establishing highly cohesive relationships with their young children. That is, they are encouraged to spend a lot of time in the classroom, to attend mothers groups, to provide home teaching, and to transport children to numerous services. When they spend all of this time with the child, what happens to their own needs and the needs of other family members? Obviously, you will want to be sensitive to the implications of your professional recommendations on a family's cohesion and disengagement. Knowing a family—the second of the eight obligations of a reliable alliance—is indispensable to creating an empowering context.

*A*daptability

Family adaptability refers to the family's ability to change in response to situational and developmental stress (Olson et al., 1980; Olson, 1988). In other words,

adaptability refers to the family's ability to plan and work out differences when change and stress occur. As with a family's cohesion, its adaptability is influenced by family values and cultural background and can also be viewed on a continuum: At one end are families who are unable or unwilling to change in response to situational or developmental stress; at the other end are families who are constantly changing, so much so that they create significant confusion in the family (Olson et al., 1979). Again, most families fall in the wide swath of balance in the center.

Ranges of Adaptability At one end of the adaptability continuum, families demonstrate a high degree of control and structure, and their interactions often are governed by many strictly enforced rules. The power hierarchy and roles in these families are firmly delineated, and negotiations are seldom tolerated. Consider the example of a son who sustains a brain injury and accompanying physical disability. The injury requires the family to deal immediately with crisis intervention in the trauma setting (Cope & Wolfson, 1994) and later with many new demanding physical, daily care, economic, and emotional needs in providing both acute and long-term care (Kreutzer, Serio, & Bergquist, 1994; Singer, Glang, & Williams, 1996). If in the past, meeting child needs was primarily the mother's role, the added demands will likely be more than she is accustomed to or perhaps can handle. If the family has difficulty sharing new responsibilities and roles with the mother and bringing in collaborators from outside the family, the added demands probably will create stress and difficulty for her and all other family members.

In addition to the general reason of knowing families (one of the eight reliable alliance obligations), there are two specific reasons why you need to take into account high degrees of control in the family power hierarchy as you propose educational programs. First, many families adapt their power hierarchies over time to support the child or adolescent in his or her evolving self-determination. As we have noted earlier, self-determination is culturally rooted, with some families placing great value on the increased autonomy of children and youth and other families considering this culturally inappropriate (Kalyanpur & Harry, 1999; Turnbull & Turnbull, 1996). As you collaborate with families, you need to be sensitive in negotiating the degree of student decision making that the family considers to be appropriate.

Second, it is helpful to identify the person or persons (for example, parent, parents, grandmother, or uncle) who have primary control over family decisions and rules. For example, if a teacher asks a mother to implement a home-based language program but does not take into account that the husband has the decision-making power in the family and rejects the program, it is unlikely that the program will be effective. Indeed, if the mother carries out the intervention against her husband's wishes, the program may create marital and parental conflict. As we suggested earlier, you should examine the impact of recommendations for home teaching on every family member, seeking to understand the family's values and goals and working with the family to develop support options that will be consistent with its values and goals and its ability and willingness to adapt. In contrast, other families demonstrate a low degree of control and structure. Their interactions often are characterized by few rules, and even these are seldom enforced and often changing. Promises and commitments are often unkept, and family members learn that they cannot depend upon one another. Frequently, there is no family leader, negotiations are endless, and roles are unsure and often changing.

All families can experience periods of chaos during stressful life events. But when chaos is a consistent way of life, the consequences can be negative for the family and the student with an exceptionality.

Consider the example of a mother with a son who has AD/HD. The child has difficulty academically and socially. The mother has a live-in boyfriend who is the family's primary source of financial support. During the last two years, the boyfriend has begun to drink heavily and abuse family members. When the boyfriend begins to fight, existing rules are suddenly harshly interpreted for the child. When the fighting escalates, the rules change; survival is the main concern. Later the remorseful boyfriend becomes extremely indulgent, creating a third set of rules. The instability and chaos continue. Because of his disability, the youngster already experiences difficulty interpreting social cues accurately, and his ever-revolving family lifestyle only exacerbates his problems.

Implications of Adaptability Well-functioning families are typically characterized by a balance between the extremes of high or low adaptability (Olson et al., 1980). A study of the adjustment of parents of adult sons and daughters with mental retardation showed that the families' adaptation is a key factor contributing to positive adjustment (Lusig & Akey, 1999). Researchers have also documented the importance of family members being able to discuss and debate a wide range of alternative choices (adaptability) while also maintaining their ties of commitment (cohesion) (Trute & Hauch, 1988).

To support those families who are dissatisfied with their current level of adaptability, you can take three actions that are generally helpful.

First, support families to plan for change. If possible, discuss schedule changes and transitions well in advance of the time they will occur. Ask yourself, "Is this change too sudden or radical for this family's current level of adaptability?" If so, some students and families may benefit from gradual transitions. When a student will be changing classrooms or school buildings, it may be helpful to start with a gradual transition such as one day a week before making the complete transition. If a child needs to learn how to ride the bus and the family is hesitant to make this change, intermediate steps (for example, riding only part of the way, riding with a friend or family member, or bringing the bus driver into the planning team) may be reassuring.

Second, encourage families to examine alternatives. Many families who lack adaptability also may not know how to examine alternatives (Shank & Turnbull, 1993; Summers, Templeton-McMann, & Fuger, 1997). They might benefit from learning a problem-solving process such as the one described in chapter 4. A service coordinator in an early intervention program described the perspectives of a parent who could benefit from problem-solving support:

> One woman finally decided to kick out her abusive boyfriend. We talked about arranging for him to pack his things and leave while she was gone. But she says to me, "What if he takes all the food with him?" And I respond, "Well, we'll have to think about things like the food pantry, or something." And then she says, "I don't know how to keep him out because he has keys." So I say, "Well, call your landlord and see if you can change the locks." (Summers, Templeton-McMann, & Fuger, 1997, p. 41)

Remember the role that the staff of the Florida Department of Child and Family Studies and Head Start played in the Benito family's life? It was to support the family to change from education that was essentially segregated and inappropriate to one that was inclusive and appropriate. And it was to support the family to move in that direction by helping the family examine alternatives to the unacceptable programs and then advocating for the admission to the more appropriate program. In short, the professional staff offered motivation and knowledge skills to the family.

Third, if a family may be interested in receiving services from the school counselor, school social worker, or other community professionals who specialize in family counseling or therapy, collaborate with the school counselor or social worker on how to approach the family and suggest these alternatives. By contrast, if a family itself asks you about possible resources, respond by referring members to those resources. Remember, however, that family dynamics are complicated and often require specialization in providing the most appropriate and personalized supports. Knowing when to refer a family to professionals with more family specialization is a critical competency for all professionals in special education.

Summary

The best way of understanding family interactions is to view the family as a system. There are three major assumptions in family systems theory. First, in a family, as in most systems, there are inputs; the family responds to and interacts with the inputs and, as a result, creates certain outputs in carrying out its family functions.

Second, the family system must be understood as a whole entity; it cannot be understood by examining only its component parts or by understanding only one or more of its members. Simply understanding the child with an exceptionality or the mother does not mean that you will understand the family; indeed, you probably will not. The family consists of subsystems (marital, parental, sibling, and extended), and the child with an exceptionality can have negative, positive, and mixed impacts on each of these subsystems.

Third, family subsystems are separated by boundaries that define the interaction that family members have with each other and with people outside the family. The family's cultural heritage and other characteristics (see chapter 5) affect the family members' interactions and the nature of boundaries.

Finally, two elements of family interaction are cohesion and adaptability. The term *family cohesion* refers to the emotional attachment that family members have toward each other and the level of independence each feels within the family. Some families are extraordinarily cohesive: Their members are enmeshed with each other. Other families are quite the opposite: Their members are disengaged from each other. Although some families are characterized by excessive degrees of closeness or disengagement, most have found (sometimes with the support of professionals such as yourself) a balance between these two extremes.

Similarly, some families are extraordinarily adaptable; they seem to have an unlimited ability to change in response to situational and developmental stress. Others, of course, are quite unadaptable; the least amount of stress is unsettling and disruptive. Again, most families strike a happy medium between these two extremes.

As Vincent and Joseph Benito enter elementary school, their family has established its pattern of interactions. Their mother Nila is the planner and organizer; their father Joe is the "deal closer" and final negotiator; their grandmother Nila and great-grandmother Francesca are the cheerleaders; and their aunt Nancy is a listening ear and reliable source of emotional support for their mother Nila. Indeed, the University of South Florida family-support staffers who have inspired and guided the Benito family on its way toward great expectations for inclusion have learned three important lessons: The Benito family is influenced by its cultural heritage (it is a large, multigenerational Italian-American family); it is highly (but not problematically) cohesive; and it is adaptable to the challenges that Vincent and Joseph pose because of their autism.

Whatever the Benito family was before it encountered the University of South Florida staff, it now is a family that wants to collaborate with the professionals in Vincent's and Joseph's schools. Indeed, as Nila has said repeatedly, without collaboration within the family and outside it with professionals, Vincent and Joseph would have little, if any, chance of being included in any aspects of general education.

Chapter Seven

Family Functions

*R*ickey Battles makes a big difference to his family—indeed, to his whole community. That's true because of, not in spite of, his disabilities. At age 13 1/2, Rickey has scoliosis and wears a brace on his back and one foot; is incontinent because of bladder and colitis problems; has mental retardation, low muscle tone, and epilepsy; and is excitable and sometimes too loud in public.

In Poultney, Vermont, where he, his father Richard, his mother Betty, and his younger brother Michael live and where Richard and Betty run a medium-sized grocery store that Richard's family established a generation ago, Rickey is fully included in his elementary school. He receives a great deal of support from special educators and various therapists and is the "hit" of a local pet shop where he is volunteering as part of his school/community access program.

Richard and Betty acknowledge that Rickey has brought the family closer together—in a family that was already very affectionate with one another. They know, too, that Rickey has influenced how his schoolmates regard people with disabilities—more welcomingly. And they delight in the fact that Rickey has made fast friends with the workers at the pet shop; his ability to tell traditional New England tall tales endears him to the owners and workers.

Yet Rickey's contributions to the family are accompanied by responsibilities the family does not have for his younger brother Michael. Richard and Betty have to be "kind of careful" about what they do with Rickey, always "figuring out and working around things" so Rickey and the family can go to parties. "Rickey's very immature for his age, and some of the questions he might ask, some of the things he might say, may not be appropriate at the time. So you really have to explain to people what's going on and why, and usually they accept it. You can never tell. You really have to be on your guard every day; you really have to know your child and what's appropriate for him."

And, yes, Rickey's disabilities require his parents to take time off from work to attend to all of Rickey's hygienic and medical needs. But over time Richard and Betty have gotten over their disappointment that Rickey was born with disabilities. "Now we really don't look at it as life with disability. We just look on it as another day with Rickey, as something we deal with. It's normal for us to deal with his disability, we guess."

Rickey's younger brother Michael "wishes that Rickey were more normal so that he could play with him more. Fortunately, we've brought Michael up so he's accepted Rickey very, very well. He knows his limits, he gets a kick out of fooling with him, and he's accepted him very well." So have Rickey's schoolmates, although their teachers have told them that Rickey has special needs and that their role is to pitch in when needed.

The socialization of Rickey's peers has been a joint endeavor between the Battles family and the Poultney educators. There's also the regular weekly meeting involving Rickey's team: his mother Betty, his classroom teacher, the school nurse, and any other educators who want to attend.

There are only two ground rules for the meetings. First, "if they have any concerns or needs, it's all right at the table; and there is a person there who will meet those needs. If not, they'll have to deal with us."

Second, "we don't allow negativism, none at all. We present Rickey in a positive way. If one of us has a problem, we have to state it in a positive way. The rest of us have to ask how we can help meet Rickey's needs."

The bottom line on Rickey? Richard and Betty sum it up as very positive: He brings affection and closeness to the family, gives them a sense of self and self-identity, and educates them and the community. Financially, he is a low-cost youngster, in large part because of a nearby Shriners' Hospital and insurance coverage. Daily care? Well, that's problematic: The constant on-guard attitude and the physical demands he places on them cannot be denied.

But those responsibilities don't weigh heavily on Richard and Betty. "Rickey's participation with the community, his schoolmates, and the teachers give meaning to his life. He gives something to other people, and his giving also gives meaning to our lives. Through Rickey, we give a different perspective, a different tolerance, a different acceptance of other people."

The Battles family: Michael, Rickey, Betty and Richard. (1995)

Families exist to meet the individual and collective needs of their members. The tasks that families perform to meet these needs are referred to as *family functions.* We identify eight categories of family functions: (1) affection, (2) self-esteem, (3) spiritual, (4) economics, (5) daily care, (6) socialization, (7) recreation, and (8) education (Turnbull, Summers, & Brotherson, 1984). The family systems framework calls these the family's *outputs* (see figure 7–1). We will briefly review each of the eight family functions and discuss some of their common themes and implications.

For each function, a family generally tries to engage in activities that reasonably satisfy its members' wants and needs. One role of the family is to show the younger members how to meet those needs and perform these functions so that these responsibilities can be transferred from the older to the younger generation, consistent with the cultural values and traditions of the family.

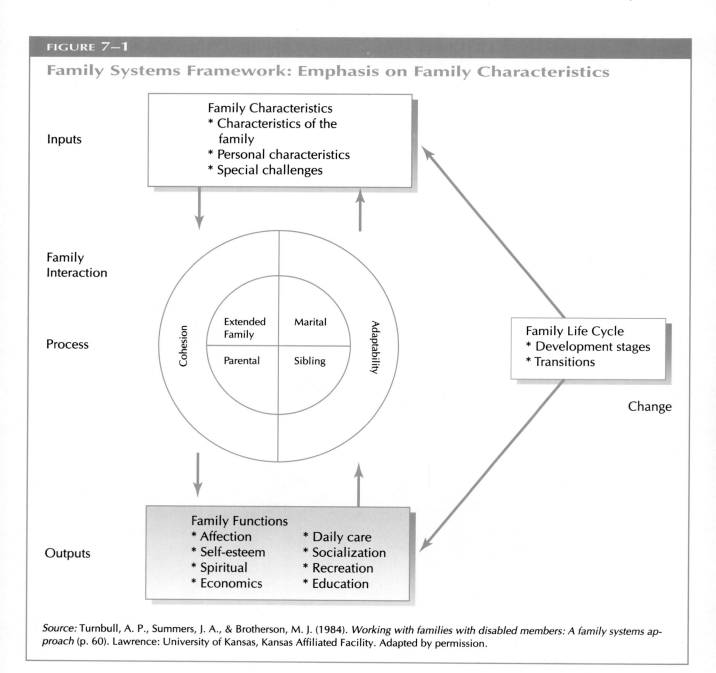

FIGURE 7–1

Family Systems Framework: Emphasis on Family Characteristics

Source: Turnbull, A. P., Summers, J. A., & Brotherson, M. J. (1984). *Working with families with disabled members: A family systems approach* (p. 60). Lawrence: University of Kansas, Kansas Affiliated Facility. Adapted by permission.

As you will learn in chapter 8, family activities and individual family member contributions are strongly influenced by the family's life cycle stage. Additionally, the family's characteristics (chapter 5) and the family's interactions (chapter 6) influence how functions are addressed within the family. Because the family is an interacting system, it is impossible to consider family functions (outputs) without taking the other portions of the family systems framework into account. Likewise, it will be futile to create an empowering context without knowing a family, the way it satisfies these eight functions, and the impact that its cultural values and traditions have on its functions.

The Impact of Exceptionality on Family Functions

Each category of family functions is distinct; in many ways, however, these functions are interrelated so that problems or benefits in one dimension of family functioning can, and usually do, impact other functions. For example, economic difficulties can have a negative impact on family members' social or recreational activities. Likewise, stress or depression related to financial worries can have a negative impact on family affection. On the other hand, a child's positive contributions to household chores (that is, daily care) can enhance self-esteem, affection, and recreational outcomes. A benefit or problem related to one family function can have ripple effects on other functions.

Each of the family functions is affected by every family member, including the presence of a family member with an exceptionality. This influence may be positive, negative, or neutral (Minnes, 1998; O'Connor, 1995; Renwick, Brown, & Raphael, 1998; Shapiro, Blacher, & Lopez, 1998; Stoneman, 1998; Summers, Behr, & Turnbull, 1989). Many people erroneously assume that a child or youth with a disability generally has a negative impact on the family. As we will point out throughout the chapter, research has documented many positive contributions that children with disabilities make to their families (Sandler & Mistretta, 1998; Scorgie, Wilgosh, & McDonald, 1998; Stainton & Besser, 1998; Summers, Behr, & Turnbull, 1989). In the Battles family and indeed throughout the community, Rickey's influence is positive. Yes, he needs accommodations in certain family functions, but his needs and the way his family functions to meet them are not especially challenging.

As you read this chapter, consider these two questions: What are the family's and your appropriate priorities for achieving family balance in carrying out family functions, and what cultural values and traditions influence these priorities? As you are able to answer these questions as you collaborate with families, you are more likely to create an empowering context.

Affection Needs

It is not surprising that studies of families that regard themselves as successful in being a family have consistently reported that these families emphasize the role of sharing affection (Mellman, Lazarus, & Rivlin, 1990; Summers, 1987a, 1987b). There are many different ways to characterize the dimensions of affection, but especially important are (1) exchanging verbal and physical affection and (2) exchanging unconditional love (Summers, 1987a, 1987b).

Exchanging Verbal and Physical Affection Much has been written about attachment, particularly between mother and child (Ainsworth, Bell, & Stayton, 1974). From a family systems perspective, attachment between and among all family members is a priority and consists of encouraging those reciprocal interactions between parents and children that deepen their emotional commitments to each other. "Human development occurs in the context of an escalating psychological ping-pong game between two people who are crazy about each other" (Bronfenbrenner, 1990, p. 31).

Cultural influences strongly determine how families deepen their emotional commitments and display affection. For example, Asian families often provide very close physical contact with infants, carrying them even during naps and having infants and toddlers sleep in the same room or bed with their parents and other siblings until they are school age or older (Chan, 1998). Middle Eastern families also are characterized as very affectionate: "Middle Eastern mothers are . . . much more permissive than their Western counterparts in allowing their babies and children to be kissed, held, or hugged" (Sharifzadeh, 1998, pp. 458).

A major but natural issue for families is their child's evolution from expressing physical affection within the family to expressing physical affection and sexuality with one or more chosen partners (see chapter 8). Read box 7–1 and consider this issue from the perspective of a 38-year-old woman with a severe learning disability. Especially note how one of the family's cultural heritages—its religion—influences the issue.

Exchanging Unconditional Love All children have basic needs for acceptance, appreciation, and love (Turnbull, 1988; Turnbull, Blue-Banning, Turbiville, & Park,

The Boyfriend Dilemma

I lived at home with my parents until three years ago when I had a chance to move here and work for my cousin. I think Mom and Dad thought I'd always live with them. Sometimes I miss them a lot. I miss their hugs and their encouragement, but I do like being on my own—feeling like a real adult. I have an apartment and a job, but what I'd really like is a husband and a family. I'm Catholic, so having children would mean a lot to me. When I'm feeling lonely I really wish that I was in love. I get depressed sometimes, because I don't think that will ever happen. I'm getting pretty old, and I hardly even know how to meet men or how to act around them. I get really nervous. I've been on about three dates in my entire life. Mom wouldn't let me go out when I was in school. She was afraid that boys would take advantage of me, because I seemed young for my age. I just didn't meet guys very often. I know that sometimes when I am around guys I act too interested and sometimes I act too shy. They frighten me a lot. I wish I could take a class somewhere on how to find a boyfriend.

1999). Exchanging unconditional love is an essential ingredient of family affection, as Harriet Rousso (1984), a social worker with a physical disability, notes:

> In particular, disabled children need to have their bodies, disability and all, accepted, appreciated, and loved. Especially by significant parenting figures. This will solidify the sense of intactness. For all children, disabled or not, the "gleam in the mother's eye" in response to all aspects of the child's body and self is essential for the development of healthy self-esteem. This includes the parent's ability to show pride and pleasure in the disabled part of the body, as one valid aspect of the child, and to communicate appreciation and respect for the child's unique, often different-looking ways of doing things. . . . Parents too often communicate to their child, directly and indirectly, that the disability should be hidden or altered, if not purged the child should strive toward appearing as "normal" and nondisabled as possible. This attitude can put the child into an identity crisis, causing him or her to push that feeling of intactness way underground. (Rousso, 1984, pp. 12–13)

Especially related to disability issues, families and professionals alike may need to examine their own values. How much do they and you tend to expect a child's achievement, normalcy, success, attractiveness, or progress to be prerequisites for his or her and your unconditional acceptance, appreciation, or love? Within a family, unconditional love for all family members, whatever their respective characteristics, cannot be taken for granted (Turnbull, 1988), nor can it be underestimated. A number of families have described their child as a major catalyst for enhancing family love (Behr & Murphy, 1993; Summers, Behr, & Turnbull, 1989).

Anyone who feels that someone else is a burden has not yet learned to love. Love feels someone else's need above their own. My son, Matthew, was not useless. . . . If he served no other purpose than to give me love, then he served that one and if he served no other purpose than to teach me love, he served that one. (Turnbull & Turnbull, 1986, p. 112)

Need we emphasize that no family role is any more important than the expression of affection? Box 7–2 lists other tips for addressing families' affection needs. The more you express unconditional love for the child, the more likely you are to encourage high quality affection within the family.

Self-Esteem Needs

Families help their members establish who they are and their worth as people (McClun & Merrell, 1998), and one member's exceptionality can have an impact on the self-esteem of all. (Self-esteem is closely related to self-efficacy. Remember that self-efficacy is one of the elements of motivation, and motivation is one of the family/professional elements of empowerment.) For example, new parents may have anticipated raising children with typical abilities. When they are confronted with raising a child who is gifted, they may feel uncertain and even threatened (Maxwell, 1998; Roedell, 1988).

Not surprisingly, parents of children with disabilities may have self-esteem challenges if they believe their own genetic makeup or their personal misconduct caused the disability. Likewise, their self-esteem may be affected when their infants do not respond readily to

Addressing Families' Affection Needs

- Recognize the needs that all family members have for affection. For example, if a parent-child home teaching program each night interferes with a busy family's only opportunities to catch up on the day's events, play games, or snuggle on the couch together, reconsider the plan to achieve a balance in meeting all family needs, not just educational needs.

- Provide materials in a resource library and arrange discussion groups involving resource persons who can help parents and students with an exceptionality gain a better understanding of sexuality and affection. Young

adults or adolescents, depending on age, type, and severity of exceptionality, benefit from accurate and sensitive information about sexuality and affection.

- Help parents identify their child's positive contributions to affection as well as other family functions. Encourage family members to discuss what positive contributions each makes. For example, at dinner encourage family members to share at least two things they appreciate about each of the other members. They can also highlight the similarities and differences in each person's list.

---

soothing or stimulation or when they deal with existential issues of why the child has a disability. Leah Ziskin (1985), mother of a daughter with a severe disability, has commented on the impact that her daughter's birth had on her own self-esteem:

> I remember feeling that I had become a completely different person, I felt that my ego had been wiped out. My superego with all of its guilts had become the most prominent part of my personality, and I had completely lost my self-esteem. Any credits of self-worth that I could give myself from any of my personal endeavors meant nothing. Graduating from college and a first-rate medical school, surviving an internship, practicing medicine, and having two beautiful sons and a good marriage counted for nil. All I knew at this point was that I was the mother of an abnormal and most likely retarded child. (Ziskin, 1985, p. 68)

A different kind of self-esteem challenge occurs for families who have frequently faced multiple challenges and have experienced low levels of self-esteem for almost their entire lives. Many women who experience poverty, especially single mothers, are highly vulnerable to demoralization, depression, and helplessness (Kaplan-Sanoff, 1996; Larner & Collins, 1996). Self-esteem is a challenge across the lifespan in addressing many challenges and is not reserved for exceptionality considerations alone. Nonetheless, some professionals who have reliable alliances with mothers who experience multiple challenges recognize the mothers'

strengths. Building on strengths is a way to create an empowering context, and one strength is the mother's persistence.

> In reality, the workers routinely recognized strengths in even the most troubled of the families served. The workers were genuinely respectful and impressed by these families' abilities to endure in the face of events which the workers did not believe they, themselves, could survive. "I see them as survivors. They go through hell and back. They can do things that I couldn't stand. They are strong. If we were suddenly thrown into their situations well, I would probably die. They don't see that, they don't see it as a strength." In addition to their tenacity, an important strength shared by most of these families was their commitment and sense of identity with their children. For many, their ability to have children was their only source of positive self-esteem. (Summers, McMann, Kitchen, & Peck, 1995, p. 15)

Not surprisingly, a family's self-esteem can depend on whether its members see the·connections between their actions and good things that happen as a result of those actions. Note, for example, how a professional supports the empowerment of one of the mothers in the "survivor" group who had not regarded herself as being strong:

> One example of the success is (a mother) who sees something happening. Not only is she getting good things in response to efforts, she is learning not to be helpless. That is helping you get rid of some of that learned helplessness. She hasn't had a lot of things

handed to her. So I talk to her. I ask her what was that a result of, can she see that was connected to her efforts? (Summers et al., 1995, p. 20)

Self-esteem is an important issue for not only parents but also young children with exceptionalities. How they come to view themselves—their own self-esteem—is influenced by families, educators, peers, and others. For example, one research study found that children who are blind who believed their parents judged them to be too thin had lower self-esteem (Pierce & Wardle, 1996). Parents and professionals play an important role in supporting the intellectual, emotional, and self-efficacy capacities of young gifted children (Maxwell, 1998) and of children and youth with learning disabilities (Gilson, Bricout, & Baskint, 1998). Individuals with learning disabilities complain that professionals often overreact to their disability and treat them as if they have limited aspirations, abilities, and rights. Students who are gifted—especially adolescent females (Dalzell, 1998) and ones who underachieve—experience challenges with self-esteem.

Very little research has been done on the self-esteem of children and youth with exceptionalities and the contributions that families make in enhancing their self-esteem (Smith-Horn & Singer, 1996). A number of studies of students with learning disabilities have focused on self-concept, but these studies do not address family factors. Nonetheless, the limited research is notable. A careful review of 20 studies indicates that by third grade, students with learning disabilities typically have substantially lower academic self-concepts (Chapman, 1988). They tend to attribute their failures to their own abilities and their successes to factors such as others' help or good luck. Aside from the particular focus on academics, students with learning disabilities had lower, but not significantly lower, general self-concepts than their classmates without exceptionalities.

Judith Heumann, Assistant Secretary of the Office of Special Education and Rehabilitative Services, U.S. Department of Education, shares her perspective:

> The most significant goal for parents of disabled students is assuring that their children maintain the sense of self-esteem with which we are all born. Parents are their children's most important role model. If disabled children know their parents have great expectations for them, they will have great expectations for themselves. (Heumann, 1997, unpaginated)

A key is ensuring that the exceptionality does not overshadow countless other individual traits, interests, and attributes (Turnbull & Turnbull, 1986). Just consider how Norman Kunc, a family therapist and a person with cerebral palsy, describes how people often see him and how he regards himself (see box 7–3).

MY VOICE BOX 7–3

Shadows or Sun on the Sundial

When people first meet me, they tend to see me as 9/10 disability, 1/10 person. What they see as paramount are the things that mark me as "different"—the way I walk, speak, and move. The disability expands in their eyes, throwing a shadow over me and my life in the same way that a shadow on a sundial widens in the afternoon light. My disability is perceived as being more influential than it actually is.

Let me counteract that view for a moment, and describe myself to you—as I see myself. First, I am a white male who grew up in Toronto, Canada. My father is Polish, my mother is English. . . . I like sailing, and used to compete in local and regional races. I'm married to Emma, and live in Port Alberni, British Columbia. I am a step-dad to Jodi, Erinn, and Evan. We live in an old house we renovated and love. Emma and I have our own business as consultants. We share a passionate interest in social justice and conflict management. I enjoy computers, classical music and Greek food. I play the drums, although not well. I have an uncanny ability to remember phone numbers and jokes. I also have cerebral palsy.

Source: Kunc, N., & Van der Klift, E. (1995). Voice: In spite of my disability. Questions, concerns, beliefs, and practical advice about inclusive education. In J. Thousand & R. Villa (Eds.), *The inclusion puzzle: Fitting the pieces together* (pp. 163–164). Alexandria, VA: Association for Supervision and Curriculum Development. Copyright © 1995 ASCD. Used by permission.

One way that the Battles family and the professional collaborators ensure that the shadow of Rickey's exceptionality does not overshadow his other attributes and his life is to focus on his strengths.

You might ask whether a program has been developed to prepare parents of children with disabilities with the motivation and knowledge/skills to enhance their children's self-esteem. One such program for parents of children with physical disabilities and mild cognitive impairments includes six weekly lessons in which parents meet as a group, and through presentations, discussions, and individual and group activities, they learn how to help their children develop independence, participate in leisure activities, interact with peers, be assertive, cope with tough situations, and practice self-advocacy (Todis, Irvin, Singer, & Yovanoff, 1993). As a result of the training, parents' self-esteem increased; children gained self-care skills, completed chores more often, and became more assertive; and the parents became more likely to support their child's request for autonomy and independence. An empowering context (in this situation) was one that provided new knowledge/skills and a caring, relational group context that fueled the parents' motivation to master the knowledge/skills.

What are the implications of these self-esteem issues for family and professional collaboration? A family's and student's self-esteem can be influenced by how you affirm their strengths in a genuine way; sadly, many families and students are much more accustomed to having their weaknesses and needs pointed out rather than their strengths. You can be an affirmer of strengths. In box 7–4 you will find other tips for addressing families' self-esteem needs.

Spiritual Needs

Although spirituality is manifested in multiple ways across different cultures (Lynch & Hanson, 1998; Uphoff, 1999), a common theme is the role of the family in transmitting cultural and personal spiritual beliefs from one generation to another (D'Antonio & Aldous, 1993). A family's religion can vastly impact family values as well as spiritual beliefs and rituals. Consider how Confucianism impacts family life in its strong emphasis on filial piety:

> Filial piety consists of unquestioning loyalty and obedience to parents and concern for and understanding of their needs and wishes. It also includes reverence for ancestors whose spirits must be appeased. Filial piety further extends to relations with all authority figures and defines a social hierarchy of allegiance in reciprocal moral obligations characterized by the "five relations" of 1) king/justice, subject/loyalty; 2) father/love, son/filiality; 3) elder brother/brotherly love, younger brother/reverence; 4) husband/initiative, wife/obedient; and 5) friends/mutual faith. (Chan, 1998, p. 258)

You might consider your own spiritual beliefs regarding these issues in terms of how similar and different they are than from Confucian principles.

Regarding the experience of having a family member with an exceptionality, a consistent finding of the research on the positive contributions of children with disabilities to their families is that their child has been a catalyst for their own increased spirituality (Behr & Murphy, 1993; Guess, Turnbull, & Turnbull, 1988; Stainton & Besser, 1998; Summers, Behr, & Turnbull, 1989). Indeed, the spiritual function of the family often comes into play

---

TIPS   BOX 7–4

Addressing Families' Self-Esteem Needs

- Affirm all family members' strengths and positive contributions.
- Underscore links between family members' actions and the positive results that accrue.
- Encourage children and youth with exceptionalities to identify and develop interests that give them pride. One strategy might be to place the student with an exceptionality in the role of helper rather than recipient of help.
- Encourage children and youth with exceptionalities to express their own choices as a strategy to enhance their self-esteem. Encouraging children and youth to choose what is important to them affords them greater control and independence.
- Ensure that children and youth have school opportunities, consistent with their preferences, to establish relationships with friends and mentors who share similar exceptionalities and ones who do not.

Source: Adapted from Stainback, S., Stainback, W., East, K., & Sapon-Shevin, M. (1994). A commentary on inclusion and the development of a positive self-identity by people with disabilities. *Exceptional Children, 60*(6), 486–90.

in terms of (1) interpreting the meaning of the child's exceptionality and (2) having a religious community that provides concrete and emotional support.

The spiritual function of the family is critically important as a basis for interpreting the meaning of disability. Some parents say that they regard their child's disability as a blessing:

> I guess God chose me to have a child with a handicap because a lot of people can't take care of handicap kids . . . You know, it was scary for a while but there is a purpose for everything in life. God never gives us more than he will help us bear. God chose me, and I feel my child is a blessing. (Rogers-Dulan, 1998, p. 98)

Kalyanpur and Harry (1999) describe the situation of a seven-year-old child, Kou, who is Hmong. Social workers brought a suit against Kou's parents for refusing corrective surgery on his two club feet. Consistent with their spiritual beliefs, however, Kou's parents interpreted Kou's condition as a "sign of good luck" and as an indication that "a warrior ancestor whose own feet were wounded in battle could be released from a sort of spiritual entrapment" (Hmong family, 1991, p. 16). As families interpret disability positively and within a spiritual framework, there are opportunities for their beliefs to be sources of motivation for them as they address the various support issues associated with the disability.

Alternatively, there are spiritual interpretations that lead families to the belief that the disability is a punishment for past sins or transgressions.

> . . . a Chinese father reported that his persistent gambling and involvement in an extramarital affair at the time of his wife's pregnancy caused his son to experience neonatal distress and subsequent cerebral palsy. A Cambodian father attributed his daughter's "club" foot to an incident when he and his pregnant wife were escaping as refuges from the jungle of Thailand; in an attempt to hunt and kill a bird with a rock, he instead only wounded its claw and leg. (Chan, 1998, p. 314)

As you develop a reliable alliance with families by honoring their cultural traditions, we encourage you to be open to their sharing with you the interpretations that they have of their child's disability. The important thing for you to remember is that their spiritual beliefs do not necessarily have to be consistent with yours and vice versa. Your role is to seek to stand in their shoes and to understand how they bring meaning to their life experiences.

Many families derive tremendous instrumental and emotional support from their religious communities. For example, Hornstein (1997) describes how the Jew-

ish religious community provides support for families of children with disabilities through Jewish day and supplemental schools, community centers, camps, and social service agencies. She describes how her own son who has autism has been supported through his synagogue.

> Joel's preparation for his Bar mitzvah was a congregational project, and today, 10 years later, the congregate still describe his Bar mitzvah as one of Temple Chai's proudest moments. When Joel attends services, he is greeted warmly by a significant portion of those attending. . . . When Joel volunteers in the synagogue library or stuffs envelopes for a mailing, he is treated just like every other adult in the group. Joel knows that Temple Chai is a second home, a "safe place" where his participation is valued, and he never questions the appropriateness of his being there. During the period of transition from school to adulthood, when all that is familiar and comforting is taken away from a young adult, being able to return to the security and regimen of weekly prayer and participation in synagogue activities becomes the reassuring anchor during this tumultuous time. (Hornstein, 1997, p. 487)

In a survey of local church support, it was reported that 81 percent of the churches had people with developmental disabilities in their congregation, with an average of five people per congregation. Most of these congregations reported that they included people with a developmental disability into their regular classes and services and made an effort to provide a social/emotional support (McNair & Swartz, 1995).

But other families may have trouble in finding a religious community that can be responsive to their child's needs. Many families report that their experiences have not been nearly as positive as they would like for them to be. As a father of a young child with autism stated:

> I just don't have the energy to look around through 30 churches in the area to find the one that is right for Jason and then make all the efforts to make all the contacts. . . . It is just one more mountain that you choose to go around instead of to climb. (Turnbull & Ruef, 1997, p. 216)

In terms of cultural strengths, much has been written about the role of the church in the lives of African American families (Willis, 1998). Many Black churches currently provide educational, recreational, and social service supports for families in addition to spiritual support.

We want to caution you that not all spiritual beliefs are tied into what many people equate with traditional religious services that occur in Protestant and Catholic churches or in Jewish synagogues. For example, there are many Native American belief systems that are highly spiritual in tying human beings to the larger universe.

> Among the Hopis (a Pueblo tribe in northern Arizona), there is a belief that the original spiritual "being" shared with the Hopi people certain rules of life and placed spiritual helpers—the Kachinas—near the tribe to protect and help them maintain a certain way of life. The Kachinas, therefore, help teach and guide the Hopis through their songs, prayers, and ceremonies (Titiev, 1972). Among the Apaches, the Mountain Spirits have a similar role. Appropriate members of the respected tribes impersonate these deities during special ceremonies. In addition, the social structures of some Pueblo tribes of the Southwest have moieties where ceremonial activities also function to ensure harmony and/or community welfare. (Joe & Malach, 1998, p. 144)

Finally, you should appreciate that not all spirituality is religious. People explore the spiritual meaning of their lives and achieve a sense of spirituality through a broad range of alternative activities. For example, a mother of a young child with a disability described her spiritual journey as follows:

> I'm getting back into my artwork, because that was a form of getting into my spirituality. Making me, you know, all one—mind, body, and soul. And it comes across. I'm happier, work is going better, things are just coming into my life, you know, happiness. (Unpublished transcript, Beach Center, 1999)

As a member of the Hindu religion, the mother of a child with a disability commented:

> I am a dancer, and Indian dance is very closely connected with religion. I like the *vilakku* (the lamp lighted for prayer) and keep the *puga* (room of worship) door open. (Raghavan, Weisner, & Patel, 1999, p. 286)

Given the constitutional separation of church and state, you may ask whether it is your role to support families in addressing their spiritual needs. We believe that because many families derive both tremendous benefit from their spiritual beliefs and also concrete and informational support from the religious communities (Hughes, 1999), you can help families if you collaborate with people within the families' religious communities to create the adaptations and accommodations that can enable the family's participation and their community. In chapter 12 you will learn in more detail about conducting comprehensive IFSP/IEP conferences. These conferences could be ideal opportunities for personnel from religious programs to learn about adaptations and accommodations for children and youth with disabilities.

Economic Needs

Nearly all families need to earn incomes; only a few have the luxury of being supported by unearned income. Whatever their sources of income, all families must decide how to spend their income and settle upon methods for handling their money.

From reading about family poverty in chapter 5, you know that family resources vary tremendously and that finances affect how families respond to the challenges of their children's exceptionality. Some can and do spend more than others, but that fact alone should not lead you to assume that the families who cannot spend much or who cannot spend at the level you want them to are not as committed to their children as more affluent families. That is the point that a Black single mother makes:

> You've got bummy blacks and bummy whites and you are saying, everybody black is stupid, and you are bums, and you are not good. That's not true. I am a single parent and I am trying to do the best I can with John. I don't send him to school dirty; he don't go hungry. When they need money and stuff for school, I do without. These are white people born with money. They are not struggling. I can't tell you what to do unless I wear your shoes. (Kalyanpur & Rao, 1991, p. 528)

What does research show about the impact of exceptionality on family economics? Data consistently show that families spend more money on their children with disabilities than on their other children; in other words, a child's disability, especially autism, mental retardation, spina bifida, cerebral palsy, and health conditions requiring technology support, creates excess costs (Aday, Aitken, & Weggener, 1988; Birenbaum & Cohen, 1993; Fujiura, Roccoforte, & Braddock, 1994; Knoll, 1992; Morris, 1987; Worley, Rosenfeld, & Lipscomb, 1991).

Data also show that the largest expense categories for families with children with autism or mental retardation are food (specialized diets), transportation (to service providers), recreation, clothing (specially adapted or tailored), durable consumer items, medical care, specialized services, personal care, and "other" (Fujiura et al., 1994). The extraordinary costs include adapted clothing, architectural modifications, climate controls and other environmental modifications, consumer electronics, dental or related needs, exercise equipment, furniture, vehicle modifications, wheelchairs or walkers, and other disability-related equipment (Fujiura et al., 1994).

In addition, many families with children with developmental disabilities, chronic health conditions, or technology support needs must administer medications, monitor medical procedures, provide specialized treatments and procedures, and carry out behavioral intervention and other habilitative programs (Aday et al., 1988; Darling & Peter, 1994; Knoll, 1992; Leff & Walizer, 1992).

It is not clear which disability creates greater excess costs than another. Data based on 1985–1986 family expenditure patterns showed that families who have children with autism spend more money on them for health care than do families with children who do not have disabilities, and families with children with severe mental retardation spend more on their health care than families with children with autism (Birenbaum & Cohen, 1993). But more recent data show that the excess costs of autism exceed those of cerebral palsy and that the costs of cerebral palsy exceed those of mental retardation (Fujiura et al., 1994).

There is another aspect of the costs of exceptionality; some families have "increased consumptive demands" and "decreased productive capacities"—also known as "lost opportunities"—because of their children's disabilities (Aday et al., 1988; Birenbaum & Cohen, 1993). Some families give up new job opportunities because they would have to move away from their present providers and service systems; they take part-time work when they could be employed full time if they did not have to care for their child; they simply leave the workforce altogether to care for their child; they change jobs to get better work hours and at-home care time; they change or refuse to change a job to get or to keep medical insurance; or they forego education that would advance their careers (Barnett & Boyce, 1995; Birenbaum & Cohen, 1993; Fujiura et al., 1994; Knoll, 1992).

Interestingly, by contrast, recent interviews with Korean parents revealed that having a child with a disability increased their financial resources through access to various benefits. For example, families in which the husbands were in the U.S. Army received free taxi services, housing priority, and medical treatment at a reduced cost. Other Korean parents emphasized how helpful it was to them to receive Medicaid benefits and social security income. Yet, a Korean father who came to the United States to be a university student lamented that lack of citizenship left him and other families without access to the common financial benefits that other families of children with disabilities might receive. He described his situation as follows:

> Doctor says that my daughter's hearing problem is progressive which means that her hearing ability gets worse and worse gradually. In this case, we were told that a hearing aid would not be useful. Doctors recommend surgery for her. Of course, we were concerned about the cost . . . approximately $40,000.

Even before discussing about the surgery, we already spent considerable money to see the audiologist. It cost us about $400 each time. (Park & Turnbull, unpublished manuscript)

A major consideration in terms of family job opportunities relates to finding satisfactory child-care arrangements. In a survey of parents with and without disabilities, 41 percent of the parents of children with disabilities reported that child-care providers had quit or let their child go because of behavioral problems as compared to only 2 percent of the parents of children without disabilities. Furthermore, only 56 percent of parents of children with disabilities reported that they had difficulty finding child care as compared to 3 percent of parents of children without disabilities (Emlen, 1998, in press).

Another research study reported that mothers of young children with developmental disabilities reported more difficulty in finding child care; and mothers of children with more severe disabilities reported more difficulty than mothers of children with milder problems (Warfield & Hauser-Cram, 1996). You might consider how you can assist families in finding successful child-care arrangements and collaborate with the child-care providers to share the adaptations and accommodations that are useful in school in successfully supporting students with special needs in child care (Brennan & Freeman, 1999; Brennan, Rosenzweig, & Ogilvie, 1999; O'Brien, 1997).

As a professional committed to providing information so that families can become more empowered, we encourage you to be prepared to provide families with general information about the financial benefits to which they might be entitled or to at least refer them to a source from which they can get that information. Generally, the local office of the Social Security Administration is a good source of information and referral; so, too, are state family support programs and the Parent Training and Information Centers that you will learn about in chapter 10. For families who have children with special health care needs, we encourage you to review the website of the international organization Family Voices and to refer families to the same resource. Family Voices provides excellent information on health care costs and benefits.

Daily Care Needs

Another basic function of families consists of meeting their members' physical and health needs. This includes the day-to-day tasks of living: cooking, cleaning, laundry, transportation, obtaining health care when needed, and so forth. A substantial portion of family life is devoted to attending to these needs. Daily care is one of the significant outputs of family interaction: Parents, children and youth, and extended family often work together to carry out their roles and responsibilities.

Research reveals how children with developmental disabilities and chronic medical conditions affect their families with respect to daily care issues (Knoll, 1992):

- Approximately 50 percent of the families gave their child extensive assistance with toileting, bathing, grooming, and medical monitoring.
- Approximately one-fourth indicated that their child needed 24-hour-a-day monitoring.
- Slightly more than half reported that they had experienced some sort of crisis requiring extraordinary intervention within the last month.

These daily care issues can manifest themselves in frequent everyday routines such as sleeping and eating. Consider the situation of the family whose child has a chronic health problem and needs special assistance while eating. His mother explains:

> I can get the most bottle into him if I start before he's totally awake. . . . I guess I spend about 1 1/2 hours in the morning and it's closer to 2 hours at lunch. That's when I get William to eat something besides just milk or formula. . . . He goes to the school in the afternoon, and I'm always late getting him there because it takes so long for him to eat. (Martin, Brady, & Kotarba, 1992, p. 10)

The child's father explains his role:

> I'm not as good as Betty when it comes to feeding William, but by 6:30 she needs a break. She eats her dinner while I feed William. I eat when I get to it. It takes about 2 hours to feed him. . . . I hadn't realized it took so long. I just know it's about 10:00 before I get to the grocery store. (Martin et al., 1992, p. 10)

Although the vast majority of children with exceptionalities do not have such extensive needs, almost every family will create family routines that are consistent with the child's needs and strengths.

Another significant daily care issue for parents of children with medical needs is dealing with the medical equipment, specialized procedures, medical appointments, and insurance paperwork (Leff & Walizer, 1992).

> Respiratory therapy 3 times a day normally. When sick or congested, 4–5 times a day, plus medications. She takes 11 different kinds of medicine, including 5 vitamins. Need to monitor stool samples daily to make sure they are solid. The inhalation therapy is not disturbing, but when we're both tired it's no fun—sometimes it's a bother. Takes a half hour 15 minutes on mask, 15 minutes pounding. It depends on her mood— if she's tired

at night, she'll sleep through it. Sometimes she'll fight all the way. (Knoll, 1992, p. 26)

Some of the issues of daily care are age related; as children with exceptionalities grow and develop, most gain an increasing and sometimes wholly independent capacity to carry out these responsibilities. You can teach children and youth daily care skills as part of their IFSP/IEP if those goals are appropriate in light of the student's strengths, preferences, and needs.

Brothers and sisters can also be collaborators. School-age children can be effective in helping their brothers or sisters with exceptionalities carry out and develop basic self-help skills (Swenson-Pierce, Kohl, & Egel, 1987). "Sometimes we ask the older girls to check the batteries in Mary Pat's hearing aid, put in new ones, help her dress or undress, monitor a bath, get her safely down the stairs. They read and sign stories, help out in a thousand other ways" (Luetke-Stahlman, Luetke-Stahlman, & Luetke-Stahlman, 1992, p. 10).

Although some children can create greater daily care needs, others do not. In fact, children with exceptionalities can make many positive contributions to this family function, helping with housekeeping, yard work, laundry, or the needs of younger siblings. As a single mother reported:

> Of my three children, the one with autism is my lifesaver when it comes to housework. He believes that everything has a place and belongs in it. His room would pass any army inspection. He organizes drawers and pulls weeds out of the flowerbeds. On the other hand, the clutter and mess in the bedrooms of my normal kids is shameful. When I ask for their help, they consider it an infringement on their social life.

Given the increasing number of "latchkey children," including those who have exceptionalities, some schools are teaming with community organizations to provide self-care instruction for parents and children. The goal of these programs is to prepare children in areas such as handling emergencies, preventing accidents and sexual abuse, managing their time, learning leisure skills, and practicing good nutrition. Staying home alone or with other siblings can be particularly challenging for students who experience exceptionalities such as learning disabilities or AD-HD because these impairments might make it more challenging for the children to make quick decisions in threatening circumstances or to use their time in a constructive and balanced way. Moreover, students who experience asthma, epilepsy, or diabetes need to know how to respond to an emergency situation, as do brothers and sisters and other people who may be close by and available to provide assistance (Koblinsky & Todd, 1991).

Socialization Needs

Socialization is vital to the overall quality of life for most individuals. Just like everyone else, persons of all ages with exceptionalities need opportunities to experience both the joys and disappointments of friendships (Meyer, Park, Grenot-Scheyer, Schwartz, & Harry, 1998). Many families experience stress in meeting the socialization needs of their child or youth with an exceptionality. In a study that involved intensive interviews with families, the majority of parents of children, youth, and adults with challenging behavior expressed disappointment and lack of hope about their son's or daughter's lack of friends (Turnbull & Ruef, 1997). In another study, parents of young children with disabilities or at risk for disabilities gave a strong priority to their children's social interactions and friendships (Guralnick, Connor, & Hammond, 1995). Forty percent of the mothers in this study expressed concern about their children being rejected by peers and the impact of that rejection on their children's self-esteem. Finally, students with learning disabilities have reported more loneliness and lower peer acceptance than their peers whose school achievement is in the average range (Malka & Meira, 1996).

Some families and professionals may welcome your encouragement and guidance in this area. Often, even empowered and supportive families and professionals may focus on other important areas of their child's development and unwittingly ignore the social dimensions of their child's life. A study of the adequacy of the IEP in documenting the students' present levels of performance related to peer interaction and in providing appropriate instruction indicated that special education and general education teachers need to know more about how their instruction can foster peer interaction (Gelzheiser, McLane, Meyers, & Pruzek, 1998). The IEPs were found to adequately describe the student's current level of performance; but, unfortunately, this accurate assessment did not lead to instruction. Teachers pointed out that the assignment of a one-on-one aide for the student appeared to limit the student's opportunities for peer and teacher interaction.

It may well be, then, that the reason that social dimensions are underemphasized is that many families and professionals are unsure of how to facilitate relationships. There are some compelling examples, however, of professionals and families who have been successful (Jamson, 1998; Meyer, Park, Grenot-Scheyer, Schwartz, & Harry, 1998). Do you remember Mr. Arias and the Cofresi family from chapter 5? You can read more about their success as well as that of other families and professionals in Turnbull, Pereira, & Blue-Banning, 1999; Turn-bull, Pereira, & Blue-Banning (in press a); and Turnbull, Pereira, & Blue-Banning (in press b). A couple of the success stories of creating friendships for students with disabilities from those articles are highlighted in box 7–5.

The Circle of Friends approach has been very successful with many students with disabilities (Falvey, 1995; Grenot-Scheyer, Abernathy, Williamson, Jubala, & Coots, 1995; O'Brien & Lyle-O'Brien, 1998; Turnbull, Pereira, & Blue-Banning, 1999). Another extremely helpful resource for preparing families and professionals to facilitate relationships is a guidebook titled *Connecting Students: A Guide to Thoughtful Friendship Facilitation for Educators and Families.* It suggests the following three steps (Schaffner & Buswell, 1992):

- Find opportunities. Bring students together so that they will have an opportunity to know each other.
- Make interpretations. Support the student, to the degree appropriate, and make connections with others in an enhancing way.
- Make accommodations. Adapt the physical environment so that individuals with disabilities have a greater opportunity to participate in a meaningful way.

Research shows how parents have been particularly successful in promoting friendships for their child with a peer who did not have a disability (Turnbull, Pereira, & Blue-Banning, 1999). Figure 7–2 highlights the friendship facilitation strategies that these families used. We encourage you to collaborate with families who are interested in friendship facilitation to support them in carrying out these facilitation strategies as well as to implement facilitation within your own educational context.

Recreation Needs

Recreation, play, and the enjoyment of leisure time are important components of life for individuals and families. Recreation includes sports, games, hobbies, or play that can be done outdoors or indoors; as a spectator or a participant; and in an independent, cooperative, or competitive manner (Dau, 1999; Moon & Bunker, 1987). A family's culture influences its views about the role of recreation and leisure. In African American culture, for example, play is regarded as necessary for promoting children's well-being:

> Play is seen as important for both social (to have friends and fun) and physical (to have a strong body) well-being. In contrast with cultures that push children toward early adulthood, in African-American families there is an attempt to give the child an opportunity to be a child and to enjoy the care and protection of responsible adults until he or she is maturationally ready for a broader role. (Willis, 1998, p. 191)

Standing Together

Angel Figueroa and Meili Quiros share two experiences. The first is demographic: They are Puerto Ricans with disabilities living in Hartford, Connecticut. Angel has a learning disability and physical impairments, and Meili has cerebral palsy and mental retardation. The second is strategic: Both have friends, but they came by them quite differently.

In Angel's case, his teacher Luis Delgado not only instructs him but also has found the way for Angel to stay out of trouble and to have a friend—a guy who is street smart where being street smart is important, given the gangs and drugs that permeate their community.

Angel's buddy is Daniel Vasquez, also from Puerto Rico, a guy who has avoided the gangs and drugs. Angel is 13, Daniel is 19, but the age difference that usually separates students in those years makes no difference to them. Daniel cautions Angel not to "look hard" or look menacing when he's around other guys. He coaches him on how to talk with girls. He encourages Angel to let off steam, and in turn he lets out his frustrations with Angel. Together, they enjoy riding bikes, playing basketball, listening to rap music, and composing their own songs.

"Of all the friends that I have, I prefer being with [Angel]," says Daniel. "Even though he's younger than my friends, I get along better with him because it's like I can do anything. I can say anything. It's okay with him. With my other friends, I gotta watch what I say."

Daniel is quick to point out, "When you live in a project, you find a way to help somebody who needs help. I knew his grandfather. My mom knew their grandmother. It was like we was family. That's the way I see it. Like we were cousins. We stand together."

Standing together isn't something that Meili, 12, and her friend Carolyn, 13, can do—not literally. Meili uses a wheelchair, even when she is competing in the Miss Puerto Rico contest in Hartford. And Carolyn herself is at a disadvantage: She and her mother Agnes are from Guyana, yet they live and work in "Spanish Hartford."

Agnes got to know Meili and her mother Lorna because she works in an agency that provides respite care for Lorna. Agnes became a close friend of Lorna and Meili.

"I do not see Lorna and her family as, well, clients. I see us as a family. That's the way I accepted her from the time I started going to her house. I tell you one thing about Guyanan culture. We are a loving people. Our motto is: Together We Stand. We go beyond friendship."

Standing together means that Agnes told her daughter Carolyn about Meili. Carolyn sought her out at school; the two became instant friends . . . and not just because Carolyn herself understands what it means to be excluded because of her traits—a black African in a brown community.

Carolyn says, "Since the first day I saw Meili, I really liked her. I've been coming [to her home] and we really got to know each other. Now it's like we are family. We visit each other. We talk and we play around. Make stuff. Sing along with tapes. Sometimes I go over and read with her."

Standing together in the streets, as Angel and Daniel do, or standing together at school assemblies, as Meili and Carolyn do—however these youngsters describe it, Luis and Agnes have played their roles as "brokers," as professionals who knew that, in spite of whatever else schools can offer, all kids need friendships.

Another cultural interpretation of recreational priorities emphasizes not so much the importance of play as the appropriate age for children or youth to participate in recreation separately from other family members. A Middle Eastern perspective illuminates this issue:

> Middle Eastern parents, particularly mothers, rarely have social and recreational activities separate from their children. Family gatherings, picnics, cinemas, and, to a lesser extent, sports events are among the most common social events in the Middle East; children are usually included in all of them. Most Middle Eastern boys do not start to have activities of their own until after puberty; for unmarried girls, this may come even later. (Sharifzadeh, 1998, p. 463)

Depending upon the nature of the child's exceptionality, the family's recreational role may be expanded, unaffected, or curtailed (Schleien & Heyne, 1998). Some children and youth have special gifts related to sports, athletics, or games (for example, chess or

Friendship Facilitation Strategies

Foundational theme
- Accepting the child/youth unconditionally (for example, loving the "disabled portion" of the child/youth and perceiving her or him as "whole" rather than "broken")

Creating opportunities
- Advocating for inclusion in the neighborhood school (for example, working to have the child/youth attend the neighborhood school rather than be bused to a school across town)
- Supporting participation in community activities (for example, enrolling the child/youth for the First Communion class and supporting the instructor to engage in comfortable interaction)
- Initiating and facilitating a Circle of Friends (for example, starting a Circle of Friends to encourage friendships within the school and community settings)

- Setting sibling-consistent expectations (for example, in light of how siblings call each other on the phone, encouraging the child/youth and his or her friends to call each other)

Making interpretations
- Encouraging others to accept the child/youth (for example, discussing their child's/youth's strengths and needs with others and supporting others to know how to communicate comfortably)
- Ensuring an attractive appearance (for example, ensuring that the child/youth is dressed and groomed in a way that is likely to draw positive and appropriate attention)

Making accommodations
- Advocating for partial participation in community activities (for example, encouraging an instructor of community activities to know how to adapt expectations to enable partial participation in completing them)

Source: Turnbull, A. P., Pereira, L., & Blue-Banning, M. J. (1999). Parents' facilitation of friendships between their children with a disability and friends without a disability. *Journal of the Association of Persons with Severe Handicaps, 24* (2), 85–99.

bridge), and a significant portion of family time may be devoted to supporting their interests and involvement.

> Because of Susan's reading disability, school has always been very hard for her. She reads slowly now but for a long time she never thought she would read at all. To make matters worse, Della and Melinda, her younger sisters, have always been star students—both of them are in the gifted program at their school. Because of these things, I really wanted to find the places where Susan could shine too. When she showed an interest in swimming, I encouraged her. She took swimming lessons at the YWCA and we all started swimming a lot as a family. Now she swims on a team for the city during the summer and next year she's decided to try out for the swim team at her high school. She has a lot of confidence in this area. She swims circles around most of her friends and all of her family! But I'm a lot better swimmer today than I would have been without her influence.

Alternatively, some families' recreation is curtailed because of the nature of their child's exceptionality, the unavailability of community resources, disapproving public reactions to their son or daughter, or general lack of ac-

commodations in making recreation possible. Families have reported substantial curtailment of activities such as going outside the home, eating in a restaurant, going on a vacation, shopping, and participating in general recreational experiences (Traustadottir, 1995). One mother has noted that she would drive her daughter with autism to the beach but would not get out of the car because of the stares and disapproving looks that her daughter would receive from other people there (Turnbull & Ruef, 1996). Similarly, a father has described issues that arise in taking his two-year-old son who is blind to a restaurant:

> We can't just pick up and go out to eat after church, our friends can't understand that. . . . Matthew doesn't sit in a highchair, and he gets overloaded by the noise in a restaurant, he gets afraid. He can't sit for one to two hours; he can't deal with the noise of the dishes, and it's hard to entertain yourself when you can't see. (Martin et al., 1992, p. 11)

Often families and professionals alike have sponsored "special populations" recreation programs rather than include children and youth with exceptionalities in typical community opportunities. A mother of a daughter with mental retardation shares how she purposely abandoned special programs in favor of inclusive ones:

> A long time ago I stopped looking at newspaper listings of special programs. . . . Now I just notice what Kathryn might like. All kinds of courses are given by community schools, YMCAs, or churches. Grandparents and teenagers, beginners, or those with some familiarity with the subject all take the same course. Though there may be beginning, intermediate, or advanced levels, nobody would notice or care if someone took the same course several times. For most of

us . . . taking enough time is more important than special techniques. (Bennett, 1985, p. 171)

Inclusive recreational opportunities help meet the recreational needs of children or youth with exceptionalities (and the family) and provide valuable experiences for their peers. Box 7–6 describes the collaborative process that was used in Iowa City, Iowa, to create an inclusive summer recreational program that responded to the preferences, strengths, and needs of all participants. This sort of collaborative process can develop a similar program in your community, and you can contribute to

TOGETHER WE CAN BOX 7–6

Hanging Out Inclusively

What do preschool and elementary school students with moderate/severe/profound mental retardation or autism do in the summer in Iowa City, Iowa? They do pretty much what their age peers without disabilities do, thanks to the collaboration of their parents, the parents of children without disabilities, the special educators in the children's schools, and the staff of the local YMCA and city parks and recreation program.

The children—all of them, those with and without disabilities—play table games, have crafts activities, play softball, fish, practice archery, enjoy free play in sandboxes and on playgrounds, and have hotdog roasts. In a word, all the children have "inclusive" summer activities.

That result occurred because a small group of committed parents, professionals, and park and recreation staffers jointly followed an eight-step process to create inclusive recreation:

- They selected the schools where the children with disabilities were enrolled to get the staff, parents, and children involved in the program.

- They surveyed community recreation programs that children without disabilities used.

- They approached the staff of those programs to solicit their participation and offer support.

- They obtained a small grant from the state department of education to pay for staff inservice, planning time, and program enrollment fees.

- They publicized the program to get participants.

- They jointly planned the program and carried it out, making sure that the children with disabilities were in age-appropriate groups, that there were "natural proportions" of those children in each group, and that the special educators served as support personnel for the recreation staff.

- They prepared the children without disabilities by formal means such as brief discussions about disabilities and informal means such as modeling inclusion.

- They carried out the recreation program; and, when the children with disabilities were not in the recreation program, they worked with the children on IEP goals.

The program evaluation was uniformly positive: The children interacted positively with each other, the recreation staff supported the program, the parents of all students—those with and without disabilities—were pleased with it, and the kids themselves had positive attitudes about their peers with disabilities.

A parent of two boys who did not have disabilities who attended the camp commented, "Our sons talked about special kids all of the time. They were the main topic at our supper table. We were pleased because our boys showed so much care. We had our eyes open because they thought of them as kids just like themselves" (Hamre-Nietupski et al., 1992, p. 73).

Source: Adapted from Hamre-Nietupski, S., Krajewski, L., Riehl, R., Sensor, K., Nietupski, J., Moravec, J., McDonald, J., & Cantine-Stull, P. (1992). Enhancing integration during the summer: Combined educational and community recreation options for students with severe disabilities. *Education and Training in Mental Retardation, 27*(1), 68–74.

that effort. But bear in mind that some individuals with exceptionalities and their families prefer special populations programs (such as Special Olympics or its "integrated sports" programs) for a variety of reasons, including a belief (with justification) that the programs provide more supervision, structure, and accommodations.

It is encouraging to note that attitudes on inclusion of individuals with disabilities into typical community recreation such as regular softball leagues appears to be moving in a positive direction. One research study investigated the attitudes of girls without disabilities, their parents, and their coaches toward the inclusion of a girl with a disability on the regular softball team. The girls and parents favored including a child with a disability in the softball league and modifying the rules to facilitate her inclusion. The five coaches were undecided in their attitude toward inclusion and toward rules modification. Regarding rules modification, two of the five coaches responded negatively to all suggested modifications, whereas three coaches responded with some combination of affirmative and probably affirmative answers (Block & Malloy, 1998).

Too often, schools have minimized educational objectives for leisure and recreation; yet leisure and recreation should be an important part of each child's curriculum (Schleien, Green, & Heyne, 1993). From a family systems perspective, you will want to find out from families what recreational hobbies and interests they particularly enjoy and where in the community they would especially like to pursue these activities. Then the student's teachers can promote the skills the child needs and help the recreation staff accommodate for the family's and the child's preferences. In addition to strengthening recreational skills, this approach can enhance self-esteem, socialization, and educational achievement. It can also ease the stress of daily care demands and not impose additional economic responsibilities on the family if the community recreational opportunities are available at no charge.

*E*ducation Needs

Across cultures, families generally place a strong emphasis on education. Within the Euro-American culture, education is typically seen as the key to success in employment, financial, and quality-of-life opportunities (Hanson, 1998). A similar Asian perspective appears in this Chinese proverb (Chan, 1998, p. 293):

> If you are planning for a year, sow rice; if you are planning for a decade, plant trees; if you are planning for a lifetime, educate people.

Families from diverse cultural and linguistic backgrounds often encounter significant educational and social barriers in attaining equal opportunities for their children (Harry, 1992a, 1992b; Harry, Allen, & McLaughlin, 1995). As a Native American grandparent stated:

> I had children and grandchildren who are really gifted. At one time they brought home a lot of high marks from school, but they learned that if they were good achievers they would be harassed at school, so they didn't want their peers to know about their good grades. The school talks about this, but they don't know what to do about it. There should be something we could do to stop this trend and turn these other kids around. Some parents, who have money or were in education and knew their child was gifted, would pull their children out of the school and send them to a white school. (U.S. Department of Education, 1990, p. 5)

Throughout this book, you will learn about families' roles in meeting their children's educational needs. Here we will emphasize the importance of families maintaining balance in family functions rather than overemphasizing education to the detriment of other functions. In chapter 8, in which we address life cycle considerations, we will describe two educational tasks that many families assume at four different life cycle stages.

One of the fundamental premises of a family systems approach is the importance of maintaining balance in carrying out family roles. As we discussed in chapter 1, sometimes professionals especially emphasize the role of parents as teachers or tutors. That emphasis is appropriate if it is consistent with a family's values, priorities, and available time. If it is not, the differences among the focus of school, other service agencies, and home can cause strain or conflict in home-school relationships and can impair the development of reliable alliances. Indeed, many parents and students with exceptionalities respond negatively to professional overemphasis on educational needs. Professionals should remember that educational needs are only one function that families must address. Maddux and Cummings (1983) warn:

> If academic learning is required in both the home and the school, a child who has difficulty learning gets very little relief. The home ceases to be a haven from scholastic pressures. Imagine how most of us would feel if the most frustrating, least enjoyable, and most difficult thing about our work were waiting for us when we came home each day. (p. 30)

We encourage you to beware of the "fix-it" approach whereby children and youth with exceptionalities are almost continuously placed in quasi-teaching situations by well-intentioned teachers, family, and friends. These perpetual educational efforts to make the child "better" may have a negative impact on self-esteem, as Harriet Rousso (1984) noted when writing about her mother's approach to her physical therapy:

> Being disabled and being intact at the same time is an extremely difficult notion for non-disabled people to make sense of. I kept thinking of my mother's words: Why wouldn't you want to walk straight? Even now, it is hard to explain that I may have wanted to walk straight, but I did not want to lose my sense of myself in the process. Perhaps the best I can say is that my perspective on disability, from the inside out, is different from my mother's, from the outside looking in. In our work with congenitally disabled clients, we must always be receptive and respectful of that difference. (Rousso, 1984, p. 12)

Professionals and families need to be keenly aware of a perspective on disability from the inside out. That is one reason why adults with disabilities can be valued mentors, role models, and consultants in assisting professionals, families, and young children with disabilities to gain this vital perspective (Turnbull & Turbiville, 1995).

Encouraging educational achievement is particularly prevalent in the homes of students who have been identified as gifted and talented (Friedman, 1994); and families especially benefit from collaboration with educators, as you will read in box 7–7.

Parents tend to place special emphasis on the particular area of their son's or daughter's special interest and to provide early and continued opportunities for growth and development (Clark & Zimmerman, 1988; Raymond & Benbow, 1989). One study reported that 70 percent of artistically talented students indicated parental support for their artwork and 65 percent had a place to do their art at home (Clark & Zimmerman, 1988). Friedman (1994) warns that many low-income parents of students who are gifted have been found not to place as much emphasis on educational achievement; however, she cautions that the additional attention that these families must devote to issues concerning housing, dangerous neighborhoods, unemployment, and other stressors should not be interpreted to mean that the families do not support their children who are gifted.

Time as a Factor in Meeting Family Functions

We encourage you to review the eight functions that we have just discussed and to imagine yourself as Rickey's parents. If you were Richard or Betty Battles seeking to raise two boys, Rickey and Michael, as well as run the gro-cery store, participate in the life of your community, have a little time for yourself, and meet the collaboration responsibilities that are required in ensuring that Rickey's great expectations come true, when would you find time to address all eight family functions? Might there be slippage when there were simply not enough hours in the day to go around for all the family functions? In these situations, how would you want Rickey's teachers to support you and your family? Would you want them to judge you as "not caring enough about Rickey to meet 100 percent of his needs," or would you hope that they would "cut you some slack," recognizing that you are juggling as many responsibilities in the finite 24-hour day as possible?

Undoubtedly, time is a major issue, if not the major issue, for many families. Just keep in mind that approximately two-thirds of all employed parents with children under 18 report that they do not have enough time to meet their children's needs (Families and Work Institute, 1994), that they often leave their children unattended at home, and that they rely on their children to be occupied by watching television. If this is the report from parents, most of whom have children without exceptionalities, what impact on the family do some of the tasks associated with exceptionality have?

In a number of studies of parents of children with disabilities, parents have reported major time limitations in attending to the needs of various family members as well as to the different family functions. Regarding interactions with family members, parents reported (1) spending less time with their spouse and children without disabilities than with their child with a disability, and (2) having almost no time for themselves (Bailey, Blasco, & Simeonsson, 1992). Regarding family functions, parents of children and adolescents with Down syndrome reported that mothers devoted less time to paid work (economics) and social activities and more time to child care (Barnett & Boyce, 1995). Fathers also increased their child care time and decreased their social activities.

In box 7–8 you will read the words of Helen Featherstone, the mother of a son with a severe disability, who had no unclaimed time in her day or night. What would you have expected of the Featherstone family if you had been Jody's parents? What if you had been his occupational therapist, teacher, or dentist? What balance should be struck between meeting the child's disability-related needs and the needs of the entire family?

In chapter 6 we discussed how mothers and fathers distribute household duties. Typically, attending to the daily care needs of family members has been "women's work," and female caring roles often expand when the child has an exceptionality (Traustadottir, 1995). Mothers expressed the commitment to maintain

Homeschool to College Quickly

I was identified as gifted before I started kindergarten, and in seventh grade I was selected to take the SAT as part of the Duke University Talent Identification Program. I qualified for national honors, and I attended the award ceremony at Duke. There we spoke with several families who had selected homeschooling as the best educational alternative.

We lived in a troubled school district, and when we looked at the high cost of private high school, homeschooling abruptly became a more viable option. My mom had left her job due to contracting cytomegalovirus and was working on freelance writing from home, and when we looked at the various pros and cons, we decided to homeschool. We continued with this program until I was a sophomore in high school.

I then decided I wanted to try college and see if I was ready to attend early. At that time my mom had just become Assistant Director of the University of Missouri-Kansas City Women's Center, so UMKC seemed like a natural choice. So in the fall of 1998, I enrolled in two junior-senior (300-level) English classes not-for-credit, and while it was tough (there was a LOT of reading) I received A's in both classes, despite having to have major surgery right before the final.

In fall 1999, after discussions with the Admissions and Financial Aid offices of UMKC, I enrolled in UMKC as a degree-seeking freshman taking 13 hours.

I was also invited to join several groups that were created for gifted students. The Circle of Excellence is a program for scholarship recipients. The Student Life Office's Emerging Leaders program teaches students leadership and teamwork skills that will help them in later life. I also joined the Honors Program, a division of the College of Arts and Sciences. And finally, I've started working part-time in the Serials Acquisitions Department of the university library. I haven't decided on a major yet, but I'm almost certainly going to be a history major. I'm young enough that I can get two bachelor's degrees by the age others have one—a definite plus when applying for a job I want. I'm also planning to join several student organizations, including the History Club and the Communication Studies Club. Perhaps a little later, I want to start a club myself for fans of Japanese animation. I plan to stay at UMKC, but spend my junior year studying abroad (either in Japan or England) because UMKC has a very good Study Abroad program, and because this may be my only chance to have the freedom to do this. I'm debating whether to

start on a master's degree after I graduate—I think I probably will.

Even though I'm younger than all of the other students, I don't particularly feel that I have trouble fitting in (despite numerous concerns by people that I was missing out on important "socialization" during my years of homeschooling). I've gotten to know people in my classes and honors group as well as other members of the Circle of Excellence and Emerging Leaders, and I hope that I'll be able to maintain these friendships throughout my life.

These opportunities would not have been possible without the help of many people: Linda Rodriguez, my mom; Ben Furnish, my stepfather, who now works on campus as well, as the Managing Editor of BkMk Press; Jan Brandow (formerly of Financial Aid, now the Assistant to the Interim Provost/Vice-Chancellor of Academic Affairs); Drs. Lois Spatz and Peter Struck, my professors during my not-for-credit semester; Dr. Harris Mirkin, head of the Honors Program; Zauyah Abdullah, Cesar Paniamogan, and Lori Byrd, my contacts in the Student Life Office and mentors during the Emerging Leaders program; Dannielle Davis, coordinator of the Circle of Excellence Program; and everyone in the Serials Acquisitions Department at the Miller Nichols Library.

---

an ordinary family life (Traustadottir, 1995), simply being able to carry out the daily routines of their life without the child's limiting those routines. Rather than assessing the severity of their child's exceptionality according to traditional standards, they more frequently interpreted severity according to the extent of limitations and constraints placed on family life routines. As one mother described, "I feel like a wishbone being pulled apart in different directions" (Renwick, Brown, & Raphael, 1998, p. 13).

There are no blanket generalizations concerning the kinds of limitations and constraints that children and

Where Will I Find the Time?

I remember the day when the occupational therapist at Jody's school called with some suggestions from a visiting nurse. Jody has a seizure problem which is controlled with the drug Dilantin. Dilantin can cause the gums to grow over the teeth; the nurse had noticed this overgrowth, and recommended innocently enough, that [his] teeth be brushed four times a day, for 5 minutes, with an electric toothbrush. The school suggested that they could do this once on school days, and that I should try to do it the other three times a day; this new demand appalled me; Jody is blind, cerebral palsied, and retarded. We do his physical therapy daily and work with him on sounds and communication. We feed him each meal on our laps, bottle him, bathe him, dry him, put him in a body cast to sleep, launder his bed linens daily, and go through a variety of routines designed to minimize his miseries and enhance his joys and his development. (All this in addition to trying to care for and enjoy our other young children and making time for each other and our careers.) Now you tell me that I should spend 15 minutes every day on something that Jody will hate, an activity that will not help him to walk or even defecate, but one that is directed at the health of his gums. This activity is not for a finite time, but forever. It is not guaranteed to help, but "it can't hurt." And it won't make the overgrowth go away but may retard it. Well, it's too much. Where is that 15 minutes going to come from? What am I supposed to give up? Taking the kids to the park? Reading a bedtime story to my eldest? Washing the breakfast dishes? Sorting the laundry? Grading students' papers? Sleeping? Because there is not time in my life that hasn't been spoken for, and for every 15-minute activity that is added one has to be taken away.

Source: Excerpted from *A Difference in the Family* by Helen Featherstone. Copyright © 1980 by Basic® Books, Inc. Reprinted by permission of BasicBooks, a division of HarperCollins Publishers, Inc.

---

youth with exceptionalities place on family living. Again, it all depends upon family characteristics, family interaction, family functions, and family lifespan issues. In the Battles family's case, they have learned to provide the support that Rickey needs and do not consider it to be a significant imposition on their family routines. In other words, they have developed routines that are compatible with his support needs.

Clearly, a significant factor is the family's level of adaptability, as you learned in chapter 6. Consider two families, one that maintains a very strict schedule and is quite frustrated by any change and another that has a balanced level of adaptability characterized by flexible rules and routines. If these two families had children with identical characteristics, the family with more balanced adaptability probably would have less difficulty in carrying out daily care responsibilities than the family whose roles and routines are strictly implemented.

In a study of family and professional perspectives toward time, parents identified four issues that served as barriers to their efficient and effective use of time—indeed, four ways in which the professional context was not empowering (Brotherson & Goldstein, 1992, p. 518):

1. The inability of professionals to coordinate their activities among themselves;
2. The overwhelming number of tasks parents were asked by professionals to complete;
3. The lack of local and accessible services; and
4. A lack of flexible and family-centered scheduling of services.

You can make a significant contribution to the quality of family life by helping to remove time barriers and by facilitating ways to use time efficiently and effectively. Parent suggestions for effective time use include the following:

Parents wanted education and therapy for their child to be part of their daily routine and environment. They wanted to work well with professionals to provide care for their children: Time was wasted if activities were learned in artificial settings or if the knowledge of parents was ignored. They wanted professionals to aid their efficiency and effectiveness by using current technology when it is applicable.

Further, they wanted to be given more time to develop rapport with professionals. (Brotherson & Goldstein, 1992, p. 515)

One of the greatest lessons that you can derive from understanding family functions is how busy family life is. We encourage you to keep in perspective that educational issues are one of eight functions; and families may or may not be able to devote the time to educational issues that you, as an educational professional, might deem desirable. As you pursue your career and your own family life, it is likely that you will experience these same time crunches. Particularly for families who have a child with a severe disability, it is critical to recognize that they are dealing with lifelong issues, ones that require the endurance of a marathon runner, not a sprinter. Professionals, however, often are tempted to urge the parents to make substantial investments of time over the short term (like a sprinter) to enhance what the child might be able to learn. "Parents think of time as daily routine, they also see the care of their child as an ongoing, life long, ever-evolving commitment, not a short-term education or therapeutic contact. This is a significant difference in time orientation that should be highlighted for professional understanding of families" (Brotherson & Goldstein, 1992, p. 523).

Summary

Families exist to meet the individual and collective needs of their members. The tasks they perform to meet those needs are referred to as family functions; in a family systems framework, they are the outputs. There are eight categories of functions or outputs: affection, self-esteem, spiritual, economics, daily care, socialization, recreation, and education.

When collaborating with families around these functions, you would do well to bear the following in mind:

- Families' cultures influence the ways they carry out these functions.
- Families may or may not spend the amount or type of time on each function that you predict you would spend if you were in their situation.
- The child with an exceptionality as well as every family member influences how the family performs each of these eight functions.
- The child's impact can be both positive and negative and will depend in part on the family's own characteristics (chapter 5), family interactions (chapter 6), and life cycle stages and transitions (chapter 8).
- The family members' motivation as well as their knowledge/skills will influence how they carry out their functions and how you can most successfully collaborate with them.
- There are some concrete steps you can take as you collaborate with families to build a reliable alliance around each of these functions.
- Family life is busy, and time is a valuable and limited resource.

Rickey Battles is beating the odds. He's not doing it alone. His family is a powerful resource for him, and each member contributes to meeting his needs in different ways. Similarly, the good citizens of Poultney, Vermont, make a positive difference in his and his family's life, whether they are the owners and customers of the pet shop where he gets his vocational education, his peers who do not have disabilities, or special and general educators and the school nurse.

Whatever Rickey's and his family's needs might be, the ground rule for the Battles family and their collaborators is clear-cut and simple: All of Rickey's needs are put onto the table so the collaboration team can begin to meet them. In meeting his needs, the team also addresses some of the functions that the Battles family, like every other family, performs. Not surprisingly, that approach to collaboration and, indeed, Rickey himself gives meaning to the collaborators' lives. In doing so, the approach meets some of each collaboration team member's needs. In a real sense, what goes around in collaboration comes around: The reciprocity and mutuality within the collaboration team creates a reliable alliance for everyone—Rickey, the Battles family, and every single team member.

Chapter Eight

Family Life Cycle

*T*here certainly was denial, that feeling that Jessica was going to get better, always that hope that she was going to get better.

To listen to Tricia Baccus-Luker was to hear that hope. But it also was to hear this: "If the seizures don't kill her, certainly all of the drugs are going to. I imagine one day her liver is just going to get tired and give up. The metabolic disorder only makes Jessica's epilepsy and cognitive impairment more complicated. Jessica's doctor simply told us that she has a degenerative disease and that he doesn't anticipate that she will live past the age of 25."

Jessica was 19 years old when she last appeared in this book. At that time, she and her family mother Tricia, her biological father Craig, and younger sisters Melissa and Lara lived time-compressed existences.

That was then.

The quotation you just read is from Tricia, speaking in 1995. Tragically, her words were pinpointedly accurate. Jessica died in September, 1999, at the age of 24 years and 29 days.

During the four years between Tricia's words about denial and hope and Jessica's death, life in her family was tumultuous. Tricia and Craig divorced. Tricia remarried to Calvin Luker, an attorney with the Michigan protection and advocacy agency. Jessica's sister Melissa graduated from high school, moved into a friend's home, then into Craig's and her stepmother's home, then into her own apartment. She now lives with her father, who divorced his second wife and moved into his daughter's apartment. Lara, Jessica's other sister, left junior high school, entered high school, and is preparing to graduate within a year. Tricia changed jobs. And Jessica—well, she too had dramatic changes.

As Jessica grew older, her seizures occurred more often and were more disabling. Changed regimens of medication seemed to be of little help. The two surgeries she endured seemed to produce no benefits until, during the spring of 1999, she had a third surgery and received a "vagus nerve stimulator." That is a battery-operated device implanted under her arm, with a wire that attaches to the vagus nerve in her neck; the nerve connects to the brain (the seat of her seizures). So, by regulating the impulses of the vagus nerve, the device regulated the part of her brain that was responsible for her seizures. For the first time in her life, Jessica was nearly seizure-free. To Tricia and Calvin, she was "doing better than she'd done in probably 12 to 15 years. She was doing so well. It was the best six weeks, I think, that she'd ever had in her whole life."

But during those "best" six weeks, Jessica kept telling Tricia and Calvin that she was going to die. Their response was incredulous: "Don't say that, honey, you're doing so well." Yet, she did indeed die.

"I think maybe she knew," Tricia says. "I think maybe for just a moment the veil parted and Jessica knew. And she was telling us that she was okay." Accompanying this "revelation" was "her mantra," her constant repetition of "I love you."

Those were weeks of joy. "We were just embracing . . . that we were conquering. . . . She was just doing so

well. . . . We had holidays. Everybody was together. She was so happy. . . . It seemed like everyone called within the last two weeks. . . . It just seemed that everything fell into place. . . . So we all said goodbye, but we just didn't know we did."

Days before she died, Jessica walked through the house singing her favorite song, from the movie *Dirty Dancing:* "I've had the time of my life, and I owe it all to you." To everybody she met, she sang out, "And I owe it all to you." She was, Tricia recalls, "just so exuberant." Those days were among the many gifts Jessica gave her family and community.

What gift may Tricia and Calvin find in Jessica's death? That is a question with which they struggle. "Do we have enough courage to go on without her? When you lose a parent, you grieve for the past. When you lose a spouse, you grieve for the present. And when you lose a child, you grieve for the future. The hard part is to walk the future without her."

Jessica "was our daily routine. To walk with her in life, that was the easy walk. Our marriage revolved around her. Now, we have time . . . time for each other, but, at the same time, we have guilt and regret that Jessica is not here. Her routine was ours."

"We felt so powerless at her death," says Tricia. "We were always focused on the present." Being focused on the present, however, means that Tricia and Calvin have no "sorries," no regrets about Jessica's life. "We pursued inclusion," Calvin says proudly. "And we never placed her into an institution or facility," says Tricia. "Home," Jessica would say after each hospitalization, "is where I belong." And that is where she lived and died, peacefully, in her sleep.

To Calvin, she "made people think differently, about what is really meaningful." To search for what is meaningful, and to find it—there is a difference between the two. One is a process, as in the "walk" that Jessica made Tricia and Calvin take. The other is a result, more elusive.

"I never expected Jessica to go at the apex of life," says Calvin. "I expected some warning so we could fight, could tell her how much we loved her. I always believed I would

Jessica Baccus. (1999)

153

have a fighting chance to say a fitting goodbye before she died. It makes you wonder, what's the purpose of all this?"

Tricia and Calvin search for the meaning of their daughter's death, but they know full well the meaning of her life. During her last IEP meeting, she, Tricia, Calvin, and Jessica's teachers and special education director made a plan to meet Jessica's ambition—a home of her own. There, she would live with three friends. "No one discouraged us," recalls Calvin. "They embraced the idea. They volunteered to make her home come true, to be part of our family, as it were."

When Jessica died, Tricia and Calvin created a trust, "Living Opportunities—

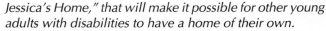

Jessica's Home," that will make it possible for other young adults with disabilities to have a home of their own.

"What's the purpose of all this?" asked Calvin. In many respects, he has answered his own question: to continue Jessica's gifts, to honor her life in a way that would meet her approval. "How we bear ourselves now and in the future," they agree, "is the measure of what Jessica gave us, of what she helped us become." What they have become is the transmitters of Jessica's own life. What a paradox! Children usually transmit their parents' lives, from one generation to another. That's the normal cycle. For Jessica, Tricia, and Calvin, it's the other way around.

In the previous three chapters, we discussed the family system and how it is affected by a member with an exceptionality. The dominant image is one of multilayered complexity. First, families differ in their characteristics to such an extent that we can truly say that every family is unique. Second, every family is an interactive system: Anything that happens to one person reverberates throughout the whole family. Third, every family is busily engaged in a variety of functions designed to fulfill a number of tangible and intangible needs.

Yet another layer of complexity—the fourth layer, called life cycle changes—affects the family system (Robinson & Stalker, 1998). The portrait of the first three layers—family characteristics, interactions, and functions—is only a snapshot of what should more accurately be portrayed as a full-length motion picture. All families progress through stages and transitions as its members are born, grow up, leave home, bring in new members through marriage or other permanent relationships, retire, and die. In addition to expected life cycle changes, families may experience unexpected or sudden changes that drastically alter their lives, such as divorce, death, separation by military service, immigration, job transfers, unemployment, a windfall inheritance, or natural catastrophes. Those are the kinds of changes that Tricia, Calvin, Jessica, Melissa, and Lara have faced over a four-year period of time. Whether the change is expected and natural so that it is "on cycle" or unexpected and unnatural so that it is "off cycle," the family changes; and as it does, so do its characteristics (chapter 5), its interactions (chapter 6), and its functions (chapter 7). The Baccus-Luker family's characteristics are much different now than four years ago: Jessica has died and Melissa has

moved out; its interactions are different, for Jessica's routine no longer becomes her parents' routine; and its functions are different, for the constant caregiving that Jessica's disability required is no longer there. In the family systems framework (figure 8–1), we show how the family system and family life cycle changes relate to each other.

Family Life Cycle Theory

Family life cycle theory seeks to explain how a family changes over time. The theory is that each family experiences certain predictable and stable stages. As the family moves from one stage to the next, it enters an interim phase known as *transition.*

For example, families typically experience a childbirth and child-raising stage. The parents learn to care for the child and understand what parenthood really entails, and the child typically learns how to talk, walk, and explore the environment of home and perhaps preschool (Carter & McGoldrick, 1989; Rodgers & White, 1993).

The exact number and character of individual life cycle stages are arbitrary. Theorists have identified as many as twenty-four and as few as six (Carter & McGoldrick, 1989). Life cycle stages are historically specific. A hundred years ago, when people tended to have large families and shorter lifespans, a post-parental life stage (when there are no dependent children in the household) was rare (Hareven, 1982).

Life cycle theorists usually regard a family as having three life cycle stages (three generations) defined by the particular life cycle stages of each member in a family (Terkelson, 1980). For example, the eldest member of a

FIGURE 8–1

Family Systems Framework: Emphasis on Family Life Cycle

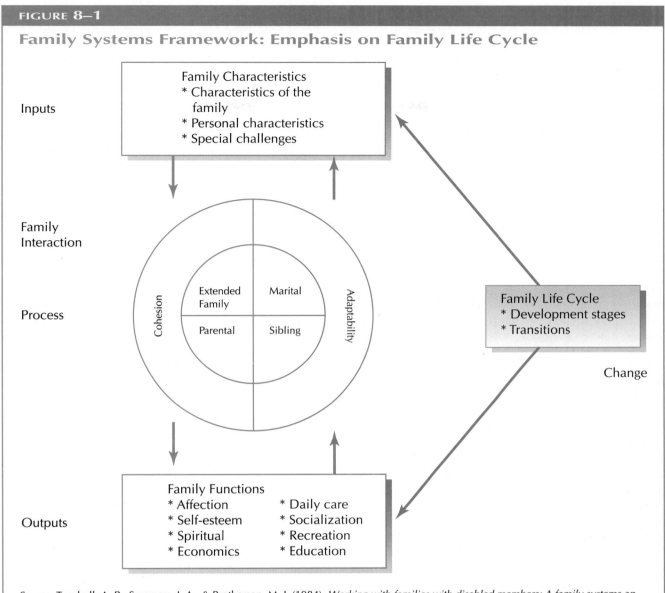

Source: Turnbull, A. P., Summers, J. A., & Brotherson, M. J. (1984). *Working with families with disabled members: A family systems approach* (p. 60). Lawrence: University of Kansas, Kansas Affiliated Facility. Adapted by permission.

family might be entering old age and facing the task of preparing for death; their children may be facing mid-career shifts or the prospect of an empty nest; and their grandchildren may be leaving home and experiencing the first travails of independent adulthood.

To describe family life cycle, however, it is not enough to say that it is the sum of each person's life cycle. A more accurate description is that it encompasses the interactions among all changes in the family (Carter & McGoldrick, 1989; Olson, 1988). In the example of the three genera-

tions, the middle generation may face responsibility for parents who have increasing needs for care while also beginning to let go of their responsibility for their own children. As family members' responsibility shifts, their values and approaches to life are transmitted across the generations, thereby preserving the basic identity of the family even while the main characters change (Carter & McGoldrick, 1989). Of course, it does not always happen that way. Some families such as Jessica's find that their values are shaped and transmitted from the younger to the older generation not, as in many families, the other way around. Expecting the unexpected is sometimes necessary, as you can learn from listening to the words of a father who was simultaneously caring for his 81-year-old mother, 21-year-old son with a developmental disability, and 13-year-old teenage daughter while also working 50 hours a week: "I felt whipsawed. No matter how much I did for one generation, there was always another whose needs cried out to me with such fervor that I felt I couldn't fulfill all of them. In a sense, my mother had become my son, because she had the greater disability and because he was becoming more independent."

Beyond the developmental tasks that the family and individual members must accomplish at each stage, there are the transitions from one stage to another. Transitions are the periods between stages when the family is adjusting its interactions and roles to meet the needs and challenges of the next developmental stage (McGoldrick & Carter, 1989; Rodgers & White, 1993). Predictably, when the child leaves the birth and early childhood stage and enters the childhood stage, the child and the family alike embark on a transition. With that transition come changes in the family's characteristics (for example, the personal characteristics of the child); the family's interactions (for example, the parental subsystem changes as the child is older and is able to communicate with the parents and contribute to the family in a different way); and family functions (for example, the child spends more time in school and on doing homework and is able to contribute more to daily care) (Carter & McGoldrick, 1989). When the transition is complete, and the transition itself may take a while, the family has reached the next stage. It performs tasks and has interactions appropriate to that stage. Thus, as a child enters adolescence, the family may need, on the one hand, to become more flexible and allow the teenager more personal freedom (adaptability). On the other hand, the family may need to maintain a family identity for all members, especially the adolescent (cohesion). That is the balancing act that Tricia and Calvin performed as they watched Jessica grow as an adolescent while she simultaneously needed more support and as they also attended to the equally legitimate needs of their two other daughters, Melissa and Lara.

Transition periods are usually briefer than the stages to which they relate. But because these shifts may result in confusion and conflict, transitions are almost always times of heightened stress (Carter & McGoldrick, 1989; Olson et al., 1983). The Baccus-Luker family admits being confused by Jessica's without-warning death: What is the purpose of that unwelcome event? And their daughter Melissa is conflicted between the love she has for Jessica and the feelings that Jessica absorbed so much of the family's attention.

Using life cycle theory to understand family change has at least two advantages: (1) It highlights families' similar rhythms over time, and (2) it aids in understanding the continuity of family life. But life cycle theory has been criticized for not sufficiently taking into account varying norms across different cultural groups, family forms, and disability-related factors (Rodgers & White, 1993; Turnbull, Summers, & Brotherson, 1986). For example, some ethnic groups place a strong emphasis on close extended families and less value on independence; thus, adults may not leave their parental home to set up a separate household (Harry & Kalyanpur, 1994; Kalyanpur & Harry, 1999; Turnbull & Turnbull, 1996).

Further, in remarried families, particularly those with older children from a previous marriage, several life cycle stages may occur simultaneously as children from the first marriage approach adulthood and as the newly married couple give birth to their own children (Sager et al., 1983).

Finally, many exceptionality-related issues affect a family. For example, youth like Jessica, whose disabilities cause progressive decline, move into the future with less capability than they had experienced at younger ages. For some families affected by disability, the future means longer but not necessarily easier lives. That was the case for the Baccus-Luker family: Jessica lived nearly the 25 years that medical predictions allotted to her, and those years were, until the very end, hardly easy.

We will concentrate on the four major life cycle stages during which the family is most likely to experience contact with schools: birth and early childhood, childhood, adolescence, and young adulthood. Then we will discuss the general issues of transition from one stage to another and how exceptionality affects and is affected by the family's ability to adjust smoothly to change. As you read, keep in mind the fluidity of the life cycle and the energy and persistence that families need as they run the marathon and face the hurdles of life cycle transitions.

Life Cycle Stages

To illustrate how family functions and their priorities change as the family moves through the life cycle, for each of the selected four stages, we will highlight two educational issues that many families typically encounter. That way, we will concentrate on one of the eight family functions about which you learned in chapter 7.

Birth and Early Childhood

For most families, the early childhood years are a period when the family is intensely absorbed with its inner workings (Olson et al., 1983). If the family is not a married family (in which new marital partners already have children), the childless couple (assuming that there is a couple and remembering that often there is a single parent only) probably has explored the parameters of its relationship, has begun to weld the norms of two families of origin into one new unit, and has learned how to respond to each other's needs. Now, sometimes quite unexpectedly, one or more small newcomers arrive on the scene, each dependent on the parents for his or her physical and emotional well-being. While the children are learning to master their bodies and their immediate environment, their parents are facing the task of nurturing their children and meeting their own needs. In addition, a family that has a member with an exceptionality faces a number of educational challenges. Two of these challenges are (1) discovering and coming to terms with the exceptionality and (2) participating in early childhood services.

Discovering and Coming to Terms with Exceptionality Infants with severe and multiple disabilities, in contrast to those with mild disabilities, typically are identified at birth as having special needs. Nowadays, however, early identification can sometimes be made prenatally, and even fetal therapy can occur in the first three or four months of pregnancy (Batshaw & Rose, 1997). With such advanced identification, some families make a decision to have an abortion while others use the advanced diagnosis to prepare for the coming birth of a child with special needs (Elkins, Stoval, Wilroy, & Dacus, 1997; Helm, Miranda, & Angoff-Chedd, 1998; Sandler, 1997).

Regardless of whether the diagnosis happens prenatally, at birth, or during the early years, the professional literature holds that families experience a "grief cycle." The cycle has been likened to stages of dealing with the death of loved ones. It includes shock, denial, guilt and anger, shame and depression, and acceptance (Kubler-Ross, 1969; Leff & Walizer, 1992; Moses, 1983). Research and clinical literature, largely based on clinical case studies in the 1960s and 1970s, has concentrated on grief stages experienced by mothers and has been described in later years as sorely lacking in empirical evidence (Blacher, 1984a, 1984b). Nonetheless, you will encounter the literature and the theory behind it, as stated by Ken Moses (1983):

> The grieving process . . . is a feeling process that permits the parent of a developmentally disabled child to separate from dreams and fantasies generated in anticipation of the birth of that child. The inability to successfully separate from such a dream is devastating to both parent and child. If the parent does not generate new dreams that the child can fulfill, then

each day the child would be experienced as a disappointment and failure in the eyes of the parent. . . . It is within this context of development that the concept of facilitating grief becomes an important tool in the intervention and habilitation of developmentally disabled children. (Moses, 1983, pp. 27–28)

A parent who had just given birth to a child with Down syndrome gives credence to the grief cycle theory when she describes her feelings:

> Shock, grief, bitter disappointment, fury, horror, my feelings were a mixture of all these after my doctor told me that our new little son, Peter, was born with Down syndrome. I was afraid to have him brought from the nursery. . . . I didn't want to see this monster. But when the nurse brought in this tiny, black-haired baby with up-tilted, almond-shaped eyes, my heart melted. . . . But the grief and fear didn't go away just because we fell in love with our son. They came in great, overwhelming waves. I felt a deep need to cry it out to cry and cry until I had worked this immense sorrow up from the center of my being and out into the open. . . . I think we should give honest and full expression to our grief. I suspect that when, in our attempts to be brave and face the future we repress our feelings, these feelings of pain and sorrow last longer. All I'm trying to say is that there's a time for weeping and then a time for pushing ahead, and I don't think you can do the second without going through the first. (Vyas, 1983, p. 17)

Although the grief-cycle conception is firmly rooted within much of the professional literature and in training programs, we encourage you to consider some alternative perspectives. The first perspective is that the clinical description of parental grief has failed to document how the "grieving" parents were initially told by professionals and what they were told about the presence of their child's exceptionality (Lee, 1994). Ruth Johnson, mother of a 15-year-old with Down syndrome, describes how she learned about her son's exceptionality: "About 8 p.m. the doctor came in and said abruptly: 'Read the numbers on the baby's ID bracelet and the one on your wrist. See, it's the same. This baby is yours. This happens to women your age. You may want genetic counseling, and you'll probably want to put it in a home.' "

In a recent study involving interviews with parents on how the prenatal diagnosis of Down syndrome was shared with them, 6 of the 10 mothers reported that their obstetrician or the obstetrical nurse reflected negative attitudes when discussing the diagnosis with them (Helm, Miranda, & Angoff-Chedd, 1998). One mother reported that the obstetrician commented, "This child will not accomplish anything. Everyone [in my practice] has aborted" (Helm et al., 1998, p. 57).

From this same research study, mothers provided advice to professionals about how they want information to be given to parents who are undergoing prenatal testing. Figure 8–2 includes this advice.

If information were shared in a supportive way and if a family were immediately linked to resources, what difference do you think those approaches might make in family members' emotional reactions? To their hope, sense of self-efficacy, perceived control, and coping skills? Diane Gerst (1991) shares her personal view of the grief process in box 8–1.

Judy O'Halloran, the mother of a son with a disability, counters the grief perspective by describing a "celebration process," a process of reflecting positively and hopefully on the emotions associated with the diagnosis of disability. She suggests that the celebration process moves beyond mere acceptance or adaptation. It emphasizes how negative emotions and behaviors can serve as catalysts for energy and persistence (the motivation elements of empowerment). She also stresses how

the celebration process affirms the positive contributions that children with disabilities make to their families (O'Halloran, 1995).

Not surprisingly, much of the literature about grieving comes from Euro-American professionals and families who are writing about their cultural peers. The initial diagnosis and the impact on families from multicultural perspectives are not yet well understood. From a Native American orientation, one might expect the following:

> When a family member has a disability or illness, traditional ceremonies are conducted to begin the healing process and to protect the individual and the rest of the home from further harm. For that reason, an Indian family may want to complete traditional ceremonies before they seek or become involved in a regime recommended by physicians or other service providers. (Joe & Malach, 1998, p. 148)

Interestingly, developmental milestones also have cultural variations. In a Euro-American culture, a major milestone occurs as the child begins to walk, whereas a first laugh, first hurt, first dance, or ear piercing may have similar priority for some native tribes (Joe & Malach, 1998; Sipes, 1993).

Children who are highly gifted are frequently identified during the infancy and early childhood years (Dalzell, 1998). Often these children show fast development in verbal and mathematics skills, which sometimes creates stress and difficulty for families and professionals alike in providing adequate educational stimulation (Dalzell, 1998; Maxwell, 1998).

In chapter 11, we will make suggestions about how to inform families about the presence of an exceptionality and how, in so doing, to foster a reliable alliance by bolstering their motivation (especially self-efficacy, perceived control, and hope). At this point, just remember that discovering the exceptionality and beginning to come to terms with it are part of a major life cycle task for many families, especially during the early childhood years. Both families and professionals benefit from its practical guidance. (A significant number of students with mild exceptionalities, however, are not identified until they are in elementary school; for their families, discovery and its associated feelings come at a much later time but pose similar challenges.) A very helpful guide with many positive suggestions for enhancing family adaptation in the early years is written by a nurse and four mothers (Miller, 1994).

FIGURE 8–2

Tips: Sharing Prenatal Testing Results with Families

- Make sure parents understand all prenatal tests.
- Give the diagnosis in person if possible.
- Give the news to both parents at the same time.
- Do not make assumptions about the parents' decision.
- Do not make judgments about the parents' decision.
- Give nonjudgmental information on all three options: continuation of pregnancy and parenting, continuation of the pregnancy and adoption placement, and termination of pregnancy.
- Give up-to-date printed material on Down syndrome.
- Make referrals to Down syndrome programs.
- Do not accentuate the negative.
- Do not use negative terminology.
- Do not pity parents, but do recognize that they may feel a loss.

Source: Helm, D. T., Miranda, S., & Angoff-Chedd, N. (1998). Prenatal diagnosis of Down syndrome: Mothers' reflections on supports needed for diagnosis to birth. *Mental Retardation, 36*(1), 55–61.

Participation in Early Childhood Services Learning about the child's exceptionality is only the first of a lifelong series of interactions with professionals. Families with young children whose exceptionalities, especially

Trevor Is a Citizen, Why Grieve?

I have never had a professional who had high expectations for Trevor tell me I was in denial or that I needed to grieve the loss of my dream. But I have had (more than once) professionals try to get me to accept a lower standard for Trevor by using denial, anger, guilt, and grief to invalidate my opinion and convince me to accept segregation and/or poor services. In the first six months of Trevor's life, I was presented with a grieving process over and over. I experienced stress over the fact that it did not represent what I felt and confusion because other parents felt that it did. I also felt anger with early intervention staff who insisted that *I was grieving* but refusing to acknowledge it.

What would have helped me during the days, weeks and months following my son's diagnosis? First, it would have been helpful if people had seen what I was going through, and helped me to see it, as a crisis, rather than as grief. I've lived through my share of crises, but no one helped me to see that the things

I had learned from previous crises could get me through this one.

It would have been helpful if someone had paid attention to what I was feeling. While judgments were abundant, careful, empathetic, respectful, nonjudgmental listening was in short supply. My feelings were often categorized, but they were not often heard and understood. . . .

And then there was the absence of "congratulations on your new baby" cards, and the "friends" that didn't come to see him. Of all the things that happened, one of the most meaningful for me was a certificate I received from a Congressman, Jack Cera. It said that Trevor was a citizen.

. . . One of the things that helped was a celebration—in spite of the disability, not in ignorance of it—because if the child is not celebrated as he/she is, the parents feel the rejection of a palpable part of the identification crisis.

Having gone through other crises in my life, I can say that during

those my thinking was not discredited or denied. Even though "things had to be worked through," people did not invalidate my ideas or reactions during times of crisis, or dismiss them because I was in an "anger stage." Trevor's a gift, as my other children are. He has never been a source of grief, either now or at his birth. I had indeed been through a crisis and had experienced pain, but he was not the source. He has many times been the consolation.

Added note: Diane wrote down these feelings when Trevor was very young. Trevor is fully included in elementary school. Trevor is not only a citizen but also a Boy Scout and a T-ball player. Diane reports that all is well with him, but the crisis more recently has focused on his younger sister who has leukemia. Diane knows how to survive and prevail when she faces crises, and her children are all the consolation.

Source: Gerst, D. (1991). *Trevor is a citizen: Why grieve?* Unpublished manuscript.

---

disabilities, have already been identified are likely to enter the world of early intervention, preschool education, and related special services. In their journey through this early childhood stage, they will encounter an early childhood service delivery system that is seeking to be family centered (McWilliam et al., 1995; Murphy, Lee, Turnbull, & Turbiville, 1995; Turnbull, Turbiville, & Turnbull, in press; Wehman, 1998). As you read in chapter 2, however, a gap sometimes exists between the family-centered philosophy and practice (Katz & Scarpati, 1995; McBride, Brotherson, Joanning, Whiddlen, & Demmit, 1993; Menke, 1991). This is not to take away from the significant progress that has been made in early childhood services

but to underscore the importance of ensuring that your practices are consistent with the espoused philosophy.

How are family-centered services incorporated into early childhood program service delivery? According to a 1994 report (Stayton & Karnes, 1994), the majority of federally funded early childhood programs offer a combined home-center option. Most (75 percent) report that they incorporate a family systems model into services for families, while the others (25 percent) describe services primarily to parents, such as providing training to be their children's teachers.

Ideally, early intervention professionals collaborate with families as they prepare for the marathon ahead, namely, the full life cycle of the family. By supporting families to focus on their long-range needs, these professionals may enable families to enhance their motivation and knowledge/skills and avoid the burnout that can occur when families exert all their efforts during the "100-yard dash" of an early intervention program (Turnbull, 1988). Box 8–2 lists tips for assisting families to develop the resilience and pace for attaining their goals over their lifetime marathons.

Childhood

Entry into elementary school, a hallmark of childhood, typically widens the horizons of both children and families. For families who have a child with an exceptionality, entry into school may mark their first encounter with many of the issues to which we have devoted whole chapters of this book (Shaw, 1998). For example, often with the support of professionals, the elementary years are a time when many parents acquire (1) a vision for their child's future and (2) a perspective on the appropriateness of inclusion.

Developing a Vision for the Future Sally Sloop, the mother of Peter, an 8-year-old who has autism, envisioned Peter's future when he is 25 years old: "He works where he wants to work, receives a decent paycheck, gets help from the job coach, and is a taxpayer. He has his own apartment and a roommate or partner so he can continue down life's road without undue loneliness" (Turnbull, Turnbull, Shank, & Leal, 1995, p. 24).

We should not be surprised that parents of children with a disability typically want the same things that al-most all parents want for their children: a home, friends, happiness, and a chance to contribute to their community (Buswell & Schaffner, 1990; Giangreco, Cloninger, Mueller, Yuan, & Ashworth, 1991).

How do families and professionals develop visions? Visions evolve from great expectations, and they often depend on hope. In chapter 2, we introduced the concept of vision (Senge, 1990). When professionals initially explain to families that their child has a disability, they can begin to instill a sense of great expectations so that families still will be able to accomplish many of their priorities. As you learned in chapter 2, an emphasis on future visions and great expectations is consistent with standard-based reform, which is emphasizing the attainment of more challenging standards for all students, including those with exceptionalities. Professionals can offer themselves as potential allies to achieve the vision (as they did when Jessica Baccus declared that she wanted to live in a home of her own), thus enhancing the family's motivation to achieve the vision, and launch the family on a great expectations journey. A parent of a son with a developmental disability described her dream for her son as follows:

> Independence, knowledge, experience life. And he's going to have that experience in life, but that's all there is to it. So is my other son. God didn't promise me that either one of my sons would be perfect. He didn't promise me my life would be perfect, and I should not expect a perfect, safe little world for my kid with a disability. It ain't gonna happen . . . there's no such thing. Bad things happen to good people. All those cliches. But, I can expect him to have a happy

TIPS

BOX 8–2

Encouraging Success Over the Family Marathon

- Meeting the basic needs for food, shelter, health, and security.
- Taking time to reflect on the strengths and limitations of the family.
- Learning to love the child with an exceptionality unconditionally.
- Establishing relationships that will provide the foundation for future support.
- Experiencing and benefiting from the wide range of emotions that accompany having a child with an exceptionality.
- Learning to collaborate to enhance the child's education and development.
- Anticipating the future and learning transitional planning.
- Establishing balance and equity in the family by learning to juggle time and attention among the members.

Source: Adapted from Turnbull, A. P. (1988). The challenge of providing comprehensive support to families. *Education and Training in Mental Retardation, 23*(4), 261–272.

life, to experience as much in life as he possibly can and to make decisions to the best of his ability with the appropriate supports.

Families of elementary students often struggle with the issue of expectations, and often they develop low expectations as a result of wholly negative thinking by professionals, other families, and outdated public attitudes. Professionals such as yourself play a critical role in igniting great expectations within a family (Turnbull & Turnbull, 1985; Turnbull, Turnbull, & Blue-Banning, 1994). So, too, do family and friends. Helping families develop positive visions of the future encourages them to push the limits of what is possible. Rather than being trapped by learned helplessness, students, families, friends, and professionals who have great expectations tend to set their sights on what is possible. It is a matter of motivating the family, of providing it with knowledge and skills, and of collaborating as a reliable ally. If Jessica Baccus' junior high school principal and teacher and her cheerleader friends had not recognized her gifts and had not entertained great expectations for her, almost surely Jessica would not have been included in so many aspects of school. Everyone has a role in creating an empowering context, just as they have a role in creating an inclusive education. And if her high school teachers had not embraced her dream of a home of her own, the chances are slim that an IEP conference would ever had focused on making that dream come true.

Developing a Perspective on the Appropriateness of Inclusion
As we discussed in chapter 2, special education reform over the last 25 years has primarily focused on (1) reshaping the provision of a free appropriate public education (through the passage, implementation, and reauthorization of the Individuals with Disabilities Education Act, called IDEA) and (2) reshaping placement (through IDEA's major emphasis on educating students in less restrictive, more inclusive environments). As children with exceptionalities enter elementary school, many parents begin to carefully weigh the benefits and drawbacks of inclusion that they perceive for their son or daughter; some families pursue issues related to the efficacy of inclusion earlier, during the early intervention and early childhood years (Erwin, Soodak, Winton, & Turnbull, in press).

Just as perspectives on inclusion vary tremendously among educators (Barnett & Monda-Amaya, 1998; Cook, Semmel, & Gerber, 1999; Coots, Bishop, & Grenot-Scheyer, 1998; Taylor, Richards, Goldstein, & Schilit, 1997), so do they vary among family members (Borthwick-Duffy, Palmer, & Lane, 1996; Green & Shinn, 1994; Palmer, Borthwick-Duffy, Widaman, & Best, 1998; Ryndak, Downing, Morrison, & Williams, 1996; York & Tundidor, 1995). A parent, JoAnn Simons, shares her perspective on inclusion in box 8–3.

An important impetus for inclusion has come from parents such as those in the Baccus family (Erwin, Soodak, Winton, & Turnbull, in press; Grove & Fisher, 1999; Soodak & Erwin, in press). Parents have reported that often their first information comes from disability-issue conferences they attend and that in pursuing inclusion, they are placed in the position of needing to convince educators that inclusion is appropriate for

MY VOICE
BOX 8–3

JoAnn Simons Speaking Out on Inclusion

I have witnessed first hand the success of full inclusion of someone with rather limited intellectual capacity. If there has been a failure to inclusion, it has not been in the area of academics, school life, or the acquisition of meaningful skills; but there is an isolation when you spend your entire day in an environment where you never see anyone quite like yourself. Whether you're the only student of color, the only gay student, or the only student with Down syndrome, there is a certain feeling that you are not quite "regular." In order to really have value, you begin to feel you must be everyone else. My hope for schools is not to run away from this challenge of inclusion but to work for even more diversity within our schools, schools where all students are celebrated and feel safe.

Source: Simons, J. A. (1998). Response to Chesley and Calaluce on inclusion. *Mental Retardation, 36*(4), August, 322–324.

their child (Grove & Fisher, 1999). The mother of a child with cerebral palsy illustrates this point:

> I felt the special education class left something to be desired; it could be a lot richer. We called a new IEP with inclusion as our goal. And the district contacted the school and they assigned an itinerant. I was the one that said, "Let's talk about what equipment he needs, can we talk about what teacher might be best for him, can I meet with the administration at the school site?" Although there was supposedly an itinerant to arrange things, I had to tell them (the school site), "You need to find out about bathroom facilities and we'll need an aide." On the whole, in terms of school information for teachers, there has been nothing. Any specific information they have about Tom has come from myself or handouts about inclusive education that I shared with them. (Grove & Fisher, 1999, p. 212)

Many parents who favor inclusion for their son or daughter say that they wish their children's educators would take more responsibility in initiating systems change and not leave so much of the "pushing" up to the parents (Erwin, Soodak, Winton, & Turnbull, in press).

As you learned in chapter 1, many parents have been political advocates in using the judicial system to bring about appropriate services for their son or daughter. A significant number of the judicial special education cases has focused on the implementation of IDEA's principle of the least restrictive environment (Lipton, 1994; Turnbull & Turnbull, 2000). One of these cases, *Oberti v. Board of Education of the Borough of Clementon School District* (1992), imposed on schools an affirmative obligation to educate students with disabilities in general education classrooms with the use of supplementary aids and services and to do so before considering more restrictive educational placements. Mr. Oberti, who had the motivation for inclusion but was faced with a context that was noninclusive and certainly not empowering, shares his perspective in box 8–4.

My Voice BOX 8–4

My Son Rafael Will Succeed

We, the parents of children with disabilities that have had the longest amount of experience working with them from birth, know the way they learn. In my family's case, my son was doing wonderfully, growing and learning in a fully inclusive environment until kindergarten when we hit the brick wall set up by an outdated system. We found that the law is not being taken seriously and that for children with severe cognitive and/or physical disabilities, the path is already written and decided—segregated classes, often very far from their hometown, or if pressed by parents, dumping in the regular class with no supports.

The demands on a child with a disability are not so extraordinary when a group of knowledgeable professionals, together with the parents, have a genuine desire to do what is correct and meet to discuss the abilities, strengths and special needs a child may have as they develop a *fully supported inclusive educational plan.* If that is done instead of "dumping" a child in the regular classroom, and if it is done on an ongoing basis, none of the "robbing" of the rest of the students will occur.

The Individuals with Disabilities Education Act, which proclaims that all children with disabilities have the right to a "free and appropriate education" in the "least restrictive environment," is very clear and still, for too many years school bureaucrats have walked all over it. They feel that based on an IQ score they have the right to label, classify, and ship out children with disabilities to a distant segregated location.

Our son, Rafael A. Oberti, went through six different placements by the time he was seven years old and there would have been many more had we followed the "professionals'" recommendations. Looking back, our only regret is not to have taken charge of the situation sooner than we did. Please remember his name, because he will succeed and he will make a great contribution in this world. Perhaps he already has, certainly in our lives.

Source: Oberti, C. (1993 September). A parent's perspective. *Exceptional Parent,* 18–21. Reprinted with the expressed consent and approval of *Exceptional Parent,* a monthly magazine for parents and families of children with disabilities and special health care needs. Subscription cost is $28 per year for 12 issues. Call 1-800-247-8080. Offices at 120 State Street, Hackensack, NJ 07601.

Alternatively, many parents oppose inclusion and believe that their son or daughter gets more individualized, expert help in special education settings. Several studies have found that parents generally tend to support the concept of placing students with disabilities in general education classrooms, but they are substantially more skeptical in terms of the reintegration of their own child from special education to general education classes, preferring special education services to having their child return to the general education classroom (Green & Shinn, 1994; Reichart et al., 1989; Simpson & Myles, 1989). As one parent said, "with the types of problems that he has, he needs one-on-one instruction. He needs someone close by to follow that he's comprehending what he's being taught. If he had the self-esteem and the motivation to learn, then he could be in the regular classroom" (Green & Shinn, 1994, p. 274).

*A*dolescence

Adolescence is the next life cycle stage in the family's development. Perhaps more than any of the life cycle stages, adolescence is strongly influenced by cultural context values (Groce, 1997). If you consider the empowerment framework in chapter 3, the emphasis in these projects is to enable students with disabilities to enhance their motivation and knowledge/skills related to self-determination. For example, many Euro-Americans generally think of their children becoming adults at around the age of 18; whereas many Navajos perceive that adulthood starts just after puberty (Deyhle & LeCompte, 1994). In addition to various ethnic/racial interpretations of adolescence, religion also has a role in defining adolescent-related rituals that signal increasing maturity during the adolescent stage. A familiar example is religious confirmation, including the Jewish religion's bar mitzvahs for boys and bat mitzvahs for girls. These ceremonies involve 13-year-old adolescents becoming full-fledged adult members of their congregations. In addition to adolescent religious rituals that tend to be more familiar, there are many associated with religions of the world that are not as familiar within our dominant culture. An example is the Hindu *upanayâna* ritual (investiture with sacred thread) signifying the transformation of brahmân (upper-class) boys into young men. As you will note here, this ceremony combines a religious perspective (Hindu) with a social class perspective (brâhman boys). The timing of the sacred thread ritual varies from between the ages of 8 and 16 to the time just before the young man is married.

> Just before the sacred thread ritual begins, the boy takes his last meal from his mother as a child. Shaving the boy's head and giving him a bath traditionally mark

symbolic distancing from childhood. Special clothes (girdle, deerskin, staff, and the sacred thread) then demarcate the liminal state. The teacher's taking the boy's "heart" into his own a symbolic father and mother ushers in a rebirth to student status. The transition from one life stage to the other is a symbolic gestation process in which the teacher becomes "pregnant" with the boy and by virtue of sacred sound (*mantra*) gives him a second birth (*Dvija*). (Forman, 1993, p. 9)

To honor a family's cultural diversity, you may need to find out the family's own interpretations and traditions associated with adolescence.

Adolescence in general can be stressful for the youth and other family members. Parents may find their authority challenged as adolescents experiment with newfound sexuality. In addition, parents may be facing problems of their own as they enter midlife. In a national study conducted with more than 1,000 families in the general population, parents reported that the life cycle stages of adolescence and young adulthood were the two stages with the highest amount of stresses and strains (Olson et al., 1983).

An exceptionality may either mitigate or compound some of the typical adolescent issues. For example, parents might be confronted with reduced rebellion and conflict because their children may have fewer peers after whom to model such behaviors, fewer opportunities to try alcohol and drugs, or decreased mobility and therefore fewer chances to take dangerous risks. In other cases, adolescence may bring greater isolation, a growing sense of difference, and confusion and fear about emerging sexuality. Some pertinent educational issues for consideration during the adolescent stage include (1) sexuality education and (2) self-determination skills.

Sexuality Education Emerging sexuality often presents family challenges. When the adolescent has an exceptionality, the challenge may be compounded (Kingsley & Levitz, 1994; O'Toole, 1996; Tilley, 1996). Unlike Tricia Baccus, who helped Jessica put on makeup and allowed her to stay overnight at a hotel after the junior-senior prom, some parents may not even recognize that it is possible for their child to have sexual needs (Brotherson, 1985). In interviews with 24 parents of adults with mental retardation, 88 percent stated that their son or daughter had no needs related to sexuality: Either the parents discouraged it or they assumed it was beyond their child's comprehension (Brotherson, Backus, Summers, & Turnbull, 1986). In fact, a challenge for many families is to address sexuality education and particularly their special concerns about the risk of sexual abuse.

A survey of female adolescents with developmental disabilities reported that a large percentage were sexually active, with half of the sample reporting vaginal intercourse and indicating that they had used a condom at least once during intercourse (Scotti et al., 1997). Similarly, research has documented that adolescents with chronic health problems (for example, diabetes or asthma) and disabilities (for example, cerebral palsy or muscular dystrophy) were found to be similar to individuals without disabilities in the proportion who had sexual intercourse, patterns of contraceptive use, age of sexual debut, pregnancy involvement, and sexual orientation (Surís, Resnick, Cassuto, & Blum, 1996).

Sexuality education has been noticeably absent from special or general education curricula in many schools (McCabe, 1993; Whitehead, 1994), and families often fail to address their children's sexuality. A survey of special education teacher-preparation programs revealed that 41 percent do not offer any course work related to sex education; and the programs that do offer content only offer an average of 3½ hours of instruction (May & Kundert, 1996).

Is there a need for sexuality education? As one teacher explained: "We see sexual problems among our students all of the time and, although we gossip about them, we do nothing to help students understand their feelings or drive. Really, we avoid getting involved. It's easier for us that way" (Brantlinger, 1992, pp. 9–10).

A professional who provides vocational preparation commented:

> The classic word around here is "redirect" to be interpreted as "you can't do it here" or "that is not appropriate here." The problem is there is nowhere where sex is appropriate. "Redirect" sounds objective, but it is really oppressive. The administrators talk out of both sides of their mouth. They sound like they are for normalization but, in truth, they're not. At least they're not when it comes to sexual behavior. (Brantlinger, 1992, p. 11)

Educators and parents would do well to include the following topics in a sexuality curriculum: anatomy and physiology, maturation and body changes, birth control, sexually transmitted diseases and their prevention, masturbation, responsibility for sexual behavior, inappropriate sexual behavior and sex offenses, same-sex and opposite-sex activity, psychosocial sexual aspects of behavior and psychosexual development, and marriage and parenthood (Monat-Haller, 1992; Walcott, 1997).

There is hardly a parent who does not worry that his or her child—especially one who has a disability—may be a victim of sexual abuse. A study that analyzed patterns of sexual abuse of adults with mental retardation over a five-year period reported that almost three-fourths of the victims were characterized as having mild mental retardation and had an average age of 30. Approximately one-fourth of the abuse incidents occurred in institutions, and another one-fourth occurred in group homes. In the remaining situations, the location of the incidents ranged among the victim's own home, a work setting, or a vehicle. The perpetrator was known to the victim in the vast majority of cases; this also is the case in sexual abuse of people who do not have an exceptionality. Although many families may expect abuse from a stranger or in an unsupervised situation in a public place, the results of this research indicate that sexual abuse is far more likely to occur from a known person in a known place (Furey, 1994).

Families and youth need accurate information about the likelihood of sexual abuse (McCarthy & Thompson, 1996; Reppucci & Haugaard, 1989); indeed, the skills and knowledge to prevent sexual abuse should be a key topic in sexuality training during the adolescent years (Lee & Tang, 1998). A recent report of a successful sexual abuse curriculum focused on Chinese females between the ages of 11 and 15 (Lee & Tang, 1998). The researchers indicated the importance of addressing sexual abuse within Chinese populations because of the usual suppression of sexuality and the Chinese pattern of socializing children into subordinate positions with adults (Ho & Kwok, 1991; Tang, Lee, & Cheung, in press). The instructional program included two 45-minute sessions using a variety of behavioral instructional techniques. While the participants demonstrated greater knowledge regarding sexual abuse and self-protective skills at the conclusion of training, some of their gains were not maintained after two months. The authors recommend providing booster sessions to continue emphasizing important skills after the completion of a sexual abuse curriculum.

Moreover, pairing adolescence with knowledge about sexually transmitted diseases is critically important (Cambridge, 1998). In a comparison of individuals who were deaf/hard of hearing and those with no disabilities, results indicated that the individuals who were deaf/hard of hearing had less knowledge about AIDS, were less likely to recognize high-risk sexual behaviors such as sexual contact with drug users and having a higher number of sexual partners, and were more likely to think that using public bathrooms and visiting an AIDS patient will increase their chance of contracting AIDS (Woodroffe, Gorenflo, Meador, & Zazove, 1998).

Although the Centers for Disease Control do not collect data on the rate of HIV/AIDS infection among individuals with disabilities, infection in this population has been reported to be escalating (Kastner, Nathanson, & Marchetti, 1992). In a survey of 25 community programs that provide services to people with developmental disabilities, 24 expressed a need for the people receiving their services to have the benefit of HIV/AIDS prevention education (Mason & Jaskulski, 1994).

A model education and skills training program to reduce the risk of HIV infection targets high school students identified as having mild developmental disabilities (Scotti et al., 1997). This program combines an AIDS training curriculum (Scotti, Speaks, Masia, Boggess, & Drabman, 1995) with role play. The authors indicated that notable improvement was made on knowledge concerning HIV transmission and in the development of risk-reduction skills. Although this program was developed for people with mild developmental disabilities, the authors noted that they were able to adapt some of the instruction for an individual with severe mental retardation. For example, the individual was not able to verbally participate in a role play to purchase a condom, but she was able to hand a clerk a wallet information card to choose the correct condom.

What is a reliable ally, the state-of-the-art professional, to do? Identifying families' concerns, providing sexuality education programs, and implementing practices to prevent sexual abuse of all kinds (chapter 10) are warranted.

Expanding Self-Determination Skills Definitions of self-determination vary depending upon the developers of various approaches (Wehmeyer, Agran, & Hughes, 1998; Wehmeyer & Sands, 1998). We define *self-determination* as living one's life consistent with one's own values, preferences, strengths, and needs. Essentially, we consider self-determination to mean the same thing as empowerment. Thus, consistent with the empowerment framework in chapter 3, we believe the enabling elements of self-determination are motivation, knowledge/skills, and a responsive context. It is interesting that within the literature of the disability field, the term *self-determination* is often used in conjunction with individuals with disability, whereas the term *empowerment* is used in conjunction with families.

Just as with empowerment, culture plays a special role with respect to self-determination and the appropriate role of children and youth in expressing their preferences and solving their problems (Kalyanpur & Harry, 1999). Some cultural norms strongly favor individualism, while other cultural norms favor collectivism, as you learned in chapter 5. Honoring families' cultural traditions is one of the eight obligations of reliable alliances.

Cultural norms aside, child development theory (Marvin & Pianta, 1992) and research (Agran, 1997; Field, Hoffman, & Spezia, 1998; Wehmeyer, Agran, & Hughes, 1998; Wehmeyer & Sands, 1998) make one fact

abundantly clear: Building on a student's interest and direction is a critical aspect of self-determination. Indeed, self-determination competence building, while especially appropriate for the adolescent, is also desirable for very young children who should be encouraged to express their choices and act on their preferences (Abery & Zajac, 1996; Cook, Brotherson, Weigner-Garrey, & Mize, 1996; Palmer, 1998; Wehmeyer, Sands, Doll, & Palmer, 1997). Increasingly, research is documenting the critical role that self-reliance competence during infancy plays in laying the foundation for later self-reliance competence during adolescence and adulthood (Greenspan & Porges, 1984; Marvin & Pianta, 1992).

Two major national initiatives have focused attention in the 1990s on self-determination for individuals with disabilities. The first is an initiative (1990–1996) by the U.S. Department of Education that funded twenty-six model demonstration programs and five curriculum-development projects for the purpose of promoting self-determination for youths with disability (Ward, 1996; Wehmeyer, Bersani, & Gagne, 2000). These projects have resulted in numerous training guides, curricula, and literature aimed at self-determination enhancements (Field, Martin, Miller, Ward, & Wehmeyer, 1998; Powers, Singer, & Sowers, 1996; Sands & Wehmeyer, 1996). Several studies on teachers' perspectives about self-determination have reported that teachers overwhelmingly support the importance of self-determination; however, there is a significant gap between that stated importance and the incorporation of self-determination instructional goals into students' IEPs (Agran, Snow, & Swaner, 1999; Hughes et al., 1997; Wehmeyer, Agran, & Hughes, 1998).

The second major self-determination initiative has been funded by the Robert Wood Johnson Foundation and involves initiatives to change state policy related to self-determination (O'Brien, 1997; Shumway, 1999). These projects encourage states to allocate federal and state Medicaid benefits directly to individuals with disabilities and their families. These funds enable individuals with disabilities and their families to have the purchasing power to access the services that particularly fit their priorities and preferences. We will discuss this self-determination funding initiative in more detail in chapter 13.

These two self-determination initiatives have been catalysts for the national movement of self-advocacy involving individuals with disabilities. Currently there are more than 700 self-advocacy groups across the country and a national organization of self-advocates, Self-Advocates Becoming Empowered (Wehmeyer, Bersani, & Gagne, 2000).

Self-advocates are increasingly expressing their preferences for eliminating stigmatizing language in the disability field, setting priorities for funding, and encouraging the development of community-inclusive services. Self-advocacy groups typically have advisors who support individuals with disabilities in becoming more empowered (taking action to get what they want and need). A role that you may want to consider at some point is being an advisor to a self-advocacy group (Cone, 1999).

How self-determined are people with mental retardation? In a study of over 4,500 adults with mental retardation, some of the findings related to self-determination are as follows:

- Thirty-three percent had a choice regarding where they lived.
- Twelve percent had a voice in hiring staff or support people to work with them.
- Twenty-one percent chose their roommate.
- Forty-four percent chose their job or day activity.
- Twenty-six percent had a chance to pay their own bills.
- Forty-two percent did at least some banking.

It is obvious from this information that these individuals had limited opportunities to control some of the major decisions in their lives (Wehmeyer & Metzler, 1995).

Such limited control is especially troubling given research indicating that students with mental retardation and learning disabilities who are more self-determined achieve more favorable adult outcomes one year after high school graduation, especially related to paid employment (Wehmeyer & Schwartz, 1998). Another important outcome of student self-determination is that it is a predictor of active student involvement in educational planning and decision making (Sands, Spencer, Gliner, & Swaim, 1999). We will discuss this concept as it relates to the development of IEPs more in chapter 12.

Mitchell Levitz, a young man with Down syndrome and many capabilities, provides his perspective related to the role of parents:

> . . . parents should not tell their children, constantly remind them, to do this, do that and also not to be protective as much. If I go out, they should not be worried or protective because I feel hurt if my parents tell me, "Don't forget to call, leave a note." Sometimes I would call just to make sure that *they're* okay and not worrying.
>
> Parents should act their own age because they know that the responsibilities are ours, not theirs. If I do my own responsibilities, and get it done without any problems, I can be independent . . . without somebody telling me what to do every single second of the day. If it's important, leave a little message saying don't forget to—only something very important. Not something idiotic. (Kingsley & Levitz, 1994, pp. 142–143)

Especially in regard to family issues, there are four obstacles that challenge parents in supporting self-determination: (1) being unclear about the extent of self-determination that is appropriate to expect, (2) being unfamiliar with instructional strategies to encourage the further development of self-determination, (3) having cultural clashes with the expression of self-determination, and (4) dealing with their child's multiple challenges and accordingly relegating self-determination to a lower priority (Powers et al., 1996). Excellent self-determination models have been developed that jointly involve students and parents in training sessions and implementation opportunities (Field & Hoffman, 1999). In chapter 12 we will discuss how to support self-determination in culturally relevant ways during IFSP/IEP conferences.

Adulthood

Adulthood is the next life cycle stage and the last one that we will consider in this chapter. Growing up (attaining the status of adulthood) is taken for granted by most adults in our society but cannot be taken for granted by people with disabilities (Ferguson & Ferguson, 1993). There are reasons why this is so. Sometimes death intervenes, as it did for Jessica Baccus. Most other times, life goes on, and with the move into adulthood comes the general expectation for meeting one's own needs in the eight categories of family functions (chapter 7); but for some adults with disabilities, carrying out these duties is problematic. In addition, although the move into adulthood typically brings opportunities for greater choice and control, those opportunities may be hard to obtain for people with disabilities. The decisions regarding how to divide independence and responsibility among the young adult, the family, and other support systems can be difficult: Letting go is hard for parents who have had to devote extra attention to meeting the extra needs of children and youth. Jessica's parents, Tricia and Calvin, honored Jessica's desire to live in a home of her own, but they found one for her just a few doors down from their own. "I could hover easily, that way," admits Tricia. And it is sometimes hard for professionals, too, to let go. Moreover, cultural values strongly influence the concept of growing up and what adulthood means to family relationships. In Euro-American culture, it may mean moving out of the house, but in a Latino culture, it may mean continuing to live with one's parents. As three Latino parents stated:

> It is against the family for the children to live alone as adults. Young married couples live at the parents' home; it is Latino tradition. Families live in the same house . . . always has been that way. (Turnbull & Turnbull, 1996, p. 200)

Figure 8–3 highlights three dimensions of adulthood: autonomy, membership, and change (Ferguson & Ferguson, 1993). For many people, especially those of Euro-American culture, moving into adulthood means finding employment and moving away from home. For the young adult, this represents a process of attaining greater independence and responsibility; for the parents, it means a process of letting go of their son or daughter. This stage can be difficult in any family, but it is especially challenging for families with young adults who have disabilities. Two issues facing the individual and his or her family involve (1) identifying post-secondary educational programs and (2) accessing supported employment and supported living opportunities. In both of these issues, motivation (such as hope and persistence) and knowledge/skills are indispensable and should be provided by the empowering professional.

Identifying Post-secondary Educational Programs and Supports The opportunity to attend post-secondary educational programs is influenced by the ability of students with disabilities to graduate from high school. Given the emphasis on school reform in general education (see chapter 2), it is not surprising that there is increased attention to graduation requirements. A survey of all 50 states revealed three graduation-requirement trends (Thurlow, Ysseldyke, & Reid, 1997):

- Increased course work requirements for students to graduate,
- Increased number of states that require the standard diploma for graduation as contrasted to alternative diplomas representing adapted standards, and
- A decrease in a number of states that require a competency test for graduation.

Given these graduation requirements, the percentage of students graduating from high school based on 1991–1992 data range from approximately one-third of students with emotional disorders to approximately three-fourth of students with hearing and visual impairments (Kaye, 1997). It is disconcerting that slightly over 20 percent of students with disabilities drop out of high

---

FIGURE 8–3

Three Dimensions of Adulthood

Autonomy
Autonomy is being one's own person. It is expressed through symbols of:

- *Self-sufficiency*—especially economic self-sufficiency, or having the resources to take care of oneself. Self-sufficiency includes emotional self-sufficiency, or the ability to "make it" on one's own. It makes a shift from economic consumption alone to production and consumption.
- *Self-determination*—assertion of individuality and independence. Self-determination is the ability to assure others that one possesses the rational maturity and personal freedom to make specific choices about how to live one's life.
- *Completeness*—a sense of having "arrived," a shift from future to present tense, no more waiting.

Membership
Membership is community connectedness, collaboration, and sacrifice. It is expressed through symbols of:

- *Citizenship*—activities of collective governance from voting and participating in town meetings to volunteering for political candidates to expressing one's position on issues with money, time, or bumper stickers to recycling to protect the shared environment.
- *Affiliation*—activities of voluntary association, fellowship, celebration, and support from greeting the new family in the neighborhood with a plate of cookies to being an active member of the church, a participant in the local service or garden club, or an entrant in area road races.

Change
Change is adulthood as an ongoing capacity for growth rather than the static outcome of childhood.

Source: Ferguson, P. M., & Ferguson, D. L. (1993). The promise of adulthood. In M. Snell (Ed.), *Instruction of persons with severe disabilities* (4th ed.) (p. 591). Englewood Cliffs, NJ: Merrill/Prentice Hall.

school and that this proportion is almost twice as large for students with emotional disorders (Kaye, 1997).

A recent national survey of over 500 post-secondary institutions provided interesting information about the nature of the participation of students with learning disabilities in those programs (Vogel et al., 1998):

- The proportion of students with learning disabilities in post-secondary institutions ranges from .5 percent to almost 10 percent.

- Between approximately one-third and one-half of the institutions use regular admissions procedures.

- When applicants disclose that they have a learning disability in the admissions process, the competitive post-secondary institutions often use additional criteria (for example, asking a knowledgeable faculty member to review the folder).

- Most post-secondary institutions provide support services solely through Disabled Student Services offices.

What are the implications of this information for you? How can you be a reliable ally in the transition process? Under IDEA, planning should begin when the student is 14 years old. At least two to three years before graduating from high school, students with post-secondary goals need information and problem-solving skills to evaluate programs at different colleges and universities and to compare the capacities of those programs with their own strengths and needs. You should assist students and families in identifying the appropriateness of post-secondary career goals, ensuring that students develop prerequisite skills and teaching students to complete applications and access services consistent with their support needs. Parents and students alike need advice about scholarship opportunities, loans, work-study programs, and disability-related funding opportunities (such as Social Security and Vocational Rehabilitation benefits). Resource guides in a school or local library and workshops on college planning and academic and financial issues can be helpful resources for families and adolescents.

Students and families will also need your support in considering a variety of other special needs when selecting a post-secondary institution. Does the post-secondary institution provide special assistance such as tutoring programs for students with learning disabilities or interpreters for students who are deaf or hard of hearing? Is the campus accessible for wheelchair users? Does the state vocational rehabilitation program provide financial assistance for personal-care attendants while the student is attending college? Does the post-secondary institution have an office that oversees the provision of reasonable accommodations for students with disabilities?

Is there a published and well-enforced plan for complying with the Americans with Disabilities Act? In other words, is the post-secondary institution the type of empowering context that you yourself try to provide?

Helpful information about post-secondary programs and disability accommodations is available from two national resources. The first is the National Clearinghouse on Postsecondary Education for Individuals with Disabilities at the American Council on Education (1 Dupont Circle, Suite 800, Washington, DC 20063-1193). The clearinghouse publishes annotated resource guides on accommodations in higher education for students with disabilities. The second is the Association on Higher Education and Disability (P.O. Box 21192, Columbus, OH 43221-0192). This association provides a journal, newsletter, and annual conferences. Share resources such as these with families and students with disabilities who are pursuing post-secondary education.

Although families are their children's primary advocates during the elementary and secondary years, colleges expect students themselves to take on this responsibility. One of the best preparations for students' success during post-secondary years is to prepare students and families throughout the elementary and secondary years for students to assume increasing responsibility to be their own disability and education advocates.

Accessing Supported Employment and Supported Living Options The 1998 National Organization on Disability/Lou Harris Poll surveyed 1,000 Americans with disabilities 16 years of age and older. Reports indicated that employment is the area where individuals with disabilities experience the widest gap between themselves and those who do not have a disability (*http://www.ichp.edu/ssi*, 1998). It is disheartening that working-age adults with disabilities today are no more likely to be employed than they were a decade ago. Some of the specific employment findings of the poll include the following:

- Approximately 30 percent of individuals with disabilities work full or part-time as compared to 80 percent of those without disabilities.

- Approximately 70 percent of individuals with disabilities who are not employed express a preference to be working.

- Approximately two-thirds of adults with disabilities say that their disability has prevented or made it more difficult for them to get the kind of job they would like to have.

Although employment barriers are significant for individuals across all types of disabilities, individuals with severe disabilities have particular challenges. Because they have pervasive needs for support, the concept of supported employment was developed in the early 1980s as a way to provide long-term support for individuals with severe disabilities in integrated work settings, work stations in industry, enclaves, and/or work crews. The goal of supported employment is the development of independent work skills and the ability to earn competitive wages in the inclusive job market (Wehman, Bricout, & Kregel, 2000).

The average hourly wages in supported employment are *at least* 2.25 times the average hourly wage in sheltered employment (Coker, Osgood, & Clouse, 1995). Although long-term studies have clearly documented the benefits of supported over sheltered employment for individuals with disabilities, their families, and taxpayers, adults with disabilities tend to still be overwhelmingly placed in sheltered workshops, day activity, or day habilitation programs rather than in supported employment (81 percent vs. 19 percent) (Braddock, Hemp, Parish, & Westrich, 1998).

A national survey of 54 state/territorial-supported employment systems in 1995 revealed the following key findings (Wehman, Revell, & Kregel, 1998):

- Increasingly, supported employment is a preferred employment option, as evidenced by its 16 percent annual growth rate between 1993 and 1995.

- Supported employment is expanding among persons with long-term mental illness.

- Typically wages for individuals in supported employment are above minimum wage; the mean wage ranges up to $7.00 per hour.

What can you do to support families who are seeking supported employment for their son or daughter with a severe disability? You can consider motivating families toward supported employment by providing them with comprehensive information about its benefits. Families can be major resources in not only helping to prepare their family member with a disability for employment but also in helping to locate employment options. One study revealed that approximately 80 percent of the jobs that were secured by former special education students were obtained through a family connection (Hasazi, Gordon, & Roe, 1985). Just as people without exceptionalities access jobs through family and friendship networks (including networks in which you, the reliable ally, participate), so do people with exceptionalities. To provide an empowering context and increase parental support for supported employment, apply the tips highlighted in box 8–5.

Supported living is a newer concept than supported employment. Ferguson and Ferguson (1993) describe supported living (as applicable to their son who has multiple disabilities) as follows:

> Simply put, supported living means that Ian should be able to live where he wants, with whom he wants, for as long as he wants, with the ongoing support needed to make that happen (Boles, Horner, & Bellamy, 1988). At a minimum, Ian's home should be the one place he will not have to worry about wheelchair accessibility. Beyond that, however, Ian should have more options than a forced choice of a five- or ten-bed group home. Indeed, supported living means that Ian should be able to find his own place (within his means), whether it be a house, an apartment, a duplex, or a cooperative, with the residential support following him to that location. (Ferguson & Ferguson, 1993, p. 602)

TIPS

BOX 8–5

Enhancing Parental Support for Supported Employment

- Obtain information on parents' needs and desires relating to placement.
- Obtain possible job leads from parents and family.
- Keep parents informed of placement activities.
- Review the details of a potential job before proceeding with placement activities.
- Provide specific suggestions for supporting and reinforcing job performance.
- Provide ongoing information about job performance and status.

Source: Sowers, J. (1993). Critical parent roles in supported employment. In G. H. S. Singer & L. K. Irvin (Eds.), *Support for caregiving families: Enabling positive adaptation to disability* (pp. 276–279). Baltimore: Brookes.

That is an ideal, but what does research say about the reality? Sadly, interviews with parents of young adults with mental retardation and physical disabilities indicate that parents in both groups report most frequently that their greatest need is for the stability and certainty that comes from finding a home that is responsive to personal preferences. Until death intervened, Tricia, Calvin, and Jessica were on their way to finding such a home for Jessica. Their memorial to her, "Living Opportunities—Jessica's Home," is the permanent reminder to Jessica's community that home and quality of life are so important to families. As one parent says, "work is not high on the hierarchy of Maslow's needs. Survival is most important. Most of all (my daughter) needs a place to live and be happy. The rest is additional" (Brotherson et al., 1986, p. 170).

Innovative adult agencies are starting exciting supported living options, and some families are pioneering supported living on their own without agency participation (Racino, Walker, O'Connor, & Taylor, 1993). In box 8–6 you will read how our son Jay experiences supported living. In chapter 13 we will describe in more detail how his "Action Group" collaborates to design and implement his specific supports.

Having reviewed two educational concerns that many families experience at each of the life cycle stages of early childhood, school age, adolescence, and early adulthood, we remind you that education is only one of the eight family functions that you learned about in chapter 7. We encourage you to develop an increasing appreciation for the challenges that families must face as they deal not only with educational issues but also with challenges associated with each of the seven other functions at each new life cycle stage.

And can you now appreciate why Tricia Baccus, contributing to this book in 1995 (four years before this edition was prepared), said that she has to believe in her family; be convinced she can affect what happens to her; and have energy, persistence, and hope? Her words at the time—"hope, becoming, and faith"—reflect the degree to which she is an empowered person, just as they reflect the important empowering roles that Jessica's health-care providers, school principals, and teachers have played in creating an empowering context for her and her family.

Life Cycle Transitions

As we noted at the beginning of the chapter, life cycle stages are like plateaus between the peaks and valleys of transitions from one life cycle stage to another, such as from adolescence to adulthood (Blalock, 1988). Transition times often are the most challenging periods for fam-

TOGETHER WE CAN   BOX 8–6

On My Own

Living "on my own" has many dimensions, many meanings.

It means having two housemates, Richard Gaeta and Anne Guthrie (a married couple), who convert his "house" into a home, replete with regular Monday night dinners to which Jay and those members of Jay's circle or people who, in Richard's and Anne's judgment, might enjoy being part of Jay's life.

Living "on my own" also means that Jay gets support from Richard and Anne in those daily life activities with which he needs help: shaving,

cooking, handling money, and transportation.

It means that Richard and Anne coordinate Jay's recreation and leisure activities, convene and run his group action planning meetings, assist him in contributing to his community by being a volunteer at the Community Mercantile Exchange—the local food coop, and provide him transportation for the many ways he participates in community life.

Finally, living "on my own" means that Richard and Anne collaborate with Jay's parents, his sister, Kate (a senior at Kansas Univer-

sity, where Jay works), and various professionals to assure that Jay receives personalized support and numerous opportunities to actualize his self-determination.

Living "on my own" is Jay's aspiration and that of his family and friends. But for hope to be realized, there must be teamwork. Living "on my own," then, involves shared lives—Jay's, Richard's, Anne's, Kate's, and Rud's and Ann's converge. Think of the Olympic Rings symbol: five circles, intertwined but still separately identifiable. That's a fitting symbol for being "on my own."

ilies because they are characterized by the most change. As Tricia and Calvin admit, they face a tremendous challenge: learning how to live without Jessica, without her routines (which became theirs), and without a sense that they are competent to control what happens to them. These are the times when you should be particularly careful to be a reliable ally and to practice the empowering context techniques that we outlined in chapter 3 and will discuss in chapters 9 through 15.

Two factors tend to reduce the amount of stress most families feel during a transition. First, in most cultures the roles of the new stages are fairly well defined. Thus, the transition may be marked by some kind of ritual such as a wedding, bar mitzvah or bat mitzvah, graduation, or funeral. These ceremonies serve as signals to the family that their relationships following the event will be changed. The interactions and roles for the new stage are modeled by other families with the same previous or present experiences. As Calvin has said, "I am afraid that, when I return to work (after two weeks of mourning), no one will ever look at me in the same way again" [he perceives that a strong aspect of his identity is being the father of a daughter with a disability]. Yet, he and Tricia know that the way in which they bear themselves in the days and months and years after Jessica's death will provide an example for other families. For those families, then, the future is not entirely unknown.

Second, the timing of transitions within various cultural contexts is also fairly well expected. In Euro-American culture, for example, children are often expected to leave home after they graduate from high school. In Latino culture, however, it is typical for children, especially daughters, to continue to live with parents until they marry (Falicov, 1996).

For families with a member who has an exceptionality, the expected roles as well as the future of the person with an exceptionality may not be clear, and a ritual to mark the change may be absent. Jessica had a wedding dress—her favorite dress. Would she ever be married? No one could foretell; this ritual, this marker, may not have happened in her life. What is for sure, however, is that she is buried in her wedding dress. Nor may the transition itself, if it does occur, happen at the expected time. Parents usually predecease their children; Jessica defied the norm (so typical of her!) and predeceased her parents. Life cycle transitions seem to be much more traumatic and stressful when they occur at times other than when expected (Turnbull et al., 1986). In this section, you will learn about (1) the implications of uncertain futures and (2) off-time transitions.

Uncertainty About the Future

For many families of children and youth with exceptionalities, the future looms like a frightening unknown. Few norms and models of expected behavior may be available for either the child or the family. The common admonition to "take things one day at a time" is particularly apt (and welcomed by many families) not only because there are more than enough responsibilities for the family in the present but also because the future is so ambiguous (Featherstone, 1980). Just reflect about Jessica's family: Tricia, Calvin, Jessica, Melissa, and Lara lived time-compressed lives, facing Jessica's earlier-than-normal death but trying to put as much joy into their lives as possible. When Jessica died, time itself decompressed, and while it seems to Tricia and Calvin that they now have all the time they need, their need, as they make clear, has always been to have Jessica's routines be theirs.

A sometimes complicating factor associated with transition challenges is that the rituals that serve as "punctuation marks" for transitions for youth without disabilities may be blurred or nonexistent in youth with disabilities. The time when a transition occurs—or should occur—may not be marked with a celebration but with chronic frustration that supports are not in place for transition to the next stage. Thus, not only is the family uncertain about exactly how their interactions might change, but they also may have no cues that the interactions will change.

A study of the perspectives of students with disabilities about the transition process revealed major lack of attention to issues of future planning (Morningstar, Turnbull, & Turnbull, 1995). The majority of students had only a very vague sense about future planning. They reported that their families were the major source of helping them develop a vision for the kinds of jobs that they would like to have and where they would like to live. Only a very small percentage of these students indicated that their school-based vocational training had been helpful in their process of future planning. Vocational and transitional support services are key needs of secondary students with exceptionalities and their families (Bullis & Cheney, 1999; Dunn, 1996; Shafer & Rangasamy, 1995).

Students living in underserved areas can encounter heightened challenges at times of transitions. A follow-up study of students who left school on the Fort Apache Indian reservation revealed than less that one-third of the school graduates were employed and most continued to reside in their parents' home (Shafer & Rangasamy, 1995). The primary reason for individuals not being employed was the lack of available employment opportunities. Two-thirds of the students reported that they experienced substance abuse, particularly alcoholism.

Almost half of the students had been arrested, mainly for driving while intoxicated. The authors pointed out the catch-22 involved in the fact that the most economic opportunity was available at the cost of leaving the reservation. Thus, many students were faced with choosing between economic self-sufficiency and confronting ". . . a world for which they are not prepared" (Shafer & Rangasmy, 1995, p. 64).

Box 8–7 is a story of a young man, his family, and his teachers who work together to make his dreams come true. Just as Gus' teacher was his ally, so can you be an ally of students and families during the transition or "uncertainty" times by working to translate their great expectations into future realities (Dunn, 1996). For example, educators can collaborate with families by creating scenarios of what might happen

TOGETHER WE CAN BOX 8–7

Gus Estrella's Dreams Come True

Gus is 34 years old. He was born in Nogales, Arizona. . . . He and his family moved to Tucson when he was a young child so that Gus could get some of the things he needed since there were no services in Mexico for children with cerebral palsy. Gus was in school before passage of IDEA law that now requires schools to include people with disabilities, yet he was fortunate enough to have good teachers who were willing to help him get ahead. They pushed him and challenged him to do more and to try different things. Gus says that this kind of instruction and encouragement really helped prepare him for his adult life. It gave him courage to try new things.

Like his teachers, Gus' parents never held him back; nor did they let people get in the way of his education. For example, when Gus entered junior high, he needed to attend school in a neighboring district. His family made the appropriate arrangements, but the district where he lived refused to pay for needed services. Without any warning, no bus was sent to pick up Gus for school on the first day. So his mother took him to school and then got on the phone with the head district official. Three days later, the

bus finally came to take Gus to school. Nine months later, the family chose to move into a different school district to get better services for Gus.

In high school, Gus really wanted to be like the other students. He took the same classes as the others, but without a power wheelchair he did not have the opportunity to make friends and to go out with his peers. In college, things changed. He discovered that having a power wheelchair was essential for getting around and for building friendships. He also lived in the dorms, putting him in the middle of a great social scene. He went regularly to the basketball and football games with his college buddies. Gus graduated from the University of Arizona in Tucson with a bachelor's degree in creative writing. He candidly explains that his Vocational Rehabilitation counselor "wasn't thrilled" about his choice of major. He says that his counselor was afraid that with a creative writing degree, the only job Gus would be able to get would be waiting tables.

Gus' creative writing degree prepared him well for speech-writing, an essential part of his job today. Gus has been working for United Cerebral Palsy in Washington, DC as a

Policy Fellow for two years. His job is to make people, especially lawmakers, aware of the value of giving the person with a disability the equipment needed in order to remove barriers from daily life. Gus was active in meetings with the people who wrote the language of the 1997 IDEA reauthorization. He says that some of those people did not even know what assistive technology was. So, Gus talked to them and showed them, too. He is articulate and skilled in using his augmentative communication device called a "Liberator . . . ."

Gus explains that having a job is one part of being successful. He says that "the rest of success includes a family who will be there no matter what you do and also to be accepted by society as a person, not as a person with a disability." With this statement, he acknowledges the impact that society has on a person's ability to be successful, and gives credit where it is due to his family. Gus wants to let parents know that "they should not hold their child back. If they want to try something, let them and if they fail, they know what not to do next time." His parents have helped him by letting him live and learn.

Source: Mish, J., & Bonesio, R. (1998). *Desert stars: Arizona stories of transition to adulthood.* Phoenix, AR: Pilot Parent Partnerships.

five years in the future and then pinpoint educational goals and objectives that will best propel the student toward that desirable future. Visits to new classrooms or community jobs, meetings with future teachers and with adults with disabilities and parents of older children with similar exceptionalities can all help to reduce the fear of the future by making it less unknown. Box 8–8 offers some suggestions for easing the transitions into and out of each of the life cycle stages discussed in this chapter.

Off-Time Transitions

Families with a member who has an exceptionality are likely to experience a life cycle transition that occurs at a time other than what is expected. Transitions are often delayed or fail to occur. For example, a young adult might remain at home with his or her parents well into the parents' elderly years (Freedman, Wyngaarden-Krauss, & Mailick-Seltzer, 1997; Magaña, 1999; Seltzer, Green-

berg, Wyngaarden-Krauss, & 1997). Although Euro-American culture generally regards this type of living arrangement as an off-time transition, research on elderly parents who have provided care across the decades of their family life indicates that these parents experience positive outcomes. A study of more than 200 aging mothers of adults with mental retardation who were living at home led the researchers to the following conclusion: "Specifically, the women in our sample were substantially healthier and had better morale than did other samples of caregivers for elderly persons and reported no more burden and stress than did other caregivers" (Seltzer & Krauss, 1989, pp. 309–310). Within the Puerto Rican culture, the role of familism (direct caregiving provided by family members) is extremely strong and families expect to take care of their members over the full lifespan (Magaña, 1999).

Whereas some transitions are delayed or do not occur, others may occur earlier than the expected time. For instance, researchers have found that placing a child in

TIPS
BOX 8–8

Enhancing Successful Transitions

Early Childhood

- Begin preparing for the separation of preschool children by periodically leaving the child with others.
- Gather information and visit preschools in the community.
- Encourage participation in Parent-to-Parent programs. (Veteran parents are matched in one-to-one relationships with parents who are just beginning the transition process.)
- Familiarize parents with possible school (elementary and secondary) programs, career options, or adult programs so they have an idea of future opportunities.

Childhood

- Provide parents with an overview of curricular options.
- Ensure that IEP meetings provide an empowering context for family collaboration.
- Encourage participation in Parent-to-Parent matches, workshops, or family support groups to discuss transitions with others.

Adolescence

- Assist families and adolescents to identify community leisure-time activities.
- Incorporate into the IEP skills that will be needed in future career and vocational programs.
- Visit or become familiar with a variety of career and living options.
- Develop a mentor relationship with an adult with a similar exceptionality and an individual who has a career that matches the student's strengths and preferences.

Adulthood

- Provide preferred information to families about guardianship, estate planning, wills, and trusts.
- Assist family members in transferring responsibilities to the individual with an exceptionality, other family members, or service providers as appropriate.
- Assist the young adult or family members with career or vocational choices.
- Address the issues and responsibilities of marriage and family for the young adult.

a living situation outside the home can create a range of emotions that include grief as well as relief (Blacher, 1994; Blacher, Baker, & Abbott-Feinfield, 1999). Another off-time transition (one that the Baccus family was obliged to anticipate) occurs at premature death. Illness and death may be expected parts of life for an older person; but when they happen to a child, they are seen as strange and cruel twists of fate.

A brother or sister of a young person who dies may be "the 'silent' family member who seems to be coping well but may be in considerable distress" (Seligman, 1985, p. 276). In the weeks just after Jessica's death, her sisters Melissa and Lara responded differently from each other. Melissa's mixed anger-and-love led her to withdraw; her distress was obvious. Lara, however, wore a "happy face," yet her parents knew how much she hurt, how much she regretted that she did not say "goodnight, I love you" on the evening of Jessica's death.

Lois Wright's 2-year-old brother had a rare form of dystrophy and died when she was 12. Lois reflects on the experience:

> Before Gary died, I tried to figure out how I was supposed to respond when he finally did die. Was I supposed to cry? Would people watch me? I periodically wanted Gary to die so Mom would stay home instead of going to the hospital and sometimes so my family could go on weekend trips and vacations. I felt guilty for thinking about the good things that would happen if Gary died.
>
> After Gary died, I experienced a deep loss and great sorrow. It was much worse than I imagined. I worried about my mom because she was so sad, and I wondered how to act when I went back to school.
>
> My parents did a good job of helping me through this hard time. They seemed to perceive almost all my feelings and tried to counteract them. They encouraged us kids to talk about how we felt and never rebuked us for expressing those feelings. They made special arrangements for me to visit Gary [at the hospital] and, thus, spend time with my mom. I will always treasure those special moments.

Finally, off-time transitions occur when students who are gifted significantly advance in grade placements, even to the point of leaving secondary schools before their peers to go to college. Although there are diverse opinions about the accelerated placements of students into higher grade levels (Feldhusen, VanWinkle, & Ehle, 1996; Southern & Jones, 1991; Tannenbaum, 1986), advancement does occur and can be in the stu-

dent's and family's best interests. A very unusual example is Michael Kearney, who entered college at age six and graduated several years later. Michael describes his experiences shortly after his college graduation at nine years of age:

> . . . Growing up, I have dealt with teachers who have never knowingly met, much less talked, to someone like me. . . . I remember going to the hallways, looking at the faces of . . . students, and listening to them refer to me as Doogie Howser. . . . Another issue that I had to deal with while attending college was the chatter of my classmates. They thought that my parents had pushed me; I beg to differ. My parents have done their best to see that I am a well adjusted and a loving human being. For example, when I decided to go to college, they had to deal with the unexpected financial cost of early college attendance. They have been behind me 100 percent.
>
> I started out, at the age of 6, as a child who thrived on learning and craved a stimulating educational system that would enhance my academic spirit. At the University of South Alabama, I was allowed the freedom to think, act independently, and pursue my educational excellence even though I was only 8. These educators believe that children like myself have the potential to excel in an appropriate education. (Turnbull et al., 1995, p. 389)

Michael's father, Kevin Kearney, adds:

> . . . We now allow Michael at age twelve to attend the graduate school in chemistry at Middle Tennessee State University in order to help him become as normal an individual as he is likely to be. Those on the teaching staff who have got to know us realize we don't consider Michael a genius. He is probably a prodigy, but on the other hand, he may in fact be the century's Aristotle, Plato, or Einstein. We still don't know. . . . We continually ask ourselves, "what does a successful person really need to know?" By success, we mean that Michael will be a happy, social, productive twenty-five-year-old. If anyone has proven ideas on how to successfully raise a possible genius, we are most ready to listen. Until then, we intend to continue with our own program of ensuring Michael is comfortable, happy, challenged, and emotionally secure about planning appropriate childhood activities for him. As a secondary issue, somewhere down the line he'll earn a master's degree or Ph.D. or two. (Turnbull et al., 1999, p. 302)

Regardless of the reason that children make off-time transitions, families deserve your support and assistance—your allegiance in creating a context that helps them get what they want in dealing with the unexpected.

Summary

Families change; the mere passage of time causes changes in their characteristics (chapter 5), interactions (chapter 6), and functions (chapter 7). The changes over a family's life cycle typically occur during four stages—birth and early childhood, childhood, adolescence, and adulthood. Sometimes these changes happen "on cycle"; sometimes they are "off cycle." Whenever they occur, the period of time leading up to and just following the change in life cycle stage is the transition time, a period when families usually experience heightened anxiety and stress. In each of these stages, however, you can support the family to take action to get what they want and need—you can be an empowering collaborator by being especially sensitive to life stages and transitions.

After Jessica Baccus's fourth birthday party had concluded and the streamers, balloons, and torn gift wrappings had been gathered up and put away, Tricia wrote her daughter a letter that reflects on the family life cycle and the meaning of that family's life.

Dear Jessica:
Sweet, sleeping child. So small, so vulnerable. This day has brought to me an aching sense of the passing of time. Just one more day of living, but with one great difference: you are one year older. Jessica, you know by now life is not all pink balloons and streamers. But all in all, life has been pretty good to you. I wish I could promise you it will always go on this way. I can't. I wish I could go ahead of you to guide, warn and protect you . . . "walk out" the hard parts for you. I can't, and even if I could, it wouldn't be right. No, I must free you to live life yourself—whatever that may involve.

Little did Tricia know at that time what freeing Jessica to live her life would mean: The transition from early childhood to childhood, marked by a fourth birthday, is significantly different than the transition from childhood to adolescence. Lip gloss and overnights replaced balloons and at-home parties. And a different-than-imagined, a different-than-wanted, future lay ahead: a truncated life. Sadly, that future—that foreshortened, truncated life— was the reality. Jessica's "walk," her journey, was brief. There is this consolation, however: On her tombstone Tricia, Calvin, Melissa and Lara have had the following inscribed: "There was joy in the journey." Not such a "hard walk," after all, despite all, despite, even, the inevitable, out-of-time, unwelcome, and sorrowful end.

Part Three

Collaborating for Empowerment

In part 3 you will learn how to collaborate for empowerment. After learning about the contexts for empowerment (chapters 1 and 2), the concepts of empowerment and reliable alliances (chapters 3 and 4), and family systems perspectives (chapters 5 through 8), you are now ready to become familiar with the seven opportunities for partnerships that form the basis of collaborating for empowerment.

In your work with families, their children, and the schools, you will invariably find opportunities for being a partner with families—for being a collaborator with them. We believe that seven opportunities for being a partner will present themselves to you, no matter what specific role you have in schools or how that role brings you into contact with families and students.

You will always need to communicate with families. Therefore, in chapter 9 we suggest how you can do that collaboratively. Because you will work with families who have great difficulties meeting their basic needs or handling special challenges such as child maltreatment, chapter 10 describes how you can enable families to meet their needs and at the same time be their partner. Every student in special education receives an evaluation and then an individualized appropriate special edu-

cation program, so chapters 11 and 12 describe how these inevitable occurrences also are opportunities for you to be a collaborator. Many families want to work with their children at home, and many children learn not only from school but also from their community activities. Thus, chapter 13 describes how you can advance their learning by collaborating with their families at home and in the community. Some families are highly involved with their children's school, often attending school events or serving as volunteers. Whenever a family member enters the school building or engages in a school activity, there is another opportunity for you to be a partner, as we show in chapter 14. Finally, parents are by nature advocates for their children; and advocacy, as we explain in chapter 15, is also an activity that generates opportunities for you to be a collaborator.

None of these seven opportunities for partnerships will lead to empowerment unless you enrich them with an affective or attitudinal dimension. In each of the chapters in part 3, we encourage you to meet your obligations to be *effective* as a partner by being *affective* in your work with families. We suggest how you can maximize the seven opportunities for partnerships by using the eight obligations of a reliable alliance that we introduced in chapter 4.

177

Chapter Nine

Communicating Among Reliable Allies

"*T*ime is our enemy. Time is our friend." That's not exactly what Sue of Frederick, Maryland, said about her son Nick. But it captured the essence of the approach she and Nick's team of teachers and administrators used to include him in regular classes from almost the very beginning of his schooling in Frederick County to now. That's no mean feat, and it is accomplished because Sue is—among other things—a communicator.

Nick is 16 and has multiple disabilities, principally cerebral palsy. After spending first grade in a segregated special school, he became the catalyst for inclusion and school teaming during his second-grade year.

It took Sue a full year to move Nick from the separate first grade to the integrated second grade. During that year, she told the county board of education that she wanted Nick to be included; then she worked out an inclusion plan with the board, district administrators, school administrators, and general and special educators.

More than that, she convinced the board and Nick's future educators that Nick would benefit from inclusion. She did this by relying on her knowledge of Nick's legal rights, citing research and demonstration models that supported her position, and by being both persistent and determined, yet willing to compromise.

Those early investments have paid big dividends for Sue and Nick. From the second grade onward, inclusion has simply been "assumed" by the county board of education. So when Nick entered Governor Thomas Johnson High School in his ninth-grade year, it was assumed that he would be included in the regular education program.

And nothing happened to change that assumption, even though he was the first student with such significant disabilities to go to that school. Nick takes general education classes throughout the day, occassionally signing up for something else that fits his needs, such as a special, intensive prevocational class. "There never was any question about Nick's inclusion in his neighborhood high-school, because I started his inclusion in elementary school." Trace inclusion to Sue and a few other parents—but recognize she got what she and Nick wanted because she could communicate.

"We set the tone (when Nick was in first grade) by letting them know that we knew what we were entitled to. . . . It is the fact that they know I persist and that I know what I'm talking about. It keeps the dialogue going. Where I see it die down with other parents is when the parents don't know what they need to know. They're not empowered, and then it's easy for the administrators to just kind of let it die, especially if it's been a difficult issue."

Sue's attitude that Nick is entitled to everything any other student can have, coupled with being self-taught about legal rights and advocacy techniques and being employed by the Maryland Coalition for Inclusive Education, have led Sue to become a "teamer." In the past, her team consisted of herself, Nick's general and special education teachers, and support staff. Now that Nick is in high school, the core team consists of Sue, the high school inclusion facilitator, a case manager provided by the local chapter of The Arc (a national support organization for children and adults with disabilities), and

Nick's special education case manager at his high school. When they believe a meeting is necessary, they convene one, and they call it an IEP meeting so they can count on Nick's teachers and school administrators to attend.

"The benefit of that teaming for the school is that now everyone in my school is comfortable with frequent meetings. . . . They've learned to team. . . . They have this wonderful teaming system for anybody with a child who is included. It requires meeting once a week, getting the entire team together."

Sue is quick to point out that it took her and the school staff many years to get to that point. Some teachers didn't think they had the time or energy for so much planning. And now that Nick is in high school and has so many general education teachers, it is even harder—but each meeting has at least one general educator and usually the assistant principal who oversees special education. Of course, it helps that Sue—the inclusion pioneer—has "history" with the county board of education and that there is top-to-bottom support for inclusion. But what really helps is that Sue remains a "high-profile" parent. "I get to know the administrators and teachers. I use all sorts of different ways to communicate with them—face to face when I need to, and daily, through Nick's notebook and "cheap talk" machine (a simple recording device that allows Nick and his buddies at school to exchange greetings or share classwork)."

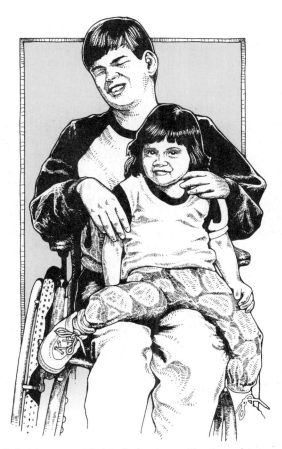

Nick Manos, with his little sister, Eleni, on his lap. (1999)

The payoff is big. With the meetings comes an energy to help Nick and other students. When the team does not meet, Nick begins to spiral down. The team members do not get feedback "on the little things that are crucial."

Naturally, some meetings also result in confrontations and disagreements. Paradoxically, however, these meetings have created a reliable alliance involving Sue, Nick, and his teachers and administrators.

By meeting so often, Sue says, "[I] thought I was destroying the relationships. Oddly, they became stronger than ever. . . . People just needed guidance back into the right direction. . . . They realized how important it was to have me there to provide continuity between home and school."

The team's efforts—sometimes painful, always candid—generated mutual respect. "I gained respect for them in many ways, even as angry or upset as I had been. They also gained some respect for me, just in terms of being able to guide them."

Now, it is Sue herself who seeks guidance. She faces a dilemma. When Nick turns 18, should she push for him to remain at Governor Thomas Johnson High School, where all his friends are; or should he transfer to another school (not his neighborhood school) with an intensive prevocational/vocational program; or should he graduate at age 18 and attend age appropriate vocational training at the local community college?

How will she make the decision? Predictably, that depends in large part on Sue and Nick.

However, unlike the times when Sue was pushing against a reluctant school system to have Nick included in the general curriculum in the second grade, Sue now has a team on which she can rely. "Future planning is automatic in Frederick County." So, Sue and Nick's team are starting it now, when Nick is 16. This will be full-blown future planning—which will include the MAPS system (McGill Action Planning System).

What a change: from being alone and pushing uphill against the school system, *to being supported to carry out inclusive education and plan for Nick's adult life in the community. "I am a communicator," Sue acknowledges. But she is quick to add: "The really big change for the school was to have this overall attitude of, 'to make it work we have to team.' The school really has become a place where everyone is interested in everyone else's best interest."*

There are seven opportunities for partnerships between families and professionals (chapters 9 through 15), but none is more important than a partnership that involves ongoing communication. Communication lies at the heart of all of the other types of partnerships. It is the initial and indispensable ingredient of the empowering context that we described in the framework discussed in chapter 3 and that we illustrate in figure 9–1.

In figure 9–1 you see that communication is one of your opportunities for creating partnerships and reliable alliances. In communicating with families, you can incorporate all eight obligations for a reliable alliance—you can come to know yourself, know them, honor their cultural diversity, affirm their strengths, promote their choices, envision great expectations, communicate positively, and warrant trust and respect. Your communication is a means by which you can create an empowering context.

More than that, your communication is a way you can affect each family's motivation and knowledge/skills. When you communicate effectively, you may affect the family's motivation, enabling them to believe in themselves (increased self-efficacy) or to acquire a greater sense of control. Likewise, you may augment their knowledge and skills by providing them with useful information or by augmenting their problem-solving, life management, or communication skills.

In this chapter, we will describe how certain strategies and skills can help you to be an effective communicator, an effective collaborator, and an empowered and empowering person.

Communication can be between two people or among more than two people. When two people are together (such as a teacher and a parent) but only one person (the teacher) speaks and does not let the other person (the parent) speak, there is not communication. Indeed, that kind of interaction can create a frustrated parent and can damage any chance for a reliable alliance between these two people. In the words of one parent, "whenever I go to school, they want to tell me what to do at home. They want to tell me how to raise my kid. They never ask me what I think. They never ask me anything" (Finders & Lewis, 1994, p. 53).

Over the last 20 years, special educators and education agencies have tried to comply with legal mandates by investing tremendous time and effort in formal team meetings, formal notices of evaluation and placement, and formal notices of legal rights (as you learned in chapter 2). Given this emphasis on formality, it is paradoxical that parents of children of various ages with various exceptionalities frequently emphasize their preference for *informal* rather than *formal* communication (Chapey, Trimarco, Crisci, & Capobianco, 1987; Stephenson, 1992; Turnbull & Winton, 1984; Turnbull, Winton, Blacher, & Salkind, 1983).

Indeed, parents regard "a 'personal touch' as the most enhancing factor in school relations" (Lindle, 1989, p. 13). Generally, families want professionals to relate to them in comfortable, nonhierarchical, positive, and relational ways. They want a reliable alliance with professionals, one based on connection and trust, one like the "Manos connection" in Maryland.

Parents also want frequent interactions with educators. Indeed, teachers who interact more frequently with parents—teachers like those who work with Sue

FIGURE 9–1

Empowerment Framework: Collaborating for Empowerment in Communicating Among Reliable Allies

Education Context Resources

Opportunities for Partnerships	Obligations for Reliable Alliances
Opportunities Arise At . . .	*Reliable Alliances Consist Of . . .*
Communicating among reliable allies	Knowing yourself
Meetings families' basic needs	Knowing families
Evaluating for special education	Honoring cultural diversity
Individualizing for appropriate education and placement	Affirming family strengths
Extending learning in home and community	Promoting family choices
Attending and volunteering at school	Envisioning great expectations
Advocating for systems improvement	Communicating positively
	Warranting trust and respect

Professional Resources

Motivation	Knowledge/Skills
Self-efficacy: Believing in our capabilities	Information: Being knowledgeable
Perceived control: Believing we can apply our capabilities to affect what happens to us	Problem solving: Knowing how to bust the barriers
Great expectations: Believing we will get what we want and need	Life management skills: Knowing how to handle what happens to us
Energy: Lighting the fire and keeping it burning	Communication skills: Being on the sending and receiving ends of expressed needs and wants
Persistence: Putting forth a sustained effort	

Family Resources

Motivation	Knowledge/Skills
Self-efficacy: Believing in our capabilities	Information: Being knowledgeable
Perceived control: Believing we can apply our capabilities to affect what happens to us	Problem solving: Knowing how to bust the barriers
Great expectations: Believing we will get what we want and need	Life management skills: Knowing how to handle what happens to us
Energy: Lighting the fire and keeping it burning	Communication skills: Being on the sending and receiving ends of expressed needs and wants
Persistence: Putting forth a sustained effort	

Collaborating for Empowerment

and her son Nick —tend to view parents as more capable and are more open to parent input (Fuqua, Hegland, & Karas, 1985; Michael, Arnold, Magliocca, & Miller, 1992; Stephenson, 1992).

In this chapter we will discuss (1) identifying and respecting family preferences, (2) written communication strategies, (3) telephone contacts, (4) technology options, and (5) face-to-face interactions.

Identifying and Respecting Family Preferences

Although most families prefer informal communication to formal communication, families still vary in their preferences. To determine a family's preferences, you need first to learn about families through a family systems perspective. Part of the family systems perspective involves the family's cultural values and traditions; you should honor those. A major aspect of honoring cultural diversity is making accommodations for linguistic diversity. You will learn about some of these linguistic accommodations in this section.

Gaining a Family Systems Perspective

You may assume that you need to conduct lengthy interviews with families to know their characteristics, interactions, functions, and life cycle. Fortunately, it will be far easier than you think to gain a systems understanding; your best approach is to develop a comfortable, trusting, authentic relationship with the family, one that begins informally. The more you genuinely connect with the family, the more its members will be eager to share their family story with you. At that point in your relationship, you can begin to fill in the different parts of the family systems framework. Coles (1989), a prominent psychiatrist and humanitarian, describes the advice that was given to him by one of his mentors: "Why don't you chuck the word 'interview.' Call yourself a friend, call your exchanges conversations!'" (p. 32).

There is wisdom in this statement. As you develop genuine relationships with families, you will find that you will not need to administer formal assessment instruments or have stiff, professionally controlled interviews. The more you think of yourself as a friend or a reliable ally and incorporate the eight obligations of a reliable alliance, the more your exchanges will be conversations. And the more conversations you have, the more likely the information that you gather will be relevant and comprehensive.

Connecting with families in a comfortable way is especially important when you work with families from cul-

turally and linguistically diverse backgrounds. The whole special education process can be overwhelming for many families, especially families from diverse backgrounds; and the more formally you present the paperwork and questionnaires, the more intimidating it is likely to be to them. We encourage you to remember that many families do not have documented status in the United States. (They are not legally documented foreign nationals.) For them, any kind of paperwork can be a special threat.

> Those families who live here on undocumented status may find the process and forms overwhelming. There are many families who simply do not participate in the education of their children for fear of their immigration status and who are uncertain about intruding on a process that they do not fully understand. (Dennis & Giangreco, 1996, p. 109)

You have learned a great deal about a family systems framework in chapters 5 through 8. You can use this framework in your conversations with families. Some families, however, do not share their family stories all neatly organized according to the family systems framework. But in practically every exchange with families, information about that family and its system will crisscross the four components (chapters 5 through 8). What components and subcomponents of the family systems framework do you detect in Armando Sellas's description of his daughter Angelica, who has Down syndrome?

> Our expectations of Angelica have been very, very little different between what we expect from her sister and what we expect from her. We take into account that they are two distinct individuals, and they're each going to have their own identity, but you know we expect Consuelo to do certain things in the way of chores around the house or homework and things like that, then we have the same expectations for Angelica to get up in the morning, make her bed, get freshened up, go to the bathroom, brush her teeth and get ready to go.

What did you learn about sibling interaction, parental expectations, the family function of daily living, or the family cultural characteristics? Now consider a passage from a different parent:

> I was raised up in my own religion, but then just recently I stopped going. My kids already know God is very important, we were all raised that way. They know right from wrong. They also already know that they are going to experience things, and I sit and tell them "I know this is wrong, because I've done it. You want to smoke a cigarette, I'll buy the pack. You know, don't do it behind my back. My daughter, if you're pregnant and you re out there, then come to me and we'll talk about it. Don't keep bringing babies be-

cause it's too hard. You want to have sexual intercourse, there's birth control. My son, you want to do drugs, I'll help you find it and then you can go through the experience with me instead out of freaking out by yourself or something. If you want to talk, we can talk. I'll try to be very open about anything you want to talk about. They want to know what it is to be street smart, and I advise that they learn streets, but be intelligent too. Stay in school, get an education, because that's the only way you're going to get by in this world."

What do you learn here about family cultural characteristics, the parental subsystems, family interaction in terms of cohesiveness and adaptability, and life cycle stages and transitions?

Appendix B is a family systems conversation guide. This guide uses the categories and subcategories of the family systems framework that you read about in chapters 5 through 8. It sets out probes and open-ended questions that you can use in your conversations with families.

Some families may take their conversation with you in a very different direction than the sequential questions on the conversation guide. Go with their lead, and listen carefully to what they are sharing with you. Even though their comments may not relate to the next question on the conversation guide, they can provide valuable and insightful information.

Another good strategy for understanding a family and its "system" is using a *portfolio.* The portfolio is a single place (folder, file, or packet) where you can keep notes of your conversations, copies of correspondence, and information. You can organize the portfolio and its contents into the family systems framework. Develop note sheets divided into the categories and subcategories of the family systems framework. Whenever you learn relevant information about a particular component of the framework, make a note in the appropriate place. As the information accumulates, you will increasingly understand and be more empowering for the family.

Although checklists and surveys can also help you collect family information (as we will describe in chapter 11), conversations permit information to emerge within the context of open-ended sharing, in contrast to a discussion specifically focused on family needs. The more you establish a reliable alliance with families, the more comfortable they will feel about sharing information informally, frequently, and over time.

*R*especting Family Preferences

To individualize your communication, you need communication skills—verbal, nonverbal, influencing, and group (as you learned in chapter 4). You are the best

judge of which approaches can best help you develop reliable alliances, and we encourage you to evaluate continually your communication effectiveness (Perl, 1995). Whenever possible, modify the strategies to suit a family's preferences and your personal style. Although individualized strategies require an initial investment of your time and energy, as the teachers and members of Nick's team learned when they started working with Nick and Sue, many of these strategies will help you to save time and energy in the long run. Indeed, good communication strategies are the means for sharing concerns between yourself and a family such as Sue and Nick and for dealing with problems while they are fresh and before they become more complex. That is one reason Sue looks forward to the future planning meetings she will have concerning Nick's options once he finishes 12th grade; now, while he is in the 10th grade, there is a certain "freshness" about planning for life after high school—there is not the same pressure of time as there would be if Nick's team were to wait until he enters 12th grade. Not surprisingly, the Sellas family also suggests addressing matters before they become time pressured and complex:

> I'll tell you one thing that we were real surprised by and this is something that we weren't aware of that was happening, but Angelica's pre-kindergarten teacher apparently had some difficulty in dealing with her, and she got Angelica in her class in the middle of the school year. She was the first teacher to receive Angelica in her home school so there was the whole novelty of it. Later on we found out that she had more concerns and more things that she wasn't in agreement with than what she had led us to believe, and I think that if we'd had an opportunity to just be able to meet on a very informal basis, where nothing is official, nothing is recorded, it's not part of the annual review meeting, let's just kind of get together and see where we're at, whether any problems need solving or just kind of come together. I think that would help people feel a little more relaxed and not so under the gun all of the time. . . . Even though I had asked this of all of Angelica's teachers, I said "Please be honest with me. Don't tell me that she is doing good in class, when you are having trouble, because maybe I can help." That's one of the things I say, if you are a parent you know where I'm coming from, please be honest.

*M*aking Accommodations for Linguistic Diversity

To accommodate a family's linguistic diversity, you will need to develop proficiency with translations of written communications and with interpretations of oral communications. Remember that many families with whom you will be working will have limited English proficiency because of their cultural and linguistic diversity. For these families, it will be essential to provide translations of written documents in the language in which they are proficient. You will need to talk with your school administrator and other professionals, such as teachers of English as a second language, to explore local and state resources for translation. Software programs that can aid this process are also available.

While some families have limited English proficiency, others are unable to read because of their own limited education or because of disabilities. That is why you should consider the reading level at which you provide written communication. Try to make it understandable and accessible to the families with whom you are working.

In face-to-face interactions with families, we encourage you to consider the occasions when you will need to have an interpreter for families who do not speak English or who are deaf. Again, you can work with your school administrators to identify local and state resources that can be used in meeting this need. Often families have preferences for interpreters with whom they have worked in the past and with whom they already have a reliable alliance. These would be natural people to include. If those types of interpreters are not available, you might provide families with some choices so that they will have some control over who does the interpretation. Some families have commented that in a conflictual situation they sometimes perceive that the interpreter is "on the side" of the school. In establishing an equal and respectful partnership, families must have confidence that the interpreter will convey both the substantive content and the emotional overtones of their messages. Box 9–1 includes tips for you to consider in working with interpreters for families who have limited English proficiency. Many of these same tips apply to communicating with families who are deaf.

Throughout the remainder of this chapter, we will focus on four communication strategies: (1) written strategies, (2) telephone contacts, (3) technology options, and (4) conferences. In addition to families varying in whether they can read English or any other language, they also vary in many other ways, including whether they have a telephone, whether they have access to and an understanding of technology, and whether they have transportation to come to school for a conference. Thus, you will need to adapt your communication strategies to respect the family's preferences and capabilities, which is one way of individualizing the education context factors of empowerment and affecting each family's empowerment.

Written Strategies for Communication

We will describe six major strategies for written communication: (1) handbooks; (2) handouts for specific situations; (3) newsletters; (4) letters, notes, and dialogue journals; (5) progress reports and report cards; and (6) occasional messages.

Handbooks

Most school handbooks for families typically outline administrative policies and procedures but do not include information about the various educational options available within the program. For this reason, it may be helpful to develop a supplemental handbook containing information specific to your program, including information about personnel, classroom procedures, classroom supplies, transportation, lunches or snacks, methods of reporting progress and sharing information, and topics unique to your program.

Content aside, you must also consider format. Handbooks are more enjoyable to read when they are concise, attractive, and written in simple and understandable language (Kroth & Edge, 1997). If families do not speak English or if they speak it as a second language, consider having the handbook printed in other languages. Translation services are becoming increasingly available, and sometimes bilingual parents may assist in producing the handbook in different languages. In fact, a San Diego school translates information to reach parents from South America, the Philippines, Cambodia, Laos, Vietnam, and other countries (National Association of Secondary School Principals, 1994).

Handouts

Handouts deal with specific matters such as resources in the community, safety and travel, preparing a child for trips to the dentist and eye doctor, accessible places of leisure and recreation, sources of college scholarships, drug prevention, violence prevention, and summer enrichment programs. To get families to read the handouts and establish communication with you, consider these issues: What are families' special interests? What are the forthcoming special ethnic occasions and celebrations? How can family strengths be affirmed as you prepare handouts? What tips or ideas from families could go into the handouts? Are any families particularly interested in desktop publishing, and would a

TIPS

BOX 9–1

Working with Interpreters

- Learn proper protocols and forms of address (including a few greetings and social phrases) in the family's primary language, the names they wish to be called, and the correct pronunciation.

- Introduce yourself and the interpreter, describe your respective roles, and clarify mutual expectations and the purpose of the encounter.

- Learn basic words and sentences in the family's language and become familiar with special terminology they may use so you can selectively attend to them during interpreter-family exchanges.

- During the interaction, address your remarks and questions directly to the family (not the interpreter); look at and listen to family members as they speak and observe their nonverbal communication.

- Avoid body language or gestures that may be offensive or misunderstood.

- Use a positive tone of voice and facial expressions that sincerely convey respect for and interest in the family. Address the family in a calm, unhurried manner.

- Speak clearly and somewhat more slowly but not more loudly.

- Limit your remarks and questions to a few sentences between translations and avoid giving too much information or long, complex discussions of several topics in a single session.

- Avoid technical jargon, colloquialisms, idioms, slang, and abstractions.

- Avoid oversimplification and condensing important explanations.

- Give instructions in a clear, logical sequence; emphasize key words or points; and offer reasons for specific recommendations.

- Periodically check on the family's understanding and the accuracy of the translation by asking the family to repeat instructions or whatever has been communicated in their own words, with the interpreter facilitating, but avoid literally asking, "Do you understand?"

- When possible, reinforce verbal information with materials written in the family's language and visual aids or behavioral modeling if appropriate. Before introducing written materials, tactfully determine the client's literacy level through the interpreter.

- Be patient and prepared for the additional time that will inevitably be required for careful interpretation.

Source: Lynch, E. W. & Hanson, M. J. (1998). *Developing cross cultural competence: A guide to working with children and their families* (2nd ed.). Baltimore: Brookes.

---

family member like to take on the task of helping to prepare handouts?

Also consider individualizing particular portions of the handouts by highlighting or placing stars next to items that are particularly pertinent to specific families or family members. Ask students to help prepare the handouts by writing, illustrating, or duplicating them; their contributions can be meaningful language arts activities.

Your time and effort in preparing handouts will undoubtedly be appreciated by many families. Often the small, thoughtful gestures show that you care and have the family's best interests in mind.

Newsletters

Newsletters can be enjoyable and useful techniques of communication. They can be developed by an individual teacher and class, an entire grade, an entire school, or families and can include "need-to-know" information as well as drawings, quotations, and essays written by the students, comic strips, announcements of upcoming special events, students' birth dates, a parent column, horoscopes, updates on ongoing school projects, an advice column, stress-reduction techniques, descriptions of adaptive devices, advertisements for toy swaps, methods of encouraging positive child behaviors, announcements of workshops and seminars, and "bragging" notes. Try to recruit families to help with all steps in publishing the newsletter, thereby affirming that their input is valued and needed. Remember that most people like to see their names in print; by sharing good news about families in the program, you highlight their strengths. Figure 9–2 includes a sample newsletter.

FIGURE 9–2

Sample Newsletter

Young Jayhawks

Volume 5, Number 6   Lois Orth-Lopes, Editor

ACTIVITIES FOR THE WEEK

We have planned large group activities that will help the children to get to know each other, including the songs, "Who Am I" and "Friends." We will also learn a new song, "Sky Bears," and play the bells as we sing.

SHARING TIME ON TUESDAY

Last week, Ryan, Tanya, and Leilani put their sharing things in paper bags and gave clues to the other children. Everybody had a great time guessing. Ryan brought in a photograph of his twin aunts. Tanya shared an animal that she calls Foozy. Leilani showed the children a book that plays music.

This week, Michael, Muhammad, Chad, Annie, and Elizabeth will have a chance to share. Remember to send the sharing item in a paper bag so that the other children can guess what is in the bag.

ARTIST CORNER

The drawing for this week is by Mark. He used felt-tipped markers to make this bear. The original work is on the wall outside our classroom.

THE ZIPPER BEARS

The children have been learning how to zip their coats without any help from their teachers or friends. When they are successful for four days, a zipper bear is hung beside their name on the art wall. Many of the children have been working very hard and will have a zipper bear by their name soon.

In Manuel's daily battle with his zipper on his coat, October 16, 1988, Manuel won! His zipper bear proudly hangs on the wall.

PARENTS' NIGHT A SUCCESS

We were very pleased to have so many parents, brothers, sisters, and grandparents come to Parents' Night last Tuesday. It was a nice opportunity for us to get to know you better even though the time was short.

If you were not able to come, or even if you were there and have questions or concerns, please feel free to call. Our number at the office is 864-3831. If it is more convenient, you can call Lois at home (842-7137).

SNACK MEAL

Our cook, Yvonne, prepares a nice variety of snacks for the children each week. The menu for this week is:

Monday:	chex mix, orange juice
Tuesday:	fresh fruit, graham crackers, water
Wednesday:	muffins, apple juice
Thursday:	mixed vegetables, crackers, water
Friday:	crackers with peanut butter, lemonade

Source: Orth-Lopes, L. (Ed.). (1988). *Young Jayhawks.* Lawrence: Assessment Learning Classroom, Edna A. Hill Child Development Laboratory Preschool, Department of Human Development. University of Kansas. Reprinted by permission.

School newspapers that include information about exceptionality issues give a positive message about inclusion and can also address substantive family concerns. Box 9–2 is an example of addressing family concerns. It is a letter written by our daughter Kate for her high school newspaper, expressing her views on using respectful language. This letter reflects her own experiences as the sister of her brother, who is 11 years older than she.

Not only did Kate express her preferences about respectful language, but she also educated her peers on the important topic of offensive language, showing them how to become more sensitive about disability discrimination.

Articles about homework, teacher profiles, "getting to know you" features, reports about special projects, and parenting tips are often well received by parents. For distribution, some schools have found that it works better to mail newsletters to homes rather than to rely on students to take them. Some communities have also found that it works well for the local newspaper to print the entire student newspaper (Loucks, 1992).

Letters, Notes, and Dialogue Journals

Letters, notes, and dialogue journals are helpful for exchanging information and strengthening relationships with families (Ellis, 1993). Sue has relied on a notebook that Nick takes to school and brings home from school each day. All sorts of useful information is contained in the notebook. Sue can let Nick's teachers know whether he is feeling up to par or not; she can share what he and his brother John, aged 14, and newly adopted 2-year-old sister, Eleni, did over the weekend or holidays. And, in turn, Nick's teachers can inform Sue about Nick; even

MY VOICE   BOX 9–2

Offensive Language Needs to Stop

The word "retard," unfortunately, has now achieved mainstream status. I have been affected by the word all my life becuase I have a brother with mental retardation and autism. When I was in elementary school and junior high I was embarrassed about my brother because people always used "retard" so lightly. Now that I am no longer embarrassed, rather, I am proud of him, I had hoped to escape the word. So far at my school, I have been unable to do so.

I frequently hear "You are such a retard!" or "Gosh, I'm so retarded!" when someone has made a mistake or has said something seemingly stupid. Every time I hear the word, I cringe. I think about my brother, my greatest teacher, and know that someone is making a mockery out of his disability.

Often times the speaker does not realize the effect of their words. What happens when lower school students,

walking down the hall to class, hear the word spoken by an upper school student? They are going to think that "retard" isn't a bad word. It is. The word itself is obviously derogatory to people with disabilities because it is never used to describe something or someone that is successful or intelligent.

People with mental retardation are not stupid; they are just slower at processing information. J. T., my brother, leads a completely normal life despite his disabilities. He works at the University of Kansas, rides the campus bus to work everyday, and lives in his own house with two graduate students. No one would want to approach him and call him a retard to his face so why is it O.K. to use the term so loosely behind his back? . . .

Some people might say that if they use "retard" or other offensive words in such a way that they don't mean them in a demeaning way, people should not take them offensively. If you know, however, that the

words have the potential to demean someone, why use them and intentionally flare up conflict or hurt someone's feelings?

"Retard" is only one example of the offensive language circulating the halls and classrooms. Our vocabulary is filled with stigmatizing words such as "faggot," "chick," and "retard." These words have the potential to deepen the factions already apparent in the human race. They cannot possibly be doing more good than bad, so why use them?

Our school is only a microcosm for the "real" world. We hear these words from our peers and even our role models everyday, but whether or not we choose to use them is solely up to us. This is a major source of conflict for students in high schools and in our everyday society. But does it have to be?

Kate Turnbull
Editor-in-Chief

general education teachers who typically are not accustomed to so much daily contact find Nick's notebook to be helpful. Over the years, many of Nick's general education teachers have become regular correspondents with Sue, quite to her delight and to Nick's benefit.

Although dialogue journals typically facilitate conversation between teachers and students (Rueda, 1992; Staton, Shuy, Peyton, & Reed, 1988), they are also useful for educators and families. Some professionals and families prefer dialogue journals over notes and letters, which may be more easily lost or misplaced. In addition, dialogue journals offer a record of communication over time and aid in end-of-the-year reports. Try to involve families in deciding how frequently to write, who will write, what kinds of information to exchange, and whether the journal will be open to all family members, not just restricted to parents.

A special education teacher's case study of her use of dialogue journals tells how she wrote a letter to parents at the beginning of the school year, describing her program and emphasizing her preference to use a daily notebook for ongoing communication (Williams & Cartledge, 1997). Being responsible for 10 students, she wrote a notebook entry every day (usually during lunch or recess) and persisted when some parents did not respond or just signed their names. As the year progressed, she indicated that parents increasingly provided written comments, to the point that the response rate from parents to the students' daily notebooks was between 90 percent and 95 percent. Impressively, she also indicated that there was 90 percent to 100 percent attendance at parent-teacher conferences. When she asked parents their reactions to the notebooks, 95 percent of their responses were extremely positive, as exemplified by the following comment:

> I am so glad for the notebook you send home daily. It is a great help to me. It enables me to plan activities that compliment the work done in school. (Williams & Cartledge, 1997, p. 33)

If you cannot use a notebook every day, you might consider alternating days or sending a notebook on a weekly or biweekly basis (Williams & Cartledge, 1997). As much as possible, use dialogue journals to communicate positive information about the student; keep negative comments to a minimum. Negative comments are best given in person, when there is an opportunity for the parents to ask questions and seek clarification. Likewise, reserve sensitive, confidential, or controversial information for private, face-to-face conferences. One parent sadly described her son's dialogue journal as a "log of sins." Each day when he got home, she dreaded pulling out the notes and reading about the 10–15 behavioral infractions in which he had participated that day. You can imagine how painful this was for her to read and what a strain it created between herself and the teacher and even between herself and her son.

Report Cards, Grading, and Progress Reports

Report cards are the traditional means of providing families with feedback about how their child is doing in school. A national survey of elementary and secondary general education teachers about their grading practices reported the following results (Bursuck, Pollaway, Plante, Epstein, Jayanthi, & McGoneghy, 1996):

- Teachers at all levels reported that pass-fail and checklist-type grades were more helpful for students with disabilities than the letter and number grades helpfully used for students without disabilities.

- Many teachers are willing to modify the criteria for grades for students with disabilities by basing grades on students' improvement in IEP objectives, giving separate grades for their effort, and adjusting their grades according to ability.

- Elementary teachers communicate more frequently with parents about grades than do junior high/middle or high school teachers.

- Approximately 40 percent of all teachers surveyed used portfolios and believe that portfolios are helpful for students with disabilities (we will discuss portfolios in chapter 11).

- Most of the students' grades are based on homework, tests, and quizzes.

- Approximately half of the time, general education teachers assume complete responsibility for grading; special and general education teachers work collaboratively on grades about 40 percent of the time.

Because more students with disabilities are in general education, grading practices and methods of reporting grades to families take on increased significance. Many students with disabilities are passing general education classes with low grade-point averages (Donahue & Zigmond, 1990). When grading systems are based on percentage cutoffs, students with cognitive disabilities are at a significant disadvantage. Given that grading of students in general education is often at the discretion of general educators, collaboration among special educators, general educators, and families is necessary for determining grading modifications and methods for reporting student progress. Indeed, communicating grades has been largely neglected within the special education body of research.

Another alternative for documenting progress and grading is authentic assessment, particularly portfolio systems (Martin, 1994; Menchetti & Bombay, 1994). In fact, many teachers use authentic assessment systems for students with disabilities.

Progress reports usually provide families with timely feedback about how their child is doing at school (Smrekar, 1993). These reports can be complex or simple; can be sent home once a day, once a week, or once every few weeks; and can communicate about a single subject or area of development or about many.

Occasional Messages

Finally, you may wish to use occasional messages to inform parents specifically about positive aspects of their child's performance. These messages can take many forms, including certificates of recognition, sticker cards, "telegrams," "happy grams," or "good news" postcards with a collage of school events on the front and space on the back for a personal message (Loucks, 1992). Box 9–3 describes how one school uses notes to home as part of a school-wide strategy for improving students' behaviors.

TOGETHER WE CAN
BOX 9–3

Being "Centralized"

If it takes a whole village to raise one child, then it takes a whole school—faculty, student body, and researchers—to improve student behavior and increase home-school communication. At least that's the lesson taught by Central Middle School, Kansas City, Kansas, its faculty, students, and Kansas University researchers in the area of positive behavioral interventions and supports (PBIS) who have worked with the school during the 1998–2000 school years.

Here was a school suddenly experiencing the effects of school redistricting and along with that, the effects of increased student misbehavior. The problem, it seemed to the staff and researchers, was that many new students—the redistricted ones—were not "centralized." They didn't know or abide by the customs and habits of the "old" Central students. And they were requiring teachers to deal with discipline rather than to offer instruction.

What does it mean to be "Centralized"? That's what the school's Positive Behavior Intervention & Support (PBIS) team wanted to know. A comprehensive survey of staff and students provided the answer. To be "Centralized" means to have—and to

measure up to—five expectations: be safe, be cooperative, be respectful, be responsible, and be ready to learn.

The five expectations underlie codes of conduct for students and teachers alike. Indeed, teachers' lesson plans incorporated each of them. And teachers also generalized them throughout the school. On one side of a matrix they wrote the five expectations. Across the top they listed the school settings in which these expectations were to be met—classroom, library, hallway, cafeteria, and transportation to and from school. Within each box they identified typical behaviors that contravened the five expectations and listed the behavior they wanted to teach through their lesson plans.

One of the problem behaviors was "hallway behavior during passing periods." The school's response: four classes that taught students how to comply with "being safe" in the hallway. The students were asked to define, demonstrate, and give a rationale for "being safe." If a student could meet those three tests, the student received a certificate as a "Certified Safe Hall Walker." The certificate listed the general steps for being safe in the hall (for example, walking and using an

"inside voice"). The students were encouraged to take their certificates home to share with their parents.

These certificates produced at least three positive outcomes throughout the entire school: something good happened for engaging in desirable behavior, parents and family members were made aware of the school's expectations, and their students exhibited the behavior of a model "Centralized" student.

But the certificates also produced another result: some of the students who had been the most "de-Centralized" and had received the greatest number of "negative office referrals" (disciplinary referrals to the assistant principal's office) changed their behavior. The consequence for them: "positive office referrals" (PORs) for being "role models/hall monitors," a notice to their parents that they won a POR, and the posting of their picture on a POR Wall of Fame in the school's main lobby for everyone to see, especially their parents on teacher-parent meeting days.

"Centralization" is more than five expectations and positive behavioral interventions and supports. It's a means for positive home-school communication.

Telephone Contacts

The telephone can be a convenient and effective means for providing both information and emotional support. Occasional telephone calls (or, as you learned in box 9–3, notes) to families may even result in improved student performance. An advantage of using the telephone is that approximately 94 percent of all American homes are equipped with telephones, whereas not all parents or other care providers are able to read or write well enough to use printed information as a communication mode (Bowe, 1995). An answering machine at the school central office lets educators receive messages from parents when it is impossible or inconvenient for school staff to answer the telephone. In-class telephones, although arguably desirable, are atypical: "The Alliance for Public Technology estimates that only 7 percent of American schools have enough electrical outlets to plug anything new into classrooms and that just 4 percent have connections such as phone jacks in the classroom" (Bowe, 1995).

As a general rule, telephone conversations with parents should be brief and to the point. Longer, more involved conversations are more effective when conducted in person. Conversing over the telephone poses some disadvantages such as not being able to see the parents' nonverbal reactions and messages. For this reason, listen carefully and check out your perceptions by asking questions and summarizing. Ask families in advance about convenient times to contact them, and also share with them times that it is possible for you to receive telephone calls. Before calling a family member at work, ask whether that person wants to receive telephone calls there. Box 9–4 contains suggestions for use of the telephone.

Families often report that they appreciate it when teachers share their telephone number with them. This often gives families a greater sense of connection; they regard the teacher as truly a reliable ally for them. It is important, however, for you to consider when it is convenient and not convenient for you to receive telephone calls. Also, when you are contacted by families, sometimes it may be hard for you to find the time to respond.

A telephone tree is an efficient way to get information to several people with relatively little effort (Heward & Orlansky, 1984). You telephone one or two parents with a message; each of them, in turn, calls two or more other parents and so on until all parents have been contacted. This system has the additional advantage of providing parents with opportunities to interact with one another.

TIPS   BOX 9–4

Using the Telephone

- Treat every message (incoming or outgoing) as an important call.
- Always identify yourself as you place a call or answer one.
- Personalize your conversation at every opportunity by using the caller's name.
- Don't use the telephone for criticism. Criticism is tricky enough even in an eye-to-eye encounter. When the parent must depend completely on your voice, criticism is doubly difficult.
- Be sure to ask parents if you have called at a convenient time. If not, ask them to name a time when they'll be free to talk.
- Jot down in advance what you want to find out from the parent and what you want to tell the parent.
- When taking down information, briefly double-check your notes.

- If it is necessary to leave the line during a call, explain the reason and excuse yourself. When you return, thank the caller for waiting. (On long-distance calls, make every effort to avoid putting a parent on "hold.")
- Always offer the caller or person being called your help or assistance.
- Allow time for parents to ask you their questions.
- Return all calls promptly; the exception, of course, is if you are involved in the classroom with students.
- Give definite information and offer positive information.
- Avoid the use of vague statements that may force the caller to dig for information. Vague statements are irritating and waste time.
- As the conversation ends, thank the caller before you say goodbye.

Source: From the Parent Center of the Albuquerque, New Mexico, Public Schools (1985). Adapted by permission.

Another way to use the telephone is to record daily messages on an automatic answering machine that parents can access. A teacher of a primary class for students with learning disabilities recorded messages such as the following:

> Good evening. The children worked very hard today. We are discussing transportation. They enjoyed talking about the airport and all the different kinds of airplanes. The spelling words for tomorrow are: train, t-r-a-i-n; plane, p-l-a-n-e; truck, t-r-u-c-k; automobile, a-u-t-o-m-o-b-i-l-e; and ship, s-h-i-p. Thank you for calling. (Heward & Chapman, 1981, p. 13)

During the six-week program, the teacher received an average of 18.7 calls per week, compared with an average of 0.16 calls per week before the program. Students' scores on daily spelling tests improved during the program.

A second option for using recorded daily messages is a call-in telephone service ("talk line") that provides developmental guidance, referral, and general information to parents (Fuller, Vandiviere, & Kronberg, 1987). A common source of telephone information is an office secretary (Stephenson, 1992). Secretaries frequently take messages from families, handle small decision making on their own, call parents when they need to pick up their child, and relay significant information. Collaborate with the school secretary in discussing family preferences for communication, such as whether parents want to be called at work or which parent to call in families in which a divorce or separation has occurred.

Technology Options

Many parents may welcome the opportunity to communicate with educators through electronic mail (e-mail). An e-mail bulletin board system for all parents or a restricted e-mail system for each family may be quite efficient and effective, especially if the child uses a computer with e-mail or Internet and World Wide Web access.

Portable microcassette recording machines have become a popular means of technology-based communication. For many years, Nick and Sue have used a device called "cheap talk," a simple recording device that allows him and his buddies at school to exchange greetings. In the past, Sue also sent Nick to school with a portable microcassette; his schoolmates could dictate "memos to Nick" that he could listen to at home and that also would inform Sue about what happened at school that day. So much technology is "low-tech," inexpensive, easy to use, and quite effective. If someone on Nick's team needs to know something or if there is simply "nice-to-know" information, "cheap talk" and microcassettes make conversation so much more accessible.

A videotape is another medium for communicating with parents. A Georgia survey documented that approximately half the parents of children with disabilities prefer to get information (including student progress reports) through videotape as opposed to other options (Alberto, Mechling, Taber, & Thompson, 1995). An elementary school in Canada used videotapes in parent information sessions to illustrate how to teach new skills to children (McDonald, Kysela, Martin, & Wheaton, 1996). Many parents indicated that they enjoyed the opportunity to view the videotape samples, although several parents requested opportunities to see their own children in the videotapes.

To reduce confusion and lack of clarity, videotapes have served as picture report cards, daily or weekly progress reports to demonstrate newly acquired skills, or illustrations of procedures the teachers are asking parents to use in the home for maintenance and generalization of new skills (Salend, 1995). This option has been especially important for working parents who cannot come into the classroom during school hours. Additionally, support personnel such as the physical therapist, occupational therapist, and speech/language pathologist can provide similar information to assist parents in following up on their suggestions (Alberto et al., 1995, p. 19).

Videotapes also can be vehicles for your cultural responsiveness in working with particular families. Native Americans have long preferred visual pathways for learning new information, a preference that may indicate interest in videotapes (Yates, 1987). Videotapes also have been recommended for families with limited English proficiency because the tapes reduce reading and writing demands on the family (Salend & Taylor, 1993).

Face-to-Face Interactions

Face-to-face interactions, one of the most effective and commonly used methods of family-professional communication and the way that Sue and Nick's school team communicate most often and effectively, give families and professionals opportunities to develop a reliable alliance. We will discuss four types of face-to-face interactions: (1) planned meetings, (2) Making Action Plans (MAPs) gatherings, (3) unplanned meetings, and (4) group family meetings.

Planned Meetings

Because of their many potential benefits, meetings should not be limited to the beginning and the end of the school year. Regularly scheduled team meetings can do much to maintain and enhance family partnerships (Lambie, 2000; Spinelli, 1999). Indeed, when Sue Manos needs to talk face-to-face with Nick's school team, she calls an IEP meeting. "Some years, the team chose to have them as often as once a month," she says, "because getting everyone to be on the 'same page' is so much harder in the middle and high school than in other grades. And we always have at least one general educator there." If Nick's inclusion is to be successful, then a team approach is necessary, and how better to secure the team's members than by an IEP meeting?

Sometimes families' cultural values conflict with professional expectations for participation in meetings (Jordan, Reyes-Blanes, Peel, Peel, & Lane, 1998): "What most people don't understand about the Hispanic community is that you come home and you take care of your husband and your family first. Then if there's time you can go out to your meetings" (Finders & Lewis, 1994, p. 51).

A major cultural barrier for families characterized by linguistic diversity is the lack of translation: "It is not easy to have a relative translate for me every time I have an appointment" (Smith & Ryan, 1987, p. 349). A study that investigated the perspectives of Chinese parents concerning their experiences with service providers concluded:

> The lack of bilingual professionals among provider agencies presented numerous problems for the parents and their children. Translation services were generally not available, and parents had to fend for themselves, using friends and family to translate complex medical and diagnostic concepts. Chinese parents simply could not communicate with professionals, which affected both their access to and use of formal services. What these parents needed most was a basic, intensive understanding. (Smith & Ryan, 1987, p. 350)

When communicating with families with limited English proficiency, it helps to explain ideas or concepts several times, to use slight variations in terminology and examples, to have more frequent checks for comprehension, and to use physical gestures and visual cues (Gersten & Woodward, 1994).

Some families will decline to take an active role in attending meetings pertaining to their children's education:

> It's her education, not mine. I've had to teach her to take care of herself. I work nights, so she's had to get up and get herself ready for school. I'm not going to be there all the time. She's got to do it. She's a tough cookie. . . . She's almost an adult, and I get the impression that they want me to walk her through her

work and it's not that I don't care either. I really do. I think it's important, but I don't think it's my place. (Finders & Lewis, 1994, p. 52)

Conscientious planning is the key to effective family-professional meetings. In planning a meeting, you will need to consider three major phases: (1) premeeting, (2) meeting, and (3) postmeeting.

Premeeting Premeeting preparation consists of three steps: (1) notify, (2) plan agenda, and (3) arrange environments (Kroth & Edge, 1997).

When notifying parents, state your reason for a meeting. Recommend whether you think that just you and the family should meet or whether it would be helpful to invite other team members. Remember that many families prefer more frequent, informal contacts. One father suggested, "Save the conferences for the big things" (Lindle, 1989, p. 13).

Many schools schedule regular teacher-parent conference days and send notice of these meetings when they distribute the school calendar at the beginning of the year. Some schedule regular team meetings like the ones for the "Manos team." Some schools only encourage "as-needed" meetings. Opportunities for ongoing communication and collaboration are especially important. Whatever the schedule, be sure to convey to parents in a clear, understandable, and nonthreatening manner the purpose of the meeting, remembering that parents' past experiences with schools and teachers may make them reluctant to attend meetings.

> They expect me to go to school so they can tell me my kid is stupid or crazy. They've been telling me that for three years, so why should I go and hear it again? They don't do anything. They just tell me my kid is bad.
> See, I've been there. I know. And it scares me. They called me a boy in trouble but I was a troubled boy. Nobody helped me because they liked it when I didn't show up. If I was gone for the semester, fine with them. I dropped out nine times. They wanted me gone. (Finders & Lewis, 1994, p. 51)

Before this father would be comfortable at a meeting, it would be essential for you to establish a reliable alliance with him, probably in a setting other than school, so that he would know that you recognize his strengths, want to affirm his choices, and want to invest your best efforts in supporting his child.

In a workshop designed to help parents and teachers develop communication skills, parents described what they thought and felt when their child's teacher called them for a conference: "I feel worried." "I feel guilty that I haven't done enough to help my child in school." "I feel nervous, I think that Roddy has done something wrong." "I think that Dorene is not doing her work" (Flake-Hobson

& Swick, 1984, p. 142). Of the group of 50 parents, not one parent described positive thoughts or feelings when asked to attend a school meeting.

By following up your written notification with a telephone call, you give family members a chance to ask questions and understand why you (and other team members) want to meet with them. You can also inquire about the family's need for child care or transportation assistance. These logistical barriers prevent many families, especially families with restricted financial resources, from participating in meetings. You might be able to persuade other educators at your school, student service clubs, or other community resources to help arrange child care and transportation assistance.

To enable families to meet with you without having to make separate child-care and transportation arrangements, consider meeting at the family's home if that is convenient for the family (Gomby, Culross, & Behrman, 1999; Jordan, Reyes-Blanes, Peel, Peel, & Lane, 1998; Klass, 1997). Box 9–5 includes tips for making home visits. Another option is to meet at a neighborhood building close to the family's home if it is more accessible and convenient than the school.

> Teachers just don't understand that I can't come to school at just any old time. I think Judy told you that we don't have a car right now. . . . Andrew catches a different bus than Dawn. He gets there a half an hour before her, and then I have to make sure Judy is home because I got three kids in three different schools. And I feel like the teachers are under pressure, and they're

turning it around and putting the pressure on me cause they want me to check up on Judy and I really can't. (Finders & Lewis, 1994, p. 51)

Some families from culturally diverse backgrounds prefer to "conduct 'business" in everyday settings or in the course of activities such as shopping, meals, visiting, or other 'unrelated' undertakings" (Rueda & Martinez, 1992, p. 98). Clearly, there is a wide range of options for conference settings, aside from school or the family's home, such as at locations within the family's natural support systems (Delgado, 1992).

Decide with the family which family members and professionals should attend the meeting and whether the student should attend. When appropriate, involving the student in discussion and problem solving (including IEP conferences) can help ensure that decisions are consistent with his or her preferences and interests (Wehmeyer & Sands, 1997). Moreover, inviting students presents them with excellent opportunities to learn and practice the decision-making skills that are so important to independent living (Wehmeyer, Agran, & Hughes, 1998). Just be sure to communicate with their family about the cultural appropriateness of their decision-making role (see chapter 12).

Providing families with a list of suggested activities to prepare for the meeting may also reduce their anxiety. Parents who receive a premeeting awareness packet (containing information about what will happen at the meeting and suggestions for preparation) have significantly higher rates of attendance than parents who do not receive premeeting suggestions (Kinloch, 1986).

TIPS   BOX 9–5

Making Home Visits

- Talk with family members about the home visit before scheduling the appointment.
- Make home visits only if they are scheduled with the family ahead of time.
- Arrive and leave on time.
- Cancel home visits only when absolutely necessary.
- Dress appropriately and comfortably.
- Respond with sensitivity to offers of food and beverages.
- Expect distractions.
- Bring activities for the children.
- Be aware of the environment, and alter the visit if your safety or the safety of the family makes you uncomfortable.
- Leave your schedule and where you will be with someone.
- If part of your visit includes working with the child, take a blanket or tablecloth and spread it on the floor for your work area.
- Parents make choices when home visitors work with their children—some choose participation in the visit, and some use it for a few minutes of respite. Do not be judgmental of their choices.

The second step in premeeting preparation is to prepare an agenda. An agenda (1) helps ensure your own preparation, (2) notifies participants about what topics are to be covered at the conference, and (3) serves as a guide for structure and sequence during the conference. The agenda should be flexible enough to accommodate last-minute additions or changes and should include topics that families have mentioned as important.

Often Euro-American professionals are eager to follow an agenda and to be as time efficient as possible in meetings. But a more indirect approach in which families and professionals engage in conversation about what they may perceive to be tangential issues as well as share humor and make self-disclosures may contribute to forming a reliable alliance with families from culturally and linguistically diverse backgrounds (Harry & Kalyanpur, 1994; Lynch & Hanson, 1998).

The third and final step in premeeting preparation is to arrange the physical environment and establish an atmosphere that will enhance communication. Start by deciding where to conduct the meeting (for example, at the family's home, the school, or a neutral location in the community such as the library or community building). Box 9–6 gives you tips on preparing the setting.

Although home visits may mean more distractions (for example, TV or telephone noise or neighbors dropping by), they also provide you with the opportunity to gather a more complete picture of the student's environment and family life and are related to teachers' improved ability to interact with parents (Fuqua et al., 1985).

In some cases, you may want to consider bringing another person (perhaps a social worker or a school nurse), particularly when the topics to be discussed are apt to cause conflict, when there is a history of misunderstandings between the family and professionals, or when you are concerned about neighborhood safety (Harden, 1997). This person may serve as a witness to events, a support person, or a mediator in case of serious disagreements.

Recognize that some parents are uncomfortable opening their homes to you and may find home visits intrusive. Families' responses to home visits are often determined by how you characterize why you want to meet at their home.

> When Kristi was first evaluated for a special education program, the school social worker called to say that she was coming to our home for a visit. She did not say why she was coming, and I did not ask. I only knew that social workers normally visit a home to see if it "passes inspection." I cleaned for days, baked cookies and had coffee, tea, and homemade lemonade ready for her visit. The joke was on me. She had only come for a social history. She did not inspect my home or even eat a cookie. How much easier my life would have been if she would have explained to me why she was making her visit.

When you hold meetings at school, you are responsible for preparing the setting. Probably the two most important considerations are privacy and comfort. An atmosphere that is confidential, comfortable, and free of interruptions can elicit open and honest communication. Meetings that are scheduled back-to-back for short periods of time can be major impediments to establishing genuine communication. "Ten minutes is ridiculous, especially when other parents are waiting right outside the door. I need time to tell the teacher about how my child is at home, too" (Lindle, 1989, p. 14).

Meeting Four major components of parent-professional meetings such as those that Sue and Nick and their inclu-

---

TIPS
BOX 9–6

Preparing the Setting

- Determine whether it is appropriate to have the meeting at school, in the family's home, or at some other location.
- Make arrangements (if the meeting is at school) for a quiet and private room, one in which the doors can be closed and the windows are not facing out to frequently used areas.
- Gather all necessary materials before the meeting and make arrangements not to be interrupted.
- Be sure that both the temperature and the lighting are comfortable.
- Choose adult-sized chairs and tables.
- Arrange the furniture in a manner that reflects equality. Avoid placing the professional's chair behind a desk or at the head of a table.
- Have tissues, beverages, papers, and pens available for all participants.
- Consider providing coffee and snacks.

sion team practice are (1) building rapport, (2) obtaining information, (3) providing information, and (4) summarizing and following up. The rapport-building phase sets the tone for the remainder of the meeting. Rapport involves making a connection in a way so that people perceive that there is interest, understanding, and respect. Your genuine (not forced or artificial) interest in, and acceptance of, the family builds rapport. Reflect on the professionals who provide services to you (such as physicians or other therapists) with whom you have a genuine rapport. What contributes to that rapport? How long did it take to develop? What could have been done to facilitate it more readily? It is likely that the factors that enhance rapport for you and your professional allies can enhance rapport for you and families. By knowing, understanding, and accepting yourself and the families and by incorporating all eight reliable alliance obligations presented in chapter 4, you will have a better chance of establishing rapport with families.

The second component of the conference entails obtaining information from the families. Obtaining information provides you the opportunity to practice many of the nonverbal and verbal communication skills such as empathetic listening that we described in chapter 4. Encourage families to share information by asking open-ended questions. When you are unclear about a family member's point of view, ask for clarification or specific examples. Respond empathetically if and when families have difficulty expressing a thought or a feeling. Provide feedback to the family regarding the ideas and, most importantly, affirm their contributions.

The third component of the conference process, sharing information with families, requires you to use jargon-free language. Jargon limits families' ability to attend to, organize, and understand information (Lavine, 1986).

> Parents are amazed by the vocabulary that interventionists use to describe their children. They are besieged by acronyms that stand for such well-known concepts as retardation and deafness. They wonder why a pronunciation problem is called a phonological disorder. They remain bemused by acronyms such as MET (Multidisciplinary Evaluation Team), IEP (Individual Education Plan), LRE (Least Restrictive Environment), and SPL (Speech-Language). The most articulate parents tell us they believe this jargon is the interventionist's way of reminding them who is in charge. (Stonestreet, Johnston, & Acton, 1991, p. 40)

When sharing information, begin on a positive note, pointing out the student's strong points before mentioning topics that concern you or the family. Provide specific examples by telling anecdotes or giving examples of the student's work. Be aware of and respond to the im-

pact of what you are saying on the family. If they are frowning or appear puzzled, stop for a moment to provide an opportunity for questions or comments. As much as possible, encourage a give-and-take atmosphere for everyone to exchange information and concerns.

Finally, when you are summarizing or planning follow-up activities, review the high points of the meeting and emphasize next-step activities. Restate who is responsible for carrying out those tasks and the date by which they are to be completed. Discuss and agree on options for follow-up strategies. If another meeting is planned, decide on the time and place. End the meeting on a positive note. Thank the family for the interest and contributions, and offer to be available should any relevant questions or issues arise.

Postmeeting Postmeeting tasks include (1) reviewing the meeting with the student, (2) sharing the outcome of the meeting with other professionals, (3) recording the proceedings, and (4) evaluating your own satisfaction.

If the student did not attend the meeting, you may want to spend some time talking with the student (with parental consent) about what was discussed there. Explain the decisions that were made and how they will affect the student's activities. Allow time for questions, and respond to any concerns.

You may also want to share the outcome of the meeting with other professionals who are involved in the student's program. Review the decisions made and any resulting changes in the student's program, thereby ensuring continuity and consistency. Those contacts can be made in person, over the telephone, or through a written report.

By recording major decisions and next steps, you can assure family-professional accountability. Complete the minutes as soon as possible after the meeting adjourns, when the information is still fresh in your mind. Include the time, the location, agenda topics, nature of interactions, decisions, and next steps. Keep a permanent file of each of your meetings so that you can access them at some later date, mark your calendar for agreed-upon follow-up dates, and list the tasks you agreed to complete as a result of the meeting. If you keep portfolios for your family contacts, the portfolio would be a good place to file the meeting minutes.

A fourth important postmeeting activity is to evaluate what happened, reflect on how you think things went, and seek reactions, feedback, and suggestions for improvement from other participants. The more you reflect and invite feedback, the more likely it is that you will be able to develop the kind of reliable alliance that will be empowering for all participants.

BOX 9–7

TOGETHER WE CAN

Six-year-old Courtnee's MAPs Process (held in the spring of her kindergarten year with Courtnee, her family, friends, and teachers)

1. What is the student's history?

Courtnee is a 6½-year-old girl with Down syndrome.

She has a brother who is 9 years old, and he attends the neighborhood school.

Had formalized assessments conducted that stated she had a vision problem as well as motor and cognitive delays in learning.

Psychologist recommended that Courtnee attend a special education preschool.

Family had to push to get help for Courtnee to attend neighborhood preschool.

Bussed to a special day class for kindergarten.

Family did not like her going away from neighborhood to attend school but didn't know what else was available for her.

Family wants Courtnee to go to first grade at the same school as her brother.

She is on medication for seizures but hasn't had one for 2 years. She gets around well but appears clumsy at times.

She has difficulty playing with other children, although she plays well with her brother at home.

2. What is your dream for the student?

Family wants Courtnee to go to first grade at the school her brother attends.

Her vision is not a problem, but her learning style and rate of learning are different.

Family wants Courtnee to learn how to play with other children, have friends, make play dates, and go to birthday parties.

Want her to be happy and take care of herself.

To feel good about herself.

To participate in extracurricular activities (Brownies, gymnastics, or soccer).

3. What is your nightmare for the student?

That people will make fun of Courtnee and not accept her.

That she will not fit in.

Because she is strong willed, afraid no one will like her.

No one to play with; often physically pushes peers.

Not able to read or write.

No one understands her when she talks.

4. Who is the student?

Courtnee is a friendly little girl who likes to run, jump, and skip.

She likes to talk, although sometimes it is difficult to understand her.

She likes adult company more than her peers.

She is learning acceptable play behavior.

She knows how to push other people's buttons to get a reaction.

She smiles a lot.

She likes to get someone (usually an adult) to do things for her, rather than do it herself.

She can be very stubborn.

She likes to dress herself and enjoys playing dress-up.

She is a people-pleaser.

She attempts to print her name.

Likes to color with crayons.

Making Action Plans (MAPs)

A special type of conference is called Making Action Plans (MAPs), a process frequently used for students with severe disabilities (Falvey, Forest, Pearpoint, & Rosenberg, 1994; Falvey, 1995). In attendance at MAPs gatherings may be the student, parents, other family members, student and family friends, educators, and others who have a substantial interest in customizing the student's school and community to be as close to the student's preferences as possible. MAPs gatherings are typically held in comfortable settings—often the student's home or some other community setting—that encourage connections and relationships.

It may seem unusual, but the Frederick County school board (the one with which Sue has worked) requires the MAPs process at each and every significant transition of a student—from preschool to early childhood education, from early childhood to elementary, from elementary to middle/junior high, from there to high school, and from high school to post-secondary education. Both the "sending" and "receiving" program representatives have to attend, along with the parents—and when appropriate, the student. The meetings are not always comfortable. Sue re-

Six-year-old Courtnee's MAPs Process (held in the spring of her kindergarten year with Courtnee, her family, friends, and teachers)

5. What are the student's strengths, gifts, and abilities?
Courtnee loves to be outside.
She loves to play on the playground equipment.
She loves animals, especially cats.
She likes to listen to music.
She loves being with people.
She is very friendly, especially with adults.
Courtnee likes to look at books.
She likes to interact with people.

6. What are the student's needs?
She needs to go to her neighborhood school with her brother and neighborhood kids.
Needs to learn not to push others when she doesn't get her way.
Needs to learn to share materials/toys.
Courtnee needs structure and consistency.
She needs help getting organized; she often forgets her school materials.
She needs her medication for seizures.
She needs to learn more appropriate ways to make and keep friends.
She needs some one-to-one attention, but not all the time.
She needs to learn her letters and numbers.
Needs to read simple sight words.

Needs to participate in more fine motor activities (prefers outside, gross motor activities).
She needs to be able to say, "I don't know," and "no."
She needs to learn not to rely on the adults around her.
She needs to have the support and reinforcement of peers.
She needs to have a contract for follow-through with tasks and activities.
Courtnee needs to assume more responsibility for herself.
She needs to get involved in after-school activities (Brownies, soccer, gymnastics).
Needs help in the lunch line.

7. What would the student's ideal day look like, and what must be done to make it happen?
Attend the neighborhood school for first grade.
Make new friends.
Play with peers on the playground.
Share toys with peers.
Schedule an IEP meeting to plan the specifics for instructional support based upon her strengths and needs in early September (see Appendix A for completed IEP and classroom schedule).
Schedule a class meeting early in September so that Courtnee can meet all the new kids and peer supports can be initiated.
Investigate after-school activities (e.g., Brownies, soccer teams, gymnastics).

Source: From Gage, T. & Falvey, M. A. (1995). Assessment strategies to develop appropriate curriculum and educational programs. In M. A. Falvey (Ed.). *Inclusive and heterogeneous schooling: Assessment, curriculum, and instruction.* Baltimore, MD: Brookes.

---

calls the first one she had with the high school staff: "I felt like an outsider and they seemed so new to this." (An outsider, because after all, Nick was now entering the ninth grade, a time when most parents are not so involved in their child's education; new to this because Nick's MAPs meeting was the first for that school.) Did the feeling of being an outsider persist? No. "I get to know the administrators and teachers, especially those who may be reluctant to do inclusion." Getting to know them—and why they are reluctant—informs them about Nick and Sue, and it brings them onto team Manos.

Seven key questions form the basis of the MAPs process (see box 9–7). The order of the questions might vary, but their purpose is to stimulate a dynamic and open-ended discussion in which people who have a major stake in the student's well-being share their cogent insights and great expectations for the student's future.

In a MAPs gathering, a facilitator is the discussion guide and encourages brainstorming to generate as many creative ideas as possible. As ideas are shared, the facilitator records them on a large poster board.

Question 1: What is the student's history or story? Typically, the student and family share the background information, highlighting the triumphs and challenges that have been associated with the student's having a way to live his or her life consistent with visions, great expectations, strengths, and preferences.

Question 2: What are your dreams? It is especially important for students to share their dreams for the future. Families also should share their dreams and supplement what the student is saying if the student cannot or chooses not to communicate with the group members. The key aspect of the MAPs process is to identify these dreams as the basis for planning the customized school schedule and extracurricular activities.

Question 3: What are your nightmares? Because students with exceptionalities and their families often have major fears that serve as barriers to their working toward great expectations, identifying nightmares lets everyone know what those are so they can put adequate supports into place. Some nightmares such as the progressive course of AIDS in a young child cannot be prevented, but sharing them can help everyone know issues around which the student will need support.

Question 4: Who is this person? The group will use as many adjectives as it takes to get behind the exceptionality label and describe the real or essential aspects of the student's personhood.

Question 5: What are the person's strengths, gifts, and talents? Many times teachers, friends, family members, and others can lose sight of the characteristics that the person can bring to bear to achieve his or her dreams. So the MAPs meeting takes the time to identify them.

Question 6: What does the person need? What will it take to make the student's and family's dreams come true? What barriers stand in the way of where the student is at the present time and having the dreams

come true? Identifying these needs can serve as the basis for educational programming.

Question 7: What is the plan of action? A plan of action includes the specific steps that need to happen to accomplish the dream. The plan of action can involve tasks, time lines, resources, and any other detailed information that will help lead to significant progress.

The MAPs gatherings can help professionals get to know the student and the family and use the information to plan a functional and relevant evaluation (chapter 11) and IFSP/IEP (chapter 12). In addition, the MAPs gatherings can benefit families because the gatherings consist of family members, friends, and professionals (not just families and professionals) and because they are carried out informally and in a familiar and comforting setting away from school, where meetings tend to be more formal and intimidating for some families. Many aspects of MAPs establish a reliable alliance, adding the personal touch that we have repeatedly emphasized. Moreover, unlike school meetings that primarily describe the student's functioning in school, the MAPs process portrays the student within the full spectrum of his or her life.

Unplanned Meetings

Unplanned meetings inevitably occur at any time and in any place. Parents may unexpectedly drop in at school before, during, and after school hours; you may receive telephone calls at home in the evenings and on weekends; or you may be approached by families with child-related concerns at unlikely places such as a movie theater or a grocery store.

Although it is probably impossible to avoid being caught somewhat off guard at such times, you can prepare for these meetings and the likelihood that parents will express their most intense thoughts and feelings at them. First, decide what is possible for you to do in response to unplanned conferences given the other demands on your time and energy. Talk with other professionals regarding their strategies for handling hard issues at impromptu meetings. You may decide, for example, that telephone calls at home on week nights are acceptable but that conferences at the shopping mall are not. Identify the options that you consider to be open or closed to consideration at unplanned meetings. Then set your priorities and seek support from the administrator at your school. This support is important both for your own sense of security and in the event that future problems arise concerning these issues. Also, some administrators wish to be alerted to this information so they can ensure consistency across programs. In addition, seek to maintain appropriate flexibility because sometimes crises or special circumstances will require an immediate meeting that can de-escalate problems.

Of course, you need to inform families of your preferences. Ideally, you should do this at the beginning of the year before any unplanned meetings have had a chance to occur. Communicate your preferences both verbally and in writing to avoid misunderstanding and to allow the families to ask questions. When stating your preferences, be sure to explain your rationale regarding unplanned meetings in noneducational settings: for example, "I want to be able to meet your needs and answer your questions as well and as completely as possible; however, I am not able to do so without sufficient preparation and access to your child's records."

It is always helpful to have well-organized and readily accessible portfolios comprised of data sheets, permanent products of the student's work, schedules, notes from previous meetings, and other pertinent materials. Other helpful resources include community guides and names, addresses, and phone numbers of other agencies, families, and professionals who may be of assistance to families. Sometimes on-the-spot referral to a school or community-based professional may be more appropriate than attempting to assist a family with a problem that may be more adequately addressed by other professionals. Last, but not least, practice positive communication. Without positive communication skills, even the best-prepared professionals can fail in their attempts to meet the needs of families.

Group Family Meetings

Sometimes, group meetings with families will be especially appropriate (see chapter 14). Almost all schools have orientation meetings at the beginning of the school year; throughout the year they also may have open houses in which families come and learn about their child's daily schedule. Although it is difficult to connect with families individually at such large meetings, group meetings provide significant quantities of information to a large number of people at one time and give families an opportunity to meet each other. Typically, attendance is optional, although a high school in Denver sent parents of incoming ninth graders a letter suggesting that they were required to participate in the orientation meeting and at least one parenting workshop during the school year. Students whose parents complied with this expectation received extra

academic credit toward graduation (National Association of Secondary School Principals, 1994).

Linking Our Themes

Having discussed the type of partnership that we call *communicating among reliable allies,* we now invite you to put that partnership into a larger context. That context is the one we call *collaborating for empowerment,* which is represented in figure 9–1 and was discussed in chapters 3 and 4.

As you see from figure 9–1 and as you read in chapters 3 and 4, empowerment occurs when the family factors of motivation and knowledge/skills connect with the education context factors of opportunities for partnerships and obligations for reliable alliances. Your first step in creating the empowering context is to communicate using the techniques we discussed in this chapter.

To create an empowering context, you need to infuse the eight obligations for reliable alliances into your communication partnerships. As you communicate (or have any other interaction with families), you will want to know yourself and know the families with whom you are communicating. Likewise, as you communicate, you will want to honor their cultural diversity, affirm their strengths, promote their choices, jointly envision great expectations, communicate positively, and thereby warrant their trust and respect.

In the rest of this chapter, we will show how you can create a reliable alliance through communication and how the communication partnership has many positive effects on the family's motivation and knowledge/skills. Indeed, as we conclude each of the chapters that follow this one, we will show you how you can infuse the eight obligations of a reliable alliance into the type of partnership we discuss in that chapter and thereby have a powerful influence on the family's motivation and knowledge/skills.

Creating a Reliable Alliance

How do you infuse each of the eight obligations of a reliable alliance into your communication partnership? Look at figure 9–3. On the left side of the figure, we list each of the eight obligations. Across from each obligation, we present an issue that may face you as you try to carry it out. In the last two columns after each obligation, we describe one action that you should not take—a disempowering action—and one action that you

FIGURE 9–3

Creating a Reliable Alliance: Disempowering and Empowering Actions

Obligations	Issues	Disempowering Actions	Empowering Actions
Knowing yourself	You feel frustrated when you talk with parents who concentrate on barriers rather than solutions.	Tell parents that you wish they would not be so negative.	Listen to the barriers, empathize, and break their and your actions down into small, manageable steps.
Knowing families Family characteristics	Parents tell you that they are going to be busy on the night of the school open house, but you sense that they are not comfortable in coming to the school.	Tell parents that they will be letting their child down if they don't come.	Invite the parents to come to the school at another time, such as when their child is performing in a music program or otherwise demonstrating a strength of which everyone can be proud.
Family interaction	A single mother asks you to meet with her in her apartment at a housing project (where there was a recent shooting) rather than her coming to school for a meeting.	Tell the mother you don't feel safe in coming into her neighborhood.	Talk with the school social worker and get advice on alternatives for home visits in this particular housing project.
Family functions	Parents of a student who is failing every subject are not showing any concern about school failure.	Tell the parents that you object to their family priorities and that they are only hurting their son.	Meet with the family and find out, from their perspective, their priorities for their son, both this year and in the future.
Family life cycle	The family has just moved to a new community, and neither the student nor parents know anyone at the child's new middle school.	Assume that the parent may be interested in coming to the school open house next year; leave them on their own to make connections in the new community and school.	Call the parents, issue a special invitation to come to the school open house, and arrange with another family to meet the new parents and student and introduce them to others.
Honoring cultural diversity	The school handbook is only available in English, yet the parents speak Mandarin.	Tell the parents that maybe their child or some friends can translate parts of the handbook to them.	Talk with your administrator about getting the handbook translated into Mandarin or securing someone to explain it to them.
Affirming and building on family strengths	A father is an accomplished photographer and particularly enjoys using his home video camera to record family activities.	Tell the father that it is impractical for him to videotape his child at school, especially interacting with other children.	Ask the father if he would be willing to get other families' consent to tape classroom activities and make the tape available to families.

FIGURE 9–3   CONTINUED

Creating a Reliable Alliance: Disempowering and Empowering Actions

Obligations	Issues	Disempowering Actions	Empowering Actions
Promoting family choices	A parent asks if a conference can be arranged before school to accommodate her work schedule.	Tell the parent it is against teacher-union policy.	Ask the parent if it would be possible to talk on the telephone early in the school day rather than to meet at school.
Envisioning great expectations	A group of parents ask you to explore the use of e-mail in communicating with families.	Dismiss their request as too far-fetched because of limited computer access.	Form a committee of families and educators to contact computer companies about the possibility of being a model site for technology demonstrations.
Using interpersonal communication skills	You are participating in a conference with parents who are extremely angry that their gifted child is making poor grades and believe that it is your fault.	Tell the parents that they have not provided proper supervision for homework and that the poor grades are their fault.	Listen empathetically and ask if they would be willing to brainstorm options that would involve them and you collaborating to promote their child's program.
Warranting trust and respect	The school administration asks parents to contribute to a fund to pay for the classroom newspaper, but the parents do not have money to contribute.	Tell them they'll not be able to get the newspaper, since they have to "pay their own way."	Identify a nonmonetary way for them to contribute to the class; tell them their classroom contribution represents their donation; keep everything confidential.

might take—an empowering action (in carrying out these actions, you would need to personalize them for each family situation). Altogether, figure 9–3 links each of the eight obligations of a reliable alliance to an issue that families may face and to a negative/disempowering action and a positive/empowering action. The obligation of knowing families separately identifies family characteristics, interactions, functions, and life cycle issues to aid you in taking a family systems approach.

*S*trengthening Family Factors

How do you know that the empowering context, the one you create by communicating among reliable allies and

that you have infused with the eight obligations for a reliable alliance, has a positive effect on the family's own empowerment? How can you have any confidence that your communications and empowering context make a difference to a family's motivation and knowledge/skills? Frankly, you may never know exactly what difference you make; but in figure 9–4 we illustrate how you can use communication to make a difference in the five elements of a family's motivation and the four elements of a family's knowledge/skills.

Finally, Remember one of the key points from chapter 3: As you enhance families' empowerment, you will likely enhance your own and your colleagues' as well.

FIGURE 9–4

Strengthening Family Factors Through an Empowering Context: Communicating Among Reliable Allies

Motivation	Enhancing Actions You Can Take	Knowledge/Skills	Enhancing Actions You Can Take
Self-efficacy	Emphasize student and family strengths in a dialogue journal and phone calls.	Information	Provide a thorough description of grading policies and procedures.
Perceived control	Ask families their communication preferences and incorporate those preferences into all communication.	Problem-solving	Hold a MAPs gathering and determine the elements of an ideal day; collaborate to put those elements into place.
Persistence	Schedule sufficient meetings to ensure that all necessary problems are resolved.	Coping skills	Empathetically listen when families need social support.
Energy	Initiate communication as soon as problems occur rather than waiting for problems to escalate.	Communication skills	Model refined verbal and nonverbal skills.
Hope	Communicate the positive gains you expect the student to accomplish by the end of the school year.		

Summary

Positive communication is the single most important key to developing a partnership between families and professionals. This is so because communication lies at the heart of all other forms of partnership and is an indispensable ingredient of the empowering context that we described in chapters 2 and 3. It also is a way to practice the eight obligations of a reliable alliance that we discussed in chapter 4.

On the whole, families typically prefer informal and frequent communication with professionals over formal and infrequent communication. To be an effective communicator, you will need to apply what you learned about family systems; this means identifying families' preferences. You also will need to know and practice specific communication strategies—written, telephone, and technology-based. In addition, you will need skills for planning, carrying out, and following up on face-to-

face interactions. Most of all, you will need to recognize that families usually want to be and can become your reliable allies.

For them to become your allies so that you and they can collaborate for empowerment, you will want to create an empowering context and infuse into it the eight obligations of reliable alliances: know yourself, know families (use the family systems perspective), honor their cultural diversity, affirm their strengths, promote their choices, jointly envision great expectations, communicate positively, and warrant their respect and trust.

Finally, you will want to link your own motivation and knowledge/skills with families' motivation and knowledge/skills. When you do this, you create an empowering context and enable families, yourself, and other professionals to become more empowered; in short, you collaborate for empowerment.

In Frederick, Maryland, Sue, Nick, and an entire team of educators involved in his inclusion can count on each other, through thick and thin, to support each other and Nick as he gets an inclusive education. It has taken a long time—nine years, beginning when Nick was in a noninclusive first-grade program—to get and then to sustain the results of a team approach and of an inclusive education. These nine years have been spent as "communicators" and have been years marked by painful but always candid conversations and by joyous times as well.

The result of the early communication—Sue's insistence on inclusion, her self-education around techniques and rights, her exploration of how to be the best talker and listener she can be—is that the Frederick County schools have changed. What once seemed unheard of—Nick's inclusion in the general curriculum—now is "assumed." It is a given, "Support from top to bottom," as Sue puts it. And so, too, is the technique of communication.

More than Nick's inclusion—and that of other students with disabilities—results from Sue's efforts. That "more" is system change: the Frederick County schools have changed: their policies, practices, personnel, and procedures differ from other Maryland counties, indeed, from other schools in many other states.

Sue doesn't use the word "empower" to describe what she does—or "empowered" to describe what she, Nick, and the schools have become. But she could and with great justification. Sue had the motivation, she acquired the skills and knowledge, and she communicated and created collaboration; and the schools took advantage of their opportunities to be partners, to become her reliable allies. As she and Nick face his adult future, one thing is certain: They won't face it alone.

Chapter Ten

Meeting Families' Basic Needs

They call New Orleans "The Big Easy." What a misnomer, at least for the families whom Ursula and DJ Markey know and help. The demographics of the families supported by their organization, Pyramid Parent Training, are stark: In one year alone, out of 174 families, 90 percent of families are African American women, 54 percent have incomes of less than $15,000 annually, and 81 percent are single parents. All of the families have one or more children with disabilities.

The litany of challenges facing these families is long and dreadful: racism, poverty, neighborhood violence, isolation, spousal abuse, single-parent family structure, limited access to health care, loss of public support as a result of welfare reform in 1994, their own language and literacy limitations, their bad memories of their own times in school, and the demise of neighborhoods.

The loss of neighborhood—of "place" and reciprocal obligation—bears heavily on families. Ursula and DJ recall that once upon a time, when they were growing up, there was a "shared sense of ownership and pride expressed in references to our children, our playground, our schools, our churches, our homes, our everything." Then there was a "long-standing silent pact between parents in the community"—a pact that each family would "check on" and even chastise another family's child, as if that child were their own.

What can be done nowadays, whether in New Orleans or in other communities consisting of traditionally underserved families? The answers are straightforward enough and surprising.

Turn back to the parents, to the families. They are the "keepers of the flame, accepting the responsibility to recall community, live community, build community."

See their strengths: "Our families are held together by love, determination, and a delicate balance of personal responsibility, disability benefits, and rights. . . . Without any one of these supports, everything could come tumbling down. We can't let that happen. As parents of children with special needs, we are already engaged in the struggle to create a society that values all children. As people who live in traditionally underserved communities, we survive and succeed against racism and discrimination daily. . . . The fighting for justice and equality is a tiresome business. Yet again, we must become as strong as we are tired."

To become as strong as one is tired! No "easy" task in the "Big Easy" or in other communities. "We tell parents, 'Your families can't afford to lose you. And your family will lose you if you are not happy with yourself!' " So, Ursula and DJ work on supporting families to meet their basic needs.

To Ursula and DJ, themselves the parents of the man to whom this book is dedicated, the first basic need is keeping the flame alive, keeping the families' dreams and visions alive, rejecting the notion that "things" will not get better. "We need to fan their sparks. We have to help them to not give up."

To endure, to prevail—it takes more than what Ursula and DJ provide through Pyramid Parent Training, more than service coordination, and more than individual advocacy and systems-change advocacy in so many different service-provider systems (education, health, "welfare" agencies, child protective services, juvenile and adult criminal justice, mental health, and developmental disabilities, to name the "usual" ones). It takes more than giving families information and training opportunities, more than sponsoring family-centered mutual support groups, more than reliance on state-of-the-art interventions.

Meeting their needs is more than a "what," more than a service. That much is necessary but not sufficient. For those families caught "between a rock and a hard place," there is a deeply affective side to meeting their needs.

"Many of us acknowledge there can be no real progress (for the family) without spiritual guidance. . . . we must celebrate ourselves and all caring parents who uphold family values by teaching their children to be lov-

ing, responsible, productive people. We must continue building communities where those values abound. . . . We laugh a lot, in spite of everything. Humor is a big factor. Humor about the happy things, about our kids and their insights and their candor in saying things we adults wouldn't dare say, like, 'it's pretty hard to sit still because the class is so boring.' "

And yet one other thing: "What sustains us across time is that we have come to understand our stress and that it is part of the process that has transformed us. There is an energy in transformation. There is power in transformation. We recognize and see it in ourselves. We've been part of two civil rights movements. And we see it and nurture it in other families. Life is a series of transitions and transformations. We have become masters of transition and transformation. We have to help other families to be the same."

The Markey family: Ursula, Duane (front), Teiko (back) and D.J. (1998)

The partnership of attending to families' basic needs involves supporting families to meet their emotional, informational, financial, safety, and health needs. Figure 10–1 offers a framework to use in helping to meet families' basic needs.

Some educators may wonder if it is appropriate for them to direct their time and attention to families' basic needs. They may well believe that their primary role—indeed, their only role—is to teach the student. Are they mistaken? The answer is yes, and the reason is fairly simple: The more you support families to address their priority personal and family needs, the more likely it is that they will be able to respond to their children's educational needs as well as their needs in other areas.

Ursula and DJ Markey put it succinctly: "The greatest need for families is that they have their basic needs met. Because if they're not able to provide stable housing, food, and decent clothing, they're never going to put special education on the front burner. . . . So the big thing is their need for economic stability." If a family has to sacrifice money to attend an IEP meeting (much less a school festival), there's little choice: It's work first and school second. That's not true of all families, of course; some are able to strike a balance, but they have different life conditions from the families with whom Ursula and DJ and many others work.

You already know from a family systems perspective that families attend to many simultaneous functions, and each demands their time and attention. Their child's education is only one of eight functions. When they have major unmet needs in some of those functions (perhaps inadequate economic resources to purchase food, shelter, and health care) or in education (such as understanding the nature of their child's exceptionality), then your assistance and support to fulfill those needs can enhance their child's well-being.

There are many different areas around which you can collaborate with families to meet their basic needs. You can connect them to health-care agencies; you can let them know where they can get benefits for their child (such as those available from a local Social Security or low-income-housing office); or you can be a witness if their child is involved in a juvenile justice proceeding or a child-protection hearing. Especially for young parents, single-parent families, or those who are already subsisting on public benefits, the key, say Ursula and DJ, is to "walk them through the problems they are experiencing." It's more than giving them information or referring them to a different provider system or a family support center such as Pyramid Parent Training, as helpful as these acts are. It's also a matter of helping them to understand that you—and others in your school—will not "lump them into groups that receive the same generic

kinds of services." Families want individual attention; each is its own entity, not a part of a conglomerate.

In this chapter we will address four topics around which families often need and want collaboration. You can collaborate with families to meet their basic needs by enabling them to (1) access social support, (2) acquire information, (3) access economic and family support, and (4) address issues associated with childhood abuse or neglect.

Accessing Social Support

By referring to the empowerment framework (see figure 10–1) and recalling specifically chapter 3, you already know the importance of the life management skill of social support.

Social support networks can provide a variety of assistance, including emotional, informational, and material support. Indeed, that's a big part of what Pyramid Parent Training and comparable groups do. Run by families and for families, especially those who are underserved, these groups (including Loving Your Disabled Child [LYDC], featured in chapter 2) sustain families with emotional support (remember LYDC and Pyramid and the importance of having and keeping faith), with information, and with material support.

Emotional support provides caring, encouragement, and understanding; informational support provides families with knowledge, skills, and connection to services; and material support provides tangible items such as money, vouchers, food, or items (for example, adaptive equipment or clothing). Extended-family networks, friends, informal neighborhood groups, coworkers, and religious groups—all of those components of the "communities" about which Ursula and DJ spoke—are examples of typical social support networks.

Many studies have shown that social support is linked to reducing stress and improving emotional well-being (Bennett, DeLuca, & Allen, 1996; Crink & Stormshak, 1997; Dunst, Trivette, & Cross, 1986; Frankel & Wamboldt, 1998; Lehman & Irvin, 1996; Lustig & Akey, 1999; Singer et al., 1999). Unfortunately, families of children with disabilities often have smaller social support networks than other families, and they often tend to get their support from nuclear and extended-family members (Herman & Thompson, 1995; Kazak & Marvin, 1984). Yet when families do have access to social support, they often report greater satisfaction as parents and more positive interactions with their children (Crnic, Greenberg, Ragozin, Robinson, & Basham, 1983; Dunst et al., 1986; Lehman & Irvin, 1996; Singer et al., 1999).

FIGURE 10–1

Empowerment Framework: Collaborating for Empowerment in Meeting Families' Basic Needs

Education Context Resources

Family Resources

Motivation

Self-efficacy: Believing in our capabilities

Perceived control: Believing we can apply our capabilities to affect what happens to us

Great expectations: Believing we will get what we want and need

Energy: Lighting the fire and keeping it burning

Persistence: Putting forth a sustained effort

Knowledge/Skills

Information: Being knowledgeable

Problem solving: Knowing how to bust the barriers

Life management skills: Knowing how to handle what happens to us

Communication skills: Being on the sending and receiving ends of expressed needs and wants

Opportunities for Partnerships

Opportunities Arise At . . .

Communicating among reliable allies

Meetings families' basic needs

Evaluating for special education

Individualizing for appropriate education and placement

Extending learning in home and community

Attending and volunteering at school

Advocating for systems improvement

Obligations for Reliable Alliances

Reliable Alliances Consist of . . .

Knowing yourself

Knowing families

Honoring cultural diversity

Affirming family strengths

Promoting family choices

Envisioning great expectations

Communicating positively

Warranting trust and respect

Professional Resources

Motivation

Self-efficacy: Believing in our capabilities

Perceived control: Believing we can apply our capabilities to affect what happens to us

Great expectations: Believing we will get what we want and need

Energy: Lighting the fire and keeping it burning

Persistence: Putting forth a sustained effort

Knowledge/Skills

Information: Being knowledgeable

Problem solving: Knowing how to bust the barriers

Life management skills: Knowing how to handle what happens to us

Communication skills: Being on the sending and receiving ends of expressed needs and wants

Collaborating for Empowerment

One way to enable families to find social support is to connect them with other families who share similar experiences (Ainbinder et al., 1998; Santelli, Turnbull, Marquis, & Lerner, 1995; 1997; Singer et al., 1999). That's how Pyramid Parent Training got started. When Ursula and DJ's son, Dwayne (also called "DJ"), was first diagnosed as having a disability, Ursula and DJ were in college. With the emotional and informational support of a caring professional ("She wouldn't let go of us. She called us, she followed through."), Ursula and DJ began to find their own strength. After hearing about them, other families began to come to them for comfort and advice. They must have felt the same way as the following parent:

> Family and friends fell by the wayside in a fantastic pattern of despair . . . like a chain of dominoes. Many of these friends were professionals that I had the utmost confidence in. Pillars of strength and guidance drifted away like straws in the wind. . . . I knew then that from that day forward my whole life must change if [my son] were to survive. His vulnerability frightened me. I knew what I must do. I could no longer go it alone. I needed other mothers, other fathers to relate to. (Pizzo, 1983, p. 25)

Like so many other parents, this mother wants to talk to others who have already walked in similar shoes down similar paths. Parents of sons and daughters with exceptionalities—parents such as those involved with Pyramid Parents and LYDC—frequently express a desire to be linked with other families whose children have similar needs (Santelli, Turnbull, Sergeant, Lerner, & Marquis, 1996; Summers et al., 1990). Making these connections is part of the self-help movement in which people who face similar experiences offer each other (1) a psychological sense of community, (2) an ideology for interpreting their experiences, (3) an opportunity for catharsis with others who understand the experience firsthand, (4) role models, (5) an opportunity to learn practical and tested life management strategies, and (6) access to a network of people for social relationships (Katz, 1993). The self-help movement offers both group and one-to-one support.

Group Support

Support groups for families whose children have exceptionalities often are organized around some base of commonality such as parents of very young children; children with a similar exceptionality; parents from a similar ethnic background; and family member roles such as groups for mothers, fathers, or grandparents (Carter & Harvey, 1996; Koroloff & Friesen, 1991; Krauss, Upshur, Shonkoff, & Hauser-Cram, 1993; Shapiro & Simonsen, 1994; Vadasy,

Fewell, Meyer, & Greenberg, 1985). What difference do these groups make?

> Empirical studies of the effects of parent group participation have produced inconsistent findings. On the one hand, there is evidence that parent groups are associated with benefits for some participants, especially those who feel a need for support and who have the skills to interact effectively in a group setting. On the other hand, there is evidence that parent groups may have equivocal or even adverse effects on some participants, especially those who have fewer needs for additional support. For parents of children with disabilities, we have little knowledge about the characteristics of those who participate in such groups or about the effects of participation on their functioning. (Krauss et al., 1993, p. 10)

What we do know from our experiences of learning from Ursula and DJ is that for families from culturally, ethnically, and linguistically diverse backgrounds, the benefits of mutual support are inestimable.

In chapter 1, you learned about families' perspectives on some of the benefits and drawbacks of parent organizations. Clearly, because family systems are diverse, no one type of support has uniform effects. Thus, your role is to individualize your efforts in meeting families' basic needs and in all other opportunities for partnerships.

One-to-One Support

A widespread and popular type of support goes by the name of *Parent to Parent*. Parent-to-Parent programs establish one-to-one matches between a trained "veteran parent"—someone who has experience as a parent of a child with a disability—and a "referred parent" who is dealing with an issue for the first time. The veteran parent provides emotional and informational support to the referred parent in personalized ways (Santelli, Turnbull, Lerner, & Marquis, 1993; Santelli, Turnbull, Marquis, & Lerner, 1997; Smith, 1993).

Parent-to-Parent programs started nearly 20 years ago in Omaha, Nebraska. Fran Porter, the young mother of a child with Down syndrome, realizing how much help she had received from parents of children who had "been there" and how many of her own experiences she had to offer, teamed with a social worker, Shirley Dean, to create a program that would foster one-to-one connections between parents. She named the model program *Pilot Parents*, symbolizing a pilot tugboat that goes out of a rocky and dangerous harbor to guide an incoming boat safely to shore. She envisioned that the veteran parent would be the pilot for the new parents in guiding them to supportive harbors. As the Omaha program grew, it hired its first paid director, Patricia McGill Smith, who was featured in the chapter 1 vignette. From that modest start has grown, informally and spontaneously, a national grassroots movement, Parent to Parent.

Local Programs In 1994 and 1995, nearly 30,000 parents were served by approximately 550 Parent-to-Parent programs. Typically, the programs serve parents without regard for the type of disability their children have, are developed and run by volunteer parents in low-budget ways, and match a veteran parent who has successfully faced a certain challenge with a parent who is just beginning to deal with that challenge. The greatest percentage of programs serve between 13 and 25 referred parents, are less than six years old, and operate in a community of more than 100,000 people (Santelli, Turnbull, Marquis, & Lerner, 1997; Santelli, Turnbull, Lerner, & Marquis, 1993).

At the heart of the Parent-to-Parent program is the one-to-one match of someone to listen and understand. The match is typically made on the basis of six factors: (1) a similar disability, (2) a family facing similar problems, (3) a veteran parent who can respond within 24 hours, (4) children with disabilities who are close to the same age, (5) families who live close by, and (6) families who have a similar family structure. In approximately three-fourths of the local programs, the veteran parent receives specific training in the communication, listening, and problem-solving skills needed to be an effective supporting parent. In approximately 80 percent of the matches, the relationship lasts for longer than one month. In about one-third of the situations, the relationship lasts for more than six months. In addition to providing emotional support, the one-to-one match is often a source of information about disability and community resources, a source of a referral to community services, a provider of advocacy training, and a source of group activities for individual and family participation.

The greatest percentage of those who participate in Parent to Parent are Caucasian (88 percent). The majority of families are two-parent households (90 percent), and approximately one-third of the families have annual incomes over $50,000. The largest single age group of children of referred parents includes those from birth to age 2 (40 percent), and the single largest age range of children of veteran parents is 6- to 11-year-olds (43 percent). Approximately two-thirds of the children have a moderate or severe disability. In about two-thirds of the matches, contact is made within the first week; and 86 percent of the first contacts are made by telephone.

The Parent-to-Parent match usually occurs just after the initial diagnosis that the child has a disability, typically within the neonatal intensive care unit of the hospital or shortly after the family leaves the hospital and begins to explore community services and supports.

> Parent to Parent has been my life-line. When I first heard the diagnosis, I was devastated. Well-meaning doctors and nurses, as well as friends and families, simply did not understand. It was only when I finally connected with another parent through the Parent to Parent program that I could begin to hope for a future for us all. My veteran parent was gently there for me whenever I needed her.

Most parents who are matched during the child's early years testify to the value of such early support, as this typical statement indicates:

> When our son with Down syndrome was born three years ago, my husband and I were shocked and devastated. We called our Parent to Parent program, which supplied us with invaluable information, as well as sending us a "support couple" to talk with. It was important to us to meet with the couple—not just the mother—since my husband takes as much responsibility for caring for our children as I do. Also important was that we were matched with a couple whose child had also been through open heart surgery (our son had major defects). The couple that our Parent to Parent program sent us were such warm, optimistic, "normal" people, they gave us hope. About a year later, my husband and I were trained by our program to be support parents. The Parent to Parent office has many requests for visits from both father and mother. My husband was one of very few men willing to go through formal training. I have also found that support for non-English speaking families is hard to come by. It has been satisfying to me to be able to serve the Spanish-speaking community.

As this mother describes, many referred parents evolve into veteran parent roles as they share their insights and practical know-how with new parents. Because it is true that "to teach is to learn twice," veteran parents have not only the benefit of knowing that they are helping others but also an opportunity to reinforce their own learning.

A participatory action research study, carried out equally by researchers and parents, investigated the efficacy of Parent-to-Parent support in a study that involved 400 parents nationally (Santelli, Singer, DiVenere, Ginsberg, & Powers, 1998; Singer et al., 1999). Over 80 percent of the parents found Parent to Parent to be helpful. Specifically, parents who use Parent-to-Parent services reported feeling better able to deal positively with their child and family situation, viewing their circumstances in a more positive light, and making progress on goals that are important to them.

What options exist if you are in a community that does not have a Parent-to-Parent program and you perceive that families might want one? You might convene a group of potential veteran parents and committed professionals to brainstorm about the possibility of starting a new local program. Box 10–1 includes tips for beginning a local program. You can also arrange for individualized matches among parents of children with disabilities and giftedness when no programs are available.

Again, no one program is uniformly helpful for everyone. One parent who did not find Parent to Parent helpful commented:

> We have different styles of dealing with our children and we realized that very quickly. I think that part of that . . . there's a personality difference. . . . She has a very different way of looking at things. . . . So in some ways I don't feel so great after talking to her sometimes. It's really important to take care of your psyche, I think, when you have a special child and to know when somebody is going to be helpful and when somebody's not. (Ainbinder et al., 1998, p. 107)

Statewide Programs Because local programs need support and coordination, statewide Parent-to-Parent programs exist in 29 states (Santelli, 1999). These statewide programs provide technical assistance to local programs and make matches on a statewide basis when a local match is not available. Statewide program models represent a continuum of services from highly centralized to highly decentralized. In some states, the statewide Parent-to-Parent program is part of the same program as the parent training and information centers about which you will read in the next section. In other states, the statewide Parent-to-Parent program is affiliated with a parent organization, an early intervention program, or a university. No two statewide programs are exactly alike. A manual that describes best practices in statewide programs is available if you would like more information (Santelli, 1999). You may order this manual from the Beach Center (see appendix A for address).

Appendix A also includes the contact information for the 29 statewide Parent-to-Parent programs. We encourage you to contact these programs if you would like to have more information about services in your state or about how you might help develop a statewide program if your state does not currently have a statewide headquarters. If you want to know about Parent-to-Parent local programs in states that do not have a statewide program, you may contact Betsy Santelli (612-525-0509), a

TIPS

BOX 10–1

Starting a Parent-to-Parent Program

- The most important first step is to identify a small group of parents who are interested in developing a Parent-to-Parent program. Parent leadership, energy, and commitment are keys to the program's success. Professionals can be important guides and offer a newly developing program many important resources.

- Decide whether your program is going to be entirely staffed by volunteers or sponsored by a service provider agency, disability organization, existing parent group, or other group. If you take the volunteer route, you may find it useful to ask people in the community for advice and assistance. Also consider asking banks, religious organizations, libraries, and other places to donate space for your meetings or office needs. If you decide to get support from sponsors, you could ask for space, donated initial costs, professional staff availability for training help, referrals, and assistance with fundraising.

- Established Parent-to-Parent programs offer excellent information and training materials. The Beach Center on Families and Disability at the University of Kansas has a list of these programs. It also has program-related materials and can provide technical assistance. Call (785) 864-7600 for further information.

- Establish a system to connect parents. You will need a local telephone number, preferably available at all times, that potential program parents can call. Use an answering machine if necessary. Appoint someone to coordinate incoming referrals and establish matches.

- Develop a record-keeping system for keeping track of referrals and matches.

- Let people know about you. Use flyers, brochures, word of mouth, parent speeches, radio, newspapers, doctor offices—anything you can to promote the program.

- Consider optional support activities, such as ongoing consultation for veteran parents, informational group activities, social gatherings, advocacy training, and instruction for others in the community.

Source: Beach Center on Families and Disability, University of Kansas, Lawrence.

staff member at the Beach Center on Families and Disability (which we codirect). She can direct you to the Parent-to-Parent programs in your area and can let you know about available resources.

Acquiring Information

As you learned in chapter 3, information is a significant element of a family's knowledge and skill and, in turn, their empowerment (Bailey et al., 1999; Hadadian & Merbler, 1995; McDonald, Kysela, Martin, & Wheaton, 1996; Scorgie, Wilgosh, & McDonald, 1998). Most studies about the information needs and priorities of families have gathered data primarily from Euro-American families; but one study interviewed more than 500 families of infants and toddlers from Hispanic, Native American, and Euro-American families to determine parents' needs for information and where they find it (Sontag & Schacht, 1994). More than anything else, these parents needed information about service availability. They also needed information about parenting, services to which their children have a legal right, their child's educational needs, expectations for children at different ages, and their child's disability. The parents reported that physicians were their most frequent sources of information. Although 75 percent of the parents indicated that they were told about their child's problem when they began receiving services, almost two-thirds indicated that they had received confusing, incomplete, or inaccurate information. Slightly more than two-thirds expressed that they had to find out many things on their own or by chance.

What are your options for acquiring information that will enhance your own empowerment, as well as sharing information with families so that all of them can become more empowered? You have already learned about one important source—Parent-to-Parent programs. In addition to providing emotional support, Parent-to-Parent programs are also valuable resources for informational support (Santelli, Turnbull, Sergeant, Lerner, & Marquis, 1996). In this section we will highlight eight additional avenues of information, including (1) parent information programs, (2) community resource programs, (3) clearinghouses, (4) family organizations, (5) adults with exceptionalities, (6) books and magazines, (7) television and radio, and (8) technology.

Parent Information Program

In this section we will consider three types of parent information programs: (1) parent training and information centers, (2) the Grassroots Consortium, and (3) community resource programs.

Parent Training and Information Centers Recognizing that parents need training and information to help their children develop to their fullest potential and to secure their rights under federal and state laws, Congress began to authorize and fund parent coalitions in the late 1960s. Currently there are approximately 70 parent training and information centers (PTIs) funded by the U.S. Department of Special Education, Office of Special Education and Rehabilitative Services. Each state has at least one PTI, and there are also centers in Palau and Puerto Rico. (See appendix A for a list of PTIs.) By law, the majority of PTI governing board members must be parents of individuals with disabilities, and each PTI must have private, nonprofit status. By tradition, PTIs typically employ parents as directors and staff members.

State PTI Programs As we have noted, there is at least one PTI in every state. We encourage you to contact the PTI in your state to learn what services it offers. You yourself may want to take advantage of these services for your own continuing education, and you certainly will want to alert families about PTI activities. In box 10–2 you can read about the Kansas PTI, Families Together.

By law, PTI projects support parents to do the following:

- Better understand the nature and needs of the disabling conditions of their children
- Provide follow-up support for their children's educational programs
- Communicate more effectively with special and general educators, administrators, related services personnel, and other relevant professionals
- Participate fully in decision-making processes, including the development of the child or youth's individualized education program (IEP)
- Obtain information about the programs, services, and resources available at the national, state, and local levels to their children and the degree to which the programs, services, and resources are appropriate to the needs of their children
- Understand the provisions for educating infants, toddlers, children, and youth with disabilities under the Individuals with Disabilities Education Act (IDEA)

In 1994, 36 PTIs provided 163,780 people with direct, person-to-person services and sent newsletters and other mailings to many more parents. Of those receiving PTI services, 46 percent were parents, and 54 percent were educators and other service providers. Of the parents who received PTI services, the greatest

Getting through the Maze

Ask Connie Zienkewicz, director of Kansas' parent information and training center, Families Together, what is the most valuable service her organization provides families, and her answer (delivered without hesitation and with a great deal of certainty) is simple: getting them through the maze of education and community services.

"We have families standing by who have the experience and expertise to help other families, one on one, in navigating the maze." Altogether, Families Together has 20 parents on its staff; each has a child with a disability. Each has experience with the schools or community providers; each has had training from experts. Each has encountered the usual problems facing families—problems about student behavior and school discipline, educational goals, least restrictive placement, transition to adult services, and community-based service provision.

Throughout the entire year, these parents operate out of four regional offices—those in Wichita, Topeka, Kansas City, and Garden City. During the school year, other families are available at regional offices (located in their homes) in Manhattan, Hays, Pratt, and Parsons.

Altogether, these four elements—statewide coverage, family experience, training from experts, and knowledge of local situations—create a network of communication among families. Need help with your child's school program? With your child's behavior? Finding an expert to treat an unusual medical condition? Finding a specialist in challenging behavior? Not a problem. Turn to the network. The network makes Families Together a force for change in Kansas.

But getting through the maze, says Connie, does not depend entirely on those four elements.

Nearly 15 years ago, Families Together began to sponsor "enrichment weekends"—times when families, including parents, the child with a disability, and brothers and sisters, uncles and aunts, grandparents and other family members—could get together to learn, problem solve, and just enjoy themselves. Tow of those weekends occur each year.

But there are eight other occasions when families—usually the parents of the child with a disability—convene. These parent networking conferences are held regionally throughout a large, sparsely populated state. They involve training and information—lots of both.

And, most useful to the families, they provide opportunities for families to find others whose situations are like their own. There's the "eureka" factor, says Connie: "You mean to say that other families in Kansas have the same kinds of challenges we have? Eureka! We can learn from each other. We can support each other."

Two factors, then, help families in "getting through the maze." There's the information that Connie, her staff, and various experts offer. And there's the family network—the reliable alliance with other Kansans, however far-flung they may be. It's not easy to negotiate the maze, but in Kansas it's not as hard as it could be, thanks to Families Together.

---

representation of disabilities was in the areas of attention deficit/hyperactivity disorder (AD/HD), learning disabilities, mental retardation, and emotional disabilities (Center for Resource Management, 1995).

National Network Congress also has authorized a national program of PTI technical assistance, Technical Assistance Alliance for Parent Centers (www.taalliance.org)—referred to within the PTI network as "the Alliance." The Alliance is located in Minneapolis, Minnesota, and is affiliated with Minnesota's PTI, which is the PACER Center (www.pacer.org). The Alliance coordinates technical assistance for all of the PTIs and has a special emphasis on enhancing the capability of PTI staff to take full advantage of computer technology for management and for the provision of educational support to families.

To ensure that state PTIs have access to other PTIs to provide them with consulting and technical assistance, the Alliance has created four regional PTI Centers:

- Northeast Regional Center—Parent Information Center, Concord, New Hampshire
- Midwest Regional Center—Ohio Coalition for the Education of Children with Disabilities, Marion, Ohio
- South Regional Center—Partners Resource Network, Inc., Beaumont, Texas
- West Regional Center—Matrix Parent Network and Resource Center, Novato, California

Each regional center is administered by a state PTI that provides technical assistance and conferences for all PTIs within the region.

In addition, the Alliance has designated nine PTIs as Centers of Expertise on priority topics, including board of directors development, cultural competency and diversity, early childhood, effective training techniques, inclusion, interagency collaboration, school reform/IDEA, self-determination, and transition from school to work. Like the regional PTI centers, the expertise centers are administered by a state PTI, but they also provide technical assistance to all other PTIs nationwide, individual parents, and professionals.

Appendix A includes the names and addresses of the Alliance, regional PTIs, state PTIs, and expertise centers. This broad national network can provide valuable information and resources to you, and we encourage you to take advantage of this support.

Grassroots Consortium The Grassroots Consortium on Disabilities is a national, multicultural alliance of community-based, parent-directed organizations that foster empowerment for families of children and young adults with disabilities in traditional underserved communities (See Appendix A). Representing over 150,000 families from diverse cultures (African American, Latino, Asian and Pacific Islander, Native American, Euro-American, urban and rural, and families dealing with migrancy and/or poverty issues), the member programs provide information and support to families who are isolated for many different reasons—racism, discrimination, cultural and linguistic differences, socioeconomic status, and/or geographic location.

The unifying concept of Grassroots is that the best solutions to social problems grow from the bottom to the top; accordingly, Grassroots' priorities include promoting leadership within underserved communities and linking the various centers, through the consortium, to each other. Grassroots' publication, *Tapestry*, highlights the activities and successful strategies of these community organizations. Ursula and DJ as well as Teresa Cooper (from chapter 3) are members of the Grassroots Consortium. All three of them excel in providing information to families. They excel because they know the families—really know them. They know the families—their members, their needs and desires for their children. This nearly familial knowledge makes it possible for Ursula, DJ, and Teresa to personalize the information they provide. Moreover, they know what language the families understand and what jargon they have not heard before. And they know what barriers they face in school-family partnerships and how other families have overcome those barriers. The bottom line is very simply that Ursula, DJ,

and Teresa can personalize the
And that ability comes from listenir
what the families tell them about tl
schools they attend.

Community Parent Resource C
Department of Education also funds co
resource centers (See Appendix A). The ...ers, created largely as a result of the advocacy of the Grassroots Consortium, work in traditionally underserved communities to provide information, training, and other assistance to families who have children with disabilities or who have limited English proficiency. Six Grassroots Consortium members have these grants—Pyramid Parents in New Orleans; a joint venture involving LYDC (see chapter 2), Vietnamese Parents of Disabled Children (VPDC), and Parents of Watts (POW), all in Los Angeles; United We Stand (UWS) in Brooklyn, New York; and Parent Power (PP), in Tacoma, Washington.

Most of Pyramid Parents' LYDC's, and POW's families are African American; most of VPDC's are Vietnamese; most of UWS's are Hispanic/Latino; and most of PP's are Korean or Vietnamese.

Despite their differences, these programs share five features. They develop new family leaders; they provide one-on-one assistance; they distribute family-friendly materials (including materials translated into languages other than English); they provide training in positive behavioral interventions and supports; and they engage in outreach to families in their communities.

Do these programs make a difference? There can be no doubt about it. Traditional agencies—often not led or staffed by families—have not sufficiently penetrated the underserved communities; they may not know how to do so, or they may be unwelcome in those communities. Moreover, some family-directed associations also have been unable to help families in those communities; again, there is a combination of ability and "fit." So, these parent resource centers—those that know who the families are, where they are, what they need, what language and customs they use, what approaches work in involving them—are invaluable. Just remember: It's all a matter of "fit."

*C*learinghouses

Clearinghouses of information for families and professionals receive federal funding to distribute information. Two different types of clearinghouses funded by the U.S. Department of Education are the National Information Center for Children and Youth with Disabilities (NICHCY) and the Beach Center on Families and Disability. The mailing addresses for these centers appear in appendix A.

prepares and disseminates free information
[...] dren and youth with disabilities and disability-
[...]d issues to families, educators, and other profes-
[...]onals (website: http://www.nichcy.org/). It has five services: (1) personal responses to questions about disability
issues such as specific disabilities, early intervention,
special education, family issues, transition, legal issues,
and multicultural issues; (2) referrals to state and national
disability groups, advocacy organizations, parent associations, and professional groups; (3) information searches
of NICHCY's databases and library; (4) free publications
such as fact sheets about disabilities and legal guides; and
(5) materials in disability-accessible formats and in Spanish. Most of NICHCY's publications can be printed off the
Internet.

The Beach Center on Families and Disability at the
University of Kansas (which is the center we codirect—
website: http://www.lsi.ukans.edu/beach/beachhp.htm)
conducts research and training to enhance families' quality
of life and to enhance public policy and professional practice. The Beach Center also disseminates information to
families, individuals with disabilities, policymakers, and
the general public. The center's information for families
covers a broad array of topics, including parent-to-parent
support, positive behavioral interventions and supports,
self-determination, family-centered policy and service delivery, and IDEA. Families find especially useful the center's
one-page "How To" and "What Research Says" fact sheets,
free newsletter, videos, and resource guides. Some of the
materials are available in Spanish, Chinese, and Korean.

Family Organizations

There are more than 2,000 family organizations nationally. Many of them also have state and local groups.
Family organizations vary in size, activities, and operating budgets. Most focus on specific disabilities; some of
those are large-population categories of disabilities such
as mental retardation, and others are concerned with a
particular rare syndrome.

One of the largest family organizations is The Arc
(formerly the Association for Retarded Citizens of the
United States—website: http://www.thearc.org). In
chapter 1, you read about The Arc's critical role in advocating for individuals with mental retardation and
their families and in stimulating state-of-the-art programs
and support systems. The Arc's newsletter is free to The
Arc's nearly 200,000 members and costs $15.00 per
year for nonmembers. Its semimonthly *Government Report* reviews the latest federal legislation, activities in
Congress and the courts, and activities of various federal
agencies. *Advocates' Voice* is a newsletter for individu-

als interested in self-advocacy. It is written at a low reading level, so it can be used very appropriately as part of
a high school curriculum in preparing students with cognitive challenges in self-advocacy skills. The Arc also
produces one-page fact sheets, pamphlets, manuals,
videotapes, and posters on a wide range of topics, including HIV/AIDS prevention, the Americans with Disabilities Act, and assistive technology devices. All of
these materials are useful to families and employers, volunteers, community citizens, and teachers.

Adults with Exceptionalities

Adults with exceptionalities have long valued the empowerment that comes through peer counseling—
connecting with another individual with a similar exceptionality for the purpose of providing information
and emotional support (Brown, 1999). As in the Parent-
to-Parent approach, an adult with an exceptionality can
provide peer counseling and information to other adults
and to children and youth with disabilities and their
families (Turnbull & Turnbull, 1993). In box 10–3 Vicki
Turbiville, a former member of the Beach Center's staff
who has expertise in early intervention and family studies, shares her perspectives (as an adult with a physical
disability) about the potential contribution that adults
with disabilities can make to young children with disabilities and their families.

Children and youth with exceptionalities and their
families can get valuable information from adults with
exceptionalities, who have "insider" knowledge (Powers, Sowers, Turner, Nesbitt, Knowles, & Ellison, 1996).
Consider adults in your own community as possible
mentors, guides, and sources of information and advocacy. You can contact them through a local or state independent living center, which is a community advocacy program for adults with disabilities.

Books and Magazines

Many books for families have been written by professionals and family members themselves. In chapter 6, when
we discussed family interactions, we specifically recommended a number of books that have been written by
mothers, fathers, and siblings. When this book was going
to press, a search of the Internet site www.Amazon.com
using the word *disability* produced a list of 1,376 books
that address disability topics. You might consider working
within your school district to set up a library of disability-
related books that parents can check out at their conve-
nience. It might be possible for parents who read the
books to write a short review in terms of what they partic-

Peers Empowering Peers

Talking to other parents when you are a new parent or to an upper classman when you are a freshman can be helpful. And children who have disabilities also have a powerful resource—we who are adults and have disabilities.

I contracted polio in 1949 when I was 3 1/2 years old. We lived in rural Iowa and were miles from anyone who knew much about polio or any disability for that matter. Although this was a time of polio epidemics, no other child in my community of 800 had polio or any other comparable disability. Once in a while, when we went to Des Moines, I would see an adult who had a disability. But most people who had a disabilities were kept at home, and there was little accommodation to provide cognitive or physical access to public places or services. At a fairly young age, 10 or 11, I remember being concerned about whether I would be able to use my crutches and braces as I got older. When I finally spotted a young adult of 20 or so who was using them, I was reassured that they were usable by older people. This search for a model has continued throughout my life (although my definition of who is old has changed as I've gotten older). Recently, I saw a woman in an airport who appeared to be in her mid-60s using crutches and braces. She's my "older" model today. I hope I see her again in about 20 years!

Everyone needs a role model, including kids who have disabilities—maybe *especially* kids who have disabilities. When a child without a disability is growing up, the parents have a reasonable idea of how their child should be when grown. Having a child who has a disability is usually a new experience for everyone in the family, and it is sometimes difficult to envision an enviable life for the child. An adult who has a disability and "has a life" can help everyone see the future and move toward it.

When you're a child or especially an adolescent (with apologies to Kermit the Frog), it isn't always "easy to be green." I remember one of my best summers was spent at the National Foundation for Infantile Paralysis in Warm Springs, Georgia. Everyone there had had polio and used a wheelchair or crutches or braces. We all had a wonderful summer being "just like everyone else." This is not to argue against inclusion. It is to suggest that students who have disabilities should have an opportunity to be included with all children, including others who have disabilities. They also need to have an opportunity to learn from adults who have disabilities and to see us in responsible and desirable positions. Then they will develop one kind of vision for the future and the knowledge needed to achieve that vision.

Just as children who have disabilities can learn from adults who have disabilities, so can those who provide services to these children learn from us. I remember talking to a parent recently about her 5-year-old who was entering kindergarten. Her daughter has cerebral palsy and uses a variety of means of mobility, including a walker and a power wheelchair. The occupational and physical therapists were not concerned that the classroom was going to be too crowded to accommodate the daughter's power chair; they wanted her to have to use the walker. I said that it was going to be most important that the child have functional mobility in the kindergarten classroom. The other kids would be moving fast; her mobility has to be adequate to permit her to move with her classmates. She was slow and awkward with the walker; the room had to be accessible for her to use the power chair. Not every event has to be an opportunity to achieve a therapeutic goal. Service providers need to remember that individuals who have disabilities have lives to lead, not just goals and objectives to accomplish. Adults with disabilities know this firsthand and can help identify the important outcomes for the children.

Getting information directly from us also affirms our own skills and abilities. We all value competence and helpfulness. When you ask for help or information from an adult with a disability, you are affirming our contribution to the well-being of others and our place in the community.

Vicki Turbiville

---

ularly like and do not like as a guide for other parents who might consider reading the book in the future.

Despite the large (and growing) market for disability-related books and "how to" guides (especially those by families for families), disability information is not systematically incorporated into popular magazines (although there has been an increase in coverage in the last several years).

A magazine that is specifically aimed at parents who have a child with an exceptionality is *Exceptional*

Parent (website: http://www.eparent.com). Published since 1971, this monthly magazine offers practical information about the day-to-day issues of living and working with a child with a disability or a special health care need. Regular features include topics such as Search (in which parents and professionals interact about specific questions), Ask the Doctor, and New Products. *Exceptional Parent* also has a library that provides easy access to a broad range of interesting and current books on disability topics. We encourage you to check out the website and to familiarize yourself with the broad resources.

Television and Radio

Increasingly, regular programming and specialized segments on television and radio highlight family and exceptionality issues. A number of regular TV shows, including "Sesame Street," routinely incorporate people with exceptionalities. Canada has even implemented the Disability Network, which has had a market share of 11 percent, or more than 1 million viewers, for the past five years.

Radio stations are also beginning to incorporate disability news and have special programs related to disability. For example, a radio station in Arizona started a "Talk Radio Show" on life and disability in 1992, and now it has grown to a satellite-delivered network of 18 markets across the country.

Technology

Technology vastly expands families' access to information. The National Rehabilitation Information Center, or NARIC (website: http://www.naric.com), will conduct computer searches for families concerning information requests, products and devices, disability organizations, and funding opportunities. NARIC has more than 20,000 products on its service list, and users can call the electronic bulletin boards to search the database, get messages, and download fact sheets. Another option for accessing the database is through CD-ROM. NARIC has a directory of national information sources on disabilities, including 42 databases, 700 organizations, and more than 100 resource directories.

Internet websites related to disability are expanding at a rapid rate. We have identified some of those websites as we have described various organizations. There are a number of other websites that offer extensive information related to families of children with disabilities. Websites that will provide you with extensive dis-

ability information and links to other relevant disability sites include:

- Linda's BookMark's—http://www.waisman. wisc.edu/~rowley/bookmark.htm
- Family Village— http://www.familyvillage.wisc.edu/index.htmlx
- Adaptz—http://www.adaptz.com
- http://www.ldonline.org

Computer bulletin boards offer interactive opportunities for families and professionals to exchange information. For example, a recent check of the autism bulletin board revealed 30 to 40 daily messages on topics such as teenagers, toilet training, the use of aversive intervention, inclusive education, research possibilities, sign language, and siblings.

Now what can you do? What steps should you take? You can build your individual and school capacity to gather information and to share it with families. Familiarize yourself with the informational resources we have discussed. Create your own library and make it available to families as well as your professional colleagues. Work with the school librarian, other educators, and community librarians to develop school and community resource libraries for families. In addition, the more you develop your computer expertise, the more you will be able to communicate readily with a number of major clearinghouses, websites, and bulletin boards that can help you get the information that you and families need. Just remember that knowledge is power, and power is at the heart of empowerment.

Accessing Economic and Family Support Services

As we discussed in chapter 5, families vary in their characteristics associated with their socioeconomic status, employment, and opportunity to earn income. One of the most basic needs that families have is for adequate economic resources in order to meet the basic needs of all of their family members as well as the specific disability needs of the family member with an exceptionality. As Ursula and DJ Markey have so correctly said, "economic stability" is the first priority for families on the margins of our wealthy nation; until they can provide themselves food, clothing, and shelter, they can hardly begin to collaborate with their children's teachers.

Households of all types that provide support to a member with developmental disabilities have less income and receive more means-tested benefits than the average U.S. household (Fugiura, 1998). Those households headed by a single parent who has a child with a developmental disability have the lowest income of any household type. In this section we will address federal and state programs that have been designed to address the economic resources as well as the employment-related opportunities of families.

Federal Programs

Among the many federal programs that provide economic resources to families, the three that are most relevant to families who have children with disabilities are the benefits available under the reformed "welfare" program and two that are available under the Social Security Act.

Welfare The Personal Responsibility and Work Opportunity Reconciliation Act of 1996 ended the former welfare entitlement assistance for eligible families with low incomes and created the Temporary Assistance for Needy Families (TANF) block grant (Blum & Berrey, 1999). TANF's goals are to provide support to poor families to care for their children, reduce the need for government benefits by promoting employment, reduce nonmarital pregnancies, and encourage two-parent families. In a nutshell, TANF requires individuals who have been welfare recipients to work and places a 5-year limit on the receipt of federal assistance. Box 10–4 describes a parent in Louisiana to whom the Markeys provide support. As you will discern in reading about Dana, she has multiple needs. Yet the TANF requirements challenge her as she addresses her many family needs.

The federal government's data emphasize TANF's success in substantially reducing the welfare role by converting welfare recipients into workers. But in examining the impact of these changes on families, family advocacy organizations report troubling data—data that coincide with the experience that Dana faces (Sherman, Amey, Duffield, Ebb, & Weinstein, 1998):

- The majority of new jobs pay substantially below the poverty line.
- Many families who leave welfare are not finding steady jobs.
- Many families who have left welfare still struggle to meet their basic needs related to food, shelter, and health care.
- Child care, health care, and transportation are major barriers to families' finding and keeping employment.

We urge you to become knowledgeable about welfare reform's impact on families and work in your own community to enhance supports for families who are falling between the cracks. Box 10–5 includes tips for how educational programs can collaborate with families and other community citizens to strengthen TANF programs, policies, and positive outcomes (Knitzer & Cauthen, 1999).

Social Security The major source of income support for low-income families of children with disabilities is Supplemental Security Income (SSI), which was started in 1974 under the Social Security Act (Title XVI—website: www.ssa.gov). SSI provides monthly payments for people who have limited income and resources (they meet the federal "poverty test") and who have a significant disability. Among those eligible are children with disabilities (those under the age of 18) whose families have limited income. Children must meet Social Security's definition of disability; they must have a physical or mental condition that results in "marked and severe functional limitations." The disabling condition must last or be expected to last at least 12 months or be expected to result in the child's death. Furthermore, the child must not be engaged in any "substantial gainful activity" (job that pays more than about $750 per month). A disability evaluation team collects evidence about the disability and makes a determination of eligibility. You may be in a position to assist a family in collecting this information to provide documentation on the nature and extent of their child's disability.

When a youth with a disability reaches 18 years of age, he or she must continue to qualify for Social Security benefits, using adult disability criteria. These criteria focus on impairments that restrict an individual from doing substantial work for at least a year or are expected to result in death.

The SSI program provides cash (in 1999, a monthly maximum of $500 for an individual and an average of $368 for each individual) so they can pay for the basic necessities for maintaining the children at home, cover the additional costs of caring for and raising the children, enhance the children's opportunities to develop, and offset the family's lost income (National Commission on Childhood Disability, 1995). A study of how families used these funds reveals that its highest areas of family utilization were clothing and shoes, diapers and related incontinence supplies, food, rent and utilities, transportation, and medicine (Pugliese & Edwards, 1995).

Research clearly documents that families need SSI and that they benefit from this economic support (Agosta & Melda, 1995). The Social Security Administration is currently funding a comprehensive survey to track children receiving SSI and the impact of welfare reform on these children. Data collection is anticipated to begin late in the year 2000.

TOGETHER WE CAN

BOX 10–4

Being Honest about Dana's Needs

Dana, a high school dropout, has entered a GED program, because under Louisiana's welfare-reform programs, she must be in school full-time. No absences are tolerated, not even to fulfill obligations to her son Marcus, age 3. A single absence automatically requires her to perform community service, beyond the community service she already must perform to remain in a welfare-to-work program. The more she does for Marcus at the expense of her own training, the more she has to do to remain in the program; and leaving the program would terminate her temporary aid for needy families (TANF, under the 1996 welfare-reform law).

The vicious circle—tend to Marcus, have to do more in the program, then have less time for Marcus—has had unhappy consequences for her and Marcus. Dana could not be present when early intervention staff determined that he has an emotional disability. She cannot consult face-to-face with teachers about his behaviors: fighting other children, crying at length when he cannot get what he wants, refusing to settle down at nap time, and pitching objects when frustrated. She was intimidated by the teacher's language—full of words she did not understand—at the only IFSP meeting she was able to attend.

When Marcus is seriously ill or agitated, Dana takes him to a hospital emergency room. There he gets same-day attention, so she misses only one day's training. But routine medical care is problematic. Her clinic basically dismisses her concerns about his behavior, advising her only to change his diet.

The welfare-to-work program provides Dana $10 per day for child care. Finding full-day care for Marcus at that price is nearly impossible as well as risky. The state does not license child care, and Marcus' disability makes him ineligible for many facilities and programs. Dana has been denied Medicaid benefits, and no state family support aid is available.

Without Dana's sister, Marcus would have no one to care for him after his early intervention program dismisses. Yet Dana's sister, too, must soon enter a welfare-to-work program.

Here, the two sisters face the same reality: The "target jobs" for which they train—such as a nursing-home assistant—pay only minimum wage, require rotating shifts, and do not offer health insurance. Moreover, the minute Dana and her sister find work, they are removed from the TANF rolls and lose the temporary aid they now receive. Trapped in the "working poor" category, Dana and Marcus then face an uncertain future.

How to help? "There's no magic wand," says DJ Markey, codirector of Pyramid Parents in New Orleans. "When a family is in crisis, we've got to be aggressive. When a family has long-term challenges, however, it's a matter of information, referral, and follow-up, especially follow-up."

Follow-up requires a large number of agencies and lots of people. But they have to be the "do right" people, says Ursula Markey, the other codirector. "You know the kind, the ones who make things happen."

And there's one other type of help: "woman-to-woman talk," the kind that only Ursula can offer. "We focus on a vision for the future. We try to expand a woman's limited vision and expectation. That limitation is internalized into them, often by schools and other programs. It's more than self-esteem. It's that they've been corralled into careers with steel ceilings—don't worry about glass ceilings, these have steel: computer school, nurses' aides, the tourist hospitality business."

Introducing Dana to mothers and fathers who have faced the same kinds of challenges but who have overcome them—that's another good technique, probably the best for raising their visions.

What's the root problem? Is it that Dana quit school? That Marcus has a disability? No, those are just symptoms.

What is truly at fault, what "corrals" Dana and limits her and Marcus, DJ and Ursula say, is the relentless effects of poverty and racism. "Are these 'intractable' facts of life?" DJ asks. No, he and Ursula think not. But they will be unless Americans—especially those at the policy-making level—refuse to have honest dialogue about them.

How to change Dana's life? Face it, honestly. Bravely. Talk about it. Better yet: Talk about her and Marcus. Don't talk about an "it," for "it" is someone; "it" is a life. Personalize Dana and Marcus. See them as you would want to be seen. Treat them as you would want to be treated. Recognize that though they are less fortunate, they are not less worthy.

TIPS

Medicaid Medicaid is a program of medical and health-care assistance for low-income people, including those with disabilities. It is commonly known as "Title XIX"—referring to the portion of the Social Security Act that sets out the Medicaid provisions. Although Title XIX was first authorized in 1965 to provide funds to pay for the health care of individuals who are poor and who have disabilities, Congress amended it in 1971 to allow federal funds to be sent to the states to improve the conditions in the state institutions for people with mental retardation and related developmental disabilities. These funds, however, created a federal "bias" in favor of institutions (Gettings, 1994), while other federal and state policy was directed at deinstitutionalization (discharging people from institutions and preventing them from being placed there). Accordingly, in 1981 Congress authorized a new program, the Home and Community-Based Services (HCBS) Waiver Program, allowing states to use Medicaid funds to provide residential and employment supports and services to individuals who would otherwise require institutional or nursing facilities if they did not receive these services (Braddock, Hemp, Parish, & Westrich, 1998). The ct of the HCBS Waiver is to reverse the bias to-ward institutional placement and to provide a catalyst for community and community supports (Lakin, Prouty, Smith, & Bock, 1995; Smith, Prouty, & Lakin, 1996). Indeed, there are twice as many individuals with mental retarda-tion receiving the HCBS Waiver as there are individuals who receive Medicaid funding for institutional and nurs-ing facilities (Lakin, Anderson, & Prouty, 1999). This change from an institutional focus to a community focus represents a revolutionary shift in service spending for in-dividuals with developmental disabilities.

One of the most exciting new developments for adults with disabilities, including students transitioning from high school into adulthood, is self-determination funding that has been initiated through the Robert Wood Johnson Foundation's leadership (Shumway, 1999). Cur-rently being implemented in 30 states, this national movement is redirecting funding streams. The redirec-tion allocates approximately the same amount of money (through the HCBS Waiver) that traditionally has gone to residential and employment agencies directly to individ-uals with developmental disabilities. The goal is to max-imize benefits for individuals with disabilities and to re-duce conflicts of interest that often exist between agency and individual priorities. Planning principles of this ap-proach include (Nerney, 1998):

- Paying for individual support and companionship to enhance community relationships rather than pro-viding 24-hour supervision
- Paying for food, transportation, and clothing consis-tent with valued preferences and lifestyle options
- Paying for job coaches to enable individuals to have real jobs that produce significant income (West, Revell, Kregel, & Bricout, 1999)
- Paying for one-time investments such as a down payment for a home, business-related equipment, and assistive technology
- Having control of the budget so that individuals and their families and friends can participate in hiring and firing support people rather than only having ac-cess to agency staff (Nerney, 1998)

All of these funding sources have complicated regu-lations and are implemented in somewhat different ways by each state. Because economic support is vital to so many families, we urge you to contact your local Social Security Office to obtain printed information and assis-tance from staff in learning the details of funding avail-ability in your state and community. As you begin to ac-quire this information, we also encourage you to seek the support of people who are experts on public benefits and who can explain information that may be hard to under-stand. Once you have a grasp of this information, we en-courage you to share it with families who are interested and to serve as a facilitator for families in finding the pos-sible funding options for which they might qualify in your community (Braddock, 1998).

State Programs

Because federal responses have been insufficient to meet families' basic needs, families have advocated for and nearly half the states have adopted family support policies and programs (Bradley, Knoll, & Agosta, 1993; Singer, Powers, & Olson, 1996; Turnbull, Garlow, & Barber, 1991; Walker, 1995). The goals for family support pro-grams are to enhance a family's ability to meet the needs of their family member with a disability within the home and community setting, including enabling the family to participate in community recreational and social activi-ties. Eligible families are typically those whose children have developmental disabilities, although some states in-clude children with emotional disorders (Bergman & Singer, 1996; Garlow, Turnbull, & Schnase, 1991).

To empower families to make and carry out the de-cisions they think are best for them, some states pay cash to the families; others give the families a voucher that they can redeem for services. Some provide both cash and a voucher. Families may use the cash or voucher to secure a wide range of services. In 1996, the average an-nual cash subsidy payment to a U.S. family was $2,331 with over 18,000 families benefiting (Braddock, Hemp, & Parish, 2000). Typically, states fund the following (Agosta & Melda, 1995; Bergman & Singer, 1996; Bradley et al., 1993; Garlow, Turnbull, & Schnase, 1991):

- Case management and service coordination
- Respite care and day care
- Other care services (for example, homemaker services)
- Medically related services (for example, home health-care services; medical and dental care not paid for by other sources; and therapeutic, habilita-tive, and nursing services)
- Assistive technology and related services (for exam-ple, vehicle and home adaptations and modifications)
- Parent education and support services (for example, parent programs, counseling services, crisis inter-vention, estate and transition planning services)
- Services for the child that are not paid for by other sources (for example, personal care attendants, spe-cialized nutrition and clothing, communication ser-vices, and self-advocacy training)

Family support programs are usually administered by the state's human resources or social/rehabilitation agency and have local councils. The local councils not only determine which families are eligible for the services but also assist them in developing and carrying out an individualized family support plan. A helpful contact for finding state-specific resources is your state's parent training and information center (see appendix A).

On the whole, families approve of family support services, and the services themselves are effective in carrying out the purposes for which they were created (Friesen & Wahlers, 1993; Herman & Thompson, 1995; Human Services Research Institute, 1995). Because families have the power to define their needs and spend the cash to satisfy the needs, they believe that they experience less stress and have an improved quality of life (Herman, 1994). Families also report an increased capability for maintaining their child at home, assisting in the child's development, and compensating to a degree for their lost income because they care for their child instead of taking a job (Agosta & Melda, 1995; Friesen & Wahlers, 1993; Herman & Thompson, 1995). Research has also documented that respite services provided to families in a way that is easy for them to access and is consistent with their preferences leads to reduced family stress (Herman & Marcenko, 1997). One of the key factors in the reduction of family stress is enabling parents to have more time for themselves. Box 10–6 includes quotations from families in Iowa, Illinois, and Louisiana who participate in their states' family support programs and describe what those programs mean to them.

A current analysis of state spending on family support revealed that states are spending slightly over $1.5 billion per year nationally; this expenditure comprises about 7 percent of the total state budget for mental retardation/developmental disability spending (Braddock, Hemp, Parish, & Westrich, 1998; Braddock, Hemp, & Parish, 1997). In chapter 15 we will discuss advocacy and roles that you might take in building family-professional partnerships in order to advocate for increased support for families. An increase in family support budgets is usually a top family priority. Helpful manuals are available on the principles and procedures of responsive family support programs (Covert, 1995).

When you begin to collaborate with a family whose child has a severe disability and who is financially needy, you may well find that they cannot meet some of their basic needs for food, shelter, clothing, medical attention, and care for themselves and especially their child. Those are precisely the families that the federal SSI, SSDI, and Medicaid programs (welfare, Social Security, and Medicaid) and the states' family support programs are designed to assist.

Meeting the families' basic needs means linking the families with the state and federal programs (as Pyramid Parent Training program does in New Orleans), or if a state does not have a family support program, advocating for one. When you take either or both of these steps, you create an opportunity to be a partner in meeting families' basic needs. And in doing so, you also affect the families' own motivation and their knowledge and skills. The bottom line is that when you link families to economic and family support resources, you are being an empowerment agent.

TIPS   BOX 10–6

What Family Support Means to Us

- Having a child who is quadriplegic is very expensive. I am a single mother and this money helps us get through everyday living.
- [We appreciate] the fact that we are able to spend the money on our child without being told what to buy. We feel that we are being trusted to meet the needs of our child.
- It is like a breath of fresh air to a drowning person.
- It is the only program that has been willing to help us financially and recognize our needs.
- The extra money helps us to keep our child at home.
- Our family member was able to get high-quality hearing aids that we would not have been able to afford.
- It gave us an opportunity to build a ramp which increased our child's safety and lessened physical stress on us.

Source: Agosta, J., & Melda, K. (1995). Supplemental Security Income for children. Boston, MA, and Salem, OR: Human Services Research Institute.

Addressing Issues of Abuse and Neglect

A fourth way to support families to meet their basic needs is to collaborate with them to prevent them from abusing or neglecting their child or to intervene if they have already maltreated their child.

Definitions

The term *maltreatment* is defined by the Congress in the Child Abuse Prevention and Treatment Act (1974), Public Law 93-247, as follows: "The physical and mental injury, sexual abuse, neglected treatment or maltreatment of a child under age 18 by a person who is responsible for the child's welfare under circumstances which indicate the child's health and welfare is harmed and threatened thereby, as determined in accordance with regulations prescribed by the Secretary of Health, Education, and Welfare" (CAPTA, 1997). Figure 10–2 includes definitions of the four major types of maltreatment—physical abuse, sexual abuse, neglect, and emotional abuse.

Maltreatment usually occurs within a pattern of similar acts; repetition usually is an essential element of maltreatment. This means that single instances usually are ex-cluded, and infrequent blowups within a family usually do not cause abuse and usually are not evidence of neglect. But a severe, especially violent single instance can cause great harm and by itself can constitute maltreatment.

Because definitions vary from state to state, it is important for you to find out how your state law defines abuse and neglect. You can do this by asking your school social worker, counselor, nurse, or principal; the local district or county attorney; or your state attorney general.

Incidence

A 1995 Gallup Poll of 1,000 parents estimated that three million U.S. children are physically abused by their parents (English, 1998). Children with disabilities seem to be at greater risk for being maltreated by their families and other caregivers (including professionals) than other children. A report by the National Center on Child Abuse and Neglect (1993) reports the following:

- Children with disabilities experienced maltreatment at a rate 1.7 times higher than children without disabilities.
- Children who have disabilities experienced emotional maltreatment at a rate 2.8 times more often than children without disabilities.

FIGURE 10–2

Definitions of Major Forms of Maltreatment

Physical abuse: An act of commission by a caregiver that results or is likely to result in physical harm, including death of a child. Examples of physical abuse acts include kicking, biting, shaking, stabbing, or punching of a child. Spanking a child is usually considered a disciplinary action, although it can be classified as abusive if the child is bruised or injured.

Sexual abuse: An act of commission, including intrusion or penetration, molestation with genital contact, or other forms of sexual acts in which children are used to provide sexual gratification for the perpetrator. This type of abuse also includes acts such as sexual exploitation and child pornography.

Neglect: An act of omission by a parent or caregiver that involves refusal or delay in providing health care; failure to provide basic needs such as food, clothing, shelter, affection, and attention; inadequate supervision; or abandonment. This failure to act holds true for both physical and emotional neglect.

Emotional abuse: An act of commission or omission that includes rejecting, isolating, terrorizing, ignoring, or corrupting a child. Examples of emotional abuse are confinement; verbal abuse; withholding sleep, food, or shelter; exposing a child to domestic violence; allowing a child to engage in substance abuse or criminal activity; refusing to provide psychological care; and other inattention that results in harm or potential harm to a child. An important component of emotional or psychological abuse is that it must be sustained and repetitive.

Source: Larner, M. B., Stevenson, C. S., & Behrman, R. E. (1998). Protecting children from abuse and neglect: Analysis and recommendations. *The Future of Children: Protecting Children from Abuse and Neglect, 8*(1), 41.

- The incidence of physical abuse among maltreated children with disabilities was 9 per 1,000, or 2.1 times the rate for maltreated children who did not have disabilities.
- Among maltreated children with disabilities, the incidence of sexual abuse was 3.5 per 1,000, or 1.8 times the rate for sexually abused children who did not have disabilities.
- Among maltreated children with disabilities, the incidence of physical neglect was 12 per 1,000, or 1.6 times the rate for maltreated children without disabilities.

In the general population of children with and without disabilities, younger children, females, premature infants, and children with more irritable temperaments are more likely to experience abuse than other children (Sedlak & Broadhurst, 1996). Research that compared children with and without disabilities, however, reported that boys with disabilities represented a larger proportion of children who experienced physical abuse, sexual abuse, and neglect (Sobsey, Randall, & Parrila, 1997). Caregivers who have a higher tendency to engage in abuse and neglect experience low self-esteem, aggressiveness, anxiety, depression, inaccurate knowledge of child development, inappropriate child expectations, and negative attitudes toward parenting (National Research Council, 1993). Some of families' special challenges such as those we discussed in chapter 5 (substance abuse and poverty, for example) also contribute to higher incidences of maltreatment (English, 1998).

A troubling finding is that decline has been documented in the number of states that are routinely collecting disability information on child maltreatment (Bonner, Crow, & Hensley, 1997). Furthermore, when a child is noted as having a disability, the specific disabling condition is rarely indicated. Also, states do not typically document the number of children whose disability has been found to be caused by maltreatment. Regarding training, states reported that typically only an average of four hours of training on disabilities is provided for child-care workers.

Pathways

There are several pathways that put children with disabilities at greater risk of maltreatment than other children. When two or more of these pathways intersect, children's risk of maltreatment increases. Thus, the context in which the child lives is extremely important (Garbarino & Kostelny, 1992).

It is essential for you to know families (one of the obligations of a reliable alliance) and the pathways that

may lead them to maltreat their child. The family systems framework will key you into each family's situation and will help you identify some of those pathways. Certain pathways are related to the family's characteristics and include the following (Ammerman, 1989, 1990; Garbarino & Kostelny, 1992; Sobsey, 1994):

- *Cultural background.* Some cultures tolerate physical punishment.
- *Socioeconomic status.* Poverty can cause stress; stress can cause abuse.
- *Geographic location.* Isolation can be a pathway to maltreatment.
- *The nature of exceptionality.* A child who is noncompliant can trigger abuse; a nonverbal child can hardly say what ails him or her and, thus, can become neglected.
- *The family's own health.* Declining health in one family member may contribute to neglect of other members.
- *Coping styles.* Poor problem-solving skills or frequent expressions of anger can be accompanied by violence to family members.

Characteristics of the child also are important in determining whether the child is on a risk pathway. A child who was born prematurely, has low birth weight or medical complications at birth, has a chronic illness or disabilities, is unable to "read" caregivers' moods and does not know when to desist difficult behaviors, or is a girl in the case of sexual abuse, clearly is at risk for maltreatment (Ammerman, 1989; Lutzker, Campbell, Newman, & Harrold, 1989).

Identification

Symptoms of abuse include bruises and injuries that the child cannot or will not explain or that the child explains implausibly. Injuries on parts of the child's body that are not usually damaged by a fall (such as the child's back or thighs) may indicate maltreatment. Signs of neglect include unkempt appearance, poor hygiene, malnutrition, and developmental delays. Sexual molestation often results in tissue damage and evidence of sexually transmitted diseases (Ammerman & Baladerian, 1993).

You probably will not be able to detect some of these symptoms. For example, unless you are a nurse, other health-care provider, provider of related services such as catheterization, or a staff member in an infants and toddlers program, you will not detect tissue damage to the child's sexual organs. But you may be able to detect others easily.

It is usually helpful to construct a history of the child's time with you. Look for sudden changes in the child's behavior, regression to earlier developmental stages, enuresis (involuntary urination), withdrawal, aggressiveness, or deterioration in academic or other performance. Ask yourself whether the child has become especially shy, hypervigilant, or resistant to being touched. Be curious about whether the child has become particularly anxious or distressed in the presence of a caregiver (Ammerman & Baladerian, 1993).

Detecting maltreatment in children with disabilities is very difficult. The children may have little or no ability to communicate or report abuse or neglect; they may be unwilling to just "say no, go, and report"—the three strategies that most professionals teach children who do not have disabilities.

Also, their very disabilities may make some children more injury-prone than others. Children with visual impairments may bump into objects more frequently than others; children with seizure disorders or physical impairments may fall down regularly; children with hyperactivity are more prone to accidental injuries than other children (Ammerman & Baladerian, 1993). So injury-proneness may lead you to overlook maltreatment or make you more apt to suspect that maltreatment has occurred.

Finally, some children and youth with disabilities are in the classic double bind of depending on the person who maltreats them to help them meet their basic needs and yet having to put up with the maltreatment because they cannot find another caregiver (Nosek, Howland, & Young, 1997): "I knew I needed this person [my caregiver] to get me up out of bed and keep me alive and do my breathing treatments. This person became my life line but was also my abuser" (National Symposium on Abuse and Neglect of Children with Disabilities, 1995).

Reporting

What should you do if you suspect that a child has been maltreated? First, make sure that your suspicions are based on facts and that you have reasonable grounds for your concern. Second, follow your school's procedures for reporting within the school. You may be required to report what you know and reasonably suspect to the school social worker, counselor, nurse, or principal depending on school procedures. Third, call the local or state child protection agency; if you do not know what agency to call, then contact your school social worker, counselor, or principal, or call your local district or county attorney. Remember that every state requires people who have any child-care responsibilities to report maltreatment. If you do not report it, you may violate the reporting law and be subject to civil or criminal punishment. Finally, do not try to intervene on your own; the techniques for preventing

and intervening almost invariably require collaborative and interdisciplinary responses.

Prevention

Prevention can include a focus on the child and family. It is a sad fact of life that when spousal abuse occurs (whether between husband and wife or two people living together as partners), the child with a disability is at higher risk for being abused than a child whose parents do not abuse each other. What Ursula and DJ see more of is spousal abuse that results in the child being neglected or abandoned; they see less of abuse of the child by adult family members. So when they encounter families where the grown-ups are engaged in spousal abuse, their antennae go up and they seek to protect the child by referring the family to services or, as a last resort, seeking to protect the child by calling in the city child protective services team or even the city police crisis intervention team.

If you suspect that a child has been abused, neglected, or maltreated, you may find the suggestions in box 10–7 to be particularly useful (and remember, they can also help a child who does not have a disability).

You can also spread your prevention efforts to the family (or other caregivers) who put the child at risk. Begin by trying to increase a family's capacities to withstand the forces that contribute to maltreatment. Recognize the family's strengths and build on them; and remember that maltreatment often occurs because the child's, the family's, and the community's characteristics intersect in ways that can lead to maltreatment (Turnbull, Buchele-Ash, & Mitchell, 1994).

Be sure to assemble a collaborative team, as the suggestions in box 10–8 point out. Work with your school social worker, counselor, or principal to get support in forming a collaborative team. Almost always, effective intervention requires people with different expertise and resources (Turnbull et al., 1994).

The cardinal rule in intervention is to protect the child. To protect the child, it may be necessary to remove the child from the family's home (often immediately) and secure placement, sometimes in a temporary foster home and sometimes in a relative's home (Berrick, 1998). This placement is followed by a thorough, interdisciplinary assessment of the causes and nature of maltreatment, and that evaluation, in turn, leads to intervention. Thereafter, the principal goal is supporting family members to be more effective in parenting the child and managing the child's behaviors and their own (assuming the child is to stay in the family home).

Teachers and other school personnel face a dilemma when confronted with maltreatment, their obligation to

Preventing Maltreatment by Working with the Child

- Help to decrease behaviors that are difficult to handle and facilitate more appropriate and adaptive behaviors through the use of positive behavioral support (discussed in chapter 13).
- Provide sexuality education that includes self-protection behaviors and assertiveness training. This one measure is particularly important because most programs train compliance by the child with a disability. Rather than allowing children to make their own choices or assert their own rights of assertiveness during appropriate situations, their goals are usually set up to develop compliance.
- Provide developmentally appropriate communication techniques so the child has an effective ability to "say no, go, and tell."
- Provide individual rights education.
- Provide social skills training.

Source: National Symposium on Abuse and Neglect of Children with Disabilities. (1995). *Abuse and neglect of children with disabilities: Report and recommendations.* Lawrence, KS: University of Kansas, Beach Center on Families and Disability and Erikson Institute of Chicago.

Preventing Maltreatment by Working with the Family

- Provide opportunities to increase parenting skills. (This includes fathers. Most training programs are targeted toward mothers only.)
- Link parents to other families for support to reduce the factor of isolation.
- Provide social and other informal positive supports.
- Provide information on positive parental responsiveness to the child.
- Increase parental awareness of resources.
- Ensure parental involvement in child-serving programs.
- Teach nonviolent strategies for handling aggressive behaviors.
- Teach techniques for positive behavioral support (see chapter 13).
- Enhance parental life management strategies.
- Arrange for home health visitors trained in detecting child maltreatment to visit families' homes following the birth of a new baby for up to one month and thereafter as needed.
- Facilitate intervention at birth to help ensure parent-child attachment and newborn care techniques.
- Provide community resource referrals to families who have substance abuse problems.
- Provide the support needed by parents when they themselves have a disability.
- Carefully select caregivers when the child is removed from the natural home.

Source: National Symposium on Abuse and Neglect of Children with Disabilities. (1995). *Abuse and neglect of children with disabilities: Report and recommendations.* Lawrence, KS: University of Kansas, Beach Center on Families and Disability and Erikson Institute of Chicago.

report it, and their desire to collaborate with a family. In box 10–9 you will read about how one of those professionals deals with this dilemma.

Collaborative interventions seem to work better if they are offered in a family-centered way over a sustained period of time and in the place (such as the home) where the maltreatment has occurred (Lutzker, 1984; Lutzker & Newman, 1986; McCroskey & Meezan, 1998). Sometimes treatment is one-on-one; sometimes it consists of involving the parent who has perpetuated the abuse in parent training, support groups (help lines, respite care, visiting nurses, or neighborhood programs), and other activities. Training and support can be responsive to the particular characteristics of parents such as those who have intellectual disabilities (Feldman, 1998). A successful parent-education program for these

Reporting Maltreatment

Iva Goodwin is the social worker at a school in Wichita, Kansas. Donna Swall is a child protective services worker in Douglas County, Kansas. The families with whom they work come from all walks of life and represent a broad spectrum of socioeconomic and racial-ethnic-cultural differences. Among them, there are those families who abuse or neglect their children.

State law requires Iva to report suspected maltreatment, just as it requires Donna to act on those reports. How do they report and investigate and, at the same time, recognize that families have strengths and that it is in their and their child's interests to regard Iva and Donna as reliable allies?

Iva starts by trying to earn families' trust, using their strengths as the basis of her relationship with them. Providing them with supports as soon as their children enter the school, educating them about what the school and other agencies can do to help them raise their child and meet their other needs, inviting personnel from outside the school to attend IEP meetings and showing families how

these personnel can support them, developing interagency collaborative teams, and showing families how to access the service provider system—these are the preventive measures Iva takes for all families.

Likewise, Donna recognizes that, while her first duty is to protect the child, she often can accomplish that if she offers to help the family. To stay connected with the families, she practices good listening skills, not only expressing her confidence in family members but also making it clear that she recognizes their frustrations. Undergirding Donna's work is her presumption that families are trying to do the best they can for their children and that they want to be good parents.

When the time comes for Iva to comply with state law and file a maltreatment report, she meets her legal obligation, telling the families that reporting is mandatory and that they should regard child protective services intervention as a source of help, not of criticism or blame.

Similarly, when Donna initiates an intervention, she makes it clear that she is offering a service, not a

form of punishment. "Proactive" characterizes her approach, not "reactive."

Some families accept these explanations. Others do not. The trust that Iva has tried to earn—by preventive steps—sometimes survives her telling the families that she will report. Sometimes it doesn't. In Donna's case, the same is true: Some families accept the services gladly. When they have a child with a disability, their feelings of guilt may make them more accepting of the offer of help.

When families do not accept Iva's offer, it is largely because the families themselves are facing multiple challenges. Iva's advice: Build the trust, recognize it takes a long time, work especially hard with disconnected or isolated families, and build on strengths. When the time comes to report, then comply with the law and say that child protective services are sources of help, not blame.

Donna's advice: Be especially sensitive to families' reactions, and work especially hard at the staying-connected tips.

---

families includes an individual plan, pictorial manuals, and weekly training sessions in the parent's home.

It is by no means easy to propose or carry out intervention strategies. The child may be out of the home. Parents may be under court order to engage in treatment but lack the intrinsic motivation to benefit from it. Parents may also deny the fact of maltreatment, be reluctant to reveal information that relates to maltreatment and reasons for it, and be unable or unwilling to establish a reliable alliance or trusting relationship with a treatment provider.

Nevertheless, you can be an effective professional in dealing with child maltreatment and a family. The key is to remember that you are a collaborator with the family, a collaborator against maltreatment.

Linking Our Themes

What action should you take to meet families' basic needs that is consistent with the empowerment framework? You can create a reliable alliance by meeting families' basic needs and by infusing into that alliance the eight obligations that enrich it. Your actions will create an empowering context, and that context, in turn, will have a positive effect on a family's own empowerment.

Creating a Reliable Alliance

In figure 10–3 we show how you can create a reliable alliance by meeting families' basic needs.

FIGURE 10–3

Creating a Reliable Alliance in Meeting Families' Basic Needs: Disempowering and Empowering Actions

Obligations	Issues	Disempowering Actions	Empowering Actions
Knowing yourself	You feel very angry and frustrated at parents who belittle their child with a learning disability.	At a conference tell them that it's imperative that they stop "putting down" their child.	Discuss learning disabilities with the parents and problem solve on information resources that would enable them to better understand their child's challenges.
Knowing families Family characteristics	The parents, who have mental retardation, are extremely fearful that their children will be put into foster care.	Assume that parents with mental retardation cannot be capable parents, and urge the parents to consider foster care.	Brainstorm with the parents about the community resources available to them, parenting information, and support; make referrals in light of their preferences, strengths, and needs.
Family interactions	The child's challenging behavior creates major frustrations for all family members.	Tell the parents that this is something that they should expect, given that their child has autism, and that they will need to learn to live with it.	If the family agrees, post a request on the autism list server describing the specific situation and asking for tips and advice that has worked for other families.
Family functions	Both parents are unemployed and are financially unable to provide basic nourishment and health care for their child with cerebral palsy.	Tell the parents that you are very worried about their child and wish that they could do more to provide for him or her.	Give the family a description and contact information for the state's family support program; put them in touch with other families who have participated.
Family life cycle	The family is very worried about the daughter with epilepsy transitioning to a large middle school and facing adolescent issues.	Tell parents to "take a day at a time" and everything will be fine.	Tell the parents about a transition workshop that the PTI is sponsoring, and ask if they would be interested.
Honoring cultural diversity	A parent wants her child with mental retardation to learn Spanish as well as English, but the language pathologist says that two languages will be too confusing.	Advise the parents to be realistic about the fact that their child will be lucky to learn English.	Network to locate the most current information on bilingual education for children with disabilities. Review information with the parents and plan next steps.
Affirming and building on family strengths	Parents of a child with spina bifida who is in an early intervention program believe that their child will have no future.	Warn the parents that they'd better make sure that their marriage is not torn apart by the child.	Suggest to the parents that they contact the local Parent-to-Parent program to be matched with parents of older children with spina bifida.

(continued)

FIGURE 10–3   CONTINUED

Creating a Reliable Alliance in Meeting Families' Basic Needs: Disempowering and Empowering Actions

Obligations	Issues	Disempowering Actions	Empowering Actions
Promoting family choices	A family has just been informed that the child has AD/HD and is invited to an IEP conference; they do not have any relevant information.	Send the parents a list of their legal rights even though you know the information is practically incomprensible.	Ask the family about their preferences for information, and review a range of resources with them. Respond to their priorities.
Envisioning great expectations	Parents of a daughter with a rare syndrome lament that they feel isolated and resentful when they hear parents of typical kids sharing their "trials and tribulations."	Suggest that they will probably have similar feelings for the rest of their lives.	Provide information about Parent to Parent. Suggest that parents could possibly be matched with a family whose child has the same syndrome.
Using interpersonal communication skills	Parents walk out of a conference when one of the participants says their adolescent daughter is too "available" to young men; they refuse to return telephone calls.	When you see them at a shopping mall, say, "Sex is part of life. Get information about it now, or become grandparents later."	Write the parents an empathetic letter and state your own discomfort with how the topic was addressed. Offer to meet with them, listen to their perspectives, and respond to their priorities.
Warranting trust and respect	A student comes to school with unexplained bruises and cuts. He has a communication impairment and will not or cannot explain why he is so frequently injured.	Call the parents, accuse them of abuse, and threaten to call the police if their son ever shows any more signs of maltreatment.	Talk with the school social worker, and get her to join you in gathering more information, filing a report if appropriate, and informing the parents.

*S*trengthening Family Resources

Remembering that the way in which you meet families' basic needs creates an empowering context, you should be able to recognize how that context, in turn, affects a family's motivation and knowledge/skills. In figure 10–4 we illustrate the link between your own resources, the resources of the context within which you are working, and the family's empowerment (enhancing their resources). This link occurs through collaboration.

Summary

Collaborating with families to meet their basic needs may not seem to be the same as educating their children, but it nonetheless is an important role for all educators. The reason is simple: The more you and other educators support families to address their critical, basic, personal, and family needs, the more likely it is that they will devote

FIGURE 10–4

Strengthening Family Resources Through an Empowering Context: Meeting Families' Basic Needs

Motivation	What You Can Do	Knowledge/Skills	What You Can Do
Self-efficacy	Encourage parents to serve as veteran parents in Parent-to-Parent programs to share their expertise and support with others.	Information	Provide information on scholarship opportunities for enrichment and postsecondary programs to all interested families.
Perceived control	Ask families facing transition what type of information on future options would be helpful and respond in their order and priority.	Problem solving	If a parent wants to discuss it, brainstorm about community resources that can help him or her escape domestic violence.
Great expectations	If you are in a state that does not have a family support program, share your vision with other families and professionals that such a program could be started through collaborative efforts and take action.		
Energy	Encourage families who experience abuse and neglect to take breaks from child care responsibility by linking with respite care programs.	Communication skills	Affirm families' positive communication skills, and let parents know how much you recognize and appreciate their skills.
Persistence	If parents get turned down for family support services, encourage them to reapply and to continue making their needs known to program administrators.	Life management skills	Encourage parents who engage in abuse to develop skills in disciplining their children that will enable them to avoid abusive interactions.

time and energy to their child's educational needs . . . and, of course, the more likely it is that you and they will develop an empowered and empowering relationship.

We have highlighted four ways you can assist families in meeting their basic needs. First, you can enable them to access social support, particularly through Parent-to-Parent networks. Second, you can assist them in acquiring information, providing a broad array of viable options.

Third, you can link families to many different economic and family support services. Fourth, you can assist families who are on one of several pathways toward maltreatment.

In all that you do, you can create a reliable alliance and take actions that empower families; remember that your job is to create a context that is empowering of the family's motivation and knowledge/skills.

Meeting families' basic needs is what Ursula and DJ Markey do in New Orleans. It is hard work, and as valued as it is by the families, it is not always valued by the larger society. That is so because, in many respects, families whose basic needs are unmet are already on the margins of society and, oddly enough, some of them have been led to believe that that is exactly where they "belong." "We have to work so hard in convincing parents that they deserve to have these rights, that their children deserve quality education. Because these are parents who didn't get that themselves, and who don't blame anybody for their not getting it. Somehow, they have internalized the notion that they are not deserving of everything that a broader society has." That sense of not being deserving is what Ursula and DJ call "the mentality of lack"—a product of racism, economic discrimination, and disability discrimination. What is certain is that this mentality is intergenerational: Grandparents, parents, and children come to accept that they are destined to "live day-to-day in the doldrums, losing their dreams and visions, accepting that 'things' will not get better." It is, of course, a massive challenge to change the causes and effects of the "mentality of lack"—but it can begin with one person, with you, or with a pair such as Ursula and DJ Markey. To talk about meeting families' basic needs is, truly, to talk about changing America so that it meets everyone's basic needs. That is a cause worth your effort, one in which you will find that collaboration with families and other professionals is essential.

Chapter Eleven

Referring and Evaluating for Special Education

"*A*gainst all odds." That's as good a description of the Lee family as you can find. There's just one thing, however: Hwa Lee, her husband In, their daughter Youmee, and their son Kyoochun (who calls himself "Samuel"—it's easier for his teachers and friends to say than his Korean name) beat the odds. But what odds they were. And how hard it was to overcome them.

In, Hwa, and their children came to America from Korea when Youmee was 3 weeks old. True, they could speak English, but their children were very young (Samuel is two years older than Youmee) and the family's at-home language was Korean.

As a graduate student at The University of Texas, Austin, they had practically no money, had even fewer friends on whom they could depend, and were understandably overwhelmed when their suspicions about Youmee were finally confirmed when she was 13 months old.

What suspicions? They suspected that she could not hear or perhaps that she had mental retardation. As Hwa recounts their early years, Youmee simply was verbally unresponsive to her parents' conversations. They would do baby talk with her; she would not respond. Facial gestures elicited a response, but words alone did not. Yet it was only after she accidentally turned the volume all the way up on the family's TV set but still did not respond to the blaring sound that they were suspicious that their daughter was profoundly deaf.

From that moment on, the Lee family has known the meaning of "against all odds." And they know what it means to reverse the odds to be in their favor. From be-

ing on the long-odds to the short-odds position in life was no easy feat for them.

Consider, for example, Youmee's early years. Neither of her parents understood anything about the American system of early intervention. Both spoke English, but their family language was Korean. Not accustomed to living in the United States, their customs, behaviors, and culture were rock-solid Korean. It was only through the intervention of an American acquaintance in the trailer park that served as graduate-student housing at the university that they learned about an early intervention program and were able to have Youmee's deafness confirmed by an audiologist. Even then, homebound instruction was all they received; their state of mind—being in an emotional and intellectual daze—was hardly helped by some members of a church who suggested that Youmee was deaf because her parents must have done something wrong and were being punished. And the Korean community at the university was not always helpful: The mythology in Korea is that deafness is contagious ("to sign is to become deaf"), so Youmee had a hard time having a playmate.

It would have been helpful if the professionals paid to help the family had indeed helped them. But that was not to be. The senior staffer of an early intervention program visited the family's home one afternoon to observe Youmee. To observe meant to play with her—toys on the floor, child and professional interacting, mother sitting and observing. Little did Hwa realize it at the time, but the professional was assessing her, not just Youmee. And the assessment was negative: "Mother does not interact with

child; goal, to get mother to interact more with child." How perverse! The Korean culture emphasizes privacy; and it commands parents to be courteous and deferential to professionals: "What I do with my child is my business. It's private." Indeed, Hwa never thought to get involved between the professional and Youmee, interpreting the professional's behavior as showing off how well she could handle a child and be an administrator, too. It didn't help, either, that Youmee had no clear idea why the professional was there; Hwa's informed consent was irrelevant. There's one more factor: "We are very shy people and we were raised not to show our emotions in public. Also, I was being humble and nice to that person." And indeed, the professional never had a formal or informal conversation with Hwa or In. "Was it appropriate for her to judge that my behavior indicated an inappropriate, inactive mother?"

The results of Youmee's evaluations—profound deafness—and the assessment the professionals made about Youmee had truly negative effects for both of them. For Youmee, it meant that she spent most of her early years in segregated, noninclusive programs; all of her peers had hearing impairments. It was not until during the third and fourth grade that she began to have partial inclusion in the general curriculum, and not until fourth grade (the 1999–2000 school year) that she was fully included. For a bright girl who taught her classmates how to sign and "finger spell," the academic exclusion and subsequent delays were inexcusable. She cannot reconcile them with her and her classmates' abilities. For Hwa, the result was that she was regarded as less than a "perfect" mother—one not worth informing, one whose aspirations for her daughter were to be disregarded. Indeed, she even began to see herself in that light; "they caused me to have low self-esteem."

So, against all odds? Yes, but not permanently. When Hwa enrolled as a doctoral student in the Department of Special Education at the University of Illinois, her and Youmee's life began to change. She began to advocate for inclusion. "I knew Youmee had to be prepared for the real world, both the hearing and the deaf world. I took a long-term view, beyond first and second and third grades. Later, she can decide whether she wants the hearing world or the deaf community. But she needed survival skills for the hearing world." Still, the schools preferred segregation, arguing that the extent of Youmee's disability was so great that inclusion was out of the question. For a while, Hwa acquiesced—but only for a while. Now

Youmee Lee, right, with her teacher, Sue. (1999)

armed with more knowledge about Youmee's rights and about techniques for accommodating her in the general curriculum, Hwa began to be successful in her pursuit of inclusion. Hwa kept asking Youmee's teachers why Youmee does not have the "readiness skills" for the general curriculum; and when will she get them? And she kept insisting that, as Youmee's evaluations showed, she was not only intelligent but also well adjusted. There was no reason, it seemed to Hwa, for her daughter to be segregated—no reason based on the evaluations or on Youmee's experiences in school.

What was especially frustrating for Hwa and In was that none of the people evaluating Youmee ever asked them about their expectations or child-rearing practices. Moreover, evaluations themselves were fake. It was not that they were misdiagnosing Youmee; it was that they were "underdiagnosing" her, missing her capabilities (intelligence and social ability), and neglecting her family's goals. "The outcomes were pre-set," Hwa recalls. Given the Korean culture of deferring to professionals and given also that for a while, Hwa and In felt that their native culture may have been inferior to the "American" culture, Youmee's segregation persisted.

But this was only for a while. With the help of evaluators who worked from their "heart, not their head" and truly cared about what Hwa and In wanted and with the additional help of a few general education teachers who wanted Youmee in their class ("she will enrich it—just think of the cultural, language, and disability teaching she can do"), Youmee moved slowly but inevitably toward inclusion in her third-grade class in Macomb, Illinois and her fourth-grade class in Livingston. There her teachers, Mrs. Natch and Sue, see a different Youmee— a bright, eager learner and a capable teacher, the youngster who helps her classmates learn how to sign or finger spell. And there Youmee has met teachers worthy of being the Lee's ally—the person who takes it on herself to look beyond just the scores on the assessments Youmee has had, to learn on her own about deafness and the language that Youmee uses. "It's not about following guidelines and strategies; it's not about what a person knows," says Hwa. That's necessary, but there is more: "It (the capability to be an evaluator and a teacher) comes from the heart, rather than the head." Just as it came from Hwa's heart and Youmee's, the will to beat the odds was the source of their pursuit of the means to beat them.

Evaluation is the gateway to special education, and referral is the path to the evaluation gate. In this chapter, we will describe both IDEA's requirements and today's best practices related to referral and evaluation; and we will explain how partnership in the referral-evaluation process can empower students, families, and professionals. Figure 11–1 depicts the empowerment model; the shaded portion pertains to referral and evaluation partnerships.

The term *referral* refers to the formal request for an evaluation of a student. IDEA defines *evaluation as follows*:

> procedures used . . . to determine whether a child has a disability and the nature and extent of the special education and related services that the child needs. The term means procedures used selectively with an individual child and does not include basic tests administered to or procedures used with all children in a school, grade, or class. (34 C.F.R. Sec. 300.500)

Traditionally, partnerships in referral and evaluation refer to professional-to-professional interaction: General or special educators collaborate with each other and with school psychologists, counselors, social workers, and related service providers to refer or evaluate or both. Also traditionally, families are on the edges of professional decision making related to referral and evaluation (Mehan, 1993; Ware, 1994).

The potential outcome of partnerships in referral and evaluation is a better understanding of the student's strengths, great expectations, preferences, and needs. That understanding is the foundation for the student's IFSP (individualized family service plan)/IEP (individualized education plan); for developing partnerships among student, family, and educators as they implement the IFSP/IEP; and for assuring that the student has long-term outcomes of independence, contribution, inclusion, and empowerment.

To show you how partnerships in referral and evaluation merge IDEA requirements, best practices, and your eight obligations for reliable alliances, we refer you to figure 11–2, which outlines eight steps in the process of referral and evaluation. In this chapter we will describe each of the steps of that process. Take note: States differ in their requirements for referring and evaluating students for gifted education. Sixty percent of states require programs

FIGURE 11–1

Empowerment Framework: Collaborating for Empowerment in Evaluating for Special Education and Community

Education Context Resources

Opportunities for Partnerships	Obligations for Reliable Alliances
Opportunities Arise At . . .	*Reliable Alliances Consist of . . .*
Communicating among reliable allies	Knowing yourself
Meetings families' basic needs	Knowing families
Evaluating for special education	Honoring cultural diversity
Individualizing for appropriate education and placement	Affirming family strengths
	Promoting family choices
Extending learning in home and community	Envisioning great expectations
Attending and volunteering at school	Communicating positively
Advocating for systems improvement	Warranting trust and respect

Family Resources

Motivation

Self-efficacy: Believing in our capabilities

Perceived control: Believing we can apply our capabilities to affect what happens to us

Great expectations: Believing we will get what we want and need

Energy: Lighting the fire and keeping it burning

Persistence: Putting forth a sustained effort

Knowledge/Skills

Information: Being knowledgeable

Problem solving: Knowing how to bust the barriers

Life management skills: Knowing how to handle what happens to us

Communication skills: Being on the sending and receiving ends of expressed needs and wants

Professional Resources

Motivation

Self-efficacy: Believing in our capabilities

Perceived control: Believing we can apply our capabilities to affect what happens to us

Great expectations: Believing we will get what we want and need

Energy: Lighting the fire and keeping it burning

Persistence: Putting forth a sustained effort

Knowledge/Skills

Information: Being knowledgeable

Problem solving: Knowing how to bust the barriers

Life management skills: Knowing how to handle what happens to us

Communication skills: Being on the sending and receiving ends of expressed needs and wants

Collaborating for Empowerment

235

FIGURE 11-2

Referral and Evaluation Process

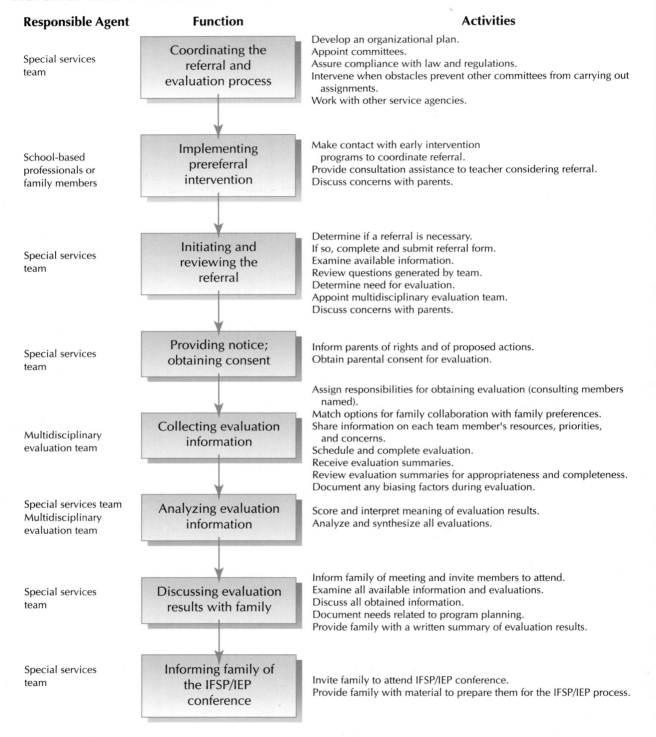

Responsible Agent	Function	Activities
Special services team	**Coordinating the referral and evaluation process**	Develop an organizational plan. Appoint committees. Assure compliance with law and regulations. Intervene when obstacles prevent other committees from carrying out assignments. Work with other service agencies.
School-based professionals or family members	**Implementing prereferral intervention**	Make contact with early intervention programs to coordinate referral. Provide consultation assistance to teacher considering referral. Discuss concerns with parents.
Special services team	**Initiating and reviewing the referral**	Determine if a referral is necessary. If so, complete and submit referral form. Examine available information. Review questions generated by team. Determine need for evaluation. Appoint multidisciplinary evaluation team. Discuss concerns with parents.
Special services team	**Providing notice; obtaining consent**	Inform parents of rights and of proposed actions. Obtain parental consent for evaluation.
Multidisciplinary evaluation team	**Collecting evaluation information**	Assign responsibilities for obtaining evaluation (consulting members named). Match options for family collaboration with family preferences. Share information on each team member's resources, priorities, and concerns. Schedule and complete evaluation. Receive evaluation summaries. Review evaluation summaries for appropriateness and completeness. Document any biasing factors during evaluation.
Special services team Multidisciplinary evaluation team	**Analyzing evaluation information**	Score and interpret meaning of evaluation results. Analyze and synthesize all evaluations.
Special services team	**Discussing evaluation results with family**	Inform family of meeting and invite members to attend. Examine all available information and evaluations. Discuss all obtained information. Document needs related to program planning. Provide family with a written summary of evaluation results.
Special services team	**Informing family of the IFSP/IEP conference**	Invite family to attend IFSP/IEP conference. Provide family with material to prepare them for the IFSP/IEP process.

Source: Adapted from Strickland, B., & Turnbull, A. P. (1990). *Developing and implementing individualized education programs* (3rd ed.) (p. 50) Englewood Cliffs, NJ: Merrill/Prentice Hall. Copyright © 1990 by Merrill Publishing Company. Adapted by permission.

for students who are gifted, but the requirements vary to some extent. Forty-three states have policies related to initial screening to identify students who are gifted (Coleman, Gallagher, & Foster, 1994). If you work with students who are gifted, you need to identify and follow local and state policies.

Coordinating the Referral and Evaluation Process

The entity with overall responsibility for referral and evaluation is the school-based special services team. (This team goes by different names in different schools.) Typically, this team consists of special services personnel (that is, teachers, psychologists, social workers, counselors, and therapists) and administrators.

Whatever these professionals can contribute, they typically lack the insights that come from living daily and closely with the students they are evaluating. Consider how little the professionals who first entered Youmee Lee's life knew—or tried to know—about her, her family, and their culture and aspirations. Thus, although it is rare for schools to include parents on the special services team, parents can provide valuable information. Parental contribution can occur if a school (1) pays a parent coordinator at the school or district level to be a permanent member of the team, (2) pays parents of children to serve rotating terms, (3) invites the parents of the student being evaluated to attend meetings whenever the team discusses the student, or (4) combines any of these steps. In addition, adults with a disability who know firsthand about the impact of labeling, the benefits and drawbacks of special and general education, and ways to accommodate to the community can assist the team in connecting the student's evaluation to the student's IEP and an appropriate education.

Implementing Prereferral Intervention

Prereferral intervention occurs *before* a formal referral for evaluation. Its primary purpose is to analyze the student's strengths and needs and then provide additional individualized assistance without providing special education (Bahr, Whitten, Dieker, Kocarek, & Manson, 1999; Bahr, Fuchs, & Fuchs, 1999; Flugum & Reschly, 1994; Safran & Safran, 1996).

The frequency of prereferral intervention increased dramatically in the mid-1980s. By the close of that decade, state educational agencies typically recommended or re-

quired some type of prereferral intervention with students (Carter & Sugai, 1989). It was anticipated that referral rates for formal evaluation would drop when general and special education teachers collaborate in modifying instruction according to individualized student needs (Fuchs, Fuchs, & Bahr, 1990; Fuchs, Fuchs, Bahr, & Stecker, 1990; Graden, Casey, & Bonstrom, 1985; Graden, Casey, & Christenson, 1985). One research study indicated that there is not a significant decrease in referrals to special education when prereferral intervention is used (Short & Talley, 1996). Another study examined the long-term impact of collaborative consultation as a prereferral intervention on referral accuracy to special education (Yocom & Staebler, 1996). (Referral accuracy was determined by computing a ratio of the number of students evaluated to the number of students whose evaluations documented that they could be appropriately served by special education.) The results of this study indicated a significant increase in referral accuracy but only after four years of training by school staff. The researchers emphasized the importance of comprehensive and long-term training in order to realize benefits from prereferral intervention.

A recent study of teams referred to as *school-based intervention teams*—teams developed to provide effective supports and services so that students will not need to be formerly referred and evaluated for special education—investigated teams' effectiveness in three states (Bahr et al., 1999). Participants in the study noted the strengths of these teams to be the assignment of specific responsibility to team members to implement intervention and the use of permanent products to evaluate academic progress. The major concerns reported were that follow-up typically was not written but relied on verbal contact and that intervention effectiveness was typically determined by teacher judgement rather than by systematic evaluation procedures. The authors noted that one of the three states—Illinois—had superior scores, which they attributed to Illinois' greater reliance on state legislation that requires prereferral intervention and investment in long-term staff development in order to ensure that educators can competently implement prereferral procedures.

Most prereferral practices involve professional collaboration and typically do not include active family and student participation in problem solving (Sindelar, Griffin, Smith, & Watanabe, 1992). In chapter 13 we show how family-professional collaboration in helping children be successful with homework and addressing issues associated with challenging behavior can be effective prereferral intervention strategies.

A different approach to preventing formal referral is the heterogeneous school and collaborative consultation model (Bauer & Shea, 1999; McGregor & Vogelsberg,

1999; Pugach & Warger, 1996; Snell & Janney, 1999; Villa, Thousand, Meyers, & Nevin, 1996). In these schools, special and general educators adapt students' instruction within general education classrooms to meet the needs of all learners. They begin with the assumption that all students belong in the general education classroom and that intensive intervention is not primarily for the purpose of preventing evaluation for and placement in separate special education programs but for enhancing the student's success in the classroom.

Initiating and Reviewing the Referral

Referral is a formal request to evaluate a student to determine whether he or she has a disability and, if so, the nature and extent of the student's special education and related services. Parents, other family members, community professionals, or school professionals may initiate a request for referral.

When does referral occur? It usually occurs after prereferral intervention but not always. Typically, children with severe congenital disabilities are identified during their infancy and increasingly are enrolled in early intervention and preschool programs. Their referral frequently comes from physicians or other professionals. That was Youmee's history—from her family's first certainty that she was deaf to the confirmation by an audiologist engaged by the local early intervention program. But children identified as having an educational exceptionality during school years typically have milder exceptionalities, experience a later onset of an exceptionality (such as a learning disability or AD/HD), or live where there is no comprehensive preschool identification program. Students who are gifted are usually identified after they enter school, although preschool identification is increasingly desirable (Sandel, McCallister, & Nash, 1993). Parents of students who are gifted often have some indication that their son or daughter has unusual abilities or potential achievement.

Why does referral occur? It happens because educators or others suspect that a student may need specially designed instruction. Often the student is performing significantly below expectation levels, as shown by classwork, homework, tests, and teacher observations. Referral also occurs because the school system itself may be ineffective; class size, teachers' lack of knowledge of education methodologies, and inappropriate instructional materials may lead staff to think that the student has special needs.

Traditionally, educators have assumed that the problem lies within the student; however, progressive educational programs recognize that problems may be attributed as much to the educational context as to the student's strengths, preferences, great expectations, and needs. Thus, rather than removing the student from general education, the intervention expands the supplementary aids and services provided in the general education classroom. In Youmee's case, however, it worked just the other way around. Perhaps because of the extent of her hearing loss and certainly in the face of her parents' aspirations and Youmee's own cognitive abilities (verified by all sorts of evaluations), they tried to keep Youmee out of the general curriculum. And for a while they succeeded. Indeed, they never even really considered that the general curriculum was an option during grades 3–5. It was, as Hwa observed, a "pre-set outcome" that they had in mind, and it was not one sanctioned by the IDEA.

Many schools have checklists that can help you identify or document your concerns and forms to complete when you ask for an evaluation, whether for a student with a disability or one who seems exceptionally capable. IDEA does not set out time lines or processes for referring students between ages 5 and 21 (Part B of IDEA), but there are special regulations regarding infants and toddlers (Part C of IDEA).

The infant and toddler regulations require states to identify and locate eligible infants and toddlers (also referred to as *child find*) and to develop procedures for evaluation and services by hospitals, physicians, parents, day-care programs, local educational agencies, public health facilities, other social service agencies, and other health-care providers. Referrals must be made two working days after a child has been identified as potentially needing or being eligible for early intervention. Once the referral is made, the evaluation and assessment activities and the development of an IFSP must be completed within 45 days. Your state's parent training and information center can provide you with a description of the state's child-find program and the procedures developed for the primary referral sources.

Although IDEA does not require parental consent for referral, some state and local educational agencies do. Even if consent is not required where you work, we encourage you to communicate with parents early on and certainly during the referral process about your concerns that their child may need specially designed instruction. By communicating, you enhance parents' understanding of their son's or daughter's current level of performance and grade-level expectations and why more extensive evaluation and intervention may be desirable.

A survey of more than 100 parents of students with learning disabilities at the elementary, junior high, and high school levels indicated that many parents are relieved when their child received special assistance:

> The most painful parental response had to do with the difficulty in getting the child appropriate help, the school's denial of parental suspicions of problems, and the "time wasted" between when the parent raised the possibility of the child's needing special help and when the child actually began to receive it. (Malekoff, Johnson, & Klappersack, 1991, p. 421)

Other parents, however, may object to a more formal referral and evaluation process: "My family is doing whatever we can to keep our adopted son's disability hidden from the school, knowing that once the disability is labeled . . . the expectations that will arise will not at all be positive" (National Council on Disability, 1995, p. 32).

The more you communicate with honesty and frequency, with a genuine interest in the student and family, and with sincere great expectations, the more families probably will see how the referral process can benefit their sons and daughters. As Hwa knows, a professional's failure to communicate with a parent—the failure to ask about the family's expectations and to take into account the family's cultural traditions of deferring to the professional—can be damaging. It was only when Hwa met Mrs. Hatch and Sue (teachers), who were eager for the contributions that Youmee could make and sought her out for her classroom, that frequent, honest, and genuine communication could occur. "Sue calls me at night to tell me what has happened in school. She also seeks information and suggestions from my family to better help Youmee. She really cares. She wants to help." It's almost as though Sue and the Lee family are on the same journey—a quest to beat the odds on Youmee's behalf.

If, however, families strongly object to referral, try to understand their rationale. Then in the spirit of partnership, try to see the situation from their point of view. They may be absolutely correct that referral would not be in the student's best interest. The bottom line is that partnership frees you from being limited by only your own perspective and enables you to benefit from family perspectives about referral for evaluation.

The school's special services team is responsible for reviewing the information on the referral form and deciding how to address the concerns stated there. The team may gather more information about the nature and results of prereferral intervention, wait several months on the suspicion that the problem is temporary, provide individualized education rather than evaluate the student for special education, or decide to pursue multidisciplinary evaluation. Based on data published in 1982 and again in 1997, it is clear that approximately 90 percent of referred students are evaluated and that approximately three-fourths of those students who receive an evaluation are determined to be eligible for special education (Christensen, Ysseldyke & Algozzine, 1982; Ysseldyke, Vanderwood & Shriner, 1997).

Are educators and families generally satisfied with the referral process? A survey of teachers in rural areas indicated that a slight majority expressed satisfaction with the referral process (Chalmers, Ortega, & Hoover, 1996). The three major concerns related to their dissatisfaction include: (a) the process moving too slowly, (b) rigid application of eligibility standards, and (c) excessive paperwork involved.

Providing Notice and Obtaining Consent

Typically, one member of the special services team is responsible for communicating with the family throughout the entire process (see figure 11–2), including the step of providing notice and obtaining consent. This person, often referred to as the service coordinator, may be the one who has already established a reliable alliance with the parents, who has had the most frequent contact with them or is likely to have such contact, whose values or communication style are most complementary to the parents', or who has enough time to work with the family and team members. The service coordinator is the hub of communication and ongoing support for the family, guiding the family through the referral and evaluation process and having a significant role in the IFSP/IEP conference (as you will learn in chapter 12). Service coordinators also ensure that necessary special education services are provided and that the services and supports are coordinated for the benefit of all team members (Friesen & Poertner, 1995; Roberts, Rule, & Innocenti, 1998; Turbiville, Turnbull, Garland, & Lee, 1996).

Providing Notice

IDEA requires schools to provide a written and timely notice to parents in their native language when the schools propose or refuse to initiate or change the student's identification, evaluation, or educational placement or the provision of a free, appropriate public education to the student (including an infant or toddler). The notice must be written at an easily understandable level and must include the following information:

1. A full explanation of all procedural safeguards available to the parent

2. A description of the proposed or refused action, an explanation of why the school proposes or refuses to take the action, and a description of any options it considered and the reasons why it rejected those options
3. A description of each evaluation procedure, test, record, or report it used as a basis for its proposal or refusal
4. A description of any other factors that are relevant to its proposal or refusal
5. A list of sources for parents to contact to gain assistance in understanding the information they have been given

The term *procedural safeguards* refers to parents' legal rights. As we noted in chapter 10, an excellent resource for obtaining information on parents' legal rights (written in family-friendly ways) is the parent training and information center in your state (see appendix A). You and the families you serve also can attend parent training and information center workshops on legal rights.

The special services team typically sends parents a written statement of their rights. Review your school's statement of rights to determine whether you believe it is easily understandable to the families with whom you work. Share it with several parents with varying levels of education, and invite their suggestions for eliminating jargon and enhancing its clarity and relevance. If it is unclear to you and your colleagues or parents, you may well conclude that it is a poor example of communication and hardly a good way to build partnerships.

The notice must describe the school's proposed course of action, rationale, and alternatives. At this point, the proposed action is to evaluate the student to determine whether he or she has an exceptionality and the nature and extent of special education necessary. Even if school staff members have already explained the reasons to the parents, they must state them in writing and explain why they rejected other possible options in favor of a full-fledged evaluation. It is a good practice to summarize the information on the referral form and to include the team's concerns and reasons.

The school's notice also must describe the assessment procedures, data, and other information the special services team used in deciding to seek an evaluation. It is a good practice to summarize information from the prereferral intervention or from the team's discussion and to include the names and especially the purposes of the tests the team plans to administer. Although the purposes of each test will probably be more meaningful to most parents than the actual names, you should give both the names and purposes.

Next, the notice must describe any relevant information the team considered in its decision to pursue an evaluation, including the student's academic performance, health status, peer relationships, or other relevant information.

Finally, the notice must provide information to families on sources for gaining more information about the information in the notice. As you have already learned, an excellent source is referring them to the parent training and information center in your state. You can also refer them to a number of other informational resources discussed in chapter 10, including technology options, books, and Parent-to-Parent programs.

The requirements for notice can help equalize the power relationship between professionals and families moving from a power-over to a power-with and power-from-within approach. The reason for this shift in power is because the notice provides information to families so that they will be on a more "even playing field" with professionals in understanding the process that is occurring. This information enables them to have an opportunity to provide input.

Sometimes a notice does not enable professionals and families to communicate with each other because it is written to satisfy legal requirements and tends to be stated in terms that lawyers or school administrators use with each other. In those instances, it is a good practice to supplement the written notice with face-to-face explanations and a clearly written notice.

Some parents will not respond to notices. There may be many reasons for their lack of response, and you should seek to determine more responsive and preferred ways to communicate with them. Follow a "touch-base" policy of telephoning, making a home visit, or consulting with other professionals involved with the family. The more you build a reliable alliance and communicate in an open way, warranting trust and respect, the more likely it is that families will respond to the notices that you send. If they do not respond, reflect on how you might personalize your communication and encourage them to respond.

Obtaining Consent

To protect parents' rights and their children's rights and to secure their participation in evaluation, IDEA requires parental consent for each proposed evaluation, reevaluation, or special education placement. Under IDEA, consent means the following:

1. The parent has been fully informed of all information relevant to the evaluation in his or her native language or other mode of communication.

2. The parent understands and agrees in writing to the evaluation, knows what activities the evaluation will involve, and knows what student records (if any) will be released and to whom.
3. The parent understands that the consent is voluntary and may be revoked at any time but not retroactively.

The 1997 IDEA revision describes a process for transferring parental rights regarding receiving a notice and providing consent to a student with a disability when that student reaches the age of majority. This is an elective IDEA provision, which means that states have the discretion of determining the age of majority for the students in their jurisdiction and also to determine whether they implement this provision of rights transfer. Assuming that a state does implement this provision, at the age of majority, students (as long as they have not been determined to be legally incompetent) are accorded all of the rights held by their parents. Parents and students must be given notice about this transfer of rights, and the student's IEP must include a statement that the student has been informed of his or her rights one year prior to the transfer. When students have been determined to be legally incompetent or when educators determine that a student does not have the ability to provide informed consent, states may establish a procedure for appointing the student's parent, or if the parent is unavailable, another appropriate individual.

It is a good practice to communicate clearly, even repeatedly, the reasons explaining how an evaluation helps determine if specially designed instruction would benefit the student. If you believe that evaluation and placement will not benefit the student, it is also good practice and ethically right to state your viewpoints. Parents who refuse to give consent may be exactly right in their perspectives that their son or daughter may be harmed rather than helped by the evaluation and placement.

If parents refuse to consent when their consent is required, they and the school must first attempt to resolve the conflict by complying with any applicable state law, such as mediation. If they still cannot agree, the school may initiate a due process hearing, which is a hearing before an independent "judge" called a *hearing officer*. If the hearing officer rules in the school's favor, the school may proceed with evaluation and notify the parents of its actions. The parents may decide to appeal the hearing officer's decision; if so, "they do so either before a state-level hearing officer (where state law so provides), a state court or a federal court (after state or local hearings)." If the hearing officer rules in favor of the parents, the school will not be able to move forward with the evaluation unless the school successfully appeals the decision.

Supplementing Written Notices and Consent Forms

Although the notice to parents and their consent must be in writing, any or all face-to-face explanations can be advantageous, so you might select one of the following options:

1. Sending parents the written notice and consent form to review and then scheduling a follow-up meeting to discuss the need for an evaluation and answer any questions
2. Giving the notice and consent form to the parents and reviewing the written information with them
3. Sharing information with parents orally and then following up the meeting with a written notice and consent form

Ask parents which option they would prefer. A face-to-face meeting with parents can be helpful in developing a reliable alliance.

When holding a face-to-face meeting with parents, you or an evaluation team member should (1) inform parents of your desire to have a meeting and state your rationale, (2) provide a thorough explanation of what will happen at the meeting, and (3) give parents information in a format of their choice so they can prepare for their role in the meeting. (We encourage you to use the information you learned in chapter 9 for premeeting, meeting, and postmeeting strategies.)

Collecting Evaluation Information

Figure 11–3 describes legal requirements for nondiscriminatory evaluation. The special services committee is responsible for appointing a multidisciplinary team to conduct the evaluation. IDEA requires the team to include at least one teacher or other specialist with knowledge in the area of the suspected exceptionality. There is no explicit requirement that family members be involved in collecting evaluation information. As you will learn later in the chapter, however, one of the 1997 IDEA revisions is that parents are now required members of the team to interpret evaluation results. If you plan to work with students who are gifted, you will need to comply with any local and state requirements related to the evaluation for gifted education.

Family members can provide valuable information from a unique perspective, but professionals do not regularly seek it (National Council on Disability, 1995). Harriet Rose, the mother of a young adult with cerebral

FIGURE 11–3

IDEA Evaluation Requirements

1. Types of tests or other evaluation materials:
   - Must be tailored to assess specific areas of the student's educational needs and not merely result in a single score.
   - Must be validated for the specific purposes for which the tests are used.
   - Must not be discriminatory on a racial or cultural basis.

2. Administration of the tests or other assessment procedures:
   - Must be by a multidisciplinary team or group of persons, including at least one teacher or other specialist who has knowledge in the area of suspected disability.
   - Must be selected and administered so as to best ensure that, when administered to a student with impairments in sensory, manual, or speaking skills, the results accurately reflect the student's aptitude or achievement level or whatever factors they purport to measure; and must not reflect the student's impairments in sensory, manual, or speaking skills unless those skills are the factors that the test or procedures themselves purport to measure.
   - Must be administered in the student's native language or other mode of communication (e.g., Braille or signing for students with visual or hearing impairments).
   - Must be administered by training personnel in conformance with instructions by the producer of the tests or material.
   - Must be administered in a manner which is nondiscriminatory on a racial or cultural basis.
   - Must include a description of the extent to which the conditions varied for any test not administered under standard conditions.

3. Number of tests:
   - Must include more than one, since no single procedure may be used as the sole basis of evaluation.

4. Breadth of the evaluation:
   - Must assess in all areas related to the suspected disability, including health, vision, hearing, social and emotional status, general intelligence, academic performance, communicative status, and motor abilities.
   - Must be comprehensive enough to identify all of the child's special education and related services needs.
   - Must, with respect to infants and toddlers, include the child's unique strengths and needs and the services appropriate to meet those needs (in the developmental areas of cognitive, physical, communication, social or emotional, and adoptive development); and the resources, priorities, and concerns of the families (if the family chooses to discuss them) and the supports and services necessary to enhance the family's capacity to meet the developmental needs of their infant or toddler.

5. Timing of the evaluation:
   - Must occur before initial placement in a program providing special education and related services. Must ensure reevaluation every three years or more frequently if conditions warrant or if requested by the student's parent or teacher.

6. Parental consent and notice:
   - Must ensure parents are fully informed and that they provide written consent prior to the evaluation or reevaluation.
   - Must include a full explanation of all due process rights, a description of what the educational agency proposes or refuses to do, a description of each evaluation procedure that was used, and a description of any factors that influenced the educational agencies' decisions.

7. Interpretation of the evaluation information:
   - Must draw upon and carefully consider a wide variety of information sources, including aptitude and achievement tests, teacher recommendations, physical status, social or cultural background, and adaptive behavior.
   - Must be made by a group of qualified professionals and parents.

Source: Turnbull, A. P., Turnbull, H. R., Shank, M., & Leal, D. (1995). *Exceptional lives: Special education in today's schools.* Englewood Cliffs, NJ: Merrill/Prentice Hall.

palsy, described her desperate attempt to get professionals to accept her opinions regarding her daughter:

> How could I convince them my daughter was bright and capable of learning? What could I say to keep them from brushing my opinions aside because I was "just a mother"? I decided I was going to have to take an aggressive approach in order to keep from being ignored.
>
> I whisked Nancy inside the center in her wheelchair, gave my interviewer a smashing smile and proceeded to tell her more than she really needed to know about Nancy, using all the technical and medical jargon I had learned over the previous 10 years. I also mentioned, very casually, that I had earned my master's degree in special education and had taught school before Nancy was born. All of which was a bare-faced lie.
>
> At first I felt a little guilty about what I had done. It really wasn't fair for me to take out my previous frustrations on those perfectly innocent professionals. But on the other hand, it was sad to think that my opinion as a pseudoprofessional was valued so much more than my opinions as a mother had ever been.

Another parent provides a compelling rationale of why collaborating with families in planning assessment can have such important outcomes. Consider the unintended consequences for Lauren when her mother's input was not welcomed:

> When Lauren was 6, the school insisted she have a standardized IQ test (Lauren has significant motor and communication challenges). I begged to be allowed to sit in on the assessment session, or at least to teach the examiner (newly out of school) how to understand Lauren's unusual way of communicating. I wasn't allowed to be there; I was told, "We don't permit parents in test sessions because they always try to help their children. It's more accurate and therefore more fair for your child if you aren't there." The outcome of the assessment was devastating to both Lauren and to us. Lauren was labeled mentally retarded and as a result, teachers expected less of her and she wasn't afforded the opportunities that she would have been given without this label. (Christy Blakely, Lauren's mother, 1997) (Lauren currently is a competent augmentative communication user, writing and speaking at grade level. She wants to be an author of children's books after college.) (Miller & Hanft, 1998, p. 55)

Family Participation in Collecting Evaluation Information

How can you create a partnership with families in evaluation and avoid creating a context in which families resort to desperate communication attempts? Invite families to choose any one or more of these options: (1) sharing their family story; (2) expressing their preferences and great expectations and describing their child's strengths and needs; (3) assisting professionals in administering assessments; (4) collaborating with professionals in constructing portfolio assessments; (5) conducting transdisciplinary assessment, and (6) especially in the case of infant and toddler evaluation, sharing their own priorities, resources, and concerns.

Sharing Their Family Story The first alternative involves having the family share its family story. Listening to family stories helps you know families—one of your obligations for creating a reliable alliance. As we have said in previous chapters, often the most relevant information evolves from informal conversations in which families share in an open-ended way their hopes, worries, successes, and questions as a basis for planning the evaluation. The conversation guide in appendix B furnishes probes for conversing with families and eliciting their family story in ways consistent with the family systems framework. You can imagine what a difference it would have made for Youmee and her family if someone—almost any professional—had asked Hwa and In about their family, their culture, and their parenting customs. If those kinds of questions had been asked and if the answers had been honored—so that professionals not only hear but also heed—it could well have been that Youmee would have been included in the general curriculum much before third grade and fourth grade. Think what a difference that could have made for her language and social development!

Expressing Preferences, Great Expectations, Strengths, and Needs The second alternative provides the student and family with an opportunity to share their preferences, great expectations, strengths, and needs. Students and families can convey their preferences—likes and dislikes related to homework, school subjects, hobbies, peer relationships, future aspirations, and any other relevant information. As you know from the empowerment model in chapter 3, perceived control is a critically important family factor in the empowerment process. When information about student and family preferences is available at the outset of the evaluation process, members of the multidisciplinary team can ensure that assessments take these preferences into account.

Likewise, students and families can be encouraged to share their great expectations for the future and to give their own perspectives on student strengths and needs related to their schoolwork and other school-related issues such as getting along with others, paying attention, and completing homework (Van Reusen, Bos, Schumaker, & Deshler, 1994). Professionals can support students and families in sharing this information directly by using probe questions and by actively listening.

Administering Assessments The third alternative involves collaborating with families in administering assessments. Although some assessment procedures have standardized instructions for administration, others are more flexible and can be adapted for family participation. Family members may join the professional who is administering the assessment, as audiologist David Luterman describes in box 11–1.

Consider the perspectives of the parent of a child with special needs. Would you prefer to participate in the assessment and discover the exact nature of your child's disability through your own observation and collaboration, or would you prefer to sit in the waiting room and receive the "verdict" from an expert? The more you collaborate with families in collecting evaluation information, the more likely you are to have accurate information and to develop a reliable alliance with them.

Maitreyi Das, a professional in the Indian government, was studying in the United States when her daughter (Moeena) was diagnosed as having a hearing impairment. Listen to what she said about working with David Luterman (the audiologist quoted in box 11–1):

> David Luterman became the guru that we, as Indians, are apt to seek out. The difference between him and an Indian guru, who directs and orders, was that he developed our capacity to decide for Moeena. In those hopeless, strained moments, he instilled hope and confidence. His team of teachers, students, and parents were our support group and fulfilled the role our extended family would have if we had been in India. Perhaps the most enduring contribution this group made was its information sharing, which enabled and empowered all the parents to become advocates for their children with hearing impairments. (Das, 1995, pp. 5–6)

Some educators may hesitate from involving families in administering assessments because they may believe that families will not be able to accurately assess their child's performance. A number of research studies have investigated the congruence between professional and parental ratings of various child performance indicators. In research focusing on the assessment of adaptive behavior, findings have generally pointed to overall correlation between parent and teacher reports; in spite

TOGETHER WE CAN BOX 11–1

Collaborating in Evaluation

After the parents have shared their concerns and their story, I enlist them as co-workers. I say something to them like, "I may be an expert on testing of hearing, but you are certainly an expert on this child; I need your help." This begins the process of empowering parents. As co-workers, we all enter the testing booth. I also bring in other family members who have accompanied the parents, including grandparents and siblings . . . I proceed to start testing the child, usually giving one parent the audiogram to fill out. In this way the information they need is being incorporated into what they are doing and seeing. The audiogram becomes much more meaningful to them because they are using it. . . .

I never overruled the parents' opinion. Although I might hold to my opinion that the child does have a hearing loss, I never impose it on the parents—they lose too much power if I did this and would not be fully invested in the child's habilitation program. . . .

Active parental involvement in the diagnostic process not only diminishes the denial mechanism, but also strengthens the bond between the audiologist and the parent. Parents have reported to me how glad they were that I was there helping them through the painful process. I was seen as an ally rather than an adversary. . . .

Another benefit of having the parents as co-diagnosticians is that they are also being educated about the audiological process. . . . Participating parents not only understand audiograms better, but they also obtain an idea of what this child can and cannot hear in the home environment, information that becomes very useful for them in the habilitation process.

Source: Luterman, D. (1991). Counseling and the diagnostic process. In *Counseling the communicatively disordered* (pp. 80–82). Austin, TX: Pro-Ed.

of similarities, some differences on domain scores have also been found (Shaw, Hammer, & Leland, 1991; Voelker, Shore, Hakim-Larson, & Bruner, 1997). When differences occur, teachers tend to rate the children as more skilled than their family caretakers. Interestingly, when teachers are able to observe children in settings other than the classroom, their ratings tend to be more consistent with parents (Foster-Gaitskell & Pratt, 1989). Educator and parental congruence on communication assessments have also revealed similar ratings (Diamond & LeFurgy, 1992; Jackson & Roberts, 1999; Snyder, Thompson, & Sexton, 1993). Higher congruence has been found for older preschool children as contrasted to infants (Gradel, Thompson, & Sheehan, 1981), families who have higher incomes (Sexton, Miller, & Rotatori, 1985) and when the child's IQ tends to be higher (Sexton, Thompson, Perez, & Rheams, 1990). Research also supports the accuracy of parental perceptions of the characteristics of their children who are gifted and the child's actual measured ability (Louis & Lewis, 1992). Thus, there is evidence to suggest that parents' involvement in collecting evaluation information will lead to accurate rather than subjective ratings.

Constructing Portfolio Assessments The fourth alternative is for schools to rely more heavily on authentic assessments and for families to participate actively in that process (as we also suggested in chapter 9). In contrast to traditional assessments that primarily rely on norm-referenced tests to provide a "snapshot" of a student at a given point in time, portfolio assessment is designed to document student progress over an extended period of time—a "videotape" rather than a "snapshot" (Gelfer & Perkins, 1998; Martin, 1994; Salend, 1998; Wesson & King, 1996). Figure 11–4 provides examples of potential items that might be included in a literacy portfolio.

In addition to the area of literacy, portfolios can address any subject area and include written products, videotape demonstrations, artwork, homework, essays, hands-on science problems, and open-ended problems. Because portfolio assessments assure a close link between typical experiences and assessment, there is a much greater role for family partnership (Flood & Lapp, 1989; Martin, 1994; Menchetti & Bombay, 1994).

For example, all parents, including those from culturally and linguistically diverse backgrounds, can nominate their children as gifted and organize a portfolio of work that best represents the student's gifts and talents (Hadaway & Marek-Schroer, 1992). An early childhood program associated with Columbia University sends parents pocket-sized "Let Me Tell You about My Child" cards that are written in the parents' primary language and contain a letter encouraging them to jot down notes and share information about their child's interests and activities. In this way, family input presents a more well-rounded picture of the child's development, and the method itself encourages

---

FIGURE 11–4

Potential Items to Include in a Literacy Portfolio

- A tape of the student reading orally from a self-selected piece of literature. The student may reread the same piece periodically, thereby allowing the viewer of the portfolio to clearly see improvement.
- A checklist of skills the student has mastered, such as phonics rules or writing conventions like capitalization and punctuation.
- A log of books read during the year, including dates completed, authors, and student's appreciation ratings of the books.
- Copies of stories the student has written, including, in some cases, copies of all the various draft stages the student has worked through.
- Pictures of a student's project, which shows understanding of a topic. For example, after studying volcanoes, the student may build a volcano and prepare a poster to illustrate how eruptions occur.
- Videotapes of students working cooperatively on language arts projects, such as putting on a skit to show understanding of a story.
- Notes the teacher makes while observing the student at work or conferencing with the student. These notes help the teacher document instructional decisions.
- A chart of progress using curriculum-based measures in reading and written expression.
- Charts the student has developed to tract bits of information collected in relation to a nonfiction theme being composed.
- Excerpts from a student's journal and learning log.

Source: Wesson, C. L., and King, R. P. (1996). Portfolio assessment and special education students. *Teaching Exceptional Children,* 44–48.

communication focused on the child's strengths. Encouraging parents' input on evaluation of culturally diverse students can be helpful in ensuring that students from culturally and linguistically diverse backgrounds are appropriately identified for special and gifted education (Artiles & Zamora-Duran, 1997; Subotnik, 1999).

Conducting Transdisciplinary Assessment Transdisciplinary assessment (sometimes called arena assessment) is a process in which professionals and families work together to simultaneously assess a child across multiple domains or areas (Foley, 1990; Linder, 1993). Most typically carried out in early childhood settings, professionals and families carry out the assessment together from planning all the way through implementation stages.

At the preassessment phase, a transdisciplinary model encourages a facilitator to provide information to families on the transdisciplinary process and to elicit their perspectives on their concerns, priorities, and resources (Crais, 1996). The facilitator plans an array of play-based activities for the child that will enable the professionals and family members to observe and draw conclusions about the child's strengths and needs.

During the actual assessment phase, professionals and families are in one room doing shared recording and observing of the child's behaviors. Typically, one person interacts with the child and then other people have an opportunity to observe and ask questions. Emphasis is on following the child's lead, eliciting the child's best performance, and being sensitive to the family's suggestions of how to get the most accurate picture possible of the child's functioning (Linder, 1993; McGonigel, Woodruff, & Roszmann-Millican, 1994). Parents may choose to be the facilitator or they may want to stay close to the child physically and provide comfort and security during the assessment process.

A research study compared a traditional, multidisciplinary assessment and a transdisciplinary play-based assessment for 40 children between the ages of birth and three (Myers, McBride, & Peterson, 1996). Children were randomly assigned to one type of assessment, and the same group of professionals completed the assessment on all children. Results indicated that the transdisciplinary assessment increased parents' satisfaction, provided a more comprehensive perspective on the child, and was a greater aid in planning intervention. Staff members also reported significantly more information obtained from the transdisciplinary assessment, with some indicating that this assessment was more useful in identifying strengths and needs as the basis of planning intervention. Overall, a transdisciplinary approach encourages collaboration and partnership.

Sharing Priorities, Resources, and Concerns
The last alternative applies particularly to parents of infants and toddlers, but it is good practice for students of any age. Families of infants and toddlers have the option, as specified by IDEA, to discuss their resources, priorities, and concerns related to enhancing the development of their child. The purpose of this provision is to plan services and supports that can promote family well-being related to the child's development. This identification of resources, priorities, and concerns must be (1) voluntary; (2) carried out by personnel trained to use appropriate methods and procedures; (3) based on a personal interview; and (4) done by incorporating the family's own description of its resources, priorities, and concerns.

Compared to other areas of family research, the area of family assessment has generated a significant body of literature (Bailey & Henderson, 1993; Garshelis & McConnell, 1993; Henderson, Aydlett, & Bailey, 1993; McGrew, 1992; Sexton, Snyder, Rheams, Barron-Sharp, & Perez, 1991). We prefer to steer away from the term *family assessment* and instead describe this process of gathering family information as the identification of family resources, priorities, and concerns. Assume that you are a parent who has just learned that your infant has a significant disability and is being referred to an early intervention program. When you find out about the process of obtaining services from the early intervention program, do you want to hear that a family assessment will be administered to you and your family? Or do you prefer to hear that you and your family will have an opportunity, if you choose, to share your own perspectives about what resources are available to support your child, your priorities for supporting your child and your family over the next year or so, and the concerns or worries that you have for the present and future? Which terminology is likely to enhance your own motivation for participating in the process? Which terminology is likely to be a catalyst for you to form a reliable alliance with early intervention staff? We encourage you to use nonclinical rather than clinical language. Clinical language tends to connote more of a power-over approach; whereas nonclinical language is more likely to suggest a power-from-within approach. Especially for families who are less educated than you or for families whose educational levels (like Hwa and In Lee's) may be as high or higher than yours but who have cultural habits that lead them to defer to you and your "power," speaking simply is one assurance that informed parents will become your allies, to the benefit of their children.

An important rationale for soliciting parents' resources, priorities, and concern is to make sure that the evaluation is customized to the particular child and family. Although likely unintentional, many professionals may proceed with assessments based on their own strengths and familiarity rather than in consideration of each unique situation.

> Recently, M., an excellent, well-trained student therapist came in for supervision. She began our session by describing her goals for Mrs. Martinis and Maria which included: reduced tactile sensitivity, increased oral motor dexterity, improved eye contact during interaction ". . . and several others." When I asked, "What was it again that Mrs. Martinis wanted?," the student . . . replied that the mother wanted Maria to get better. When prodded to consider the mother's perspective, we finally began a dialogue that enabled the student to see that she was providing a program for the child focused on what she herself knew, and not on what Mrs. Martinis wanted for Maria. (Fieldwork supervisor, 1997) (Miller & Hanft, 1998, pp. 53–54)

Just as this student therapist was proceeding with intervention based on what she knew, many professionals do the same thing in collecting evaluation information. When you take the time to clearly understand the parents' resources, priorities, and concerns from the outset, this dilemma can be avoided.

Furthermore, it is important at this stage to start formulating the collaborative team that will administer the evaluation and will be involved in developing and implementing the IFSP/IEP, should it be found that the student has a disability and qualifies for special education. The major value of collaboration is that it brings together people whose collective resources can be the basis for planning an evaluation that will enable team members to implement individualized appropriate special education. After all, the basis of evaluation should be to address the resources, priorities, and concerns of team members in a way that most effectively builds on each collaborator's unique resources. Thus, we recommend not only that families have an opportunity to share resources, priorities, and concerns but also that this same opportunity be extended to all team members (as we will discuss in more detail in chapter 12).

During the evaluation phase, every interaction with a family can help identify its resources, priorities, and concerns. As you learned in chapters 4 and 9, communication is the key to all interactions; and you can continually evolve a family's systems understanding by listening and organizing what you hear using the family systems framework. Again, as you develop reliable alliances with families, it is likely that they will increasingly trust you and will share more and more information on resources, priorities, and concerns with you.

In addition to open-ended and conversational sharing, you can offer families the option of completing checklists. A number of these have been developed at the early childhood level, including the *Family Interest Survey* (Cripe & Bricker, 1993), *Parent Needs Survey* (Seligman & Darling, 1997), *Family Needs Survey* (Bailey & Simeonsson, 1988), *How Can We Help* (Child Development Resources, 1989), and the *Family Needs Scale* (Dunst, Cooper, Weeldreyer, Snyder, & Chase, 1988). These checklists provide an opportunity for families to rate the extent to which the items, almost all of them related to needs, apply to their family situation. These scales are not nearly as focused on family resources that the family members have to offer as they are on family needs. We encourage you to consider the cultural appropriateness of various checklists and the preferences that all families have, including those from culturally and linguistically diverse backgrounds, about the use of checklists (Dennis & Giangreco, 1996). For families with limited English proficiency, a checklist can be especially daunting and often inappropriate.

The Family Needs Survey (Bailey & Simeonsson, 1988) lets families share their needs with professionals. Approximately 60 percent of mothers reported that they would prefer to share information through conversations, whereas 60 percent of fathers preferred the written survey. Here are some guidelines to keep in mind when using surveys (Bailey & Henderson, 1993):

1. Families should have the choice whether or not to share family information.
2. Items should be worded so that they are not deficit-oriented or judgmental.
3. Open-ended formats should supplement a written survey.
4. Because family preferences vary, family members should be given a choice about how they share information.

Some families may be interested in identifying other people who have ongoing relationships with and commitments to their child. If so, the team can invite them and get different perspectives on resources, priorities, and concerns. This is a very different process than is typical nowadays. In programs for infants and toddlers, typically only families share this information. In programs at the elementary and secondary levels, this step of the process also is typically omitted. Indeed, evaluation too often becomes a "canned" process of administering a package of assessment instruments. Instead, it should be a way for everyone to reflect about the student and about resources, priorities, and concerns that can be collected to enhance the student's education (Mehan, 1993; Ware, 1994).

Each of the six ways for involving families in collecting evaluation information can contribute to developing partnerships. They also produce a more robust understanding of the student. Rather than having a limited view of the child's skills and abilities on a given assessment day, the team has a comprehensive understanding of the student's and family's lives. It then is more able to individualize supports and services to make meaningful and sustainable differences in family members' lives.

Right of Parents to Obtain Independent Evaluations

Under IDEA, parents have the right to obtain an independent evaluation, and the school must take it into account in the evaluation process. This right applies even if the school's evaluation has already been completed. The school must provide parents with information about where they can obtain an independent evaluation; indeed, the school must pay for the evaluation unless it can prove through a due process hearing that its own evaluation was appropriate.

Why would parents seek an independent evaluation? They may be concerned about the appropriateness, accuracy, completeness, or timeliness of the agency's evaluation; or they may be concerned about the implications of the evaluation. In either case, it is important for professionals, with parental consent, to communicate their findings and recommendations to each other (Hepner & Silverstein, 1988). Unfortunately, that type of collaboration does not always occur, as a father recounts:

> We invited one of the evaluators, who had a Ph.D., at our expense to come to Dubuque to observe Alex in a school setting. . . . We were told later that the independent evaluation was considered, when honestly, it was ignored. (Testimony by Greg Omori, in National Council on Disability, 1995, p. 46)

Analyzing Evaluation Information

The evaluation team must (1) determine whether the student qualifies for special education and (2) if so, determine what the student's education needs are. This second step basically determines the nature and extent of the student's special education. Under IDEA, the team achieves this goal by (1) scoring, analyzing, and interpreting the results of each evaluation instrument or procedure and (2) synthesizing all the separate evaluations in order to obtain an overall understanding of the student. The first task typically is done individually or collaboratively by team members who administered the evaluation procedures, and the second typically takes place at a full-team meeting.

It is rare to find family-professional partnerships in analyzing evaluation information. Many professionals assume that the scoring, analysis, and synthesis of evaluations require technical expertise that most families do not have. Family members can, however, be partners in evaluation as was demonstrated in box 11–1, which recounted the audiological assessment in which the parents and other family members were co-diagnosticians. True, some assessment procedures such as an IQ test are standardized and may be administered and scored only by people with special training. But many assessment procedures such as the audiological examination can be carried out collaboratively with family members.

Some families participate in the analysis of evaluation information, but others prefer to not be involved. Some families appreciate being present at any discussion related to their child, perhaps because they perceive that the best way to ensure that their perspective is considered is to be part of the decision-making process from its beginning and at all later points. Others will opt out of the process. Particularly for them, but indeed for all families, the interpretations should not be considered final until they are reviewed and commented on by the families. Thus, lack of family involvement at the stage of analyzing evaluation data should lead to only tentative interpretations. If you want partnerships, respect the families' perspectives and insights and be careful about reaching conclusions without their involvement.

Discussing Evaluation Results with Parents

This section will discuss five aspects related to discussing evaluation results with parents: (1) notifying parents, (2) taking the families' perspective, (3) fostering a reliable alliance, (4) considering the student's role in discussing evaluation results, and (5) following an agenda for discussing results.

Notifying Parents

IDEA requires schools to notify parents in writing any time a school team proposes or refuses to change a student's identification, evaluation, educational placement, or the provision of a free, appropriate education. Thus, schools must give parents written notification (or a written summary) of the initial and all later evaluation results.

Full disclosure frequently enhances family trust and increases the probability of informed decisions. In addition, because evaluation information can be highly technical and written explanations may not be fully informative, it is good professional practice to explain the results face-to-face. These discussions can elicit family perspectives that can be extremely helpful in validating or dispelling tentative interpretations. Parents can share information about their son's or daughter's special needs, confirm whether the performance described by the professionals is typical, and make connections between the evaluations completed by persons outside the school (such as pediatricians and preschool teachers).

One option for interpreting evaluation findings for families is to convene a conference with the parents; another is to review the evaluation during the IEP conference. The advantages of a separate conference, particularly for the initial evaluation, is that it allows more time to discuss findings in depth and enables the parents to assimilate evaluation information before immediately making program and placement decisions. On the other hand, the advantage of incorporating the discussion of evaluation results into the IFSP/IEP conference is that it eliminates an additional meeting. Generally we recommend inviting parents to a separate conference to discuss the initial and all subsequent reevaluations. It is practically impossible to review and discuss the formal evaluation data and also plan an IFSP/IEP in one meeting. Further, most families and professionals have a hard time simultaneously receiving and then immediately translating evaluation information into decisions about their child's or family's goals, objectives, placement, and services.

Taking the Families' Perspective

How do families respond to evaluation results? From relief to pain, the gamut of their responses is long and varied. However sensitively you convey the information, many families—particularly those who strongly value academic achievement, success, and conformity—will be sorely disappointed by the confirmation of a disability. Many parents want hopeful information. That kind of information can enhance families' motivation, just as negative expectations can dispel families' hope:

> My frustration is with professionals in the field who say "she'll plateau"; she'll "like to do only routine things"; "don't expect too much"; "she's already doing better than I ever expected," etc., etc. . . . These individuals are very dangerous in the predictor's status quo that individuals [with disabilities] all fit in a neat nutshell. In fact, I often see them no differently than those who characterize a race, those of a specific religion, those of a specific sport, etc. The thing that is very troubling is

that these are young graduates in special education and those who have lots of contacts with parents.

Some parents may feel that in some ways they have contributed to their child's exceptionality or that they should have attended to it earlier. They may worry about their child's future and fear that their child's and family's challenges will necessarily and inevitably escalate. They may doubt the credibility or expertise of the evaluation team; and some will need more time than others to come to grips with the reality of the evaluation results.

> Fourteen years ago, when my son was in junior high, I remember walking into the room with five teachers, a guidance counselor, a vice principal, a psychologist, a social worker and a learning consultant. I was told that my child was a behavior problem, dyslexic, hyperactive and a general "pain in the neck." He was always clowning and disrupting classes. This child was the light of my life, yet no one had anything positive to say about him. No one suggested that his clowning was a need to cover for his feelings of inadequacy. No one realized that it is easier to let others think he was funny than reveal that he couldn't do the work. I looked up and saw the eyes of all ten people upon me. I felt that each of them had not only judged my son but was judging me as a parent. I was a working mother, which elicits some guilt under any circumstances, but in this situation, I believed they were questioning why I was working when my son had problems. I felt guilty, inadequate, angry, frustrated, and most of all helpless. (Halperin, 1989, p. 6)

Other families will feel justified and relieved (Mallow & Bechtel, 1999). Justified because they, unlike the schools, believed all along that their children had real needs, that they were not just lazy or uncooperative students. Relieved because at last they have an evaluation that they hope can lead to an effective intervention.

Consider family perspectives about labeling. Parents' opinions range widely. Some object to labels as demeaning to their children:

> My young son . . . must learn, build his own self-esteem, and learn his valuable role in society. He doesn't need to be singled out by receiving a label and all these self-fulfilling prophecies that attach themselves to that label . . . so please advocate . . . for changes that will stop the identification, segregation, and isolation of students with disabilities. (Testimony by Fran Maiuri, in National Council on Disability, 1995, p. 32)

This view is supported by adults with learning disabilities who report that professionals treat them as though they categorically have more limited abilities and aspirations (Gilson, Bricout, & Baskink, 1998).

Other parents believe that a noncategorical, nonlabeling approach will limit the services and supports their children need:

> We also have concerns about proposed changes in disability categories which may result in denial of services for some students with disabilities or may result in dumping them in regular classes without appropriate support services. (Testimony by Charlotte Des Jardins, in National Council on Disability, 1995, p. 33)

Still other parents favor new disability categories, believing that their children will get better services when their special needs are identified with a high degree of precision:

> I would like to speak about these children that we like to call children with neurobiological disorders. Our children are very stigmatized when they are served under the category of SED [serious emotional disturbance]. . . . As their parents, many times, when we go to try to work with the schools, our advice and our input is discounted because we are seen as the cause of their disturbance. . . . The families that we represent would like to see a change in the SED category, to truly talk about what's going on in the brains and central nervous systems of children with special learning needs . . . because research has shown that many of the behaviors and the learning needs of children are generated because of . . . the brain dysfunction, and so we would like to see that reflected in the law. (Testimony of Sara Gonzales, in National Council on Disability, 1995, pp. 49–50)

Not surprisingly, different cultures ascribe different connotations to standard terminology. For example, a Puerto Rican mother described the distinction, from her cultural and language perspective, between "retarded" and "handicapped":

> For me, retarded is crazy; in Spanish that's "retardado." For me, the word "handicapped" means a person who is incapacitated, like mentally, or missing a leg, or who is blind or deaf, who cannot work and cannot do anything . . . a person who is invalid, useless. . . . But for Americans, it is a different thing—for them "handicapped" is everybody! (Harry, 1992, p. 31)

Many traditional Native American languages do not have words for retardation, handicap, and disability (Robinson-Zañartu & Majel-Dixon, 1996). Not only is there lack of language but a lack of the overall disability concept.

> If . . . [a] Navajo child is diagnosed with Down syndrome and is from a more traditional Navajo family, the family may disagree with school officials when their child is said to have a disability. They may welcome the child's placement in special education, but from the family's perspective, they feel that their child functions well at home and exhibits no physical evidence of a disability. In other words, all the body parts are there and are in their appropriate places. The child walks, eats, and helps others at home. (Joe, 1997, p. 254)

Kalyanpur and Harry (1999) provide an excellent discussion of how the concept of disability is alternatively interpreted in various cultures.

Some people assume that enhanced parent-professional communication and understanding will occur if the child is offered noncategorical services. They think that by avoiding the use of disability labels they will be able to communicate better with parents. Unfortunately, in many school districts ambiguous language is used in place of more definitive disability terminology. Ambiguity does not enhance understanding. In some cultures, such as American Indians, no words for *disability* are reported in many Native languages (Joe, 1997; Marshall & Largo, 1999).

> The disposition for 5-year-old Tyrone indicated that his disability category was "04" (speech and language impaired) and that he would continue in his present placement of "Level III services" until the new academic year, at which time he would be moved to a "Level IV" (more restrictive) placement. At the end of the meeting, after the disposition was signed, the mother, . . . asked the professional team what Level IV meant, and was told it meant that the child would have more hours of service, which meant a smaller class and more one-to-one attention. When we asked the mother in an interview what she thought the other "04" designation on the record meant, she replied: "I think that's what they call Level IV: it means 4 hours of special education a week." (Harry, Allen, & McLaughlin, 1995, p. 369)

The similarity in the two types of codes and the fact that the 04 code was never explained led the mother to confuse the two and thereby remain unaware that her child had been assigned a categorical code. Although the professionals had assigned the diagnostic category of mental retardation to the child, they did not communicate that fact to the mother. Thus, in an attempt to be noncategorical, they increased their power-over approach by not communicating to the mother.

Another issue relates to cultural challenges and language. Consider the situation of Chinese families (most of whom had low income and all but one of whom used Chinese as their primary language) who reported to a researcher how they received evaluation information. Sixty percent of them said that none of the professionals involved in the diagnosis of their child spoke Chinese: "It was hard for us to understand because we were confused. We did not know how to start or who to turn to. We felt alone and helpless" (Smith & Ryan, 1987, pp. 347–348).

When asked to describe their feelings about the initial evaluation of their child, parents reported "confusion, anger, guilt, shame, and being upset, overwhelmed, heart-broken, sorry, depressed, helpless, worried, and embarrassed" (Smith & Ryan, 1987, p. 348). They continued (p. 348):

- I was afraid that my in-laws would blame me for producing a problem child. They felt that I brought them bad luck with my first son.

- My husband at first could not understand why my son would not speak, then, slowly he began to feel I didn't bring him up properly.

In all of your communication with families, particularly those from culturally and linguistically diverse backgrounds, there is no time when your sensitivity, personalization, and respect is more important than when you are sharing evaluation information (Miller & Hanft, 1998). Beth Harry and her colleagues, national leaders in developing culturally sensitive services, provide tips in box 11–2 for assessing students from diverse cultures.

Fostering a Reliable Alliance

An early intervention professional on a Native American reservation has described far better than we can the importance of a reliable alliance in pursuing infant assessment:

I felt that the families were a little bit reluctant. [Even though] I'm a member of their own tribe, . . . they still considered me an intruder of some type, because a lot of other times when programs came in, they felt there were too many people hounding them or hovering over them and wanting them to do this or do that, but as I explained to them, I'm also the parent of a child with disabilities, and that made it a little bit easier. I share their culture and beliefs, and I encourage them to use traditional medicines, never doubting that, and that always comes first, but at the same time, getting them to believe that in reality, too, there is something different. And that's how I've gained a lot of the parents' trust. (Testimony of Norberta Sarracino, in National Council on Disability, 1995, p. 38)

You can build a reliable alliance by responding to parents' questions, clearly describing and giving concrete examples of their child's performance, demonstrating a genuine interest and commitment to their child's success, and highlighting their child's strengths and abilities. In chapter 4, we emphasized the importance of empathetic listening, expressions of empathy, and empathetic reciprocity in building reliable alliances. Especially when parents are dealing with evaluation information, display empathy in all of your communications. Linda Mitchell, a parent and speech-language pathologist whose son experiences a developmental disability, characterizes the critically important role of empathy:

I don't want someone to feel sorry for me. Sorrow sets me up to grieve for a loss, but I don't feel that my son, John, is any kind of a loss. He is truly a source of great happiness and a huge contributor to our family. Empathy says I feel for you because I care about you. Sympathy says I feel sorry for you. Empathy connects, sympathy disconnects. If you want to really begin to build a relationship with me, empathize with me, and then help me move on.

TIPS   BOX 11–2

Assessing Students from Diverse Cultures

- Include parents in the assessment process by inviting them to observe and/or participate in all assessment procedures, following their lead in identifying which family members to involve, and arranging meetings at convenient times and places.

- Provide extended time for explaining assessment results to parents who hold very different values and beliefs about the meaning of disability.

- Provide an independent person who is familiar with the family's culture to interpret during conferences and encourage families to bring friends or advocates who share their cultural beliefs with them to the conference.

- Ensure that children are assessed in their native language.

- Consider using alternative assessment approaches, such as authentic assessment, that will best enable students to demonstrate their capabilities, strengths, and needs.

Source: Adapted from Harry, B., Grenot-Scheyer, M., Smith-Lewis, M., Park, H., Xin, F., & Schwartz, I. (1995). Developing culturally inclusive services for individuals with severe disabilities. *Journal of the Association for Persons with Severe Handicaps, 20*(2), 99–109.

How can families learn to trust? Families learn to trust when professionals learn and practice ways to warrant their trust. For Hwa and In Lee, trust came slowly. They certainly experienced competent professionals, but by the Lees' standard, they were misdirected professionals; family and professional goals diverged without any basis in Youmee's evaluation for the divergence. Yet the Lees also encountered professionals whom they learned to trust. Youmee's teacher Sue is one of them. And why is that so? What has Sue done to earn the Lees' trust? It is primarily that she works from her heart, and then when she finds that she lacks the knowledge to put her heart-felt instincts into operation, she works from the head, learning on her own about deafness and the language of the deaf.

Many professionals still think their main role is to interpret evaluation results for parents, but that role can involve one-way communication—professionals telling parents how their child is performing. On the contrary, the conference's other and more valuable function is for professionals and families (and others whom they invite, including—when families and professionals agree—the child) to discuss the evaluation findings and to reach the most complete understanding possible of the student's instructional needs. Some parents prefer to be passive recipients of information, while others want to be actively involved in making evaluation decisions. It is best for you to honor those preferences.

Sometimes professionals are frustrated by parents who do not immediately accept the evaluation results. But by taking into account the parents' perspectives, you may realize how much they love their child and how strong their parental need is to "stack the deck" in their child's favor. Your support and patience will pay off in the end.

Some parents seek additional information, perhaps from one specialist and then another, in a search for answers to their questions. These parents have been unkindly labeled "shoppers" who have failed to accept their child's exceptionality (Blacher, 1984a). But consider this: They may be seeking full and complete information so that they can make the best decision. They may be investigating the fullest possible range of professional resources so that they will be able to make an informed decision about their child and about the professional team, one with whom they might want to form a reliable alliance.

Unfortunately, some professionals interpret families' desire to get a second opinion or to question evaluation results as a personal challenge to their expertise. Any family who needs or wants additional information or resources related to evaluation deserves immediate referrals. If you affirm them in taking action rather than criticize them for refusing to accept the diagnosis, you can be a catalyst for their further empowerment.

Considering the Student's Role in Discussing Evaluation Results

Sharing evaluation results with children and youth can help them make decisions about themselves, provide them with accurate estimates about their abilities, and contribute to their esteem (Sattler, 1988). A student can be involved in conferences at many different levels (Teglasi, 1985). First, the parents may share the evaluation results and recommendations with their son or daughter. Second, the student may participate at the end of a conference held initially only with the parents. Third, one or more members of the evaluation team may hold a separate conference with the parents and/or the student. Separate conferences also can be followed by a joint conference where the results are reviewed on the student's level. This approach may prevent the student from becoming overpowered by the presence of many adults. Finally, students can participate in the regular evaluation team meeting. In that event, prepare the student in advance, and be sure that the discussion at the conference is clear to the student; affirm the student's strengths, and discuss the student's needs. It does not matter which approach is used as long as you are sensitive to the family's and student's preferences and needs about how to receive evaluation information.

Following an Agenda for Discussing Results

There are at least three goals of the conference at which the team discusses evaluation results (Teglasi, 1985):

1. Ensuring a clear understanding of the student's strengths, preferences, great expectations, and needs
2. Empathetically supporting families and students in the emotional adjustment to the evaluation information
3. Interpreting and communicating information to facilitate an appropriate education for the student and collective empowerment for the student, family, and all team participants. One broad way of structuring the agenda to accomplish these goals is to include the following four components (Rockowitz & Davidson, 1979):

   1. Initial proceedings
   2. Presentation of findings
   3. Recommendations
   4. Summary

Initial Proceedings Whatever the agenda, families should have the opportunity according to their preferences to provide their own input and to react to and reflect upon others' input. For example, during the initial proceedings, it is important for families to describe their perspectives about their child's functioning. Their comments will give you clues to their current level of understanding about their child. Perhaps you can incorporate some of the words they use (such as "lagging behind") in subsequent explanations.

Presentation of Findings

You should be as concrete and specific as you can and follow the following four suggestions (Hirsch, 1981):

1. Introduce the domain/subject area being discussed and include examples.
2. State the student's current level of functioning within that domain/subject area and how it compares to chronological age peers.
3. Give examples of skills (within the domain/subject area) that the student can and cannot perform.
4. Address the importance of any discrepancy between age and achievement and how the discrepancy may affect the student's development now or in the future.

You also should incorporate the communication skills that you learned in chapters 4 and 9. Many families have had clues that their child may have problems, and they usually appreciate direct yet sensitive communication. For example, use jargon-free language, offer suggestions for follow-up reading material, and clearly convey the message that you have the child's and family's interests in mind.

The evaluation team should present a composite of the student's strengths, preferences, great expectations, and needs, not just list a string of separate and isolated discipline-specific reports. The family is dealing with the whole child, not a child segmented into discrete parts.

> Specialists see [my daughter] from their own point of view. I guess the hardest thing is that I want answers. I wanted them to say she is going to make it or she isn't going to make it. I guess the hardest thing is not getting answers and everyone looking at their particular area and no one giving me the whole picture. Everyone is just looking at one area and forgetting she is a whole child. (author unknown)

The evaluation conference should seek to do more than present a composite; it should also stimulate discussion and assist in addressing the priorities and concerns of family and other team members.

> Feedback of test results inevitably affects the way in which a family conceives their child's problem. It may serve to answer questions the family has already framed, such as "is he able to perform his school-

work?" It may also serve to introduce whole new viewpoints from which to see a certain behavior. That is, a child whom the parents see as "bad" or "disobedient" may be reframed by the consultant as "disabled." One who is seen as "lazy" may be reframed as "depressed." The main purpose of "reframing" a child's problem is to "construct a workable reality" (Liebman, 1975) for the family. That is, to state the problem in a way that permits a solution. (Fulmer, Cohen, & Monaco, 1985, pp. 145–146)

Different families will have different reframing perspectives and schedules (Gill & Maynard, 1995). Most will need time to absorb the evaluation information and develop new understandings about their child. These new understandings often create conflicting emotions—disappointment as well as hopefulness/well-being (Larson, 1998).

Switzer (1985) describes a cognitive problem-solving seminar she offered for parents of children who recently received the diagnosis of learning disabilities. The seminar's purpose was to provide them with factual knowledge, to decrease their feelings of anxiety, and to increase their receptivity to remediation. She reported a positive evaluation by families. Interestingly, parents recommended that such a seminar be delayed until about two months after diagnosis so that they could have some necessary distance and time for reflection from the initial evaluation before learning more about their child.

The evaluation team should discuss the student's performance and the type of exceptionality, particularly at the initial evaluation conference (Gill & Maynard, 1995). Categorical labels are often painful for some parents, but others are relieved to have a name to call a condition that has created so many concerns for them. Thus, merely discussing conditions (without the significance of the label) can create tension for families and professionals alike.

> Many professionals have difficulty discussing mental retardation in a straightforward manner. These professionals are usually extremely sensitive to the social stigma associated with mental retardation and/or to the parents' distress, . . . usually this phenomenon is seen among young professionals, but occasionally even experienced professionals have identified so closely with the parents that to cause them pain is extremely difficult. When professionals are uncomfortable with mental retardation, they have been observed to ramble around the topic and "forget" that the term has not been used, become dysfluent and almost incoherent as they approach the use of the term, or to report that they had to "force" themselves to say it. Unfortunately, these reactions on the part of the professionals usually increase the stress and tension felt by the parents. (Shea, 1984, p. 275)

Professionals should explain that mental retardation means that the child has slower-than-average development. Because many families associate mental retardation with negative societal stereotypes, team members should talk about the different degrees of mental retardation and the positive outcomes that many individuals, whatever their degree of mental retardation, experience when they have access to appropriate services. They should offer to connect the parents with local or regional parent organizations (such as The Arc, a parent training and information center, Parent to Parent, or other disability-specific groups about which you read in chapter 10) so that they can talk with other parents whose children also experience mental retardation, learn about services, and get emotional support.

Remember that many of the information sources that you learned about in chapter 10 (such as parent support groups, internet sites, books, criteria for access to funding, and a range of other resources) are organized by category of disability. Thus, when families have a label for the condition, they are likely to have a much easier time with getting information about their child's strengths and needs.

Recommendations After discussing evaluation results, professionals have to make recommendations. The more that parents have been partners in the evaluation process, the more they are apt to generate and follow through on professionals' and their own recommendations. Traditionally, evaluation conferences have been characterized by professionals' agreeing in advance about their recommendations and then presenting them to families. A partnership model, however, encourages families and professionals to reflect collaboratively about the evaluation data and to generate recommendations for action. The recommendations should, of course, enhance the student's appropriate education and, at best, help both the child and family.

Many evaluation conferences tend to do nothing more than recommend that the student be placed in a special education program. In that respect, they do not comply with IDEA. Instead, as IDEA requires, they should describe the specially designed instruction, related services, assistive technology, extracurricular activities, and other school activities (including those in the general curriculum) that can benefit the student. Given that the purpose of evaluation is to lead to an appropriate education, recommendations logically must provide families, teachers, and related service providers with *detailed* information about the child's participation and progress in all aspects of school, including the general curriculum. They should also show how best to promote preferences, build on strengths, and remediate needs.

Parents are most apt to carry out recommendations when they have the following experiences (Teglasi, 1985):

- They perceive their child's needs and strengths in a manner similar to the professionals'.
- Both parents attend the conference, particularly if there are two or more conferences.
- The professionals are precise and clear in their presentations.
- Families perceive professionals as caring.

To assure that all recommendations are implemented, it is helpful to recommend a specific plan of action, specifying who is responsible for following through on each recommendation, when those people will begin and finish their duties, the necessary resources for the job, and how people will know the work has been done. This plan can help make sure that team members and parents alike act in an empowered way, taking action in light of the conference recommendations. It also is useful to engage in continuous reflection in subsequent evaluation or IFSP/IEP conferences about the extent to which a reliable alliance has been developed and how team members interact with each other and with families.

Finally, two major outcomes should result from discussing evaluation results. First, if the team and the family determines that the student does not qualify for special education, they should find other services to address the child's needs; and parents must then receive the legally required notice that the student does not qualify for special education. Or second, if the team and family determine that the student is eligible for special education (that is, specially designed instruction), they must develop an individually appropriate program for the child (see chapter 12).

As we conclude this section on discussing evaluation results with parents, we want to underscore what a formative moment it is for most parents when they first learn about the nature of their child's disability (Miller & Hanft, 1998). As you share evaluation results, you need to be always mindful that the parents' expectations for the future—great or small—may be largely determined by the words and messages that they receive at this crucial time. We concur with the parent of a child who expressed her perspectives as follows:

> . . . If I could say one thing to doctors, educators and all professionals who work with families of children with disabilities it's this: they need to know their power and the effect their words can have on these families. Predictions about the child's future should not be given without great circumspection and an extraordinary degree of sensitivity for the parents' feelings. If parents lose hope, everything is lost. (Sullivan, 1995, p. 70)

You can be the catalyst for the long-term positive outcomes that this parent experienced through your reliable alliances with families in the referral and evaluation process:

> The remembrance of Haley's first assessment will always linger in my mind as one of the gentle reminders that there are kind, supportive, and caring service providers who are there to give true service and support to families in times of great trial and adversity. With this session as a foundation to our experiences, we were able to weather the sporadic intense "storms" that many, many surgeries and long recuperative periods in numerous hospitals created for our family. As a parent, I know that bright beginnings are a great forecast of future happenings, and ours was certainly hopeful of what our unexpected journey might have in store for us. (Tracy Price-Johnson, Haley's mother, 1997) (Miller & Hanft, 1998, p. 57)

Informing Parents of the Individualized Program Conference

In chapter 12, we will discuss in detail IDEA's requirements for an individualized program for every child from birth through age 21 who receives special education. At this point, we simply call your attention to the IDEA requirement that schools must take steps to ensure that the child's parents are present or are given the opportunity to participate in each meeting related to their child's individualized program. This means that schools must (1) notify (in writing or orally) the parents about the meeting early enough to allow them to make arrangements to attend; (2) indicate the purpose, the time, and the location as well as the persons who will attend; (3) inform the parents that they may bring other individuals to the IEP meeting who have knowledge or special expertise about their child; and (4) schedule the conference at a mutually agreed-upon time and place. The schools also must provide a written notice to students when they become 14 years old and also at age 15, inviting them to the meeting and describing that one purpose of the meeting is to state what the student needs for transition to post-secondary activities. When the student reaches age 16, the schools must give a notice that the meeting will develop a plan of transition services.

Linking Our Themes: Building a Reliable Alliance

By now, you should realize that the eight reliable alliance obligations can be infused into every partnership opportunity. Just as you have already learned about infusing these obligations into the partnerships of communicating among reliable allies (chapter 9) and meeting families' basic needs (chapter 10), so you can learn to infuse obligations into the partnership opportunity of referring and evaluating for special education. Figure 11–5 provides an example of issues

---

FIGURE 11–5

Creating a Reliable Alliance: Referring and Evaluating for Special Education

Obligations	Issues	Disempowering Actions	Empowering Actions
Knowing yourself	You feel highly frustrated with students who have behavior disorders, and you have a tendency to want their parents to know how much they disrupt your class.	Recount to the parents a litany of all the irritations that you have experienced with their son.	Identify the student's strengths and let the student and family know that you appreciate those strengths. Stop dwelling on frustrations and irritations.
Knowing families Family characteristics	A Vietnamese family with whom you have scheduled an evaluation conference does not speak English.	Ask the student to come to the conference and interpret for his parents.	In advance of the conference, confirm with family members their need for an interpreter. Ask whether they would like to recommend a specific interpreter. If possible, act on their recommendation in getting the interpreter of their choice. *(continued)*

FIGURE 11–5 CONTINUED

Creating a Reliable Alliance: Referring and Evaluating for Special Education

Obligations	Issues	Disempowering Actions	Empowering Actions
Family interaction	Divorced parents attend a meeting to devise jointly prereferral strategies. They argue with each other, and the father abruptly leaves in the middle of the conference.	Tell the mother that it will be impossible for you to communicate with them until they can work out a way to be in a conference without experiencing such conflict.	When it is obvious that stress is escalating, ask the parents if they would like to reschedule the meeting. After the father leaves, solicit the mother's preferences for next steps. Telephone the father after the meeting and solicit his preferred next steps.
Family functions	A family does not understand its legal rights and is totally confused by the formal notice and consent form. Family members are extremely overextended with multiple challenges.	Send the parents a notice of a workshop on legal rights as well as the school district's legal rights handbook.	Ask the family members what you and other educators can do that would be the most supportive to them given the multiple challenges that they are facing. Offer to give them explanations in a time-efficient fashion.
Family life cycle	Family members of a gifted girl in your class are distressed that their daughter wants to pursue a career in mathematics rather than be a homemaker, which is the traditional role for women in their culture.	Reprimand the family members for not having a stronger feminist orientation toward the education of their daughter.	Invite family members to share with you their visions of their daughter's future and seek to understand their values about women's roles and career options. Invite the student to do the same.
Honoring cultural diversity	Asian family members tell you that they believe their son's learning disability is a punishment to them for not adequately honoring their ancestors.	Tell the family to discount nonscientific interpretations as groundless and foolish.	Listen empathetically to the family's perspectives and ask members what information or support you could provide that they might find helpful.
Affirming and building on family strengths	A mother with AIDS comes to a diagnostic conference to hear the latest educational report on her child, who also has AIDS.	Tell the mother that nothing would make you feel as guilty as giving AIDS to your child.	Share with the mother one or more things that she has done that has made a positive difference in the child's educational progress and tell her you appreciate her efforts.

FIGURE 11–5   CONTINUED

Creating a Reliable Alliance: Referring and Evaluating for Special Education

Obligations	Issues	Disempowering Actions	Empowering Actions
Promoting family choices	Parents are highly dissatisfied with the evaluation that you believe has been done very appropriately. They request an independent evaluation, but you do not believe one is needed.	Defend the school's evaluation and tell the parents that their request is unwarranted.	Encourage the parents to discuss with you their concerns and ask them to describe an evaluation process that they would find satisfactory. Inform them of the process for initiating an independent evaluation.
Envisioning great expectations	Parents have just received the diagnosis that their infant is legally blind.	Encourage the parents to be realistic and to recognize that it is too much of a burden for community preschools to adapt their programs.	Ask the parents what information would be especially helpful for them as they consider their next steps. Let them know that you look forward to collaborating with them and watching their child grow and develop. Tell them that you are available to help make their dreams for their child come true.
Using interpersonal communication skills	In the evaluation conference, the parents seem to want to "kill the messenger." They are angry at the professionals for "creating" their child's problem.	Point out to the parents that they have displaced anger and that you and other professionals are doing all that you know how to do to help them.	Listen empathetically to the parents' perspective and reflect on whether any of the communication used in the conference could unintentionally come across as representing a "we-they" orientation.
Warranting trust and respect	In your noncategorical program, parents ask you what "functional placement" means. You know that the professional interpretation is "severe disability," but the school district forbids you to use that classification.	Tell parents that "functional placement" really does not have a meaning, and that the professionals do not associate any kind of diagnostic label with it.	Explain to parents the rationale for noncategorical programming and share your own values. Also tell them that sometimes noncategorical labels have other connotations, and honestly share those connotations with them.

related to each of the eight obligations as well as disempowering and empowering actions that you can take.

Linking Our Themes: Strengthening Family Resources

Ultimately, the empowering context that you help create can provide an opportunity for students to flourish in their educational outcomes and an opportunity for families to enhance their motivation and knowledge/skills. It bears repeating that a family's empowerment can contribute to collective empowerment; thus, as you contribute to enhancing families' empowerment, it is likely that the synergy created will have the outcome of also enhancing your own empowerment. How can you enhance families' empowerment through the process of referring and evaluating students for special education? Figure 11–6 provides some examples.

FIGURE 11–6

Strengthening Family Factors Through an Empowering Context: Referring and Evaluating for Special Education

Motivation	What You Can Do	Knowledge/Skills	What You Can Do
Self-efficacy	Emphasize to parents how helpful their ideas on instructional accommodations have been in enhancing the success of the prereferral process.	Information	Provide information to families in their preferred language and/or at their preferred reading level to ensure that they gain a meaningful understanding of evaluation results.
Perceived control	Brainstorm with family members about the roles that they would like to have in collecting and interpreting evaluation results.	Problem solving	When evaluation results are mixed and even conflictual, brainstorm with families on their interpretations and plan a strategy to gain a clearer picture of the student's strengths, great expectations, preferences, and needs.
Great expectations	As evaluation results are interpreted, consistently point out hopeful indications that the student is progressing and that educational challenges are being resolved.		
Energy	When parents share their priorities, resources, and concerns, emphasize the importance of their taking time for themselves and enhancing their own wellness to the greatest degrees possible.	Communication skills	Point out to parents how their questions about the evaluation report end up pinpointing ambiguous areas and clarifying information for all team members. Encourage them to keep asking such excellent questions.
Persistence	Encourage parents to pursue an independent evaluation if they are dissatisfied with the school's evaluation.	Life management skills	Encourage parents to share their disappointment over their child's lack of progress and brainstorm with them about what kind of support would be helpful in addressing their emotional and information needs.

Summary

The steps in the referral and evaluation process and the activities associated with them for school-age children are summarized in figure 11–2. The process is long, with many component parts: (1) coordinating the referral and evaluation process, (2) implementing prereferral intervention, (3) initiating and reviewing the referral, (4) providing notice and obtaining consent, (5) collecting evaluation information, (6) analyzing evaluation information, (7) discussing evaluation results with the family, and (8) informing the family of the IFSP/IEP conferences. When you accomplish referral and evaluation soundly and humanely, you build a collaborative relationship among families and other professionals. It is upon this strong foundation that you can develop the student's individualized education program.

In Livingston, New Jersey, in the last year of the millennium, there are a few people who have beaten the odds. There are Hwa, In, Youmee, and Samuel Lee, immigrants whose culture, language, and early life circumstances were bleak, at least in this country and in some of its schools. And there is Sue, a person whose heart and mind, in sync with each other, met the challenge that Youmee's deafness poses. If you had to write another scenario about the odds, it would have to be this one: Youmee and her family are odds-on favorites to make a difference in America. As professors at Seton Hall University in New Jersey, Hwa and In already are members of one of America's elites, the academics. And as a student in her school, Youmee represents the fruition of what nondiscriminatory evaluation is all about: recognizing the true person, strengths and needs alike, and building on that essential person.

Chapter Twelve

Individualizing for Appropriate Education

"*T*he meeting was a good thing because I needed help with the things (written) on the board"—things such as staying in his seat, keeping his hands to himself, taking tests, and improving his grades. That's Greg Motley, a high school freshman, talking about his individualized education program (IEP) meeting. The IEP process "helped me to understand what I needed to do to get better, to do better."

Now listen to what his mother, Sherry, says about the same meeting: "We discussed as a group the goals we wanted my son to achieve. As a group, we came to the same conclusions as far as strategies to implement the goals we wanted my son to attain. The whole process was very beneficial to me as a parent. We all know what our role would be to help my son attain his goals. The program was a complete success as far as I'm concerned." That was her judgment in the academic year 1998–99. Does she have the same judgment about the next year's IEP process for Greg? Yes! "It's just wonderful, really. Amazing. Greg's had two great teachers. And a great IEP."

The perspective of Stephen D. Kroeger, Greg's teacher at Turpin High School in the Forest Hills School District in suburban Cincinnati, rounds out the picture: "What is the most effective way to create a sense of ownership on the part of all who have gathered? How can this student . . . become an authentic participant in writing this document? . . . The IEP is a useless document unless the student buys it."

In Greg's, Sherry's, and Stephen's case, as well as in the case of his other teachers at Turpin, including his pre-sent teacher, Donna Owens, the buy-in is authentic on everyone's part. Why is that so? It's simply because of "vision": "To keep the (IEP writing) process positive, we needed to be anchored by our vision" for Greg, says Stephen Kroeger. "From our vision, the team could prioritize needs and challenges. After a process of analysis, the goals and objectives appear to write themselves."

From vision—that Greg would, as he puts it, graduate and "work outdoors," perhaps as a forester—to goals and objectives is but one step in the IEP process. The bottom line is not writing goals and objectives but achieving them. And that's what Greg Motley has done, not just by receiving support from his teachers and parents but also by becoming self-knowledgeable and self-directed. For example, he knew he needed accommodations in taking tests. "I wanted to take the test in a room all by myself, so I could concentrate." No problem: that's an IEP-approved procedure. "I knew I needed to have certain kinds of teachers." Also no problem: Greg could say what teachers he wanted to avoid, so the school agreed not to assign him to those teachers. "I knew I needed to keep my hands to myself and not yell at other students." No problem here either: "I'm getting along better with my classmates. I don't do what I used to do." And finally, Greg knew he had academic problems; a string of "F" grades has turned into a string of "C" or better grades. "I like school more, it's not so hard, and I'm getting better grades." And his vision: It's unimpaired—the outdoors still beckons, and Greg marches toward graduation confident of himself. "This is as good as it's going to get, and it's good to begin with."

It's not been all peaches and cream for Greg, Sherry, and his teachers. "The day of the IEP meeting, I was scared. There were at least 15 adults in the room." Reduce the number of people, Greg says. No, disagrees Sherry: Without all those participants (from his "sending" junior high school and from his "receiving" senior high school), she and Greg would not have had the "positive, nice picture" of Greg's needs and of how the school would respond to them.

Responding to Greg's needs—that's an important element of the IEP. And combining his academic needs (for example, test taking that would improve his grades), his behavioral needs (keep his hands to himself, stay in his seat), and his "community service" needs (playing centerfield on the varsity baseball team) is the holistic way of responding. Greg's not a young man of several parts; he's a whole person, and a whole-person response is what he, Sherry, and his teachers sought. And it's what they achieved.

Greg Motley. (1999)

Whenever you develop and implement an individualized program for any student, you have a ready-made opportunity to be a partner and to create a reliable alliance with the student and the family. That's exactly what Stephen Kroeger and Donna Owens have done with Greg and Sherry Motley. Figure 12–1 highlights this opportunity.

Evaluating students is of little value unless educators then provide them with an appropriate education. The cornerstone of an appropriate education for students ages 3 through 21 is the IEP. When students turn 14 years old, their IEPs must contain plans for their transition to post-school activities. For children from birth through age 2, the cornerstone is the individualized family service plan (IFSP). Every student who receives special education (ages 3 through 21) or early intervention services (from birth through age 2) must have an IEP or IFSP, as appropriate. The legal requirements and research related to IFSP/IEP partnerships provide you with many opportunities for forming reliable alliances related to individualizing a student's appropriate education.

Legal Requirements

Because there are differences in IEP and IFSP legal requirements, we will review them separately.

Individualized Education Program (IEP)

The IEP is a written document setting forth the nature of the student's specially designed instruction, "related services," and "supplementary aids and services." Regarding the IEP, we will discuss required (1) components and timelines, (2) participants, and (3) considerations. (We will define these terms later in this chapter.)

Required Components and Timelines The IEP must contain statements concerning eight different factors:

- The student's present levels of educational performance, including how the student's disability affects his or her involvement in the general curriculum; or, for a preschool child, his or her participation in appropriate activities
- Measurable annual goals, including benchmarks or short-term instructional objectives, related to (a) meeting the child's needs that result from the disability to enable the child to be involved in and progress in the general curriculum, and (b) meeting each of the child's other educational needs that result from the child's disability

- Special education, related services, supplementary aids and services, program modifications or supports that will be provided to advance the student toward attaining the annual goals, to be involved and progress in the general curriculum, to participate in extracurricular and other school activities, and to enable the child to participate in activities with children without disabilities
- An explanation of the extent, if any, to which the child will not participate with children without disabilities in the regular class and in extracurricular and other school activities with children who do not have disabilities
- Any individual modifications in the administration of statewide or district-wide assessments of student achievement that are needed so the child can participate in those assessments
- The projected date for beginning the services and the anticipated frequency, location, and duration of services and modifications
- Beginning at age 14 and updated annually thereafter, a statement of the services the child needs for transition to post-secondary activities
- How the child's progress toward meeting annual goals will be measured; how parents will be regularly informed of their child's progress toward meeting the annual goals; how the child's parents will be regularly informed, at least as often as parents are informed of their nondisabled children's progress, of the child's progress toward the annual goals and the extent to which that progress is sufficient to achieve the goals by the end of the year

Each of these eight statements must contain still further details. For example, the statement concerning transition services must also contain statements about the child's transition needs (this must be included when the child attains age 14) and the child's needed transition services, including interagency services (this must be included when the child attains age 16). In addition, one year before the child attains the age of majority (in most states, age 18), the IEP must contain a statement that the child has been informed of the rights that will transfer to him or her—from the parents—when the child reaches the age of majority. This provision—the so-called "devolution" provision (the rights devolve from the parent to the child)—can be problematic if the child lacks the mental capacity to exercise those rights. Thus, the law provides that if the child has not been determined to be "incompetent" by a court of law but is determined not to have the ability to provide informed consent with respect to his or her educational program, then the state has to have

FIGURE 12—1

Empowerment Framework: Collaborating for Empowerment in Individualizing for Appropriate Education

Education Context Resources

	Opportunities for Partnerships	Obligations for Reliable Alliances
	Opportunities Arise At . . .	**Reliable Alliances Consist of . . .**
	Communicating among reliable allies	Knowing yourself
	Meetings families' basic needs	Knowing families
	Evaluating for special education	Honoring cultural diversity
	Individualizing for appropriate education	Affirming family strengths
	Extending learning in home and community	Promoting family choices
	Attending and volunteering at school	Envisioning great expectations
	Advocating for systems improvement	Communicating positively
		Warranting trust and respect

Professional Resources

Motivation	Knowledge/Skills
Self-efficacy: Believing in our capabilities	Information: Being knowledgeable
Perceived control: Believing we can apply our capabilities to affect what happens to us	Problem solving: Knowing how to bust the barriers
Great expectations: Believing we will get what we want and need	Life management skills: Knowing how to handle what happens to us
Energy: Lighting the fire and keeping it burning	Communication skills: Being on the sending and receiving ends of expressed needs and wants
Persistence: Putting forth a sustained effort	

Family Resources

Motivation	Knowledge/Skills
Self-efficacy: Believing in our capabilities	Information: Being knowledgeable
Perceived control: Believing we can apply our capabilities to affect what happens to us	Problem solving: Knowing how to bust the barriers
Great expectations: Believing we will get what we want and need	Life management skills: Knowing how to handle what happens to us
Energy: Lighting the fire and keeping it burning	Communication skills: Being on the sending and receiving ends of expressed needs and wants
Persistence: Putting forth a sustained effort	

Collaborating for Empowerment

some procedures for appointing the student's parent, or some other person if the parent is not available, to represent the child's educational interests so long as the child is entitled to any benefits under IDEA.

The IEP must be reviewed and, if appropriate, revised annually; it may be reviewed and revised more often if warranted in the judgment of professionals or parents.

If a public school enrolls a student in a private school at public expense, the public and private schools must jointly develop an IEP and ensure that it is carried out. But if a student's parents enroll the student in a private school at their expense, the local education agency has only limited obligations: It must see to it that the student has access to special education and related services. Note that the student has no individual right to any particular service or services that he or she would receive if enrolled in a public school.

Required Participants
The participants in IEP meetings must include the following individuals:

- The student's parents
- At least one regular education teacher of the child (this teacher must assist in determining not only appropriate positive behavioral interventions and strategies for the child but also supplementary aids and services, program modifications, or supports for school personnel that will be provided for the child)
- At least one special education teacher of the child or, where appropriate, at least one special education provider of the child
- A representative of the local educational agency who is qualified to provide or supervise the provision of specially designed instruction, is knowledgeable about the general curriculum, and is knowledgeable about the availability of agency resources
- An individual who can interpret the instructional implications of the evaluation results (this role may be covered by one of the other participants such as one of the teachers or the representative of the local educational agency)
- At the discretion of the parents or school district, other individuals who have knowledge or special expertise regarding the child, including related services personnel
- The student, whenever appropriate

When Greg Motley had his first IEP meeting, there were at least 15 people present—teachers from the school he was leaving, teachers from the school he was entering, a psychologist who had tested him to determine whether he had a disability, administrators from his "old" school

and from his "new" school, his parents, and, of course, Greg himself. It is possible for the IEP meeting to have many people. That can be intimidating to some parents or to the student; as Greg says, he was "scared." But it also can be helpful; as Sherry and Greg say, the more the people, the better the picture of what Greg needs and how he will get it. And, as Stephen Kroeger, his teacher, points out, the IEP was no longer his "draft" but became a document owned by everyone, "as co-equals."

The IEP has been characterized as a written commitment of agency resources, a management tool to ensure that the student's needs are being addressed, a compliance/monitoring document for determining if the student is receiving an appropriate education, an evaluation device for gauging the student's progress, and a communication vehicle between parents and school personnel (U.S. Department of Education, 1981). IDEA does not require that schools, teachers, or any other person be held accountable if the child does not achieve the IEP annual goals. Educators are required, however, to make a good faith effort to assist the child in mastering the IEP goals and objectives. By heeding Greg's preferences for his goals (working outdoors), by allowing him to select his teachers, by letting him say how he wants to take tests, and by allowing him to do a variety of things such as going to a separate room to study and participating in baseball, his IEP team—skillfully guided by Stephen Kroeger—collectively made a good faith effort and succeeded in helping Greg achieve his goals.

Given IDEA's purposes, educators must take steps to assure that a student's parents have a chance to attend the IEP conference and that they receive a free copy of the IEP following the conference. Steps to take before the IEP conference include providing advance notice of the meeting, scheduling a mutually convenient time, and arranging interpreters for parents who are deaf or non-English speaking. If parents are unable to attend the IEP conference, they may still participate through individual or conference telephone calls.

IEP meetings may be held without parents present only if schools have unsuccessfully attempted to have the parents participate. Educators must document their efforts to secure parent participation through detailed records of telephone calls, copies of letters to or from the parents, and detailed records of visits made to the parents' home or place of work and the results of those visits.

IDEA provides that students may attend the IEP meeting whenever appropriate. While they could begin attending at a very early age, it is more likely that they will attend as they grow older and certainly should attend beginning a year before they reach the age of majority and each year thereafter. Greg Motley attended his first IEP meeting when he was in the 9th grade, at age 15. When students are over age 14 and they do not attend their IEP meeting to discuss their transition services, the school must take steps to ensure that the student's preferences and interests are considered. They must also invite representatives of other agencies that will likely be providing or paying for transition services.

As you learned in chapter 11, when the student reaches age 14, the school must send a notice to the student as well as to the student's parents, explaining that the purpose of the IEP meeting will be to develop a statement concerning transition services.

The student's right to attend the IEP conference affirms that a student can contribute to the meeting by ensuring that (1) the student's perspective is taken into account and (2) the other participants focus on the student's strengths, needs, preferences, and great expectations, not on what they themselves want or find convenient. Greg Motley, for example, has attended his two IEP meetings (9th and 10th grades) and early in his 10th-grade year, is part of a team that is considering whether he should enroll in a vocational education program that is separate from the school he attends now. In having to choose between the vocational program and his present program, Greg and his team will have to weigh the relative advantages and disadvantages of each—the academic, extracurricular (varsity baseball), and vocational (outdoors work, perhaps as a forester). That may be heavy duty for some students; for others who have a good appreciation of their interests and abilities, as Greg does, that seems entirely proper. After all, it's Greg's life. Just as families and professionals can become more empowered through collaborative decision making, so can the student. That was the case for Greg: he learned that the school was there to help him, he sought out and accepted the help, and the consequences are that he is a more capable student and more well-adjusted young man.

Required Considerations in the IEP When developing the IEP, the IEP team must consider the child's strengths, the initial or most recent nondiscriminatory evaluation of the child, the parents' concerns, and, as appropriate, the results of the child's performance on general state or district-wide assessment programs.

There are also special factors that IEP teams must take into account:

- When a child's behavior impedes his or her learning or that of others, the IEP team must consider (when appropriate) strategies, including positive behavioral interventions, strategies, and supports to address the impeding behavior.

- In the case of the child with limited English proficiency, the IEP team must consider the language needs of the child as those needs relate to the IEP.

- In the case of the child who is blind or has a visual impairment, the IEP team must provide for instruction in the use of Braille unless after an appropriate evaluation of the child's reading and writing skills, needs, and media (techniques for reading and writing), the team determines that Braille is not appropriate for the child.

- In the case of the child who is deaf or hard of hearing, the IEP team must consider the child's language and communication needs, opportunities for direct communications with peers and professional personnel in the child's language and communication mode, the child's academic level, and the full range of needs, including opportunities for direct instruction in the child's language and communication mode.

- In the case of each child, the IEP team must consider whether the child requires assistive technology devices and services.

The team must indicate in the child's IEP whether any of these special considerations are relevant to the child and, if so, how the IEP will take them into account.

Individualized Family Service Plan (IFSP)

Like the IEP, the IFSP is a written document; but it specifies the services for infants and toddlers, from birth up to age 3, and their families. Whereas the IEP focuses on the needs of the individual student, the IFSP focuses on services and supports for the *family* as well. The IFSP has the dual goals of enhancing the child's development while simultaneously enhancing the family's capacity to meet the child's special needs.

Required Components Accordingly, the IFSP must contain statements concerning each of the following eight factors:

- The child's present levels of physical, cognitive, communicative, social or emotional, and adaptive development, all based on professionally acceptable objective criteria

- The family's resources, priorities, and concerns related to enhancing their child's development

- The major outcomes for the child and family and the criteria, procedures, and timelines for determining the degree of their progress and whether modifications or revisions of outcomes or services are necessary

- The specific early intervention services necessary to meet the child's and the family's unique needs, including the frequency, intensity, location, and method of service delivery

- The natural environments in which early intervention services shall be provided, including a justification of the extent, if any, to which services will not be provided in the natural environment

- The projected dates for initiating the services and the duration of each

- The name of the service coordinator from the profession most immediately relevant to the child's or family's needs (or who is otherwise qualified) who will be responsible for IFSP implementation and coordination with other agencies and persons

- A statement of steps to be taken to support the child's transition from early intervention services to preschool or other appropriate services

The initial meeting to develop the IFSP must take place within 45 days after the child or family is referred for early intervention services. Thereafter, periodic review is available in two ways: (1) Every six months the IFSP must be reviewed for progress and appropriate revision, by a meeting or other means agreeable to the participants, and (2) a meeting must be held annually to evaluate the IFSP and to revise it as appropriate.

If the parents agree, early intervention services may begin before evaluation and assessment. In that event, an interim IFSP is developed (naming the service coordinator and demonstrating that the services are needed immediately by the child and family), and the evaluation and assessment must be completed within the 45-day period.

Required Participants

The IFSP uses the term *family,* whereas the IEP uses the term *parent*. This difference reflects the evolving recognition within the field of special education of the importance of a family systems perspective. Accordingly, early intervention providers must explain to parents what the IFSP contains and must secure the parents' informed written consent to those services; the parents may consent to some services and receive them but object to other services and not have to accept those.

The participants in the initial and in each annual IFSP meeting must include the following:

- The child's parent or parents
- Other family members as requested by the parent(s), if it is feasible to include them
- The service coordinator

- The person(s) directly involved in conducting the child and family evaluations and assessments
- As appropriate, persons who will provide services to the child or family

If a required person is not available to attend the meeting, other means for participation must be used; for example, telephone conference calls, attendance by a knowledgeable representative, or pertinent records must be made available at the meeting. All meetings must be scheduled at times and places convenient to the family. The family's native language or other mode of communication must be used. (For the IEP, the requirement is for an interpreter to be present. However, for the IFSP, IDEA instead requires that the meeting be conducted in the family's native language or other communication mode.) The meetings must be arranged to allow the families enough time to plan to attend.

Review of Research on IEP/IFSP Partnerships

What are IDEA's intentions regarding family-professional partnerships? The U.S. Department of Education clearly states the intent:

> Throughout the process of developing and implementing IFSPs for an eligible child and the child's family, it is important for agencies to recognize the variety of roles that family members play in enhancing the child's development. It also is important that the degree to which the needs of the family are addressed in the IFSP process is determined in a collaborative manner, with the full agreement and participation of the parents of the child. Parents retain the ultimate decision in determining whether they, their child, or other family members will accept or decline services under this part. (U.S. Department of Education, 1999)

Note the language in this policy interpretation—". . . collaborative manner with the full agreement and participation of the parents. . . ." The federal expectation is that there will be a collaborative process characterized by having a reliable alliance. That's exactly what happened in Greg Motley's case. Although the IEP process was "foreign" to Greg's mother, Sherry, she found it to be a "complete success." Greg's teacher, Stephen, had an IEP format outlined on the classroom chalkboard; the outline defined the process the IEP team would follow. Sherry says, "We discussed as a group the goals we wanted my son to achieve. Everyone had input, including my son. As a group, we came to the same conclusions as far as strategies to implement the goals we wanted my son to attain. The whole process was very beneficial to me as a parent" (Kroeger, Liebold, & Ryan, 1999).

How has the expectation of a collaborative partnership been incorporated into educational practices? Sadly, but typically, there is a great shortcoming: The expectation is usually unfulfilled.

One of the earliest research studies was conducted within the first several years after schools began to implement IDEA (Goldstein, Strickland, Turnbull, & Curry, 1980). The researchers observed IEP conferences of 14 elementary students with mild disabilities and analyzed the topics of discussion and the frequency of contributions by each conference participant. After each conference, all participants completed a questionnaire to rate their satisfaction with their role in the conference and the decisions made. The researchers concluded the following:

- Parental contributions (mothers in 12 of 14 conferences) accounted for less than 25 percent of the total conference contributions.
- The mean length of conferences was 36 minutes.
- The most frequently discussed topics were the student's curriculum, behavior, and performance.
- The topics of placement, related services, legal rights and responsibilities, individual responsibility for implementing goals and objectives, the child's health, future contacts among parents and professionals, and future plans for the child were each discussed (on average) less than once per conference.
- Parents, resource teachers, classroom teachers, and principals were overwhelmingly positive.
- Overall, these conferences consisted of the resource teachers describing a previously developed IEP to the student's mother.

Did IEP conferences change over time? Eight years later, other researchers evaluated 26 conferences of students with learning disabilities (Vaughn, Bos, Harrell, & Lasky, 1988), determining the length, composition, parental participation, and parental attitudes of each. They reported the following:

- On average, 6.5 participants met for 41 minutes.
- Parent interactions accounted for only 14.8 percent of the conference time, or 6.5 minutes.
- More than one-fourth of the parents thought the term *learning disability* meant that their child was slow. To 12 percent, the term implied that their child had

a physical problem. Some merely responded, "Learning disabled is what my child is" (Vaughn et al., 1988, p. 86). Twenty-three percent had no explanation or had an unrelated explanation.
- Nearly two-thirds (59 percent) of the parents were positive and appreciative of the meeting. Some mentioned being nervous and cautious, while others said they felt confused and overwhelmed. In spite of these descriptions, 65 percent believed that all of their questions had been answered.

How do IFSP practices differ from IEP practices? A researcher who observed 25 IFSP conferences and conducted 50 interviews with parents and professionals to examine their overall satisfaction with the IFSP process (Able-Boone, 1993) reported the following:

- The average number of conference participants was 6, with 24 mothers and only 3 fathers attending.
- All conferences were held during the work week and during typical working hours, but one was held at 5:30 P.M.
- The average conference lasted for one hour.
- Professionals spoke more often than parents.
- Only four of the conferences focused on family-centered outcomes such as respite care, parent support groups, and counseling services.
- Parents and professionals reported equally high satisfaction with the conferences.
- The typical conference focused primarily on child development rather than on the child within the context of the family.

One of the more recent IEP studies reported data on 24 families whose children were in special education. Twelve families participated for three years: six for the first year only, and six for the second and third years only (Harry, Allen, & McLaughlin, 1995). The researchers interviewed families and observed conferences over a three-year period and reported the following:

- Although 16 of 18 parents attended the IEP conference during the first year, only 11 of 18 attended in the third year. Parents' reasons for not attending included conflicts with work schedules, late notice of the meeting, the routine nature of the meeting in which they felt their input was discounted, and the fact that the school tended to send papers home for signatures, whether or not parents attended.
- Six parents indicated that they were able to influence decisions in the conference.

- The length of a conference ranged from 20 to 30 minutes. (In one school, conferences were always terminated at the end of 30 minutes regardless of whether they were complete. Parents were advised that they could continue discussions with the teacher after the meeting.)
- The main activity was securing parents' signatures on IEP documents rather than encouraging genuine participation in the meeting.
- Extensive special education jargon was evident in all meetings.

The researchers commented:

As professionals identify with the culture of the school bureaucracy, most become entrenched in a "we-they" posture by which parents are seen as potential adversaries, rather than allies. . . . In this study, professional role identification seemed to become the dominant ethic driving how most educators, regardless of race, interacted with parents. (Harry et al., 1995, p. 374)

Although we have highlighted only these four studies, Smith (1990) summarized the body of IEP literature from IDEA's initial enactment in 1975 through 1990 and categorized IEP implementation into three phases. (These phases also apply to research conducted from 1990 through the present time as well as the research conducted during the period reviewed by Smith.)

- *Normative phase.* During the early years of IDEA implementation, research focused on explaining IEP components and expectations for their implementation (Abeson & Weintraub, 1977; Morissey & Safer, 1977; Turnbull, Strickland, & Hammer, 1978).
- *Analytic phase.* In this phase, research focused on development of the IEP (similar to the four studies reported earlier in the chapter), particularly related to special education teacher perceptions, parent and student involvement, extent of individualization, team approach, nature of service coordination, and general education teacher participation (Espin, Deno, & Albayrak-Kaymak, 1998; Farel, Shackelford, & Hurth, 1997; Gerber, Banbury, Miller, & Griffin, 1986; Getzel & deFur, 1997; Goldstein & Turnbull, 1982; Lewis, Busch, Proger, & Juska, 1981; Lynch & Stein, 1982; Nadler & Shore, 1980; Pyecha et al., 1980; Salembier & Furney, 1998; Smith & Simpson, 1989). There was also an analytic phase of IFSP research (Bailey, Winton, Rouse, & Turnbull, 1990; Boone, McBride, Swann, Moore, & Drew, 1999; Farel, Shackelford, & Hurth, 1997; DeGangi, Royeen, & Wietlisbach, 1992; Gallagher & Desimone, 1995; Minke & Scott, 1993).

- *Technology-reaction phase.* Research focused on computer-managed instructional systems to reduce time and paperwork hassles associated with the IEP. The shift of attention moved from the quality of the process to the logistical management of the process (Davis, 1985; Enell & Barrick, 1983; Glutting, 1987; Johnson, Proctor, & Corey, 1995; Minick & School, 1982; Ryan & Rucker, 1986).

Based on this extensive literature review, Smith concluded:

After more than a decade of implementation, research, and subsequent recommendations for improvement, substantive IEP change has not ensued. In consequence, we may have been ignoring "specially designed instruction" for special needs students, and thus, the very students the law was designed to protect and educate with their individual needs in mind. (Smith, 1990, p. 11)

In some states, students who are gifted have a right (under state law) to an IEP. The parents of students who are gifted may have a less positive attitude about the IEP process than parents of students classified as having a disability (Lewis et al., 1981).

That [IEP process, including the IEP meeting] was about as much of nothing as one could imagine. They, at that time and I'm afraid still now, had the same goal plan for every student; they really did not know how to run a program, although there were some very talented teachers working with gifted students. The meeting merely consisted of reporting the score (99+ on the Wechsler) and passing around a form, which everyone at the table signed.

In 1994, the National Council on Disability took testimony in ten states from families and individuals with disabilities concerning their perspectives about IEPs. The following quotations illustrate this grassroots testimony:

In regard to the IEP process itself, I wish it stood for Individual Encouragement to Parents. . . . In many ways this Public Law has become our enemy. Educators are being consumed by accountability and the IEP process itself. . . . The IEP process is so labor-intensive that it actually drives us away from the child instead of closer to the child. It has become a burden to our professionals. You may have five to eight professionals on a team and not one of those people really possess a true trusting relationship with the parents. Not one sees that big picture of this child's life, because they are caught up in the accountability, they are caught up in time, which also becomes their enemy. (Testimony by Kathy Davis, in National Council on Disability, 1995, pp. 56–57)

We have set up a system that I believe creates almost a tremendous bureaucracy in terms of making sure that we comply with hundreds and hundreds of rules, but there is no rule that says that we must have any kind of real successful outcomes for these kids. So we spend all of our lives making sure we cross all our "T"s and dot all our "I"s and people don't look to see whether the kids are doing better, whether they are being more successful. (Testimony by Diego Gallegos, National Council on Disability, p. 64)

The dominant theme of the research and the testimony is that schools try to comply with legal mandates and procedures, but they do not make an effort to foster empowerment through collaboration (Rodger, 1995; Smith, 1990; Smith & Brownell, 1995). There is scant evidence that the process enhances the motivation and knowledge/skills of families and professional participants or that an empowering context has been developed—one that is characterized by the eight obligations of a reliable alliance. Finally, there is little evidence that a collaborative process bridges either individual factors (motivation and knowledge/skills) or the context factors associated with collaborating for empowerment in individualizing for appropriate education.

It is entirely possible, however, to develop and implement IFSPs/IEPs in an empowering way. In Greg's case, for example, his teacher, Stephen Kroeger, used a simple "low tech" process. Using colored chalk, he outlined the components of an IEP on the chalkboard—a practice with which he and the team were most pleased. "Chalk, it turns out, was my biggest ally. Colored chalk was even better. The very nature of chalk is transitional and temporary. Chalk writing is easy to change, erase, circle, underline, and emphasize" (Kroeger, Leibold, & Ryan, 1999). He asked the participants to describe their visions for Greg, he found consensus in the vision, and he used the vision as an anchor for the subsequent discussion about goals and objectives. He also wrote the goals and objectives into the IEP format, making the IEP writing process "open-ended and flexible."

He also encouraged the team to prioritize the goals and objectives and kept them focused on the vision and on Greg's gifts, abilities, and strengths. Using these positive aspects as a "list in progress" and as a way to enable Greg to face the challenges of his learning needs with more confidence, the team prioritized two to four of Greg's challenging behaviors and then applied a collaborative problem-solving process to them.

As in Greg's case, success can come in IEPs if the student, parents, and professionals getting to know each other emphasize what each does that is helpful, support each other in their respective roles, meet often, plan collaboratively, and then implement the individualized program rigorously. As box 12–1 shows, this is an achievable result. (The box highlights the IFSP process but can be and should be just as easily adapted to the IEP process.)

For most participants, the IEP process has tended to be a disempowering experience. Although research generally indicates that the IFSP process comes closer than the IEP process to creating a reliable alliance, the IFSP process, too, generally still falls short of being a reliable alliance that fosters collaboration, leading to empowerment. By moving from a disempowering to an empowering partnership with families, as you and they individualize for appropriate education, you can be part of the team that supports students' success.

Opportunities for Collaboration

The IFSP/IEP conference should consist of the following nine components:

1. Preparing in advance
2. Connecting and getting started
3. Sharing visions, great expectations, and strengths
4. Reviewing formal evaluation and current levels of performance
5. Sharing resources, priorities, and concerns
6. Developing goals and objectives (or outcomes)
7. Specifying placement, supplementary aides/services, and related services
8. Specifying assessment modifications and special factors
9. Summarizing and concluding

Before reading about each component of the IFSP/IEP process and our suggestions for collaborating with families, study our summary of these suggestions in box 12–2. We encourage you to remember what you learned in chapters 5–8 regarding the individuality of families. The four components of the family system—characteristics, interactions, functions, and life cycle—all individually and collectively influence families' preferences regarding IFSP/IEP team participation. Thus, we will offer a broad range of issues for you to consider; but you will need to apply this information to every individual family situation. We especially want to highlight the important role of culture in influencing family preferences regarding the IFSP/IEP process (Hyun & Fowler, 1995; Kalyanpur & Harry, 1999; Nelson, Smith, & Dodd, 1992; Rhodes, 1996).

A Family-Friendly IFSP

Developing a family-friendly IFSP—or, for that matter, an IEP—is never a hurried matter; you can't hurry and listen at the same time. Making the process and goals family-friendly, however, can create collaboration between professionals and families. This Beach Center model of collaboration, in turn, can empower all of the participants, in the sense that each gets some of what each wants.

For Leslie Jones, her husband David, and her daughter Natalie (who has multiple disabilities and significant health problems), the collaboration begins when they tell, and professionals empathetically listen to, the Jones family story—their background, concerns, people to whom and places where they are most connected. Developing a "to do" list—services that respond to the Jones family and Natalie's specific needs, preferences and great expectations that become outcome-based goals—is the second stage.

Both the first and second stages are designed for the family and professionals to "get onto the same wavelengths" and even develop an interim IFSP. There follows an evaluation of Natalie; a discussion with Leslie and David about the evaluation results and their implications for Leslie, David, Natalie, and her sisters; the development of the IFSP, and the delivery of services to Natalie and her family.

Leslie describes the unhurried and whole-family approach of the Beach Center's family-friendly IFSP as "very sensitive to the well-being of the family as a whole and to the individual family members. No one is overlooked. Natalie's needs were balanced with the family's needs, recognizing that the family must be strong to meet her needs adequately. We talked a lot about me and whether I felt I could handle the work demanded by the various potential programs in her service plan."

Two problems emerged. The first one was getting Natalie dressed every day for preschool while also dressing and spending time with her sisters. The second problem was transporting Natalie directly to preschool rather than making her sit on a school bus for a long time, something that would be hard on her physically.

The Joneses' friends—whom they had invited to the IFSP meeting—and the professionals voluntarily developed a simple solution. They would help with both tasks, splitting the responsibilities among themselves.

Rather than being a "heavy weight" like other IFSPs that "created demands" on Leslie—demands for her time, energy, planning, and money—the family-friendly approach "looked at ways to provide services for Natalie without interrupting everything that was happening at home. This way, our needs were met, as well as Natalie's."

Most of all, the family-friendly process and services changed the Joneses' perspectives, helping them to "think about our relationship with Natalie and to view her as a part of the larger community . . . as someone who has a place in the community."

"Now that we realize that Natalie can give as well as receive in these relationships, we do not feel hopelessly indebted to others who help in Natalie's care. We recognize that they benefit from this 'togetherness,' just as much as we do. This new attitude toward our circle of friends has relieved our fear, and we are more willing to ask others to help. Now our approach is to encourage others to see our vision and to become part of the team effort."

[The Beach Center publication *Handbook for the Development of a Family-Friendly IFSP* (Turbiville, Lee, Turnbull, & Murphy, 1993) describes this process; its *Parent Handbook for Individualized Family Service Plans* (Turbiville, 1995) includes suggestions for families as they prepare for IFSP meetings. Both are available from the Beach Center; see appendix A for the Center's address.]

Source: Turnbull, A. P., Turbiville, V., Jones L. & Lee, I. (1992, Summer). A family-responsive approach to the development of the individualized family service plan. *OSERS News in Print,* pp. 12–15.

Collaborating with Parents in IFSP/IEP Conferences

Preparing in Advance

- Appoint a service coordinator to organize the conference.
- Make sure that the evaluation has included all relevant areas, is complete, and has clearly synthesized results.
- Reflect on what you know about the family's characteristics, interactions, functions, and life cycle. Individualize your planning according to the family systems consideration.
- Ask the family about its preferences regarding the conference.
- Discuss the conference with the student, and consider his or her preferences for participation.
- Decide who should attend the conference, and include the student if appropriate.
- Arrange a convenient time and location for the conference.
- Assist the family with logistical needs such as transportation and child care.
- Inform the family and students who are at least 14 years of age (in straightforward, jargon-free language) verbally and/or in writing about the following:
  - Purpose of the conference
  - Time and location of the conference
  - Names and roles of participants
  - Option to invite people with special expertise to attend the conference
- Give the family and student the information they want before the conference.
- Encourage and arrange for the student, family members, and their advocates to visit optional educational placements for the student before the conference.
- Encourage the student and family members to talk with each other about the conference.
- Encourage the family to share information and discuss concerns with all participants.
- Review the student's previous IFSP/IEP and ensure that school records document the extent to which each of the goals and objectives (or outcomes) have been accomplished.
- Identify the factors that have most contributed to the attainment of those results and the factors that have been the most significant barriers.
- Request an informal meeting with any teachers or related service providers who will not attend the conference. Document and report their perspectives at the conference.
- Consider whether providing snacks would be appropriate and possible. If so, make necessary arrangements.
- Prepare an agenda to cover the remaining components of the conference.

Connecting and Getting Started

- Greet the student, family, and their advocates.
- Share informal conversation in a comfortable and relaxed way.
- Serve snacks, if available.
- Share an experience about the student that was particularly positive or one that reflects the student's best work.
- Provide a list of all participants or use name tags if there are several people who have not met before.
- Introduce each participant, briefly describing his or her role in the conference.
- State the purpose of the conference. Review the agenda, and ask if additional issues need to be covered.
- Ask the participants how long they can stay, discuss the conference time frame, and offer to schedule a follow-up conference if necessary to complete the agenda.
- Ask if family members want you to clarify their legal rights. If so, do so.

Sharing Visions, Great Expectations, and Strengths

- If a MAPs process has been completed, share the results with everyone.
- If a MAPs process has not been completed, consider incorporating it into the conference.
- Encourage the student and family to share their visions and great expectations for the future, as well as the student's strengths. Then encourage all committee members to share their visions of the most desirable future for the student, based on the student's preferences, strengths, and needs.
- Affirm the excitement about the visions, great expectations, and strengths and about the commitment with the goals and objectives (or outcomes) that will be planned at the conference.

Reviewing Formal Evaluation and Current Levels of Performance

- Give family members a written copy of all evaluation results.

Collaborating with Parents in IFSP/IEP Conferences

- Avoid educational jargon as much as possible, and clarify any terms that seem to puzzle the family, student, or their advocates.

- If a separate evaluation conference has not been scheduled, discuss the evaluation procedures and tests and the results of each.

- Invite families and other conference participants to agree or disagree with the evaluation results and to state their reasons.

- Discuss the meaning and implications of the results in terms of the student's appropriate education, preferences, strengths, great expectations, and needs.

- Review the student's developmental progress and current levels of performance in each subject area or domain.

- Ask families if they agree or disagree with the stated progress and performance levels.

- Strive to resolve any disagreements among participants.

- Proceed with the IFSP/IEP only after all participants agree about the student's current levels of performance.

Sharing Resources, Priorities, and Concerns
- Identify the student's and family's visions, great expectations, strengths, preferences, and needs, as well as those of the professionals (those attending and absent).

- Ask participants to share their priorities, and reach consensus on the most important issues.

- Encourage all participants to express their concerns about their own roles in supporting the student, especially in areas where they believe they will need support or assistance.

- Plan how all participants can share expertise and resources to create the most comprehensive support system possible in addressing priorities and responding to concerns.

Developing Goals and Objectives (or Outcomes)
- Generate appropriate goals and objectives for all subject areas requiring specially designed instruction consistent with stated great expectations, strengths, and priorities, as well as for social relationships, nonacademic subjects, and extracurricular activities.

- Discuss goals and objectives for the student's future educational and career options.

- Identify goals and objectives to expand the positive contributions the student can make to family, friends, and community.

- Prioritize all goals and objectives in light of student and family visions, great expectations, needs, strengths, and preferences.

- Clarify who—student, family, professionals—is responsible for reaching the goals and objectives and ensuring their generalization or mastery.

- Determine evaluation criteria, procedures, and schedules for goals and objectives and how parents will be regularly informed.

- Explain that the IFSP/IEP is not a guarantee that the student will attain the goals and objectives but that it represents a good-faith effort among all participants to work toward the goals and objectives.

Determining Placement, Supplementary Aids/Services, and Related Services
- Discuss the benefits and drawbacks of less restrictive, more inclusive placement options. Consider the resources that all committee members can bring to bear,

Preparing in Advance

In far too many situations, families and educators do not adequately prepare for IFSP/IEP conferences. Indeed, the primary work for the conference usually starts once everyone sits down. This is much too late.

As you prepare for the conference, implement the suggestions we made in chapter 4 regarding a reliable alliance. From the outset, start communicating with families in ways consistent with what you have already learned in chapter 4 and chapter 9 about communication skills and strategies. By using a family systems perspective, you will contribute to meaningful IFSP/IEP preconference preparation.

For example, when you work with a family such as Greg Motley's, you will want to know that Greg wants to work outdoors, excels at baseball, has a mother who volunteers her time to provide care for elderly citizens of Cincinnati, has three older sisters (one of whom still lives at home), has a father who excels as a sales representa-

Collaborating with Parents in IFSP/IEP Conferences

especially supplementary aids/services and related services, in inclusive settings.

- Select a placement option that enables the student to receive appropriate individualized instruction and to develop a sense of belonging with peers with and without exceptionalities.

- Agree on a tentative placement until the student and family can visit and confirm its appropriateness.

- Specify the supplementary aids/services and related services that the student will receive to ensure the appropriateness of the educational placement.

- If the student is to be placed in a special education program, state why supplementary aids/services and related services are not capable of assisting the student within a general education setting.

- Explain the extent to which the child will not participate in the regular education program.

- Document and record the time line for providing the supplementary aids/services and related services that will enable the student to make the transition to the general education setting.

- Discuss the benefits and drawbacks of types, schedules, and modes of providing related services that the student needs.

- Specify the dates for initiating supplementary aids/services and related services, frequency, and the anticipated duration.

- Share the names and qualifications of all personnel who will provide instruction, supplementary aids/services, and related services.

Addressing Assessment Modifications and Special Factors

- Determine necessary modifications for the student to participate in state or district-wide assessments of student achievement.

- If the student is not able to participate in the state or district assessment, provide a rationale and specify how the student will be assessed.

- Consider the five special factors identified in IDEA (for example, positive behavioral support, limited English proficiency, use of Braille, language and communication modes for people who are deaf or hard of hearing, and assistive technology), and make plans as needed for the student.

- Identify any other modifications or special factors that apply to the student, and develop appropriate plans to address those.

Concluding the Conference

- Assign follow-up responsibility for any task requiring attention.

- Summarize orally and on paper the major decisions and follow-up responsibilities of all participants.

- Set a tentative date for reviewing IFSP/IEP implementation.

- Identify preferred options for ongoing communication among all participants.

- Reach a consensus decision with the parents of how they will be regularly informed of the student's progress toward the annual goals and the extent to which that progress is sufficient in achieving the goals by the end of the year.

- Express appreciation to all team members for their collaborative decision making.

- Affirm the value of a reliable alliance, and cite specific examples of how having an alliance enhanced the quality of decision making.

tive, and (perhaps most importantly to Greg's senior high school program), came to a high school of 1000 students (where the average class size is 35) from a small Lutheran school (where the average class size was 10 and where the staff was especially tolerant of a child's preferences and needs).

It is not clear exactly what role all these factors might play in Greg's education or what contributions they may make to his challenging behaviors (Greg is classified as "SBH"—having a severe behavioral handicap); but it is clear that they should be taken into account as possible explanations of his behavior and as possible clues to what will help him attain his goals.

Even before a conference, you can refer interested families to Parent to Parent and to Parent Training and Information Centers so they can obtain the emotional and informational support they may need to come to conferences in a more confident and empowered manner. For students who are initially evaluated for special education, how you and other educators carry out the referral and evaluation process will also significantly contribute to preconference preparation. The more you collaborate with families and respect their preferences in the referral and evaluation process, the more likely it is that a reliable alliance will be well under way before the IFSP/IEP meeting is even scheduled.

If you will pause to take stock of what you have already learned, everything that we have discussed in chapter 1 through chapter 11 can become part of your preconference preparation. But you should also consider four other issues: (1) designating a service coordinator, (2) inviting participants, (3) taking care of logistical considerations, and (4) attending to advance preparation.

Designating a Service Coordinator You have already learned about the important role of a service coordinator in supporting families throughout the prereferral, referral, and evaluation processes. A service coordinator can be just as useful during the IFSP/IEP process. The service coordinator's primary responsibility at this stage is to ensure that preconference preparation is adequately carried out and guided by students' and families' strengths, preferences, great expectations, and needs. The service coordinator can and should continue as the primary team facilitator throughout IFSP/IEP implementation. Some families may find that the service coordinator blocks their access to and communication with other professionals. That is not good practice. If anything, the coordinator should ensure access and communication.

A study of service coordinators across different agencies in developing IFSPs reveals that service coordinators from mental health programs were generally far more positive about the IFSP process as contrasted to service coordinators from health departments (Farel, Shackelford, & Hurth, 1997). Thus, the nature of the service coordinator's training and agency affiliation can strongly influence his or her role.

Inviting Participants To determine families' preferences, you should discuss their preferences with them in a conference or over the telephone or ask for advice from professionals who have worked successfully with a family in the past (such as teachers) or who have a positive current relationship (such as a social worker or a public health nurse). Find out families' preferences concerning the family members, friends, and professionals who should attend the conference, convenient times and places for scheduling, whether assistance with transportation or child care would be helpful, and the kinds of information they would like to have in advance. Give them a chance to have evaluation reports, a summary of the student's strengths and needs in each subject area, information on legal rights, descriptions of various placement options and related services, draft goals and objectives from the professionals' perspective, options of extracurricular activities, and information on transition services. Gather this information early enough so you can carry through on it in making the necessary arrangements.

Most IFSP/IEP conferences have been composed of three to five professionals and the mother (Able-Boone, 1993; Campbell, Strickland, & La Forme, 1992; Goldstein et al., 1980; Vacc et al., 1985). From a family systems perspective, take stock of which family members may want to participate—fathers, grandparents, brothers and sisters, cousins, live-in significant others, godparents, or other people within the family's culture who have family-like relationships. In addition to family members, friends of the student or family, people who are in strategic positions to foster community inclusion (such as soccer coaches, scout leaders, and religious education teachers), and people who can be mentors in supporting the student to explore preferences for hobbies or careers (such as musicians, business leaders, and mechanics) are all potential participants who can enhance the quality of a student's education (Turbiville, Turnbull, Garland, & Lee, 1996). Encourage families to identify not only people they have typically included in IFSP/IEP conferences but also any others who may have unique resources and expertise to offer their son or daughter.

Empowerment involves making choices, including students' making choices about their own participation in conferences. Under IDEA, all students may participate in IEP meetings "whenever appropriate"; and students who are 16 years of age and older must have their preferences and interests taken into account when developing transition services. The legal presumption is that the transition-age student will participate.

Greg's teacher, Stephen Kroeger, emphasizes how strongly he believes in student participation. In fact, he describes the student as the most important person participating in the meeting and will reschedule conferences in order to accommodate student schedules so that he or she can attend. As you will recall, Greg said that he was "scared" by his first IEP conference: too many people there. But he also was satisfied by it: "I needed help . . . they were specific about the things they wanted to help me with."

The majority of students in special education still are not participating in the development of their own IEPs (Van Reusen & Bos, 1994). Interviews with 74 students with disabilities revealed that only approximately one-third had attended their IEP meeting and only about 10 percent reported that they were prepared in advance for the meeting (Shellady, Hendrickson, Reisen, Sampson, & Vance, 1994).

Even students at the transition age are typically not attending their IEP meetings (Getzel & deFur, 1997). A study of transition-age students indicated that only one-third attended their transition planning IEP meetings. It is not surprising that students with more significant disabilities were less likely to attend; it was surprising, however, that students who had three or more years remaining in school were more likely to attend their conference than students who are in their last year at school.

Some students have described experiences that prevent them from wanting to participate again in the future:

> When I go to them meetings, I get really frustrated because it seems like if you do something wrong, you know, which everybody does, they exaggerate it. I mean you tell them the basic of what happened, but they, like, exaggerate it. Teachers are good at that. They should be salesmen. (Morningstar, Turnbull, & Turnbull, 1995)

There are many different approaches for involving students in educational planning and decision making (Snyder & Shapiro, 1997; Wehmeyer & Sands, 1998). One approach is an educational planning strategy referred to as I-PLAN (Van Reusen, 1998; Van Reusen & Bos, 1990; 1994; Van Reusen, Bos, Schumaker, & Deshler, 1987). The five steps of this planning process are illustrated in box 12–3. The I-PLAN steps involve working with students and parents in advance, teaching them how to complete one or more student inventories, and using those inventories as a basis for generating goals. Students make more contributions and generate more IEP goals with this training than without it (Van Reusen, Deshler, & Schumaker, 1989; Van Reusen & Bos, 1990). Furthermore, conferences have more positive communication, especially in affirming students' strengths (Van Reusen & Bos, 1994).

As we have pointed out before, it is critically important to recognize cultural values associated with special education practices, including practices such as student participation in IEP conferences. Some cultures value child and adolescent autonomy more than others. The Taiwanese mother of a high school student who is gifted described her frustration at the IEP conference when the professionals were more concerned with having her daughter express her preferences than with giving the mother an opportunity to express her own opinions:

> When my daughter, Jean, was in junior high school, the gifted education counselor, she never asked me and then she never gave me eye contact. During the meeting she only asked my daughter what she wanted to do in the next year, and she didn't ask me. After she asked my daughter, then she give me the papers and say, "Okay, sign your name." That was really frustrating.

A Hispanic mother concurred with this view when she added her comments:

> We felt the same, and I think that basically the cultural differences are not being considered in these IEP

TIPS   BOX 12–3

I-PLAN to Enhance Student Participation

- The first step is the *Inventory* step. This provides the student an opportunity to list his or her perceived strengths, areas that need improvement, goals and choices for learning. The information is listed on an Inventory sheet, which the student can take to a conference. The students use the remaining steps of the strategy for communicating during the conference.

- The second step, *Provide Your Inventory Information*, focuses on knowing how and when to provide information during a conference.

- The third step, *Listen and Respond*, includes procedures for effectively listening and knowing how and when to respond to statements and questions made by other individuals at the conference.

- The fourth step, *Ask Questions*, enables the student to know how and when to ask questions.

- The fifth and final step, *Name Your Goals*, requires the student to name the goals that were agreed upon before the end of the conference.

Source: Van Reusen, A. K. (1993). Learning disabled adolescents and motivation. In *Their World* (pp. 28–31). New York: National Center for Learning Disabilities (p. 697A). Reprinted with the permission of the National Center for Learning Disabilities, 381 Park Avenue South, New York, NY 10016.

meetings. And here in the United States it is like you always ask the child first, and for us it's very important for us as a parent to participate. And so the way that they handle those IEP meetings is like the American people, and they're not considering Chinese or Hispanic or any other culture. I know that it's not on their mind, but it really hurts our feelings. . . . We tell our children more what to do, what's wrong, what's right, and maybe we don't develop that independence . . . and maybe we start doing that after they turn 19 or 20. When we came to the United States five years ago, my children felt that difference in their education from school and home. They didn't understand very well what was going on; why we were one way at home (in asserting parental authority) and the teachers treated them in a different way (offering them more choices).

Clearly, you need to consider the cultural appropriateness of involving students in conferences (when it is appropriate to do so), then support students to develop participation skills using strategies such as the I-PLAN. Honoring cultural diversity, which includes determining the appropriateness of self-determination, is one of the eight objectives of establishing a reliable alliance.

Taking Care of Logistical Considerations A third task takes into account logistical considerations such as scheduling, committee size, transportation, and child care. We discussed these same logistical considerations in chapter 9 as they pertained to other school conferences, and the tips we suggested there also apply here.

The more you work with families on these issues from the outset, the more families will be able to participate meaningfully. Addressing the logistical barriers can foster creative school-community partnerships, as when employers provide time off from work for parents, or when community groups assist with transportation and child-care needs.

Let's consider the size of the IEP team. Some parents prefer a minimum number of people at the conference, and others want everyone who has a stake in the quality of the child's education to attend. Marion (1979) warned that "the single greatest deterrent to minority parent participation is that they might feel overwhelmed when they walk into a meeting and see all the school people are lined up against them" (p. 9). He suggests having in attendance only those people who are most familiar with the child. Other professionals should be on call to join the meeting upon request. The benefit of smaller conferences is that they can be less intimidating and more focused.

By contrast, a survey of 243 parents (whose ethnicity was not identified) in Colorado showed that the presence of large numbers of professionals at conferences did not make it difficult for parents to ask questions and did not prevent good discussions. Indeed, some parents view the large numbers as evidence of concern and interest (Witt, Miller, McIntyre, & Smith, 1984). The more people present, the greater the breadth of expertise and the chance of including all persons who have responsibility for implementing the IFSP/IEP.

Time is a major logistical issue. It requires systematic and creative problem solving. Many professionals feel harried by the time requirements needed to complete IFSP/IEP-related paperwork.

> I cannot ask my wife and children to put up with me, depressed and tense for months each spring because I must finish my testing, must begin testing with the new kids we've identified, must get the reports in on time, must complete reams of papers (the law says so, and tells me how much time I have to do it), and can't teach. When I am in class, I am tense and harried because the testing isn't getting done on time. I don't have any time to plan, to diagnose, to remediate, and I can't get on top. (Katzen, 1980, p. 582)

One research study underscores that compared to five other variables, allowing enough time for the conference was the most important variable associated with parent satisfaction (Witt et al., 1984). Clearly, the place to cut time corners is not during the conference itself. To address time barriers, some schools hire a permanent floating substitute to free teachers to attend to IFSP/IEP-related tasks, hire aides, or use volunteers to provide educators with additional release time. Others assign specific times each week for staff collaboration and set aside one day in each grading period as a collaboration day in which no other activities can be scheduled. Still others purchase laptop computers for all teachers to use in IEP development (Johnson, Proctor, & Corey, 1995; West, 1990).

Attending to Advance Preparation

Box 12–2 includes suggestions for work to complete in advance of IFSP/IEP meetings. Consider exchanging advance information, such as tentative or draft goals and objectives. Families frequently find it helpful to reflect in advance on information such as current levels of performance, goals, objectives, placement, supplementary aids/services, and related services so they can feel confident about agreeing or disagreeing with professionals' opinions and recommendations. Other families may find it empowering to draft their own version of an IFSP/IEP and then have professionals respond to it.

By exchanging information in advance, families and professionals can use the conference time to clarify issues and make decisions. Without advance information, they are likely to spend most of their time reviewing information and generating ideas and rushing to decisions. When families prefer to not receive advance written information, two meetings—one to review information, and one to make instrumental decisions—may be useful, taking into account both personal preference and time efficiency.

It is important not to predetermine the IFSP/IEP. Distinguish between preparation and predetermination. Parents report being dissatisfied when decisions are predetermined by educators (Salembier & Furney, 1997).

Advance planning also can eliminate or minimize cultural differences between families and professionals. A sometimes overlooked component of cultural difference is a family's religious beliefs, as one teacher noted:

> Sam's expression was wide-eyed when the psychologist who was to test him walked through the door. Sam was not going to perform well for this man, I could tell. I was teaching in a private Christian school, and Sam's parents were fundamentalist Christians. The psychologist was dressed, to put it kindly, casually and very differently from the dress code we had at our school. . . . A simple phone call to Sam's administrator, myself, or his parents to ask what might prove offensive to the family's religious beliefs would have established a better rapport with all concerned and provided Sam with an opportunity to perform to his capacity during assessment.

Connecting and Getting Started

The initial conference proceedings can set a "reliable alliance ambience" for the entire meeting, one of welcoming, valuing, trusting, respecting, listening to, and collaborating with families to enhance the student's appropriate education. Stephen Kroeger emphasizes how helpful it has been for him to use the chalkboard to write the IEP as a way to keep the process open-ended and flexible. The chalkboard directs the focus of the individual or participants from the group away from themselves and toward their common goal of constructing the IEP. He also believes it is important to introduce all people present and to describe the format that will be used and the time line that will be followed. In polling team members to verify that they can accommodate the time frame, it helps people to know what to expect and to have confidence in the overall "game plan." People genuinely working with other people, not just role-playing prescribed parts, is a key ingredient in both an appropriate education and in mutual empowerment. Many factors can help family members believe that professionals have a power-with/power-from-within orientation toward them rather than a power-over orientation.

An early consideration is to ensure that members of the IFSP/IEP team genuinely value the contributions of families and the opportunities to form partnerships. In a study of 145 special education teachers in six states, only slightly more than half of the teachers valued parents' participation. Seventy-one percent of them agreed to an option to waive parents' rights to attend and instead give decision-making authority to professionals. Moreover, 44 percent of the teachers regarded the IEP conference as little more than a formality. A parent commented about the differential power structure, saying: "One group has power and the other doesn't. I think the ultimate lack of power is to have a child who has special needs" (Ferguson, 1984, p. 44).

To equalize power and move from a professionally dominated process to a reliable alliance, try to create a warm and relaxed atmosphere in which all committee members use the positive communication skills that we discussed in chapter 4. In a study of parent participation in IEP/transition planning team meetings, parents identified the importance of communication in enhancing their participation (Salembier & Furney, 1997). Betsy Santelli, a parent of two daughters enrolled in a gifted program, described the importance of informal sharing:

> Although anxious at first about what our roles might be, Jim and I were delighted to find a real willingness and genuine interest on the part of the staffing team to learn from us about Maren and Tami's unique and special qualities as well as those of our family. Before any assessment results were shared or questions were asked, time was allowed for informal sharing among all of us as people—not professionals, not parents—just people. Those few minutes helped set the stage for the comfortable sharing of information that followed and continues to this day.

Researchers have assessed the impact of interpersonal communication by measuring the effect of school counselors serving as parent advocates (Goldstein & Turnbull, 1982). The counselors were asked to engage in five communication skills: (1) introduce parents, (2) clarify jargon, (3) ask questions, (4) reinforce parental contributions, and (5) summarize decisions at the end of the conference. Significantly more parent contributions occurred in conferences in which a counselor/parent advocate was present (using the five communication skills) than in the control group that lacked a parent advocate.

Regrettably, some parents believe that school personnel blame them for their child's disability. Indeed, parents' satisfaction with conferences depends to a large degree on professionals' behavior in attributing blame to sources other than the parents (Witt et al., 1984). As we stated in chapter 1, you need to be particularly sensitive to direct comments or innuendoes that families might interpret as blaming them for their child's special needs. In addition, you should affirm the positive contributions that parents make to their son or daughter. Empathetic reciprocity will be one of your best guides during the initial portion of the conference and throughout the whole conference. Ask yourself, "How would I want to be treated at this conference? How would I want others to support me? To what extent would I be feeling insecure or vulnerable? What could others do to minimize my vulnerability and maximize my empowerment?"

By taking this perspective, you can make substantial progress toward establishing a reliable alliance. If you invest time and energy in genuinely connecting with families, conveying to them your authentic interest in their son or daughter and in them and expressing your unconditional regard and respect for their opinions and suggestions, you will do more toward having a successful IFSP/IEP conference than anything else you could do. Remember, far too many professionals have erred on the side of formal compliance with legal mandates and have failed to build a reliable alliance (Gallagher & Desimone, 1995; Harry et al., 1995; Lovitt & Cushing, 1999). To build a reliable alliance, positive interpersonal communication practices are an indispensable obligation.

*S*haring Visions, Great Expectations, and Strengths

In chapter 9 you learned about the MAPs process as a technique for providing an open-ended, intimate, and personalized view of the student and family. If the family has already completed a MAPs process, the initial portion of the IFSP/IEP meeting is an appropriate time to review that information with the group. If the family has not had an opportunity to engage in a MAPs process, you might want to incorporate that into the initial conference proceedings, recognizing that you will not be able to complete that activity as well as the full IFSP/IEP all at one occasion. Educators often report that the MAPs process contributes positively to IFSP/IEP development. One teacher described the impact of MAPs on school personnel as follows:

> Since we're dealing with students with disabilities, you know, so often you've looked at that student with a list of they can't do this, this, this, this, and this. So it's enabled the whole group, including the school personnel, I think more than anybody, to be able to see that student in a different light, which has been extremely valuable. (Grigal, Quirk, & Manos, 1998)

From an administrative point of view, a principal commented on the benefits of MAPs also:

It's not learning just sterile facts. When you hear parents talk about their hopes and their dreams for their child, its just like any other parent talking about their hopes and dreams. When you listen to the fears, it's the same as any other parent talking about the fears they have. The difference is that you're talking about a child with a disability. And how are we going to help this child feel good about being in a situation in a school setting and make sure that the child is viewed as other children are. (Grigal, Quirk, & Manos, 1998)

If the family and professionals decide to forego the complete MAPs process, they still need to set aside time for sharing visions and great expectations and strengths. Stephen Kroeger firmly believes in the importance of this phase. He describes the process of envisioning as the "anchor element" and "heart and soul" of the IEP process. Figure 12–2 illustrates the documentation of gifts, capacities, and strengths, as well as challenges and learning needs that his IEP team believed are the basis of developing a vision for Greg's future. Stephen Kroeger calls this a "list in progress" because he gathers contributions from people who are not able to attend the conference and encourages all team members to continually add to the list. He shared the comment of one student who participated in this process:

> I have never in my life heard a group of adults sit around and say anything positive about me. That list is exactly right. (Kroeger, Leibold, & Ryan, 1999, p. 6)

Sharing visions, great expectations, and strengths can generate enthusiasm and motivation for the future. Typically, people become more excited and have higher levels of motivation when they are working for something that genuinely sparks their hopes and dreams. Within the empowerment framework, great expectations are a way to enhance the individuals' motivation.

Figure 12–3 includes a framework for families to start writing down their visions and great expectations for their child. These visions and great expectations should build on the child's strengths and preferences. Of course, students, educators, and other IFSP/IEP members can join in this process. As everyone's perspectives of visions, great expectations, and strengths become more concrete, the next step is to identify the goals or outcomes that will most likely transform the vision to a reality.

*R*eviewing Formal Evaluation and Current Levels of Performance

The IEP must include the student's current levels of performance. This information derives directly from the nondiscriminatory evaluation of the student and pro-

FIGURE 12–2

Developing a Vision

Gifts, Capacities, and Strengths	Challenges and Learning Needs

Gifts, Capacities, and Strengths

- Alert
- Asks questions
- Neat handwriting
- Reading comprehension above average
- Good visual memory
- Appropriate one-on-one behavior
- Easily redirected
- Seems happy
- Concrete self-expression
- Likes to sing and act
- Enjoys cooking
- Has a good sense of humor
- Has lots of energy
- Many friends

Challenges and Learning Needs

- Skips class frequently
- Reading below grade level
- Grades are poor due to behavior
- Concentration is a big problem
- Very distractible
- Does not take school seriously
- Impulsive behaviors
- Can be oppositional and defiant
- Can distort the picture
- Interrupts
- Physically and verbally aggressive
- Argues
- Does not take responsibility
- Feels isolated

FIGURE 12–3

My Vision for My Child as a Young Adult

1. Home Environment—I envision my child will
   a. live in:
   b. live with:
   c. be able to:
2. Work Environment—I envision my child will
   a. work in:
   b. be employed as:
   c. be able to (responsibilities):
3. Community Environment—I envision my child will participate in
   a. places:
   b. activities:
   c. social events:

4. I hope that my child will develop relationships/friendships with:

   _____

5. I would also like my child to:

   _____

6. I think that my child will probably need the following supports and/or environmental modifications:

   _____

   _____

Source: Parker, D., with Moore, C. (1991). *Achieving inclusion through the IEP process: A handbook for parents.* Hanover, MD: Maryland Coalition for Integrated Education.

vides the foundation for the student's IFSP/IEP and appropriate education. Two options are available. First, the IFSP/IEP conference can be used to review formal evaluation results and to develop the IFSP/IEP. Second, a separate meeting (before the IFSP/IEP conference) can be held for the sole purpose of reviewing the evaluation results. (We discussed both options in chapter 11.) The decision about when to report evaluation results should be based on family and professional preferences.

Sharing Resources, Priorities, and Concerns

The referral and evaluation process can be a time for families, teachers, related service providers, friends, and other interested people (such as physicians) to identify their respective resources, priorities, and concerns. As we pointed out in chapter 11, the process of identifying and agreeing to share resources, priorities, and concerns should start during the evaluation process and continue during the IFSP/IEP conference. The goal is to link the evaluation information to priority outcomes for student and families.

Thus, at the IFSP/IEP conference, after reviewing the evaluation and performance information, you should review each participant's resources, priorities, and concerns. Make sure that sufficient information is available to decide about goals, objectives, placement, supplementary aids/services, related services, assessment modifications, and "special considerations." Remember that the "special considerations" are positive behavioral interventions to address impeding behavior, language accommodations to address limited English proficiency, use of Braille, appropriate instruction in language and communication modes, and the use of assistive technology devices and services. (As we said in chapter 11, IFSP regulations specify that families should have the opportunity to share their resources, priorities, and concerns. We certainly endorse this option for families; but we also believe that collaboration best occurs when *all* participants share their resources, priorities, and concerns.)

Participants should begin by focusing on their resources—the special contributions that they can make in best supporting the student. Remember the definition of collaboration: the opportunity to pool diverse resources in the problem-solving process. Each team member (family members and professionals) brings different resources and strengths to the IFSP/IEP process. Only by sharing their own unique resources can they combine these resources to benefit the student and each other.

Next, team members should identify their priorities based on their visions, great expectations, and the student's current levels of performance. Discuss priorities at the outset, before identifying goals and objectives, to help ensure that goals and objectives reflect individual and collective priorities.

Finally, the team should discuss concerns or what worries them; the student's most significant needs; how the school can enhance the student's educational outcomes; and whether resources are available within the group or from other people within the family, school, or community to accomplish the agreed-upon outcomes. For example, a general educator who has concerns about individualizing the curriculum for a student with a learning disability can collaborate with a special education consulting teacher. Teachers who are fearful about having students who are supported by medical technology can receive instruction and support from parents, the school nurse, and other specialists on how to maintain the medical equipment and attend to the student's special needs (Clatterbuck & Turnbull, 1996).

By discussing resources and concerns, the team can match some people's concerns with other resources. Remember, collaboration means individual members are not left to address their concerns alone.

Developing Goals and Objectives (or Outcomes)

Goals and objectives are the substance of a student's educational program. All participants must address the central issue: What are the most important goals and objectives (or outcomes) for this student based on the student's as well as the family's current and future visions, great expectations, strengths, preferences, and needs? Identify the criteria that are most important to the family, student, and professional team members for determining appropriate goals and objectives. Some criteria for consideration include:

- Student and family visions, great expectations, strengths, preferences, and needs
- The likelihood that the goal and objective will promote access to the general curriculum and successful participation in inclusive settings
- Opportunities to participate in extracurricular activities
- Enhancement of friendships and social opportunities
- The connection to career and other post-secondary outcomes
- Age-appropriateness

We encourage the team to add to or modify these criteria based on professional and family recommendations. The team's members can rank draft goals and objectives, then discuss the rankings, and finally select priority goals and objectives. Consider nonacademic and extracurricular opportunities, and also consider other school activities (for example, field trips, dances, and so on), not just academic skills, as goals and objectives. Areas that are often overlooked in formulating goals and objectives include friendships and other social relationships (Fisher, Pumpian, & Sax, 1998; McConnell, McEvoy, & Odom, 1992; Michnowicz, McConnell, Peterson, & Odom, 1995) and participation in extracurricular activities (Lovitt & Cushing, 1999; Morningstar, Turnbull, & Turnbull, 1995). Additionally, nonacademic opportunities related to a student's leisure skills are important.

Tony is a 17-year-old student with autism. His major needs relate to independent living and career education. Considering his many deficits, it would be easy to identify more than enough goals and objectives for the year in these two areas alone. But Tony also has a special interest and talent in music. He believes that "music is magic." Music was identified as an important subject to include on Tony's IEP. One of the objectives was to teach Tony to play a guitar. As the year progressed the music program and the guitar, as contrasted to the independent living and career-education programs, provided the spark for Tony to turn off the alarm clock and get out of bed every morning.

If the team makes the goals and objectives specific, educators, families, and students will be more accountable to each other for student progress.

> Regarding IEPs, more often than not parents are presented with what is more or less a completed IEP at their planning placement team meeting. . . . The goals and objectives are generally very, very vague, nonspecific and often don't have an appropriate way to evaluate whether the child is making progress in his or her program. (Testimony by Laura Glomb, in National Council on Disability, 1995, p. 57)

We have been discussing IEP goals and objectives, but what about IFSP outcomes? Some people regard goals, objectives, and outcomes as relatively synonymous. The original intention of IFSP outcomes was to encourage writing these outcomes in the language of the family—in terms of what changes they want to see—rather than being stated in the format of a behavioral objective (McGonigel, Kaufmann, & Johnson, 1991). For example, this might be a "professionally stated" behavioral objective:

> The siblings will attend a siblings support group for at least 80% of the meetings in order to gain a developmentally appropriate understanding of Down syndrome.

But a "family-stated" outcome might be worded like this:

> We want some assistance in knowing how to help our other children understand why their little sister is slow, so they can answer the questions of their friends at school. (McGonigel, Kaufmann, & Johnson, 1991, p. 58)

Are outcomes typically stated in more family-friendly language? A recent study of IFSP practices in two states reveals that the majority of outcome statements are written in professional language (Boone, McBride, Swann, Moore, & Drew, 1998). The study also found that the majority of outcome statements were child-focused, even though the IFSP must state outcomes for both the child and family (if the family agrees to having outcomes stated). Furthermore, there was only a 50 percent match between the concerns and priorities stated, on the one hand, and the outcomes, on the other hand. Typically, the concern/priority statements that did not have matching outcomes were related to family concerns. Unlike the IEP, the IFSP must state outcomes for both the child and the family (if the family agrees to having outcomes stated), whereas IEP goals and objectives focus only on the student.

An early IFSP study noted that the majority of family outcomes were primarily written by staff and stated what a parent was responsible for doing—for example, "parent will attend scheduled classes" (Bailey, Winton, Rouse, & Turnbull, 1990). Remember, the purpose of family outcomes is not so that staff assigns duties to families but so the early intervention programs will provide supports and services to families and their infants and toddlers. Figure 12–4 includes a framework for thinking about outcomes: child outcomes that are primarily child- or family-related and family outcomes that are primarily child-related but that also address the family's general well-being (Beckman & Bristol, 1991).

To state and implement outcomes related to the family's general well-being, early intervention program planners will need to collaborate with other professionals and agencies. (In chapter 13, we discuss comprehensive school-linked services, which is one model for supporting diverse family priorities and needs.) There are differences between the outcomes that educators and related service providers are prepared to address and the ones that require special expertise or training from social workers, psychologists, and counselors to ensure that appropriate services are offered.

The more you create a reliable alliance with families, the more they will trust you, share their concerns, and brainstorm about the most appropriate child and family outcomes. As you establish this reliable alliance, we encourage you to remember to use the posture of cultural reciprocity (discussed in chapter 4) to address discrepancies in priority goals, objectives, and outcomes that professionals may perceive are appropriate, as contrasted to the ones that families perceive are appropriate. This process will enable you to enhance your understanding of these discrepancies and to find a common ground on which everyone can reach consensus. While being guided by the eight obligations for establishing reliable alliances, honor the family's cultural diversity, affirm his or her strengths, and build on his or her choices as you develop family outcomes.

FIGURE 12–4

Framework for Distinguishing Child and Family Outcomes

Component	Child Outcomes	Family Outcomes
Child-related	Child intervention related to physical, cognitive communication, social or emotional development, and adaptive skills	Family intervention to help family life be easier—respite care, assistive technology, sibling support
Family-related	Child intervention to help family life be easier—eating, sleeping, behavior	Family intervention focused on general family needs (which will likely have positive spin-off effects on child)—marital counseling, financial support, GED education

Source: Adapted from "Issues in Developing the IFSP: A Framework for Establishing Family Outcomes" by P. J. Beckman and M. M. Bristol, 1991, *Topics in Early Childhood Special Education,* 11, pp. 19–31. Copyright © 1991 by PRO-ED, Inc. Reprinted by permission.

Specifying Placement, Supplementary Aids/Services and Related Services

Few aspects of educational decision making are more important than placement, supplementary aids/services, and related services. This is because placement and related services that are set out in the student's IFSP/IEP must be made available, but those that are not stated need not be made available.

Specifying Placement Families who are unfamiliar with placement options have a right to a specific description of the various options available. Yet, based on observations of 34 conferences, a team of researchers concluded that the concept of least restrictive placement was neither explicitly stated nor used as a basis for making placement decisions in any of the conferences (Ysseldyke, Algozzine, & Mitchell, 1982). The authors observed: "In general, teams presented data, and then someone on the team recommended a placement. The efficacy of the placement was seldom discussed" (p. 311). Consistent with this finding, a parent advocate recently commented:

> I've been to 57 IEP meetings. Not once, not ever once, did the school offer regular class placement as a placement for a child. Beyond that, they never offered, never discussed, never considered what kinds of supports, modifications, options would be necessary for a child to succeed in a regular class environment. Children are placed within existing programs, they're placed categorically and/or into existing programs. (Testimony by Laura Glomb, in National Council on Disability, 1995, p. 59)

In addition, a survey of parents of children who are deaf and enrolled in residential schools revealed that about two-thirds of the parents had been given information about residential schools. However, almost half of those who had received information had not received information on any other educational option (Bernstein & Martin, 1992). Approximately one-third of the parents who were surveyed were not satisfied with the information that they had received about placement. Consistent with this research, some parents feel that they do not have real choices about less restrictive options:

> One parent was told from an administrator, "[Your son] can either go to his neighborhood school, where he will be teased and humiliated, or he can continue to go to the segregated school, where he will have the opportunity to be class president and captain of the basketball team." (Testimony by E. J. Jorgensen, in National Council on Disability, 1995, p. 84)

You have already learned about the Regular Education Initiative and the inclusion movement in chapter 2, and you have learned about parent perspectives on inclusion in chapter 8. Sadly, many parents receive an explicit or implicit message that their children will be a burden to their teachers and classmates (Barber & Brophy, 1993). One such parent, Carmen Ramirez, shares her experiences in box 12–4.

Carmen and Alfredo Ramirez did "go for it" by winning a major lawsuit that compelled their school district to include Danny in some general education programs. This lawsuit, *Daniel R.R. v. State Board of Education* (1989), is cited in chapter 15. Listen to what Charles Fields, Danny's general education language arts teacher,

Who Wants Danny

The discrimination I felt was rich to poor, but racist also. I wondered if it would ever end. First, because I was poor and brown and of Mexican descent, and then because I had a child with a disability. With Danny, I felt like I was being discriminated against all over again. One of the things that stands out in my mind is our not being allowed to belong; we were called "dirty Mexican greasers."

When Danny was in pre-kindergarten, we saw that the kids were separated. They had an early childhood classroom next to the pre-kindergarten classroom—the kids were the same age but one class was for kids with disabilities and the other one was for typical kids. I'd come home and I'd tell Alfredo, "You know, this isn't right. I mean the other kids—they get to eat in the cafeteria and go out on the playground, and Danny's class doesn't. I want that for Danny. When he turns 4, I want that for him."

So then we asked for Danny to be included, and they were very offended. The school people were very offended. How dare we ask that. You don't do that. I mean, "Don't you see we're giving you all the best here with these kids, and you got the best teacher and whatever. We're sorry, but we don't think it's best for him."

The special education teacher, when she found out that she was going to have a child with Down syndrome in her classroom, did not want him there, because her classroom was for "high-functioning kids." She told me, "I've never taught kids with Down syndrome and this is for kids that function very high, and I think your son is going to end up at that other school that's three miles from here. That's the one that takes the kids with severe challenges."

Well, it ended up being that Danny got in her class, but, not because we pushed it, but because of the IQ scoring. She didn't like it at all. So we had trouble with her, because she was always dragging her feet in educating him, because it was going to be all this work. I remember I would get so frustrated and I would tell Alfredo, "What is so wrong with even special education? They're supposed to be so prepared and so perfect and so wonderful, and they don't want Danny. Who's going to want him?" So for us, he was being rejected from both sides. What the hell, let's go for it!

Carmen Ramirez, 1994

---

says (five years after the lawsuit was concluded) about teaching him:

> The definitive nature of teaching is to be accepting of anybody who is willing to learn and if you have that person there, you are supposed to have the talents and creativity in order to produce some type of objective where that person can grow from it. . . . One of the things I try to stress is the process of learning, and I have to utilize my resources. I don't try to do it all myself. I work with other teachers, and we get together and we modify lesson plans. If I have a particular problem, I go to the person who's the expert on that problem. . . . Danny just belongs, because he wants to belong. . . . You know he's not combative; he's not a behavioral problem. He's hard not to like. . . . I can see ideas in his eyes. Danny has his dreams, I'm sure he does. You know, even though he can't express them right now, we need to get as many people involved as we can to make his dreams come true.

Carmen and Alfredo's description of their reaction to teachers who do not want Danny in their classes underscores how important it is for teachers to *welcome* students into general education placements, not just to ensure that special education supports and services are provided. Families yearn to hear that their children are wanted, and they are alienated from professionals who describe their children as being a burden to teachers and classmates. "The teacher that honestly believes that a child is an asset to the class and is a privilege to teach communicates much to that child, and sets an example for the rest of the class to value all people" (Testimony by Gayle Underdown, in National Council on Disability, 1995, p. 82).

Danny's teacher, Charles Fields, underscores an important point: He doesn't have all the answers himself, but his success depends on collaboration with others to help to make Danny's dreams come true. When discussing placement options, everyone should try to draw upon the resources that each participant can offer. Concentrate on mutual support to implement the IFSP/IEP. Remember that the goal is mutual empowerment for all.

As you learned in chapter 8, families vary in their support for inclusion (Erwin, Soodak, Winton, & Turnbull, 2000; Fisher, Pumpian, & Sax, 1998; York & Tundidor, 1995): "I have some serious concerns about the current movement to adopt inclusionary practices as a single, universal concept to meet the needs of deaf and hard of hearing" (Testimony by Timothy Jaech, in National Council on Disability, 1995, p. 92). Parents of deaf children often cite "the lack of language education in many integrated settings, isolation from peers because of communication barriers, and underdeveloped self-esteem due to a lack of role models" (National Council on Disability, 1995, p. 94). That is why IDEA now requires the IEP team to deal with the "special consideration" of deaf and hard-of-hearing children's access to professionals and peers who communicate in the same language as the student.

Educators have questioned the meaning of the least restrictive environment for students who are gifted, given their likelihood of benefiting from an accelerated or enriched curriculum (Gallagher, 1997; Gallagher & Gallagher, 1994). Almost 900 academically gifted students in elementary through secondary levels responded to a survey indicating that over half of them did not perceive their social studies and language arts classes to be challenging (Gallagher, Harradine, & Coleman, 1997). Furthermore, educators have pointed out that there are some distinct differences in the IEPs for students with learning disabilities, mental retardation, and emotional and behavioral disorders who are placed in resource rooms versus general education classrooms (Espin, Deno, & Albayrak-Kaymak, 1998). They concluded that teachers in resource rooms are more likely to individually tailor IEP goals and objectives to the students' level of performance.

The National Council on Disability recognizes the legitimacy of different perspectives on placement but underscores the need for systemic school reform in developing greater capacity for individualization in general education programs through high-quality support services:

> There will be situations where parents will want substantially separate placements, usually because school districts have not offered appropriate supports within the regular school environment. Other times, parents might require such placements based on the nature of their child's disability (e.g., deafness). At this point in history, such requests might be appropriate. However, this should not obstruct the overall process of rebuilding special education as a high-quality support service available in every public school building in America. The problem at present is not a lack of options to segregate students with disabilities from their peers; rather, it is a lack of options to include students with disabilities in the ongoing lives of their schools and communities. (National Council on Disability, 1995, p. 98)

Specifying Supplementary Aids and Services

IDEA's 1997 amendments give stronger emphasis to the preference of placing students in the general curriculum (defined as academic, extracurricular, and other school activities). One of the new requirements is to provide a statement of the supplementary aids and services that will be provided to students to enable them to attain their annual goals, to be involved in the general education curriculum, and to participate with other children, including those with and without disabilities. This new requirement demands much more specificity in terms of considering the supplementary aids and services—the nature of the specially designed instruction—that will be provided in the general curriculum. This requirement is consistent with parental concern about program modifications and teacher competency that are necessary in order for children with exceptionalities to be successful in inclusive placements (Erwin, Soodak, Winton, & Turnbull, in press; Fisher, Pumpian, & Sax, 1998).

A new process has been proposed for making these decisions. It encourages educators to consider what physical, instructional, social-behavioral, and collaborative dimensions may be necessary for individualization. Figure 12–5 outlines factors and sample questions related to each of these dimensions.

Only after the IFSP/IEP team has carefully considered these dimensions should the team put into the IFSP/IEP a statement about those services and identify the individuals responsible for providing the supplementary aids and services. For example, Greg Motley has difficulty with English and math; he has no such difficulty with science or social studies. So when he is in English class and having difficulty reading, he can ask for permission to leave class, go to the resource room, and do his reading there, often with the one-on-one help of his English teacher. Greg knows what he needs by way of accommodations, he has asked for them, they have been set out in his IEP, and they are implemented. The result: His failing grades have turned to passing grades. He's a learner, not a nonlearner.

One of the newest developments in the provision of supplementary aids and services is an emphasis on "universal design." This concept comes from the field of architecture; it focuses on access for individuals with disabilities to the "built" environment. Today, universal design in school means creating instructional materials and activities (or supplementary aids and services) to provide full and meaningful access to students with exceptional learning needs (CEC, 1999). Box 12–5 provides an example of some of the exciting developments in using technology to provide an increasing number of options for textbook instruction. Given the fast-paced development of

FIGURE 12–5

Sample Factors and Questions for the Physical, Instructional, Social-Behavioral, and Collaborative Dimensions of Specifying Supplementary Aids and Services

Factors	Sample Question(s)
Physical Dimension	
Mobility	Could the classroom be made more accessible to the student?
Room arrangement	Could a round table be available in the classroom for small-group work?
Seating	Does the student's desk need to be placed close to the blackboard and the teacher?
Instructional Dimension	
Lesson presentation	Does the student need visual aids, large print, or alternative media?
Skill acquisition	Could the student be provided process-of-reading guides, highlighted or tape-recorded?
Assignments and worksheets	Could the student be allowed extra time for completion of assignments, have alternative assignments, or be provided a calculator or word processor?
Test taking	Could the student have take-home or alternative (e.g., oral) tests? Could the student use a study guide during the test? Could tests be divided into parts and taken over a series of days?
Evaluation	Could the student be graded pass/fail or receive IEP progress grading? Could the resource teacher and regular teacher use shared grading? Could contracting be used? Could portfolio evaluation be used?
Learning structures	Could cooperative learning or reciprocal teaching be incorporated? Could the student be assigned a partner?
Organization	Does the student need an assignment notebook or home copies of texts?
Parallel activities	Could the student work on related activities such as illustrating?
Parallel curriculum	Could the student work on alternative, functional skills (e.g., coin recognition during the unit on metric conversion)?
Assistive technology	Could the student be provided computer-assisted instruction, communication switches, or software? Does the student require electronic aids or services?
Social-Behavioral Dimension	
Skill training	Could the student be involved in social skill instruction? Does the student need counseling?
Behavior management plan	Does the student need a behavioral management plan that describes a reinforcement system, supportive signals, and corrective options?
Self-management	Could the student use self-monitoring of target behaviors?
Peer support	Could peers be used to monitor and/or redirect behavior? Could peers be used to take notes, help prepare for exams, and so on?
Class-wide systems	Could the teacher implement an interdependent group contingency for the class? Could a "Circle of Friends" be initiated?
Collaborative Dimensions	
1:1 Aide	Does the student need a paraprofessional to assist him or her?
Co-teaching	Could the regular educator and special educator team-teach? Do teachers need additional time for planning and problem-solving?
Resource room assistance	Does the student need additional strategy or study skill instruction (e.g., memory strategies, test-taking skills)?
Teacher consultation	Could the teacher receive assistance from a curriculum consultant, strategist, or behavioral specialist?
Teacher training	Could a workshop or inservice on behavior management strategies or certain topics (e.g., autism, ADHD) be provided?

Source: Etscheidt, S. K., & Bartlett, L. (1999). The IDEA amendments: *A four-step approach for determining supplementary aids and services, Exceptional Children 65*(2), 163–174.

Universal Design to Increase Access to the General Curriculum

"Current textbook materials and teaching practices typically fail to effectively provide support that can be individualized for students who need help," explains Bart Pisha of Center for Applied Special Technology (CAST) . . . Pisha and his colleagues are using universal design principles to develop and research a software tool and instructional approach that will improve cognitive access for students with special needs to the general education curriculum.

A focus of the project is refining the CAST-developed ULTimate Reader (Universal Learning Technology, *http://www.cast.org*). This software uses an electronic version of the textbook or materials that the teacher is already using, and provides a rich variety of highly flexible reading supports such as adding spoken voice and visual highlighting to the electronic text. It is designed to support students as they learn about social studies from textbooks and the World Wide Web. This support is scaffolded—that is, it is gradually reduced as students develop more independence in the curriculum.

Pisha and his colleagues also are creating features for the ULTimate Reader that will support stu-

dents as they identify patterns in text, develop effective strategies, and learn to sustain motivation and effort. They are creating text layouts that are clearer and easier to understand. "We have tried to integrate into the software strategies that make the content patterns more evident, build in strategies for comprehension, and make the presentation of information less intimidating and more engaging," Pisha describes. Among the many accommodations are highlighting words, phrases, and paragraphs to help readers focus on text; controlling speed of presentation; changing size of text; offering advanced organizers; providing definitions; allowing text to be read out loud; and changing the gender of the voice . . .

Pisha and his colleagues are working with students and teachers at Wakefield High School in Massachusetts. Pisha chose a social studies text that was difficult for students with limited reading skills. With the blessing of the publisher, the text was digitized and loaded into the ULTimate Reader program. From there Pisha and his colleagues began studying how students interacted with the new features . . .

One of the resource room teachers who is providing customer input is Terry Fuller. "It really changes the way that students learn material," Fuller tells us. For example, the technology changes the traditional practice of having students answer questions at the end of the chapter. With the text in digital form, students can simply drag and drop whole paragraphs for use in their answers. Or, they can access definitions by hitting a key. Fuller says this raises issues about how teachers teach. "As teachers, this challenges us to have students go beyond tasks that can be mechanically handled by the computer and engage them in more higher level thinking activities."

Although it is too early in the development process to ascertain student outcome results, teachers and students alike give the universally designed approach high marks. For one, Fuller sees the effort as supporting Massachusetts State learning standards. For example, students who cannot read the book can gain the information, and students who cannot write legibly can communicate.

Source: ERIC/OSEP Special Project (1999). Universal design in action: Building in access right from the start. From *Research Connections in Special Education*, No. 5, Fall.

new technologies, increasingly families and educators will have enhanced options for providing creative, interesting, and individualized options for the delivery of supplementary aids and services.

Specifying Related Services In addition to the program and placement decisions, the IFSP/IEP addresses related services. IDEA defines related services as transportational and developmental, corrective, or other supportive services that are necessary for students with disabilities to benefit from special education. Related

services for students ages 3 through 21 are audiology, counseling services, early identification, medical diagnostic services, occupational therapy, parent counseling and training, physical therapy, psychological services, recreation, school health services, social work services, speech/language therapy, and transportation. In addition, the IFSP/IEP should specify any assistive technology services and devices that the child needs.

Additional related services for infants and toddlers include family training, counseling, and home visits; certain health services, limited medical services, vision ser-

FIGURE 12–6

Summary of Assessment Methods

Assessment Method	Explanation
Observations—Watching the student exhibit the behavior	Staged or natural Live or taped Continuous or in segments Observed by teachers or third party
Interview/surveys—Gathering information by interviews or surveys with people who know the student	Source can be the parent, caregiver, student, teacher, therapist, work-study coordinator If interviews, can be face-to-face or by phone Surveys are almost always by mail Can use standard checklists, rating scales, adaptive behavior checklist
Record reviews—Using a structured procedure to extract information	Cumulative file/IEPs Databases Student products Teacher/therapist anecdotal records Nonschool records (e.g., parents' files and medical records)
Tests—Putting a challenge in front of students and having them solve the problem	Adaptations of the state assessment Battery of published instruments Performance events Portfolios Closed- or open-ended Norm- or criterion-referenced Variety of options for communicating responses

Source: Ysseldyke, J., & Olsen, K. (1999). *Putting alternate assessments into practice: What to measure and possible sources of data,* Exceptional Children 65(2), 175–185.

vices, and nursing services; service coordination; and services related to special instruction. The special instruction skills include learning environments and activities designed to promote the child's skill acquisition; curriculum planning related to IFSP outcomes; provision of information, skills, and support to families; and working with children to enhance their development. If related service providers cannot attend IFSP/IEP meetings, the team should secure their written recommendations or generate recommendations but not finalize this portion of the IFSP/IEP until the absentees have an opportunity to respond.

Many parents and professionals are concerned about the unavailability of necessary related services. In a survey of parents of students who are ventilator-assisted, parents reported that they were most satisfied with the schools' success in the areas of academics, health care, and socialization but most dissatisfied with the provision of related services (Jones, Clatterbuck, Marquis, Turnbull, & Moberly, in press). Parents wanted more therapy than the schools were providing, and they had expectations different from the schools' concerning school responsibility for providing related services.

The IFSP/IEP must specify the nature of the services to be provided and the amount of time devoted to each. Team members may choose among a variety of service delivery models, including consultation to general education teachers, provision of therapy within general education classrooms, and pull-out services—that is, working with students in a one-to-one arrangement or in small groups (Fey, Windsor, & Warren, 1993; Rainforth & York-Barr, 1997). School systems also may develop cooperative agreements with private related service providers or other school districts.

If their child is entitled to related services, the parents have a right not to be charged for them (Rogers, 1994). When the IFSP/IEP committee agrees that a related service is necessary, the school is responsible for the full cost of the related service even if the school does not provide it and must obtain it from a private agency. In some instances, related services might be reimbursable by the family's insurance provider. Many insurance policies provide coverage for medically related services such as physical therapy, occupational therapy, and speech therapy. The parents' insurance may be used to pay for related services but only if the parents agree to have their insurance charged. The school district may not require parents to use their insurance to pay for related services. If, however, parents choose to obtain related services that are not part of the IFSP/IEP, they are responsible for paying for them and may use any available insurance or they may use any federal benefits to which they are entitled. For example, if they qualify for Medicaid (health-related services for parents who meet federal low-income standards and who have children who have qualified for Medicaid because of the extent of their disabilities), then the parents may seek reimbursement from the Medicaid agency. But they would do this only if the services are not provided for in their child's IEP. If they are provided for in the child's IEP, if the child has been declared eligible for Medicaid services, and if the services are reimbursable under the state's Medicaid plan, then the school district may seek to have the state Medicaid agency pay for the services. Under IDEA, the state educational and Medicaid agencies must enter into an agreement concerning when the Medicaid agency will pay; the state educational agency is the payor of last resort—the agency that ultimately must pay for the related services if the state Medicaid agency does not.

A student's educational needs should be the only basis for determining which services are needed and the amount of service. If you find yourself in conferences in which school personnel are trying to avoid their responsibility for related services, we encourage you to ask yourself, "What would I want school personnel to do if I were the student's parents?" The bottom line for you to remember is that the student's needs are the primary consideration, not the availability or cost of related services.

Specifying Assessment Modifications and Special Factors

For the first time, IDEA now specifies that the IEP must include a statement of how statewide or district-wide assessments of student achievement will be modified in or-der for the student to participate in those assessments. If the team determines that the student will not participate in the statement, the team must include in the IEP its rationale and alternative ways for assessing the child's progress. You will recall our discussion in chapter 2 of the school-reform movement and the emphasis on standards-based accountability. The purpose of including students with disabilities in assessments is to hold the school accountable for improving the results for students—results that have not been sufficiently favorable in the past (Erickson, 1998; McLaughlin, 1998).

A major problem with educational reform initiatives related to national and state assessments is that, typically, students with disabilities have been omitted from them (Vanderwood, McGrew, & Ysseldyke, 1998). The exclusion rate at the national level has been estimated to be 40 percent to 50 percent of school-age students with disabilities.

Teachers of students with severe disabilities have suggested how alternative assessments might be carried out (Ysseldyke & Olsen, 1999). They proposed that assessments should include observations, interviews or surveys, record reviews, and tests. Figure 12–6 summarizes these methods. For example, teachers suggested that students' academic or functional literacy skills could be assessed by interviewing or surveying people who are regularly involved with them, using checklists of student functional skills. They emphasize that assessment should be geared to meaningful community environments, measured across time, and provide an integration of skills rather than testing discrete and isolated skills.

At the beginning of this chapter we discussed IDEA's requirements, and we identified five special factors that must be addressed on IEPs. These factors include issues associated with positive behavioral support (Horner, 2000; Horner, Albin, Sprague, & Todd, 2000; Quinn, Gable, Rutherford, Nelson, & Howell, 1998), limited English proficiency (Banks & McGee-Banks, 1999), the use of Braille (Koenig & Holbrook, 1993), the use of appropriate language and communication modes for students who are deaf or hard of hearing (Boutté, 1997; Corrado, 1995; King, 1996; North, 1997), and the use of assistive technology devices and services (Beukelman & Mirenda, 1998; Gray, Quatrano, & Lieberman, 1998; Parette & Angelo, 1996). If any of these is a priority or concern for a student, the IEP team must consider these special factors and relate each one to the nine components of the IEP.

Summarizing and Concluding

The concluding portion of the conference should synthesize recommendations and develop an action plan for follow-up responsibility as specified in box 12–2. As the conference concludes, it is especially important for the participants to acknowledge and affirm the value of the family's and each other's contributions, express great expectations for ongoing collaboration in implementing the IEP or IFSP, and encourage the family to contact the other members with any follow-up questions or suggestions. The suggestions in box 12–2 will help the team reach closure and identify next steps. A goal is to end the conference with the recognition that the reliable alliance is stronger and that there is an enhanced appreciation for the likelihood of getting what is wanted and needed (empowerment) through collaboration.

Linking Our Themes

Creating a Reliable Alliance

By now you are becoming well prepared to infuse the eight obligations of a reliable alliance into each partner-

ship opportunity. As you collaborate with families to individualize for an appropriate education, we encourage you to do what you have learned to do on all previous opportunities for partnerships: to develop the values, knowledge, and skills to build a reliable alliance with families. Figure 12–7 summarizes tips for how you can do just that.

Strengthening Family Factors

In the four previous chapters on developing partnerships with families, you have learned a myriad of ways to enhance family empowerment. In the partnership opportunity on which we have focused in this chapter, individualizing for appropriate education, you will have numerous additional opportunities to contribute to family empowerment. To stimulate your thinking, study figure 12–8.

FIGURE 12–7

Creating a Reliable Alliance: Disempowering and Empowering Actions for Individualizing for Appropriate Education

Obligations	Issues	Disempowering Actions	Empowering Actions
Knowing yourself	You realize you do not have sufficient time to listen to families.	Ask only closed-ended questions that can be answered quickly.	Work with other school personnel to create innovative options for release time.
Knowing families			
Family characteristics	Parents have a low educational level and find the IFSP/IEP process confusing and intimidating.	Tell the parents that it really isn't important for them to attend the conference.	Contact the PTI, ask about available resources, and brainstorm options with the parents.
Family interactions	A grandparent and mother (who has a history of chronic drug abuse) attend the conference; the grandmother criticizes her daughter and preempts her contributions.	Assume that a mother with a history of drug abuse probably does not care about her child and is not capable of making worthwhile contributions.	Reflect on the mother's strengths and let her know the positive things that she is doing or can do. Affirm the grandmother's strengths and express your desire to work together as a team.
Family functions	The parents' major priority is facilitating friendships for their child with multiple disabilities. They are very worried and sad that their child has no friends.	Inform the parents that the IFSP/IEP focuses only on preacademic and academic skills.	Have all IFSP/IEP committee members share visions, goals, objectives, and strategies for increasing the child's social connections.

(continued)

FIGURE 12–7　CONTINUED

Creating a Reliable Alliance: Disempowering and Empowering Actions in Individualizing for Appropriate Education

Obligations	Issues	Disempowering Actions	Empowering Actions
Family life cycle	The parents of a toddler who is reaching her third birthday are worried about leaving a specialized early intervention program and entering the early childhood program at the neighborhood public school.	Inform the parents that they'll never have it so good again and suggest that they be realistic about inclusion.	Arrange to visit preschool classrooms with the parents and share impressions about the benefits and drawbacks of each in terms of the child's preferences, great expectations, strengths, and needs.
Honoring cultural diversity	You need to develop an IEP with parents who are deaf.	Hold the IEP meeting and have the student sign for his parents.	Ask the parents in advance whom they would prefer to have as an interpreter; make necessary arrangements.
Affirming and building on family strengths	You are developing an IFSP with parents whom you believe emotionally neglect their toddler.	Scold parents in the conference for being the cause of their child's low self-esteem.	Highlight one or more positive contributions that the parents make to their child; alert them to community resources (including Parent to Parent) that provide parenting support and information.
Promoting family choices	A family wants an adolescent with mental retardation to attend a community college; you and other team members do not think it is a feasible transition goal.	Ignore family members' preferences and talk with them only about vocational training.	Contact community colleges and find out about their admission policies and accommodations for persons with disabilities.
Envisioning great expectations	A gifted student says her goal is to get a scholarship to Harvard.	Discourage the student by emphasizing the excess expense that the scholarship is unlikely to cover.	Collaborate with the student and family to research scholarship options; locate a community mentor who graduated from Harvard to provide admissions advice.
Using interpersonal communication skills	You are working with parents who have had past negative professional interactions; they're angry.	Tell parents that you are not the one who committed past mistakes, and you do not appreciate their taking it out on you.	Listen emphatically to their experiences; invite suggestions on making the IEP conference as supportive as possible.
Warranting trust and respect	A family shares concerns during the IEP conference about his or her child's sexuality.	Confront the student and probe for more information.	Obtain sexuality information, curriculum guides, and community resources and review them with the family and student.

FIGURE 12–8

Strengthening Family Factors Through an Empowering Context: Individualizing for Appropriate Education

Motivation	What Team Members Can Do	Knowledge/Skills	What Team Members Can Do
Self-efficacy	Point out to participants their contributions in IFSP/IEP conferences that are especially helpful to other team members.	Information	Brainstorm about services after high school and encourage participants to visit future options before making career-education decisions.
Perceived control	Listen to each participant's preferences regarding goals, objectives, placement, supplementary aids/services, and related services and ensure that his or her priorities are incorporated into the IFSP/IEP.	Problem-solving	Brainstorm about helpful supplementary aids and services in inclusive settings.
Great expectations	Incorporate great expectations into the IFSP/IEP discussion and ensure that goals and objectives are providing the foundation for accomplishing great expectations.	Life management skills	Encourage participants to network with others who have had empowering IFSP/IEP meetings and to get their suggestions.
Energy	Ensure that IFSP/IEP meetings are energizing rather than draining by having comfortable communication, highlighting progress, serving snacks, and respecting participants' time frames.	Communication skills	Encourage the facilitator to summarize the most important next steps that should be taken based on the participants' consensus.
Persistence	If any participant is dissatisfied with the recommended plan for related services, do not finalize the IFSP/IEP until exploring satisfactory options.		

Summary

It is by no means easy to individualize for a student's appropriate education, but it also is not terribly difficult. First, there is the team's commitment to the student, to the concept of teaming and collaboration, and to bringing the eight opportunities for a reliable alliance to bear on the opportunity to develop a partnership through individualizing. Within this commitment, there is a strong affective element. We call it "getting to know families" and letting families get to know you. That's part and parcel of collaboration for empowerment.

Second, there is the team's adherence to process following the logical steps of preparing; connecting and getting started; sharing visions, great expectations, and strengths; reviewing the nondiscriminatory evaluation and using it as a springboard to delivering services; sharing resources, priorities, and concerns; developing goals and objectives; specifying placement, supplementary aids/services, and related services; and addressing assessment modifications and special factors; summarizing and concluding.

Is it possible to create a reliable alliance while individualizing for an appropriate education? Yes, of course it is, as we have suggested. Is it possible to strengthen a family, to make it more empowerful, while following the process? Yes, and we have shown how you can do just that. Predictably, individualizing for the student also involves individualizing for the team members.

In the Forest Hills suburb of Cincinnati, Ohio, there exists a remarkable team of reliable allies. The team's "founder" was Stephen Kroeger—the teacher with colored chalk, a firm commitment to vision, an eye for Greg Motley's strengths and gifts, and an open-ended and flexible approach to writing and implementing an IEP. The "charter members" are Greg and Sherry Motley—the student and parent who recognized that they needed help, who participated as full partners in identifying the challenges that Greg faced, and who are delighted with the results. The "new members" are all those at Turpin High School who are part of Greg's education—special educators, general educators, psychologists, administrators, and case managers.

Together, they form a reliable alliance—a team that uses a collaborative process to reach mutually owned results. In the jargon of the world of business, they plan the work and work the plan. But they don't do so mechanically; there is, in Stephen Kroeger's words, something "lively" going on—a discussion that had a single and wonderful result: "Everyone was on the same page. . . . We were standing on the solid ground that this IEP had meaning, and that each member had brought her or his insights into it" (Kroeger, Liebold, & Ryan, p. 8).

Chapter Thirteen

Extending Learning into Home and Community

Ask Jim Antos, the principal of Central Middle School in Kansas City, Kansas, what one wish he would make for the students in his school, no matter how far-fetched the wish might seem. He answers, without hesitation: "For each student to have one responsible adult in their life on a daily basis." Then he laughs, a bit skeptically, and says, "Of course, you didn't place any limits on my wish. You didn't say to wish what might actually come to be."

So, ask him a second question: Within the realm of the possible, what one wish would you make for your students. And he answers, also without hesitation: "To have an array of social workers and psychologists for first period every day for all of my students, so the kids can get over the effects of their life outside of school and then be ready to learn."

He explains that most of his children face extraordinary challenges outside of Central: homelessness and other aspects of poverty; abuse and neglect; and exposure to the drug trade and gangs, alcoholism, and prostitution at home. The list goes on and on. And then your conversation with him ends abruptly; he walks over to a boy (later identified as being one who faces many challenges), wraps his arms around the boy's shoulders, and asks, "How are you today, Mike?"

Now shift your focus to Dustin Neil, age 14. Dustin is a student at Central and a special attention-getter for Jim Antos and his staff. Dustin is a tall (5'7"), lithe (a mere 116 lbs.), clean-shaven, clean-cut, tee-shirted active kid. In the pocket of his baggy blue jeans he carries a paper-

back. He engages your eyes when he shakes hands, says "yes, sir" and "no, sir," uses a complex and complimentary vocabulary ("Your handwriting is exquisite, sir"), is inquisitive ("What's the meaning of that word you just used?"), jovial ("I'd better not mess with Candi: she cuts my hair and has the shears"), and intelligent (he knows how to avoid written work by acting out just a little bit).

To meet Dustin, you go to his family's home. There you also meet his mother and father, Karen and Juan Gonzalez; his 15-year-old brother, Jeremy, a high school special education student; his 16-year-old sister, Candi, who has dropped out of school; and her daughter, Cierra, age 2.

Now, ask Karen and Juan Gonzalez what they want for themselves and their children. Karen answers, tearfully: "To have a better life than I've had." Juan nods his head in silent agreement. She fills in the details: complete high school (she didn't), get and hold a job (she can't), avoid substance abuse (she didn't), overcome depression (hers is chronic), and plan your life and work your plan (she has problems following through on her plans). And though she does not say it, she conveys it: "Live with dignity. Be able to respect yourself."

That's not easy to do, given the poverty that affects every aspect of the family's life. Take their home, for example. Within a few months of each other, one part of the roof caved in under heavy rains; the water heater rusted away; a furnace went out of commission; the utility company threatened a cutoff because the landlord (Karen's father) has not paid the bill on that and other slum-houses

he owns; window frames lacked glass panes; wood floors creaked when even a lightweight adult walked on them; and two parents, three children, one grandchild, and two other relatives crowded into a three-room, one-bath, wood-frame, single-story house.

To have a better life than Karen has had could be a dim prospect for Dustin, Jeremy, and Candi. Dustin has a long history of school disciplinary problems and is being evaluated for placement into special education. Jeremy is already placed into special education as having an emotional disability. After giving birth to her baby, Candi dropped out of school at age 14. Karen and her three children receive treatment from a local mental health center and are on medication for various illnesses. And Juan is seasonally employed in the lawn-and-garden business, Karen cannot work, and Candi quit her work because the pressure of work, being a mother, and trying to get her GED was too great.

Yet this family still hopes; Karen still wishes for that "better-than-mine life." The prospect could be dim, but it isn't. The reason is simple: Central Middle School and Karen's family are connected—very, very tightly.

Connecting them, indeed, connecting Mr. Antos' aspirations, Karen's aspirations, and the family's needs and strengths, is a team of passionately committed individuals representing the key stakeholders (Karen, Dustin, their family members, and the Central staff) and specialists (the University of Kansas team members), offering different but complementary perspectives and talents.

At one level, the team's principal focus is on Dustin, but on another its focus is on Central Middle School and on Karen and her family as a whole.

Not only does the connection exist at different levels, but it also exists through at least four different but complementary strategies. Each extends into the home what Dustin learns at Central. The challenge and the key to that "better-than-mine life" is to extend what Dustin learns at school to his home. Dustin's education—the academic part of it and the behavior-changing part of it—and his future cannot be separated from the environment where he spends the greatest amount of his time.

What difference can it make that Central, Dustin, and Karen and their family are linked to each other? One might say, without stretching the point, that it is a step—nothing more, but nothing less, either—in helping Jim Antos' dream come true and in helping Karen's come true, too. He wanted each child to have at least one committed adult. Dustin now has several of those

Karen Gonzalez with her son, Dustin Neil. (1999)

adults: Karen, with her renewed commitment buoyed by the team; the administrators and teachers at Central; and the members of the KU research and technical assistance team.

He wanted every child to have the chance to debrief and switch gears—to put behind them, if only for a while, what happens outside of school so they can benefit from what can happen inside of school; and Karen wanted to get her life together by earning her GED and becoming an interpreter for the deaf so that, in the long run, her children would have a better life than hers. Now both of them find some help—some, but not enough— in Dustin's team of educators, family members, and researchers. They are the debriefing team. More than that, they have *become a support system for Karen and through her for the whole family.*

Extending Dustin's learning to home and community means connecting his school and his home—in his case, through the team. Mr. Antos knows that to do that means that he and his faculty have to look at Dustin, but they also have to look beyond him. They have to reach from the polished corridors of Central to the paint-peeled rooms where Karen, Dustin, and their family seek that "better-than-mine life." It's a daunting but doable challenge. Curiously, to know the challenge exists and to take action to meet it is exactly what gives Mr. Antos, his colleagues, Karen, Dustin, and their family that which Karen seeks: a life—indeed, many lives—characterized by dignity.

The partnership of extending students' learning into their homes and communities involves building links among the many activities and environments in which students participate. Figure 13–1 reminds you how the partnership focus of this chapter—extending learning into home and community—relates to the overall empowerment process.

Given the special challenges of giftedness or disability, students need learning opportunities that cut across their school, home, and community experiences. Their progress in achieving educational outcomes should not depend wholly on their six-hour school day. This is particularly true for students with cognitive or behavioral challenges; they often have difficulty generalizing what they learn at school to home and community settings. (In chapter 7, we emphasize the importance of collaborating with recreational and leisure-time service providers, and in chapter 8 we emphasize providing students with opportunities for a variety of job experiences. Both topics relate to extending learning beyond school.)

Four opportunities to extend learning involve (1) incorporating person-centered planning, (2) fostering homework collaboration, (3) implementing positive behavioral supports, and (4) integrating services.

Incorporating Person-Centered Planning

Person-centered planning has primarily developed within the field of developmental disabilities as a method for enhancing quality of life of individuals with disabilities and their families. Additionally, there has been increasing recognition that formal systems, including schools and vocational rehabilitation agencies, are, by and of themselves, not fully able to enhance a quality lifestyle that is consistent with the preferences of the individual with the disability and of the person's family (O'Brien & O'Brien, 1996, 1998; Mount, 1995; Risley, 1996; Turnbull & Turnbull, 1996).

Person-centered planning is a process that was created to *listen* to the great expectations of individuals with disabilities and their families and to *tailor* lifestyle support to *actualize* those great expectations. There are a number of planning strategies that have been developed that go by different names, but they share a common philosophical base. These planning strategies include Community Building (O'Brien & O'Brien, 1996), Personal Futures Planning (Mount, 1995), MAPs (Falvey, Forest, Pearpoint, & Rosenberg, 1997; Forest & Lusthaus, 1990), Essential Lifestyle Planning (Smull & Harrison, 1992), PATH (Falvey, Forest, Pearpoint, & Rosenberg, 1994), Choosing Options and Accommodations for Children (Giangreco, Cloninger, & Iverson, 1993), and Group Action Planning (Turnbull & Turnbull, 1996; Turnbull, Turbiville, Schaffer, & Schaffer, 1996; Turnbull, Turnbull, & Blue-Banning, 1994).

Regardless of the particular person-centered process, five general outcomes are associated with person-centered planning approaches (Kincaid, 1996, pp. 440–441):

- Being present and participating in community life
- Gaining and maintaining satisfying relationships
- Expressing preferences and making choices in everyday life

FIGURE 13–1

Empowerment Framework: Collaborating for Empowerment in Extending Learning into Home and Community

Education Context Resources

Professional Resources

Knowledge/Skills	Motivation
Information: Being knowledgeable	Self-efficacy: Believing in our capabilities
Problem solving: Knowing how to bust the barriers	Perceived control: Believing we can apply our capabilities to affect what happens to us
Life management skills: Knowing how to handle what happens to us	Great expectations: Believing we will get what we want and need
Communication skills: Being on the sending and receiving ends of expressed needs and wants	Energy: Lighting the fire and keeping it burning
	Persistence: Putting forth a sustained effort

Education Context Resources

Obligations for Reliable Alliances — Reliable Alliances Consist of . . .	Opportunities for Partnerships — Opportunities Arise At . . .
Knowing yourself	Communicating among reliable allies
Knowing families	Meetings families' basic needs
Honoring cultural diversity	Evaluating for special education
Affirming family strengths	Individualizing for appropriate education and placement
Promoting family choices	Extending learning in home and community
Envisioning great expectations	Attending and volunteering at school
Communicating positively	Advocating for systems improvement
Warranting trust and respect	

Family Resources

Knowledge/Skills	Motivation
Information: Being knowledgeable	Self-efficacy: Believing in our capabilities
Problem solving: Knowing how to bust the barriers	Perceived control: Believing we can apply our capabilities to affect what happens to us
Life management skills: Knowing how to handle what happens to us	Great expectations: Believing we will get what we want and need
Communication skills: Being on the sending and receiving ends of expressed needs and wants	Energy: Lighting the fire and keeping it burning
	Persistence: Putting forth a sustained effort

Collaborating for Empowerment

- Having opportunities to fulfill respective roles and to live with dignity
- Continuing to develop personal competencies

The particular form of person-centered planning with which we have had the most experience is Group Action Planning—a form of person-centered planning that involves creating great expectations for the future, establishing an interdependent group of committed people, and engaging in creative problem solving in order to accomplish great expectations (Turnbull & Turnbull, 1996; Turnbull, Turbiville, Schaffer, & Schaffer, 1996; Turnbull, Turnbull, & Blue-Banning, 1994). You have already learned about the Making Action Plans (MAPs) process in chapter 9. Group Action Planning extends MAPs by giving special attention to *implementing the vision* that is created in MAPs gatherings. Although both Group Action Planning and IFSP/IEP approaches focus on long-term goals and short-term objectives, they are radically different, as figure 13–2 illustrates.

Significant lifestyle changes are typically necessary before great expectations can be achieved. Within a life cycle perspective (as you learned in chapter 8), these changes are particularly necessary at transition times, when children, youth, young adults, and their families are moving from one service system to another (such as early intervention to preschool or high school to employment) or from one school to another (such as middle school to high school). Although all transitions are times of special challenge, the transition from high school to adulthood can be particularly problematic because so many new supports and services need to be put into place. That's when Group Action Planning may be especially useful. In box 13–1, Martha Blue-Banning, the mother of Ryan, describes the experiences and outcomes of Ryan's Action Group. Ryan was a pioneer for other students with disabilities in seeking inclusive educational experiences at his junior and senior high schools.

Action Groups consist of family members, professionals, and friends who are especially committed to the individual and can be strategically helpful. Typically, Action Groups might start with 4 to 6 people, but it is not unusual for 12 to 15 people to be involved within 12 to 24 months after an Action Group begins. Because Action

---

FIGURE 13–2

Comparison of Traditional IFSP/IEP Conferences and Person-Centered Planning Approaches

IFSP/IEP Conferences—Traditional Planning	Group Action Planning—Person-Centered Planning
Professionally directed, unequal ratio of professionals to family members and friends	Approximately equal proportion of participants from the groups of friends, community citizens, family members, and professionals
Individual with a disability is typically absent	Individual with a disability is typically present
Structured, formal process	Reflective, creative process that focuses on divergent problem solving
Regulated by mandated paperwork for monitoring compliance	Not mandated or regulated; facilitated by an individual skilled in collaborative communication
Held in professional setting (e.g., conference room)	Held in an informal setting, most often the home of family or friends
Serious atmosphere in which the focus of attention is on the student's developmental needs	Relational, fun, affirming atmosphere in which the strengths, capabilities, contributions, and dreams are the focus of attention
Meets once or twice a year	Meets regularly (usually monthly) to accomplish next steps
Developmental assessment and outcomes guide the process	Visions and relationships guide the process
Professionals and agencies are primarily responsible for implementing programs to accomplish developmental outcomes	Group members form a reliable alliance with every member, assuming responsibility for transforming visions to reality

Source: Turnbull, A. P., H. R., & Blue-Banning, M. J. (1994). Enhancing inclusion of infants and toddlers with disabilities and their families: A theoretical and programmatic analysis. *Infants and Young Children,* 7(2), 1–14. Copyright © 1994 Aspen Publishers, Inc.

Ryan's Mother, Martha, on Group Action Planning

During the first 15 years of Ryan's life, Bob and I learned to actively advocate for Ryan's right to "a life." Our hopes and visions for Ryan have always been that he would live in his own home with supports, have a job, and one day get married if that is what he wanted. We truly believed that having opportunities with his same-age peers in general education classes and extracurricular activities was the type of education that would lead to the achievement of our visions for Ryan. Our efforts at advocating for him to have inclusive education and a true sense of belonging at his schools were met with much resistance from the educational system. Frequently, it seemed that educational personnel saw us as the "opponent" rather than true partners in Ryan's education. Bob and I both had a profound sense of isolation.

This all changed seven years ago when we began an action group for Ryan. Our action group started as a result of our realization that Ryan's life was filled with family, professionals, and peer "helpers" but was bereft of friends. I was taking with a friend about our concerns, and she suggested that we use a planning process called Group Action Planning to increase Ryan's social network. We invited people to the first meeting who were really committed to Ryan's future. I vividly remember two things from that meeting. First, I remember thinking that we had accomplished more in one meeting toward increasing Ryan's social network than in ten years of meeting with school staff alone. Second, I experienced an incredible sense of relief that we weren't alone in our efforts to achieve our visions for Ryan's future. This immediate feeling of success was really motivating.

The connections that were started at that meeting seven years ago are now stronger than ever. Many of our current action group members have been with us since the beginning. They have truly become our reliable allies, our cherished friends, members of our extended family. We have met each month to help create a lifestyle for Ryan that is consistent with his preferences and visions for the future. Ryan now has a job that he enjoys and where he is proud to be a good employee. He has co-workers who provide the natural supports he needs to be successful. Ryan recently moved into his own home and lives with three housemates who do not have disabilities. Ryan's visions have become a reality because we've had a committed group of friends who shared the vision with us, who planned with Ryan rather than for him, and who supported Ryan, the person, rather than Ryan, the disability.

The focus of our action group has broadened over the years from increasing Ryan's social network to his full inclusion at the high school to living successfully in his own home. We've had our ups and downs over the years, but when the down times came, we always had our reliable allies to problem solve with us. Problems become more a challenge than a threat.

Ryan has now aged out of the public school system. Our focus changed as we faced Ryan's transition from high school to adulthood. Ryan has had a right to a free appropriate education. This right to supports and services has changed because after high school there are no mandated services for young adults with disabilities. We are now faced with the next fifty years of Ryan's life in a community where many adult service agencies believe that sheltered workshops and congregate living comprise an acceptable way of life. If it were not for the members of our action group, we would feel more frightened and alone than ever before. They make all the difference in the world to us. We know that we aren't making this journey alone. I recognize that we have only taken first steps in a long journey that will involve a lot of risk and faith. It is frightening to let go of Ryan to live in his own home in a community where many others do not share our great expectations for individuals with disabilities. But, risks are a part of life, and being an active participant is what it's all about. And with our reliable allies I have no doubt that the journey will be a successful one.

Martha Blue-Banning
Lawrence, KS
Summer, 1997

Source: Adapted from Turnbull, A., Turnbull, R., Shank, M., Leal, D. (1997). *Exceptional lives: Special education in today's schools* (2nd ed.); p. 347. Upper Saddle River, NJ: Merrill/Prentice Hall.

ngs tend to be especially enjoyable and are
y a strong sense of social connectedness
mpowerment, people who get involved
h their commitment over a long period of
rovides tips for the each of the five com-
Group Action Planning process.

A growing body of research highlights some of the
key process considerations in successfully implementing
person-centered planning (Blue-Banning, Turnbull, &
Pereira, in press; Hagner, Helm, & Butterworth, 1996;
Malette et al., 1992; Timmons & Whitney-Thomas,
1998; Whitney-Thomas & Timmons, 1998). One recent
study investigated perspectives of nine participants who
had been involved in five different person-centered plan-

ning groups (Everson & Zhang, 2000). After conducting
in-depth interviews, the researchers reported that all participants expressed positive changes in the lives of the focus persons and satisfaction with the person-centered
process. Groups consisted of an average number of 4
participants with a range between 3 and 11. The future
visions of the groups primarily centered around seeking
(1) inclusive educational programs and (2) opportunities
for more friendships and social activities. The difficulty
of communicating with the person with a disability or of
accommodating to his or her limited social skills were
barriers for the group. One of the group participants
commented: "It's very difficult to get him [individual
with a disability] to say what he really wants. A lot of

Tips

BOX 13–2

Implementing the Five Components of the Group Action Planning Process

1. **Invite Support.**
   - Before you ask anyone to join the group, determine where to meet. Someone's home could be ideal because you want a casual setting so people will be at ease. Or use a restaurant, community building, or other accessible, comfortable place. Find a convenient day and time. Then invite people.
   - Explain to potential members what Group Action Planning is, why they would be a welcome addition, and that they do not have to make a definite commitment to the group before coming to a meeting. You only want them to experience the Group Action Planning meeting.
   - Before you have an actual meeting, choose a facilitator—someone who can listen well, connect well with people, make others feel valued, set a comfortable discussion pace, maintain a positive tone, keep comments relevant, identify key points, summarize discussions, and assign tasks (if needed).

2. **Create Connections.**
   - Leave ample time before and after the meeting for members to visit.
   - Offer food.
   - Be alert to each other's special days and recognize those days (such as birthdays or other anniversaries).

3. **Share Great Expectations.**
   - Think big. Everyone needs to have a dream for his or her future.

   - Think of the ideal job, home, friends, recreation, etc.
   - Think "what if" and "why not." Push the limits of possibility.

4. **Solve Problems.**
   - Treat problems as questions.
   - Brainstorm to solve problems—that is, to answer questions.
   - Address one specific problem at a time.
   - Seek quantity, not quality, of ideas.
   - Encourage everyone to speak up. Expand on each other's ideas.
   - Discourage negative and critical remarks.
   - Decide on the best ideas; discard the impracticable or nearly impossible ones.
   - Discuss each idea's possibilities and problems; then pick the strongest.
   - Develop an action plan specifying next steps, persons responsible, and time lines.

5. **Celebrate Success.**
   - Get together once in a while for pure enjoyment. Consider watching a sporting event, having a backyard cookout, or doing whatever you can do to have fun and feel positive about the group's successes.
   - Have food and drink and let members know how much their support is appreciated.

times he goes along with what the group says; and then when we try to implement it, he doesn't want to go, and he doesn't want to participate . . ." Everson & Zhang, 2000

Even though we have pointed out how Group Action Planning is different from the IFSP/IEP process (figure 13–2), you may be wondering if these two types of planning processes can be merged. In a sense, Group Action Planning is the same as an *ideal* IFSP/IEP conference process. Once Group Action Planning gets underway, the resulting reliable alliance can be carried over into IFSP/IEP planning. Although some merger can occur, we recommend Group Action Planning as a process to be carried on primarily outside of school (even though educators participate) because it differs from the school-based, curriculum/placement-focused process that is typical of schools.

Most of the writing about person-centered planning has focused on Euro-American families. Does this mean that Group Action Planning is culturally unresponsive to the preferences of families and individuals with disabilities from culturally and linguistically diverse backgrounds? Not necessarily. One research study involved presenting a workshop on Group Action Planning to Hispanic parents and then involving them in focus groups to get their perspectives on their perceived advantages and disadvantages of implementing Group Action Planning (Blue-Banning, Turnbull, & Pereira, in press). Thirty-eight Hispanic parents of youths and young adults with developmental disabilities participated and identified far more advantages than disadvantages. They particularly emphasized the benefits of teamwork and flexibility. As one mother stated:

> That [sharing the responsibility] would be so relaxing . . . because I have so much tension . . . it's almost like everything is on me, everything, and if I let somebody else in the family and the community in it, I can relax a little, sit back and say, 'Wow, it's not all on me now and everybody is helping me.' Everson & Zhang, 2000

They also identified some disadvantages, especially a sense of vulnerability in being so open with a group of people and the time commitment that would be involved (Blue-Banning, Turnbull, & Pereira, in press).

Do educators have the time to participate in Action Groups that meet on a monthly basis? Clearly, it would not be possible for them to have an Action Group for every student. But in our experience, and judging from the comments we have received from educators and families throughout the United States who use Group Action Planning (and other forms of person-centered planning), many educators look forward to Action Groups because they tend to be enjoyable, socially con-

nected, and mutually empowering. As one teacher commented:

> When I'm at Action Group meetings, I'm reminded of why I went into the field of special education in the first place. Sometimes in the hectic pace of day-to-day responsibilities in dealing with all of the system rules and regulations, it's easy to forget what this field is really all about. Sitting there and looking around the room, it does my heart good to get flooded with feelings that what my work is really all about is making sure students and families have the best life possible.

Group Action Planning creates a context of belonging and reciprocity among Action Group members. This is one of its goals and benefits. Even though individuals originally decide to join an Action Group to provide emotional, social, and problem-solving support to the individual with an exceptionality, the Action Group can foster reciprocal relationships (Turnbull et al., 1994). Mike Ruef, a former member of JT's (our son) Action Group, said:

> As Americans, we are raised to be independent and self-sufficient. What we often don't realize (in my case I was over 35 before I realized it) is that we need each other; we need community. While I know some members of JT's GAP [Group Action Planning] better than I know others, I have the feeling that I can go to any of them for help, because we are all on the same wavelength. These people are my safety net, my reliable alliance. Although I have been a contributor, GAP has never felt like an "obligation." Rather, it enriches me and has become an essential part of my life.

Fostering Homework Collaboration

Traditionally, homework has been one of the activities that families, students, and schools have shared most often. School reform efforts (see chapter 2) aimed at raising standards for students have also raised expectations for homework (U.S. Department of Education, 1992). Nonetheless, special education teacher training programs seem to disregard the positive outcomes of homework in building a home-school partnership. A review of five of the most commonly used curriculum and methods texts for special education teachers reported that only one discusses homework (Epstein, Polloway, Foley, & Patton, 1993).

Does homework have a positive effect on the academic achievement of students? It is difficult to answer this question definitively, given the current research base. Research from approximately 1960 to 1989 reached variable conclusions, including ". . . homework having positive effects, no effects, or complex effects to the suggestion that the research was too sparse or poorly conducted to allow trustworthy conclusions" (Cooper, Lindsay, Nye, & Greathouse, 1998, p. 70). A comprehensive research synthesis of the research literature (mostly related to students without disabilities) concluded that higher grade-level students who do more homework have better achievement in terms of test scores or class grades (Cooper, 1989b). A follow-up study concluded that a positive relationship exists between homework assignments completed by students and their achievement (Cooper et al., 1998a, 1989b). The relationship is stronger at upper rather than lower grades and stronger for teacher-assigned grades than for standardized tests. The authors of this research drew the following implications for homework at early grades:

> Thus, we suggest that the present study supports the assignment of homework in early grades, not necessarily for its immediate effects on achievement but rather for its potential long-term impact. The impact of early-grade homework is mediated, through time, by its facilitation of the development of proper study skills, which, in turn, influence grades. (Cooper et al., 1998, p. 82)

Generally, homework has a desirable effect on school achievement for students with mild disabilities; but there has been only limited research on the role of homework for students with severe disabilities, particularly those who are in inclusive settings (Epstein et al., 1993). Often students with exceptionalities have more problems with homework than classmates who do not have special needs (Epstein et al., 1993; Gajria & Salend, 1995; Polloway, Epstein, & Foley, 1992; Salend & Schiff, 1989). For example, students with disabilities in resource rooms and self-contained programs have reported that homework is boring, a waste of time, and too difficult for them to complete without the assistance of others (Bryan, Nelson, & Mathur, 1995; Bryan & Nelson, 1995). Adolescents with behavior disorders have far more significant homework problems (for example, failing to bring home assignment materials, denying they have homework, producing sloppier homework, responding poorly when told by parents to correct homework) than their classmates without disabilities (Soderlund, Bursuck, Polloway, & Foley, 1995). Moreover, 50 percent of teachers of students with learning disabilities have reported that they do not discuss, review, and regularly grade homework assignments (Salend & Schiff, 1989).

For Dustin, homework—and help at home with his work—basically consists of working on his own. But Karen and the family help in an unexpected way: They help Dustin find a quiet place where he can work, a place not already occupied by others in the family. Though that may seem to be not much help, given the large family in a small house, it is important and useful help. In his special place, Dustin devours Animorph books, diligently studies Spanish, and struggles with the physical act of writing. Where does his mother, Karen, fit in? She does her own homework, pursuing her GED and studying American Sign Language so she can be an interpreter. Candi is studying to pass the last two examinations for her own GED, and Jeremy also has homework. This is a family where work at home consists of reinforcing each other for good behavior, of pursuing its own education, and of caring for a large family, one that is poor only in the economic sense of "poor" but that is committed to learning, together, how to have a different and better life.

In this section we will discuss (1) family concerns about homework and (2) suggestions for homework collaboration.

Family Concerns about Homework

Research on the perspectives of parents of academically gifted students indicates that their children complete homework with limited negative responses and without a great deal of help from their parents (Worrell, Gabelko, Roth, & Samuels, 1999). Indeed, homework increases during elementary grades, but the amount of parental assistance decreases. In this section, we will focus on the concerns of families who have children and youth with disabilities. Because homework rarely is given to students with severe disabilities, our focus will be on what has been learned from research about the following concerns of parents of students with mild disabilities (Kay, Fitzgerald, Paradee, & Mellencamp, 1994):

- They feel inadequate to help their children with homework.
- They want more information about the classroom teacher's expectations and approach to homework.
- They want homework to be individualized and to respect student and family needs.
- They prefer homework to be related to life skills.
- They want comprehensive, two-way communication between home and school.

Parents Feel Inadequate Parents may feel inadequate for three reasons: (1) changes in instructional methods since they were students, (2) a lack of information about what is being taught at school, and (3) their belief that specialized training is needed for them to be able to help their children.

If I could actually see once in a while how they're teaching him, then it might spill over into how I could do it at home. . . . When it comes to teaching my child, I feel like times have changed since I was in school, and I hate to teach him wrong. (Kay et al., 1994, p. 555)

Parents Want More Information about a Teacher's Homework Expectations Parents' concerns center on (1) end-of-the-year expectations, (2) a teacher's expectations for parents' roles and contributions, and (3) ensuring consistency and structure between home and school. Their ambiguity about expectations causes them to worry that they will do the wrong thing.

Last year with my son I was told by the teacher that I could help him with math. This year I don't know if I can help with math so I am very hesitant to help or correct. I want to show him the right way, but how much should I be helping or pushing him? I need clarification from the teacher on what she expects. (Kay et al., 1994, p. 555)

Box 13–3 includes diary entries of a parent, Connie, who has a family that includes three sons: David (eighth grade), Fred (fourth grade), and Ethan (third grade). The log entries focus on issues associated with Fred's homework. At age 10, Fred was receiving services for students who have an IQ of 76 or less or whose performance falls 1.5 standard deviations below the norm on standardized aptitude and achievement tests. He spent 80 percent of his time in a general education fourth-grade classroom and received direct special education services within the classroom in a small-group setting and reading instruc-

tion in a resource room. His homework was assigned by his general classroom teacher.

Consider Connie's perspectives. What would your response be to these homework issues? What kind of partnership would you want to establish with the teacher to alleviate some of these concerns? Think back to chapter 6 and chapter 7 on family interaction and functions. What impact do homework and stress associated with homework have on parental and sibling interactions? What spillover might there be to marital and extended family interactions? What impact does this situation have on family functions? If Connie spends more time on the family function of education by assisting Fred with his homework, what is the impact on other family functions? Has the teacher tried to individualize homework assignments, considering that what may be easy for one student is difficult for another?

Parents Prefer Experiential Homework Related to Life Skills Many parents and students prefer hands-on, practical homework that involves project activities rather than paper-and-pencil tasks (Bryan & Sullivan-Burstein, 1998). Contrast Connie's perspectives in box 13–3 with her perspectives about the benefit of experiential homework described in box 13–4.

Compare both "My Voice" figures. What differences are evident in Fred's motivation? What differences are evident in the family support available to Fred? One thing that is particularly interesting to note is the number of times that "I" is used in box 13–3 and the number of times that "Fred" is used in box 13–4. In which instance do both Fred and Connie appear to be more empowered?

MY VOICE
BOX 13–3

Homework Concerns

9/10: [He had four subjects for homework.] Fred didn't want to read today. The math seemed way over his head, even after I tried to explain it. I still feel that Fred brings home some inappropriate homework for his level. I think this is discouraging for him.

9/24: I am feeling swamped with the homework. Even though each subject takes a reasonable amount

of time, I feel the total time spent on homework is too much . . . I wonder how other fourth grade parents feel.

9/30: Fred seems to be forgetting homework lately. I can't seem to figure out if he is really forgetting it, or if he is sick of doing it and is doing this on purpose.

Source: From "Making Homework Work at Home: The Parent's Perspective" by P. J. Kay, M. Fitzgerald, C. Paradee, and A. Mellencamp, 1994, *Journal of Learning Disabilities, 27,* pp. 550–561. Copyright © 1994 by PRO-ED, Inc. Reproduced by permission.

Parents Want Communication In communicating with parents about homework, you can use many of the communication strategies you learned about in chapter 9, including telephone calls, written notes, and dialogue journals (which they find useful because journals have specific information about homework assignments).

Suggestions for Homework Collaboration

Educators and families have communication problems pertaining to homework (Epstein, 1987; Epstein, Munk, Bursuck, Polloway, & Jayanthi, 1999; Jayanthi, Sawyer, Nelson, Bursuck, & Epstein, 1995). Yet there are at least three ways to enhance homework collaboration (Epstein et al., 1999; Jayanthi et al., 1995):

- Create more opportunities for students, parents, general education teachers, and special education teachers to communicate with each other.
- Minimize family responsibility for homework.
- Provide a potpourri of ideas to improve practice.

Create Communication Opportunities Lack of time and communication opportunities present major challenges for both families and educators. To address these challenges, the Manzanita Elementary School in Arizona uses communication folders as a way for students to carry information back and forth between school and home (Bos, Nahmias, & Urban, 1999). This information includes announcements, notes, weekly school newsletters, and weekly homework packets. The

homework packets for students with disabilities are sometimes adapted in light of a particular student's strengths and needs. Students take the folders home on Friday, and they return them to the teacher the following Friday with their parent's signature. At higher grade levels in the same school district, some students with disabilities are provided with a homework "coach" who meets with the student to address organizational, study, time-management, and self-advocacy skills. The coach assists the student with communication with the various content teachers as well as with parents. This district has also found that "contracts" for longer assignments are helpful to students and parents in planning long-term time lines and responsibilities.

That approach—the sustained linking of school and home for long-term results—is what Central, Dustin and Karen, and the Central teachers practice. Dustin loves to read; Karen encourages it; and together with the administrators and teachers at Central Middle School and with the guidance of the Action Group, they have secured in-school activities that keep Dustin engaged academically and that have significantly reduced his disciplinary problems. These include easy access to the computer classroom and to the school and community library, and a "contract" for good behavior at school and home to improve Dustin's behavior in both places.

Consider what you learned in chapter 9 about various communication strategies. Each of the strategies about which you learned has relevance for homework collaboration. Listen to what a single mother says about how helpful an answering machine might be in exchanging information related to homework:

I am a single parent. I work all day long. By the time I ever get home, the teachers are gone. Why couldn't there be some sort of an answering machine at the school, so [that I could] dial this number to leave a message for the math teachers [and] dial this number for the English teachers. Answering machines are cheap. I have an answering machine. [The teachers] could probably answer me back and that might solve [these communication problems]. (Jayanthi et al., 1995, p. 217)

Many families would like to have more information about the best way to contact teachers:

I have a very hard time catching these teachers. I would like to know at the beginning of the year what are the break hours for each teacher. I could call them during that time period instead of [the office workers] always telling me [that the teacher] is in class. (Jayanthi et al., 1995, p. 217)

Here are some suggestions for providing increased communication:

- Provide parents with teachers' names and their preferred times and methods for being contacted (Jayanthi et al., 1995).
- Establish systems that enable teachers to put homework assignments on audiotapes that parents can access by telephone/voicemail with the option for parents to leave messages if they have questions (Epstein et al., 1999).
- Increase communication among all teachers to avoid homework overload and to increase the likelihood of consistent homework modifications (Jayanthi et al., 1995).
- Ensure that general education teachers have access to information on student preferences, great expectations, strengths, and needs related to homework modification (Jayanthi et al., 1995).
- Ask families and educators to share their homework expectations with each other and to agree on the consequences for incomplete homework (Jayanthi et al., 1995).
- Teach students to use homework planners as a way to keep up with their assignments and to communicate between school and home (Bryan & Sullivan-Burstein, 1997, 1998; Epstein et al., 1999; Stormont-Spurgin, 1997).
- Teach the students to graph their homework completion and to use these graphs at parent-teacher-student conferences to report their progress to their parents (Bryan & Sullivan-Burstein, 1997, 1998).

One of the most comprehensive parent partnership homework approaches reported in the literature provided an opportunity for parents and students to learn about self-management skills (Callahan, Rademacher, & Hildreth, 1998). This approach included a self-management program that involved daily math assignments. Students received a checklist and matching sheet in their homework folders, and they were required to do the following:

- *Self-monitoring*—the student monitored and recorded the starting and ending times of homework, total time spent, whether or not homework was completed, and the location of completing homework
- *Self-recording*—the student recorded the number of correct and incorrect problems
- *Self-reinforcement*—the student determined and recorded the number of matching points earned for accuracy for the homework completion
- *Self-instruction and goal setting*—the student evaluated his or her score and determined whether an alternative form of the same assignment or progressing to a new assignment was indicated

The students and parents were given procedures for how to go through these steps with the parents supporting the student's accurate completion. Parents were provided with two informational sessions so the program could be explained to them, and a separate meeting was held for students. Results of the program indicated that homework completion and quality were significantly higher when the parents facilitated this self-management approach than before the intervention was started. Math achievement increased at a greater-than-anticipated rate, and students and parents were extremely positive about their involvement with the program.

Create Options to Minimize Family Responsibility for Homework Sometimes it may be advantageous to consider options for a student to complete homework outside the family setting, as one special education teacher pointed out:

I have a situation where the mom cannot read and the girl wants to do her homework. She cannot help, so I modify her assignments. If I have a parent who either cannot read or chooses not to read, I take the responsibility on myself and modify things, so that the child can feel successful, feel like they are doing homework. (Jayanthi et al., 1995, p. 221)

Another teacher emphasized the importance of considering community resources: "Another thing might be having copies of major assignments, research projects, and all of that in your local library, so that the parents have a way to see those, because the libraries are open until 10 o'clock at night" (Jayanthi et al., 1995, p. 221). Because Dustin can write so much better with a computer (but his family cannot afford to buy one), the Action Group (with Dustin and Karen) is exploring ways to find resources to purchase a computer for him.

Other options include the following (Epstein et al., 1999; Jayanthi et al., 1995):

- Provide less homework, particularly on weekends.
- Provide more supervised study halls and after-school sessions to support students in doing their homework. (Dustin benefits from after-school programs.)
- Arrange for peer tutoring and support.
- Arrange for community volunteers to be in study hall or to be at after-school sessions as homework aides.
- Arrange for after-school sessions where students can go to get assistance on their homework.

Provide a Potpourri of Ideas to Improve Practice

A broad range of additional ideas follows (Bryan & Sullivan-Burstein, 1997; Epstein et al., 1999; Jayanthi et al., 1995; Stormont-Spurgin, 1997):

- Encourage families to designate a study area and regular study time at home.
- Develop a regular routine for giving assignments, and be consistent about when and how information is given (for example, assignments always written on the board in the same place and at the same time).
- Use game and fun activities at home (for example, card games or board games).
- Use homework assignments that involve families and students carrying out projects at home, such as reading the newspaper, reviewing and commenting on television programs, cooking, and measuring things around the house (or, in Dustin's case, using the same behavioral interventions at both home and school).
- Develop a school-wide policy on homework, and consider providing incentives to teachers who create individualized modifications.
- Ensure that homework expectations and modifications are discussed in the IEP meeting and incorporated into the IEP document.
- Teach students to manage their time more effectively.

A research study asked students with learning disabilities to provide their perspectives on what made homework easy and hard for them (Sawer, Nelson, Jayanthi, Bursuck, & Epstein, 1996). Students empha-

sized the importance of their parents supporting and encouraging them in a patient way to complete their homework, buying aids to enhance their accuracy (for example, a spellchecker, dictionary, or computer), and helping them set up a routine of completing their homework as soon as they get home from school. Another study of middle school students, including students with disabilities (learning disabilities and/or behavior disorders) and without, indicated that students prefer the following homework adaptations: being able to finish homework at school, having extra-credit assignments, having an opportunity in school to begin homework and to check it for understanding, and having reminders about due dates (Polloway, Bursuck, Jayanthi, Epstein, & Nelson, 1996).

When students have special learning challenges and needs, consider the impact on the parent-child relationship of expecting a parent to help the child with homework or teach specific objectives at home. Parents can experience stress when working with their child at home, and this pressure may escalate when the child with a disability is in a general education rather than special education setting.

There are comparable concerns with early childhood services. Working with children on developmental outcomes (often called home teaching instead of homework) still requires families to devote substantial time to accomplishing educational objectives. Judy O'Halloran looks back on the time when her son Casey was in early intervention: "I could get really angry thinking about how early intervention intruded into our lives. Until he was eight, Casey never had a bath that wasn't an educational experience" (Turnbull, 1993, p. 2).

In chapter 7 we discussed the importance of the family's role in supporting the child to develop positive self-esteem. Simply stated, you should be cautious about the downside of home teaching and homework: Home can become a second school.

For example, one research study reported that mothers' teaching interaction with their children with learning disabilities tends to be more adult-centered and does not incorporate much encouragement or negotiation (Lyytinen, Rasku-Puttonen, Poikkeus, Laakso, & Ahonen, 1994). The students apparently participated in learning tasks out of a sense of obligation rather than internal motivation. When compared to students who did not have disabilities and who were working with their mothers, the students with learning disabilities did not cooperate as much. On the other hand, both Dustin and Karen benefit from a team approach to extending Dustin's academic and behavioral skill development to home. Each encourages the other to learn, and both encourage Dustin's sister, Candi, as she pursues her GED and his brother, Jeremy, as he goes through school. Everyone also reinforces everyone else for positive behaviors, even when they disagree about something.

What are the possible implications for the parent-child relationship? Given that students with disabilities often experience learning challenges, interactions based on parent teaching may not be as satisfying and may be more stressful than those between parents and children with typical learning characteristics. Clearly, individual variations exist: Some parents do extremely well when working with their child at home, and others find it highly stressful. To create a responsive context around homework issues, you will need to individualize your approach for each family. For Karen, Dustin, and the other members of their family, work at home is welcomed, for it benefits everyone in the family.

Implementing Positive Behavioral Support

Let's stay with Dustin, Karen, and their family, and let's return to Central Middle School in Kansas City, Kansas. Then, let's use all of them as prisms for learning about positive behavioral supports.

Many factors have converged to place high priority on addressing impeding behaviors of students with and without disabilities. Two of the primary factors are (1) national concern over the alarming rate of discipline problems and (2) IDEA's new emphasis on positive behavioral support. Figure 13–3 provides a summary of current national data pointing to the extreme discipline upheaval in schools that involve office referrals, suspensions, and expulsions. These national data do not capture the picture in each school or each school district; variations exist there. At Central Middle School, for example, 36 percent of the students (just over a third of them) are responsible for 80 percent (four-fifths) of all office disciplinary referrals.

This national concern with impeding behavior and discipline led to new IDEA provisions related to the role of schools in addressing these challenges. IDEA states that "in the case of a child whose behavior impedes his or her learning or that of others, the child's IEP team must consider, when appropriate, strategies, including positive behavioral intervention strategies and supports, to address that behavior" (Sec. 1414 (d)(3)(B)(i)).

Although IDEA does not define *impeding behavior,* a definition has emerged. Researchers who have conducted a policy analysis of positive behavioral support

FIGURE 13–3

Current Disciplin

- A rural middle school with over 2,600 office referrals least one referral, 136 stu referrals, 34 students had and one student had 87 Greene et al., 1997).

- In one state, expulsions increased from 426 to 2,088 and suspensions went from 53,374 to 66,914 over a four-year period (Juvenile Justice Fact Sheet).

- In another state, expulsions increased from 855 to 1,180 between the 1994–95 and 1995–96 school year—a 200 percent increase from the 1991–92 school year (Juvenile Justice Fact Sheet).

- Being suspended or expelled from school is reported by students as one of the top three school-related reasons for leaving school (National Association of Child Advocates, 1998).

- In one state, 10.7 percent of students who had been suspended or expelled also were found in the state's Department of Juvenile Justice Database; 5.4 percent of suspended students were arrested while on suspension; and 18.7 percent were arrested while on expulsion (National Association of Child Advocates, 1998).

- Thirty-six percent of general public school parents fear for the physical safety of their oldest child at school, and 31 percent fear for the physical safety of their oldest child while playing in the neighborhood (Gallup, Elam, & Rose, 1998).

- The general public rated fighting/violence/gangs, lack of discipline, lack of funding, and use of drugs/dope as the top four biggest problems facing local schools. These same four have been the top four for over 15 years (Gallup, Elam, & Rose, 1998).

- Fifty-five percent of teachers report that students fail to do their homework (Farkas, Johnson, & Duffett, 1999).

- Sixty-nine percent of teachers indicate that the most serious problem they face is with students who try to get by doing as little work as possible (Farkas, Johnson, & Duffett, 1999).

Source: Applying Positive Behavioral Support and Functional Behavioral Assessment in Schools (pp. 1–23), by G. Sugai, R. H. Horner, G. Gunlap, M. Hieneman, T. J. Lewis, C. M. Nelson, T. Scott, C. Liaupsin, W. Sailor, A. P. Turnbull, H. R. Turnbull, D. Wickham, M. Ruef, and B. Wilcox, 1999, Washington, DC: U.S. Department of Education.

owing definition (Turnbull, Turnbull, e, 1999):

impeding behavior means those behaviors t that:

impede the learning of the student or of others and include those behaviors that are externalizing (such as verbal abuse, aggressions, self-injury, or property destruction), are internalizing (such as physical or social withdrawal, depression, passivity, resistance, social or physical isolation, or noncompliance), are manifestations of biological or neurological conditions (such as obsessions, compulsions, stereotypes, or irresistible impulses), or are disruptive (such as annoying, confrontational, defiant, or taunting behavior);

2. could cause the student to be disciplined pursuant to any state or federal law or regulations or could cause any consideration of a change of the student's educational placement; and

3. are consistently recurring and therefore require functional behavioral assessment and the systematic and frequent application of positive behavioral interventions and supports.

The IDEA provision is remarkable for at least this reason: For the first time in its history, IDEA requires educators to consider using a specific intervention for students with disabilities. In this section we will define positive behavioral support and describe how it can be implemented in collaboration with families at the school-building level.

Definition of Positive Behavioral Support

Positive behavioral support is a problem-solving, data-based, and proactive orientation to maximizing students' successful behavioral outcomes. Whereas the traditional behavior management approach views students as "the problem," positive behavioral support views systems, settings, and skill deficiencies as "the problem." Thus, the focus is shifted from "fixing" the individual to "fixing" the systems, settings, and skills so that they will be more enhancing of students' appropriate behavior.

The outcomes of positive behavioral support are supportive systems, settings, and skill attainment enabling students to maximize their potential (Carr et al., 1999; Horner & Carr, 1997; Horner, Albin, Sprague, & Todd, 2000; Koegel, Koegel, & Dunlap, 1996; Weigle, 1997). In other words, positive behavioral support is an approach for maximizing great expectations, preferences, and strengths while simultaneously responding to needs.

School-Wide Positive Behavioral Support

The National Center for Positive Behavioral Interventions and Supports (*www.pbis.org*) is taking the lead nationally in creating successful school-wide models. We encourage you to visit the website and learn about the latest research.

Figure 13–4 illustrates a school-wide framework for positive behavioral support. This framework's horizontal columns illustrate the varying levels of positive behavioral support that characterize a school-wide model. The three levels include: (1) clear expectations and positive feedback, (2) functional assessment and individualized interventions in the school environment, and (3) functional assessments and comprehensive services across multiple environments. In this section you will learn about the nature of positive behavioral support intervention at each of these three levels.

Level 1 Support Level 1 support in a comprehensive school-wide model provides clear expectations and positive feedback for all students throughout all classrooms and nonclassroom settings (for example, halls, cafeteria, playgrounds, buses). Schools that have been successful in building school-wide systems found the following procedures to be useful (Horner, 2000; Lewis & Sugai, 1999; Lewis, Sugai, & Colvin, 1998; Todd, Horner, Sugai, & Sprague, 1999):

- *Behavioral expectations are clearly defined*—These expectations are typically simple, positively framed, and few in number.

- *Behavioral expectations are taught*—Each of the behaviorally stated expectations must be explicitly taught so that students will know exactly what is expected of them.

- *Appropriate behaviors are acknowledged*—Schools need to build a positive culture in which students are positively affirmed at least four times as often as they are negatively sanctioned.

- *Program evaluations and adaptations are made by a positive behavioral support team*—School-wide systems need guidance, and that guidance can best come from a collaborative team comprised of administrators, teachers, parents, students, and community representatives. The team frequently tallies and reviews data on behavioral incidences, attendance rates, detentions, and suspension rates.

At Central Middle School, for example, the school-wide expectations for all students were developed by a positive behavioral support team, are known to all, and

FIGURE 13-4

School-Wide Framework for Positive Behavioral Support

Nature of Support	Level 1: Clear expectations and positive feedback	Level 2: Individualized support in school settings	Level 3: Comprehensive support across home, school, and community settings
1. Target group	All students	Some students	Fewer students
2. Settings	Classrooms and other school settings	Classrooms and other school settings	Classrooms, other school settings, multiple environments (including home and community settings)
3. Data gathering	Descriptive group statistics	Functional assessment in school settings	Fuctional assessment in multiple settings
4. Intensity	Limited	Moderate	Pervasive

are carried out school-wide. In box 13–5, you can read about how Central Middle School addressed some of the school-wide issues through positive behavioral support.

How are families and communities involved in level 1 support? Families are important members of the school's positive behavioral support team in helping to develop, teach, and monitor the school-wide behavioral expectations. Parents are also important collaborators in following through in the home setting with the school's clear expectations. In a national survey of over 1,000 parents, one-half reported that they would be "very comfortable" in helping the school decide its policy on school behavior and discipline, but only 20 percent have actually participated in this activity. Thus, there appears to be many more families available to assist in level 1 support as contrasted to those who have been invited or who have participated (Farkas, Johnson, & Duffett, 1999).

Consider the five expectations for being "centralized." These same expectations can readily be expected and positively reinforced in home and community settings. A recent national survey of parents and teachers regarding their perspectives toward parental involvement in public schools underscores the importance of family collaboration in level 1 support (Farkas, Johnson, & Duffett, 1999).

> Yet the most serious and pervasive problem, according to teachers, is that too many parents are failing at the most fundamental and traditional elements of parenting-teaching their children the discipline, perseverance, and good manners that allow them to work within the classroom structure. Fully 81% of teachers cite as a serious problem parents who refuse to hold their kids accountable for their behavior or academic performance. More than 8 in 10 (83%) complain about parents who fail to set limits and create structure at home for their kids. (Farkas, Johnson, & Duffett, 1999, pp. 24–25)

It is clear that educators strongly support the need for home-school collaboration on the very critically important topic of school discipline. Actively involving families in developing and implementing level 1 support for all students is an ideal way to build this collaboration.

Community representatives can also serve on the school-based team, incorporating the same behavioral expectations in various community environments in which many of the school's students participate—recreation programs, scouting, restaurants, religious organizations, and others. The more students receive consistent expectations across home, school, and community settings, the more likely they are to incorporate behavioral expectations across all aspects of their lives.

Level 1 support is limited but nevertheless is sufficiently intense to meet the needs of a substantial number of students in decreasing their impeding behaviors and maximizing successful student behavioral outcomes (Horner, 2000; Lewis & Sugai, 1999; Lewis, Sugai, & Colvin, 1998; Todd, Horner, Sugai, & Sprague, 1999).

The actual proportion of students who respond successfully to level 1 varies from school to school. In some schools, this type of support might be appropriate for 90 percent of the school population; in other schools, level

BOX 13–5

TOGETHER WE CAN

Being Centralized

If it takes a whole village to raise one child, then it takes a whole school—faculty, student body, and researchers—to improve student behavior and to extend learning into home and community. At least that's the lesson taught by Central Middle School in Kansas City, Kansas, its faculty, students, and Kansas University researchers in the area of positive behavioral support who have worked with the school during the 1998–2000 school years.

Here was a school suddenly experiencing the effects of school redistricting and along with that, the effects of increased student misbehavior. The problem, it seemed to the staff and researchers, was that many of the new students who came from other districts were not "Centralized." They didn't know or abide by the customs and habits of the "old" Central students. And they were requiring teachers to deal with discipline rather than to offer instruction.

What does it mean to be "Centralized"? That's what the school's positive behavioral support team wanted to know. A comprehensive survey of staff and students provided the answer. To be "Centralized" means to have—and to measure up to—five expectations: Be safe, be cooperative, be respectful, be responsible, and be ready to learn.

The five expectations underlie codes of conduct for students and teachers alike. Indeed, teachers' lesson plans incorporated each of them, and teachers also generalized them throughout the school. On one side of a matrix they wrote the five expectations. Across the top they listed the school settings in which these expectations were to be met—classroom, library, hallway, cafeteria, and transportation to and from school. Within each box they identified typical behaviors that contravened the five expectations and listed the behaviors they wanted to teach through their lesson plans.

One of the impeding behaviors was "hallway behavior during passing periods." The school's response was to create four classes that taught students how to comply with "being safe" in the hallway. The students were asked to define, demonstrate, and give a rationale for "being safe." If a student could meet those three tests, the student received a certificate as a "Certified Safe Hall Walker." The certificate listed the general steps for being safe in the hall (for example, walking and using an "inside voice"). The students were encouraged to take their certificates home to share with their parents.

These certificates produced at least three positive outcomes throughout the entire school: something good happened for engaging in desirable behavior, parents and family members were made aware of the school's expectations, and the student exhibited the behavior of a model "Centralized" student.

But the certificates also produced another result: Some of the students who had been the most "de-Centralized" and had received the greatest number of "negative officer referrals" (disciplinary referrals to the assistant principal's office) changed their behavior. The consequence for them was positive office referral slips for being "role models/hall monitors," a notice to their parents that they earned a positive office referral slip, and the posting of their picture on a Positive Office Referral Wall of Fame in the school's main lobby for everyone to see, especially their parents on teacher-parent meeting days.

1 support may be appropriate for less than half of the students. As we indicated previously, just slightly more than one-third of the students at Central Middle School are responsible for four-fifths of the disciplinary office referrals. At that school, then, level 1 support is useful for the entire school. As box 13–5 showed, level 1 support there consists of establishing similar expectations among all teachers and peers; everyone knows what is expected of them. It then consists of enforcing those expectations in all areas of the school—from classroom to lunchroom to hallway to the "in-school suspension" room.

Another important consideration is that students vary in their needs for positive behavioral support, depending upon their histories with school success and failure, health, environmental factors, and a host of other considerations. Thus, students move back and forth across various levels of support according to their circumstances at any given time. As with all students, students with disabilities vary in their needs. Some students with disabilities will operate successfully at level 1; others will require more intensive support at levels 2 or 3. For example, Dustin benefits from knowing what is expected of him: being respectful of teachers, administrators, and peers, and completing his writing assignments. He's perfectly capable of the former but has chronic difficulty with the latter. Indeed, when faced with assignments that call for him to write, he consistently avoids them, often by skipping school or acting out. It's his repetitive truancy and in-school disciplinary problems that prevent level 1 support from being effective for him. He needs more; he needs level 2 support.

Level 2 Support

As we said earlier, school-wide positive behavioral support enables all students in the school to receive level 1 support. When level 1 support is not sufficient to deter a student from engaging in impeding behavior, the student's need for support justifies level 2 support. Level 2 support involves moving beyond the universal support to interventions that are implemented on an individual basis in both classroom and nonclassroom settings. The intensity is stepped up from limited to moderate support. As illustrated in figure 13–4, level 2 support involves group and individual interventions—primarily at the classroom and individual level. Dustin receives level 2 support.

Typically, the first step in providing level 2 support is for the student's school-based team (the IEP team, as augmented by specialists in positive behavioral support) to conduct a functional assessment. In Dustin's case, his IEP team has conducted a functional behavioral assessment, which begins by gathering information to determine the function or the purpose of the student's impeding behavior. Why does Dustin do what he does? Students' impeding behavior usually serves a particular function (for example, gaining attention; gaining access to preferred tasks; expressing frustration, insecurity, or anxiety; avoiding tasks; asserting control; seeking revenge). A functional assessment enables educators and families to gain an understanding of why the student is engaging in the impeding behavior.

A functional assessment typically involves collecting information through direct observation of the student and through interviews with the student and others who spend significant amounts of time with the student. The purpose of the observations and interviews is to develop summary statements (hypotheses or hunches) that describe specific behaviors, specific types of situations in which they occur, and the consequences that maintain the behaviors (Gable, 1996; Horner & Carr, 1997; Lewis-Palmer, Sugai, & Larson, 1999; O'Neill et al., 1996; Reed, Thomas, Sprague, & Horner, 1997).

Information about the student's overall patterns of behavior, the conditions that seem to predict that the behavior will occur, and the possible reasons for the behavior then becomes the foundation for planning individualized intervention at the levels of moderate (and intensive) support.

It seems, for example, that one reason Dustin acts out at school is to avoid doing writing assignments. As you learned, he is a voracious reader and has a highly developed vocabulary; he also enjoys studying Spanish and working on the computer. But he intensely dislikes having to write; when classwork requires him to do written work, he finds a way out—by misbehaving. However, there's more to the matter than simply acting out. For a good part of a school year, Dustin has no place of his own at home, no place where he can do his homework or even sleep in his own bed without another family member being there, too. It's the lack of family resources, then, that causes him to fall behind in his homework or to fall asleep at school. Moreover, the lack of family resources helps explain why he sometimes needs a haircut or comes to school without having had a morning shower. Among his peers, style and hygiene are important, and Dustin knows that. So when he comes to school sleepy and disheveled, with his eyes downcast and his chin on his chest, it is almost certain that he will have some acting-out behaviors—not complying with teachers' instructions or requests, yelling at them, slamming doors, banging lockers, and shouting epithets at his peers. By contrast, when he is well rested, showered, clean, and with his hair cut, he's a different young man—positive, energetic, cooperative, and even a leader among his peers when he and they are engaged in cooperative learning activities. It is not farfetched to say that in Dustin's case (and in the case of other students, too, as Mr. Antos, the school principal, pointed out), impeding behavior is a function of the interaction between home environment and school expectations.

Students with disabilities who have impeding behavior often need the moderate intensity of level 2 support. For these students, it is good practice to incorporate a functional assessment into their nondiscriminatory evaluation (see chapter 11) and their IEP (see chapter 12—you might consider how the IEP process implemented by Stephen Kroeger with Greg Motley that you learned about in the chapter 12 vignette incorporated a plan to enhance Greg's positive behavior). Many intervention strategies have been used successfully with students who need level 2 positive behavioral support. Box 13–6 includes tips for implementing these interventions.

What does research say about the effectiveness of level 2 positive behavioral support? A substantial body of research has accumulated over the last decade. A group of researchers recently synthesized over 100 research articles published between the years of 1985 and 1996 to investigate the behavioral outcomes for the 230 individuals with impeding behavior who were part of this database (Carr et al., 1999). Some of the conclusions of this research synthesis are as follows:

- Positive behavioral support was successful in achieving at least an 80 percent reduction in impeding behavior for approximately two-thirds of the behavioral outcomes that were studied.

Individualized Strategies in Providing Level 2 Support

- Alter the environment.
  - Accommodate students' environmental needs (e.g., attend to noises, light, and other sensory stimuli that may be distracting; provide quiet learning area).
  - Consider room arrangements and traffic patterns.
- Increase predictability and scheduling.
  - Use visual or written schedules to provide structure.
  - Prepare students in advance for changes and transitions.
- Increase choice making.
  - Encourage students to express their preferences and take them into account in planning instruction and environment supports.
  - Teach students specific skills in decision making and self-determination.
- Make curricular adaptations.
  - Adjust tasks and activities so that they are presented in formats that are consistent with students' strengths, needs, and preferences.

- Appreciate positive behaviors.
  - "Catch the student being good," and provide affirmation to students and families.
  - Teach students to use self-monitoring as a way to track their own success.
  - Maintain a 4-to-1 ratio of positive to negative statements.
  - Embed rewards within difficult activities.
- Teach replacement skills.
  - Teach students a different way to accomplish their purpose without needing to engage in the impeding behavior.
  - Teach students problem-solving skills so that they will know how to generate appropriate alternatives when they encounter problems.
- Change systems.
  - Work with other educators and families to develop state-of-the-art services and supports.
  - Work within your community to create inclusive opportunities in which students with impeding behavior can participate in a successful way.

- The success of positive behavioral support is substantially enhanced when a functional assessment is carried out as the basis for planning the intervention(s).

- Positive behavioral support is more effective when significant people (for example, educators and families) change their behavior as contrasted to when only the individual with impeding behavior changes.

- Positive behavioral support is more effective when the environment is reorganized as contrasted to when the environment is not reorganized.

- Positive behavioral support is more effective when it is carried out by significant people in the individual's life (for example, educators and families) than by people who do not have ongoing relationships with the individual (for example, researchers and clinicians).

- Positive behavioral support works just as effectively with individuals who have multiple disabilities as with individuals who have a single disability.

In light of these findings, it is obvious that positive behavioral support enables students needing level 2 support to make important, durable change in a positive direction. When the Central team first started to work with Dustin,

the school administration, his teachers, and his family (especially his mother Karen), Dustin's rate of discipline was unacceptably high; he was among the 36 percent of the students who had 80 percent of the disciplinary office referrals. As a result of nearly a year of teamwork, his disciplinary problems are significantly lower. His attendance has improved; now it is rare for him to be truant. Instead of resisting his schoolwork, Dustin seeks out the Spanish and computer classes. That's progress and evidence that his dysgraphia (problems in writing) are not holding him back in classes where he can use a keyboard or display his subject-matter mastery by speaking (Spanish) or by reporting orally on what he has read (English).

Indeed, Dustin's Action Group has helped create and solidify relationships between him and two of his favorite teachers/subjects—computers and Spanish; and it has helped Dustin learn how to behave with other students—less assertively, less aggressively, and more friendly. The consequence: Dustin has adult allies at school, and he is developing better relationships with his peers (as a leader in cooperative learning and as a person who has learned that fighting is not a means for solving problems and making friends).

How are families and community members involved in level 2 support? When students require individualized interventions characterized by a functional assessment and a behavioral plan, it is especially important to involve families as partners in carrying out the functional assessment and in developing, implementing, and monitoring the plan. For example, Karen has formally and in writing requested that Dustin be evaluated for special education; she has given her consent to a functional behavioral assessment; she has met weekly with the Kansas University members of the school's PBIS team, usually at her home (since transportation to school is a problem for her); she has explained Dustin's behavior at home, allowed the PBIS team representatives to come into her home so that they will have a full understanding of that environment, told and showed them how she and Dustin and the other family members interact, specified what the family's expectations are at home and what she hopes the school can do for Dustin when he is there and when he is at home, and discussed Dustin's regimen of medication (what drugs he takes, why, how often, and what their effects seem to be). In short, she helps the team understand at least one environment and its effect on Dustin's school and home behaviors.

As we stated earlier, when a student has a disability, this process can be meaningfully integrated into the nondiscriminatory evaluation and IEP process. The more that educators and families can agree on behavioral expectations, rewards, and other important elements of positive behavioral support, the more likely it will be that students will be successful in overcoming their behavioral challenges. That's certainly the lesson that the Dustin team provides.

In terms of community involvement, one of the key themes in many of the suggestions in box 13–6 is building on the student's interests and fostering meaningful relationships. Although level 2 positive behavioral support focuses on interventions within the school, there may be many opportunities for students to work on generalizing the skills they are learning in school to community settings. Indeed, members of valued community settings (for example, park supervisors, scout leaders, merchants, and community service providers) might be members of the student's IEP team and might be helpful in encouraging the student to carry out the same positive behaviors in community settings that are demonstrated at school.

An excellent way to involve community members is to implement person-centered planning—an ideal process for implementing level 2 support.

For Dustin and Karen, level 2 simply is not sufficient to change his behaviors. The reason is simple enough:

No matter how much Dustin and Karen want to change and understand the reason for Dustin's behaviors, change cannot occur unless the environment in which they live can also be changed, even if only a little. When poverty, family health and educational challenges, and neighborhood distress play such a large role in shaping Dustin's behavior and his opportunities, it is unreasonable to expect that level 2 support will be effective. As Mr. Antos observed, many of his students (Dustin among them) need a whole lot more than they can get at school, even such a positively-oriented one as Central Middle School.

Level 3 Support What distinguishes level 2 from level 3 support? Although the precise demarcation is blurry, level 3 support is provided to students when a functional assessment and individualized support, characterized by the moderate intensity of level 2, are not sufficient in eliminating impeding behavior and maximizing appropriate behavior. Typically (although not always), students requiring level 3 support have disabilities and experience impeding behavior across multiple environments, including home, neighborhood, and community settings, in addition to school environments.

Level 3 support incorporates all of the interventions that we have discussed related to level 1 and level 2 supports. Thus, students who require level 3 support already are receiving the clear expectations and positive feedback that characterize level 1 support. Furthermore, they receive a functional assessment and individualized interventions in school settings (level 2) using many of the approaches identified in box 13–6.

The fact remains, however, that this support is not always sufficient. Some students require functional assessments and comprehensive interventions across multiple environments to optimize their success. In the next and final section of this chapter, you will learn about best practices in integrating services across numerous service sectors. When schools have integrated services, it is an ideal context in which to embed level 3 positive behavioral support. Unfortunately, most schools do not have comprehensive services; but we are hoping that you will find a role in the schools where you teach to be agents for systems change in order to transform current discrete, segmented programs into ones that meet the holistic needs of students and families.

When schools do not have integrated services in order to provide comprehensive supports, an approach that pools services for individual students has emerged from the mental health field and is referred to as the *wraparound* model. This model is a process—driven by the needs of children, youth, and families—for providing services to meet priority needs (Burns & Goldman, 1999; Clark et al., 1998; Eber, Nelson, & Miles, 1997; VanDenBurg & Grealish, 1996). A unique feature of the wraparound approach is that it brings together families, professionals, and other interested stakeholders to "think outside of the box" in seeking to integrate and transform services in a way that has typically not been available. Wraparound team members generally consider needs and a broad variety of life domains, including residence, social, emotional/psychological, educational/vocational, safety, legal, medical, spiritual, cultural, behavioral, and financial (VanDenBerg & Grealish, 1996, 1998). (As you consider this list, bear in mind its parallels with the eight family functions about which you learned in chapter 7. Thus, wraparound can address each of those family function areas to consider child and family needs and put together an array of services and supports that are responsive to those needs.) A critical dimension of wraparound is that people from various service sectors agree to blend their otherwise separate resources to create a single fund that, in turn, pays for a comprehensive service and support plan (Eber, Nelson, & Miles, 1997; VanDenBerg & Grealish, 1996).

One of the first programs to use wraparound services was a Chicago child welfare agency (Kaleidoscope), which was a joint effort to combine education, mental health, corrections, child welfare, and family services (Goetz, 1994). More than 20 years ago, the agency began to develop alternatives for children and youth with emotional and behavioral disorders who had been institutionalized and were returning to the community.

School districts are now adopting this approach, especially in facilitating inclusion of students with emotional and behavioral disorders. In the LaGrange Area Department of Special Education outside of Chicago, the school-based wraparound model, directed by Dr. Lucile Eber, offers creative and personalized services as identified in figure 13–5.

From data collected from the initial implementation of the wraparound approach, the LaGrange Department of Special Education has reported the following results:

> Some interesting trends . . . include a drastic reduction in self-contained placements, a substantial drop in psychiatric hospitalizations during the first year, and consistently low use of psychiatric hospitals or other out-of-home placements . . . the teachers report satisfaction with the supports they are receiving, and academic outcomes are improving. (Goldman & Faw, 1999, p. 47)

Additional evaluation findings on wraparound approaches include the following (Handron, Dosser, McCammon, & Powell, 1998):

- When discharged from a residential treatment program, 32 percent of those who did not have wraparound services were reinstitutionalized within 12 months of discharge; by contrast, only 10 percent of those who had had wraparound services were reinstitutionalized (Brown & Greenbaum, 1994).

- One hundred thirty-two foster children who received wraparound services rather than traditional foster care services were more likely to be placed in a permanent home (Clark, Lee, Prange, & MacDonald, 1996).

- Children served through the Wraparound Milwaukee Project in community services, as contrasted to those provided with only traditional residential services, had service plans that were substantially less expensive (Wraparound Milwaukee Project Staff, 1996).

- One year after a wraparound service program, children experiencing emotional and behavior problems had a significant decrease in negative behaviors, and 89 percent were maintained in the community, with the cost being less than that of out-of-state residential care (Bruns, Burchard, & Yoe, 1995).

- Children who were referred to out-of-home placement who were provided wraparound services had more favorable outcomes from multiple indicators including externalizing behavior, social problems, thought problems, and family adaptability/cohesion as compared to children in similar circumstances who received family-based treatment (Evans, Armstrong, & Kuppinger, 1996).

Interestingly, while there has been a heavy emphasis on person-centered planning within the developmental disability field, there has been very little incorporation of wraparound approaches. The wraparound model has been primarily limited to children and youth with mental health needs, although it is highly applicable to any student who has intensive and chronic needs across a number of different areas. One of the primary differences between how person-centered planning and wraparound approaches have been implemented is that person-centered planning typically has not involved the merger of funding from various service sectors; it has concentrated more on informal networks—classmates, friends, coworkers—in building support systems. The wraparound approach has given more emphasis to the merger of services from various formal agencies.

In Dustin's case, community support is forthcoming from the local mental health agency where Dustin, Karen, and Candi all receive various treatments. Among the treatments is medication: Each takes a different medication for different reasons, and each reinforces the other to remember to take their medications regularly.

FIGURE 13-5

Examples of Wraparound Services

Student Services	School Services	Family Services	Community Services

• Develop behavior change programs
 	
• Develop transition plans for high school
 	
• Medication management
 	
• Secure peer buddies
 	
• After-school training
 	
• Develop home/school homework plans
 	
• Develop transition plans into regular education
	• Coverage for in-school to prevent out-of-school suspensions
	
	• In-school respite:
	  • Lunchrooms
	  • Physical education class
	  • Recess
	  • Computers
	  • Library
	  • Art
	
	• Technical assistance:
	  • Changing roles of school-based staff
	  • Inclusion of students with emotional and behavioral disorders
	  • Clinical consultation
	  • Case review opportunities
	  • Behavioral programming
	  • Dealing with resistance
	  • Developing school wraparound plans
	
	• Provide substitutes to assure teacher participation at meetings
	
	• Crisis intervention at school
	
	• Individual observations and behavior programming
	
	• Academic testing
	
	• Coordinate out-of-school supports
		• Home visits
		
		• Accompany parents and students to court
		
		• Facilitate the completion of needed neurological and psychiatric evaluations
		
		• Facilitate communication between home and school
		
		• Support for families in crisis
		
		• Provide transportation to needed appointments
		
		• Secure before-school child care
		
		• Accompany parents and students to doctor's appointments
		
		• Referral to the local area networks
		
		• Develop home behavior plans
			• Recreational coaching
			
			• Develop transition plans for high school
			
			• Business partnerships:
			  • Subway Sandwiches
			  • Brookfield Zoo
			  • Bank One
			  • Target Store
			  • Sign Source
			
			• Community service liaison to provide:
			  • Christmas tree and gifts
			  • Rent waiver to avoid eviction
			  • Funds to pay utilities
			  • Drug screening
			  • Recreation activities
			  • Mentoring by police
			  • Mental health agencies
			
			• Develop community resource directory

What is the role of families and community members at level 3 support? Obviously, their involvement is pervasive—significantly more so than at level 1 and level 2. For level 3 support, it is essential to link with families and communities as closely as possible in being involved in intensive planning, implementation, and monitoring of comprehensive approaches (see figure 13–4). Pervasive family and community collaboration is a distinguishing characteristic of level 3 support.

Students who require level 2 support often need assistance in "getting a life," in having places to go, things to do, and valued relationships throughout the school day and outside of school (Risley, 1996; Turnbull & Ruef, 1996, 1997).

As we stated earlier, the ideal arrangement is for schools to have integrated, comprehensive services for all students, including those with the most intense behavioral challenges. You will learn about this approach in the next section.

FIGURE 13–6

Continuum of Service Partnerships

Service
Cooperation — Service Coordination — Service Collaboration — Service Integration

Integrating Services

Throughout this book we have emphasized the importance of partnerships among individuals—primarily families and educators. Partnerships also occur at the systems level when agencies providing different types of services work together to accomplish mutual goals. In terms of the broad concept of partnerships among different agencies, some people have described a service organization continuum, which is illustrated in figure 13–6.

From this continuum we see a movement from simply having cooperation among various services that might be offered to families such as Dustin's to the point of integrating services. Schools around the country are making great strides in working to move to the right end of the continuum—toward service integration (and ultimately having service transformation).

Consider the challenges that face Dustin and his family. If they have to go to every separate agency that might offer them support, they would spend an inordinate amount of time filling out "intake forms," providing information, and trying desperately to fill in the holes of service gaps. An alternative to that discrete, piecemeal approach is the integration of multiple services—all with the goal of offering integrated, seamless support for children and families.

The general education literature of the last decade has described various models for accomplishing service integration. Two of the most frequently used terms are *school-linked services* and *full-service schools*. Many other terms, however, are also used, including inter-professional collaboration, coordinated services, community-linked services, community schools, and others (Adelman & Taylor, 1997; Amato, 1996; Calfee, Wittwer, & Meredith, 1998; Coltoff, 1998; Comer, Haynes, Joyner, & Ben-Avie, 1996; Doktor & Poertner, 1996; Dryfoos, 1996, 1997, 1998; Dupper & Poertner, 1997; Franklin & Streeter, 1995; Gardner, 1992; Briar-Lawson, Lawson, Collier, & Joseph, 1997; Lawson, 1998, in press; Lawson & Briar-Lawson, 1997; MacKenzie & Rogers, 1997; Raham, 1998; Sailor, in press; Skrtic & Sailor, 1996; U.S. Department of Education, 1999). These approaches to service integration are substantial improvements over the typical situation of having

services spread throughout the entire community and requiring families and even wraparound teams to try to access and coordinate services on their own.

Full-service or community schools seek to provide quality education (for example, school-based management, individualized instruction, and team teaching) and to link their students and staff to a vast array of other services provided by the school (for example, comprehensive health education and social skills training) and by community agencies with school-based location (for example, immunizations, social services, and substance abuse treatment) (Calfee, Wittwer, & Meredith, 1998; Dryfoos, 1996; Raham, 1998).

The distinguishing characteristics of full-service schools are that they have a single point of delivery, meet the holistic needs of the students within the context of their families, and provide whatever services are needed to enhance a child's success in school and in the community (Calfee, Wittwer, & Meredith, 1998). That is the second wish that Jim Antos, the principal at Central Middle School, made: to have the specialized staff that can help students debrief from their life outside of school, receive services there, and then be ready to learn.

Figure 13–7 includes a service matrix for a truly comprehensive, full-service school. We encourage you to carefully review all of the different services reflected in this service matrix.

Figure 13–7 shows services available in one community at the four feeder school sites, ranging from pre-kindergarten through grade 12. Most of the 24 services are located on one of the four school campuses; students from one school go to the other school for particular services. Additionally, some of these services are offered at a community center, a student's home, a child-care center, or a family service center linked to the school. In addition to students and their families being able to use these services, they are also available to other community citizens.

The middle school is open six days a week from 7:00 A.M. to 9:30 P.M. and on Sunday from 8:00 A.M. to 1:00 P.M. At this particular location, the following services are available (Calfee, Wittwer, & Meredith, 1998, p. 21):

- Adult basic education and college-level course work (evening hours)

FIGURE 13–7

Service Matrix for a Real Full-Service School

Service	Description/Clientele	Location/Hours	Funding Sources
Adult education	Basic education and remediation for those adults aged 161 Undergraduate and graduate coursework	Middle School, Monday and Thursday, 5–8 PM College and enrichment classes by semester	• Adult Learning Center • Community schools • Community college • State university
Case work	Protective services, Project Vision Referrals for delinquency, foster care, developmental and economic services, alcohol/drug abuse, mental health, counseling, home visits	Middle School, weekdays	• State Department of Children and Families (DCF)
Child care	Free or reduced, subsidized child care for children aged 3 months to 12 years (some restrictions apply)	Appointments taken for location convenient to parent	• Children's Services
Community use of school facilities	Civic and parent groups apply for permission Available to all, free	Primary, Intermediate, and Middle Schools	• County School Board
Economic services	AFDC, Medicaid, food stamps: intake, screening, application, review Referrals to other community resources	Middle School, Monday through Friday, 8 AM–5 PM Appointments preferred; walk-ins accepted	• DCF
Educational opportunity center	Career options counseling and financial aid for students aged 191	Community Center, Tuesdays, 1–4 PM	• Community college
First call for help	Toll-free community resource information hotline	Available district-wide	• Center for Community Mental Health • United Way • Retired senior volunteers
Graduation enhancement program	Technology-based early intervention to promote student learning	Intermediate and Middle Schools	• County School Board

(continued)

FIGURE 13–7   CONTINUED

Service Matrix for a Real Full-Service School

Service	Description/Clientele	Location/Hours	Funding Sources
Health services	RN and psychologist: prevention, early detection, early intervention, and community referrals Mobile health unit Emergency food and clothing Affordable health insurance for school-age children	Intermediate and Middle Schools, Monday through Friday, school hours	• Supplemental School Health Grant: DCF and State Department of Education • Sacred Heart Hospital • Community resources • Healthy Kids Corp.
Healthy kids	Affordable health insurance for children ages 3 to 19	Available district-wide Enrollment by toll-free number	• State legislature • Healthy Kids Corp. • County School Board • County commissioners • Blue Cross/Blue Shield Health Options
Home visitor high-risk infant program	Home visits by social worker for at-risk infants Training in parenting skills, immunizations, etc.	South end of county	• DCF
Job services	Employment services for job training and placement with computer access to regional job listings	Middle School, Monday through Friday, 8 AM–5 PM	• DCF • Private Industry Council (PIC) • Job Training Partnership Act
Juvenile Alternative Services Program (JASP)	Meaningful sanctions and services for certain juvenile offenders and their families, designed to divert from judicial processing and to reduce incidence of law violations	Intermediate and Middle Schools	• DCF
Latchkey	State-licensed after-school programs until 6 PM school days and some holidays Summer camp program, 7:30 AM–6:30 PM	Primary, Intermediate, and Middle Schools Campers picked up and returned to Intermediate School	• Community schools • Parent tuition • Title XX funding for qualified families
Mental health counseling	Counseling for students and families Exceptional student education specialist Full-time therapist for emotionally or severely emotionally handicapped	Primary, Intermediate, and Middle Schools	• Center for Community Mental Health • Medicaid • Private Insurance

FIGURE 13–7 CONTINUED

Service Matrix for a Real Full-Service School

Service	Description/Clientele	Location/Hours	Funding Sources
Parent involvement center	Educational and counseling materials available for checkout by parents for use with students at home	Primary, Intermediate, and Middle Schools	• Project Vision • National Foundation for the Improvement of Education (NFIE) • Junior League • Community resources • Parent-teacher association (PTA) • Parent advisory boards
Parent workshops	Hosted periodically during the school year for all interested persons	Primary, Intermediate, and Middle Schools	• Project Vision • Community resources • PTA • Parent advisory boards
Prekindergarten	Head Start or early intervention programs for 4-year-olds Placement on space-available basis Some restrictions	Intermediate school	• Federal and state funding in collaboration with County School Board
Private Industry Council (PIC)	Employability skills for middle school, students aged 161, and adults	Middle School	• PIC
Protective services	On-site investigator for abuse or neglect complaints through State Protective Services System's Abuse Registry	Middle School	• DCF
Research	Ongoing research activity supervised by state university	Primary, Intermediate, and Middle Schools	• Full-service schools • State university
Sheriff's department	On-site duty available for assistance with law enforcement issues, education, and prevention activities	Primary, Intermediate, and Middle Schools	• County Sheriff's Department • Full-service schools
Volunteers	Volunteers act as tutors, teacher helpers, mentors, etc.	Primary, Intermediate, and Middle Schools	• Retired senior volunteers • County School Board • Community Organizations
Women, infants, and children program	Offers nutrition counseling and supplemental food for prenatal and postnatal care and for children from birth to 5 years	Community Center, 1st Wednesday and 2nd Friday each month, 9 AM–3 PM	• PIC • Federal funding through County Public Health Unit

Source: From *Building a Full-Service School: A Step-by-Step Guide* (pp. 18–20), by C. Calfee, F. Wittwer, & M. Meredith, 1998, San Francisco: Jossey-Bass.

Benefiting from Full-Service Schools

Meet the Young family. They live two miles from the site of our full-service school, and they have been involved with the program for about four years. Alice and Sam Young have two children. Amy, twelve, is a seventh grader with multiple physical and educational challenges; she has been in the exceptional student education class since second grade. John, ten, is a handful; he performs poorly, disrupts the class, and may fail the fifth grade. His teacher has tried numerous interventions, unsuccessfully. It is because of John's classroom behavior—and the rumor that he recently broke into a neighbor's home—that John's teacher refers the Youngs to an interagency problem-solving "care team" by way of the school counselor. The care team consists of members of the child's family, the classroom teacher, the school counselor and social worker, a project psychologist, an administrator, a registered nurse, a resource officer, a caseworker specializing in child abuse and neglect, and other members of the

community support system as needed. The care team meets to help the family decide on a course of action to promote student success.

The school counselor tells the other team members about John's classroom problems. The sheriff's department resource officer explains John's recent brush with the law. The health nurse voices her concerns about Amy. Having considered the facts, the team decides that the school's onsite social worker should join the health nurse for a home visit and conference with Mr. and Mrs. Young.

The visit provides evidence that the Youngs are struggling, both economically and emotionally, and John's acting-out behaviors are symptomatic of high levels of stress at home. Sam, a truck driver, is in and out of work and rarely at home. There is very little food in the Youngs' dilapidated two-bedroom trailer. Alice, overwhelmed and confused by the family's circumstances, shows signs of stress and depression. She has no job, no car, and few friends; her health is poor.

Daughter Amy is obviously unhappy, and John's behavior at school is getting worse.

When the team meets with Alice, they discover some important strengths. Alice is very eager to participate in any available services, she has significant support from her extended family, her family unit is intact and her husband is currently employed. There are critical deficits as well: Alice did not finish high school, she worries because Amy had not had a physical exam in over four years, she confides that John tried to run away from home last month, and she admits she frequently argues with her husband over family finances.

Together, the team and the Youngs work to develop the *family care coordination plan*. The plan includes health services for Amy, counseling for John, career counseling for Alice, and economic and educational services for the family.

With the plan in place, the Youngs' situation starts to improve. After talking with the full-service

---

- Protective services case work (week days)
- Civic and parent groups (after hours)
- Economic services (weekdays, walk-in, or by appointment)
- Graduation enhancement program
- Health services: registered nurse, psychologist, mobile health unit (school hours)
- Juvenile Alternative Services program (school hours)
- Parent involvement center and workshops
- Sheriff's department prevention activities
- Volunteer tutors

Box 13–7 provides a description of comprehensive support for two children with special needs and their par-

ents. From reading this description, can you envision how Dustin and his family would benefit from such comprehensive support?

Fortunately, Central Middle School has a strong school-linked, community-linked program. Through it, for example, Dustin receives the opportunity to participate in after-school activities and to enroll in summer school. The moving word is *opportunity*. Dustin is not compelled to take advantage of these opportunities, and in fact he has not done so. The reason is that he and his family lack the transportation necessary for him to stay after school or to attend summer school and be brought home safely. Karen, Juan, and the family have a car but not the money to pay for it to be insured or even to run reliably. The school bus schedule accommodates

Benefiting from Full-Service Schools   continued

school's adult career options counselor, Alice enrolls in night-time adult basic education classes. She also volunteers in the school's computer lab and signs up for dance lessons on Wednesday nights, all on site at the full-service school. The school's onsite registered nurse assesses Amy's condition and refers her to Children's Medical Services for a complete physical exam. Amy is also found eligible for a Private Industry Council program that pays students while they learn practical job skills. Through the school's onsite child care referral office, John is certified for an after-school latchkey program—instead of after-school mischief. He is placed in an onsite early intervention program that incorporates technology into the curriculum, and the health service psychologist provides insight into effective behavioral interventions for his teacher.

Alice and Sam begin family counseling sessions with a mental health professional who offers evening ap-pointments at the full-service school, and at the suggestion of John's teacher they check out educational materials from the parent involvement center. At the school's economic services office, the Youngs apply for and are approved for food stamps. Alice attends a parenting workshop on adolescents, sponsored by the school counselors.

Where are the Youngs today? Four years after becoming involved with the full-service school, Alice has received her GED and is employed as a data entry clerk. Amy, diagnosed with a rare disorder, is undergoing a regimen of medication designed to help her body develop normally. She recently won a gold medal at the Special Olympics. John has had no further brushes with the law, and his grades, attendance, and attitude improved so much he was mainstreamed to regular education classes. Sam, still a truck driver, recently began more stable employment, thanks to information he re-ceived from the full-service school's new job services terminal. The family no longer receives, or needs, food stamps. When the family became ineligible for Medicaid because of its increased income, Amy and John were able to enroll in a new school-based, affordable, comprehensive health insurance plan called Healthy Kids, for a fee of $5 each per month.

The Youngs' story is true; only their names and identifying details have been changed to ensure confidentiality. Alice in involved with school and school-related issues every day. She works with the classroom teacher to keep both children on track. She attends parenting sessions and checks out educational materials for use at home. Her new interest in education for herself has made her a powerful role model for her children. The Youngs grow and learn—as a family—every day because of their involvement with a full-service school.

Source: From *Building a Full-Service School: A Step-by-Step Guide,* by C. Calfee, F. Wittwer, and M. Meredith, 1998, San Francisco: Jossey-Bass.

Dustin for regular school hours during the fall and spring but not for after-school or summer school. And walking home can be perilous: Dustin has to pass through urban jungles—those places ripe with drug trade, crack houses, drive-by shootings, gang wars, and teen-on-teen violence. Whatever the school-linked services has done (such as providing Dustin with new clothes or a referral to the local mental health clinic), it cannot surmount the total effects of the environment in which Dustin and Karen live. And it is, as we have said, the totality of that environment that plays such a devastating role in Dustin's life at school. To ask Central Middle School to be effective in Dustin's life is to ask for a radical change in the world in which he—and so many other of Mr. Antos' students—live. Schools have their

limits; the consequence is that Dustin, other students, and faculty are limited.

Linking Our Themes

Creating a Reliable Alliance

By now, you know how important it is to infuse the eight obligations of a reliable alliance into all of your partnership opportunities. Figure 13–8 provides suggestions for how best to create this reliable alliance. Review the figure carefully, and generate additional ideas for empowering actions that you can take and disempowering actions to avoid.

FIGURE 13–8

Creating a Reliable Alliance: Emphasis on Extending Learning into Home and Community

Obligations	Issues	Disempowering Actions	Empowering Actions
Knowing yourself	You are interested in Group Action Planning, but you know that you have a tendency to overcommit yourself and then experience stress because you are so busy.	Even though it's not feasible, commit to starting an Action Group for six students.	Commit to starting an Action Group for one student and encourage a colleague or friend who may be a potential facilitator of another group to join you. After she has learned the process, encourage her to start a group for another student.
Knowing families Family characteristics	A family who has just recently moved to the community where you teach is interested in starting an Action Group but doesn't know anyone to invite.	Suggest to the family that they wait until they meet people and have a social network from which to draw.	Facilitate a MAPs gathering to learn more about the student and family. Brainstorm with the family about community resources to consider (such as Big Brother/Big Sister Programs, religious organizations, and community recreation programs).
Family interaction	A mother's partner (who is gay) is interested in helping the student in your class with homework, but she doesn't know the best way to go about it.	Ignore the partner because of your own values related to gay lifestyles.	Set up a dialogue journal to send notes home with homework suggestions.
Family functions	A student in your class has asthma and is getting inadequate medical care; the family has no money or health insurance.	Send a note home and suggest to family members that they need to take their child to the doctor.	Contact the coordinator of integrated services who is at another school in your district and ask how a student in your school might be able to get services.
Family life cycle	Parents refuse to allow their teenager to go out during evenings or weekends because they are afraid of the impeding behavior that might occur.	Consider out-of-school issues to be outside of the realm of your professional responsibility.	Facilitate friendships at school with peers, support them in using positive behavioral support with the student, and encourage them to include the student in evening and weekend classes.

FIGURE 13–8   CONTINUED

Creating a Reliable Alliance: Emphasis on Extending Learning into Home and Community

Obligations	Issues	Disempowering Actions	Empowering Actions
Honoring cultural diversity	A family who has been contacted to be involved in integrated services will not answer the door when someone makes a home visit, fearing loss of family privacy.	Decide that the family has "lost its chance" and drop them from a list of potential participants.	Arrange for someone from the family members' own cultural group to make contact with them and recognize that building a trusting relationship may take significant time and effort.
Affirming and building on family strengths	A parent of one of your students is particularly successful in modifying homework assignments and making homework sessions motivating and enjoyable.	When she makes suggestions, ignore them because you are the expert and you do not want her to think that she can influence school actions.	Brainstorm with her to elicit as many ideas as possible that you can incorporate into homework modifications and arrange for her to share her ideas with other families.
Promoting family choices	Parents of a student with AD/HD are worried about the problems that their child is having during after-school hours when they both are working and there is no one to provide child care.	Tell them that you strongly encourage them to take action before there is a serious problem with neighbors or others who live close by.	Provide them with information on the comprehensive school-linked services program and ask if they would like to receive information on community resources for after-school child care.
Envisioning great expectations	Parents have requested that their child with serious impeding behavior be fully included.	Tell the parents that full inclusion is out of the question and that if the student doesn't improve he will likely be transferred to a special school.	Get information from www.pbis.org about successful inclusion for students with impeding behavior.
Using interpersonal communication skills	In an Action Group, the father of a student in your class repeatedly criticizes his daughter for being overweight.	Tell the father that you think his comments are rude and that he is contributing to a negative atmosphere within the meetings.	Invite the father to share what he perceives to be his daughter's strengths and needs as well as his concerns about her. Brainstorm with him about ways that his concerns can be addressed in a constructive manner.
Warranting trust and respect	Family members share with you that they feel very embarrassed when they are in public and their child with impeding behavior goes up to strangers and makes inappropriate remarks.	Tell the family that you are not embarrassed, and they should not be either.	Listen empathetically to what they are saying and ask what they think would be helpful in becoming more comfortable; ask if they have ever had the opportunity to talk with other families who face similar situations.

FIGURE 13–9

Strengthening Family Resources: Emphasis on Extending Learning into Home and Community

Motivation	What You Can Do	Knowledge/Skills	What You Can Do
Self-efficacy	Encourage parents who have been particularly successful with their own Action Group to consider being facilitators for a family who needs the support of an Action Group.	Information	Provide families with information on Action Groups and ask them to consider whether they would be interested in starting one.
Perceived control	Encourage family members to suggest the amount of homework they believe is reasonable for their son or daughter to complete on a regular basis.	Problem solving	Problem solve with families about the triggers of their child's impeding behavior and make environmental adaptations to eliminate or reduce those triggers.
Great expectations	Encourage families who live in a violent neighborhood and are receiving integrated services on violence prevention to maintain hope that their neighborhood can become a safety rather than a danger zone.	Life management	Encourage families to help their child develop time-management skills for completing homework assignments. Provide concrete and practical tips.
Energy	Ask the parents how integrated services can help relieve them of anxiety about providing for their son or daughter and give them a break from assuming so much logistical and emotional responsibility.	Communication skills	Use an answering machine at school to leave messages about homework completion.
Persistence	When episodes of impeding behavior occur, remind the parents how much progress has been made and how you will be a reliable ally with them until the problem behavior is practically nonexistent.		

Strengthening Family Factors

Your own actions in creating an empowering context can enhance family motivation as well as the motivation of yourself and all team members. As you reflect on figure 13–9, we encourage you to make the link in your own thinking and actions between what you do and the impact that it has on others.

Summary

It is by now common knowledge that children are full-time learners; they need not be six-hour students, restricted to schools as the only source of their development.

Extending children's learning into their homes and communities does not always occur incidentally. A haphazard approach will produce haphazard results. Because children and youth with disabilities, more than other students, need systematic approaches to learning in order to help them generalize what they learn and make their learning durable over time, schools and families have developed several approaches to extend their learning.

Group Action Planning puts into effect an action-oriented process whereby family members, the student with a disability, family friends, and professionals all collaborate to arrange the student's environment so that it satisfies the student's needs and preferences. It is a five-step process that converts the "great expectations" visioning of other future-planning techniques (for example, MAPs—see chapter 9) into an implementation plan addressed by all members of the group.

Homework need not be onerous for students or their families, but it often is. Collaboration between schools and families can make homework beneficial; here, the key is for schools and families to be sensitive to each other's and the student's preferences, strengths, and needs. Indeed, when schools and parents collaborate around homework, they develop the habit and techniques of collaborating around other issues and challenges.

A challenge of extending learning into home and community is finding ways to develop positive behavioral support approaches for impeding behaviors. New models are being developed that address positive behavioral support on a school-wide basis—clear expectations and positive feedback available to all students, individualized interventions in school settings available for students who need moderately pervasive support, and comprehensive services across multiple environments for students requiring intense support. Research has been particularly encouraging of the successful results that can accrue when positive behavioral support is implemented systematically.

Integrated services provide a single point of access to the wide variety of services that children and youth with disabilities (and those who do not have disabilities) and their families need. They consolidate services and then ensure that the services comprehensively and holistically address student and family needs.

To meet Dustin Neil is to be delighted. The raw material is all there; sure, his dysgraphia is a problem, and, sure, his behaviors are a problem. But those are not—at this point in his life—insurmountable barriers; at least, they aren't if Central and other federal, state, local, and private agencies can be more effective in addressing the environmental challenges facing Dustin and his family.

And to meet his mother, Karen, is also a delight. True, she is a recovered abuser of alcohol and drugs; true, she has unmet health care needs, especially dental needs; true, she never finished high school (but had three children, each a year apart); and true, she has been up and down, and up and down again, always starting something (such as her GED) but finding that her own mental health challenges block her from completing what she knows she must do. But she has a dream and is working toward it, by studying for the GED, instructing herself in American Sign Language (ASL), and investigating how to attend community college to become more proficient at ASL.

To be invited to their home is to be invited into a family steeped in economic poverty. Yet it is also to be invited into a home full of what Karen calls "determination"—"self will that comes from within, that says that we're tired of living as we've been living and are going to change."

And to go to their home after talking with Jim Antos at Central Middle School and hearing his dreams ("just one solid adult for each child," "a team of people who can buffer life outside of school from life within school"), and to do that in the company of the Action Group team is to realize how essential—yes, essential—is the linkage between home and school.

It is no exaggeration to say that if it were not for Central educators and the Action Group, Dustin and Karen would be headed down a long and winding road, one that ultimately and almost invariably would lead to an unfortunate door, the door of lost opportunities and desperate lives.

That is not the case, however: A powerful connection exists between Central on the one hand and Dustin, Karen, and their family on the other. That connection is the best assurance any of them have that the long and winding road will lead to a different door: It is not inevitable that Dustin will drop out of school and live on the economic margins of society. Karen's dream can come true: A better life for her family can result. But it takes a school and home connection to support her, Dustin, and Central in pursuing that dream.

Chapter Fourteen

Attending and Volunteering at School

If you were to put Pat Boyd and John and Jane Hoyt into the same room and ask only one question—"What do you truly have in common?" the most correct answer would not be "Andrew, Nick, and Grace Hoyt." That would be correct enough: Pat taught Andrew (now 16), is teaching Nick (14), and will teach Grace (11) in the gifted-talented program at Central Junior High School in Lawrence, Kansas.

But the most correct answer would be "We are restoring parents' rights to be involved in their children's education."

Pat believes something has gone wrong in American schools. "The schools have removed families from teaching. We haven't built on the overlapping environments of home and school. We have set ourselves up as the experts. We have treated parents as phenomena to be set aside, as people whom we have to deal with, reluctantly."

To counterbalance what has gone wrong, Pat has her own creed about schools, professionals, and families. It goes something like this:

"Parents and teachers are invested partners, invested in each other and the children. Teachers are not giving families anything new. We are returning to them what was taken from them. Parents, the school belongs to you."

As director of the Excalibur Choir and a teacher in the gifted-talented program at Central, Pat puts that creed into effect in the most remarkable way. When Andrew and then Nick expressed an interest in participating in Excalibur, together with John and Jane, they met the creed head on.

Pat told the boys that they had to keep a certain grade-point average, that they had to attend 7:00 A.M. rehearsals (with no "ifs/ands/buts" about it), and that they had to help raise money for the choir's activities. "Raising the standard," the Hoyts noted, "created an instant positive peer group for the boys, because the discipline thinned the ranks of the uncommitted kids."

Pat's creed did more than raise the standards for the students. It set a high one for their parents, too.

"Pat invited us to participate in Excalibur. Well, 'invite' is not exactly it. Truth be told, she expected our participation."

To participate meant that parents and students set the agenda for the choir's performances and decided how to raise money and to which local charity it should be donated.

"Partnership with Pat is a myriad of little instances," Jane and John say. It consists of her knowing the names of all the children in the choir and their parents' names, too. It entails understanding how and why family members respond to their children in certain ways. It means being interested in the details of the family's life. It means singing at the weddings and funerals. It means treating families such as the Hoyts as competent and trustworthy people.

Ask Pat how she goes about her work, and she replies, "I am passionate about investing in the families. I am honest with them. I give parents tasks to do. I ask them to write the home-school handbook. I get families into the art rooms and photography dark rooms, and on the stage with their kids. I give them something tactile to

do. I help families, their kids, and the school work alongside each other. We get to see each other as people, not as role-holders. We reduce the remoteness between us. I ask upper-grade parents to guide lower-grade parents. Teachers guide families. Families guide us. We bring each other along."

Bringing each other along has a curious effect on families. "We become real to our children and their friends, and they become real to us." Becoming real occurs because John and Jane are disc jockeys at the winter formal, invite their children's friends to learn how to garden, show them how to weave, make uniforms for them, help them build mazes for their science projects, teach them dance steps from the 1960s, and push them around school in their wheelchairs. "Pat articulates and practices what we feel inside, that we are part of our children's education," say the Hoyts.

Pat's parent-empowerment approach means the Hoyts get to become friends with other families. "There is a community that wants us. That is healing. It is restorative. We see our children are happier than we were. The pain of our school years vanishes, and we have a peace about our own pasts. It's all because we have had the opportunity to be involved. It is because we are valued and respected as co-educators. She expected our participation, and she demanded it. That's how we came to trust each other. We are part of a trusting community . . . a community that begins with Pat and extends to our children, their friends, and their friends' families."

Ask Pat about a trusting community, and she says that "we" is its central word. But "we" and community can't exist where authority is the value that drives the schools and where "we" has a unilateral meaning, referring only to educators who have and want to keep authority.

"We" is a trilateral "we." It consists of the students, their families, and the teachers. "We" comes alive because of the highly participatory experiences of co-educating children and each other writing handbooks, developing photos, and singing together.

When the parents cleaned out a room at Central, painted it, and designated it as "our place," they engaged in the tactile act of empowering themselves: They invited themselves into school.

Who found the unused room? Yes, it was Pat Boyd. And who filled it up? Yes, it was eager families like the Hoyts and creative teachers like Pat. Filling up a place, a room that's a metaphor for co-educating each other, for collective empowerment.

Andrew, Nick and Grace Hoyt. (1995)

You have already learned about five opportunities for partnerships. This chapter will present a sixth opportunity: attending and volunteering at school. Figure 14–1 highlights this opportunity within the empowerment framework.

What are parents' views on attending and volunteering at school? A nationwide telephone survey of adults with at least one child in public school reported that 91 percent of parents agreed that it is "extremely important" for parents to be involved in their children's school, in order for their children to get a quality education (Bennett, Petts, & Blumenthal, 1998). Approximately half of the parents indicated that they believe that most parents do not know what is going on at school, and over half of the parents indicated that schools do not do a good job of keeping parents well informed about what is going on. In another national opinion survey of over 1,000 parents of children in public school, 83 percent of the parents reported that their most important job is attending to their child's learning at home as contrasted to being actively involved in school activities (Farkas, Johnson, & Duffett, 1999).

What special issues arise if and when parents of children with exceptionalities attend and volunteer at their children's schools? The answer depends on the school and its staff; that is, it depends on the *context*. For Jane and John Hoyt, the issue is meeting Pat Boyd and her creed head on: the invitations, expectations, and demands for their participation and coeducation. For families whose children have disabilities or are gifted, the issue depends on the degree to which their children are being educated in inclusive settings. When parents attend functions at special schools attended by only other students with similar special needs or talents, the context differs greatly from that of a typical elementary, middle, or secondary school. Given that the vast majority of students with exceptionalities do not attend special schools and that students with disabilities or special gifts/talents are in the minority in nearly all schools, their families will find that the majority of parents attending inclusive school events do not have children with special needs.

Two research studies have focused on the interactions of parents of children with and without exceptionalities in inclusive settings, and both of these studies report on families whose children are at the preschool level. One study indicated that there is limited interaction between families whose children have disabilities and those whose children do not have disabilities (Blacher & Turnbull, 1983). A later study investigated patterns of friendship and acquaintance among families in an integrated day-care program, when children first entered the program and again nine months later (Bailey

& Winton, 1989). Parents of the preschoolers with disabilities reported that they tended to interact about equally with parents of children with disabilities and parents of children without disabilities. The majority of parents of preschoolers without disabilities, however, reported that they were more likely to interact with other parents of children without disabilities than with parents of children with disabilities. Additionally, the parents of children with disabilities indicated that they were less satisfied with their knowledge of other parents than were parents of children without disabilities. Also, families of children with disabilities were more likely to become friends with families of other children with disabilities and were not as satisfied with their relationships with families whose children do not have disabilities.

How might a school facilitate intermingling among families? How might a school accomplish the coeducation of its students and create a trusting community such as the one that Pat Boyd accomplishes through her parent-empowerment efforts and the Excalibur Choir at Central Junior High School? Professionals can create partnerships around families' (1) attending school events, (2) contributing to classroom instruction, (3) contributing to other school tasks, (4) attending classes of their own, (5) participating in the parent-teacher organization, and (6) participating in family resource centers.

Attending School Events

Many schools have been creative in arranging a broad array of school events that attract families' interest and participation (Aronson, 1996; Carey, Lewis, & Farris, 1998; Daniels, 1996; Fowler & Corley, 1996; Funkhouser & Gonzales, 1997; Moles, 1996; Otterbourg, 1994). In our discussion, we will focus first on families' attending general school events. Then we will address issues associated with families attending extracurricular activities in which their children participate.

Attending General School Events

Schools typically offer various options for parents to attend general school events such as book fairs, school carnivals, and seasonal parties. Probably the most typical school event is the open house at the beginning of the school year, when families learn about their child's educational program. A national survey of public elementary schools indicated that 97 percent hold an open house or back-to-school night and approximately half of the schools report that most or all of the parents attend

FIGURE 14–1

Empowerment Framework: Collaborating for Empowerment in Attending and Volunteering at School

Education Context Resources

Family Resources

Motivation	Knowledge/Skills
Self-efficacy: Believing in our capabilities	Information: Being knowledgeable
Perceived control: Believing we can apply our capabilities to affect what happens to us	Problem solving: Knowing how to bust the barriers
Great expectations: Believing we will get what we want and need	Life management skills: Knowing how to handle what happens to us
Energy: Lighting the fire and keeping it burning	Communication skills: Being on the sending and receiving ends of expressed needs and wants
Persistence: Putting forth a sustained effort	

Opportunities for Partnerships	Obligations for Reliable Alliances
Opportunities Arise At . . .	*Reliable Alliances Consist of . . .*
Communicating among reliable allies	Knowing yourself
Meetings families' basic needs	Knowing families
Evaluating for special education	Honoring cultural diversity
	Affirming family strengths
Individualizing for appropriate education and placement	Promoting family choices
Extending learning in home and community	Envisioning great expectations
Attending and volunteering at school	Communicating positively
Advocating for systems improvement	Warranting trust and respect

Professional Resources

Motivation	Knowledge/Skills
Self-efficacy: Believing in our capabilities	Information: Being knowledgeable
Perceived control: Believing we can apply our capabilities to affect what happens to us	Problem solving: Knowing how to bust the barriers
Great expectations: Believing we will get what we want and need	Life management skills: Knowing how to handle what happens to us
Energy: Lighting the fire and keeping it burning	Communication skills: Being on the sending and receiving ends of expressed needs and wants
Persistence: Putting forth a sustained effort	

Collaborating for Empowerment

331

(Carey, Lewis, & Farris, 1998). In schools that offer a departmentalized curriculum, families frequently follow their child's schedule from class to class, having an opportunity to listen to each teacher describe the curriculum and to ask questions.

One of the particular issues to keep in mind for students with exceptionalities in inclusive settings is that some of the families' questions may differ from those of families whose children do not have special needs. For example, parents of a child with impeding behavior might attend their child's classes and worry about the teachers' frustration related to their child's behavior as well as about the frustration of other parents because their child's behavior is disrupting the class. On the other hand, parents of students who are gifted may listen to an overview of the year's curriculum knowing that their son or daughter mastered similar materials several years earlier.

Be sensitive to families' exceptionality-specific issues and concerns and develop approaches to respond to them. In meeting with a group of families, it is extremely difficult to address individual concerns; however, let families know that you will be available to meet with them separately at a later time to address their individual issues specifically.

A second issue to consider when families of children with exceptionalities attend general school events is that they may not know many of the other families. Often, families come to know other families because their own children are friends with children of other families. Have you noticed that families of students who are friends sit together at school events and experience a sense of having more in common with each other than with other families in the school? Indeed, many students with exceptionalities, particularly significant disabilities, often have fewer close friends and even acquaintances (Malka & Meira, 1996; Turnbull & Ruef, 1997). Just as they often feel on the periphery of student life, their isolation makes them feel on the periphery of family life at general school events. To welcome families into the school, increase the social relationships and friendships that their children experience. As schools welcome and include children and youth with exceptionalities in schools, their families may have the similar experience of being welcomed and included in the school at large. At general school events, introduce the families of students with exceptionalities to others and highlight their children's positive contributions to peers.

*A*ttending Extracurricular Activity Events

A national survey of public elementary schools reported that over 80 percent of the schools provided activities for parent attendance such as art events (for example, plays,

dances, and musical performances), sporting events, and science fairs or other academic events. Approximately one-third of the schools reported that most or all of the parents attended art events, and fewer schools reported that most or all of the parents attended science fairs/other academic events (19 percent) or sporting events (12 percent) (Carey, Lewis, & Farris, 1998). As compared to these figures representing the families of all students, it is likely that families of students with disabilities are underrepresented in attending such activities because many of their children have not had the same opportunities to participate in extracurricular events as their classmates who do not have disabilities (Falvey, Coots, & Terry-Gage, 1992; Harris, 1994; Morningstar, Turnbull, & Turnbull, 1995).

There are many reasons why this is so, including (1) an overemphasis on academic goals to the exclusion of other important student outcomes, (2) an assumption that students with exceptionalities will not be able to compete or participate successfully, (3) the placement of special classes in schools where the students in these classes do not match the age ranges of the students without exceptionalities and the resulting extracurricular activities are not as appropriate for the students with exceptionalities, and (4) schools' failure to have the necessary supplementary supports and services to enhance the student's success in extracurricular activities.

In our own family experience, it was not until our son, J. T., was in his last year of high school (at the age of 20) that he had his first opportunity to participate in an inclusive sports activity. He served as a manager for the school's football team, so our attendance at football games was a regular Friday night activity. Box 14–1 describes the collaboration that J. T.'s teacher and others at his school practiced to include him and us in school activities.

Why not earn a letter, not as a manager of the football team, but as a player? You may assume that some students with disabilities are not able to compete as players, but additional supports can help make that possible. For example, David Cain, a high school student with a severe emotional and behavioral disability, has had an incredibly successful experience as a member of his high school's football team. After spending most of his elementary and middle school years in a state residential facility, David came back home to live with his family and attend his local school. Although he very much wanted to participate in football, people feared that his unpredictable behavior and quick temper would escalate in a competitive contact sport such as football. To make football a successful experience for him, the local mental health center hired a paraprofessional who served as an assistant football coach, recognizing that it is far more economical to hire a

J. T.'s Letter Jacket

When Walt Whitman High School opened its doors for the fall 1987 semester, there walked, rolled, and was pushed into the building a much different group of students than ever before had attended the Bethesda, Maryland, school. For the first time, Whitman was including students with disabilities among its student body. Now, instead of just the college-bound sons and daughters of members of Congress and diplomats, lawyers and lobbyists, physicians and physicists, Whitman counted among its number students for whom supported employment and supported living were appropriate goals.

Among that group of students was J. T., our 20-year-old son. And as lead teacher of a special education class, there was Mary Morningstar. Mary's first goal for J. T. was his placement among the most high-status students in school—the football players, cheerleaders, and band members.

She figured that if J. T. could demonstrate his abilities as an assistant manager of the football team, he would meet all these youngsters and their families, show that he and his classmates belonged, and create a network of friends. Just as important, she calculated that if J. T. could do all that and also pick up the first-period roll from each classroom, he would have a positive impact on the faculty.

Mary's gamble paid off, big time. J. T. handed out towels to every player at every game, whether they needed a towel or not. His loyalty to the team, his insistence on traveling on the team bus to away games, and his school spirit and friendliness with the supporting crew of cheerleaders and musicians all opened up a world of inclusion for him.

Little did anyone know how much J. T. was included, and how successful he and Mary had been, until the fall sports banquet in mid-December. The banquet proceeded rather predictably, with a few speeches and the awarding of letters, "player of the week" mugs, and certificates to the junior varsity players and managers.

When, however, it came time for the varsity awards to be given, J. T.'s name was the first one called. "Jay Turnbull, assistant manager, has been with us for only one year, but he has made a significant contribution to our program. J. T., come up for your letter."

As J. T. walked toward the elevated platform where the coaches, school board members, and superintendent and principal sat, his awkward gait was faster than usual. His pride in himself was evident. So evident that, instead of allowing the letter to be handed down to him, he tried to mount the platform. Seeing that he was determined to stand with the dignitaries, some of them pulled him up, and players at nearby tables pushed him up.

Standing on the platform, he now received his letter. In his typical fashion, he patted himself on the back. Only then did the parents, players, and supporting crew notice, "That's J. T. up there. That's that young man with the towels."

The usual polite applause turned into a crescendo, peaked, abated, and rose again. That night, J. T. got more applause than any other player or manager, coach or volunteer.

A few minutes later, J. T., now seated at his table with his beaming parents and Mary Morningstar, had an unexpected visitor. The mother of the team's quarterback came to him, a jacket in her hand.

"J. T., all of us want you to know how much we appreciated your help. It will be a long while before you get your own letter jacket. So here's my son's. We want you to wear it until you get your own. You belong, and we want everyone to know that."

With this one simple gesture, J. T. was more than included; he was welcomed. Not by the players and supporting crew: They had already taken him in. No, he was welcomed by the parents of those academically elite young people. And we ourselves confirmed the direction for J. T.: inclusion now, inclusion forever . . . whatever it takes, however long it takes, with whoever will be our reliable allies.

---

paraprofessional than to pay over $100,000 per year to keep him in a state residential facility.

When David demonstrated inappropriate behavior during practices or games, the assistant coach immediately responded by providing him with the supports to redirect his behavior appropriately. Participating on the team was a major ticket to acceptance for David in terms of establishing a network of friends and status among his classmates as a school contributor. Likewise, his football participation is a major source of family pride and a catalyst for his family's developing a vision of greater hope for his future (Turnbull, Turnbull, Shank, & Leal, 1999).

On the other hand, families can participate in a wide range of extracurricular activities, whatever their children's exceptionalities. The Excalibur Choir at Central Junior High includes students who have physical disabilities and who are blind; it also includes their parents as contributors in one way or another. And because Pat Boyd insists on good grades and regular attendance, it includes students who are competent, disciplined, and committed.

You can create an empowering context for families to attend school events by including students with exceptionalities as full members of extracurricular activities. When children participate in events, it is far more likely that their family members will take an interest in the event, attend the special functions associated with the event, and experience for themselves a feeling of genuine membership in the school community. To enhance extracurricular involvement, supplementary aids and services may be necessary, just as they are for a student's academic program. (You will recall that you learned about the IDEA requirement to specify supplementary aids and services as part of the IEP.) Indeed, the curriculum adaptations that enable students to participate in regular physical education programs also can enable them to engage in extracurricular sports activities (Block, 1994; Block & Malloy, 1998). Box 14–2 includes tips for increasing successful participation of students in extracurricular activities.

As you attend extracurricular activities, introduce parents or students with disabilities to other families. Ask the "experienced" families to mentor the new ones, as Pat Boyd asks the upper-grade families to set examples for and bring along the lower-grade families at Central Junior High. Work to build a trusting and inclusive community, as Pat and the families have.

Contributing to Classroom Instruction

Families have expertise that can enhance the breadth and depth of classroom instruction. Frequently, educators have concerns about how much time it takes to individualize instruction and attend to their many instructional responsibilities. Families can contribute to classroom instruction by developing instructional materials, adaptive equipment, or games; copying and collating instructional materials; grading papers; tutoring individual students during or after class; and serving as instructional aides (Vatterott, 1994). As instructional aides, families can participate in field trips, volunteer to come into the classroom and serve in the capacity somewhat similar to a paraprofessional's, and make guest presentations to classes in their particular area of expertise. Jane Hoyt teaches her children's schoolmates about weaving and gardening, and John teaches them about renovating houses and doing the "twist and shout" dances of 30 years earlier. Individualizing for students means individualizing for the participation of their families.

A Massachusetts elementary school implemented an innovative approach by having a Friday Club in which

TIPS

BOX 14–2

Including Students with Exceptionalities in Extracurricular Activities

- Identify activities based on the student's preferences and strengths. Involve the sponsor, coach, or teacher of the extracurricular activities in collaborative decision making to share a vision of the student's participation and develop a plan for supplementary aids and services.

- Consider the appropriateness of providing peer support.

- If necessary, provide additional training and skill development to help ensure that the student has the expertise and capability for meaningful participation.

- Encourage the parents to make friends with other parents whose children are participating and to be an active contributor to the group effort.

- Encourage the parents to initiate invitations to the other children who participate in the activities to have additional time for companionship outside of school activities.

- Encourage the parents to contribute to the extracurricular activity by providing transportation, snacks, supervision, fundraising, or other needed support.

- Incorporate the student's experience into academic subjects such as writing a story during language arts about the extracurricular activity or integrating it into other subject areas as appropriate.

many parents and other community members participated (Fowler & Corley, 1996). Teachers were freed up every Friday from 8:00 to 10:00 A.M. while parent and community activities engaged students in creative learning opportunities such as building doll houses, learning to play soccer, cooking, designing stage sets, solving problems, learning Spanish, and participating in martial arts. It was a win-win situation in that benefits accrued for students, families, community members, and teachers.

Within the special education field, volunteering in the classroom has been more prevalent during early childhood services (Stayton & Karnes, 1994) than during elementary and secondary years. One of the most prominent examples of parents as classroom instructors within the early childhood special education field is the Regional Intervention Program, which started in Nashville, Tennessee, and has been expanded to communities throughout the United States and several other countries (Timm, 1993). The Regional Intervention Program incorporates parents of young children with behavioral disorders and developmental delays as the primary teachers of their children as well as trainers of other parents and evaluators of program effectiveness. This program model provides extensive training for parents in behavioral intervention, with all parents being expected to acquire skills enabling them to be effective teachers of their own children and other children in the program.

A useful approach for securing parents to contribute to classroom instruction is a model that takes a "funds-of-knowledge perspective" (Moll, 1992, p. 21). Figure 14–2 describes a sample of the household funds of knowledge of just one class.

By interviewing families and asking about the resources and expertise they might share to supplement the teacher's curriculum (Moll, 1992), teachers become aware of the wealth of knowledge and information from which they can draw. A particular strength of this approach is that it builds on families' cultural values, traditions, and diversities (Gallimore, Weisner, Kaufman, & Bernheimer, 1989).

FIGURE 14–2

A Sample of Household Funds of Knowledge

Agriculture and Mining	Economics	Household Management	Material & Scientific Knowledge	Medicine	Religion
Ranching and farming	Market values	Budgets	Construction	Contemporary medicine	Catechism
Horsemanship (cowboys)	Appraising	Child care	Carpentry	Drugs	Baptisms
Animal husbandry	Renting and selling	Cooking	Roofing	First aid procedures	Bible studies
Soil and irrigation systems	Loans	Appliance repair	Masonry	Anatomy	Moral knowledge and ethics
Crop planting	Labor laws		Painting	Midwifery	
Hunting, tracking, dressing	Building codes		Design and architecture	Folk medicine	
Mining	Consumer knowledge		Repair	Herbal knowledge	
Timbering	Accounting		Airplane	Folk cures	
Minerals	Sales		Automobile	Folk veterinary cures	
Blasting			Tractor		
Equipment operation and maintenance			House maintenance		

Source: From p. 22 of Moll, L. C. (1992). Bilingual classroom studies and community analysis: Some recent trends. *Educational Researcher, 21*(2), 20–24. Copyright 1992 by the American Educational Research Association. Reprinted by permission of the publisher.

"Professor" Jimmy Pérez

Jimmy Pérez is an unlikely candidate to be a "courtesy professor" or co-teacher at his daughter's school. But Jimmy is an unusual man, and the teacher, Jo-Anne Wilson Keenan, is an unusual teacher.

As the school year was coming to a close, Blanca Pedraza, her father Jimmy, and her mother Evelyn had not yet visited school together. That's curious, thought Jo-Anne, because Evelyn had come into school the year before, albeit briefly, and seemed to support Blanca to learn to read and write; Did Blanca's parents care about her?

The answer was an unequivocal *yes.* When they appeared at school for the dress rehearsal for the spring performance, Jo-Ann told Jimmy, "I'd love to have your family come in and spend time in the classroom. It would mean a lot to Blanca if you'd come. Many of the families have joined us. You could tell about some things your family does together. You could show us some of your photographs. What are your hobbies?

An hour later, Jimmy entered his daughter's classroom, a portfolio of his artwork under his arm. To an increasingly admiring crowd of students, he displayed the cartoons he had drawn and told why he draws. "Drawing is like your feelings. You know, you're feeling sad, you're feeling happy, you're feeling bad; you know, some things come out the way you feel."

There soon appeared another facet of Jimmy—his career as a martial artist. Over a 13-year period of study, he had earned three black belts. He spoke with spiritual respect for this ancient art, telling how the art form blends mind, body, and spirit into a disciplined whole, stressing that the students should never use the martial arts for aggression, and debunking the cartoon ninjas as inaccurate caricatures.

Discipline, Jimmy said, is the key to painting and to martial arts. That lesson—from a gentle and immensely talented man—showed again how valuable parents are as teachers. He was the expert that day, the person to whom the students turned for approval and assistance. His was an important lesson, not just that discipline is necessary for all endeavors, but that parents can be great allies for their children's teachers.

Source: Adapted from Keenan, J. W., Willett, J., & Solsken, J. (1993). Focus on research. Constructing an urban village: School/home collaboration in a multicultural classroom. *Language Arts, 70,* 204–214. Copyright 1993 by the National Council of Teachers of English. Used with permission.

An excellent example of using a funds-of-knowledge approach is Jo-Anne Wilson Keenan's first- and second-grade classroom (Keenan, Willett, & Solsken, 1993). Before Jo-Anne used a funds-of-knowledge approach, parents of her students typically only attended open houses, parent-teacher conferences, and special performances. To change the school so it would support families, rather than expecting the families to change to support the school, Jo-Anne invited her student's families to participate in classroom instruction, and 20 out of 24 children's parents accepted her invitation. An example of one father's presentation is included in box 14–3.

The student body in this school was approximately 75 percent Puerto Rican and African American students and 25 percent Euro-American students. Many of them were regarded as "at risk," and 86 percent qualified for free or reduced-fee school lunches. Within Jo-Anne's class of 24, 20 students had a family member who visited the class at least once. Like Jimmy Pérez, these parents had a wealth of valuable information to share, especially about multicultural traditions.

The visitors brought into the classroom the languages and cultures of the diverse community served by the school. The children heard each of these—Spanish, Polish, Arabic, Hebrew, Italian, French, and various dialects of English spoken; and they learned about the different ways that families lived, ate, worked, played, and celebrated. (Keenan et al., 1993, p. 205)

Jo-Anne offers some tips in box 14–4 about how to incorporate the funds-of-knowledge approach.

Jo-Anne highlights the reciprocal benefits to herself and the families as they create a reliable alliance with each other. In terms of teacher benefits, she comments:

English is the predominant language in our classroom, but home languages include Spanish and Polish. Home cultures are Polish, Puerto Rican, Irish American, Italian American, and African American. Since many of the students are Puerto Rican, I have recently been attempting to read in Spanish, and I employ the assistance of my students and their families in doing so. The children and their parents seem to enjoy helping me. They can also help us to understand whether or not information found in our books

Families' Contributions to Classroom Instruction

- Inviting parents to become curriculum partners allows us to discover the often unsuspected knowledge and teaching capabilities of parents and to tap them as valuable resources for classroom learning.

- Collaborating with parents requires that we confront our own fears of difference and open our classrooms to discussions of topics that may raise tensions among the values of different individuals, groups, and institutions.

- In co-teaching with parents, the curriculum often emerges in the give and take of what may appear to be noninstructional conversation, as the children make connections to the visitor, the teacher, school subjects, and each other through stories.

- Constructing equitable relations with parents and students requires that we acknowledge our limitations, share our vulnerabilities, and take the risk of letting them teach us about their languages and cultures.

Source: Keenen, J. W., Willett, J., & Solsken, J. (1993). Focus on research. Constructing an urban village: School/home collaboration in a multicultural classroom. *Language Arts, 70,* 204–214. Copyright 1993 by the National Council of Teachers of English. Used with permission.

is authentic to their upbringing and culture. (Keenan et al., 1993, p. 211)

In terms of family benefits, she comments:

In almost every family visit, especially those of low-income and minority families, there have been signs that the parents did not expect to be seen as capable teachers of children. They did not expect the cultural knowledge and practices of their families to be valued in the classroom, and they did not expect to be treated as partners in the education of their own children and children of other cultural backgrounds. It is hard for a "village" to raise a child well, unless each member of the community is an equal among equals. (Keenan et al., 1993, p. 212)

Reflect on what it means to view families as equals among equals and how that view contributes to the motivation and knowledge/skills components of their own empowerment. What impact might being a valued classroom contributor have on Mr. Pérez's self-efficacy, perceived control, great expectations, information, and communication skills?

Finally, what difference does such a collaborative instructional partnership have on the reliable alliance that you might have with families? This is one of the benefits that Jo-Anne pointed out:

The most satisfying part of the families' visits to our classroom is that they lead to a greater appreciation and understanding of each other as people, and this understanding generates an intimate level of communication that was unattainable in the past. Just before Miriam's mother left, she apologized for not having been able to come in the previous week. She then told me about a tragedy that had befallen the family.

I told her that we had experienced a similar sorrow in my family. We spent the next few minutes sharing details and consoling each other. The stories of our families have become common ground in my classroom. The support we give each other once we share the joys and sorrows of those stories is the common bond of our community. (Keenan et al., 1993, p. 211)

Describing the "trusting community" that they entered through the Excalibur Choir and the parent-empowerment project that Pat Boyd directs, the Hoyts recalled that, when one of their children was involved in a minor incident with the local police, they confided their concerns to not only Pat but also other families. Alarmed that they would be so candid about something that most families would hide, some of their friends asked, in effect, how they could be so open. The answer: We can trust each other because we have come to know each other through the choir and other activities.

That common ground is the basis of experiencing the synergistic communities we discussed in chapter 3. Once synergy among participants is present, it is very likely that there will be collective empowerment for all.

Contributing to Other School Tasks

Families can make meaningful contributions to other school tasks. They can be involved in activities as volunteers, committee members, and full- or part-time employees. Their noninstructional volunteer activities can include activities that enliven everyone (such as John Hoyt's being a disc jockey or Jane Hoyt's being a member of the school choir), or they can include typical ones such as substituting for teachers during lunch duty, bus duty, or planning time; collecting money and student forms associated with various school activities; handling lunch money; organizing the library; raising money; or engaging in a broad range of other activities (Vatterott, 1994). A national survey of parents reported that of 10 different types of parent involvement in school activities, the three activities in which over half of the parents reported that they would be "very comfortable" included volunteering to help supervise and guide students in after-school activities, helping with school events such as a career day or book sale, and volunteering to chaperone their child's class trip or party (Farkas, Johnson, & Duffett, 1999).

Families of students with disabilities often have extensive expertise related to exceptionality-specific issues. They can be extremely helpful in providing information for educators about the nature of a child's exceptionality and specific ways that the child needs to be supported. They can also provide assistance with supplementary aids and services, such as providing sign-language interpretation for school plays and musical performances (Luetke-Stahlman, Luetke-Stahlman, & Luetke-Stahlman, 1992).

School districts find it helpful to have one or more parent liaisons who can identify family preferences, provide a broad range of opportunities, and offer networking support to make such volunteer efforts especially beneficial (Moles, 1996; Rich, 1993). Working collaboratively with parent liaisons or other educators and families, you can identify the full range of responsibilities you will have as an educator. Consider the ones where you would especially appreciate family assistance. Work with others to coordinate family contributions in a systemic way. If the administration of the school where you teach is not interested in setting up a systemic program, consider how the families of the students you teach might collaborate to accomplish various school tasks. In building on the preferences, interests, and time availability of parents and other family members, you might discover a whole reservoir of assistance that would be empowering not only for you but also for them. That is Professor Jimmy Pérez's lesson to you.

Attending Classes of Their Own

Closely related to integrated services (which you learned about in chapter 13) are the opportunities that many schools provide for parents to come to school to participate in classes of their own. For example, at Paul Robeson High School in Chicago, computer training and stress-reduction classes are available to families in a class titled, "Strategy to Empower Parents and Students." A group of parents who received computer instruction became interested in writing and printing a school newsletter; that interest in turn improved home-school communication. Parents also have the opportunity to participate in classes to learn to write proposals, and several of the proposals were funded to benefit the school. Another class teaches families how to obtain community services. All these classes invited parents to come to the school to expand their own information and problem-solving skills (Lynn, 1994). Other examples of innovative practices of parents attending classes include the following:

- Buhreh Elementary School in Cleveland offers family math and science workshops in which children and families spend an evening at school working collaboratively on math and science.
- The Highlands Elementary School in Shawnee Mission, Kansas offered an evening program of classes for parents, children, and families, including resume writing and stock investing (for adults), exploring the Internet and discussing exotic pets (for students), and cooking and entertaining Italian-style (for adults and children). Classes were taught by parents and community members for other parents and community members (Funkhouser & Gonzales, 1998; National PTA website).
- Ferguson Elementary School in Philadelphia offers an adult evening school in conjunction with a nearby university. Classes are offered in computer literacy, self-esteem, English as a second language, and Spanish literacy. The university provides stipends for baby-sitters to provide care for the participants' children (Funkhouser & Gonzales, 1998).
- The Alamo Navajo Community School in Magaleno, New Mexico, broadcast programs in Navajo to parents from a local radio station operated by the reservation's school board (Funkhouser & Gonzales, 1998).

Box 14–5 includes a description of a literacy program for families who are homeless.

On a less formal basis, families can be colearners with their children, becoming involved as Pat Boyd insists they must in learning the rudiments and refinements of photography, all the way from loading a camera, framing and composing the photograph, and developing the negatives, to displaying the finished product.

In terms of exceptionality-specific issues, families may be interested in attending workshops on topics such as legal rights, planning for life after high school, aug-

One Family at a Time

If you are a homeless parent, your child's education and even your own makes less of a difference to you than some basic necessities such as having a place to live, food on the table, and a reliable relationship with at least one adult who is involved with you and your child.

That's what Karen McGee learned in her role as reading coordinator of the Washoe County School District in Reno, Nevada. Naturally, Karen was concerned about the ability of district students to read.

She was especially worried about children whose families move frequently. These families are regarded as homeless because they do not have a single permanent address. They live in shelters or in trailer parks that rent on a week-by-week basis; they come to be known as "motel mothers."

It is often the case, Karen believed, that not only were her students deficient in their reading ability but so too were their parents. Their combined illiteracy, she was convinced, perpetuated a cycle of poverty. A solution, she hoped, would be to involve the students and

their parents together in a reading program.

What she learned is that her aspiration was realistic but her strategies were ill-conceived. She had planned to provide transportation to school, reading instruction by teachers and volunteers, and guidance on how the parents could encourage their children to read at home. None of those strategies worked as planned.

Instead, parent involvement occurred and was sustained when Karen and her colleagues provided food; when they solicited parents' participation by advertising an after-school program that was not focused on parent illiteracy (which stigmatizes parents) but was advertised and conducted as a "family fun night" in which reading instruction was only one of the activities; and when they established a personal relationship with the parents.

"We were dealing with survivors, and we had to admire their strengths," Karen concluded. To deal and to admire, Karen learned, resulted in a single bottom line: "Perhaps our most important discovery

was that human relationships must precede academic pursuits."

Unless the district's staff could see that their challenge was not one of education but of seeing life through a different prism, then there would be no benefit to the children or their parents. These were, after all, parents who would say that they "can't distinguish between the living experience and the learning experience."

Accordingly, the district's staff faced a job of persuasion—persuading the parents to become involved in a school system. Given that they themselves were illiterate and on the economic margin of society, the staff's first task was to listen to the parents talk about "their living conditions, their children, their relationships (with other adults), and problems with the law." Then, and only then, did they offer something that was fun for both the parents and their children: reading strategies that kept the parents involved and that taught them to read and to guide their children to read.

It's really a matter of relationships, food, and fun. But mostly, relationships.

Source: Adapted from "One family at a time." by K. McGee, April 1996, *Educational Leadership,* pp. 30–33.

---

mentative communication, and inclusion. Workshops on helping children develop talents, take tests, and improve behavior are also popular among families of general education students (Dauber & Epstein, 1993) and probably also would be of interest to many families of students with exceptionalities.

How can you find people to lead the workshops? Using a collaborative approach, survey possible speakers in terms of their unique expertise and resources. Create a pool of collaborators from among school staff members, families of students, and community citizens who have special interests in contributing to the life of the

school. A useful resource on exceptionality-specific information is the Parent Training and Information Program (see appendix A) and other exceptionality-related programs in your communities, such as Parent-to-Parent programs and parent support groups.

Participating in the Parent-Teacher Organization

Started in 1897 as the National Congress of Mothers, the Parent-Teacher Association (PTA) now has a membership of more than 6 million members in approximately 26,700 local units in each of the 50 states (National PTA website http://www.pta.org). The mission of the PTA is:

- to support and speak on behalf of children and youth,
- to assist parents in developing skills needed to be effective parents, and
- to encourage parents and other community citizens to be actively involved in the public schools.

The national PTA encourages local chapters to form committees for children and youth with exceptionalities. These committees can provide current information on the needs of students who receive special education and can network with organizations (such as the Council for Exceptional Children and other exceptionality-specific organizations), including those representing children who have disabilities as well as those who are gifted and talented.

PTAs have developed excellent materials on general topics related to enhancing self-esteem, expanding student participation in volunteer activities, participating in cultural arts, and becoming more knowledgeable on topics such as HIV/AIDS and drugs and alcohol. Additionally, they have helpful materials related to special education, including tips on how to advocate for children with special needs and descriptions of IDEA rights and responsibilities.

Some PTAs such as the PTA at the St. Michaels Elementary/Middle School in Maryland have taken particular interest in disability issues. This PTA organized a Disability Awareness Week, led by parents who had first-hand experience with individuals with disabilities. The program involved having speakers share disability-related information with students, demonstrating computer hardware and software that improves the daily life of people with disabilities, and having an improvisational youth theater group perform skits dealing with the emotional issues associated with having a disability. Students also participated in disability simulations that were followed by panel discussions with people with disabilities in which students shared their experiences. This PTA also sponsored a school-wide poster and essay contest in which students were asked to express their perspectives about the activities involved in the Disability Awareness Week. Of the 72 student entries, 20 received special recognition; and all entries were displayed in the school hallway. This is an excellent example of how a PTA can be a catalyst for educating the school community about disability and also involving families of students with disabilities in the process (PTA website).

Related to the general topic of family partnerships, it is noteworthy that the National PTA is working collaboratively with Dr. Joyce Epstein (see chapter 2) to develop standards for schools to follow in implementing Epstein's six-step parent partnership framework (National PTA, 1998). These PTA standards emphasize the importance of family-educational partnerships and are being promoted by not only the National PTA but also by state and local units. The PTA has distributed more than 180,000 copies of the national standards related to Epstein's framework.

Participating in Family Resource Centers

Many schools have organized family resource centers within the school building, where families may come to learn about volunteer activities and meet other families (Arson, 1996; Doktor & Poertner, 1996; Fowler & Corley, 1996; Funkhouser & Gonzales, 1998; Moles, 1999). Approximately one-third of all schools report having a parent resource center; another 12 percent indicate that they are in the process of developing a resource center (Carey, Lewis, & Farris, 1998). Of the schools that currently have parent resource centers, approximately one-third report that the center is infrequently or never used, almost half report somewhat frequent usage, and 14 percent report very frequent usage. Pat Boyd and the families at Central Junior High School have their own room, a physical and symbolic presence as coeducators.

Kentucky state legislation mandates family resource centers for all elementary schools in which 20 percent or more of the student body is eligible for free school meals (Doktor & Poertner, 1996). An example of the Kentucky network of parent resource centers is the Family Resource Center associated with the Cane Run Elementary School in Louisville, Kentucky (Funkhouser & Gonzales, 1998). A full-time coordinator is employed by the Family Resource Center and is assisted by an average of four parent volunteers each day. These volunteers help with data entry, telephones, and administrative work. In addition to helping to coordinate numerous volunteer activities, the Family Resource Center sponsors an affordable after-school program from 3:30 to 6:00 P.M. every day. Parent volunteers and paid staff provide tutoring, access to computers, karate classes, games, and other activities to the participating children. Families are charged $10 a week for the program; however, families unable to pay the weekly fee can waive it by volunteering their time at the school or the center. The principal commented, "We create an atmosphere where parents are truly comfortable to come into the school building. They want to come back, and they feel that they are part of the school" (Funkhouser & Gonzales, 1998, p. A-17).

A Comprehensive Program

Many schools that genuinely embrace families' attendance and volunteer efforts at school apply some or all five of the options we described. To illustrate how a range of different options can be merged within a single school, we will highlight the model developed by Professor James Comer at Yale University. The Comer model encourages schools to integrate collaboration options into the life of the school rather than just use them as adjunct programs to the school (Comer & Haynes, 1991; Comer, Haynes, Joyner, & Ben-Arie, 1996).

Comprising the Comer model are the following three components: *on text*

1. *School Planning and Management Team.* This team represents families, professional staff, and all nonprofessional support staff to carry out the three management operations of (a) developing and implementing a comprehensive school plan, including a focus on school climate and academics; (b) staff development to implement the plan; and (c) evaluation and modification of the school program as needed. The major goals include creating a sense of direction and providing a sense of program ownership and purpose to all stakeholders.

2. *Student and Staff Support Team.* This team is comprised of staff who have child development and mental health expertise, including the school psychologist, counselor, school nurse, special education teacher, pupil personnel workers, attendance officers, and others. The major goal is to address psychosocial issues, individual student concerns, and school-wide climate.

3. *Parent Team.* This team involves parents in all types of partnerships throughout the school. Parents are members of the PTA, serve as volunteers or as paid assistants in school functions, and select their fellow parents to represent them on the School Planning and Management Team. The program developers describe the essence of this approach as follows:

> In order to sustain a learning and caring community in which all adults feel respected and all children feel valued and motivated to learn and achieve, the work of the teams is driven by *three guiding principles—* consensus, collaboration, and no-fault—that nurture

a positive climate. (Comer, Haynes, & Joyner, 1996, p. 9)

The Parent Program has three levels. Level 3 includes five or six parents who are elected by other parents to represent them on the School Planning and Management Team. Working with other stakeholders on the Management Team, parent representatives contribute a strong community perspective and an important link to other parents. When parents expressed interest in learning more about how to access community services, the School Planning and Management Team planned a "Share Night," enabling community service providers to discuss their services with families. A large number of parents attended, primarily because the program directly responded to their top priority. Many families experience difficulty in school participation because of work schedules; therefore, the principal contacted employers, sought their collaboration in supporting families to attend school meetings, and received it.

Level 2 involves encouraging parents to attend and volunteer in school activities. Parents and staff work together in establishing the school calendar and participating in school events such as assemblies, parties, field trips, and athletic programs. Extending the volunteer work of families, a "Parent Assistant in the Classroom" program pays parents the minimum wage for 10 hours of work each week, with arrangements made so that deductions were not made from their welfare checks. On top of the 10 hours of paid work, parents frequently volunteered an additional 20 to 30 hours a week. Tips for carrying out level 2 activities are included in box 14–6.

> They were not assigned the clean-up or "dirty work" in the classroom or school; rather, they helped carry out the academic and social program of the classroom, assisted on field trips, and supported desirable behaviors of students within the school. Between 8 and 12 classroom parents, one in each class, became the core of the parent organization within the school. When they invited two friends each to help sponsor a school activity, 30–50 parents were then involved. (Comer & Haynes, 1991, p. 274)

Level 1 involvement is characterized by parents' attending the general activities of the school. Over a four-year period, as this program was implemented, attendance went from 15 to 30 parents at an activity such as a Christmas program to 400 parents. Approximately 250 parents, representing a student body of 300 students (with a majority of these being single parents), regularly attended most school activities. Program leaders placed special emphasis on student performances so that parents could take pride in their children's participation. These leaders also communicated positive news to parents. The program developers commented:

> Recently we visited one of the lowest-income schools in New Haven unannounced, on a warm fall day. Over 100 parents from the three housing projects in the area had arrived to pick up their children. Many of the teachers were visiting with the parents, discussing both school and home happenings. Such interaction is possible when parents view school as a good place, the product of a process that integrates the parent program with the overall program of the school. (Comer & Haynes, 1991, p. 276)

Do you remember our discussion in chapter 2 about the general education reform movement and site-based management? In chapter 2, we also described the Comer model and included a vignette on Dwight Fleming, a principal at a Comer school in Connecticut. Reread box 2–1 and reflect on the important role of the school principal in setting the tone for parents' attending and volunteering at school. Reflect also on Pat Boyd, John and Jane Hoyt, the three Hoyt children, and Excalibur Choir. Like Dwight Fleming in New Haven, Pat Boyd in Lawrence, Kansas, sets the tone for the families and students. The tone is simple: "This school belongs to you."

So she goes beyond inviting the families and students to participate. She expects it. And the families and students become coeducators and coempowerers.

Linking Our Themes

Creating a Reliable Alliance

By now you know the significance of infusing the eight obligations for reliable alliances into the partnership opportunity of families attending and volunteering at school. Throughout the chapter, we have emphasized ways you can do just that. Figure 14–3 highlights examples of this infusion.

Strengthening Family Factors

Just as with every other partnership opportunity, families, professionals, and all who participate in collaborative decision making have opportunities to expand individual and collective empowerment. Figure 14–4 illustrates how attending and volunteering at school can enhance motivation and knowledge/skills components in the empowerment equation.

FIGURE 14–3

Creating a Reliable Alliance: Emphasis on Attending and Volunteering at School

Obligations	Issues	Disempowering Actions	Empowering Actions
Knowing yourself	You would like to invite a parent in your classroom to volunteer, but she speaks Russian and you don't know how to bridge the language barrier.	Rationalize that the parent would probably not have time to participate anyway.	Locate the people in your district with the strongest bilingual expertise and invite their collaboration in learning how best to approach this parent.
Knowing families Family characteristics	The parent of one of your students has a chronic mental illness, and you are hesitant to include her as a classroom volunteer.	You ask the student if he thinks his mother is up to coming to school.	You call the mother, invite her perspectives on the kinds of school activities that would be especially meaningful to her, and make arrangements to respond to her priorities.
Family interactions	A grandmother of one of your students has the predominant decision-making role in the family.	You assume that it would usurp the parents' role to invite the grandmother to chaperone a field trip.	Share your idea to include the grandmother with the parents and solicit their reactions.
Family functions	A mother of one of your students is a computer executive and seems to always work overtime when school events occur.	Write the mother a note and tell her that she is neglecting her child.	Share your vision of how technology could be incorporated into your instruction and invite the mother to share her expertise with you and other school colleagues on options for expanding technology.
Family life cycle	Parents of a student with a severe disability are very anxious about their daughter's transition from junior high to high school.	Encourage them to consider having their daughter stay another year in your class so that they will not have to deal with the transition.	Six to nine months before the transition, ask if they would like to attend an open house at the high school so that they can begin to get a picture of what it will be like and what kinds of plans need to be made. Accompany them to the open house.
Honoring cultural diversity	All PTA materials are in English, but the family of one of your students speaks Hindi.	Encourage the parents to come to the meetings anyway because it might help them learn English more quickly.	Find an interpreter who speaks Hindi who could accompany the parents to the meetings and provide simultaneous translation.

(continued)

FIGURE 14–3   CONTINUED

Creating a Reliable Alliance: Emphasis on Attending and Volunteering at School

Obligations	Issues	Disempowering Actions	Empowering Actions
Affirming and building on family strengths	A father has gone far beyond the call of duty in the number of volunteer hours that he has contributed to the school.	Suggest to the father he back off some and encourage his wife to be more involved.	Create a special award for parent contributions and present a certificate to this father at an assembly program.
Promoting family choices	A parent is interested in starting a grandparent volunteer day, which has never been done in your school before.	Tell the parent that she will need to prepare a written proposal and submit it to the district office.	Arrange a collaborative meeting with the school principal and other key school leaders and invite them to support this mother in implementing her idea.
Envisioning great expectations	Parents would like to set up a family resource center within the school, but there is no available space.	Tell the families that it simply is not feasible given space limitations.	Convene a group of educators and PTA leaders and brainstorm about how space might be rearranged to free up a location for the family resource center.
Using interpersonal communication skills	A parent volunteering in your classroom expresses concern to you about how you discipline students.	Tell the parent that you are the professional and that it is not her place to make suggestions about classroom discipline.	Encourage the parent to share examples with you and brainstorm with her about the pros and cons of your approach versus other approaches that you might take.
Warranting trust and respect	You encourage parents to allow their son to try out for the wrestling team, but the parents are afraid he will be hurt and ridiculed.	Concede that wrestling team participation is probably unrealistic.	Listen empathetically to the parents' concerns, brainstorm a plan for addressing their concerns, and consider ways that their son could be involved in extracurricular activities even though some risks must be addressed.

FIGURE 14–4

Strengthening Family Resources Through an Empowering Context: Emphasis on Attending and Volunteering at School

Motivation	What You Can Do	Knowledge/Skills	What You Can Do
Self-efficacy	Provide feedback to parents on how helpful their instructional contributions are in expanding learning opportunities for the students.	Information	When parents are volunteers in the classroom, provide them with information on how to respond most effectively to challenging behavior.
Perceived control	Invite parents to prioritize the ways that they would like to attend and volunteer at school and create opportunities based on their preferences.	Problem solving	Meet with highly involved parents to have them come up with new ways to attract the interest of parents who have not attended or volunteered at school in the past.
Great expectations	Consider all of the extracurricular opportunities in which a student and parents could participate and brainstorm with parents about the benefits that could accrue.		
Energy	Help create a family resource center in the school for parents to relax, have coffee, and provide support to each other.	Communication skills	Provide opportunities for parents to present to the class and develop more self-confidence in making group presentations.
Persistence	Provide encouragement to parents who plan PTA activities when few parents participate.	Life management skills	Invite parents' ideas in resolving student conflicts that arise during field trips when parents are chaperoning.

Summary

Attending and volunteering at school can take five different but mutually compatible forms: attending school events, contributing to classroom instruction, contributing to other school tasks, attending classes for families alone, and participating in parent-teacher organizations. Because these are not and should not be mutually exclusive activities, schools are using comprehensive approaches (such as the model that James Comer at Yale University developed and that Dwight Fleming in New Haven is practicing) or they can do as Pat Boyd does in Lawrence, Kansas.

Talking to Pat Boyd, one learns that she has been teaching for almost 20 years. You might expect some sense of fatigue, some slight hint of burnout. But you won't find it.

To listen to Pat is to hear not just the language of family participation, coeducation, and empowerment. It is to detect, easily and early on, her fierce and passionate commitment to returning the schools and education to the families. "Invested partners" is the phrase that she uses over and over again: invested in the same sense that she is invested, which is deeply and permanently; and partners in the same sense that she is a partner, one who is reciprocal with families and students alike.

Listening to the Hoyts, one learns that their own school experiences were less than ideal. Jane describes her education as isolated, not just in the geographic sense that her homes in southern Minnesota and mountainous Colorado were isolated, but in the sense that she herself was a loner in school. John talks freely about growing up in the wealthy suburbs in lower Connecticut, about being afraid to do anything in a community of "expert throat cutters," and about not being able to find his own niche when he was sent off to boarding school.

That was then—some 30 years ago. Now Jane and John speak in much different words about their involvement in school, in the Excalibur Choir and the empowerment approach that Pat Boyd directs. Jane uses the word healing and attributes that turnaround to her opportunity to be involved. John uses the word restorative and is clearly delighted that he is "valued as a parent and coeducator, a respected collaborator" with Jane, Pat, and his three children.

"It's a trust thing," they say, "we're members of a trusting community." It's quite clear whom they trust—Pat, each other, their children, and other families. And it's quite clear whom Pat trusts—the Hoyts and other families, too.

With trust comes power—the educator's power to return education to the families and the families' power to accept that responsibility.

Chapter Fifteen

Advocating for Systems Improvement

*T*here's a paradox in the lives of Delfy and James Roach. The paradox is this: Being destructive is being constructive. At least sometimes that's the case.

It certainly was the case when James, who has been diagnosed with a bipolar disorder, was expelled from special education when he was in the second grade. The trigger for his expulsion was his behavior: Placed in a time-out room because he acted out so much, he simply destroyed the room.

When Delfy asked how long he would be out of school, she was told, "Until we fix the room."

"How long will that take?" she asked.

"We aren't sure."

What would happen in the meanwhile? James would get one hour a day of homebound instruction, four days a week.

"That was not acceptable. I was a full-time working person, I'm a single parent, my husband committed suicide several years before, and that's when my advocacy started. I found a support group and learned that James had a right to an appropriate public education and the supports to be successful in school."

So Delfy began her advocacy career because James destroyed the time-out room. That makes sense, Delfy reasons. "I came in fighting at that time, and I think I made a few enemies then, but I didn't know what else to do at the time. I was so upset that they had totally destroyed James. Here was a kid who had been doing okay in the program he was in before. Now we were talking hospitalization, because his disorders are so severe. I

guess what's so depressing about that and so agonizing is that I knew that hospitalization wasn't the answer for him. I truly felt like I was up against the wall and could go no other place except to come out fighting. So I did."

Delfy hasn't stopped fighting, but now she fights not just for James but for other families whose children have severe emotional problems. "My advocacy has been a process," from being helped by Parents for Behaviorally Different Children, a statewide parent-directed advocacy program in New Mexico, to being its executive director. "I didn't want other families to have to go through what I had to go through."

Delfy's statewide advocacy is for parents like her whose children have emotional challenges, especially for parents who, like her, are members of a culturally diverse group.

As part of her advocacy, Delfy was instrumental in changing New Mexico's laws governing parents' decisions to hospitalize their children. Parents and children needed services not available in schools or community mental health centers, so hospitalization or outpatient services were needed. Civil rights advocates opposed easier hospitalization, while providers and parents wanted easier hospitalization.

"As parents, we took a lot of abuse at those meetings. There was so much blaming going on, people saying that the reason the kids are the way they are is because of the parents. People said that there's nothing wrong with the kids; it's the parents, and they should be hospitalized, not the kids."

So not only do Delfy and others have to bear the stigma of mental health disorders, but they also have to do so as a culturally underrepresented group. The schools do not print forms in Spanish. The Spanish-speaking parents have a cultural heritage of respecting the teachers and not asking questions of people in authority. "You just accept what is being given you."

Acceptance is not only natural but necessary for those families who do not have legal citizenship status. They fear the immigration services and believe the schools will "use retribution and have them or their child deported."

So advocacy for the Spanish-speaking families means holding conferences in only Spanish, in their communities, in collaboration with their community leaders, and at times when their religious holidays or fiestas are not in process. It means teaching them about their rights and respecting their preferences to use the medicine man (the Curandero) or the witch doctor (the Brujo), not just the teachers, therapists, or physicians that schools or the state hire.

And when school restructuring is the issue, it means recognizing that the schools will restructure themselves without consulting with the families in advance. "Right now, we aren't exactly involved in the restructuring the schools are doing around inclusion. We were invited to hear the reform after it was already done, so the school people could run it by us."

"Principals normally don't want our children in there (in school, much less in inclusive programs). I don't think they want kids with disabilities. Period. But especially kids with behaviors."

So advocacy means reaching the families in family-friendly and culturally appropriate ways, letting them know their rights, and constantly monitoring the principals and the whole school.

It means showing respect for the educators. "We don't need to bash or blame professionals for everything. We're going to have to come together and work in the best interests of our kids. Professionals are going to need the commitment the families have." It means asking the professionals to ask themselves a simple but difficult question: "If this were my family, what would I want to see happen?"

After all, as Delfy says, "Our kids are with us for a lifetime. The professionals may be in our kids' lives and our families' lives for an hour a week for a whole year, but we are with our kids the rest of our lives. They need to understand and respect that."

James Roach. (1995)

The seventh and last partnership opportunity is advocating to improve school systems. We present the empowerment framework in figure 15–1 with the last partnership opportunity advocating for systems improvement shaded. As you advocate for systems improvement, you will have opportunities to implement all of the seven opportunities for partnerships.

This chapter focuses on (1) becoming an advocate, (2) advocating for change through school reform, (3) advocating for change in parental participation, and (4) advocating for change through legislative and judicial processes.

Becoming an Advocate

Have you ever had to stand up for something you believed in? Of course you have. Sometime and some place in your family, school or college, or workplace, you have asserted your interests or those of another person. What you did then is a form of advocacy. Although it is a very natural behavior of families and professionals, that does not mean it is easy to be an advocate.

Definition

Advocacy is defined as taking one's own or another's perspective to obtain a result not otherwise available. Advocacy is closely aligned to empowerment; and as you know, empowerment means taking action to get what you want and need. Advocacy is a strategy for taking action, and it consists of presenting, supporting, or defending a position. Advocacy can be for yourself (self-advocacy) or for another (representational advocacy).

For example, a student who is engaged in supported employment may not want to learn a particular job or have a particular job coach; and through words or behavior, the student communicates that choice. This is self-advocacy. In a curious way, James Roach's destructive behaviors were a form of self-advocacy: He was saying he wanted out of the time-out confinement. Alternatively, parents who challenge the curriculum or placement that a school proposes for their child engage in representational advocacy (on their child's behalf). Delfy Roach engaged in representational advocacy when she "came out fighting" for her son James and for other parents of children with emotional challenges. Finally, advocacy is purposeful; it seeks a particular outcome from a situation in which at least one person perceives that a change is needed. Accordingly, when Delfy sought more appropriate education for James and differ-

ent laws pertaining to commitment and residential programs, she was advocating purposefully arguing for change.

Places, People, Issues, and Orientations for Advocacy

Advocacy occurs in many different places. It occurs when a team (including the student's family) meets to evaluate the student (especially to conduct a functional behavioral assessment; see chapter 13) or to develop an IEP. In that case, the place probably is a conference room at the school, the issue concerns the student's needs and IDEA rights, and the people are professionally and family oriented. Advocacy can occur in a hearing before a judge in a lawsuit between a student's parents and the local school system. In that case, the place will be a courtroom, the issue is legal, and the people are rights-and-duties oriented. It can occur when a group of parents present their concerns to a local or state superintendent of education. In that case, the venue will be an office; the issue concerns the development or implementation of special or general education policies; and the people have a policy, political, and family orientation. Likewise, advocacy can occur when parents and professionals testify before a state or congressional committee. In that case, the venue is a legislative committee room; the issue is the development or implementation of state or federal law; and the people have a policy, political, family, and professional orientation.

Delfy Roach has engaged in each of these types of advocacy. Like many other family members, she has found that she cannot limit her advocacy to simply one place, one issue, and one forum. Delfy is not the only parent who cannot limit her advocacy. There are many others. Among them is Valerie Burrell-Muhammed, a community activist in Richmond, Virginia and the mother of four children—Daryl, now 25 and married, who was classified as having a learning disability when he was in school; Flora-Daisy, now 16 and in the 11th grade, an honors student who survived a brain tumor and neurosurgery at the age of 3 years and 11 months; Kahadijah, now 14 and in the 9th grade; and Ibrahim, now 9 and in the 4th grade. Box 15–1 tells about Valerie, her perspectives on advocacy, and her alliances.

So advocacy involves all kinds of people (including students, parents or other family members, professionals, lawyers, judges, policymakers, and local and state agency administrators) who struggle with all kinds of issues (such as professional, student-related, family-related, community-related, legal, policy, and fiscal) in all kinds of places

FIGURE 15—1

Empowerment Framework: Collaborating for Empowerment in Advocating for Systems Improvement

Education Context Resources

Opportunities for Partnerships	Obligations for Reliable Alliances
Opportunities Arise At . . .	*Reliable Alliances Consist of . . .*
Communicating among reliable allies	Knowing yourself
Meetings families' basic needs	Knowing families
Evaluating for special education	Honoring cultural diversity
Individualizing for appropriate education and placement	Affirming family strengths
Extending learning in home and community	Promoting family choices
Attending and volunteering at school	Envisioning great expectations
Advocating for systems improvement	Communicating positively
	Warranting trust and respect

Professional Resources

Motivation	Knowledge/Skills
Self-efficacy: Believing in our capabilities	Information: Being knowledgeable
Perceived control: Believing we can apply our capabilities to affect what happens to us	Problem solving: Knowing how to bust the barriers
Great expectations: Believing we will get what we want and need	Life management skills: Knowing how to handle what happens to us
Energy: Lighting the fire and keeping it burning	Communication skills: Being on the sending and receiving ends of expressed needs and wants
Persistence: Putting forth a sustained effort	

Family Resources

Knowledge/Skills	Motivation
Information: Being knowledgeable	Self-efficacy: Believing in our capabilities
Problem solving: Knowing how to bust the barriers	Perceived control: Believing we can apply our capabilities to affect what happens to us
Life management skills: Knowing how to handle what happens to us	Great expectations: Believing we will get what we want and need
Communication skills: Being on the sending and receiving ends of expressed needs and wants	Energy: Lighting the fire and keeping it burning
	Persistence: Putting forth a sustained effort

Collaborating for Empowerment

The Community Activist

Like so many parents of children with disabilities, Valerie Burrell-Muhammed is an accidental advocate: "I didn't choose my work, it chose me." And it did so through a combination of two factors.

One was an undeniable reality of her family life. Her son Daryl was in special education because of a specific learning disability, and the life of her daughter Flora-Daisy was threatened at the age of only 3 by a brain tumor. The other was an undeniable reality of urban life, namely, the "oppressive conditions" and "violent community" that "wreck havoc" to the mental and physical health of residents of Richmond, Virginia's inner city.

What was the first reality? What happened to Valerie as she, Daryl, and Flora-Daisy were caught up in the special education and health-care service delivery systems? In a word: disempowerment. "No one said it out loud, but I was led to feel that I was at fault for my children's conditions. There were a lot of subtle suggestions and innuendoes. So we learned to blame ourselves. The professionals have the specialized knowledge and training. I couldn't sit at their tables, understand their jargon. I was intimidated. Their translations were condescending. I was not trusted. I was dismissed. I was demeaned. I even questioned whether I have the right to question professionals."

Deep in her heart, Valerie believed in a different reality, a reality of dignity and justice. "I am a woman of discipline and dignity. To have to ask questions, to have to seek services, was to be put upon and ultimately was humiliating. I am intelligent, ra-

tional, and understanding. But I was not so regarded." Nor were her children dignified: "Daryl and Flora-Daisy were not 'cases' because a human being is not a 'case.' So their human-ness was lost."

That second reality is personal, but also societal. "Society has changed in the last 25 years, but the injustice has become worse because of the increasing gap between the 'haves' and the 'have-nots.'" The more Valerie worked for her son and daughter, the more she became recognized by her own community as a go-to activist who was no longer afraid to ask for quality services for her family and for other families, too. "People in the systems (education, health, mental health, social service, and juvenile justice) began to recognize my metamorphosis."

The metamorphosis—from being put upon to being a stand-up advocate—attracted the attention of the Annie Casey Foundation and the Federation of Families for Children's Mental Health as they worked within the inner cities of Richmond, Houston, Boston, and Miami to create a system of care for children with disabilities and their families.

That joint effort is called the "Urban Mental Health Initiative." It recognizes that toxic urban environments create mental health problems for families and children. One response is to empower the residents of the inner cities. "We have to engage the systems to get them to change. We have to insist on pro-family policy and practice."

By pro-family, Valerie means something more than *family centered*. "Pro-family practice recognizes

the need for everyone to come together—professionals and families alike. We have a duty to create good outcomes for all of the partners. We have to come together. No one system can do it alone. The empowerment piece belongs to us all. We must acknowledge this in a pro-family way. As difficult as it may be to overlook the facts about some people (they are not bathed, are unkempt, or have unusual mannerisms—they aren't 'your kind'), if we are one with the universe, with God, whatever our spiritual preferences may be, then we must draw on our experiences with our own Creator, with the universe, and our own family. Every person deserves the same opportunity and has the same human needs. Our circumstances may vary but God didn't reject the sinner. We, no less than God, create and serve. So we have no right to violate another person because they do not 'measure up.' If that is not enough, then I say, 'Go examine your school of thought.' All schools of thought value people. We must attach the whole human family to these values. As Nelson Mandela said, 'The struggle continues.' And as Frederick Douglass said, 'How can we not appreciate the struggle? We all struggle.'"

There it is: We all struggle. We all advocate. That's Valerie's message. That, and this one, too: "The empowerment piece belongs to us all." To struggle together, not against each other; to advocate for each other, not against each other: That's a good way to "create and serve."

It's Valerie's way. It's the Casey Foundation's. And it's the Federation's.

(including schools, offices, courtrooms, committee rooms, and so on). Advocacy involves you.

When you identify barriers that are blocking you, other educators, students, and families from getting what you and they want and need, your role is to be an advocate, taking action to eliminate those barriers and to produce a more empowering context. Remember what Valerie said: "We all struggle." You do not have to be stuck with the status quo or work around problems that could be solved if someone would take the initiative to solve them. Valerie again is on point: "The empowerment piece belongs to us all." As a professional, it is your duty to advocate to improve the capacity of school systems to empower students and families. A parent recently described her frustration with the perception on the part of many professionals that they do not have a duty to advocate:

> It's really . . . I always tell people its sort of like incest within the family. Everybody at the school knows that things are not being done right for special education students . . . the teachers, most of all, they know. But they know they can't say anything and so they keep a secret and our children continue to not get educated. It's really, really sick. It's a sick, sick thing. I can't tell you how many teachers and principals I've talked to who say, "Well, I KNOW that its not really right, but I'm powerless to do anything." (Beach Center focus group transcripts, 1999)

We implore you to recognize that you indeed can have the power to make a difference, to "create and serve," if you develop and refine your advocacy skills. It can be very difficult for teachers to advocate within school systems that are more system-focused than student- or family-focused. Sometimes advocacy can create conflict with colleagues who do not share an advocacy orientation; in the most difficult circumstances, assuming advocacy roles might even result in a threat to job stability or even job loss. Some educators have found that they are able to indirectly advocate when direct advocacy might result in extensive punitive consequences for them. As one teacher stated:

> I think sometimes in my job, there are things that conflict . . . I don't want to tell parents to go against the system because the system employs me so I really appreciate having a program to refer them to and I usually say, "Call [name of program]. Tell them what the situation is. And I know there will be a parent there who will advocate—who will come and advocate with you at the IEP meeting or point you in the right direction." (Beach Center focus group transcripts, 1999)

This teacher was referring parents to the parent training and information center in her state (see appendix A for the contact information of the parent training and information center in your state). Ensuring that parents have access to information on their educational rights and have advocates who can attend meetings with them is a valuable advocacy contribution you can make.

Sources and Levels of Advocacy

Advocacy can occur at the federal/national, state, regional, or local levels. Patricia McGill Smith's work as executive director of the National Parent Network on Disability (chapter 1 vignette) is an example of advocacy at the national level; her job requires her to be an advocate for families and the national, state, and local family organizations to which they belong. The work that Delfy and Valerie carry out and the work of families advocating in IFSP/IEP conferences for their children's rights under IDEA are examples of advocacy at the local level. Advocacy can also be somewhere in between, as the following situations illustrate:

- The volunteer president of a state family organization for students with learning disabilities testifies before a state legislative committee.
- You poll your professional colleagues and families to determine the extent of their concern about the unavailability of sufficient supplementary aides and services to include students successfully in general education classrooms.
- People such as Delfy and Valerie work simultaneously at the local, regional, and state levels.

Sometimes there is the expectation that families of children with exceptionalities should be advocates for their own child and for others. As we have discussed throughout this book, many families like Delfy's and Valerie's embrace the role of advocacy and eagerly work for systems improvement (Cunconan-Lahr & Brotherson, 1996). From a research study that focused on how parents of children and youth with disability effectively managed their lives from day to day, we learn about the personal transformation parents have experienced in terms of their advocacy effectiveness (Scorgie, Wilgosh, & McDonald, 1996). Parents in this study emphasized their new roles as ". . . parent group leaders, conference speakers, advocates, teachers, writers, or members of advisory counsels for schools, hospitals or agencies representing persons with disabilities. A parent spoke, 'I've been changed. I've had opportunities I never would have dreamed possible by being involved in advocacy . . .' " (Scorgie, Wilgosh, & McDonald, 1996, p. 83).

Parents who have benefited from their advocacy roles emphasize that they need support to be successful advocates. These supports include (Cunconan-Lahr &

Brotherson, 1996; Friesen & Huff, 1990; Searcy, Lee-Lawson, & Trombino, 1995)

- developing communication skills related to how, to whom, what, and when to communicate;
- benefiting from the mentoring of parents with strong advocacy track records,
- developing an extensive network with other advocates and policymakers;
- being provided with financial compensation for the time that they invest in advocacy; and
- having the support of professionals, family, and friends related to their ever-evolving motivation and knowledge/skills.

But even families who embrace this role often tire of the laborious job of advocacy and retaliatory issues:

> When you have to advocate for your child, you pay a high price for that in many ways. It's very stressful on the family . . . . Because of the kind of advocacy work that I've had to do . . . . I'm not able to teach anywhere locally. I actually teach school in Texas, which is a 30-mile drive in the time difference away from my home . . . . My son suffers from bipolar disorder and numerous other difficulties. That illness itself is stressful, but when you have a vindictive, harassing, retaliatory school district to deal with, it makes your life completely miserable . . . that's what I've had to deal with. (Testimony of Edris Klucher, quoted in National Council on Disability, 1995, p. 124)

A research study that explored advocacy experiences of parents and individuals with disabilities reported that some of the problems associated with advocacy include the amount of time it takes, the expenses that are involved, and the emotional drain it exacts (Cunconan-Lahr & Brotherson, 1996).

Parents' advocacy burden would be significantly lessened if every single educator saw himself or herself as an advocate. Mark A. Mlawer, a professional who works for inclusive education, shares his perspective on advocacy expectations for families and professionals in box 15–2. He reminds us that the expectation that every parent should be an advocate may be inconsistent with what some parents want (Mlawer, 1993; Turnbull & Turnbull, 1982).

This warning concerning parental advocacy preferences is particularly important to remember in terms of families from culturally and linguistically diverse backgrounds. The expectation to advocate can be completely countercultural to one's values regarding the expectation for equity, individual rights, and individual/family choice (Kalyanpur, Harry, & Skrtic, 2000). It's important, however, to not overgeneralize this point and simplisti-

cally assume that all families from culturally and linguistically diverse backgrounds do not subscribe to parental advocacy roles. Delfy Roach is an excellent example of a Latino parent who is a strong and successful advocate, and Valerie Burrell-Muhammed is an equally excellent example of an African American parent who is a strong and successful advocate.

Monitoring and Advisory Committees

Often advocacy occurs when a group of individuals is responsible for monitoring or advising educators. These groups perform various types of functions, but the most usual are to assure themselves, families and students, and educators that the educational agency is delivering the services in the manner required by law or good professional practice.

Monitoring involves inspecting the educational agency's records; holding hearings; interviewing families, students, and agency employees; and seeking peer review from wholly disinterested individuals or associations. In a very real sense, this work is more than quality control; it is advocacy for the people for whom the services are intended.

Monitoring teams, often constituted by the state education agency or sometimes by the U.S. Department of Education, may come into your school system and carry out the monitoring roles that were just described. Present to them the strengths and needs of the program; do not try to emphasize only strengths and minimize some of the real needs that exist. As you develop collaborative relationships with other educators and administrators, the goal of that collaboration should be to provide the highest-quality program possible, not merely to put an unjustified favorable light on something that needs improvement. Remember that the purpose of the special education program is to enhance educational outcomes for students and to provide support to families. By keeping focused on this goal, you can participate in the monitoring process in an ethical and honest way.

Another form of advocacy occurs when a group of individuals is constituted as an advisory committee for a state or local education agency or other provider. The role of the advisory committee is to give advice to the educational agency that created it. The advisory committee seeks to improve the quality of service delivery according to good professional standards. Many school districts have a special education advisory committee composed of families, teachers, and administrators, whose role is to review the special education program and to make recommendations for improvement. As inclusive school practices are being implemented, some school districts

Advocacy Expectations for Families and Professionals

The answer, therefore, to the question "Who should fight?" is: professionals. Those of us who enter the special education and disability "fields" by choice rather than necessity, those of us who ask for the duties and responsibilities of working on behalf of students with disabilities, are those with the obligations of advocacy. No matter what our job, advocacy must be part of it.

It is impossible to avoid one implication of this point of view: by engaging in advocacy, special education and disability professionals risk making their employers angry and may even risk their jobs. While the risks are usually overestimated, it cannot be denied that they exist. Nevertheless, it is time to accept that working on behalf of students with disabilities entails risks; and as with many other professions, one should not enter this profession without ac-

cepting its values and all the risks that living in accordance with those values entails. And, in fact, some special education and disability professionals—particularly some classroom teachers—take these risks and have for some time. Parents will be spared the burdens of advocacy when others, especially more of those in administrative positions, join these courageous professionals.

Moreover, in order to truly empower parents, programs must be developed that are capable of engaging in advocacy along with and on behalf of parents; programs that are available regardless of income; programs that are well publicized and easy to access; and programs that have available a corps of independent, uncompromised special educators to serve as experts on behalf of students. Only by creating a true balance of power between par-

ents and school systems, not just between some middle- and upper-class parents and school systems, will *all* parents be given the opportunity of empowerment. "Empowerment" without real power is an empty concept, a cruel sham that results in disempowerment for many. . . .

We can best assist children and youth with disabilities if we stop pushing their parents to become advocates and simply allow them to be parents. But this will only happen if we expand the ranks of, and access to, qualified advocates, and start doing our jobs as professionals; this can begin once we accept the responsibilities our roles entail, and once funding priorities are set based on the real needs of parents and families, rather than upon what we wish those needs were.

Source: Mlawer, M. A. (1993). Who should fight? *Journal on Disability Policy Studies, 4*(1), 112–114.

---

are eliminating a separate special education advisory committee and having an educational advisory committee whose responsibility includes the education of students with and without exceptionalities.

Of course, some school districts are uncommitted to parent participation in school reform; they create a situation in which the students' families have yet another challenge. That new challenge is to advocate for a fair process for school reform. If families can open up the process, then they confront the challenge of advocating for more appropriate and inclusive special education.

In all of these kinds of activity, advocacy is almost always unavoidable. This is because most monitoring and advisory committees will find one or more ways in which the educational agency can improve its services and make one or more recommendations on how the agency can do its job better.

The risk for both professionals and families in any of these groups is that they will be co-opted by the educational agency and persuaded to be the advocate for the agency against students and families. The issue of dual allegiance arises and requires you and other professionals to be very clear about your loyalties: Are you loyal to protecting the educational agency or to ensuring an appropriate education for students?

Advocacy, Collaboration, and Empowerment

Advocacy can and should be a collaborative undertaking between families and professionals (Friesen & Huff, 1990). That is an idealized view. In reality, when parents and professionals clash, as they often do, collaboration withers away and adversarial, even irreparable, relationships take its place.

There are many reasons to avoid adversarial relationships between yourself and families. Adversarial relationships often cause lingering hard feelings and great emotional and financial costs (especially to a family); they also risk retaliation against the student (Fiedler, 1985; McGinley, 1987). Moreover, adversarial positions create a "win-lose" world, an environment in which one side must gain and the other must lose. In that environment, collaboration is nearly impossible.

Recognizing that adversarial positions have great limitations, many people now advocate for a form of alternative dispute resolution involving mediation (Fisher & Ury, 1991). A "win-win" approach to advocacy emphasizes "enlarging the pie" so that everyone gains and no one loses much or at all. Whether a student, parent, teacher, or bureaucrat takes the "win-win" approach, the advocate who wants to "get to yes" (Fisher & Ury, 1991) stands a much better chance of having a long-term collaboration and a mutually empowering context than does one who approaches advocacy as an adversarial confrontation. When all stakeholders have something to gain, their effectiveness in supporting families and educating students seems to improve (Allen & Petr, 1996; Clatterbuck & Turnbull, 1996; Jones, Garlow, Turnbull, & Barber, 1996).

That is one reason why Congress, in reauthorizing IDEA in 1997, added a provision concerning mediation. Under IDEA, a school district must establish procedures to ensure that the parties (parents and school) may resolve their dispute through a mediation process. The process must be voluntary on the part of the parents and school; neither can compel the other to enter mediation. Moreover, if both use mediation, that process may not delay the parents' right to a due process hearing or to any other rights. The mediation must be conducted by an impartial and trained person. If the parents do not want to enter mediation, the school district may establish procedures to require them to meet, at a time and place convenient to them, with a disinterested party, under contract with the district; that contracted party must encourage the parents to use mediation and must explain the benefits of the mediation process.

Unfortunately, advocacy is not always collaborative, and mediation is not always successful. Sometimes parents or professionals or both need to develop other ways for securing systems change. For Delfy Roach, the solution was to join the New Mexico organization Parents for Behaviorally Different Children and later to rise to its executive directorship. For Valerie-Burrell Muhammed, the solution was to affiliate with the Casey Foundation and Federation of Families for Children's Mental Health. But not everyone wants to do what they did, nor can everyone follow their paths. They have to find other vehicles for systems change.

One popular approach to systems advocacy involves a program called Partners in Policymaking. Developed by the Minnesota Governor's Planning Council on Developmental Disabilities, this program provides information, training, and resources to the parents of children, youth, and adults with disabilities and to adults with disabilities. Some of the program components include having 128 hours of instruction over the course of a program year (eight weekend training sessions), benefiting from the perspectives of national speakers, and engaging in experiential learning in which participants immediately apply the information from their weekend sessions.

The program has been immensely successful in developing a cadre of well-informed and skillful advocates for disability policies, programs, and funding (Cunconan-Lahr & Brotherson, 1996; Zirpoli, Wieck, Hancox, & Skarnulis, 1994). Currently, Partners in Policymaking has been or is currently being implemented in all but four states and the District of Columbia within the United States, in six sites in the United Kingdom, and in increasing sites with recent UNICEF funding (Barenok & Wieck, 1998). Graduates of the program have increased contact with national, state, and local elected and appointed officials; they have testified at public hearings, have given presentations at state and national conferences, have appeared on TV and radio shows, have been appointed to state and local disability-policy committees, and have published articles and letters in newspapers or professional journals. As stated by the Partners in Policymaking program designers, "perhaps most profoundly, there are literally thousands of people in the United States and the United Kingdom who share the same expertise and are able to make their own lives and the lives of others better" (Barenok & Wieck, 1998, p. 8). Clearly, when family members and adults with disabilities are motivated and then gain the knowledge/skills to be effective advocates, they collaborate in systems change.

Similarly, parent training and information centers (see chapter 10) provide advocacy training for families. In Kansas, for example, the parent training and information center, incorporated as Families Together, Inc., provides training to families about their children's rights to an education and the families' rights to various health and family support services. It also mobilizes families to write letters, make telephone calls, send faxes, and make personal contacts with their state and national representatives, advocating for or against policy changes.

The parent training and information centers are not the only family advocacy groups. In nearly every state, disability-specific associations that are affiliated with national organizations (such as The Arc or United Cerebral Palsy Associations) regularly engage in systems advocacy. One of the most effective—and newest—of those organizations is the Federation for Children's Mental Health, which we described in chapter 1 (Bryant-Comstock, Huff, & VanDenBerg, 1996). Its local chapters (such as Delfy Roach's Parents for Behaviorally Different Children in New Mexico) and its activities (such as the inner-city work in Richmond involving Valerie Burrell-Muhammed) have played major roles in reforming policy and practice.

What if there is no family advocacy organization in your state? What are your choices? You might network with the family organizations that do exist to see what role they might assume in addressing the issue that is most important to you. Or you might be a founder of a new family advocacy organization specifically directed at your priorities. That was the choice of Kathy Berg, a graduate student at Boise State University, a mother of a young man with an emotional disorder, and a person who filled an advocacy void in her state, Idaho. Box 15–3 describes how one person can make a big difference.

TOGETHER WE CAN   BOX 15–3

Internet Idaho

To imagine Idaho, if you don't live there, is to imagine wide open space. Vastness comes to mind. And no problems of population density: People are not crowded together. But there's a lot more to Idaho than you might imagine.

You'd almost never think this: 31,974 children, ages birth through 18, with emotional disabilities. OK, that's using a high estimate. Use the more conservative one and get a different figure: 17,421 who not only have emotional disabilities but also have extreme impairments in their functioning.

Get a different picture of Idaho?

Now, think about the families of these young people: scattered across the high plains of the west; culturally different—rural, Anglo, Native American; desperate (like many other families, wherever they may be) for information about emotional disabilities—categories and types of disabilities, services to which they may be entitled, location and cost of services and of specialists, ideas and emotional support from other families. And facing not just the vastness of open spaces and distance from each other, but also the unforgiving and long winters that make intrastate travel risky.

Think again. Think about those families linked by a website that is operated by a nonprofit corporation organized and directed by families whose children have emotional disabilities. Think about them being "netted" to a national organization and their own state departments of education and child services.

Think all that. And then—then, imagine Internet Idaho!

Now, you've got the picture. It's the same picture that Kathy Berg had. And that she created—created because she is not only the mother of a young man with an emotional disorder but is also a master's student at Boise State University, and in that role, she undertook a project (later written up as her master's thesis). The project included Internet Idaho and more.

A statewide, family-directed, state and privately supported corporation, Idaho Federation of Families for Children's Mental Health, Inc., is affiliated with the national Federation of Families for Children's Mental Health and is supported by Idaho state agencies.

Its most useful service? That's hard to say. But the vehicle for that service is readily identifiable. It is the Internet website that the Idaho Federation has created. It is what Idaho's families said they needed: one means of communication. It is what responds to their capacities; so many have computers. And it is what links them to each other and to other web-based resource sites where they can obtain the particular information they seek.

The Together We Can moral of this short story—of Kathy Berg's imagination and dedication and work—is simple to tell: When one fully committed person has an idea, and when that person persuades families and state agencies to come together to respond to families' known needs, the solutions can be effective if they are tailored to the families' life circumstances.

In Idaho, families' life circumstances consist of distances that the "net" eliminates; for that reason, high tech is in so many families' homes. And for that same reason, the Federation and the Idaho Department of Health and Welfare, Bureau of Family and Children's Services can together respond to families' needs. In Idaho, function and form merge. That's a consequence of "netting."

Source: Adapted from Berg, K. M. (1999). *Developing a statewide family network for families of children with emotional, behavioral, and mental disorders.* Unpublished thesis, Boise State University.

When you or the families you work with want to advocate, consider going to the parent training and information centers or other family advocacy associations. Or do what Delfy, Valerie, and Kathy did: Do it on your own.

Advocating for Change through Standards-Based School Reform

Current Status

In chapter 2 you learned about the highlights of general and special education school reform over the last 20 years. You also read about Goals 2000: the Educate America Act passed in March 1994, which established the eight National Education Goals included in figure 15–2.

The National Education Goals derive from the grave concern of many professionals, parents, and citizens at large that educational quality has declined to unacceptable levels and that bold and ambitious new efforts are needed to advocate for systems change. Empowerment is at the heart of the process for achieving these goals. School, family, and community participants need to take action to get what they need and want—namely, higher standards and achievement for all students. An underlying theme of the National Education Goals is great expectations for all:

All students can learn at significantly higher levels, given the proper tools and resources. Yet our system sorts children almost from the beginning of grade school into advanced vs. slow tracks. We test children against a bell-shaped curve essentially against each other rather than against any standard of what it is they need to know and be able to do to get jobs or maintain a high standard of living. . . .

To turn this around, we need a revolution in our thinking. We must shape a system of teaching and learning based on the philosophy that all students can learn at higher levels, that achievement is as much a function of expectations and effort as it is of innate ability.

Perhaps the greatest barrier of all to achieving equity is that we have not made clear to our students what it is they need to know and be able to do to be successful. If we have not thought through this clearly and cannot articulate it, then we are guaranteeing that our system cannot be held accountable for providing a high-quality and equitable education for all children. (U.S. Department of Education, 1995, p. 14)

The National Education Goals set high standards for all students, emphasizing the following three:

1. *Content standards:* defining the knowledge, skills, and understandings that students should accomplish in the broad range of subject areas

---

FIGURE 15–2

National Education Goals

Ready to Learn
By the year 2000, all children in the United States will start school ready to learn.

School Completion
By the year 2000, the high school graduation rate will increase to at least 90 percent.

Student Achievement and Citizenship
By the year 2000, all students will leave grades 4, 8, and 12 having demonstrated competency in challenging subject matter including English, mathematics, science, foreign languages, civics and government, economics, arts, history, and geography; and every school in the United States will ensure that all students learn to use their minds well, so they may be prepared for responsible citizenship, further learning, and productive employment in our nation's modern economy.

Mathematics and Science
By the year 2000, U.S. students will be the first in the world in mathematics and science achievement.

Adult Literacy and Lifelong Learning
By the year 2000, every adult American will be literate and will possess the knowledge and skills necessary to compete in a global economy and exercise the rights and responsibilities of citizenship.

Safe, Disciplined, and Drug-Free Schools
By the year 2000, every school in the United States will be free of drugs, violence, and the unauthorized presence of firearms and alcohol and will offer a disciplined environment conducive to learning.

Teacher Education and Professional Development
By the year 2000, members of the nation's teaching force will have access to programs for the continued improvement of their skills and the opportunity to acquire the knowledge and skills needed to instruct and prepare all American students for the next century.

Parental Participation
By the year 2000, every school will promote partnerships that will increase parental involvement and participation in promoting the social, emotional, and academic growth of children.

2. *Performance standards:* defining the levels of student achievement in the subject matter that must be met to exemplify proficiency
3. *Opportunity-to-learn standards:* defining the conditions in schools that will enable all students to achieve the content and to perform at an acceptable proficiency level

Although the intention of Goals 2000 and the National Education Goals was to shore up educational accountability for all students (including those with and without exceptionalities), states have been slow to establish standards and even slower to develop accountability systems for meeting those standards. The American Federation of Teachers (1996) collected information from 48 states on their progress in establishing standards. Approximately one-third of the states have clear, specific standards in the content areas of language arts, mathematics, science, and social studies. Approximately three-fourths of the states anticipate assessing student achievement in these four areas at some point in the future. Approximately 15 percent of the states anticipate offering differentiated diplomas as a way to motivate students to reach higher standards. Approximately one-third of the state special education directors reported that they were not involved in the creation of academic content standards in their states (Erickson, 1998), which causes one to question the participatory process of ensuring that the needs of these students were represented in the standard-setting process.

Some states have developed separate standards for students with disabilities despite the clear direction of the country toward establishing core standards expected of all students—those with and without disabilities (Erickson, 1998). Typically, the arguments in favor of using the same standards point to the need to raise expectations for students with disabilities and to assure that their needs are not overlooked in an effort to improve performance of all students. The argument against having the same standards is that students with disabilities might be particularly penalized for not meeting standards and the standards-based curricula may be in conflict with their individualized needs.

Currently there is a major need for advocacy in bringing together general and special education stakeholders to ensure that the needs of students with disabilities are adequately addressed in the standards-based school-reform movement.

In the future, IEP teams will need a great deal of information about standard-setting efforts within their local or state school systems. Policy expectations will need to be clearly articulated to students, parents, and both general and special educators. Decision-making guidelines and training will be needed by IEP committees to assist them in making their choices. In particular, students with disabilities and their families must know whether modifications to either content or performance standards will lead to diminished expectations, a narrowing of curricular offerings, or a different graduation status. (Erickson, 1998, p. 19)

Roles in Advocating for School Reform

Research data on preferences of parents and educators for parental roles in advocating for standards-based school reform are mixed. A 1998 Gallup Poll of the Public's Attitudes Toward the Public Schools reported that Americans believe that public school parents should have more say than in the past in aspects of school operations such as selecting and hiring administrators, principals, and teachers; setting teacher and administrator salaries; selecting books and instructional materials; and identifying books for school libraries (Rose & Gallup, 1998).

Schools, however, report that parent input on key decisions occurs to a small extent. The U.S. Department of Education carried out a national study to assess the extent to which schools were complying with the National Education Goals (Carey, Lewis, & Farris, 1998). Only 9 percent of public elementary schools reported considering parent input to a great extent on issues associated with the curriculum or the overall instructional program, and only 1 percent considered parent input to a great extent on the topic of monitoring or evaluating teachers. Almost 80 percent of the schools reported having an advisory group or policy counsel that includes parents; thus, one can assume that the parents in these groups did not have significant input.

Another national survey conducted by Public Agenda involved interviews with 1,000 public school teachers and over 1,200 parents of children in public school (Farkas, Johnson, & Duffett, 1999). Approximately one-third of the parents indicated that they would be "very comfortable" with deciding how to spend the school's money or helping to evaluate the quality of teachers; similarly, about this same percentage of teachers indicated that those roles would be appropriate for parents. Only about 12 percent of the teachers indicated that parents were involved in their schools in helping to evaluate teachers, and only 7 percent of the teachers indicated that parents currently proposed changes to teaching methods. As compared to other options for parent involvement, involvement in decision making related to school reform tended to have lower priority. The researchers concluded:

The pronounced lack of parental enthusiasm may arise from a deference to professional educators, an

Essential Steps in the Goals Process

- Adopt the National Education Goals or similar goals that reflect high expectations for all and cover the entire breadth of focus from prenatal care to lifelong learning.
- Assess current strengths and weaknesses and build a strong accountability system to measure and report regularly on progress toward the goals over time.
- Set specific performance benchmarks to make progress along the way and guide the change process.

- Identify the barriers to and opportunities for goal attainment in the many systems that support teaching and learning.
- Create and mount strategies to overcome the barriers, seize the opportunities, and meet the performance benchmarks.
- Make a long-term commitment to continuously reevaluate your accomplishments and shortcomings in meeting the community goals and be willing to modify your strategy as needed.

awareness of their own limited knowledge, or simply having their "hands full" with the demands of everyday life. Whatever the reason, there is no surge of parents knocking on closed school doors, anxious to assert control. Advocates of government reform must confront the reality: Only a small segment of parents have any real desire to pitch in on this front. The rest admit that it is simply not their current priority. (Farkas, Johnson, & Duffett, 1999)

In spite of these data, a collaborative process among all stakeholders is at the heart of implementing the National Education Goals (Buswell, 1993; Buswell & Schaffner, 1994; Erickson, 1998; Trammill, in press). It is just what Delfy Roach sought but did not find in her school district in New Mexico. And it is just what underlies the work that Valerie Burrell-Muhammed, the Casey Foundation, and the Federation do in Richmond and other inner cities. The U.S. Department of Education (1995) recommends the steps listed in box 15–4 as methods to address the National Education Goals within schools and communities. You will recognize these steps as the key steps of the problem-solving process about which you learned about in chapter 4. Once you master the basic steps of the problem-solving process, you can apply them to almost any problem, whether it be at the individual-student level or the system level.

Discuss the National Education Goals with your principal and find out about the planning process within your school and community. Many schools are appointing a school-improvement team that brings together stakeholders for collaborative planning and implementation. If you are interested, ask to become a member of the school-improvement team. The more you participate actively in the change process, the more empowered you are likely to be.

How have families of students with exceptionalities participated in the school-reform process? Research answers the question from the perspectives of parents (of students with disabilities) who have been members of school-improvement teams (Wade, 1994).

1. *Do school improvement teams make important decisions?* Approximately half the participants stated that no important decisions had been made by their school-improvement team. Decisions focused on curriculum, technology, physical plant, and parent involvement. Two different opinions about progress represent the range of perspectives:

   We're talking about the six weeks we spent on getting the extra bulletin board for the teacher's lounge so that they could get communication. That was the biggest waste of time.

   I have only been here one year, but my experience has been that the school improvement committee has an incredible amount of power. (Wade, 1994, p. 7)

2. *Do they feel like empowered members of the team?* Slightly more than half of the participants (53 percent) described themselves as being equal members of the team, but slightly fewer than half (47 percent) stated that they were not equal members. Empowered members attributed their equal role to the leadership of the principal (context resource) or to their own personal attributes (family resources related to motivation and knowledge/skills). Contrasting perspectives include the following:

   It's almost like you're part of the family when you go in and sit down and talk.

Enhancing Family Participation in School Reform and School-Improvement Teams

- Become familiar with the groups in your school and district that are studying school-reform issues and join the one that interests you the most.
- Look at education reform broadly rather than with a narrow, specialized focus that might serve only one group of students.
- Learn the issues.
- Ask students for feedback as new practices are implemented in their schools.
- Locate and build allies in your school, school district, or state with people who have vision, who are informed

about quality education, and who are open to exploring new ideas.
- Assist people to view students with disabilities as whole children who happen to have particular challenges.
- Provide key decision makers with information and reading material on educational issues.
- Encourage ongoing training for a wide variety of participants, a key to successful school reform.
- Talk with university leaders in the community and state.
- Understand the process of change.

Source: Buswell, B., & Schaffner, B. (1994). Parents in school reform. *Coalition Quarterly (published by the Federation for Children with Special Needs), 12*(1), 16–19.

[At] my school it's the principal. They don't start anything until the queen bee comes in, and nothing can be finalized until she is there. [If] she comes in late or doesn't come that just sets the whole thing off for the entire school. (Wade, 1994, p. 9)

3. *Do school-improvement teams deal with issues concerning disability? Do decisions made directly affect children with disabilities?* Three-fourths of the respondents indicated that the needs of students with a disability were not a concern of the school-improvement team.

We're not per se at the top of the list and maybe not really mentioned, you know, in the meeting because I think they are probably looking at the majority. (Wade, 1994, p. 13)

4. *What type of training and information do participants receive? What type of training and information do they and others need?* Participants who had attended training believed that it was beneficial and indicated that more training and advanced planning would be helpful.

There needs to be a method developed where I get the same information everybody else does. My son is right there with a backpack that goes home everyday, but no one is able to figure out how to get the same information to me that the staff have. This lends to the feeling of this is "just a parent" so it isn't important. (Wade, 1994, p. 14)

Discussion of important issues that might lead to school improvement was families' most favorable perspective about the process; their least favorable perspectives related to providing adequate training for parent involvement activities and addressing the needs of students with disabilities.

These data show that in attempting to address the needs of all students in the school, school-improvement teams may advertently or inadvertently overlook the needs of students with exceptionalities. As a professional with a special interest in this area, you should advocate for school-improvement teams to solicit and consider family and professional perspectives related to exceptionality. In other words, do not abandon Delfy Roach, Valerie Burrell-Muhammed, Kathy Berg, and other families by keeping them on the outside of school-reform discussions. If you do, you will simply perpetuate the power-over posture that impairs collaboration and empowerment.

The second major concern relates to providing adequate preparation for families. Consider family resources in the empowerment framework, especially the knowledge/skills component. You and other educators should provide opportunities for families to expand their information, problem-solving skills, coping skills, and communication skills related to school-reform issues. When you create that kind of empowering context, there is every reason to be optimistic about families' contribution to the accomplishment of the National Education Goals. Box 15–5 includes tips to help families enhance their meaningful participation in school-reform efforts, including school-improvement teams.

Advocating for Change in Parental Participation

The National Education Goal related to parental participation (see figure 15–3) has three objectives:

1. Every state will develop policies to assist local schools and local educational agencies to establish programs for increasing partnerships that respond to the varying needs of parents in the home, including parents of children who are disadvantaged or bilingual and parents of children with disabilities.
2. Every school will actively engage parents and families in a partnership that supports the academic work of children at home and shared educational decision making at school.
3. Parents and families will help to ensure that schools are adequately supported and will hold schools and teachers to high standards of accountability.

What are the key themes of these objectives? What have you learned that can prepare you, as an educational professional, to implement these objectives? We hope that you note the strong emphasis on increasing partnerships. You have learned a great deal about the seven different opportunities for partnerships, each one infused with the eight obligations for a reliable alliance. Advocating for systems improvement related to the National Education Goal of increasing parental participation means that you can be an advocate within your school to carry out these partnerships yourself and to help create a plan for your entire school and even your entire school district in implementing the seven opportunities for partnerships and eight obligations for a reliable alliance. As Delfy Roach was working to reform her state's hospitalization laws, she found that some professionals were her partners and others were not. Those who were her partners had a very clear understanding of the difficulties that she and other families face in raising a child who has emotional disabilities and is also from a culturally diverse background. They had infused into their alliances with the families their understanding of the families and the cultural traditions the families followed, affirming their strengths, promoting their choices, and warranting the families' trust and respect.

Joyce Epstein (1995) and Mavis Sanders (1999) are implementing a process for creating comprehensive school-family-community partnerships at school, district, and state levels. During the 1996–1997 school year, they initiated the National Network of Partnership Schools. In fall 1999, the membership included 1,144 schools, 135 districts, and 12 state departments of education. A school may join the network with or without its

---

FIGURE 15–3

Identifying Starting Points

- *Present strengths.* Which practices of school, family, and community partnerships are now working well for the school as a whole? For individual grade levels? For which types of involvement?

- *Needed changes.* Ideally, how do we want school, family, and community partnerships to work at this school three years from now? Which present practices should continue, and which should change? To reach school goals, what new practices are needed for each of the major types of involvement?

- *Expectations.* What do teachers expect of families? What do families expect of teachers and other school personnel? What do students expect their families to do to help them negotiate school life? What do students expect their teachers to do to keep their families informed and involved?

- *Sense of community.* Which families are we now reaching, and which are not yet reaching? Who are the "hard-to-reach" families? What might be done to communicate with and engage these families in their children's education? Are current partnership practices coordinated to include all families as a school community? Or are families whose children receive special services (e.g., Title I, special education, bilingual education) separated from families?

- *Links to goals.* How might family and community connections assist the school in helping more students reach higher goals and achieve greater success? Which practices of school, family, and community partnerships would directly connect to particular goals?

Source: Epstein, J. L. (1995, May). School/family/community partnerships: Caring for the children we share. *Phi Delta Kappan,* p. 709.

district or state, but Dr. Epstein and Dr. Sanders are very interested in schools, districts, and states collaboratively joining in order to provide the most pervasive support for implementing the partnership model. At the school level, the National Network membership requires the creation of a partnership action team in each school to plan and implement a comprehensive partnership program. It might be a subgroup of the school-improvement team, which has responsibility for implementing all six National Education Goals. The partnership action team has the responsibility of focusing specifically on the goal related to parental participation. There are five implementation steps to apply (Epstein, 1995; Epstein, Coates, Salinas, Sanders, & Simon, 1997):

1. *Create a partnership action team.* The team should be composed of at least one administrator, one member from the community, three teachers from different grade levels, and three parents of children in different grade levels. Nonprofessional staff, including custodians and cafeteria workers, can also be included. We would add the caveat that the number of parent representatives might be increased and should include families of typically developing children, children with disabilities, and children who are gifted and talented. A chairperson or facilitator of the action team needs to be strong in the family factors associated with empowerment, five elements of motivation, and four elements of knowledge/skills. An empowered leader can be a critical factor in the overall success of the partnership action team.

   One method of organization is to have a subcommittee for each of the seven opportunities for partnerships. The subcommittee membership should represent the broad range of stakeholders.

2. *Obtain funds and other support.* Epstein et al. (1997) suggest that partnership action teams have at least $1,000 per year for three to five years (with additional summer supplements) to invest in staff development, demonstration programs, consultants, and special materials. Another key aspect of support is having sufficient release time so that careful thinking can be invested in the process of developing and implementing action plans for each of the opportunities for partnerships.

3. *Identify starting points.* Conducting a self-assessment of present strengths, needed changes, expectations, and a sense of community can provide a starting point for specifying goals, objectives, and time lines for implementation. Figure 15–3 includes a list of questions that can serve as the basis for planning (Epstein, 1995).

   Strategies for assessing the school's current level of performance related to school-family-community partnerships include interviews, focus groups, questionnaires, panel discussions, and self-assessments.

4. *Develop a three-year plan.* Epstein et al. (1997) suggest developing a three-year plan of the specific action steps for implementing partnerships. After the three-year general plan is developed, the subcommittees can develop a more detailed one-year plan. This one-year plan should specify the activities, time line, persons responsible, resources needed, cost, and method of evaluation. These plans need to be presented to all stakeholders (for example, school faculty, families of students in the school, and community) through school newsletters; stakeholder assemblies; and the community's local radio, television, and newspapers.

5. *Continue planning and working.* The partnership action team should recommend a plan for close monitoring of the implementation of each annual plan and ensure that the monitoring process provides opportunities for troubleshooting, refinement, and a review of evaluation results. As each one-year plan is implemented, subcommittees should develop more detailed plans for the second and third years. As the hard work of implementation goes forward, the partnership action team should celebrate its success and recognize people who have been key contributors. At the end of three years, it will probably be necessary to develop another three-year plan for ongoing implementation and refinement.

> Progress in partnerships is incremental, including more families each year in ways that benefit more students. Like reading or math programs, assessment programs, sports programs, or other school investments, partnership programs take time to develop, must be periodically reviewed, and should be continuously improved. The schools in our projects have shown that three years is a minimum time needed for an action team to complete a number of activities on each type of involvement and to establish its work as a productive and permanent structure in a school. (Epstein, 1995, p. 710)

At the district level, each school district that joins the National Network must agree to the following conditions:

- Assign one full-time-equivalent facilitator to work with from 15 to 30 schools to create their Action

Teams for Partnerships, to develop and implement their plans using the partnership framework, and to share their activities.

- Allocate an annual budget for the work and activities of the district staff.
- Communicate annually with the National Network to share plans and progress.

Similarly, state requirements for National Network membership include:

- Identify a department or office within the State Department of Education and one full-time-equivalent professional to provide leadership in coordinating activities for partnerships across schools and districts.
- Allocate an annual budget for the work and activities of the state, including the facilitator's salary and competitive grants for schools or districts to implement their partnership activities.
- Communicate annually with the National Network to share plans and progress.

The National Network provides extremely valuable support to schools, districts, and states in offering them free materials, semiannual training workshops at no cost to members (except their expenses), a semiannual newsletter, technical assistance through technology options, and research/evaluation opportunities.

An evaluation of the 1997 National Network participants yielded both descriptive and experiential findings (Sanders, 1999). Highlights of the descriptive findings include the following:

- Eighty-four percent of schools joined the National Network along with districts or states.
- Approximately two-thirds of the respondents reported linking partnership activities with school-improvement goals.
- Approximately half of the action teams reported sharing information about the school's partnership program with all families, and almost two-thirds indicated they shared partnership information with all teachers and school improvement or planning teams.
- School budgets for Action Teams during the 1996–1997 school year ranged from under $100 to $70,000, with a mean of $4,065.
- Half of the respondents reported lacking time to plan and carry out partnership activities.

The experimental findings from this same research study identified five key ingredients for a successful partnership program:

The ingredients include (a) an active and supportive Action Team for School, Family, and Community Partnerships, (b) appropriate funding, (c) time, (d) guidance, and (e) leadership. Schools with adequate funding (the level varies by school) and with Action Team members who support one another's efforts are more likely than other schools to have well-implemented programs. A well-implemented program is the key element to overall program quality, along with adequate time to expand and improve partnership activities. (Sanders, 1999, p 228)

You can and should be a key contributor to the development of regularized opportunities for partnerships in the school where you are employed, and you can and should be a key advocate for empowered family involvement. To do this, you will need to enhance your own development on the family factors of empowerment and then contribute to the process of creating an empowering context for systemic planning to take place. As plans are developed and implemented and as partnerships begin to flourish, you probably will find that you are part of the synergistic community we discussed in chapter 3. When the energy of all participants contributes to a coordinated and comprehensive planning process, the whole becomes greater than the sum of the parts, and empowerment for all becomes the reality.

Advocating for Change through Legislative and Judicial Processes

National Influence

Nowhere is the advocacy role more obvious than with respect to the federal special education law known as the Individuals with Disabilities Education Act, or IDEA (Turnbull & Turnbull, 2000). When, between 1972 and 1975, Congress was first considering whether or not to help the states educate students with disabilities, its members discovered just how effective families can be.

With direction from a national coalition of family-run disability advocacy organizations and professional groups such as the Council for Exceptional Children, parents mounted a highly organized grassroots advocacy effort. Families visited their representatives in their Washington, DC, and local offices. They invited legislators to tour the schools where children and youth with disabilities were educated and to see also the institutions where other children and youth were deprived of an education and any meaningful treatment. Parents were witnesses at congressional hearings held throughout the country and in Washington, DC. They pleaded with state representatives, governors, and school officials to join their cause in getting federal money to educate students. They skillfully used the media to publicize their cause and elicit public support. And most important of all, they secured the strategic help of passionately committed insiders—family members of individuals with disabilities who were also members of Congress or members' staff as well as appointees to high positions in the administrations of Presidents Nixon and Ford (Turnbull & Turnbull, 1996).

Even today, families and their advocacy organizations, in collaboration with some (but not all) professional organizations, are using the same strategies that their predecessors used 20 years earlier. Few things are so constant and effective as families' systems advocacy. This is because many families are highly motivated to create favorable policies and programs and because they have the knowledge/skills to be effective.

State/Local Influence

It should not come as a surprise that families such as Delfy Roach's, Valerie Burrell-Muhammed's, or Kathy Berg's also engage in systems change advocacy at the state and local levels. After all, most service delivery systems are operated by state and local government agencies or by private agencies under the supervision of state and local governments.

A sterling example of effective state-level advocacy during the early to mid 1990s relates to family support laws and programs. We described family support in chapter 10; it is a program that provides cash, vouchers, or both to families of children with developmental or emotional disabilities. During the late 1980s and early 1990s, families (assisted by researchers and policy analysts) developed a grassroots movement to secure family support laws. This movement was organized nationally but was carried out locally; its targets were governors, state representatives, and state bureaucrats. It was, without doubt, enormously successful: The number of states with family support laws increased over a period of five years or so from a handful to more than half the states (Bergman & Singer, 1996; Braddock, Hemp, Parish, Westrich, & Park, 1998; Powers, 1996; Yuan, Baker-McCue, & Witkin, 1996). In the family support advocacy movement, there is a recurring theme: the collaboration among families, professionals, and other interested individuals and organizations for systems change. This is the same kind of collaboration that produced the reforms in New Mexico's mental health laws that Delfy Roach and other families and professionals wanted. It is the same kind of collaboration that is changing the hostile environment of inner city Richmond so that families like Valerie Burrell-Muhammed's will be better served. And it is the same kind of collaboration that resulted in Kathy Berg's Internet Idaho success.

Influencing Policy through the Courts

Finally, families have advocated for systems change by suing state or local educational agencies for more appropriate and more inclusive education for children with disabilities. To a very large degree they have been successful.

As early as 1972, parents and their skilled civil-rights lawyers persuaded federal courts in Pennsylvania and the District of Columbia that their children have a constitutional right to go to school (*Mills v. DC Board of Education,* 1972; *PARC v. Commonwealth,* 1971, 1972). Armed with these victories, the parents then persuaded Congress to put some teeth behind that right to education; the result of their advocacy was, of course, IDEA.

When state and local educational agencies were reluctant or unable to discharge their duty to educate children with disabilities, parents sued. Sometimes they got what they wanted, such as clean intermittent catheterization (*Irving Independent School District v. Tatro,* 1984) or school nursing services (*Garret F. v. Cedar Rapids,* 1999). Sometimes they did not get what they wanted (such as an interpreter) but instead benefited from a decision holding that the state and local agencies must provide some benefit to the students and cannot get away with simply opening the schoolhouse doors and admitting them to the building (*Board of Education v. Rowley,* 1982).

Over time, parents became increasingly dissatisfied with the schools' refusal to comply with the doctrine of least restrictive placements. Impelled by the Regular Education Initiative and later the full inclusion doctrine (chapter 2), families sued for and won the rights to have their children included in the same schools and same academic and extracurricular programs as children who do not have disabilities (*Roncker v. Walters,* 1983; *Daniel R. R. v. State Board of Education,* 1989; *Greer v. Rome City School District,* 1990; *Oberti v. Board of Education,* 1992; *Board of Education v. Holland,* 1994). You may want to reread box 8–4, which features Carlos Oberti talking about his fight for his son's inclusion.

When the U.S. Supreme Court interprets IDEA, its decision is binding throughout the country. When a federal court of appeals or trial court interprets IDEA, its opinion is binding on all educational agencies within its jurisdiction. Clearly, then, a victorious lawsuit can have system-wide implications. It sets into motion change for the one student whose rights were defined by the court. Additionally, it generates system-wide changes because many other students now have acquired the same rights as the child in the lawsuit.

Although system change often requires lawsuits, many parents cannot afford to hire a lawyer. One parent state the necessity for money to engage in systems advocacy as follows:

> You have no rights actually unless you're wealthy enough to defend yourself in court. That's what it boils down to. If you don't have the money to challenge the system, they don't care about your complaining; they don't care that you're unhappy. You can sit in the IEP meeting, fine, so what are you gonna do about it? Like, "We're not doing what you want Ms. C, what ARE you gonna do about it? Unless you take us to court, we're finished talking to you." So, now the laws are only in place to defend the people who are wealthy enough to hire an attorney and take them to court over that. (Beach Center focus group transcripts, 1999)

Congress has created two programs of legal services to protect the rights of parents who cannot afford legal services. The first system is called Protection and Advocacy and is responsible for advocating for families or individuals with developmental disabilities or mental illness. Much of the work of Protection and Advocacy agencies deals with the rights of students under IDEA. Each state has a Protection and Advocacy agency; contact your governor's office to find out its address and telephone number.

The second system is organized under the Legal Services Corporation, a public corporation created by Congress for the purpose of providing legal aid to poor or low-income families. Every state has one or more Legal Services Offices; most large cities have an office. Contact the administrative offices of the state bar association or state supreme court or check the local telephone directory (white or yellow pages) for the listings for the local or regional legal services corporation.

In most states, parent training and information centers should know the name, address, and location of the Protection and Advocacy and Legal Services Corporation offices or should be able to help you find low-cost legal aid (such as aid usually provided under the auspices of state or county bar associations). In addition, those bar associations should be able to assist families to locate lawyers who will do pro bono work. (The term *pro bono* is short for *pro bono publico* and means "for the public good.") A lawyer or firm that does pro bono work usually charges a reduced fee or no fee at all if it takes a case that it determines will be in the public interest. This is the kind of case that usually will achieve system-wide changes.

In concluding our discussion on advocacy, we encourage you to reflect upon and remember the following parental perspective concerning the ultimate accountability of advocacy decision making:

> I do recall sitting at an IEP meeting one time and it was in the middle of my very big advocacy and I was quite prepared and I had three doctors requesting what I wanted, actually there on my behalf. I would say leaders in their field. . . . Truly, they should have been highly respected for what they had to say. We did about five hours of advocacy in this IEP meeting and at the end of it we were told, "We don't agree with anything you said for the last four hours and we intend to do exactly what we intended to do when you first sat down." When it was all said and done, I remember telling the representative of the school system, "Your opinion is to do this and my opinion and my support professionals' opinion is to do this. You intend to do this regardless of what we say. If you made the wrong mistake, what will happen to you? Nothing. I have to live with the outcome of any erroneous decision for the rest of my life because I will be caring for my child until I'm gone from this planet and I have to reap the consequences. If a wrong decision is going to be made, I'd rather suffer the consequences of making it myself than knowing I'm suffering the consequences of your mistake. I want to make the decisions about my child, and I'll live with the consequences if I happen to make the wrong one. But it's difficult to live with the consequences for the decision you made that I was against." (Beach Center focus group transcripts, 1999)

Creating a Reliable Alliance

The eight obligations of a reliable alliance need to be infused into the partnership opportunity of advocating for systems improvement in the same way that you infuse them into the six other opportunities for partnerships. By this point, this infusion should seem like second nature for you. Figure 15–4 highlights issues that are likely to arise and disempowering and empowering options that you have in creating the reliable alliance obligations.

Strengthening Family Factors

Your partnerships with families can make all the difference in either enhancing or detracting from their motivation and knowledge/skills related to empowerment. Figure 15–5 suggests how your actions can make a meaningful difference in family empowerment as well as the empowerment of yourself and your professional colleagues.

FIGURE 15–4

Creating a Reliable Alliance: Emphasis on Advocating for Systems Improvement

Obligations	Issues	Disempowering Actions	Empowering Actions
Knowing yourself	As a new teacher you think you might be "out-of-place" to express your interest in being a member of the school-improvement team.	Decide to wait several years until you have more credibility before you let others know of your interest in systems improvement.	Ask the principal to bring you up to date on how the school is implementing the National Education Goals and express your interest in being an active participant in the process.
Knowing families Family characteristics	A father from a lower socioeconomic background has a special commitment to partnerships and could represent a whole segment of families who do not currently have a voice in school planning.	Conclude that this father would likely not be available to hold his own in serving on the partnership action team and recommend a parent who is a university professor in his place.	Advocate for the father to be a parent representative on the team. Stress the importance of parents from all backgrounds being represented.
Family interactions	A mother of one of your students is so involved in organizing a letter-writing campaign to influence state policy that she is unavailable to help her child with homework assignments. Her child is falling further and further behind.	Suggest to the mother that her child's progress needs to take precedence over her advocacy efforts and that it is not fair to neglect him.	Brainstorm with the mother about how she might be able to get others to help with the letter-writing campaign so that she will not have so much to do herself. Also, consider who else might be available to help with homework.
Family functions	Parents of one of your students want to know about the latest court cases on inclusion, but they don't have access to this information and don't know where to get it.	Conclude that sharing information about court cases is just encouraging parents to sue you. Tell them there is nothing that you can do to help.	Encourage parents to contact a parent training and information center to gather the latest information on inclusion court cases.
Family life cycle	Parents of one of the students who is graduating from your high school class are very frustrated by only having a sheltered workshop as a post-secondary option. Your director of special education encourages them to be realistic about their son's potential.	Accept what the director of special education says so that you can be sure to protect your job.	Convene a meeting of high school teachers and families and invite people to share great expectations of the kinds of services they would like to have after high school. Develop an action plan for professionals taking more responsibility to advocate for appropriate services.

(continued)

FIGURE 15–4   CONTINUED

Creating a Reliable Alliance: Emphasis on Advocating for Systems Improvement

Obligations	Issues	Disempowering Actions	Empowering Actions
Honoring cultural diversity	As you review the roster of members of the school-improvement team, you realize that all are Euro-American.	Assume that the principal knew what he or she was doing when these appointments were made and that it is none of your business to make any suggestions.	Reflect on possible school, family, or community participants from culturally diverse backgrounds. Make recommendations to the principal of additional participants representing diverse backgrounds.
Affirming and building on family strengths	A parent of a student in your class is an attorney who has a particular interest in disability policy.	Assume that it is better for parents of students in your classroom not to know much about disability policy because they may start making too many unreasonable demands on you.	Ask the parent who is a lawyer if he or she would be willing to provide an update to all parents in your classroom of the process the state uses to monitor IDEA implementation and how they might be able to contribute to the process.
Promoting family choices	A parent of one of your students suggests activities that the school might undertake to improve the IEP process.	Acknowledge that the parent has a good idea but dismiss it because it would require change in the procedures that the school has always followed.	Give the parent the name of the person who is in charge of the partnership action team subcommittee related to individualizing education. Encourage the parent to meet with the subcommittee and share the good idea.
Envisioning great expectations	You develop your own vision for how the opportunities for partnerships might permeate every professional and family in your school.	Assume that you are only responsible for yourself and that all you can do is to take care of your own classroom.	Share your vision with professional colleagues and families and encourage them to start a partnership action team.
Using interpersonal communication skills	During meetings of the school-improvement team, you notice that the principal dominates the discussion and cuts off family contributions.	Assume that the principal has the prerogative to dominate decision making.	Discuss with the principal the fact that you have heard many good ideas raised by families in private conversations and brainstorm about what might be done to ensure that these ideas come up at the school-improvement team meetings.

FIGURE 15–4   CONTINUED

Creating a Reliable Alliance: Emphasis on Advocating for Systems Improvement

Obligations	Issues	Disempowering Actions	Empowering Actions
Warranting trust and respect	You are intimidated by parents of one of your students who are making adversarial threats.	When parents try to schedule a meeting, tell them that you do not have any available time.	Listen empathetically to the parents' concerns and consider ways that their concerns can be taken into account by the school-improvement team and by your own advocacy efforts.

FIGURE 15–5

Strengthening Family Factors Through an Empowering Context: Emphasis on Advocating for Systems Improvement

Motivation	What You Can Do	Knowledge/Skills	What You Can Do
Self-efficacy	Provide feedback to parents on partnership action teams to reinforce their contributions. Cite specific examples of how they help the team be effective.	Information	Keep families informed of proposed changes in national and state legislation and contact information for how they can make their viewpoints known to key policymakers.
Perceived control	When many changes are needed to ensure an appropriate education for the student, identify families' priorities and advocate for those priorities to be addressed first.	Problem solving	Ensure that the partnership action teams incorporate a systematic problem-solving process so that detailed action plans are developed and implemented.
Energy	Help identify empowerful professionals and families to serve on the school-improvement team so the full responsibility will not fall on a few individuals.	Communication skills	Emphasize to families how important it is to be assertive in school-improvement team meetings to make sure that issues associated with special education are included on the agenda.
Persistence	If initial efforts fail to influence appropriate state and local policies, encourage advocates to keep working until the goal is reached.	Coping skills	Encourage families who are heavily involved in advocacy to work closely with others who have similar interests so that mutual support can be shared.
Hope	When funds are being cut back at the national and state levels, emphasize the importance of advocacy and the possibility that the cuts might be restored.		

Summary

Advocacy simply means taking one's own or another's perspective to obtain a result not otherwise available. Standing up for one's own rights and interests (self-advocacy) or for the rights and interests of another (representational advocacy) occurs at the local, regional, state, and national levels. Indeed, many families have to engage in local advocacy at one time or another, and many who have become advocates for change at the local level have also become advocates at the state or national level.

Advocacy seeks to make a difference not only in the education of a single student but also in the way a school system educates all students; this is systems advocacy. Many parents welcome the chance to be single-student or even systems change advocates; others do not care to be advocates.

Advocacy is typically most effective when it involves collaboration among families and professionals. And advocacy often involves efforts to change laws or win lawsuits.

The agencies that seem most helpful to families and their professional allies are the Partners in Policymaking programs, the parent training and information centers, disability-specific organizations at the national/state/local levels, Protection and Advocacy agencies, Legal Services Corporation law firms, and pro bono lawyers.

The national emphasis on school reform gives parents a chance to advocate for the effective implementation of the National Education Goals. Many schools have created school-improvement teams, comprised of a full range of stakeholders, to collaborate for educational improvement. In those teams, issues associated with students who have exceptionalities often have taken a back burner to other issues that have priority with typically developing students. One of your roles can be to ensure that family and professional perspectives related to exceptionality are kept at the front of the school-reform movement.

Of the eight National Education Goals, one focuses on parent participation. We suggested a process developed by Epstein (1995) and Sanders (1999) that your school, district, and state can follow in creating partnership action teams to plan for the effective implementation of all seven opportunities for partnerships. This process is associated with the National Network of Partnership Schools, which provides training, technical assistance, and resource materials to enhance the likelihood of success. Research underscores the successful elements of the National Network.

Finally, many families and professionals have been effective in advocating for systems change through the legislative process at national and state levels and through judicial processes.

There are connecting threads in the lives of Delfy Roach, Valerie Burrell-Muhammed, and Kathy Berg. They are parents: Whatever their idiosyncratic experiences, they share a common cause—passionate commitment to their children and to the children of other families. They are advocates: They stand up for themselves and their children, and they stand up for other families, too. And they are collaborators: They may have started out alone, but they created networks of other families and of professionals, knowing that there is strength in numbers.

In creating those networks, they appealed to professionals and policy leaders in two ways. First, they appealed to their heads: Do what is smart, do what benefits the children and families, do what makes your systems better. Second, they appealed to their hearts: "If this were your child, if this were your family, what would you want?"

In asking that question, they did more than appeal to their empathy. They created a common thread of humanity and tied this to their own lives and to the lives of other families.

We all struggle. We all advocate. The empowerment piece belongs to us all.

Technical Assistance Alliance

National Coordination

PACER Center
4826 Chicago Avenue South
Minneapolis, MN 55417-1098
612-827-2966 voice
612-827-7770 TTY
612-827-3065 fax
1-888-248-0822 (toll-free nationally)
alliance@taalliance.org
www.taalliance.org

Regional Coordination

Northeast Regional Center

Parent Information Center
P.O. Box 2405
Concord, NH 03302-2405
603-224-7005 voice
603-224-4379 fax
picnh@aol.com
CT, DE, DC, ME, MD, MA, NH, NJ,
    NY, PA, Puerto Rico, RI, US VI, VT

Midwest Regional Center

**Ohio Coalition for the Education of
    Children with Disabilities (OCECD)**
Bank One Building
165 West Center Street, Suite 302
Marion, OH 43302-3741
740-382-5452 voice
740-383-6421 fax
ocecd@gte.net
CO, IL, IA, IN, KS, KY, MI, MN, MO,
    NE, ND, OH, SD, WI

South Regional Center

Partners Resource Network, Inc.
1090 Longfellow Drive, Suite B
Beaumont, TX 77706-4819
409-898-4684 voice
409-898-4869 fax
txprn@pnx.com
AL, AR, FL, GA, LA, MS, NC, OK, SC,
    TN, TX, VA, WV

West Regional Center

**Matrix Parent Network and Resource
    Center**
94 Galli Drive, Suite C
Novato, CA 94949
415-884-3535
415-884-3555 fax
matrix@matrixparents.org
AK, AZ, Department of Defense
    Dependent Schools (DODDS), CA,
    HI, ID, MT, NV, NM, OR, Pacific
    Jurisdiction, UT, WA, WY

This list of federally funded Parent
Centers was generated by the
Alliance Coordinating Office at the
PACER Center. If there are any
corrections please notify the Alliance
Office.
The Alliance Grant Project Officer is
Donna Fluke, Office of Special
Education Programs.

Parent Training and Information Centers

Alabama

**Special Education Action Committee,
    Inc.**
P.O. Box 161274
Mobile, AL 36616-2274
334-478-1208 voice & TDD
334-473-7877 fax
1-800-222-7322 AL only
seacofmobile@zebra.net
www.home.hiwaay.net/~seachsv/

Alaska

PARENTS, Inc.
4743 E. Northern Lights Blvd.
Anchorage, AK 99508
907-337-7678 voice
907-337-7629 TDD

907-337-7671 fax
1-800-478-7678 in AK
parents@parentsinc.org
www.parentsinc.org

American Samoa

American Samoa PAVE
P.O. Box 3432
Pago Pago, AS 96799
011-684-699-6946
011-684-699-6952 fax
SAMPAVE@samoatelco.com
www.taalliance.org/ptis/amsamoa/

Arizona

Pilot Parents of Southern Arizona
2600 North Wyatt Drive
Tucson, AZ 85712
520-324-3150
520-324-3152
ppsa@pilotparents.org
www.pilotparents.org
Southern AZ

RAISING Special Kids
4750 N. Black Canyon Hwy, Suite
    101
Phoenix, AZ 85017-3621
602-242-4366 voice & TDD
602-242-4306 fax
1-800-237-3007 in AZ
Central and Northern AZ

Arkansas

Arkansas Disability Coalition
1123 University Ave., Suite 225
Little Rock, AR 72204-1605
501-614-7020 voice & TDD
501-614-9082 fax
1-800-223-1330 AR only
adc@alltel.net
www.adcpti.org
Statewide
With FOCUS AR

FOCUS, Inc.
305 West Jefferson Ave.
Jonesboro, AR 72401
870-935-2750 voice
870-931-3755 fax
888-247-3755
focusinc@ipa.net
www.grnco.net/~norre/
With Arkansas Disability Coalition AR

California

DREDF
2212 Sixth Street
Berkeley, CA 94710
510-644-2555 (TDD available)
510-841-8645 fax
1-800-466-4232
dredf@dredf.org
www.dredf.org
Northern California
With Parents Helping Parents, Santa
Clara

**Exceptional Family Support, Education
and Advocacy Center**
6402 Skyway
Paradise, CA 95969
530-876-8321 voice
530-876-0346 fax
sea@sunset.net
www.sea-center.org

Exceptional Parents Unlimited
4120 N. First St.
Fresno, CA 93726
559-229-2000
559-229-2956 fax
epul@cybergate.com
www.exceptionalparents.org
Central California

Matrix
94 Galli Drive, Suite C
Novato, CA 94949
415-884-3535
415-884-3555 fax
1-800-578-2592
matrix@matrixparents.org
www.matrixparents.org
Northern California
With Parents Helping Parents, Santa
Clara

**Parents Helping Parents of San
Francisco**
594 Monterey Blvd.
San Francisco, CA 94127-2416
415-841-8820
415-841-8824 fax
sfphp@earthlink.com
Nine counties in the San Francisco
Bay area

Parents Helping Parents of Santa Clara
3041 Olcott St.
Santa Clara, CA 95054-3222
408-727-5775 voice
408-727-7655 TDD
408-727-0182 fax
info@php.com
www.php.com
Northern California
With Matrix and DREDF

**Support for Families of Children with
Disabilities**
2601 Mission #710
San Francisco, CA 94110-3111
415-282-7494
415-282-1226 fax
sfcdmiss@aol.com
San Francisco

TASK, Anaheim
100 West Cerritos Ave.
Anaheim, CA 92805
714-533-8275
714-533-2533 fax
taskca@aol.com
Southern California

TASK, San Diego
3750 Convoy St., Suite 303
San Diego, CA 92111-3741
619-874-2386
619-874-2375 fax
tasksd1@aol.com
City of San Diego and Imperial
Counties

Colorado

PEAK Parent Center, Inc.
6055 Lehman Drive, Suite 101
Colorado Springs, CO 80918
719-531-9400 voice
719-531-9403 TDD
719-531-9452 fax
1-800-284-0251
info@peakparent.org
www.peakparent.org

Connecticut

Connecticut Parent Advocacy Center
338 Main Street
Niantic, CT 06357
860-739-3089 voice & TDD
860-739-7460 fax (Call first to
dedicate line)

1-800-445-2722 in CT
cpacinc@aol.com
members.aol.com/cpacinc/cpac.htm

Delaware

Parent Information Center (PIC)
700 Barksdale Road, Suite 16
Newark, DE 19711
302-366-0152 voice/302-366-0178
(TDD)
302-366-0276 fax
picofdel@picofdel.org
www.picofdel.org

District of Columbia

Advocates for Justice and Education
2041 Martin Luther King Ave., SE,
Suite 301
Washington, DC 20020
202-678-8060
202-678-8062 fax
1-888-327-8060
justice1@bellatlantic.net
www.aje.qpg.com/

Florida

Family Network on Disabilities
2735 Whitney Road
Clearwater, FL 33760-1610
727-523-1130
727-523-8687 fax
1-800-825-5736 FL only
fnd@fndfl.org
fndfl.org

Georgia

**Parents Educating Parents and
Professionals for All Children
(PEPPAC)**
6613 East Church Street, Suite 100
Douglasville, GA 30134
770-577-7771
770-577-7774 fax
peppac@bellsouth.net
www.peppac.org

Hawaii

AWARE
200 N. Vineyard Blvd., Suite 310
Honolulu, HI 96817
808-536-9684 voice
808-536-2280 voice & TTY
808-537-6780 fax
1-800-533-9684
1dah@gte.net

**Palau Parent Network/Center on
Disability Studies, University of
Hawaii**
1833 Kala Kaua Avenue, #609
Honolulu, HI 96815
808-945-1432

808-945-1440 fax
dotty@hawaii.edu
patric@palaunet.com

Idaho

Idaho Parents Unlimited, Inc.
4696 Overland Road, Suite 568
Boise, ID 83705
208-342-5884 voice & TDD
208-342-1408 fax
1-800-242-4785
ipul@rmci.net
home.rmci.net/ipul

Native American Parent Training and Information Center
129 East Third
Moscow, ID 83843
208-885-3500
famtog@moscow.com
Nationwide resource for Native American families, tribes, and communities as well as parent centers and others needing information on this subject

Illinois

Designs for Change
6 North Michigan Ave., Suite 1600
Chicago, IL 60602
312-857-9292 voice
312-857-1013 TDD
312-857-9299 fax
1-800-851-8728
dfc1@aol.com
www.dfc1.org

Family Resource Center on Disabilities
20 E. Jackson Blvd., Room 300
Chicago, IL 60604
312-939-3513 voice
312-939-3519 TTY & TDY
312-939-7297 fax
1-800-952-4199 IL only
frcdptii1@ameritech.net
www.ameritech.net/users/frcdptii1/index.html

Family T.I.E.S. Network
830 South Spring
Springfield, IL 62704
217-544-5809
217-544-6018 fax
1-800-865-7842
ftiesn@aol.com
www.taalliance.org/ptis/fties/
Central and Southern Illinois

National Center for Latinos with Disabilities
1915-17 South Blue Island Ave.
Chicago, IL 60608
312-666-3393 voice
312-666-1788 TTY
312-666-1787 fax

1-800-532-3393
ncld@ncld.com
homepage.interaccess.com/~ncld/

Indiana

IN*SOURCE
809 N. Michigan St.
South Bend, IN 46601-1036
219-234-7101
219-239-7275 TDD
219-234-7279 fax
1-800-332-4433 in IN
insourc1@aol.com
www.insource.org

Iowa

Access for Special Kids (ASK)
321 E. 6th St.
Des Moines, IA 50309
515-243-1713
515-243-1902 fax
1-800-450-8667
ptiiowa@aol.com
www.taalliance.org/ptis/ia/

Kansas

Families Together, Inc.
3340 W Douglas, Ste. 102
Wichita, KS 67203
316-945-7747
316-945-7795 fax
1-888-815-6364
fmin@feist.com
www.kansas.net/~family/

Kentucky

Kentucky Special Parent Involvement Network (KY-SPIN)
2210 Goldsmith Lane, Suite 118
Louisville, KY 40218
502-456-0923
502-456-0893 fax
1-800-525-7746
spininc@aol.com

Louisiana

Project PROMPT
4323 Division Street, Suite 110
Metairie, LA 70002-3179
504-888-9111
504-888-0246 fax
1-800-766-7736
fhfgno@ix.netcom.com
www.projectprompt.com

Maine

Special Needs Parent Info Network
P.O. Box 2067
Augusta, ME 04338-2067
207-582-2504
207-582-3638 fax
1-800-870-SPIN in ME

jlachance@mpf.org
www.mpf.org

Maryland

Parents Place of Maryland, Inc.
7484 Candlewood Rd., Suite S
Hanover, MD 21076-1306
410-859-5300 voice & TDD
410-859-5301 fax
info@ppmd.org
www.ppmd.org

Massachusetts

Federation for Children with Special Needs
1135 Tremont Street, Suite 420
Boston, MA 02120-2140
617-236-7210 voice and TTY
617-572-2094 fax
1-800-331-0688 in MA
fcsninfo@fcsn.org
www.fcsn.org/

Michigan

CAUSE
3303 W. Saginaw, Suite F-1
Lansing, MI 48917-2303
517-886-9167 voice & TDD & TDY
517-886-9775 fax
1-800-221-9105 in MI
info-cause@voyager.net
www.pathwaynet.com/cause/

Parents Are Experts
23077 Greenfield Road, Suite 205
Southfield, MI 48075-3745
248-557-5070 voice & TDD
248-557-4456 fax
1-800-827-4843
ucp@ameritech.net
www.taalliance.org/ptis/mi-parents/
Wayne County

Minnesota

PACER Center, Inc.
4826 Chicago Avenue South
Minneapolis, MN 55417-1098
612-827-2966 voice
612-827-7770 TTY
612-827-3065 fax
1-800-537-2237 in MN
pacer@pacer.org
www.pacer.org

Mississippi

Parent Partners
1900 North West St., Ste. C-100
Jackson, MS 39202
601-714-5707
601-714-4025 fax
1-800-366-5707 in MS
ptiofms@misnet.com
www.taalliance.org/ptis/ms/

Missouri

Missouri Parents Act
2100 S. Brentwood, Suite G
Springfield, MO 65804
417-882-7434
417-882-8413 fax
1-800-743-7634 (in MO only)
mpactsm@axs.net
www.crn.org/mpact/

Montana

Parents Let's Unite for Kids
516 N. 32nd Street
Billings, MT 59101
406-255-0540
406-255-0523 fax
1-800-222-7585 in MT
plukinfo@pluk.org
www.pluk.org

Nebraska

Nebraska Parents Center
1941 South 42nd St., #122
Omaha, NE 68105-2942
402-346-0525 voice & TDD
402-346-5253 fax
1-800-284-8520
gdavis@neparentcenter.org
www.neparentcenter.org

Nevada

Nevada Parents Encouraging Parents (PEP)
2810 W. Charleston Blvd., Suite G-68
Quall Park IV
Las Vegas, NV 89102
702-388-8899
702-388-2966 fax
1-800-216-5188
nvpep@vegas.infi.net
www.nvpep.org

New Hampshire

Parent Information Center
P.O. Box 2405
Concord, NH 03302-2405
603-224-7005 voice & TDD
603-224-4379 fax
1-800-232-0986 in NH
picnh@aol.com
www.taalliance.org/ptis/nhpic/

New Jersey

Statewide Parent Advocacy Network (SPAN)
35 Halsey Street, 4th Floor
Newark, NJ 07102
973-642-8100
973-642-8080 fax
1-800-654-SPAN

span@bellatlantic.net
www.taalliance.org/ptis/nj/

New Mexico

Parents Reaching Out, Project ADOBE
1000-A Main St. NW
Los Lunas, NM 87031
505-865-3700 voice & TDD
505-865-3737 fax
1-800-524-5176 in NM
nmproth@aol.com
www.parentsreachingout.org

New York

The Advocacy Center
277 Alexander St., Suite 500
Rochester, NY 14607
716-546-1700
716-546-7069 fax
1-800-650-4967 (NY only)
advocacy@frontiernet.net
www.advocacycenter.com
Statewide except for NY city

Advocates for Children of NY
151 West 50th Street, 5th Floor
Brooklyn, NY 10001
212-947-9779
212-947-9790 fax
info@advocatesforchildren.org
www.advocatesforchildren.org
Five boroughs of New York City

Resources for Children with Special Needs
200 Park Ave. S., Suite 816
New York, NY 10003
212-677-4650
212-254-4070 fax
resourcesnyc@prodigy.net
www.resourcesnyc.org
New York City (Bronx, Brooklyn, Manhattan, Queens, Staten Island)

Sinergia/Metropolitan Parent Center
15 West 65th St., 6th Floor
New York, NY 10023
212-496-1300
212-496-5608 fax
Sinergia@panix.com
www.panix.com/~sinergia/
New York City

North Carolina

ECAC, Inc.
P.O. Box 16
Davidson, NC 28036
704-892-1321
704-892-5028 fax (Call first to dedicate line)
1-800-962-6817 NC only
ECAC1@aol.com
www.ecac-parentcenter.org/

North Dakota

ND Pathfinder Parent Training and Information Center
Arrowhead Shopping Center
1600 2nd Ave. SW, Suite 19
Minot, ND 58701-3459
701-837-7500 voice
701-837-7501 TTY
701-837-7548 fax
1-800-245-5840 ND only
ndpath01@minot.ndak.net
www.pathfinder.minot.com

Ohio

Child Advocacy Center
1821 Summit Road, Suite 303
Cincinnati, OH 45237
513-821-2400
513-821-2442 fax
CADCenter@aol.com
Southwestern Ohio, Northern Kentucky, Dearborn County, Indiana

OCECD
Bank One Building
165 West Center St., Suite 302
Marion, OH 43302-3741
740-382-5452 voice & TDD
740-383-6421 fax
1-800-374-2806
ocecd@gte.net
www.taalliance.org/PTIs/regohio/

Oklahoma

Parents Reaching Out in OK
1917 S. Harvard Avenue
Oklahoma City, OK 73128
405-681-9710
405-685-4006 fax
1-800-759-4142
prook1@aol.com
www.taalliance.org/ptis/ok/

Oregon

Oregon COPE Project
999 Locust St. NE
Salem, OR 97303
503-581-8156 voice & TDD
503-391-0429 fax
1-888-505-COPE
orcope@open.org
www.open.org/~orcope

Pennsylvania

Hispanos Unidas para Niños con Impedimentos
(Hispanics United for Special Needs Children)
Buena Vista Plaza
166 W. Lehigh Avenue, Suite 101

Philadelphia, PA 19133-3838
215-425-6203
215-425-6204 fax
hupni@aol.com
City of Philadelphia, occasional
service to surrounding counties

Parent Education Network
2107 Industrial Hwy.
York, PA 17402-2223
717-600-0100 voice & TTY
717-600-1801 fax
1-800-522-5827 in PA
1-800-441-5028 (Spanish in PA)
pen@parentednet.org
www.parentednet.org

Parents Union for Public Schools
1315 Walnut Street, Suite 1124
Philadelphia, PA 19107
215-546-1166
215-731-1688 fax
ParentsU@aol.com
City of Philadelphia, occasional
service to surrounding counties

Puerto Rico

APNI
P.O. Box 21301
Ponce de Leon 724
San Juan, PR 00928-1301
787-250-4552
787-765-0345 fax
1-800-981-8492
1-800-949-4232
apnipr@prtc.net
Island of Puerto Rico

Rhode Island

RI Parent Information Network
175 Main Street
Pawtucket, RI 02860
401-727-4144 voice
401-727-4151 TDD
401-727-4040 fax
1-800-464-3399 in RI
collins@ripin.org
http://www.ripin.org/

South Carolina

Advocacy Coalition for Youth with Disabilities
c/o Family Resource Center
135 Rutledge Ave.
PO Box 250567
Charleston, SC 29425
843-876-1519
843-876-1518 fax
mccarthyb@musc.edu
Tri-county: Charleston, Berkeley, and
Dorchester

PRO-PARENTS
2712 Middleburg Drive, Suite 203
Columbia, SC 29204
803-779-3859 voice & TDD
803-252-4513 fax
1-800-759-4776 in SC
pro-parents@aol.com
community.columbiatoday.com/realc
ities/proparents

South Dakota

South Dakota Parent Connection
3701 West 49th St., Suite 200B
Sioux Falls, SD 57106
605-361-3171 voice & TDD
605-361-2928 fax
1-800-640-4553 in SD
bpete@dakota.net
www.sdparent.org

Tennessee

Support and Training for Exceptional Parents, Inc. (STEP)
424 E. Bernard Ave., Suite 3
Greeneville, TN 37745
423-639-0125 voice
636-8217 TDD
423-636-8217 fax
1-800-280-STEP in TN
tnstep@aol.com
www.tnstep.org

Texas

Grassroots Consortium
6202 Belmark
P.O. Box 61628
Houston, TX 77087
713-643-9576
713-643-6291 fax
speckids@pdq.net
Comprised of various community
groups nationwide

Partners Resource Network, Inc.
1090 Longfellow Drive, Suite B
Beaumont, TX 77706-4819
409-898-4684 voice & TDD
409-898-4869 fax
1-800-866-4726 in TX
txprn@pnx.com
www.PartnersTX.org

Project PODER
1017 N. Main Ave., Suite 207
San Antonio, TX 78212
210-222-2637
210-475-9283 fax
1-800-682-9747 TX only
poder@tfepoder.org
www.tfepoder.org
San Antonia, Hondo, & Catroville,
Cameron, Hidalgo, Willacy, and
Starr Counties

Utah

Utah Parent Center
2290 East 4500 S., Suite 110
Salt Lake City, UT 84117-4428
801-272-1051
801-272-8907 fax
1-800-468-1160 in UT
upc@inconnect.com
www.utahparentcenter.org

Vermont

Vermont Parent Information Center
1 Mill Street, Suite A7
Burlington, VT 05401
802-658-5315 voice & TDD
802-658-5395 fax
1-800-639-7170 in VT
vpic@together.net
homepages.together.net/~vpic

Virgin Islands

V.I. FIND
#2 Nye Gade
St. Thomas, US VI 00802
340-774-1662
340-775-3962 fax
vifind@islands.vi
www.taalliance.org/ptis/vifind/
Virgin Islands

Virginia

Parent Educational Advocacy Training Center
6320 Augusta Drive
Springfield, VA 22150
703-923-0010
703-923-0030 fax
1-800-869-6782 VA only
partners@peatc.org
www.peatc.org

Washington

PAVE/STOMP
6316 South 12th St.
Tacoma, WA 98465
253-565-2266 voice & TTY
253-566-8052 fax
1-800-572-7368
wapave9@washingtonpave.org
washingtonpave.org/stomp.html
U.S. Military installations; and as a
resource for parent centers and
others needing information on this
subject

Washington PAVE
6316 South 12th
Tacoma, WA 98465-1900
253-565-2266 voice & TDD
253-566-8052 fax
1-800-572-7368 in WA

wapave9@washingtonpave.org
washingtonpave.org

West Virginia

West Virginia PTI
371 Broaddus Ave
Clarksburg, WV 26301
304-624-1436 voice & TTY
304-624-1438
1-800-281-1436 in WV
wvpti@aol.com
www.iolinc.net/wvpti

Wisconsin

**Native American Family
Empowerment Center**
Great Lakes Inter-Tribal Council, Inc.
2932 Highway 47N, P.O. Box 9
Lac du Flambeau, WI 54538
715-588-3324
715-588-7900
1-800-472-7207 (WI only)
drosin@newnorth.net

Parent Education Project of Wisconsin
2192 South 60th Street
West Allis, WI 53219-1568
414-328-5520 voice
414-328-5525 TDD
414-328-5530
1-800-231-8382 (WI only)
PMColletti@aol.com
members.aol.com/pepofwi/

Wyoming

Parent Information Center
5 North Lobban
Buffalo, WY 82834
307-684-2277 voice & TDD
307-684-5314
1-800-660-9742 WY only
tdawsonpic@vcn.com
www.wpic.org

Expertise Centers

**Board of Directors and Board
Development**
Parents Helping Parents (PHP) of
Santa Clara
3041 Olcoit Street
Santa Clara, CA 95054
408-727-5775

Cultural Competency and Diversity
Pro-Oklahoma–Parents Reaching Out
in Oklahoma
1917 S. Harvard Avenue
Oklahoma City, OK 73128
405-681-9710

Early Childhood
Resources for Children with Special
Needs, Inc.
200 Park Avenue South, Room 816
New York, New York 10003
212-677-4650

Effective Training Techniques
Utah Parent Center
2290 East 4500 S., Suite 110
Salt Lake City, UT 84117
801-272-1051

Inclusion
PEAK Parent Center, Inc.
6055 Lehman Drive, Suite 101
Colorado Springs, CO 80918
719-531-9400

Interagency Collaboration
EPICS
P.O. Box 788
Bernalillo, NM 87004
505-881-0185

School Reform/IDEA
Statewide Parent Advocacy Network
of New Jersey, Inc.
35 Halsey Street, 4th floor
Newark, NJ 07102
973-642-8100

Self-Determination
RAISING Special Kids
4750 N. Black Canyon Hwy. (#101)
Phoenix, AZ 85017
602-242-4366

Transition (School to Work)
Nebraska Parents Center
194 South 42nd Street, Ste. 122
Omaha, NE 68105-2942
402-346-0525

Community Parent Resource Centers (CPRCs)

*The National Information Center
for Children and Youth with
Disabilities (NICHCY)*
P.O. Box 1492
Washington, DC 20013-1492
1-202-884-8200 voice
1-800-695-0285 voice
1-202-884-8441 fax
nichcy@aed.org
www.nichcy.org

California (CPRC)

Loving Your Disabled Child
4528 Crenshaw Boulevard
Los Angeles, CA 90043
323-299-2925
323-299-4373 fax
lydc@pacbell.net
www.lydc.org
Most of LA County

Florida (CPRC)

Parent to Parent of Miami, Inc.
c/o Sunrise Community
9040 Sunset Drive, Suite G
Miami, FL 33173
305-271-9797
305-271-6628 fax
PtoP1086@aol.com
Miami Dade and Monroe Counties

Kansas (CPRC)

Families ACT
555 N. Woodlawn
Wichita, KS 67203
316-685-1821
316-685-0768 fax
nina@mhasck.org
www.mhasck.org
Sedgwick County and outlying area

Louisiana (CPRC)

Pyramid Parent Training Program
4101 Fontainbleau Dr
New Orleans, LA 70125
504-827-0610
504-827-2999 fax
dmarkey404@aol.com

Mississippi (CPRC)

Project Empower
136 South Poplar Ave.
Greenville, MS 38701
601-332-4852
601-332-1622 fax
1-800-337-4852
empower@tecinfo.com

New York (CPRC)

United We Stand
c/o Casa del Barrio

728 Driggs Ave.
Brooklyn, NY 11211
718-302-4313, ext.562
718-302-4315 fax
uwsofny@aol.com
www.taalliance.org/ptis/uws/

Texas (CPRC)

El Valle Community Parent Resource Center
530 South Texas Blvd., Suite J
Weslaco, TX 78596
956-969-3611
956-969-8761 fax
1-800-680-0255 TX only
texasfiestaedu@acnet.net
www.tfepoder.org
Cameron, Willacy, and Starr Counties

Texas (CPRC)

The Arc of Texas in the Rio Grande Valley
Parents Supporting Parents Network
601 N. Texas Blvd.
Weslaco, TX 78596
956-447-8408
956-973-9503 fax
1-888-857-8688
dmeraz@gtemail.net
www.thearcoftexas.org

Virginia (CPRC)

PADDA, Inc.
813 Forrest Drive, Suite 3
Newport News, VA 23606
757-591-9119
757-591-8990 fax
1-888-337-2332
webmaster@padda.org
www.padda.org

Washington (CPRC)

Parent to Parent Power
1118 S 142nd St.
Tacoma, WA 98444
253-531-2022
253-538-1126 fax
ylink@aa.net

Wisconsin (CPRC)

Wisconsin Family Assistance Center for Education, Training and Support
2714 North Dr. Martin Luther King Dr., Suite E
Milwaukee, WI 53212
414-374-4645
414-374-4635 TTD
414-374-4655 fax
wifacets@execpc.com

Grassroots Consortium on Disabilities

Loving Your Disabled Child
4528 Crenshaw Blvd.
Los Angeles, CA 90043
323-299-2925
323-299-4373 fax
lydc@pacbell.net

COFFO, Inc.
305 South Flager Avenue
Homestead, FL 33030
305-237-5093
305-237-5013 fax

VI-FIND
P.O. Box 11670
St. Thomas, VI 00801
340-774-1662
340-775-3962 fax
ae712@virgin.usvi.net

Parents of Watts
10828 Lou Dillion Avenue
Los Angeles, CA 90059
323-566-7556
323-569-3982 fax

Lakota Tiwahe Tokata Ho
P.O. Box 937
Pine Ridge, SD 57770
605-867-1392
605-867-2761 fax

SKI/Grassroots PTI
P.O. Box 266958
Houston, TX 77207-6958
713-643-9576
713-643-6291 fax
speckids@pdq.net

IPEST
202 Lake Street, P.O. Box 4081
Vineyard Haven, MA 02586
508-693-8612
508-693-7111 fax
ckennedy@tiac.net

Parent to Parent Power
1118 South 142nd Street
Tacoma, WA 98444
253-531-2022
253-538-1126 fax
ylink@aa.net

Pyramid Parent Training
4101 Fountainbleau Drive
New Orleans, LA 70125
504-827-0610
504-827-2999
dmarkey404@aol.com

United We Stand
312 S. 3rd Street
Brooklyn, NY 11211
718-302-4313
718-302-4315 fax
uswofny@aol.com

UPBEATT
9950 Fielding
Detroit, MI 48228
313-835-6898
313-837-1164 fax

Mentor Parent Program
P.O. Box 47
Pittsfield, PA 16340
814-563-3470
814-563-3445 fax
gal97@penn.com

Vietnamese Parents of Disabled Children
831 Park Vine Street
Orange, CA 92686
310-370-6704
310-542-0522 fax
luyenchu@aol.com

Statewide Parent to Parent Programs

Arizona

Raising Special Kids
4750 Black Canyon Highway, Suite 101
Phoenix, AZ 85017-3621
602-242-4366
602-242-4306 fax
mfslaugh@aol.com

Arkansas

Parent to Parent
2000 Main
Little Rock, AR 72206

501-375-7770
501-372-4558 fax

California

Parents Helping Parents
3041 Olcott Street
Santa Clara, CA 95054-3222
408-727-5775
408-727-0182 fax
trudy@php.com

Colorado

Parent to Parent of Colorado
c/o UCP of Colorado
2200 S. Jasmine Street
Denver, CO 80222
303-627-8888
303-627-1265 fax
diannedmc@aol.com

Connecticut

Parent to Parent Network of CT
The Family Center
282 Washington
Hartford, CT 06106
860-545-9021
860-545-9201 fax

Florida

Family Network on Disabilities of Florida
2735 Whitney Road
Clearwater, FL 34520
727-523-1130
727-523-8687 fax
eileen@aol.com

Georgia

Parent to Parent of Georgia
2872 Woodcock Blvd., Suite 230
Atlanta, GA 30341
770-451-5484
770-458-4091 fax
parenttoparentofga.org

Indiana

Indiana Parent Information Network
4755 Kingsway Drive, Suite 105
Indianapolis, IN 46205
317-257-8683
317-251-7488 fax
familynetw@aol.com

Kansas

Families Together, Inc.
501 SW Jackson, Suite 400
Topeka, KS 66603
785-233-4777
785-233-4787 fax
family@inland.net

Kentucky

Parent Information Network of Kentucky
3002 Taylorsville Road
Louisville, KY 40205
502-479-7465
502-452-2145 fax
vwb511@aol.com

Louisiana

Families Helping Families
4323 Division Street, Suite 110
Metairie, LA 70002-3179
504-888-9111
504-888-0246 fax
fhfgno@ix.netcom.com

Massachusetts

Family Ties—MA. Dept. of Public Health
DCSHCN, 4th Floor
250 Washington Street
Boston, MA 02108
617-624-5979
617-624-5990 fax
rosalie.edes@state.ma.us
polly.sherman@state.ma.us

Michigan

Family Support Network of Michigan
1200 6th Street, 3rd Floor, South Tower, # 316
Detroit, MI 48226-2495
313-256-2183 or 800-359-3722
313-256-2605 fax
jordandasilvaf@state.mi.us

Nevada

Nevada Parent Network—UAP
College of Education/285
Reno, NV 89557-0082
775-784-4921
775-784-4997 fax
cdinnell@scs.unr.edu

New Hampshire

Parent to Parent of New Hampshire
12 Flynn Street
Lebanon, NH 03766
603-448-6393
603-448-6311 fax
parent.to.parent@dartmouth.edu

New Jersey

New Jersey Statewide Parent to Parent
c/o SPAN, 35 Halsey Street, 4th Floor
Newark, NJ 07102
973-642-8100
973-642-8080 fax
njptp@ptd.net

New Mexico

Parents Reaching Out
1000A Main Street
Los Lunas, NM 87031
505-865-3700
505-865-3737 fax
proth@swcp.com

New York

Parent to Parent of New York State
Balltown and Consaul Roads
Schenectady, NY 12304
800-305-8817
518-382-1959 fax
parent2par@aol.com

North Carolina

Family Support Network of NC
CB#7340, Chase Hall
University of North Carolina
Chapel Hill, NC 27699-7340
919-966-2841
919-966-2916 fax
shgeiss@med.unc.edu
karen_leclair@med.unc.edu

North Dakota

Family to Family Project
UND School of Medicine and Health Science
P.O. Box 9037
Grand Forks, ND 58202
701-777-2359
701-777-2353 fax
feist@daktel.com

Ohio

The Family Information Network
143 Northwest Avenue, Bldg. A
Tallmadge, OH 44278
330-633-2055
330-633-2685 fax

Pennsylvania

Parent to Parent of Pennsylvania
Gateway Corporate Center
6340 Flank Drive, #1200
Harrisburg, PA 17112
717-540-4722
717-657-5983 fax
ksbrill@aol.com

South Carolina

Family Connection of South Carolina
2712 Middleburg Drive, Suite 103-B
Columbia, SC 29204
803-252-0914
803-799-8017 fax
connieg@mindspring.com

Tennessee

Parents Encouraging Parents
5th Floor, C. Hull Building, 426 Fifth
   Avenue N.
Nashville, TN 37247-4850
615-741-0353
615-741-1063 fax
srothacker@mail.state.tn.us

Utah

HOPE-A Parent Network
2290 East 4500 South, Suite 110
Salt Lake City, UT 84117
801-272-1051
801-272-8907 fax
upc@inconnect.com

Vermont

Parent to Parent of Vermont
1 Main Street, 69 Champlain Mill
Winooski, VT 05404
802-655-5290
802-655-3507 fax
nancy.divenere@partoparvt.org

Virginia

Parent to Parent of VA
c/o Arc of VA
6 North 6th Street, Suite 403
Richmond, VA 23219
804-222-1945
804-222-3402 fax
ptopofva@aol.com

West Virginia

Common Bonds of West Virginia
1101 Hospital Drive
Hurricane, WV 25526
304-757-8465
304-757-1003 fax
rwright@inetmail.att.net

Washington

Parent to Parent Support Program
10550 Lake City Way NE, Suite A
Seattle, WA 98125
206-364-3814
206-364-8140 fax
jrhv7@aol.com
statep2p@aol.com

Other National Family Resources

The National Information Center for Children and Youth with Disabilities (NICHCY)
P.O. Box 1492
Washington, DC 20013-1492
1-202-884-8200 voice
1-800-695-0285 voice
1-202-884-8441 fax
nichcy@aed.org
www.nichcy.org

The Beach Center on Families and Disability
3111 Haworth
University of Kansas
Lawrence, KS 66045
913-864-7600 (phone/TDD)
913-864-7605 (FAX)
Beach@dole.lsi.ukans.edu
www.beachcenter.org

Appendix B

Conversation Guide

We hope you will use this document as a guide to a natural and relaxed conversation with families. If you follow our guide, trying to move away from *interviewing* families and toward *conversing* with them instead, you will want to use as much spontaneity as possible—just as you do with your friends or family when you have conversations with them.

Conversations are more enlightening when questions or issues are open-ended. That means that you will not follow a strict order of questions; rather, you will be sensitive to the family's lead, following the issues that they are most interested in addressing. Just as you read in chapter 9, families do not organize their conversations to be consistent with the family systems framework. Rather, they might talk first about the family function of recreation and then immediately go to a discussion about siblings. We hope you will *go with their flow* rather than with the order of questions/probes that you find here.

Family Characteristics

- Who are the members of your family? Who lives together in your home? Who is interested in supporting _____'s education?
- We all have certain cultural characteristics that especially influence our families. These might be related to the part of the country where we grew up or to our jobs, religion, race, or financial resources. I've always considered one of the major cultural influences on my family to be _____ . How do you characterize your family's culture?
- What are the most important things that parents should teach their children? What are the most important things that schools should teach children?
- Has any particular type of advice about how people ought to live their lives been handed down through the generations of your family? What is it, and do you think it has implications for _____'s educational program?
- Are there issues related to your family's financial resources that are important for the school to take into account?
- What is one of the major strengths of your family?
- Is there a particular challenge or struggle that your family is having now that might influence _____'s educational program?

Personal Characteristics

- I'm eager to get to know _____ . Tell me about _____'s typical day and especially about the things that _____ most likes and dislikes about the day.
- What are things that seem to be going especially well for _____ ?
- What are some of the particular challenges that _____ is facing now?
- So much of _____'s day is spent in school. What's your view of how things are going at school?
- How do _____'s strengths and needs influence schoolwork? How do _____'s strengths and needs influence _____'s relationships with classmates?
- What is the nature of _____'s exceptionality? What have others told you about it? Do you agree or disagree about what you have been told? Why?
- What do you most enjoy about _____ ?
- How does _____ contribute to the family in a positive way?
- What issues about _____'s exceptionality pose the greatest challenges to your family?
- We all have different ways of dealing with problems when they arise. As you think back over the last 6 to 12 months and the problems that various members of your family have faced, what are some of the things that you and other family members do that particularly help you meet these challenges?
- What are some of the less effective ways that you have tried to meet the challenges?
- Do any particular health concerns of family members influence your daily and weekly routines? What do you want to tell me about them?
- Who are the people most available to participate in school activities and to help _____ with homework?

Special Challenges

- All families face times when things seem to be a bit easier and other times when things seem to be more difficult. Is your family now facing any particular challenges that impact the time, energy, and resources that you can invest in _____'s educational program? What do you want to tell me about them?
- On a long-term basis, are there family issues or circumstances that make life more challenging? Do you feel comfortable sharing these with me?

Family Interaction

Marital Interactions

- What is your current marital status?
- How would you describe _____'s impact on your marriage?
- Has there been a time in the past when _____'s educational program somehow caused stress on your marriage? How could we work together to make sure to avoid such situations in the future?

- Are there any custody issues associated with your separation or divorce about which the school needs to be aware?
- If you have joint custody of _____ with another person, what does the court decree provide about communication and participation in conferences? What are your preferences about who should receive communication from the school and participate in conferences?

Parental Interactions

- How do you and your spouse share parental roles? Given this pattern, what are your preferences for how you participate this year in _____'s educational program?
- Sometimes in families there are adults who take on some parental responsibilities even though they are not actually parents. Are there people like that involved with _____? Who are they? What do they do? How might we best involve them in his or her educational program?
- What do you find to be the most and least enjoyable aspects of interacting with _____? Given those aspects, how can we best ensure that we respect your preferences as we offer educational activities for you and _____ to do in your home?
- Over time, has there been a fairly consistent pattern for your parental responsibilities or has this changed because of some kind of special circumstances? If it has changed, what is the change and why did it occur?

Sibling Interactions

- What are the most and least enjoyable ways that your other children interact with _____?
- In what ways might _____'s brothers or sisters provide educational support to _____?
- What challenges are your other children experiencing that are taking a large amount of your family's time, energy, and resources right now?
- What approach is right in terms of spreading your time and attention across all your children's interests? Do you think any of your children feel that _____'s exceptionality has taken undue time and attention from them? Are there ways the school staff can be helpful?
- What do you think about the idea of having _____'s brothers and sisters attend conferences to plan his or her educational program? What would _____'s brothers or sisters think about attending those conferences?

Extended Family Interactions

- Who is in your extended family? How often do you see them?
- In what ways have extended-family members provided you with support and assistance in raising _____?
- Do you think your extended-family members would be interested in having additional information about how they might best support _____? What information would be helpful, and how do you want to share it with them?
- Would you like us to extend an invitation to your extended family to participate in educational conferences or school events?

Family Functions

Affection

- In what ways does _____ particularly like to have affection expressed by family members toward him or her?
- How important do you think it is to express affection to _____ and your other children?
- Are there other people outside of the family on whom _____ depends for affection?

Self-Esteem

- Standing in _____'s shoes, how do you think _____ sees himself or herself in terms of personal strengths and weaknesses?
- What are your family beliefs about how best to help your family members feel good about themselves?
- What have been some school experiences in the past that have particularly helped _____ feel good about himself or herself?
- What have been some school experiences in the past that have had a negative impact on _____'s self-esteem?
- What do you think are the most significant ways that we can work together to support _____ to develop a stronger self-esteem?

Economics

- To what extent do family economics influence the kind of support that you can provide to _____ ?
- Has _____ required more or fewer economic resources than other family members?
- Are you interested in _____'s learning job skills so that he or she might get a part-time job after school or during the summer to contribute to family income?
- Because of _____'s exceptionality, have there been special family responsibilities for dealing with insurance or other reimbursement programs?

Spiritual

- Is it important to your family to participate in a spiritual or religious community? If so, are there any special issues to address to ensure that _____ is able to participate, consistent with his or her preferences and your own?
- When we get together to plan _____'s IFSP/IEP, we could invite anyone from your religious community that might benefit from knowing more about how to best support _____ . Do you have any interest in considering this?
- Are there any special celebrations associated with your religion that are important for us to consider as part of _____'s educational program?

Daily Care

- What is a typical day like in your family?
- What are the most challenging aspects of the day?

- Do you have time built in throughout the day for relaxation and rest?
- As a family, how do you divide the daily tasks related to meeting each individual's needs?
- What (if any) tasks does _____ assume, and how can we work together to teach him or her skills that make the family's daily routine easier?

Recreation

- As a family, what do you do for fun?
- In what way does _____'s exceptionality influence family recreation and leisure?
- What recreation or leisure skills might _____ learn at school that would make family recreation and leisure more enjoyable?

Socialization

- Whom does _____ hang out with when he or she is not at school?
- What are your perspectives on _____'s friendship network? What would be an ideal friendship network for _____ ?
- How has _____'s exceptionality influenced his or her opportunities for friends?
- How do you characterize the extent to which your family friends support _____ ?

Education/Vocation

- Of all the teachers who have worked with _____ , who had an especially good relationship with him or her and you? What can we learn from that situation that we can incorporate into the school year?
- Now, don't give me a name, but please just describe a situation that was really difficult when a teacher was not especially helpful at all to _____ and your family. What can we learn from that situation to make sure that we don't repeat any of it?
- What do you see _____ doing after graduating from high school in terms of where he or she works and lives? Does _____ have the same vision for himself or herself?
- In what ways do you most enjoy participating with _____ in his or her educational program?
- There are many different ways that we could communicate throughout the school year, such as through home visits, school conferences, telephone calls, notes, or a notebook. What are your preferences for communication? What do you think will work best for you and your family?
- In terms of _____'s vocational development, are there family members or friends who might be especially good resources in helping to create job opportunities? How might we best capitalize upon their contributions?

Family Cycle

Early Childhood

- Tell me about _____'s early years. What stands out in terms of some of your happiest memories? What about your most troublesome memories?

- Did you find out during the early years that _____ has an exceptionality? If so, how did you find out? Looking back, in what ways would you like to have improved the manner in which it was communicated to you?
- Did _____ participate in an early childhood program? What did you think of the program?

School Age

- What have been the highs and lows of _____'s educational experiences?
- If you found out about _____'s exceptionality during school years, what was that process like? Looking back, how would you have improved it?
- How do you think _____ is or has been best prepared for his or her future by school experiences?
- Try to create a picture in your mind of an ideal situation for _____ when he or she is an adult. Describe that situation to me. What are your great expectations for his or her future?

Adolescence

- When you look to the future, what are your great expectations for _____'s life? What are your greatest concerns?
- As you look ahead to adolescence, what do you anticipate to be the easiest and most difficult aspects?
- Now that _____ is a teenager, how would you describe the highs and lows of adolescence?
- How does _____'s adolescence compare with the adolescence of his or her brothers and/or sisters?
- What do you see as the priorities that need to be addressed in school to best prepare _____ for life as an adult?

Abbott, D. A., & Meredith, W. H. (1986). Strengths of parents with retarded children. *Family Relations, 35,* 371–375.

Abel, E. L. (1995). An update on incidence of FAS: FAS is not an equal opportunity birth defect. *Neurotoxicology and Teratology, 17,* 437–443.

Abery, B., & Zajac, R. (1996). Self-determination as a goal of early childhood and elementary education. In D. J. Sands & M. L. Wehmeyer (Eds.), *Self-determination across the life span: Independence and choice for people with disabilities* (pp. 169–196). Baltimore: Brookes.

Abeson, A., & Weintraub, F. (1977). Understanding the individualized education program. In S. Torres (Ed.), *A primer on individualized education programs for handicapped children* (pp. 3–8). Reston, VA: Foundation for Exceptional Children.

Able-Boone, H. (1993). Family participation in the IFSP process: Family or professional driven? *Infant-Toddler Intervention, 3*(1), 63–71.

Able-Boone, H., Sandall, S. R., Stevens, E., & Frederick, L. (1992). Family support resources and needs: How early intervention can make a difference. *Infant-Toddler Intervention, 2*(2), 93–102.

Abudabbeh, N. (1996). Arab families. In M. McGoldrick, J. Giordano, & J. K. Pearce (Eds.), *Ethnicity and family therapy* (2nd ed., pp. 333–346). New York: The Guilford Press.

Aday, L. A., Aitken, M. J., & Weggener, D. H. (1988). *Pediatric homecare:*
Results of a national evaluation of programs for ventilator assisted children. Chicago: Pluribus Press and the Center for Health Administration Studies, University of Chicago.

Adelman, H. S., & Taylor, L. (1997). Addressing barriers to learning: Beyond school-linked services and full-service schools. *American Journal of Orthopsychiatry, 67*(3), 408–419.

Affleck, G., Tennen, H., Rowe, J., Roscher, B., & Walker, L. (1989). Effects of formal support on mothers' adaptation to the hospital-to-home transition of high-risk infants: The benefits and costs of helping. *Child Development, 60,* 488–501.

Agosta, J. M., & Bradley, V. J. (Eds.). (1985). *Family care for persons with developmental disabilities: A growing commitment.* Cambridge, MA: Human Services Research Institute.

Agosta, J., & Melda, K. (1995). *Supplemental security income for children with disabilities.* Washington, DC: Human Services Research Institute.

Agran, M. (1997). *Student-directed learning: Teaching self-determination skills.* Pacific Grove, CA: Brooks/Cole.

Agran, M., Snow, K., & Swaner, J. (1999). Teacher perceptions of self-determination: Benefits, characteristics, strategies. *Education and Training in Mental Retardation and Developmental Disabilities, 34,* 293–301.

Agran, M., & Wehmeyer, M. (1999). *Innovations.* Washington, DC: American Association of Mental Retardation.

Ahl, V. (1999). Untitled [Review of the book *Fetal alcohol syndrome: A guide for communities and families*]. *American Journal on Mental Retardation, 104*(1), 100–102.

Ainbinder, J., Blanchard, L., Singer, G. H. S., Sullivan, M., Powers, L., Marquis, J., & Santelli, B. (1998). How parents help one another: A qualitative study of Parent to Parent self-help. *Journal of Pediatric Psychology, 23,* 99–109.

Ainge, D., Covin, G., & Baker, S. (1998). Analysis of perceptions of parents who have children with intellectual disabilities: Implications for service providers. *Education and Training in Mental Retardation and Developmental Disabilities, 33*(4), 331–341.

Ainsworth, M. D. S., Bell, S. M., & Stayton, D. (1974). Infant-mother attachment and social developing. In M. P. Richards (Ed.), *The introduction of the child into a social world.* London: Cambridge University Press.

Akey, T. M., Marquis, J. G., & Ross, M. E. (in press). Validation of scores on the psychological empowerment scale: A measure of empowerment for parents of children with a disability. *Educational and Psychological Measurement.*

Alameda, T. (1993–1994). The healthy learners' project. *Family Resource Coalition Report, 12*(3 & 4), 20–21.

Alan Guttmacher Institute. (1996). *Facts in brief: Teen sex and pregnancy.* Washington, DC: Author.

Alberto, P. A., Mechling, L., Taber, T. A., & Thompson, J. (1995, Spring). Using videotape to communicate with parents of students with severe disabilities. *Teaching Exceptional Children,* pp. 18–21.

Allen, M., & Larson, J. (1999). *Healing the whole family.* Washington, DC: Children's Defense Fund.

Allen, R. I., & Petr, C. G. (1996). Toward developing standards and measurements for family-centered practice in family support programs. In G. H. S. Singer, L. E. Powers, & A. L. Olson (Eds.), *Redefining family support: Innovations in public-private partnerships* (pp. 57–86). Baltimore: Brookes.

Alsop, G. (1997). Coping or counseling: Families of intellectually gifted students. *Roeper Review, 20*(1), 28–34.

Althen, G. (1988). *American ways: A guide for foreigners in the United States.* Yarmouth, ME: Intercultural Press.

Altshuler, S. J. (1997). A reveille for school social workers: Children in foster care need our help! *Social Work in Education, 19*(2), 121–127.

Amato, C. (1996). Freedom elementary school and its community: An approach to school-linked service integration. *Remedial and Special Education, 17*(5), 303–309.

Ammerman, R. T. (1989). Child abuse and neglect. In M. Hersen (Ed.), *Innovations in child behavior therapy* (pp. 353–394). New York: Springer.

Ammerman, R. T., & Baladerian, N. J. (1993). *Maltreatment of children with disabilities* [Invited Working Paper No. 860]. Chicago: National Committee for the Prevention of Child Abuse.

Ammerman, R. T., Hersen, M., & Lubetsky, M. J. (1990). Assessment of child maltreatment in special education settings. *International Journal of Special Education, 5*(1), 51–65.

Anastopoulos, A. D., Guevremont, D. C., Shelton, T. L., & DuPaul, G. J. (1992). Parenting stress among families of children with attention deficit hyperactivity disorder. *Journal of Abnormal Child Psychology, 20,* 503–520.

The Arc. (1988, September). A status report on waiting lists for community services [Fact sheet]. Arlington, TX: Author.

The Arc. (1990, November). Position statement on education. Arlington, TX: Author.

Artiles, A. J., & Zamora-Duran, G. (Eds.). (1997). *Reducing disproportionate representation of culturally diverse students in special and gifted education.* Reston, VA: The Council for Exceptional Children.

Ashton, P. A., & Webb, R. B. (1986). *Making a difference: Teachers' sense of efficacy and student achievement.* White Plains, NY: Longman.

Atkins, S. P. (1991). Siblings of learning disabled children: Are they special, too? *Child and Adolescent Social Work, 8*(6), 525–533.

Audette, B., & Algozzine, B. (1997). Re-inventing government? Let's re-invent special education. *Journal of Learning Disabilities, 30*(4), 378–383.

Avis, D. W. (1985). Deinstitutionalization jet lag. In H. R. Turnbull & A. P. Turnbull (Eds.), *Parents speak out: Then and now* (2nd ed., pp. 181–200). Englewood Cliffs, NJ: Merrill/Prentice-Hall.

Baca, L. M., & Almanza, E. (1991). *Language minority students and disabilities.* Reston, VA: Council for Exceptional Children.

Bahr, M. W., Fuchs, D., & Fuchs, L. S. (1999). Mainstream assistance teams: A consultation-based approach to prereferral intervention. In S. Graham & K. Harris (Eds.), *Teachers working together: Enhancing the performance of students with special needs* (pp. 87–116). Cambridge, MA: Brookline Books.

Bahr, M. W., Whitten, E., Dieker, L., Kocarek, C. E., & Manson, D. (1999). A comparison of school-based intervention teams: Implications for educational and legal reform. *Exceptional Children, 66*(1), 67–83.

Bailey, D. B., Blasco, P. M., & Simeonsson, R. J. (1992). Needs expressed by mothers and fathers of young children with disabilities. *American Journal on Mental Rehabilitation, 97*(1), 1–10.

Bailey, D. B., Buysse, V., Edmondson, R., & Smith, T. (1992). Creating family-centered services in early intervention: Perceptions of professionals in four states. *Exceptional Children, 58,* 298–309.

Bailey, D. B., & Henderson, L. W. (1993). Traditions in family assessment: Toward an inquiry-oriented, reflective model. In D. Bryant & M. Graham (Eds.), *Implementing early intervention: From research to effective practice.* New York: Guilford.

Bailey, D. B., & Simeonsson, R. J. (1988). Assessing needs of families with handicapped infants. *Journal of Special Education, 22,* 117–127.

Bailey, D. B., Skinner, D., Correa, V., Arcia, E., Reyes-Blanes, M. E., Rodriguez, P., Vázquez-Montilla, E., & Skinner, M. (1999). Needs and supports reported by Latino families of young children with developmental disabilities. *American Journal on Mental Retardation, 104*(5), 437–451.

Bailey, D., & Winton, P. (1989). Friendship and acquaintance among families in a mainstreamed day care center. *Education and Training of the Mentally Retarded, 24,* 107–113.

Bailey, D. B., Winton, P. J., Rouse, L., & Turnbull, A. P. (1990). Family goals in infant intervention: Analysis and issues. *Journal of Early Intervention, 14,* 15–26.

Baker, B. L., with Ambrose, S. A., & Anderson, S. R. (1989). Parent training and developmental disabilities [Special issue]. *Monographs of the American Association on Mental Retardation, 13.*

Baker, D. B. (1994). Parenting stress and ADHD: A comparison of mothers and fathers. *Journal of Emotional and Behavioral Disorders, 2*(1), 46–50.

Baker, J. A., Bridger, R., & Evans, K. (1998). Models of underachievement among gifted preadolescents: The role of personal, family, and school factors. *Gifted Child Quarterly, 42*(1), 5–15.

Bandura, A. (1997). *Self-efficacy.* New York: W. H. Freeman.

Bandura, A., Barbaranelli, C., Caprara, G. V., & Pastorelli, C. (1996). Multifaceted impact of self-efficacy beliefs on academic functioning. *Child Development, 67,* 1206–1222.

Banks, J. A., & McGee-Banks, C. A. (Eds.). (1997). *Multicultural education: Issues and perspectives* (3rd ed.). Needham Heights, MA: Allyn & Bacon.

Banks, J. A., & McGee-Banks, C. A. (Eds.). (1999). *Multicultural education.* New York: Wiley and Sons.

Barakat, L., & Linney, J. (1992). Children with physical handicaps and their mothers: The interrelation of social support, maternal adjustment, and child adjustment. *Journal of Pediatric Psychology, 17,* 725–739.

Barbell, K. (1996). *Foster care today: National and South Carolina perspective. Council on Child Abuse and Neglect. Foster Parent Recruitment and Retention Workshop.* Washington, DC: Child Welfare League of America.

Barber, L., & Brophy, K. (1993). Parents' views on school placement procedures for their children with special needs. *Journal on Developmental Disabilities, 2*(1), 100–111.

Barbetta, P. M. (1995). Emotional or behavioral disorders. In A. P. Turnbull, H. R. Turnbull, M. Shank, & D. Leal, (Eds.), *Exceptional lives: Special education in today's schools* (pp. 186–235). Englewood Cliffs, NJ: Merrill/Prentice-Hall.

Barenok, T., & Wieck, C. (1998). Partners in policymaking: Far more than the object of policy. *Focal Point, 12*(1), 1, 6–8.

Barnes, K. (1986). Surviving as a single parent. *Exceptional Parent, 16*(3), 47–49.

Barnett, C., & Monda-Amaya, L. E. (1998). Principals' knowledge of and attitudes toward inclusion. *Remedial and Special Education, 19*(3), 181–192.

Barnett, W. S., & Boyce, G. C. (1995). Effects of children with down syndrome on parents' activities. *American Journal on Mental Retardation, 100*(2), 115–127.

Barr, M. W. (1913). *Mental defectives: Their history, treatment, and training.* Philadelphia: Blakiston.

Barrera, M. (1986). Distinctions between social supports concepts, measures, and models. *American Journal of Community Psychology, 14*(4), 413–445.

Batshaw, M. L., & Conlon, C. J. (1997). Substance abuse. In M. L. Batshaw (Ed.), *Children with disabilities* (4th ed., pp. 143–162). Baltimore: Brookes.

Batshaw, M. L., Conlon, C. J., & Rustein, R. M. (1997). HIV and AIDS. In M. L. Batshaw (Ed.), *Children with disabilities* (4th ed., pp. 163–181). Baltimore: Brookes.

Batshaw, M. L., & Perret, Y. M. (1992). *Children with handicaps: A medical primer* (3rd ed.). Baltimore: Brookes.

Batshaw, M. L., & Rose, N. C. (1997). Birth defects, prenatal diagnosis, and fetal therapy. In M. L. Batshaw (Ed.), *Children with disabilities* (4th ed., pp. 35–52). Baltimore: Brookes.

Bauer, A. M., & Shea, T. M. (1999). *Inclusion 101: How to teach all learners.* Baltimore: Brookes.

Baumeister, A. A., Kupstas, F. D., & Woodley-Zanthos, P. (1993). *The new morbidity: Recommendations for actions and an updated guide to state planning for the prevention of mental retardation and related disabilities associated with socioeconomic conditions.* Washington, DC: U.S. Department of Health and Human Services.

Beckman, A. A., & Brent, R. L. (1986). Mechanism of known environmental teratogens: Drugs and chemicals. *Clinics in Perinatology, 13,* 649–687.

Beckman, P. D., Newcomb, S., Frank, N., Brown, L., Stepanek, J., & Barnwell, D. (in press). Preparing professionals to work with families on early intervention teams. In D. Bricker & A. Widerstrom (Eds.), *Preparing personnel to work with infants, young children, and their families: A team approach.* Baltimore: Brookes.

Beckman, P. J. (1991). Comparison of mothers' and fathers' perceptions of the effect of young children with and without disabilities. *American Journal of Mental Retardation, 95*(5), 585–595.

Beckman, P. J., & Bristol, M. M. (1991). Issues in developing the IFSP: A framework for establishing family outcomes. *Topics in Early Childhood Special Education, 11*(3), 19–31.

Beckman, P. J., & Pokomi, J. L. (1988). A longitudinal study of families of preterm infants: Changes in stress and support over the first two years. *Journal of Special Education, 22,* 55–65.

Beckman, P. J., Robinson, C. C., Rosenberg, S., & Filer, J. (1994). Family involvement in early intervention: The evolution of family-centered services. In L. J. Johnson, R. J. Gallagher, M. J. LaMontagne, J. B. Jordan, J. J. Gallagher, P. L. Hutinger, & M. B. Karnes (Eds.), *Early intervention for children and their families: Providing services from birth to three.* Baltimore: Brookes.

Behr, S. K., & Murphy, D. L. (1993). Research progress and promise: The role of perceptions in cognitive adaptation to disability. In A. P. Turnbull, J. M. Patterson, S. K. Behr, D. L. Murphy, J. G. Marquis, & M. J. Blue-Banning (Eds.), *Cognitive coping, families, and disability* (pp. 151–164). Baltimore: Brookes.

Benjamin Darling, R. (1991). Initial and continuing adaption to the birth of a disabled child. In M. Seligman (Ed.), *The family with a handicapped child* (2nd ed., pp. 55–89). Boston: Allyn & Bacon.

Bennett, J. M. (1985). Company, halt! In H. R. Turnbull & A. P. Turnbull (Eds.), *Parents speak out: Then and now* (2nd ed., pp. 159–173). Englewood Cliffs, NJ: Merrill/Prentice-Hall.

Bennett, L. A., Wolin, S. J., & Mcavity, K. J. (1988). Family identity, ritual, and myth: A cultural perspective in life cycle transitions. In C. J. Falicov (Ed.), *Family Transitions* (pp. 211–234). New York: The Guilford Press.

Bennett, T., DeLuca, D. A., & Allen, R. W. (1996). Families of children with disabilities: Positive adaptation across the life cycle. *Social Work in Education, 18*(1), 31–44.

Bennett, T., Lee, H., & Lueke, B. (1998). Expectations and concerns: What mothers and fathers say about inclusion. *Education and Training in Mental Retardation and Developmental Disabilities, 33,* 108–122.

Benson, B. A., & Gross, A. M. (1989). The effect of a congenitally handicapped child upon the marital dyad: A review of the literature. *Clinical Psychology Review, 9*(6), 747–758.

Benson, H. A., & Turnbull, A. P. (1986) Approaching families from an individualized perspective. In R. H. Horner, L. H. Meyer, & H. D. Fredericks (Eds.), *Education of learners with severe handicaps: Exemplary service strategies* (pp. 127–157). Baltimore, MD: Brookes.

Benton Foundation. (1998). *About foster care, take this heart: The foster care project.* [On-line] Available: *http://www.kidscampaigns.org/hot/fostercare/started/about/about1.html*

Bergman, A. I., & Singer, G. H. S. (1996). The thinking behind new public policy. In G. H. S. Singer, L. E. Powers, & A. L. Olson (Eds.), *Redefining family support: Innovations in public-private partnerships* (pp. 435–464). Baltimore: Brookes.

Bernbaum, J. C., & Batshaw, M. L. (1997). Born too soon, born too small. In M. L. Batshaw (Ed.), *Children with disabilities* (4th ed., pp. 115–139). Baltimore: Brookes.

Bernstein, M. E., & Martin, J. (1992). Informing parents about educational options: How well are we doing? *American Annals of the Deaf, 137*(1), 31–39.

Berres, M. S., Ferguson, D. L., Knoblock, P., & Woods, C. (Eds.). (1996). *Creating tomorrow's schools today.* New York: Teachers College Press.

Berrick, J. D. (1998). When children cannot remain home: Foster family care and kinship care. *The Future of Children, 8*(1), 72–87.

Betson, D. M., & Michael, R. T. (1997). Why so many children are poor. *The Future of Children, 7*(2), 25–39.

Bettelheim, B. (1950). *Love is not enough.* Glencoe, NY: Free Press.

Bettelheim, B. (1967). *The empty fortress: Infantile autism and the birth of the self.* London: Collier-Macmillan.

Beukelman, D. R., & Mirenda, P. (1998). *Augmentative and alternative communication.* Baltimore: Brookes.

Billingsley, B. S., & Cross, L. H. (1991). Teachers' decisions to transfer from special to general education. *Journal of Special Education, 24,* 496–511.

Billingsley, F. F. (1993). Reader response in my dreams: A response to some current trends in education. *Journal of the Association for Persons with Severe Handicaps, 18*(1), 61–63.

Birenbaum, A., & Cohen, H. J. (1993). On the importance of helping families: Policy implications from a national study. *Mental Retardation, 31*(2), 67–74.

Blacher, J. (1984a). Sequential stages of adjustment to the birth of a child with handicaps: Fact or artifact? *Mental Retardation, 22,* 55–68.

Blacher, J. (Ed.). (1984b). *Severely handicapped young children and their families: Research in review.* New York: Academic Press.

Blacher, J. (1994). Placement and its consequences for families with children who have mental retardation. In J. Blacher (Ed.), *When there's no place like home: Options for children living apart from their natural families* (pp. 211–212). Baltimore: Brookes.

Blacher, J., Baker, B. L., & Abbott-Feinfield, K. (1999). Leaving or launching? Continuing family involvement with children and adolescents in placement. *American Journal on Mental Retardation, 104*(5), 452–465.

Blacher, J., & Turnbull, A. P. (1983). Are parents mainstreamed? A survey of parent interactions in the mainstreamed preschool. *Education and Training of the Mentally Retarded, 18,* 10–16.

Black Community Crusade for Children. (1993). *Progress and peril: Black children in America.* Washington, DC: Children's Defense Fund.

Blackorby, J., & Wagner, M. (1996, March–April). Longitudinal post-school outcomes for youth with disabilities: Findings from the national longitudinal transition study. *Exceptional Children, 62*(5): 399–413.

Blalock, G. (1988). Transition across a life span. In B. Ludlow, A. P. Turnbull, & R. Luckasson (Eds.), *Transition to adult life for people with mental retardation: Principles and practices* (pp. 1–20). Baltimore: Paul H. Brookes.

Block, M. E. (1994). *A teacher's guide to including students with disabilities in regular physical education.* Baltimore: Brookes.

Block, M. E., & Malloy, M. (1998). Attitudes on inclusion of a player with disabilities in a regular softball league. *Mental Retardation, 36*(2), 137–144.

Bloom, B. S. (1985). *Developing talent in young people.* New York: Ballantine Books.

Blue-Banning, M. J. (1995). [Unpublished raw data.] Lawrence: University of Kansas, Beach Center on Families and Disability.

Blue-Banning, M. J., Santelli, B., Guy, B., & Wallace, E. (1994). *Cognitive coping project: Coping with the challenges of disability.* Lawrence: University of Kansas, Beach Center on Families and Disability.

Blue-Banning, M. J., Turnbull, A. P., & Pereira, L. (in press). Group action planning as a support strategy for Hispanic families: Parent and professional perspectives. *Mental Retardation.*

Blum, B. B., & Berrey, E. C. (1999). *Welfare research perspectives: Past, present, and future.* New York: National Center for Children in Poverty, Columbia University.

Blum, N. J., & Mercugliano, M. (1997). Attention-deficit/hyperactivity disorder. In M. L. Batshaw (Ed.), *Children with disabilities* (4th ed., pp. 449–470). Baltimore: Brookes.

Board of Education of Sacramento Unified School District v. Holland, 14 F.3d 1398 (9th Cir., 1994).

Board of Education v. Rowley, 458 U.S. 176, 102 S. Ct. 3034, 73 L. Ed., 2d 690 (1982).

Boggs, E. M. (1985). Who is putting whose head in the sand? (Or in the clouds, as the case may be). In H. R. Turnbull & A. P. Turnbull (Eds.), *Parents speak out: Then and now* (2nd ed., pp. 39–55). Englewood Cliffs, NJ: Merrill/Prentice-Hall.

Boggs, S. T. (1965). An interactional study of Ojibwa socialization. *American Sociological Review, 21,* 191–198.

Boles, S., Horner, R. H., & Bellamy, G. T. (1988). Implementing transition: Programs for supported living. In B. L. Ludlow, A. P. Turnbull, & R. Luckasson (Eds.), *Transitions to adult life for people with mental retardation: Principles and practices* (pp. 101–117). Baltimore: Brookes.

Bond, M., & Keys, C. (1993). Empowerment, diversity, and collaboration: Promoting synergy on community boards. *American Journal of Community Psychology, 21*(1), 37–57.

Bonner, B. L., Crow, S. M., & Hensley, L. D. (1997). State efforts to identify maltreated children with disabilities: A follow-up study. *Child Maltreatment, 2*(1), 52–60.

Boone, H. A., McBride, S. L., Swann, D., Moore, S., & Drew, B. S. (1999). IFSP practices in two states: Implications for practice. *Infants and Young Children, 10*(4), 36–45.

Borthwick-Duffy, S. A., Palmer, D. S., & Lane, K. L. (1996). One size doesn't fit all: Full inclusion and individual differences. *Journal of Behavioral Education, 6,* 311–329.

Bos, C. S., Nahmias, M. L., & Urban, M. A. (1999, July/August). Targeting home-school collaboration for students with ADHD. *Teaching Exceptional Children,* 4–11.

Boutté, V. (1997, September/October). Life after high school. *Volta Voices,* 21–23.

Boutte, G. S., & DeFlorimonte, D. (1998). The complexities of valuing cultural differences without overemphasizing them: Taking it to the next level. *Equity and Excellence in Education, 31*(3), 54–62.

Bowe, F. G. (1995). *Birth to five: Early childhood special education.* New York: Delmar.

Boyce, S. (1992, April). Coping well with the labellers of Down syndrome. *Down Syndrome News, 37.*

Braddock, D. (1998). Mental retardation and developmental disabilities: Historical and contemporary perspectives. In D. Braddock, R. Hemp, S. Parish, & J. Westrich (Eds.), *The state of the states in developmental disabilities* (pp. 3–22). Washington, DC: American Association on Mental Retardation.

Braddock, D., Hemp, R., & Parish, S. (1997). Emergence of individual and family support in state service-delivery systems. In K. C. Lakin, D. Braddock, & G. Smith (Eds.), *Mental Retardation* (pp. 497–498). Washington, DC: American Association on Mental Retardation.

Braddock, D., Hemp, R., & Parish, S. (2000). Transforming service delivery systems in the states. In M. L. Wehmeyer & J. R. Patton (Eds.), *Mental retardation in the 21st century* (pp. 259–378). Austin, TX: Pro-ed.

Braddock, D., Hemp, R., Parish, S., Westrich, J., & Park, H. (1998). *The state of the states in developmental disabilities: Summary of the study.* In D. Braddock, R. Hemp, S. Parish, & J. Westrich (Eds.), *The state of the states in developmental disabilities* (5th ed., pp. 23–54). Washington, DC: American Association on Mental Retardation.

Bradley, V., Knoll, J., & Agosta, J. (1993). *Emerging issues in family support* (Monograph No. 18). Washington, DC: American Association on Mental Retardation.

Brammer, L. (1988). *The helping relationship.* Englewood Cliffs, NJ: Prentice-Hall.

Brantlinger, E. (1992). Professionals' attitudes toward the sterilization of people with disabilities. *Journal of the Association for Persons with Severe Handicaps, 17*(1), 4–18.

Brennan, E., & Freeman, L. (1999). Inclusive child care. *Focal Point, 13*(1), 1, 8–9.

Brennan, E. M., Rosenzweig, J. M., & Ogilvie, A. M. (1999). Support for working caregivers. *Focal Point, 13*(1), 1, 3–5.

Briar-Lawson, K., Lawson, H. A., Collier, C., & Joseph, A. (1997). School-linked comprehensive services: Promising beginnings, lessons learned, and future challenges. *Social Work in Education, 19*(3), 136–145.

Bricker, W. A., & Bricker, D. D. (1976). The infant, toddler, and preschool research and intervention project. In T. D. Tjossem (Ed.), *Intervention strategies for high risk infants and young children* (pp. 545–572). Baltimore: University Park Press.

Briggs, H. E. (1994). Promoting adoptions by foster parents through an inner-city organization. *Research on Social Work Practice, 4*(4), 497–509.

Bristol, M. M., Gallagher, J. J., & Schopler, E. (1988). Mothers and fathers of young developmentally disabled and nondisabled boys: Adaptation and spousal support. *Developmental Psychology, 24*(3), 441–451.

Broderick, C., & Smith, J. (1979). The general systems approach to the family. In W. R. Burr, R. Hill, F. I. Nye, & I. L. Reiss (Eds.), *Contemporary theories about the family* (vol. 2, pp. 112–129). New York: Free Press.

Brodzinsky, D. M. (1993). Long-term outcomes in adoption. *The future of children, 3*(1), 153–166.

Bronfenbrenner, U. (1990). Discovering what families do. In D. Blankenhorn, S. B. Ayme, & J. B. Elshtain (Eds.), *Rebuilding the nest: A new commitment to the American family* (pp. 27–38). Milwaukee, WI: Family Service American.

Brookes-Gunn, J., & Chase-Lansdale, P. L. (1991). Children having children: Effects on the family system. *Pediatric Annals, 20*(9), 467–481.

Brotherson, M. J. (1985). *Parents self report of future planning and its relationship to family functioning and family stress with sons and daughters who are disabled.* Unpublished doctoral dissertation, University of Kansas, Lawrence.

Brotherson, M. J., Backus, L., Summers, J. A., & Turnbull, A. P. (1986). Transition to adulthood. In J. A. Summers (Ed.), *The right to grow up:*

Introduction to developmentally disabled adults (pp. 17–44). Baltimore: Brookes.

Brotherson, M. J., & Goldstein, B. L. (1992). Time as a resource and constraint for parents of young children with disabilities: Implications for early intervention services. *Topics in Early Childhood Special Education, 12*(4), 508–527.

Brown, E., & Greenbaum, P. E. (1994). Reinstitutionalization after discharge from residential mental health facilities: Competing-risks survival analysis. In C. Liberton, K. Kutash, & R. Friedman (Eds.), *The 7th annual research conference proceedings. A system of care for children's mental health: Expanding the research base* (pp. 271–276). Tampa, FL: University of South Florida.

Brown, K. R. (1993–1994). Building beacons for children and families in New York City. *Family Resource Coalition Report, 12*(3 & 4), 39–41.

Brown, S. (1999a). *Advocacy-oriented peer support part two: Moving from talk to action* (H133B50003). Silver Spring, MD: Rehabilitation Research and Training Center on Independent Living Center Management and Services, Independent Living Research Utilization at the Institute for Rehabilitation.

Brown, S. (1999b). *Peer counseling: Advocacy-oriented peer support-part one* (H133B50003). Silver Spring, MD: Rehabilitation Research and Training Center on Independent Living Center Management and Services, Independent Living Research Utilization at the Institute of Rehabilitation.

Bruder, M. B., Anderson, R., Schultz, G., & Caldera, M. (1991). Niños especiales program: A culturally sensitive early intervention model. *Journal of Early Intervention, 15*(3), 268–277.

Bruns, E. J., Burchard, J. D., & Yoe, J. T. (1995). Evaluating the Vermont system of care: Outcomes associated with community-based wraparound services. *Journal of Child and Family Studies, 4*(3), 321–339.

Bryan, T., & Nelson, C. (1995). Doing homework: Perspectives of elementary and middle school students. *Journal of Learning Disabilities, 27,* 488–499.

Bryan, T., Nelson, C., & Mathur, S. (1995). Doing homework: Perspectives of primary students in mainstream, resource, and self-contained special education classrooms. *Learning Disabilities Research and Practice, 10,* 85–90.

Bryan, T., & Sullivan-Burstein, K. (1998). Teacher-selected strategies for improving homework completion. *Remedial and Special Education, 19*(5), 263–275.

Bryant-Comstock, S., Huff, B., & VanDenBerg, J. (1996). The evolution of the family advocacy movement. In B. A. Stroul (Ed.), *Children's mental health* (pp. 359–376). Baltimore: Brookes.

Buck v. Bell, 274 U.S. 200 (1927).

Buck, G. H., Bursuck, W. D., Polloway, E. A., Nelson, J., Jayanthi, M. J., & Whitehouse, F. A. (1996). Homework-related communication problems: Perspectives of special educators. *Journal of Emotional and Behavioral Disorders, 4*(2), 105–113.

Bulgatz, M., & O'Neill, R. E. (1994). *Teacher perceptions and recommendations concerning students with challenging behaviors in the regular classroom: An initial survey.* Unpublished manuscript.

Bullis, M., & Cheney, D. (1999). Vocational and transition interventions for adolescents and young adults with emotional or behavioral disorders. *Focus on Exceptional Children, 31*(7), 1–24.

Burchard, J., Burchard, S., Sewell, C., & VanDenBerg, J. (1993). *One kid at a time: Evaluative case studies and description of the Alaska Youth Initiative Demonstration Project.* Juneau: State of Alaska, Division of Mental Health and Mental Retardation.

Burns, B. J., & Goldman, S. K. (Eds.). (1999). *Systems of care: Promising practices in children's mental health.* Washington, DC: Center for

Effective Collaboration and Practice, American Institutes for Research.

Bursuck, W. D., Rose, E., Cowen, S., & Yahaya, A. (1989). Nationwide survey of postsecondary education services for students with learning disabilities. *Exceptional Children, 56,* 236–245.

Bursuck, W., Pollaway, E. A., Plante, L., Epstein, M. H., Jayanthi, M., & McConeghy, J. (1996). Report card grading and adaptions: A national survey of classroom practices. *Exceptional Children, 62*(4), 301–318.

Burton, S. L. (1988). *Serving the needs of grandparents and siblings of the handicapped in rural America: A preservice/in-service curriculum module for preparation of rural special educators.* Bellingham: Western Washington University, National Rural Development Institute.

Burton, S. L., & Parks, A. L. (1994). College-aged siblings of individuals with disabilities. *Social Work Research, 18*(3), 178–185.

Buswell, B. (1993, November). *School reform and students with disabilities. Discussions about school reform: Strategies for families of students with disabilities.* Washington, DC: U.S. Department of Education, Office of Special Education and Rehabilitative Services.

Buswell, B. E., & Schaffner, C. B. (1990). Families supporting inclusive schooling. In W. Stainback & S. Stainback (Eds.), *Support networks for inclusive schooling: Interdependent integrated education* (pp. 219–230). Baltimore: Brookes.

Buswell, B., & Schaffner, B. (1994). Parents and school reform. *Coalition Quarterly, 12*(1), 16–20.

Butera, G., & Maughan, G. (1998). A place in the mountains: Rural homeless families in West Virginia. *Zero to Three, 19*(1), 24–30.

Buyse, M. L. (1990). *Birth defects encyclopedia.* Dover, MA: Center for Birth Defects Information Services.

Calfee, C., Wittwer, F., & Meredith, M. (1998). Why build a full-service school? In C. Calfee, F. Wittwer, &

M. Meredith (Eds.), *Building a full-service school* (pp. 6–24). San Francisco: Jossey-Bass.

Calfee, R. C., & Perfumo, P. (1993). Student portfolios: Opportunities for a revolution in assessment. *Journal of Reading, 36*(7), 532–537.

Callahan, K., Rademacher, J. A., & Hildreth, B. L. (1998). The effect of parent participation in strategies to improve the homework performance of students who are at risk. *Remedial and Special Education, 19*(3), 131–141.

Callahan, M., & Mank, D. (1998). Choice and control of employment for people with disabilities. In T. Nerney & D. Shumway (Eds.), *The importance of income* (pp. 15–33). Concord, NH: The Robert Wood Johnson Foundation.

Cambridge, P. (1998). Challenges for safer sex education and HIV prevention in services for people with intellectual disabilities in Britain. *Health Promotion International, 13*(1), 67–74.

Campbell, P. H., Strickland, B., & La Forme, C. (1992). Enhancing parent participation in the individualized family service plan. *Topics in Early Childhood Special Education, 11*(4), 112–124.

Caplan, P. J., & Hall-McCorquodale, I. (1985). Mother-blaming in major clinical journals. *American Journal of Orthopsychiatry, 55*(3), 345–353.

Carandang, L. A. (1992). Family dynamics of the gifted. *Gifted Education International, 8*(2), 117–120.

Carey, N., Lewis, L., & Farris, E. (1998). *Parent involvement in children's education: Efforts by public elementary schools* (NCES 98-032). Washington, DC: U.S. Department of Education, National Center for Education Statistics.

Carnes, P. (1981). *Family development I: Understanding us.* Minneapolis, MN: Interpersonal Communications Programs.

Carr, J. (1988). Six-weeks to twenty-one years old: A longitudinal study of children with Down's syndrome and their families. *Journal of Child Psychology and Psychiatry, 29*(4), 407–431.

Carr, E. G., Horner, R. H., Turnbull, A. P., Marquis, J. G., Magito-McLaughlin, D., McAtee, M. L., Smith, C. E., Ryan, K. A., Ruef, M. B., & Doolabh, A. (1999). *Positive behavior support as an approach for dealing with problem behavior in people with developmental disabilities: A research synthesis.* Washington, DC: American Association on Mental Retardation Monograph Series.

Carta, J. J. (1997). Caregiving interventions for children affected by prenatal substance abuse. *Advances in Early Education and Day Care, 9,* 203–222.

Carta, J. J., McConnell, S. R., McEvoy, M. A., Greenwood, C. R., Atwater, J. B., Baggett, K., & Williams, R. (1997). Developmental outcomes associated with *in utero* exposure to alcohol and other drugs. In M. R. Haack (Ed.), *Drug-dependent mothers and their children* (pp. 64–90). New York: Springer.

Carter, E. A., & McGoldrick, M. (Eds.). (1980). *The family life cycle: A framework for family therapy.* New York: Gardner.

Carter, E. A., & McGoldrick, M. (Eds.). (1989). *The changing family life cycle: A framework for family therapy* (2nd ed.). Boston: Allyn & Bacon.

Carter, J., & Sugai, G. (1989). Survey on prereferral practices: Responses from state departments of education. *Exceptional Children, 55*(5), 298–302.

Carter, N., & Harvey, C. (1996). Gaining perspective on parenting groups. *Zero to Three, 16*(6), 1, 3–8.

Cauce, A. M., Paradise, M., Embry, L., Morgan, C. J., Lohr, Y., Theofelis, J., Heger, J., & Wagner, V. (1998). Homeless youth in Seattle: Youth characteristics, mental health needs, and intensive care management. In M. H. Epstein, K. Kutash, & A. Duchnowski (Eds.), *Outcomes for children and youth with behavioral and emotional disorders* (pp. 611–632). Austin, TX: Pro-ed.

Center for Resource Management. (1995). Summary of data from annual PTI reports FY'95 [Report]. South Hampton, NH: Author.

Chalmers, L., Ortega, J. C., & Hoover, J. H. (1996). Attitudes of rural and small-town educators toward special education referral. *Case-in-Point, 10*(1), 21–28.

Chan, S. (1998). Families with Asian roots. In E. W. Lynch & M. J. Hanson (Eds.), *Developing cross-cultural competence: A guide for working with young children and their families* (2nd ed., pp. 251–354). Baltimore: Brookes.

Chapey, G. D., Trimarco, T. A., Crisci, P., & Capobianco, M. (1987). School-parent partnerships in gifted education: From paper to reality. *Educational Research Quarterly, 11*(3), 37–46.

Chapman, J. W. (1988). Learning disabled children's self-concepts. *Review of Educational Research, 58*(3), 347–371.

Chen, T. Y., & Tang, C. (1997). Stress appraisal and social support of Chinese mothers of adult children with mental retardation. *American Journal on Mental Retardation, 103*(2), 473–482.

Cheney, D., & Osher, T. (1997). Collaborate with families. *Journal of Emotional and Behavioral Disorders, 5*(1), 36–44, 54.

Chesapeake Institute. (1994, September). *National agenda for achieving better results for children and youth with serious emotional disturbance.* Washington, DC: Department of Education, Office of Special Education and Rehabilitative Services, Office of Special Education Programs.

Child Abuse Prevention and Treatment Act, 42 U.S.C. 5106 (Supp. 1992).

Child Abuse Prevention and Treatment Act, Pub. L. No. 93-247, 42 U.S.C. 5101 § 3 (1974).

Child Abuse Prevention and Treatment and Reform Act, 42 U.S.C., Sec. 5106a.

Child Development Resources. (1989). How can we get help? In B. H. Johnson, M. J. McGonigel, & R. K.

Kaufmann (Eds.), *Guidelines and recommended practices for Individualized Family Service Plan* (pp. D9–D11). Washington, DC: Association for the Care of Children's Health.

Children's Defense Fund. (1991). *The state of America's children: 1991.* Washington, DC: Author.

Children's Defense Fund. (1993). *The state of America's children: 1993.* Washington, DC: Author.

Children's Defense Fund. (1995). *The state of America's children yearbook, 1995.* Washington, DC: Author.

Christenson, S., Ysseldyke, J. E., & Algozzine, B. (1982, July). Institutional constraints and external pressures influencing referral decisions. *Psychology in the Schools, 19*(3), 341–345.

Christiansen, J. B., & Barnartt, S. N. (1995). *Deaf president now!: The 1988 revolution at Gallaudet University.* Washington, DC: Gallaudet University.

Christmon, K. (1996). A descriptive study of adolescent fathers and their mothers. *Journal of Health and Social Policy, 7*(3), 75–82.

Cigno, K., & Burke, P. (1997). Single mothers of children with learning disabilities: An undervalued group. *Journal of Interprofessional Care, 11*(2), 177–186.

Ciotti, P. (1989, May 9). Growing up different: When the retarded become parents, perhaps their children know best how it works. *Los Angeles Times,* pp. V–1, V–4, V–10.

Clark, G. A., & Zimmerman, E. D. (1988). Views of self, family background, and school: Interviews with artistically talented students. *Gifted Child Quarterly, 32*(4), 340–346.

Clark, H. B., Lee, B., Prange, M. E., & McDonald, B. A. (1996). Children lost within the childcare system: Can wraparound service strategies improve placement outcomes? *Journal of Child and Family Studies, 5,* 39–54.

Clatterbuck, C., & Turnbull, H. R. (1996). The role of education and community services in supporting families of children with complex health care needs. In G. H. S. Singer, L. E. Powers, & A. L. Olson (Eds.), *Redefining family support: Innovations in public-private partnerships* (pp. 389–412). Baltimore: Brookes.

Cochran, M. (1992). Parent empowerment: Developing a conceptual framework. *Family Science Review, 5*(1 & 2), 3–21.

Cohen, H. J., Grosz, J., Ayoob, K. T., & Schoen, S. (1997). Early intervention for children with HIV infection. In M. J. Guralnick (Ed.), *The effectiveness of early intervention* (pp. 193–206). Baltimore: Brookes.

Cohen, S., & Wills, T. A. (1985). Stress, social support, and the buffering hypothesis. *Psychological Bulletin, 98,* 310–357.

Coker, C. C., Menz, F. E., Johnson, L. A., & McAlees, D. C. (1998). *School outcomes and community benefits for minority youth with serious emotional disturbances: A synthesis of the research literature.* Menomonie, WI: The Rehabilitation Research and Training Center, Stout Vocational Rehabilitation Institute, College of Human Development, University of Wisconsin-Stout.

Coker, C. C., Osgood, K., & Clouse, K. R. (1995). *A comparison of job satisfaction and economic benefits of four different employment models for persons with disabilities.* Stout, WI: University of Wisconsin, Rehabilitation Research and Training Center on Improving Community-Based Rehabilitation Programs.

Coleman, M. R., Gallagher, J., & Foster, A. (1994). *Updated report on state policies related to the identification of gifted students* [Report]. Chapel Hill: University of North Carolina, Gifted Education Policy Studies Program.

Coles, R. (1989). *The call of stories.* Boston: Houghton Mifflin.

Coley, R. L., & Chase-Lansdale, P. L. (1998). Adolescent pregnancy and parenthood. Recent evidence and future directions. *American Psychology, 53*(2), 49–65, 152–166.

Coltoff, P. (1998). *Community schools: Education reform and partnership with our nation's social service agencies.* Washington, DC: Child Welfare League of America.

Comer, J. P. (1986). Parent participation in the schools. *Phi Delta Kappan, 67*(6), 442–446.

Comer, J. P., & Haynes, N. M. (1991). Parent involvement in schools: An ecological approach. *Elementary School Journal, 91*(3), 271–277.

Comer, J. P., Haynes, N. M., Joyner, E. T., & Ben-Avie, M. (Eds.). (1996). *Rallying the whole village.* New York: Teachers College Press.

Commission on the Education of the Deaf. (1988). *Toward equality: Education of the deaf.* Washington, DC: U.S. Government Printing Office.

Cone, A. A. (1999). Profile of advisors to self-advocacy groups for people with mental retardation. *Mental Retardation, 37*(4), 308–318.

Conoley, J. C., & Sheridan, S. M. (1996). Pediatric traumatic brain injury: Challenges and interventions for families. *Journal of Learning Disabilities, 29*(6), 662–669.

Cook, B. G., Semmel, M. I., & Gerber, M. M. (1999). Attitudes of principals and special education teachers toward the inclusion of students with mild disabilities. *Remedial and Special Education, 20*(4), 199–207, 243.

Cook, C. C., Brotherson, M. J., Weigner-Garrey, C., & Mize, I. (1996). Homes to support the self-determination of children. In D. J. Sands & M. L. Wehmeyer (Eds.), *Self-determination across the life span: Independence and choice for people with disabilities* (pp. 91–110). Baltimore: Paul H. Brookes.

Cook, L. H., & Boe, E. E. (1995). Who is teaching students with disabilities? *Teaching Exceptional Children, 28*(1), 70–72.

Cooper, C. S., & Allred, K. W. (1992). A comparison of mothers' versus fathers' needs for support in caring for a young child with special needs. *Infant-Toddler Intervention, 2*(2), 205–221.

Cooper, H. M. (1989a). *Homework.* White Plains, NY: Longman.

Cooper, H. M. (1989b). Synthesis of research on homework. *Educational Leadership, 47*(3), 85–91.

Cooper, H., Lindsey, J. J., Nye, B., & Greathouse, S. (1998). Relationships among attitudes about homework, amount of homework assigned and completed, and student achievement. *Journal of Educational Psychology, 90*(1), 70–83.

Coots, J. J., Bishop, K. D., & Grenot-Scheyer, M. (1998). Supporting elementary age students with significant disabilities in general education classrooms: Personal perspectives on inclusion. *Education and Training in Mental Retardation and Developmental Disabilities, 33*(4), 317–330.

Cope, D. N., & Wolfson, B. (1994). Crisis intervention with the family in the trauma setting. *Journal of Head Trauma Rehabilitation, 9*(1), 67–81.

Corcoran, J. (1998). Consequences of adolescent pregnancy/parenting: A review of the literature. *Social Work Health Care, 27*(2), 49–67, 152–156.

Corcoran, M. E., & Chaudry, A. (1997). The dynamics of childhood poverty. *The Future of Children, 7*(2), 40–54.

Cornell, D. G., & Grossberg, I. N. (1987). Family environment and personality adjustment in gifted program children. *Gifted Child Quarterly, 31*, 59–64.

Cornell Empowerment Group. (1989). Empowerment through family support. *Networking Bulletin: Empowerment and Family Support, 1*(1), 1–3.

Corrado, C. (1995). The IEP: Once more, with meaning. *Perspectives, 13*(3), 22.

Coulter, D. L. (1987). The neurology of mental retardation. In F. J. Menolascino & J. A. Stark (Eds.), *Preventative and curative intervention in mental retardation* (pp. 113–154). Baltimore: Brookes.

Council for Exceptional Children, U.S. Office of Special Education Programs. (1999, Fall). Universal design: Ensuring access to the general education curriculum. *Research Connections in Special Education, 5*, 1–7.

Countryman, L. L., & Schroeder, M. (1996). When students lead parent-teacher conferences. *Educational Leadership, 53*(7), 64–68.

Cousins, N. (1989). *Head first: The biology of hope.* New York: Dutton.

Covert, S. B. (1995). *Excellence in family support.* St. Augustine, FL: Training Resource Network.

Covey, S. R. (1990). *The seven habits of highly effective people: Restoring the character ethic.* New York: Fireside/Simon & Schuster.

Cowger, C. (1994). Assessing client strengths: Clinical assessment for empowerment. *Social Work, 39*, 262–268.

Cox, S. (1996). The birth of intercountry adoptions. *Focal Point, 10*(1), 22–23.

Craft, A., & Craft, J. (1979). *Handicapped married couples.* London: Routledge & Kegan Paul.

Crago, M. B., & Eriks-Brophy, A. A. (1993). Feeling right: Approaches to a family's culture. *Volta Review, 95*(5), 123–129.

Craig, C., & Herbert, D. (1997). *The state of the children: An examination of government-run foster care. NCPA Policy Report N. 210.* [On-line] Available: http://www.public-policy.org/~ncpa/studies/s210/s210.html.

Craig, J. H., & Craig, M. (1974). *Synergic power: Beyond domination and permissiveness.* San Rafael: Pro-Active Press.

Crais, E. R. (1996). Applying family-centered principles to child assessment. In P. J. McWilliam & E. R. Crais (Eds.), *Practical strategies for family-centered intervention* (pp. 69–96). San Diego, CA: Singular.

Crinc, K., & Stormshak, E. (1997). The effectiveness of providing social support for families of children at risk. In M. Guralnick (Ed.), *The effectiveness of early intervention.* Baltimore: Brookes.

Cripe, J., & Bricker, D. (1993). Family interest survey. In D. Bricker (Ed.), *Assessment, evaluation, and programming system (AEPS) for infants and children* (pp. 1–6). Baltimore: Brookes.

Crnic, K., & Booth, C. (1991). Mothers' and fathers' perceptions of daily hassles of parenting across early childhood. *Journal of Marriage and the Family, 53*, 1042–1050.

Crnic, K. A., Greenberg, M. T., Ragozin, A. S., Robinson, N. M., & Basham, R. (1983). Effects of stress and social support on mothers and premature and full-term infants. *Child Development, 54*, 209–217.

Crowson, R. L., & Boyd, W. L. (1993, February). Coordinated services for children: Designing arks for storms and seas unknown. *American Journal of Education, 101*, 140–179.

Cummings, S. T. (1976). The impact of the child's deficiency on the father: A study of fathers of mentally retarded and of chronically ill children. *American Journal of Orthopsychiatry, 46*, 246–255.

Cunconan-Lahr, R. & Brotherson, M. J. (1996). Advocacy in disability policy: Parents and consumers as advocates. *Mental Retardation, 34*(6), 352–358.

Cuskelly, M., & Gunn, P. (1993). Maternal reports of behavior of siblings of children with Down syndrome. *American Journal on Mental Retardation, 97*(5), 521–529.

Dagirmanjian, S. (1996). Armenian families. In M. McGoldrick, J. Giordano, & J. K. Pearce (Eds.), *Ethnicity and family therapy* (2nd ed., pp. 376–391). New York: The Guilford Press.

Dalzell, H. J. (1998, May–June). Giftedness: Infancy to adolescence—A developmental perspective. *Roeper Review, 20*(4), 259–264.

Damiani, V. B. (1999). Responsibility and adjustment in siblings of children with disabilities: Update and review. *Families in Society: The Journal of Contemporary Human Services, 34*–40.

Daniel, R. R. v. State Board of Education, 874 F.2d 1036 (5th Cir. 1989).

D'Antonio, W. V., & Aldous, J. (Eds.). (1983). *Families and religions.* Beverly Hills, CA: Sage Publications.

D'Apolito, K. (1998). Substance abuse: Infant and childhood outcomes.

Journal of Pediatric Nursing, 13(5), 307–316.

Darling, R. B., & Peter, M. I. (1994). *Families, physicians, and children with special health needs: Collaborative medical education models.* Westport, CT: Auburn House.

Das, M. (1995). Tough decisions: One family's experience crosses cultures and continents. *Volta Voices, 2*(3), 5–7.

Dash, L. (1996). *Rosa Lee.* New York: Basic Books.

Dau, E. (Ed.). (1999). *Child's play.* Baltimore: Brookes.

Dauber, S. L., & Epstein, J. L. (1993). Parents' attitudes and practices of involvement in inner-city elementary and middle schools. In N. F. Chavkin (Ed.), *Families and schools in a pluralistic society.* Albany: State University of New York Press.

Davis, B. (1985). *IEP management programs.* Reports to Decision Makers, 7. (ERIC Document Reproduction Service No. ED 266 610). Northwest Regional Educational Lab, Portland, OR.

Dearholt, D. R. (drd@ichp.edu). (1998, July 28). Summary of NOD/Lou Harris Poll: E-mail to *CSHCN-L@LISTS.UFL.EDU.*

DeChillo, N., Koren, P. E., & Schultze, K. H. (1994). From paternalism to partnership: Family and professional collaboration in children's mental health. *American Journal of Orthopsychiatry, 64*(4), 565–576.

DeGangi, G., Royeen, C. B., & Wietlisbach, S. (1992). How to examine the Individualized Family Service Plan process: Preliminary findings and a procedural guide. *Infants and Young Children, 5*(2), 42–56.

Delgado, M. (1992). *The Puerto Rican community and natural support systems: Implications for the education of children* (Report No. 10). Boston: Boston University, School of Social Work, Center on Families, Communities, Schools, and Children's Learning.

DeMoss, A., Rogers, J., Tuleja, C., & Kirshbaum, M. (1995). *Adaptive parenting equipment: Idea Book One.* Berkeley, CA: Through the Looking Glass.

Dempsey, I. (1996). Facilitating empowerment in families with a member with a disability. *Developmental Disabilities Bulletin, 24*(2), 1–19.

Denby, R. W. (1996). Resiliency and the African American family: A model of family preservation. In S. L. Logan (Ed.), *The black family* (pp. 144–163). Boulder, CO: Westview Press.

Dennis, R. E., & Giangreco, M. F. (1996). Creating conversation: Reflections on cultural sensitivity in family interviewing. *Exceptional Children, 63*(1), 103–116.

Deslandes, R., Royer, E., Potvin, P., & Leclerc, D. (1999). Patterns of home and school partnership for general and special education students at the secondary level. *Exceptional Children, 65*(4), 496–506.

Deyhle, D., & LeCompte, M. (1994). Cultural differences in child development: Navajo adolescents in middle schools. *Theory into Practice, 33*(3), 156–166.

Diamond, K. E., & LeFurgy, W. G. (1992). Relations between mothers' expectations and the performance of their infants who have developmental handicaps. *American Journal on Mental Retardation, 97*(1), 11–20.

Diamond, S., (1981). Growing up with parents of a handicapped child: A handicapped person's perspective. In *Understanding and working with parents of children with special needs.* New York, NY: Holt, Rinehart, and Winston.

DiBella-McCarthy, H., McDaniel, E., & Miller, R. (1995). How efficacious are you? *Teaching Exceptional Children, 27*(3), 68–72.

Doktor, J. E., & Poertner, J. (1996). Kentucky's family resource centers. *Remedial and Special Education, 17*(5), 293–302.

Dolnick, E. (1993). Deafness as a culture. *The Atlantic, 272*(3), 37–53.

Donahue, K., & Zigmond, N. (1990). Academic grades of ninth-grade urban learning disabled students and low-achieving peers. *Exceptionality, 1,* 17–27.

Donahue-Kilburg, G. (1992). *Family-centered early intervention for communication disorders: Prevention and treatment.* Gaithersburg, MD: Aspen.

Dowdney, L., & Skuse, D. (1993). Parenting provided by adults with mental retardation. *Journal of Child Psychology and Psychiatry, 34*(1), 25–47.

Dryfoos, J. (1998). *Safe passage: Making it through adolescence in a risky society.* New York: Oxford University Press.

Dryfoos, J. G. (1996). Full-service schools. *Educational Leadership, 57*(3), 18–23.

Dryfoos, J. G. (1997). Adolescents at risk: Shaping programs to fit the need. *Journal of Negro Education, 65*(1), 5–18.

Dubus, P., & Buckner, J. (1998). A shelter is not a home: Homeless urban mothers and their young children. *Zero to Three, 19*(1), 18–23.

Dunifon, R. (1999). Recent evidence on adolescent pregnancy has implications for future research. *Poverty Research News, 3*(1), 19–22.

Dunn, C. (1996). A status report on transition planning for individuals with learning disabilities. *Journal of Learning Disabilities, 29*(1), 17–30.

Dunst, C. J., Cooper, C. S., Weeldreyer, J. C., Snyder, K. D., & Chase, J. H. (1988). Family needs scale. In C. J. Dunst, C. M. Trivette, & A. G. Deal (Eds.), *Enabling and empowering families: Principles and guidelines for practice.* Cambridge, MA: Brookline.

Dunst, C. J., Johnson, C., Trivette, C. M., & Hamby, D. (1991). Family-oriented early intervention policies and practices: Family-centered or not? *Exceptional Children, 58*(2), 115–126.

Dunst, C. J., Trivette, C. M., & Cross, A. H. (1986). Mediating influences of social support: Personal, family, and child outcomes. *American Journal of Mental Deficiency, 90,* 403–417.

Dunst, C. J., Trivette, C. M., & Deal, A. G. (1988). *Enabling and empowering families: Principles and guidelines for practice.* Cambridge, MA: Brookline.

Dunst, C. J., Trivette, C. M., Gordon, N. J., & Starnes, L. (1993). Family-centered case management practices: Characteristics and consequences. In G. H. S. Singer & L. E. Powers (Eds.), *Families, disability, and empowerment: Active coping skills and strategies for family interventions* (pp. 89–118). Baltimore: Brookes.

Dunst, C. J., Trivette, C. M., & Jodry, W. (1997). Influences of social support on children with disabilities and their families. In M. J. Guralnick (Ed.), *The effectiveness of early intervention* (pp. 499–522). Baltimore: Brookes.

Dunst, C. J., Trivette, C. M., & LaPointe, N. (1992). Toward clarification of the meaning and key elements of empowerment. *Family Studies Review, 5* (1 & 2), 111–130.

Dupper, D. R., & Poertner, J. (1997). Public schools and the revitalization of impoverished communities: School-linked, family resource centers. *Social Work, 42*(5), 415–422.

Dyson, L. L. (1993). Responding to the presence of a child with disabilities: Parental stress and family functioning over time. *American Journal on Mental Retardation, 98,* 207–218.

Dyson, L. L. (1996). The experiences of families of children with learning disabilities: Parental stress, family functioning, and sibling self-concept. *Journal of Learning Disabilities, 29,* 280–286.

Dyson, L. L. (1997). Fathers and mothers of school-age children with developmental disabilities: Parental stress, family functioning, and social support. *American Association on Mental Retardation, 102*(3), 267–279.

Dyson, L. L. (1998). A support program for siblings of children with disabilities: What siblings learn and what they like. *Psychology in the Schools, 35*(1), 57–63.

Dyson, L., Edgar, E., & Crnic, K. (1989). Psychological predictors of adjustment by siblings of developmentally disabled children. *American Journal on Mental Retardation, 94*(3), 292–302.

Dyson, L., & Fewell, R. R. (1989). The self-concept of siblings of handicapped children: A comparison. *Journal of Early Intervention, 13*(3), 230–238.

Eber, L. (1994). *The wraparound approach toward effective school inclusion.* Alexandria, VA: Federation of Families for Children's Mental Health.

Eber, L., Nelson, C. M., & Miles, P. (1997). School-based wraparound for students with emotional and behavioral challenges. *Exceptional Children, 63*(4), 539–555.

Eber, L., Osuch, R., & Redditt, C. A. (1996). School-based applications of the wraparound process: Early results on service provision and student outcomes. *Journal of Child and Family Studies, 5,* 83–99.

Eber, L., Wilson, L., Notier, V., & Pendell, D. (1994). The wraparound approach. Inclusion: A many-sided issue. *Illinois Research and Development Journal, 30*(2), 17–24.

Education Flexibility Partnership Act of 1999 (P.L. 106-25) 113 Stat.41.

Education for All Handicapped Children Act of 1975, Pub. L. No. 94-142, amending Education of the Handicapped Act, renamed Individuals with Disabilities Education Act, as amended by P.L. 98-199, P.L. 99-457, P.L. 100-630, & P.L. 100-476, 20 U.S.C., §§1400–1485.

Edwards, M. (1986). Effects of training and self-evaluation upon special educators' communication and interaction skills when discussing emotion-laden information with parents of handicapped infants (Doctoral dissertation, University of Idaho). *Dissertation Abstracts International, 47,* 2996A.

Edwards, O. W. (1998). Helping grandkin—Grandchildren raised by grandparents: Expanding psychology in the schools. *Psychology in the Schools, 35*(2), 173–180.

Elkins, T. E., Stoval, T. G., Wilroy, S., & Dacus, J. V. (1997). Attitudes of mothers of children with Down syndrome concerning amniocentesis, abortion, and prenatal genetic counseling techniques. *Obstetrics and Gynecology, 68,* 181–184.

Elliot, D. J., Koroloff, M. I., Koren, P. E., & Friesen, B. J. (1998). Improving access to children's mental health services: The family associate approach. In M. H. Epstein, K. Kutash, & A. Duchnowski (Eds.), *Outcomes for children and youth with behavioral and emotional disorders* (pp. 581–609). Austin, TX: Pro-ed.

Ellis, C. L. (1993). *Dialogue journal communication between parent and teacher to describe a parent involvement program.* Unpublished doctoral dissertation, University of Kansas, Lawrence.

Emlen, A. C. (1998). *AFS consumer survey: From parents receiving child care assistance.* Portland, OR: Regional Research Institute for Human Services, Portland State University.

Emlen, A. C. (in press). *Quality of child care and special needs of children who have emotional or behavioral problems.* Paper presented at Building on Family Strengths: A National Conference on Research and Services in Support of Children and their Families, Portland, OR.

Enell, N. C., & Barrick, S. W. (1983). *An examination of the relative efficiency and usefulness of computer-assisted individualized education programs.* Carmichael, CA: San Juan Unified School District. (ERIC Document Reproduction Service No. ED 236 861).

English, D. J. (1998). The extent and consequences of child maltreatment. *The Future of Children, 8*(1), 39–53.

Epstein, J. L. (1987). Parent involvement: What research says to administrators. *Education and Urban Society, 19,* 119–136.

Epstein, J. L. (1987). Toward a theory of family-school connections: Teacher practice and parent involvement. In K. Hurrelman, F. Kaufman, & F. Losel (Eds.), *Social intervention: Potential and constraints* (pp. 121–136). New York: DeGruyter.

Epstein, J. L. (1992). School and family partnerships. *Encyclopedia of Educational Research, 6,* pp. 1139–1151. New York: MacMillan.

Epstein, J. L. (1994). Theory to practice: School and family partnerships lead to school improvement and student success. In C. L. Fagnano & B. Z. Werber (Eds.), *School, family, and community interaction: A view from the firing lines* (pp. 39–52). Boulder, CO: Westview.

Epstein, J. L. (1995, May). School/family/community partnerships: Caring for the children we share. *Phi Delta Kappan, 701–712.*

Epstein, J. L. (1996). Perspectives and previews on research and policy for school, family, and community partnerships. In A. Booth & J. F. Dunn (Eds.), *Family-school links* (pp. 209–246). Mahwah, NJ: Lawrence Erlbaum Associates.

Epstein, J. L. (still in press). A call for action: Improving school-family-community partnerships in the middle grades. In J. Ball & T. Erb (Eds.), *This we believe.* Columbus, OH: National Middle School Association.

Epstein, J. L. (in press-b). School, family, and community connections: New directions for social research. In M. Hallinan (Ed.), *Handbook of sociology of education.* New York: Plenum Press.

Epstein, J. L., Coates, L., Salinas, K. C., Sanders, M. G., & Simon, B. S. (1997). *School, family, and community partnerships.* Thousand Oaks, CA: Corwin Press.

Epstein, J. L., & Sanders, M. G. (1996). *School, family, community partnerships: Overview and new directions.* Baltimore: Johns Hopkins University.

Epstein, J. L., & Sanders, M. G. (in press-a). Family, community partnerships: Overview and new directions. In D. L. Levinson, A. R. Sadovnik, & P. W. Cook (Eds.), *Education and Sociology: An Encyclopedia.* New York: Garland Publishing.

Epstein, J. L., & Sanders, M. G. (in press-b). School, family, and community connections: New directions for social research. In M. Hallinan (Ed.), *Handbook of Sociology Education.* New York: Plenum Press.

Epstein, M. H. (1999). The development and validation of a scale to assess the emotional and behavioral strengths of children and adoles-

cents. *Remedial and Special Education, 20*(5), 258–262.

Epstein, M. H., Kutash, K., & Duchnowski, A. (Eds.). (1998). *Outcomes for children and youth with behavioral and emotional disorders.* Austin, TX: Pro-ed.

Epstein, M. H., Munk, D. D., Bursuck, W. D., Polloway, E. A., & Jayanthi, M. M. (1999). Strategies for improving home-school communication about homework for students with disabilities. *The Journal of Special Education, 33*(3), 166–176.

Epstein, M. H., Polloway, E. A., Foley, R. M., & Patton, J. R. (1993). Homework: A comparison of teachers' and parents' perceptions of the problems experienced by students identified as having behavioral disorders, learning disabilities, or no disabilities. *Remedial and Special Education, 14*(5), 40–50.

ERIC/OSEP Special project. (1999, Fall). Universal design: Ensuring access to the general education curriculum. *Research Connections in Special Education, 5.*

Erickson, R. (1998). *Accountability, standards, and assessment.* Washington, DC: Federal Resource Center, Academy for Educational Development.

Erickson-Warfield, M., & Hauser-Cram, P. (1996). Child care needs, arrangements, and satisfaction of mothers of children with developmental disabilities. *Mental Retardation, 34*(5), 294–302.

Erickson-Warfield, M., Wyngaarden-Krauss, M., Hauser-Cram, P., Upshur, C. C., & Shonkoff, J. P. (1999). Adaption during early childhood among mothers of children with disabilities. *Developmental and Behavioral Pediatrics, 20*(1), 9–16.

Erwin, E. J., & Rainforth, B. (1996). Partnerships for collaboration: Building bridges in early care and education. In E. J. Erwin (Ed.), *Putting children first* (pp. 227–251). Baltimore: Brookes.

Erwin, E. J., & Soodak, L. C. (1995). I never knew I could stand up to the system: Families' perspectives on pursuing inclusive education. *Journal of the Association for Persons*

with Severe Handicaps, 20(2), 136–146.

Erwin, E., Soodak, L., Winton, P., & Turnbull, A. (still in press). "I wish it wouldn't all depend upon me": Research on families and early childhood inclusion. In M. J. Guralnick (Ed.), *Early childhood inclusion: Focus on change* (pp. 5–12). Baltimore: Brookes.

Espin, C. A., Deno, S. L., & Albayrak-Kaymak, D. (1998). Individualized education programs in resource and inclusive settings: How "individualized" are they? *The Journal of Special Education, 32*(3), 164–174.

Etscheidt, S. K., & Bartlett, L. (1999). The IDEA amendments: A four-step approach for determining supplementary aids and services. *Exceptional Children, 65*(2), 163–174.

Evans, M., Armstrong, M., & Kuppinger, A. (1996). Family-centered intensive case management: A step toward understanding individualized care. *Journal of Child and Family Studies, 5*(1), 55–65.

Fagan, J., & Schorr, D. (1993). Mothers of children with spina bifida: Factors related to maternal psychological functioning. *American Journal of Orthopsychiatry, 63,* 146–152.

Falicov, C. J. (1996). Mexican families. In M. McGoldrick, J. Giordano, & J. K. Pearce (Eds.), *Ethnicity and family therapy* (2nd ed., pp. 169–182). New York: The Guilford Press.

Falvey, M., Coots, J., & Terry-Gage, S. (1992). Extracurricular activities. In S. Stainback & W. Stainback (Eds.), *Curriculum considerations in inclusive classrooms: Facilitating learning for all students* (pp. 229–238). Baltimore: Brookes.

Falvey, M. A., Forest, M., Pearpoint, J., & Rosenberg, R. (1994). Building connections. In J. S. Thousand, R. A. Villa, & A. I. Nevin (Eds.), *Creativity and collaborative learning: A practical guide to empowering students and teachers* (pp. 347–368). Baltimore: Brookes.

Falvey, M. A., Forest, M., Pearpoint, J., & Rosenberg, R. L. (1997). *All my life's a circle.* Toronto, Ontario: Inclusion Press.

Families and Work Institute. (1994). *Employers, families, and education: Facilitating family involvement in learning.* New York: Author.

Fantuzzo, J. W., Wray, L., Hall, R., Goins, C., & Azar, S. (1986). Parent and social-skills training for mentally retarded mothers identified as child maltreaters. *American Journal of Mental Deficiency, 91*(2), 135–140.

Farber, B., & Ryckman, D. B. (1965). Effects of severely mentally retarded children on family relationships. *Mental Retardation Abstracts, 2,* 1–17.

Farel, A. M., Shackelford, J., & Hurth, J. L. (1997). Perceptions regarding the IFSP process in a statewide interagency service coordination program. *Topics in Early Childhood Special Education, 17*(2), 234–249.

Farkas, S., Johnson, J., Duffett, A., Aulicino, C., & McHugh, J. (1999). *Playing their parts: Parents and teachers talk about parental involvement in public schools.* New York: A Report from Public Agenda.

Featherstone, H. (1980). *A difference in the family: Living with a disabled child.* New York: Basic Books.

Federal Register. (1981, January 19). Washington, DC: U.S. Government Printing Office.

Feitel, B., Margetson, N., Chamas, J., & Lipman, C. (1992). Psychosocial background and behavioural and emotional disorders of homeless and runaway youth. *Hospital and Community Psychiatry, 43*(2), 155–159.

Feldhusen, J., Van Winkle, L., & Ehle, D. A. (1996). Is it acceleration or simply appropriate instruction for precocious youth? *Teaching Exceptional Children, 28*(3), 48–51.

Feldman, M. A. (1997). The effectiveness of early intervention for children of parents with mental retardation. In M. L. Guralnick (Ed.), *The effectiveness of early intervention* (pp. 171–191). Baltimore: Brookes.

Feldman, M. A. (1998). Preventing child neglect: Child-care training for parents with intellectual disabilities. *Infants and Young Children, 11*(2), 1–11.

Feldman, M. A., Case, L., Rincover, A., & Betel, J. (1989). Parent Education Project III: Increasing affection and responsivity in developmentally handicapped mothers: Component analysis, generalization, and effects on child language. *Journal of Applied Behavior Analysis, 22,* 211–222.

Feldman, M. A., & Walton-Allen, N. (1997). Effects of maternal mental retardation and poverty on intellectual, academic, and behavioral status of school-age children. *American Journal on Mental Retardation, 101*(4), 352–364.

Ferguson, D. L. (1984). Parent advocacy network. *Exceptional Parent, 14,* 41–45.

Ferguson, P. M. (1994). *Abandoned to their fate: Social policy and practice toward severely retarded people in America, 1820–1920.* Philadelphia: Temple University Press.

Ferguson, P. M., & Ferguson, D. L. (1993). The promise of adulthood. In M. Snell (Ed.), *Instruction of persons with severe disabilities* (4th ed., pp. 588–607). Englewood Cliffs, NJ: Merrill/Prentice-Hall.

Fewell, R. R. (1986). Supports from religious organizations and personal beliefs. In R. R. Fewell & P. F. Vadasy (Eds.), *Families of handicapped children: Needs and supports across the life span* (pp. 297–316). Austin, TX: Pro-ed.

Fey, M. E., Windsor, J., & Warren, S. F. (Eds.). (1995). *Language intervention: Preschool through the elementary years.* Baltimore: Brookes.

Fiedler, C. R. (1985). *Conflict prevention, containment, and resolution in special education due process disputes: Parents' and school personnel's perception of variables associated with the development and escalation of due process conflict.* Unpublished doctoral dissertation, University of Kansas, Lawrence.

Field, S., & Hoffman, A. (1999). The importance of family involvement for promoting self-determination in adolescents with autism and other developmental disabilities. *Focus on Autism and other Developmental Disabilities, 14*(1), 36–41.

Field, S., Hoffman, A., & Spezia, S. (1998). *Self-determination strategies for adolescents in transition.* Austin, TX: Pro-ed.

Field, S., Martin, J. E., Miller, R. J., Ward, M. J., & Wehmeyer, M. L. (1998). *A practical guide for teaching self-determination.* Reston, VA: Council for Exceptional Children.

Finders, M., & Lewis, C. (1994, May). Why some parents don't come to school. *Educational Leadership,* 50–54.

Fine, M. (1990). Facilitating home-school relationships: A family-oriented approach to collaborative consultation. *Journal of Educational and Psychological Consultation, 1*(2), 169–187.

Fisher, D., Pumpian, I., & Sax, C. (1998). Parent and caregiver impressions of different educational models. *Remedial and Special Education, 19*(3), 173–180.

Fisher, R., & Ury, W. (1991). *Getting to yes: Negotiating agreement without giving in* (2nd ed.). Boston: Houghton Mifflin.

Fishman, K. D. (1992). Problem adoptions. *The Atlantic Monthly, 270*(3), 37–69.

Fitzpatrick, J. P. (1987). *Puerto Rican Americans: The meaning of migration to the mainland.* Englewood Cliffs, NJ: Prentice-Hall.

Flach, F. (1988). *Resilience: Discovering a new strength at times of stress.* New York: Fawcett Columbine.

Flaherty, M. J., Facteau, L., & Garner, P. (1994). Grandmother functions in multigenerational families: An exploratory study of black adolescent mothers and their infants. In R. Staples (Ed.), *The black family: Essays and studies* (5th ed., pp. 195–203). Belmont, CA: Wadsworth.

Flake-Hobson, C., & Swick, K. J. (1984). Communication strategies for parents and teachers, or how to say what you mean. In M. L. Henniger & E. M. Nesselroad (Eds.), *Working with parents of handicapped children: A book of readings for school personnel* (pp. 141–149). Lanham, MD: University Press of America.

Flood, J., & Lapp, D. (1989, March). Reporting reading progress: A comparison portfolio for parents. *Reading Teacher,* 508–515.

Florin, P. & Wandersman, A. (1984). Cognitive social learning and participation in community development. *American Journal of Community Psychology, 12,* 689–708.

Flugum, K. R., & Reschly, D. J. (1994). Prereferral interventions: Quality indices and outcomes. *Journal of School Psychology, 32*(1), 1–14.

Flynn, L., & Wilson, P. (1998). Partnerships with family members: What about fathers? *Young Exceptional Children, 2,* 21–29.

Flynt, W., & Wood, T. A. (1989). Stress and coping of mothers of children with moderate mental retardation. *American Journal on Mental Retardation, 94,* 278–283.

Foley, G. M. (1990). Portrait of the arena assessment. In E. D. Gibbs & D. M. Teti (Eds.), *Interdisciplinary assessment of infants: A guide for early intervention professionals* (pp. 271–286). Baltimore: Brookes.

Forest, M., & Lusthaus, E. (1990). Everyone belongs with the MAPs action planning system. *Teaching Exceptional Children, 22*(2), 32–35.

Forman, R. K. C. (Ed.). (1993). *Religions of the world* (3rd ed.). New York: St. Martin's Press.

Foster-Gaitskell, D., & Pratt, C. (1989). Comparison of parent and teacher ratings of adaptive behavior of children with mental retardation. *American Journal on Mental Retardation, 94,* 177–181.

Fowler, R. C., Corley, K. K. (1996). Linking families, building community. *Educational Leadership, 53*(7), 24–26.

Fox, S. (1997). The controversy over ebonics. *Phi Delta Kappan, 79* (3), 237–240.

Frankel, K., & Wamboldt, M. Z. (1998). Chronic childhood illness and maternal mental health—Why should we care? *Journal of Asthma, 35*(8), 621–630.

Franklin, C., & Streeter, C. L. (1995). School reform: Linking public schools with human services. *Social Work, 40*(6), 773–782.

Freedman, R. I., Wyngaarden-Krauss, M., & Mailick-Seltzer, M. (1997). Aging parents' residential plans for adult children with mental retardation. *Mental Retardation, 35*(2), 114–123.

French-Gilson, S., Bricout, J. C., & Baskind, F. R. (1998, March/April). Listening to voices of individuals with disabilities. *Families in Society: The Journal of Contemporary Human Services,* 188–195.

Frey, K. S., Fewell, R. R., & Vadasy, P. F. (1989). Parental adjustment and changes in child outcome among families of young handicapped children. *Topics in Early Childhood Special Education, 8*(4), 38–57.

Frey, K. S., Greenberg, M. T., & Fewell, R. F. (1989). Stress and coping among parents of handicapped children: A multidimensional approach. *American Journal of Mental Retardation, 94*(3), 240–249.

Friedman, E. H. (1980). Systems and ceremonies: A family view of rites of passage. In E. A. Carter & M. McGoldrick (Eds.), *The family life cycle: A framework for family therapy* (pp. 429–460). New York: Gardner.

Friedman, R. C. (1994). Upstream helping for low-income families of gifted students: Challenges and opportunities. *Journal of Educational and Psychological Consultation, 5*(4), 321–338.

Friedman, R. C., & Gallagher, T. (1991). The family with a gifted child. In M. J. Fine (Ed.), *Collaboration with parents of exceptional children* (pp. 257–276). Brandon, VT: Clinical Psychology Publishing.

Friesen, B. J., & Huff, B. (1990). Parents and professionals of advocacy partners. *Preventing School Failure, 34*(3), 31–35.

Friesen, B. J., Koren, P. E., & Koroloff, N. M. (1992). How parents view professional behaviors: A cross-professional analysis. *Journal of Child and Family Studies, 1*(2), 209–231.

Friesen, B. J., & Koroloff, N. M. (1990). Family-centered services: Implications for mental health administration and research. *Journal of Mental Health Administration, 17*(1), 13–25.

Friesen, B. J., & Poertner, J. (Eds.). (1995). *Case management to service coordination for children with emotional, behavioral, or mental disorders.* Baltimore: Brookes.

Friesen, B. J., & Wahlers, D. (1993). Respect and real help: Family support and children's mental health. *Journal of Emotional and Behavioral Problems, 2*(4), 12–15.

Fuchs, D., Fuchs, L. S., & Bahr, M. W. (1990). Mainstream assistance teams: A scientific basis for the art of consultation. *Exceptional Children, 57,* 128–139.

Fuchs, D., Fuchs, L. S., Bahr, M. W., & Stecker, P. M. (1990). Prereferral intervention: A prescriptive approach. *Exceptional Children, 56,* 493–513.

Fujiura, G. T. (1998). Demography of family households. *American Journal on Mental Retardation, 103*(3), 225–235.

Fujiura, G. T., Roccoforte, J. A., & Braddock, D. (1994). Costs of family care for adults with mental retardation and related developmental disabilities. *American Journal on Mental Retardation, 99*(3), 250–261.

Fujiura, G. T., & Yamaki, K. (1997). Analysis of ethnic variations in developmental disability prevalence and household economic status. *Mental Retardation, 35*(4), 286–294.

Fuller, C., Vandiviere, P., & Kronberg, C. (1987). TALKLINE: An evaluation of a call-in telephone source for parents. *Journal of the Division for Early Childhood, 11*(3), 265–270.

Fulmer, R. H., Cohen, S., & Monaco, G. (1985). Using psychological assessment in structural family therapy. *Journal of Learning Disabilities, 18*(3), 145–150.

Funkhouser, J. E., & Gonzales, M. R. (1998). *Family involvement in children's education.* Washington, DC: U.S. Department of Education, Office of Educational Research and Improvement.

Fuqua, R. W., Hegland, S. M., & Karas, S. C. (1985). Processes influencing linkages between preschool handicap classrooms and homes. *Exceptional Children, 51*(4), 307–314.

Furey, E. M. (1994). Sexual abuse of adults with mental retardation:

Who and where. *Mental Retardation, 32*(3), 173–180.

Furstenberg, F. F., Brooks-Gunn, J., & Morgan, S. P. (1987). *Adolescent mothers in later life.* Cambridge, MA: Cambridge University Press.

Gable, R. A. (1996). A critical analysis of functional assessment: Issues for researchers and practitioners. *Behavioral Disorders, 22,* 36–40.

Gage, S. T., & Falvey, M. A. (1995). Assessment strategies to develop appropriate curricula and educational programs. In M. A. Falvey (Ed.), *Inclusive and heterogeneous schooling* (pp. 59–110). Baltimore: Brookes.

Gajria, M., & Salend, S. (1995). A comparison of homework practices of students with and without learning disabilities. *Journal of Learning Disabilities, 28,* 291–296.

Gallagher, J. J. (1997). Least restrictive environment and gifted students. *Peabody Journal of Education, 72* (3&4), 153–165.

Gallagher, J., & Desimone, L. (1995). Lessons learned from implementations of the IEP: Applications to the IFSP. *Topics in Early Childhood Special Education, 15*(3), 353–378.

Gallagher, J. J., & Gallagher, G. G. (1985). Family adaptation to a handicapped child and assorted professionals. In H. R. Turnbull & A. P. Turnbull (Eds.), *Parents speak out: Then and now* (2nd ed., pp. 233–244). Englewood Cliffs, NJ: Merrill/Prentice-Hall.

Gallagher, J., & Gallagher, S. (1994). *Teaching the gifted child.* (4th ed.). Boston: Allyn & Bacon.

Gallagher, J., Harradine, C. C., & Coleman, M. R. (1997). Challenge or boredom? Gifted students' views on their schooling. *Roeper Review, 19*(3), 132–136.

Gallimore, R., Weisner, T., Bernheimer, L., Guthrie, D., & Nihira, K. (1993). Family responses to young children with developmental delays: Accommodation activity in ecological and cultural content. *American Journal on Mental Retardation, 98,* 185–206.

Gallimore, R., Weisner, T. S., Kaufman, S. Z., & Bernheimer, L. P. (1989). The social construction of ecocultural niches: Family accommodation of developmentally delayed children. *American Journal of Mental Retardation, 94,* 216–230.

Gallivan-Fenlon, A. (1994). "Their senior year": Family and service provider perspectives on the transition from school to adult life for young adults with disabilities. *Journal of the Association for Persons with Severe Handicaps, 19*(1), 11–23.

Gans, L. (1997). *Sisters, brothers, and disability.* Minneapolis, MN: Fairview Press.

Garbarino, J., & Kostelny, K. (1992). Neighborhood-based programs [Manuscript prepared for U.S. Advisory Board on Child Abuse and Neglect]. Chicago: Erikson Institute.

Garcia-Preto, N. (1996). Latino families: An overview. In M. McGoldrick & J. Giordano (Eds.), *Ethnicity and family therapy* (2nd ed., pp. 65–87, 141–145). New York: The Guilford Press.

Garlow, J. E., Turnbull, H. R., & Schnase, D. (1991). Model disability and family support act of 1991. *Kansas Law Review, 39*(3), 783–816.

Garshelis, J. A., & McConnell, S. R. (1993). Comparison of family needs assessed by mothers, individual professionals, and interdisciplinary teams. *Journal of Early Intervention, 17*(1), 36–49.

Gath, A. (1977). The impact of an abnormal child upon the parents. *British Journal of Psychiatry, 130,* 405–410.

Gath, A., & Gumley, D. (1987). Retarded children and their siblings. *Journal of Child Psychology and Psychiatry, 28,* 715–730.

Gaventa, W. C. (2000). Defining and assessing spirituality and spiritual supports: Moving from benediction to invocation. In S. Greenspan & H. Switzky (Eds.), *What is mental retardation: Ideas for the new century.* Washington, DC: American Association on Mental Retardation.

Gee, K. (1996). Least restrictive environment: Elementary and middle school. In *National Council on Disability, Improving the implementation of the Individuals with Disabilities Education Act: Making schools work for all of America's children.* Supplement (pp. 395–426). Washington, DC: National Council on Disability.

Gelfer, J. I., & Perkins, P. G. (1998). Portfolios: Focus on young children. *Teaching Exceptional Children, 31*(2), 44–47.

Gelzheiser, L. M., McLane, M., Meyers, J., & Pruzek, R. M. (1998). IEP-Specified peer interaction needs: Accurate but ignored. *Exceptional Children, 65*(1), 51–65.

George, J. D. (1988). Therapeutic intervention for grandparents and extended family of children with developmental delays. *Mental Retardation, 26*(6), 369–375.

George, R. M., VanVoorhis, J., Grant, S., Casey, K., & Robinson, S. (1992). Special education experiences of foster children: An empirical study. *Child Welfare, 71*(5), 419–437.

Gerber, P. J., Banbury, M. M., Miller, J. H., & Griffin, H. D. (1986). Special educators' perceptions of parental participation in the individual education plan process. *Psychology in the Schools, 23,* 158–163.

Gerry, M. (in press). Service integration and achieving the goals of school reform. In W. Sailor (Ed.), *Inclusive education and school/community partnerships.* New York: Teacher's College Press.

Gerst, D. (1991). *Trevor is a citizen: Why grieve?* Unpublished manuscript.

Gersten, R., & Woodward, J. (1994). The language-minority student and special education: Issues, trends, and paradoxes. *Exceptional Children, 60*(4), 310–322.

Gervasio, A. H. (1993). How TBI affects the family. *TBI Transmit, 4*(1), 1–3.

Gettings, R. M. (1994). The link between public financing and systematic change. In V. J. Bradley, J. W. Ashbaugh, & B. C. Blaney (Eds.), *Creating individual supports for people with developmental disabilities* (pp. 155–170). Baltimore: Brookes.

Getzel, E. E., & deFur, S. (1997). Transition planning for students with significant disabilities: Implications for student-centered planning. *Focus on Autism and Other Developmental Disabilities, 12*(1), 39–48.

Giangreco, M. F., Cloninger, C. J., Mueller, P. H., Yuan, S., & Ashworth, S. (1991). Perspectives of parents whose children have dual sensory impairments. *Journal of the Association for Persons with Severe Handicaps, 16*(1), 14–24.

Gill, B. (1997). *Changed by a child.* New York: Doubleday Publishers.

Gill, V., & Maynard, D. W. (1995). On "labeling" in actual interaction: Delivering and receiving diagnoses of developmental disabilities. *Social Problems, 42*(1), 11–37.

Gilson, S. F., Bricourt, J. C., & Baskind, F. R. (1998, March–April). Listening to the voices of individuals with disabilities. *Families in Society: The Journal of Contemporary Human Services, 79*(2), 188–196.

Glascoe, F. P. (1999). Communicating with parents. *Young Exceptional Children, 2*(4), 17–25.

Glidden, L. M. (1989). *Parents for children, children for parents: The adoption alternative.* Washington, DC: American Association on Mental Retardation.

Glidden, L. M., & Johnson, V. E. (1999). Twelve years later: Adjustment in families who adopted children with developmental disabilities. *Mental Retardation, 37*(1), 16–24.

Glidden, L. M., Kiphart, M. J., Willoughby, J. C., & Bush, B. A. (1993). Family functioning when rearing children with developmental disabilities. In A. P. Turnbull, J. M. Patterson, S. K. Behr, D. L. Murphy, J. G. Marquis, & M. J. Blue-Banning (Eds.), *Cognitive coping, families, and disability* (pp. 173–182). Baltimore: Brookes.

Glidden, L. M., & Pursley, J. T. (1989). Longitudinal comparisons of families who have adopted children with mental retardation. *American Journal of Mental Retardation, 94*(3), 272–277.

Glutting, J. J. (1987). The McDermott multidimensional assessment of children: Contribution to the development of individualized educational programs. *The Journal of Special Education, 20,* 431–445.

Goddard, H. H. (1912). *The Kallikak family: A study in the heredity of feeblemindedness.* New York: Macmillan.

Goetz, K. (1994, Spring–Summer). Kaleidoscope: Hope at the end of the road. *Family Resource Coalition Report,* 20–21.

Goldenberg, I., & Goldenberg, H. (1980). *Family therapy: An overview.* Monterey, CA: Brooks/Cole.

Goldenson, L. H. (1965, March). *Remarks on the occasion of United Cerebral Palsy Associations' 15th anniversary.* Paper presented at the 15th annual meeting of the United Cerebral Palsy Associations, Los Angeles.

Goldstein, H. (1990). Strength or pathology: Ethical and rhetorical contrasts in approaches to practice. *Families in Society, 71,* 267–276.

Goldstein, S., Strickland, B., Turnbull, A. P., & Curry, L. (1980). An observational analysis of the IEP conference. *Exceptional Children, 46*(4), 278–286.

Goldstein, S., & Turnbull, A. P. (1982). The use of two strategies to increase parent participation in IEP conferences. *Exceptional Children, 46*(4), 360–361.

Gomby, D. S., Culross, P. L., & Behrman, R. E. (1999). Home visiting: Recent program evaluations—Analysis and recommendations. *The Future of Children, 9*(1), 4–26.

Gowen, J. W., Christy, D. S., & Sparling, J. (1993). Informational needs of parents of young children with special needs. *Journal of Early Intervention, 17*(2), 194–210.

Gradel, K., Thompson, M. S., & Sheehan, R. (1981). Parental and professional agreement in early childhood assessment. *Topics in Early Childhood Special Education, 1*(2), 31–39.

Graden, J. E., Casey, A., & Bonstrom, O. (1985). Implementing a prereferral intervention system. Part II: The data. *Exceptional Children, 51,* 487–496.

Graden, J. E., Casey, A., & Christenson, S. L. (1985). Implementing a prereferral intervention system. Part I: The model. *Exceptional Children, 51,* 377–384.

Grant, T., Ernst, C., & Streissguth, A. (1996). An intervention with high-risk mothers who abuse alcohol and drugs: The Seattle advocacy model. *American Journal of Public Health, 86*(12), 1,816–1,817.

Gray, D. B., Quatrano, L. A., & Lieberman, M. L. (Eds.). (1998). *Designing and using assistive technology.* Baltimore: Brookes.

Greene, B. F., Norman, K. R., Searle, M. S., Daniels, M., & Lubeck, R. C. (1995). Child abuse and neglect by parents with disabilities: A tale of two families. *Journal of Applied Behavior Analysis, 28*(4), 417–434.

Green, S. K., & Shinn, M. R. (1994). Parent attitudes about special education and reintegration: What is the role of student outcomes? *Exceptional Children, 61*(3), 269–281.

Greenfield, P. M. (1994). Independence and interdependence as developmental scripts: Implications for theory, research, and practice. In P. M. Greenfield & R. R. Cocking (Eds.), *Cross-cultural roots of minority child development* (pp. 1–37). Hillsdale, NJ: Erlbaum.

Greenspan, S., & Porges, S. (1984). Psychopathology in infancy and early childhood: Clinical perspectives on the organization of sensory and affective-thematic experience. *Child Development, 55,* 49–70.

Greenwald, R. (1997). *My son, my gentle son.* Tallmadge, OH: Family Child Learning Center.

Greenwood, R. (1997). *My son, my gentle son.* Talmadge, OH: Family Child Learning Center.

Greer v. Rome City School District, 762 F. Supp. 936 (N.D. Ga. 1990).

Grenier, M. E. (1985). Gifted children and other siblings. *Gifted Child Quarterly, 29,* 164–167.

Grigal, M., Quirk, C., & Manos, S. (1998). *MAPS as a planning tool: What works? What doesn't? Says who?* Paper presented at the TASH Conference, Seattle, WA.

Groce, N. E. (October 6, 1997). *Adolescence and disability.* Paper presented at the Thematic Discussion on Childhood Disability, Sixteenth Session of the Committee on the Rights of the Child, Palais des Nations, Geneva.

Grotevant, H. D., & McRoy, R. G. (1990). Adopted adolescents in residential treatment: The role of the family. In D. Brodzinsky & M. Schechter (Eds.), *The psychology of adoption* (pp. 167–186). New York: Oxford University Press.

Grove, K. A., & Fisher, D. (1999). Entrepreneurs of meaning. *Remedial and Special Education, 20*(4), 208–215, 256.

Groves, B. (1997). Growing up in a violent world: The impact of family and community violence on young children and their families. In J. J. Carta (Ed.), *Topics in early childhood special education* (pp. 74–102). Austin, TX: Pro-ed.

Gruber, J., & Trivette, E. J. (1987). Can we empower others? The paradox of empowerment in the governing of an alternative public school. *American Journal of Community Psychology, 15*(3), 353–371.

Guralnick, M. J. (1994). Mothers' perceptions of the benefits and drawbacks of early childhood mainstreaming. *Journal of Early Intervention, 18*(2), 168–183.

Guralnick, M. J., Conner, R. T., & Hammond, M. (1995). Parent perspectives of peer relationships and friendships in integrated and specialized settings. *American Journal on Mental Retardation, 99,* 457–476.

Gutiérrez, L., & Nurius, P. (Eds.). (1994). *Education and research for empowerment practice* (Monograph No. 7). Seattle, WA: University of Washington, School of Social Work, Center for Policy and Practice Research.

Hackney, H. L., & Cormier, L. S. (1996). *The professional counselor.* (3rd ed.). Boston: Allyn & Bacon.

Hadadian, A., & Merbler, J. (1995). Parents of infants and toddlers with special needs: Sharing views of desired services. *Infant-Toddler Intervention, 5*(2), 141–152.

Hadaway, N., & Marek-Schroer, M. F. (1992). Multidimensional assessment of the gifted minority student. *Roeper Review, 15*(2), 73–77.

Hagborg, W. J. (1989). A comparative study of parental stress among mothers and fathers of deaf school-age children. *Journal of Community Psychology, 17,* 220–224.

Hagner, D., Helm, R. T., & Butterworth, J. (1996). "This is your meeting": A qualitative study of person-centered planning. *Mental Retardation, 34*(3), 159–171.

Hall, E. T. (1966). *The hidden dimension.* Garden City, NY: Doubleday.

Hallahan, D. P., Keller, C. E., McKinney, J. D., Lloyd, J. W., & Bryan, T. C. (1988). Examining the research base of the Regular Education Initiative: Efficacy studies and the adaptive learning environments model. *Journal of Learning Disabilities, 21,* 29–35.

Haller, E. J., & Millman, J. (1987). *A survey of Arc members* [Internal report]. Arlington, TX: The Arc.

Halperin, L. (1989). Encounters of the closest kind: A view from within. *National Association of School Psychologists Communiqué, 17,* 6.

Hammond, H. (1999). Identifying best family-centered practices in early-intervention programs. *Teaching Exceptional Children, 31*(6), 42–46.

Handron, D. S., Doser, D. A., McCammon, S. L., & Powell, J. Y. (1998). "A wraparound"—the wave of the future: Theoretical and professional practice implications for children and families with complex needs. *Journal of Family Nursing, 4*(1), 65–86.

Hannah, M. E., & Midlarsky, E. (1999). Competence and adjustment of siblings of children with mental retardation. *American Journal on Mental Retardation, 104*(1), 22–37.

Hanson, M. J. (1998). Families with Anglo-European roots. In E. W. Lynch & M. J. Hanson (Eds.), *Developing cross-cultural competence: A guide for working with young children and their families* (2nd ed., pp. 65–87, 93–126). Baltimore: Brookes.

Harden, B. J. (1997). You cannot do it alone: Home visitation with psychologically vulnerable families and children. *Bulletin of Zero to Three: National Center for Infants, Toddlers, and Families, 17*(4), 10–16.

Hare, J. (1994). Concerns and issues faced by families headed by a lesbian couple. *Families in Society: The Journal of Contemporary Human Services, 75,* 27–35.

Hareven, T. K. (1982). American families in transition: Perspectives on change. In F. Walsh (Ed.), *Normal family processes* (pp. 446–466). New York: Guilford.

Harris, T. (1994). Christine's inclusion: An example of peers supporting one another. In J. S. Thousand, R. A. Villa, & A. I. Nevin (Eds.), *Creativity and collaborative learning: A practical guide to empowering students and teachers* (pp. 293–304). Baltimore: Brookes.

Harris, V. S., & McHale, S. M. (1989). Family life problems, daily caregiving activities, and psychological well-being of mothers of mentally retarded children. *American Journal on Mental Retardation, 94,* 231–239.

Harrison, F., & Crow, M. (1993). *Living and learning with blind children.* Toronto, NY: University of Toronto Press.

Harry, B. (1992a). An ethnographic study of cross-cultural communication with Puerto Rican-American families in the special education system. *American Educational Research Journal, 29*(3), 471–494.

Harry, B. (1992b). *Cultural diversity, families, and the special education system: Communication and empowerment.* New York: Teachers College Press.

Harry, B. (1992c). Developing cultural self-awareness: The first step in values clarification for early interventionists. *Topics in Early Childhood Special Education, 12*(3), 333–350.

Harry, B. (1992d). Making sense of disability: Low-income, Puerto Rican parents' theories of the problem. *Exceptional Children, 59*(1), 27–40.

Harry, B., Allen, N., & McLaughlin, M. (1995). Communication versus compliance: African-American parents' involvement in special education. *Exceptional Children, 61*(4), 364–377.

Harry, B., & Anderson, M. (1999). The social construction of disability: African American males and the special education system. In V. Polite (Ed.), *African American males in school and society: Policies and practices for effective education.* New York: Teachers College Press.

Harry, B., Day, M., & Quist, F. (1998). "He can't really play": An ethnographic study of sibling acceptance and interaction. *JASH, 23*(4), 289–299.

Harry, B., & Kalyanpur, M. (1994). Cultural underpinnings of special education: Implications for professional interactions with culturally diverse families. *Disability and Society, 9*(2), 145–165.

Harry, B., Kalyanpur, M., & Day, M. (1999). *Building cultural reciprocity with families.* Baltimore: Paul H. Brookes.

Harry, B., Rueda, R., & Kalyanpur, M. (1999). Cultural reciprocity in sociocultural perspective: Adapting the normalization principle for family collaboration. *Exceptional Children, 66*(1), 123–136.

Hasazi, S., Gordon, L., & Roe, C. (1985). Factors associated with the employment status of handicapped youth exiting from high school from 1979 to 1983. *Exceptional Children, 51*(6), 455–469.

Hasazi, S. B., Johnston, A. P., Liggett, A., & Schattman, R. (1994). A qualitative policy study of the least restrictive environment provision of the Individuals with Disabilities Education Act. *Exceptional Children, 60*(6), 491–507.

Hauser-Cram, P., Erickson-Warfield, M., Shonkoff, J. P., Wyngaarden-Krauss, M., Upshur, C. C., & Sayer, A. (1999). Family influences on adaptive development in young children with Down syndrome. *Child Development, 70*(4), 979–989.

Haworth, A. M., Hill, A. E., & Glidden, L. M. (1996). Measuring religiousness of parents of children with developmental disabilities. *Mental Retardation, 34*(5), 271–279.

Hayden, M. F., & Heller, T. (1997). Support, problem-solving/coping ability, and personal burden of younger and older caregivers of adults with mental retardation. *Mental Retardation, 35*(5), 364–372.

Heflin, L. J., & Rudy, K. (1991). *Homeless and in need of special education.* Reston, VA: Council for Exceptional Children.

Heflinger, C. A., Bickman, L., Northrup, D., & Sinnichsen, S. (1997). A theory-driven intervention and evaluation to explore family caregiver empowerment. *Journal of Emotional and Behavioral Disorders, 5*(3), 184–191.

Hehir, T. (1994). *Improving the individuals with disabilities education act: IDEA reauthorization.* U.S. Department of Education, Office of Special Education Programs, Unpublished manuscript. Washington, DC.

Helge, D. (1991). *Rural, exceptional, at risk.* Reston, VA: Council for Exceptional Children.

Heller, K. (1990). Social and community interventions. *Annual Review of Psychology, 41,* 141–168.

Heller, K. W., Gallagher, P. A., & Frederick, L. D. (1999). Parents' perceptions of siblings' interactions with their brothers and sisters who are deaf-blind. *The Journal of the Association for Persons with Severe Handicaps, 24*(1), 33–43.

Helm, D. T., Miranda, S., & Angoff-Chedd, N. (1998). Prenatal diagnosis of Down syndrome: Mothers' reflections on supports needed from diagnosis to birth. *Mental Retardation, 36*(1), 55–61.

Helsel Family. (1985). The Helsels' story of Robin. In H. R. Turnbull & A. P. Turnbull (Eds.), *Parents speak out: Then and now* (2nd ed., pp. 81–100). Englewood Cliffs, NJ: Merrill/Prentice-Hall.

Henderson, L. W., Aydlett, L. A., & Bailey, D. B. (1993). Evaluating family needs surveys: Do standard measures of reliability and validity tell us what we want to know? *Journal of Psychoeducational Assessment, 11,* 208–219.

Hepner, P., & Silverstein, J. (1988). Seeking an independent evaluation. Part II: What will the assessment involve? *Exceptional Parent, 18*(2), 48–53.

Herman, S. E. (1994). Cash subsidy program: Family satisfaction and need. *Mental Retardation, 32*(6), 416–421.

Herman, S. E., & Marcenko, M. O. (1997). Perceptions of services and resources as mediators of depression among parents of children with developmental disabilities. *Mental Retardation, 35*(6), 458–467.

Herman, S. E., & Thompson, L. (1995). Families' perceptions of their resources for caring for children with developmental disabilities. *Mental Retardation, 33*(2), 73–83.

Hernandez, M., & Isaacs, M. R. (Eds.). (1998). *Promoting cultural competence in children's mental health services.* Baltimore: Brookes.

Hetherington, E. M., & Arasteh, J. D. (Eds.). (1988). *Impact of divorce, single parenting, and stepparenting on children.* Hillsdale, NJ: Lawrence Erlbaum.

Heumann, J. (1997, Spring). Assistant secretary Judith E. Heumann. The parent movement: Reflections and Directions. *Coalition Quarterly, 14*(1).

Heward, W. L., & Chapman, J. E. (1981). Improving parent-teacher communication through recorded telephone messages: Systematic replication in a special education classroom. *Journal of Special Education Technology, 4,* 11–19.

Hill, J., Seyfarth, J., Banks, P., Wehman, P., & Orelove, F. (1985). Parent/guardian attitudes toward the working conditions of their mentally retarded children. *Exceptional Children, 54*(1), 9–24.

Hilton, A., & Henderson, C. J. (1993). Parent involvement: A best practice or forgotten practice? *Education and Training in Mental Retardation, 28*(3), 119–211.

Hirsch, G. P. (1981). *Training developmental disability specialists in parent conference skills.* Unpublished doctoral dissertation, University of Kansas, Lawrence.

Hirsch, G., & Altman, K. (1986). Training graduate students in parent conference skills. *Applied Research in Mental Retardation, 7*(3), 371–385.

Hmong family prevents surgery on son. (1991, January). *Omaha World Herald,* p. 16.

Ho, T. P., & Kwok, W. M. (1991). Child sexual abuse in Hong Kong. *Child Abuse and Neglect, 15,* 597–600.

Hocutt, A., & McKinney, D. (1995). Moving beyond the regular education initiative: National reform in special education. In J. L. Paul, H. Rosselli, & D. Evans (Eds.), *Integrating school restructuring and special education reform* (pp. 43–62). Fort Worth, TX: Harcourt Brace.

Hodapp, R. M., & Krasner, D. V. (1995). Families of children with disabilities: Findings from a national sample of eighth-grade students. *Exceptionality, 5*(2), 71–81.

Hodge, J. P., & Shriner, J. G. (1997). Special education mediation: A workable solution to impasses between parents and school districts. *Beyond Behavior, 8*(2), 20–24.

Holman, L. J. (1997). Working effectively with Hispanic immigrant families. *Phi Delta Kappan, 78*(8), 647–649.

Homes for the Homeless. (1992). Who are homeless families? A profile of homelessness in New York City [Report]. New York: Author.

Hoover-Dempsey, K. V., Bassler, D. C., & Brissie, J. S. (1992). Explorations in parent-school relations. *Journal of Educational Research, 85*(5), 287–294.

Hoover-Dempsey, K. V., & Sandler, H. M. (1995). Parental involvement in children's education: Why does it make a difference? *Teachers College Record, 95,* 310–331.

Hoover-Dempsey, K. V., & Sandler, H. M. (1997). Why do parents become involved in their children's education? *Review of Educational Research, 67*(1), 3–42.

Horner, R. H. (2000). Positive behavior supports. In M. L. Wehmeyer & J. R. Patton (Eds.), *Mental retardation in the 21st century* (pp. 181–196). Austin, TX: Pro-ed.

Horner, R. H., Albin, R. W., Sprague, J. R., & Todd, A. W. (2000). Positive behavior support. In M. E. Snell & F. Brown (Eds.), *Instruction of students with severe disabilities.* (5th ed., pp. 207–244). Upper Saddle River, NJ: Merrill Publishing.

Horner, R. H., & Carr, E. G. (1997). Behavioral support for students with severe disabilities: Functional assessment and comprehensive intervention. *The Journal of Special Education, 31*(1), 84–104.

Horner, R. H., Diemer, S., & Brazeau, K. (1992). Educational support for students with severe problem behaviors in Oregon: A descriptive analysis from the 1987–1988 school year. *Journal of the Association for Persons with Severe Handicaps, 17*(3), 154–169.

Horner, R. H., Dunlap, G., & Koegel, R. L. (1988). *Generalization and maintenance: Lifestyle changes in applied settings.* Baltimore: Brookes.

Horner, R. H., Dunlap, G., Koegel, R. L., Carr, E. G., Sailor, W., Anderson, J., Albin, R. W., & O'Neill, R. E. (1990). Toward a technology of "nonaversive" behavioral support. *Journal of the Association for Persons with Severe Handicaps, 15*(5), 125–132.

Hornstein, B. (1997 December). How the religious community can support the transition to adulthood: A parent's perspective. *Mental Retardation, 36*(6), 485–487.

Houle, G. (1996). Violence and the changing universe of disabilities. *Early Childhood Education Journal, 23*(4), 197–200.

Hudson, P., & Glomb, N. (1997). If it takes two to tango, then why not teach both partners to dance? Collaboration instruction for all educators. *Journal of Learning Disabilities, 30*(4), 442–448.

Hughes, C., Kim, J., Hwang, B., Killian, D. J., Fischer, G. M., Brock, M. L., Godshall, J. C., & Houser, B. (1997). Practitioner-validated secondary transition support strategies. *Education and Training in Mental Retardation and Developmental Disabilities, 32,* 201–212.

Hughes, R. S. (1999). An investigation of coping skills of parents of children with disabilities: Implications for service providers. *Education and Training in Mental Retardation and Developmental Disabilities, 34*(3), 271–280.

Human Resources Report Number 105–177, 105th Cong. 2d Sess. (1997).

Human Services Research Institute. (1995, May). *Supplemental security income for children with disabilities: An exploration of child and family needs and the relative merits of the cash benefit-program.* Salem, OR: Author.

Humphrey, K. R. (1999). *Research Comprehensive Paper.* Lawrence: University of Kansas.

Hunt, J. (Ed.). (1972). *Human intelligence.* New Brunswick, NJ: Transaction Books.

Hyun, J. K., & Fowler, S. A. (1995). Respect, cultural sensitivity, and communication. *Teaching Exceptional Children, 28*(1), 25–31.

Indian Nations at Risk & National Advisory Council on Indian Education. (1990, October). *Joint issues sessions proceedings summary: Education of exceptional children.* National Indian Education Association 22nd Annual Conference, San Diego, CA. (ERIC Document Reproduction Service No. ED 341 529).

Individuals with Disabilities Education Act (IDEA). 20 U.S.C. Secs. 1400 et. seq.

Irving Independent School District v. Tatro, 468 U.S. 883, 104 S. Ct. 3371, 82 L. Ed. 2d 664 (1984).

Isbell, H. (1983). He looked the way a baby should look. In T. Dougan, L. Isbell, & P. Vyas (Eds.), *We have been there: Families share the joys and struggles of living with mental retardation* (pp. 19–23). Nashville, TN: Abingdon.

Ivey, A. E. (1994). *Intentional interviewing and counseling.* (3rd ed.). Pacific Grove, CA: Brooks/Cole.

Ivey, A. E., Ivey, M. B., & Simek-Morgan, L. (1993). *Counseling and psychotherapy: A multicultural perspective.* (3rd ed.). Boston: Allyn & Bacon.

Jackson, S. C., & Roberts, J. E. (1999). Family and professional congruence in communication assessments of preschool boys with Fragile X syndrome. *Journal of Early Intervention, 22*(2), 137–151.

Jalali, B. (1996). Iranian families. In M. McGoldrick, J. Giordano, & J. K. Pearce (Eds.), *Ethnicity and family therapy* (pp. 347–363). New York: The Guilford Press.

Jameson, C. (1998). Promoting long-term relationships between individuals with mental retardation and people in their community: An agency self-evaluation. *Mental Retardation, 36*(2), 116–127.

Jamieson, J. R. (1995). Interactions between mothers and children who are deaf. *Journal of Early Intervention, 19*(2), 108–117.

Jayanthi, M., Sawyer, V., Nelson, J. S., Bursuck, W. D., & Epstein, M. H. (1995). Recommendations for homework-communication problems. *Remedial and Special Education, 16*(4), 212–225.

Jenkins, J. R., Pious, C. G., & Peterson, D. L. (1988). Categorical programs for remedial and handicapped students: Issues of validity. *Exceptional Children, 55,* 147–158.

Joe, J. R. (1997). American Indian children with disabilities: The impact of culture on health and education services. *Families, Systems, and Health, 15*(3), 251–261.

Joe, J. R., & Malach, R. S. (1992). Families with Native American roots. In E. W. Lynch & M. J. Hanson (Eds.), *Developing cross-cultural competence: A guide for working with young children and their families* (pp. 89–120). Baltimore: Brookes.

Johnson, S. D., Proctor, W. A., & Corey, S. E. (1995). A new partner in the IEP process: The laptop computer. *Teaching Exceptional Children, 28*(1), 46–56.

Jones, D. E., Clatterbuck, C. C., Barber, P., Marquis, J., & Turnbull, H. R. (1995). *Educational placements for children who are ventilator assisted.* Lawrence: University of Kansas, Beach Center on Families and Disability.

Jones, D. E., Clatterbuck, C. C., Marquis, J., Turnbull, H. R., & Moberly, R. L. (in press). Educational placements for children who are ventilator assisted. *Exceptional Children.*

Jones, T. M., Garlow, J. A., Turnbull, H. R., & Barber, P. A. (1996). Family empowerment in a family support program. In G. H. S. Singers, L. E. Powers, & A. L. Olson (Eds.), *Redefining family support innovations: Innovations in public-private partnerships* (pp. 87–114). Baltimore: Brookes.

Jordan, L., Reyes-Blanes, M. E., Peel, B. B., Peel, H. A., & Lane, H. B. (1998). Developing teacher-parent partnerships across cultures: Effective parent conferences. *Intervention in School and Clinic, 33*(3), 141–147.

Joselevich, E. (1988). Family transitions, cumulative stress, and crises. In C. J. Falicov (Ed.), *Family Transitions* (pp. 273–292). New York: The Guilford Press.

Kagan, S. L., & Neville, P. R. (1993a). Family support and school-linked services. *Family Resource Coalition Report, 12*(3 & 4), 4–6.

Kagan, S. L., & Neville, P. R. (1993b). *Integrating services for children and families: Understanding the past to shape the future.* New Haven, CT: Yale University Press.

Kairys, S. (1996). Family support in cases of child abuse and neglect. In G. H. S. Singer, L. E. Powers, & A. L. Olson (Eds.), *Redefining family support* (pp. 171–188). Baltimore: Brookes.

Kalyanpur, M. (1998). The challenges of cultural blindness: Implications for family-focused service delivery. *Journal of Child and Family Studies, 7*(3), 317–332.

Kalyanpur, M. (1999). Special education epistemology as a product of western culture: Implications for non-western families of children with disabilities. *International Journal of Rehabilitation Research, 22*(2), 1–7.

Kalyanpur, M., & Harry, B. (1999). *Culture in special education.* Baltimore: Paul H. Brookes Co.

Kalyanpur, M., Harry, B., & Skrtic, T. (in press). Equity and advocacy expectations of culturally diverse families' participation in special education. *International Journal of Disability, Development and Education, 47*(1).

Kalyanpur, M., & Rao, S. S. (1991). Empowering low-income black families of handicapped children. *American Journal of Orthopsychiatry, 61*(4), 523–532.

Kanner, L. (1949). Problems of nosology and psychodynamica of early infantile autism. *American Journal of Orthopsychiatry, 19,* 416–426.

Kaplan, L., & Girard, J. L. (1994). *Strengthening high-risk families.* New York: Lexington Books.

Kaplan-Sanoff, M. (1996). The impact of maternal substance abuse on young children: Myths and realities. In E. J. Erwin (Ed.), *Putting children first* (pp. 79–103). Baltimore: Brookes.

Karnes, M. B., & Teska, J. A. (1980). Toward successful parent involvement in programs for handicapped children. In J. J. Gallagher (Ed.), *New directions for exceptional children: Parents and families of handicapped children* (Vol. 4, pp. 85–109). San Francisco: Jossey-Bass.

Karp, N. (1996). Individualized wrap-around services for children with emotional, behavior, and mental disorders. In G. H. S. Singer, L. E. Powers, & A. L. Olson (Eds.), *Redefining family support* (pp. 291–312). Baltimore: Brookes.

Kastner, T. A., Nathanson, R., & Marchetti, A. (1992). Epidemiology of HIV infection in adults with developmental disabilities. In A. C. Crocker, H. J. Cohen, & T. A. Kastner (Eds.), *HIV infection and developmental disabilities: A resource for service providers* (pp. 127–132). Baltimore: Brookes.

Katsiyannis, A., Conderman, G., & Franks, D. J. (1995). State practices on inclusion: A national review. *Remedial and Special Education, 16*(5), 279–287.

Katz, A. H. (1993). *Self-help in America: A social movement perspective*. New York: Twyane Publishers.

Katz, L., & Scarpati, S. (1995). A cultural interpretation of early intervention teams and the IFSP: Parent and professional perceptions of roles and responsibilities. *Infant-Toddler Intervention, 5*(2), 177–192.

Katz, R. (1984). Empowerment and synergy: Expanding the community's healing resources. *Prevention in Human Services, 3*(2 & 3), 201–226.

Katzen, K. (1980). To the editor: An open letter to CEC. *Exceptional Children, 46*(8), 582.

Kauffman, J. M., Gerber, M. M., & Semmel, M. I. (1988). Arguable assumptions underlying the Regular Education Initiative. *Journal of Learning Disabilities, 21*, 6–11.

Kay, P. J., Fitzgerald, M., Paradee, C., & Mellencamp, A. (1994). Making homework work at home: The parent's perspective. *Journal of Learning Disabilities, 27*(9), 550–561.

Kaye, H. S. (1997). *Education of children with disabilities* (Disability Statistics Abstract 19). Washington, DC: U.S. Department of Education.

Kazak, A. E., & Marvin, R. S. (1984). Differences, difficulties and adaptation: Stress and social networks in families with a handicapped child. *Family Relations, 33*, 67–77.

Keenan, J. W., Willett, J., & Solsken, J. (1993). Focus on research. Constructing an urban village: School/home collaboration in a multicultural classroom. *Language Arts, 70*, 204–214.

Keum Cox, S. S. (1996). The birth of intercountry adoptions. *Focal Point, 10*(1), 22–23.

Kieffer, C. H. (1984). Citizen empowerment: A developmental perspective. *Prevention in Human Services, 3*(2 & 3), 9–36.

Kiernan, W. E. (2000). Where we are now: Perspectives on employment of persons with mental retardation. In M. L. Wehmeyer & J. R. Patton (Eds.), *Mental retardation in the 21st century* (pp. 151–164). Austin, TX: Pro-ed.

Kim, U., & Choi, S. H. (1994). Individualism, collectivism, and child development: A Korean perspective. In P. M. Greenfield & R. R. Cocking (Eds.), *Cross-cultural roots of minority child development* (pp. 226–257). Hillsdale, NJ: Erlbaum.

King, J. (1996). Program and IEP: Meeting students' needs. *Perspectives, 15*(2), 6–7.

Kingsley, J., & Levitz, M. (1994). *Count us in: Growing up with Down Syndrome*. New York: Harcourt Brace Publishers.

Kinloch, D. (1986). *An investigation of the impact of a preparation strategy on teachers' perceptions of parent participation in the IEP review conferences of learning disabled and educable mentally retarded students*. Unpublished doctoral dissertation, University of Missouri, Columbia.

Kirk, S. A. (1984). Introspection and prophecy. In B. Blatt & R. J. Morris (Eds.), *Perspectives in special education: Personal orientations* (pp. 25–55). Glenview, IL: Scott, Foresman.

Kit-shan-Lee, Y., & So-kum-Tang, C. (1998). Evaluation of a sexual abuse prevention program for female Chinese adolescents with mild mental retardation. *American Journal on Mental Retardation, 103*(2), 105–116.

Klass, C. S. (1997). The home visitor-parent relationship: The linchpin of home visiting. *Bulletin of Zero to Three: National Center for Infants, Toddlers, and Families, 17*(4), 1–9.

Kleinhammer-Tramill, J., & Gallagher, K. (in press). The implications of goals 2000 for inclusive education. In W. Sailor (Ed.), *Inclusive education and school/community partnerships*. New York: Teachers College Press.

Knackendoffel, E. A., Robinson, S. M., Deshler, D. D., & Schumaker, J. B. (1992). *Collaborative problem solving: A step-by-step guide to creating educational solutions*. Lawrence, KS: Edge Enterprises.

Knitzer, J., & Cauthen, N. K. (1999). *Enhancing the well-being of young children and families in the context of welfare reform*. New York: National Center for Children in Poverty, The Joseph L. Mailman School of Public Health, Columbia University.

Knoll, J. (1992). Being a family: The experience of raising a child with a disability or chronic illness. In V. J. Bradley, J. Knoll, & J. M. Agosta (Eds.), *Emerging issues in family support* (pp. 9–56). Monographs of the American Association on Mental Retardation, 18.

Knoll, J., Covert, S., Osuch, R., O'Connor, S., Agosta, J., Blaney, B., & Bradley, V. (1990). *Family support services in the United States: An end of decade status report [Summary report]*. Cambridge, MA: Human Services Research Institute.

Koblinsky, S. A., & Todd, C. M. (1991, Spring). Teaching self-care skills. *Teaching Exceptional Children*, 40–44.

Kocinski, J. M. (1998). Foster care. *State Government News, 41*(4), 16–19.

Koegel, L. K., Koegel, R. L., & Dunlap, G. (Eds.). (1996). *Community, school, and social inclusion through positive behavioral support*. Baltimore: Brookes.

Koenig, A. J., & Holbrook, M. C. (1993). *Learning media assessment of students with visual impairments: A resource guide for teachers*. Austin, TX: Texas School for the Blind and Visually Impaired.

Kohl, M. A., Parrish, J. M., Neef, N. A., Driessen, J. R., & Hallinan, P. C. (1988). Communication skills training for parents: Experimental and social validation. *Journal of Applied Behavior Analysis, 21*(1), 21–30.

Kolstoe, O. P. (1970). *Teaching educable mentally retarded children*. New York: Holt, Rinehart, & Winston.

Koppelman, J. (1995). *SSI for children: Looking at enrollment concerns and program intent and chronic illness*. Washington, DC: George Washington University.

Koren, P. E., DeChillo, N., & Friesen, B. (1992). Measuring empowerment in families whose children have emotional disabilities: A brief questionnaire. *Rehabilitation Psychology, 37*, 305–321.

Koren, P. E., Paulson, R. I., Kinney, R. F., Yatchemenoff, D. K., Gordon, L. J., & DeChillo, N. (1997). Service coordination in children's mental health: An empirical study from the caregiver's perspective. *Journal of Emotional and Behavioral Disorders, 5*(3), 162–172.

Koroloff, N. M. (1990). Moving out: Transition policies for youth with serious emotional disabilities. *Journal of Mental Health Administration, 17*(1), 78–86.

Koroloff, N. M., & Friesen, B. J. (1991). Support groups for parents of children with emotional disorders: A comparison of members and non-members. *Community Mental Health Journal, 27*(4), 265–279.

Kortering, L. J., & Braziel, P. M. (1999). School dropout from the perspective of former students. *Remedial and Special Education, 20*(2), 78–83.

Koyanagi, C., & Gaines, S. (1993a). *All systems failure: An examination of the results of neglecting the needs of children with serious emotional disturbance.* Alexandria, VA: National Mental Health Association.

Koyanagi, C., & Gaines, S. (1993b). *A guide for advocates for "all systems failure": An examination of the results of neglecting the needs of children with serious emotional disturbance.* Alexandria, VA: Federation of Families for Children's Mental Health.

Kozol, J. (1988). *Rachel and her children: Homeless families in America.* New York: Fawcett Columbine.

Kozol, J. (1995). *Amazing grace.* New York: Crown Publishers.

Krauss, M. W. (1993). Child-related and parenting stress: Similarities and differences between mothers and fathers of children with disabilities. *American Journal on Mental Retardation, 97,* 393–404.

Krauss, M. W., Mailick-Seltzer, M., Gordon, R., & Haig-Friedman, H. (1996, April). Binding ties: The roles of adult siblings of persons with mental retardation. *Journal on Mental Retardation, 34*(2), 83–93.

Krauss, M. W., Upshur, C. C., Shonkoff, J. P., & Hauser-Cram, P. (1993). The impact of parent groups on mothers of infants with disabilities. *Journal of Early Intervention, 17*(1), 8–20.

Kreutzer, J. S., Serio, C. D., & Bergquist, S. (1994). Family needs after brain injury: A quantitative analysis. *Journal of Head Trauma Rehabilitation, 9*(3), 104–115.

Kroeger, S. D., Leibold, C. K., & Ryan, B. (1999, Sept./Oct.). Creating a sense of ownership in the IEP process. *Teaching Exceptional Children,* 4–9.

Kroth, R. L. (1985). *Communicating with parents of exceptional children: Improving parent-teacher relationships* (2nd ed.). Denver, CO: Love.

Kroth, R. L., & Edge, D. (1997). *Strategies for communicating with parents and families of exceptional children.* (3rd ed.). Denver, CO: Love.

Kubler-Ross, E. (1969). *On death and dying.* New York: Macmillan.

Lake, R. (1990). An Indian father's plea. *Teacher Magazine, 2,* 48–53.

Lakin, K. C., Anderson, L., & Prouty, R. (1999). Medicaid HCBS "waiver" recipients are now twice the number of Medicaid ICF/MR residents. In K. C. Lakin, D. Braddock, & G. Smith (Eds.), *Mental Retardation* (pp. 341–343). Washington, DC: American Association on Mental Retardation.

Lakin, K. C., Prouty, R., Smith, G., & Braddock, D. (1995). Places of residence of Medicaid HCBS recipients. *Mental Retardation, 33,* 406.

Lamb, M. (1983). Fathers of exceptional children. In M. Seligman (Ed.), *The family with a handicapped child* (pp. 125–146). New York: Grune & Stratton.

Lambie, R. (2000). *Family systems within educational contexts* (2nd ed.). Denver, CO: Love.

Lane, H., Hoffmeister, R., & Bahan, B. (1996). *A journey into the deaf world.* San Diego, CA: Dawn Sign Press.

Langdon, C. A. (1997). The fourth Phi Delta Kappan poll of teachers' attitudes toward the public schools. *Phi Delta Kappan, 79*(3), 78–83.

LaPlante, M. P., Carlson, D., Kaye, H. S., & Bradsher, J. E. (1996). *Families with disabilities in the United States* (Disability Statistics Report 8). Washington, DC: U.S. Department of Education, National Institute on Disability and Rehabilitation Research.

Larner, M., & Collins, A. (1996). Poverty in the lives of young children. In E. J. Erwin (Ed.), *Putting children first* (pp. 55–75). Baltimore: Paul H. Brookes.

Larner, M. B., Stevenson, C. S., & Behrman, R. E. (1998). Protecting children from abuse and neglect. *The Future of Children, 8*(1), 4–22.

Larson, E. (1998). Reframing the meaning of disability to families: The embrace of paradox. *Social Science Medical Journal, 47*(7), 865–875.

Lavine, J. (1986). De-mystifying professional evaluations. *Academic Therapy, 21*(5), 615–617.

Lawson, H., & Briar-Lawson, K. (1997). *Connecting the dots: Progress toward the integration of school reform, school-linked services, parent involvement and community schools. Unpublished manuscript,* The Danforth Foundation and the Institute for Educational Renewal, Miami University, Oxford, OH.

Lee, G. R. (1982). *Family structure and interaction: A comparative analysis.* Minneapolis: University of Minnesota Press.

Lee, I. M. (1994, June). *Collaboration: What do families and physicians want?* Paper presented at the international conference on the Family on the Threshold of the 21st Century Jerusalem: Trends and Implications.

Lee, Y. K., & Tang, C. S. (1998). Evaluation of a sexual abuse prevention program for female Chinese adolescents with mild mental retardation. *American Journal on Mental Retardation, 103*(4), 105–116.

Leff, P. T., & Walizer, E. H. (1992). *Building the healing partnership: Parents, professionals, and children with chronic illnesses and disabilities.* Cambridge, MA: Brookline Books.

Lehman, C. M., & Irvin, L. K. (1996). Support for families with children who have emotional or behavioral disorders. *Education and Treatment of Children, 19*(3), 335–353.

Lehmann, J. P., & Roberto, K. A. (1996). Comparison of factors influencing mothers' perceptions about the futures of their adolescent children with and without disabilities. *Mental Retardation, 34*(1), 27–38.

Levine, J. A., Murphy, D. T., & Wilson, S. (1993). *Getting men involved: Strategies for early childhood programs.* New York: New York Scholastic.

Levine, J. A., & Pitt, E. W. (1995). *New expectations: Community strategies for responsible fatherhood.* New York: Families and Work Institute.

Levine, M., & Perkins, D. V. (1987). *Principles of community psychology.* Oxford: Oxford University Press.

Levine, P., & Nourse, S. W. (1998). What follow-up studies say about postschool life for young men and women with learning disabilities: A critical look at the literature. *Journal of Learning Disabilities, 31*(3), 212–233.

Lewis, C. L., Busch, J. P., Proger, B. B., & Juska, P. J. (1981). Parents' perspectives concerning the IEP process. *Education Unlimited, 3*(3), 18–22.

Lewis, T. J., & Sugai, G. (1999). Effective behavior support: A systems approach to proactive school-wide management. *Focus on Exceptional Children, 31*(6), 1–24.

Lewis, T. J., Sugai, G., & Colvin, G. (1998). Reducing problem behavior through a school-wide system of effective behavioral support: Investigation of a school-wide social skills training program and contextual interventions. *School Psychology Review, 27*, 446–459.

Lewis-Palmer, T., Sugai, G., & Larson, S. (1999). Using data to guide decisions about program implementation and effectiveness. *Effective School Practices, 17*(4), 47–53.

Li, J., & Bennett, N. (1998). *Young children in poverty* (A Statistical Update). New York: National Center for Children in Poverty.

Lichtenstein, J. (1993). Help for troubled marriages. In G. H. S. Singer & L. E. Powers (Eds.), *Families, disability,*

and empowerment (pp. 259–283). Baltimore: Brookes.

Liebman, R. (1975). *Constructing a workable reality* [Videotape]. Philadelphia: Philadelphia Child Guidance Clinic.

Lightburn, A., & Pine, B. A. (1996). Supporting and enhancing the adoption of children with developmental disabilities. *Children and Youth Services Review, 18*(1–2), 139–162.

Lin, M. C. (1999). *Child maltreatment.* Unpublished manuscript, University of Kansas.

Linder, T. W. (1993). *Transdisciplinary play-based assessment: A functional approach to working with young children.* Baltimore: Brookes.

Lindle, J. C. (1989, October). What do parents want from principals? *Educational Leadership,* 12–14.

Lipton, D. (1994). The "full inclusion" court cases: 1989–1994. *National Center on Educational Restructuring and Inclusion Bulletin, 1*(2), 1–8.

Little Soldier, L. (1997, April). Is there an 'Indian' in your classroom? *Phi Delta Kappan,* 650–653.

Lobato, D., Barbour, L., Hall, L. J., & Miller, C. T. (1987). Psychosocial characteristics of preschool siblings of handicapped and nonhandicapped children. *Journal of Abnormal Child Psychology, 15,* 329–338.

Logan, S. L. (Ed.). (1996). *The black family.* Boulder, CO: Westview Press.

Lombana, J. H. (1983). *Home-school partnerships: Guidelines and strategies for educators.* New York: Grune & Stratton.

Lonsdale, G. (1978). Family life with a handicapped child: The parents speak. *Child Care, Health, and Development, 4,* 99–120.

Lopez, S. J. (1999). *Contemporary issues in psychological assessment.* Paper presented at the 107th Annual Convention of the American Psychological Association, Boston.

Lortie, D. C. (1975). *Schoolteacher: A sociological study.* Chicago: University of Chicago Press.

Loucks, H. (1992). Increased parent/family involvement: Ten ideas that work. *National Association of Sec-*

ondary School Principals Bulletin, 76, 19–23.

Louis, B., & Lewis, M. (1992). Parental beliefs about giftedness in young children and their relation to actual ability. *Gifted Child Quarterly, 36,* 27–31.

Lovitt, T. C., & Cushing, S. (1999). Parents of youth with disabilities. *Remedial and Special Education, 20*(3), 124–142.

Lovitt, T. C., Plavins, M., & Cushing, S. (1999). What do pupils with disabilities have to say about their experience in high school? *Remedial and Special Education, 20*(2), 67–76, 83.

Lucito, L. J. (1963). Gifted children. In L. M. Dunn (Ed.), *Exceptional children in the schools* (pp. 179–238). New York: Holt, Rinehart, & Winston.

Lucyshyn, Dunlap, and Albin (in press) (Eds.), *Families and positive behavioral support: Addressing the challenges of problem behaviors in family contexts.* Baltimore: Brookes.

Luetke-Stahlman, B. (1992, May–June). Yes, siblings can help. *Perspectives in Education and Deafness, 10*(5), 9–11.

Luetke-Stahlman, B., Luetke-Stahlman, B., & Luetke-Stahlman, H. (1992). Yes, siblings can help. *Perspectives, 10*(5), 9–11.

Lustig, D. C., & Akey, T. (1999). Adaptation in families with adult children with mental retardation: Impact of family strengths and appraisal. *Education and Training in Mental Retardation and Developmental Disabilities, 34*(3), 260–270.

Lutzker, J. R. (1984). Project 12-ways: Treating child abuse and neglect from an ecobehavioral perspective. In R. F. Dangel & R. A. Polster (Eds.), *Parent training: Foundations of research and practice* (pp. 260–297). New York: Guilford.

Lutzker, J. R., Campbell, R. V., Newman, M. R., & Harrold, M. (1989). Ecobehavioral interventions for abusive, neglectful, and high-risk families. In G. H. S. Singer & L. K. Irvin (Eds.), *Support for caregiving families* (pp. 313–326). Baltimore: Brookes.

Lutzker, J. R., & Newman, M. R. (1986). Child abuse and neglect:

Community problem, community solutions. *Education and Treatment of Children, 9,* 344–354.

Lynch, E. W. (1998). Developing cross-cultural competence. In E. W. Lynch & M. J. Hanson (Eds.), *Developing cross-cultural competence* (2nd ed., pp. 47–86). Baltimore: Brookes.

Lynch, E. W., & Hanson, M. J. (1998). *Developing cross-cultural competence: A guide for working with children and their families* (2nd ed.). Baltimore: Brookes.

Lynch, E. W., & Stein, R. (1982). Perspectives on parent participation in special education. *Exceptional Children, 3*(2), 56–63.

Lynn, L. (1994). Building parent involvement. *National Association of Secondary School Principals Practitioner, 20*(5), 1–4.

Lyytinen, P., Rasku-Puttonen, H., Poikkeus, A. M., Laakso, M. L., & Ahonen, T. (1994). Mother-child teaching strategies and learning disabilities. *Journal of Learning Disabilities, 27*(3), 186–192.

MacDonald, W. S., & Oden, C. W., Jr. (1978). *Moose: A very special person.* Minneapolis, MN: Winston Press.

MacKenzie, D., & Rogers, V. (1997). The full service school: A management and organizational structure for 21st century schools. *Community Education Journal, 25*(3–4), 9–11.

MacMurphy, H. (1916). The relation of feeblemindedness to other social problems. *Journal of Psycho-Asthenics, 21,* 58–63.

Maddux, C. D., & Cummings, R. E. (1983). Parental home tutoring: Aids and cautions. *Exceptional Parent, 13*(4), 30–33.

Magana, S. M. (1999). Puerto Rican families caring for an adult with mental retardation: The role of familism. *American Journal on Mental Retardation, 104*(5), 466–482.

Mailick-Seltzer, M., Greenberg, J. S., Wyngaarden-Krauss, M., Gordon, R. M., & Judge, K. (1997). Siblings of adults with mental retardation or mental illness: Effects on lifestyle and psychological well-being. *Family Relations, 46*(4), 395–405.

Mailick-Seltzer, M., Greenberg, J. S., Wyngaarden-Krauss, M., & Hong, J. (1997). Predictors and outcomes of the end of co-resident caregiving in aging families of adults with mental retardation or mental illness. *Family Relations, 46*(1), 13–22.

Mailick-Seltzer, M., Wyngaarden-Krauss, M., & Janicki, M. P. (Eds.). (1994). *Life course perspectives on adulthood and old age.* Washington, DC: American Association on Mental Retardation.

Malekoff, A., Johnson, H., & Klappersack, B. (1991, September). Parent-professional collaboration on behalf of children with learning disabilities. *Families in Society,* 416–424.

Malette, P., Mirenda, P., Kundborg, T., Jones, P., Bunz, P., & Rogow, S. (1992). Applications of a lifestyle development process for persons with severe intellectual disabilities: A case study report. *Journal of the Association for Persons with Severe Handicaps, 17,* 179–191.

Mallow, G. E., & Bechtel, G. A. (1999). Chronic sorrow: The experience of parents with children who are developmentally disabled. *Journal of Psychosocial Nursing, 37*(7), 31–35.

Man, D. (1999). Community-based empowerment programme for families with a brain injured survivor: An outcome study. *Brain Injury, 13*(6), 433–445.

Man, D. W. K. (1998). The empowering of Hong Kong Chinese families with a brain damaged member: Its investigation and measurement. *Brain Injury, 12*(3), 245–254.

Marcenko, M. O., & Smith, L. K. (1991). Post-adoption needs of families adopting children with developmental disabilities. *Children and Youth Services Review, 13,* 413–424.

Marcus, L. M. (1977). Patterns of coping in families of psychotic children. *American Journal of Orthopsychiatry, 47*(3), 388–399.

Margalit, M., & Efrati, M. (1996). Loneliness, coherence and companionship among children with learning disorders. *Educational Psychology, 16*(1), 69–79.

Marion, R. (1979). Minority parent involvement in the IEP process: A systematic model approach. *Focus on Exceptional Children, 10*(8), 1–16.

Marshall, C. A., & Largo, H. R., Jr. (1999). Disability and rehabilitation: A context for understanding the American Indian experience. *Lancet, 354,* 758–760.

Martin, A. (1993). *The lesbian and gay parenting handbook.* New York: HarperCollins.

Martin, S. (1994). *Take a Look: Observation and portfolio assessment in early childhood.* Don Mills, Ontario: Addison-Wesley.

Martin, S. S., Brady, M. P., & Kotarba, J. A. (1992). Families with chronically ill young children: The unsinkable family. *Remedial and Special Education, 13*(2), 6–15.

Marvin, R. S., & Pianta, R. C. (1992). A relationship-based approach to self-reliance in young children with motor impairments. *Infants and Young Children, 4*(4), 33–45.

Masino, L. L., & Hodapp, R. M. (1996). Parental educational expectations for adolescents with disabilities. *Exceptional Children, 62*(6), 515–523.

Mason, C. Y., & Jaskulski, T. (1994). HIV/AIDS prevention and education. In M. Agran, N. E. Marchand-Martella, & R. C. Martella (Eds.), *Promoting health and safety: Skills for independent living* (pp. 161–192). Baltimore: Brookes.

Maton, K. L., & Salem, D. A. (1995). Organizational characteristics of empowering community settings: A multiple case approach. *American Journal of Community Psychology, 23*(5), 631–656.

Maxwell, E. (1998). "I can do it myself!" Reflections on early self-efficacy. *Roeper Review, 20*(3), 183–187.

May, D. C., & Kundert, D. K. (1996). Are special educators prepared to meet the sex education needs of their students? A progress report. *The Jour-*

nal of Special Education, 29(4), 433–441.

Maynard, R. (Ed.). (1996). *Kids having kids: A Robin Hood Foundation special report on the costs of adolescent child bearing.* New York: Robin Hood Foundation.

McArnarney, E. R., & Hendee, W. R. (1989). Adolescent pregnancy and its consequences. *Journal of the American Medical Association, 262,* 74–77.

McBride, S. L., Brotherson, M. J., Joanning, H., Whiddon, D., & Demmit, A. (1993). Implementation of family-centered services: Perceptions of families and professionals. *Journal of Early Intervention, 17,* 414–430.

McCabe, M. (1993). Sex education programs for people with mental retardation. *Mental Retardation, 31,* 377–387.

McCarthy, M., & Thompson, D. (1996). Sexual abuse by design: An examination of the issues in learning disability services. *Disability and Society, 11*(2), 205–217.

McClun, L. A., & Merrell, K. W. (1998). Relationship of perceived parenting styles, locus of control orientation, and self-concept among junior high age students. *Psychology in the Schools, 35*(4), 381–389.

McConnell, S. R., McEvoy, M. A., & Odom, S. L. (1992). Implementation of social competence interventions in early childhood special education classes: Current practices and future directions. In S. L. Odom, S. R. McConnell, & M. A. McEvoy (Eds.), *Social competence of young children with disabilities: Nature, development, and intervention* (pp. 277–306). Baltimore: Brookes.

McCroskey, J., & Meezan, W. (1998). Family-centered services: Approaches and effectiveness. *The Future of Children, 8*(1), 54–71.

McDonald, L., Kysela, G., Martin, C., & Wheaton, S. (1996). The Hazeldean project. *Teaching Exceptional Children, 28–32.*

McDonnell, L. M., McLaughlin, M. J., & Morison, P. (Eds.). (1997). *Educating one and all: Students with disabilities and standards-based reform.* Washington, DC: National Academy Press.

McGill, D. W., & Pearce, J. K. (1982). British families. In M. McGoldrick, J. K. Pearce, & J. Giordano (Eds.), *Ethnicity in family therapy* (pp. 457–482). New York: Guilford.

McGill, D. W., & Pearce, J. K. (1996). American families with English ancestors from the colonial era: Anglo Americans. In M. McGoldrick & J. Giordano (Eds.), *Ethnicity and family therapy* (2nd ed., pp. 451–466). New York: The Guilford Press.

McGinley, K. H. (1987). *Evaluating the effectiveness of mediation as an alternative to the sole use of the due process hearing in special education.* Unpublished doctoral dissertation, University of Kansas, Lawrence.

McGoldrick, M., Giordano, J., & Pearce, J. K. (Eds.). (1996). *Ethnicity and family therapy* (2nd ed.). New York: The Guilford Press.

McGonigel, M. J., Kaufmann, R. K., & Johnson, R. H. (Eds.). (1991). *Guidelines and recommended practices for the Individualized Family Service Plan* (2nd ed.). Bethesda, MD: Association for the Care of Children's Health.

McGonigel, M. J., Woodruff, G., & Roszmann-Millican, M. (1994). The transdisciplinary team: A model for family-centered early intervention. In L. Johnson, R. Gallagher, M. LaMontagne, J. Jordon, J. Gallagher, P. Huntinger, & M. Karnes (Eds.), *Meeting early intervention challenges, issues from birth to three* (2nd ed., pp. 95–131). Baltimore: Brookes.

McGregor, G., & Vogelsberg, T. (1999). *Inclusive schooling practices: Pedagogical and research foundations.* Baltimore: Brookes.

McGrew, K. (1992). A review of scales to assess family needs. *Journal of Psychoeducational Assessment, 10,* 4–25.

McHale, S. M., & Gamble, W. C. (1989). Sibling relationships of children with disabled and nondisabled brothers and sisters. *Developmental Psychology, 25*(3), 421–429.

McLaughlin, M. (1996). School restructuring. *In National Council on Disability, Improving the implementation of the Individuals with Disabilities Education Act: Making schools work for all of America's children. Supplement* (pp. 635–660). Washington, DC: National Council on Disability.

McLaughlin, M. J., Leone, P., Warren, S. H., & Schofield, P. F. (1994). *Doing things differently: Issues and options for creating comprehensive school-linked services for children and youth with emotional or behavioral disorders.* College Park, MD: University of Maryland and Westat.

McLaughlin, M. L. (1998). *Special education in an era of school reform: An overview.* Washington, DC: Federal Resource Center, Academy for Educational Development.

McNair, J., & Swartz, S. L. (1995). Local church support to individuals with developmental disabilities. *Education and Training in Mental Retardation and Developmental Disabilities, 304*–312.

McRoy, R. G., & Grotevant, H. D. (1996). Emotional disorders in adopted children and youth. *Focal Point, 10*(1), 9–12.

McRoy, R. G., Grotevant, H. D., & Zurcher, L. A. (1988). *Emotional disturbance in adopted adolescents: Origins and development.* New York: Praeger.

McWilliam, R. A., Lang, L., Vandiviere, P., Angell, R., Collins, L., & Underdown, G. (1995). Satisfaction and struggles: Family perceptions of early intervention services. *Journal of Early Intervention, 19*(1), 43–60.

Mehan, H. (1993). Beneath the skin and between the ears: A case study in the politics of representation. In S. Chaiklin & J. Lave (Eds.), *Understanding perspectives on activity and context* (pp. 241–268). Cambridge, MA: Cambridge University Press.

Melaville, A. I., & Blank, M. J. (with Asayesh, G.). (1993). *Together we* can: A guide for crafting a profamily system of education and human services. Washington, DC: U.S. Government Printing Office.

Melberg-Schwier, K., & Hingsburger, D. (in press). Sexuality. Baltimore: Brookes.

Mellman, M., Lazarus, E., & Rivlin, A. (1990). Family time, family values. In D. Blankenhorn, S. Bayme, & J. B. Elshtain (Eds.), Rebuilding the nest: A new commitment to the American family (pp. 73–92). Milwaukee, WI: Family Service America.

Menchetti, B. M., & Bombay, H. E. (1994). Facilitating community inclusion with vocational assessment portfolios. Assessment in Rehabilitation and Exceptionality, 1(3), 213–222.

Meyer, D. (Ed.). (1997). Views from our shoes. Bethesda, MD: Woodbine House.

Meyer, D. J. (Ed.). (1995). Uncommon fathers. Bethesda, MD: Woodbine House.

Meyer, D. J., & Vadasy, P. F. (1986). Grandparent workshops: How to organize workshops for grandparents of children with handicaps. Seattle: University of Washington Press.

Meyer, D. J., & Vadasy, P. F. (1994). Sibshops: Workshops for siblings of children with special needs. Baltimore: Brookes.

Meyer, L. H., Park, H. S., Grenot-Scheyer, M., Schwartz, I. S., & Harry, B. (Eds.). (1998). Making friends. Baltimore: Brookes.

Michael, M. G., Arnold, K. D., Magliocca, L. A., & Miller, S. (1992). Influences on teachers' attitudes of the parents' role as collaborator. Remedial and Special Education, 13(2), 24–30, 39.

Michnowicz, L., McConnell, S. R., Peterson, C. A., & Odom, S. L. (1995). Social goals and the objectives of preschool IEPs: A content analysis. Journal of Early Intervention, 19(4), 273–282.

Miller, L. J., & Hanft, B. E. (1998). Building positive alliances: Partnerships with families as the cornerstone of developmental assess-

ment. Infants and Young Children, 11(1), 49–60.

Miller, N. B. (1994). Nobody's perfect. Baltimore: Brookes.

Mills v. DC Board of Education, 348 F. Supp. 866 (D. D.C. 1972); contempt proceedings, EHLR 551: 643 (D. D.C. 1980).

Milstein, G., Guarnaccia, P., & Midlarsky, E. (1995). Ethnic differences in the interpretation of mental illness: Perspectives of caregivers. Research in Community and Mental Health, 8, 155–176.

Minick, B. A., & School, B. A. (1982). The IEP process: Can computers help? Academic Therapy, 18, 41–48.

Minke, K. (1991). The development of individualized family service plans in three early intervention programs: A data-based construction. Dissertation Abstracts International, 52(06), 2077A. (University Microfilms No. 9134817)

Minke, K. M., & Scott, M. M. (1993). The development of Individualized Family Service Plans: Roles for parents and staff. Journal of Special Education, 27(1), 82–106.

Minnes, P. (1998). Mental retardation: The impact upon the family. In J. A. Burack, R. M. Hodapp, & E. Zigler (Eds.), Handbook of mental retardation and development (pp. 693–712). Cambridge, MA: Cambridge University Press.

Minuchin, S., & Fishman, H. C. (1981). Family therapy techniques. Cambridge, MA: Harvard University Press.

Minuchin, S. (1974). Families and family therapy. Cambridge, MA: Harvard University Press.

Mirfin-Veitch, B., Bray, A., & Watson, M. (1997). We're just that sort of family: Intergenerational relationships in families including children with disabilities. Family Relations, 46(3), 305–311.

Mish, J., & Bonesio, R. (1998). Desert stars (1st ed.). Phoenix, AZ: Pilot Parent Partnerships.

Mlawer, M. A. (1993). Who should fight? Parents and the advocacy expectation. Journal of Disability Policy Studies, 4(1), 105–115.

Mokuau, N., & Tauili'ili, P. (1998). Families with native Hawaiian and Pacific Island roots. In E. W. Lynch & M. J. Hanson (Eds.), Developing cross-cultural competence: A guide for working with young children and their families (2nd ed.). (pp. 409–440). Baltimore: Brookes.

Moles, O. C. (1993). Collaboration between schools and disadvantaged parents: Obstacles and openings. In N. F. Chavkin (Ed.), Families and schools in a pluralistic society (pp. 21–51). Albany: State University of New York Press.

Moles, O. C. (Ed.). (1996). Reaching all families: Creating family-friendly schools. Washington, DC: U.S. Department of Education, Office of Educational Research and Improvement.

Moles, O. C. (Ed.). (1999). Reaching all families. Washington, DC: The U.S. Department of Education, U.S. Government Printing Office.

Moll, L. C. (1992). Bilingual classroom studies and community analysis: Some recent trends. Educational Researcher, 21(2), 20–24.

Monat-Haller, R. K. (1992). Understanding and expressing sexuality: Responsible choices for individuals with developmental disabilities. Baltimore: Brookes.

Moon, M. S., & Bunker, L. (1987). Recreation and motor skills programming. In M. E. Snell (Ed.), Systematic instruction of persons with severe handicaps (pp. 214–244). Englewood Cliffs, NJ: Merrill/Prentice-Hall.

Moore-Hines, P., & Boyd-Franklin, N. (1996). African American families. In M. McGoldrick, J. Giordano, & J. K. Pearce (Eds.), Ethnicity and family therapy (2nd ed., pp. 66–84). New York: The Guilford Press.

Morgan, S. B. (1988). The autistic child and family functioning: A developmental-family systems perspective. Journal of Autism and Developmental Disorders, 18(2), 263–281.

Morissey, P. A., & Safer, N. (1977). The Individualized Education Program: Implications for special education. Viewpoints, 53, 31–38.

Morningstar, M. E., Turnbull, A. P., & Turnbull, H. R. (1995a). [Unpublished raw data]. Lawrence: University of Kansas, Beach Center on Families and Disability.

Morningstar, M. E., Turnbull, A. P., & Turnbull, H. R. (1995b). What do students with disabilities tell us about the importance of family involvement in the transition from school to adult life? *Exceptional Children, 62*(3), 249–260.

Morris, M. W. (1987). Health care: Who pays the bills? *Exceptional Parent, 17,* 38–39.

Moses, K. I. (1983). The impact of initial diagnosis: Mobilizing family resources. In J. A. Mulick & S. M. Pueschel (Eds.), *Parent-professional partnerships in developmental disability services* (pp. 11–34). Cambridge, MA: Ware.

Mount, B. (1995). *Capacity works.* New York: Graphic Futures.

Mount, B., & Zwernik, K. (1988). *It's never too early, it's never too late: A booklet about personal planning for persons with developmental disabilities, their families and friends, case managers, service providers, and advocates.* St. Paul, MN: Metropolitan Council.

Murphy, A. T. (1982). The family with a handicapped child: A review of the literature. *Developmental and Behavioral Pediatrics, 3*(2), 73–82.

Murphy, D. L., Lee, I. M., Turnbull, A. P., & Turbiville, V. (1995). The family-centered program rating scale: An instrument for program evaluation and change. *Journal of Early Intervention, 19*(1), 24–42.

Myers, C. L., McBride, S. L., & Peterson, C. A. (1996). Transdisciplinary, play-based assessment in early childhood special education: An examination of social validity. *Topics in Early Childhood Special Education, 16*(1), 102–126.

Myerson-O'Neill, A. (1985). Normal and bright children of mentally retarded parents: The Huck Finn syndrome. *Child Psychiatry and Human Development, 15*(4), 255–268.

Nadler, B., & Shore, K. (1980). Individualized Education Programs: A look at realities. *Education Unlimited, 2,* 30–34.

Nagy, S., & Ungerer, J. (1990). The adaptation of mothers and fathers to children with cystic fibrosis: A comparison. *Children's Health Care, 19*(3), 147–154.

Naseef, R. A. (1997). *Special children, challenged parents.* Secaucus, NJ: Carol Publishing Group.

Natiello, P. (1990). The person-centered approach, collaborative power, and cultural transformation. *Person-Centered Review, 5*(3), 268–286.

National Association of Secondary School Principals (NASSP). (1994). Building parent involvement. *NASSP Practitioner, 20*(5), 1–4.

National Center for Children in Poverty. (1995). Number of poor children under six increased from 5 to 6 million, 1987–1992. *National Center for Children in Poverty News and Issues, 5*(1), 1–2.

National Center on Child Abuse and Neglect. (1993). *A report on the maltreatment of children with disabilities* [Report No. 20-10030]. Washington, DC: U.S. Department of Health and Human Services.

National Commission on Childhood Disability. (1995). *Supplemental security income for children with disabilities: Report to Congress of the National Commission on Childhood Disability.* Washington, DC: Author.

National Commission on Children. (1991). *Beyond rhetoric: A new American agenda for children and families.* Washington, DC: U.S. Government Printing Office.

National Commission on Excellence in Education. (1983). *A nation at risk: The imperative for educational reform.* Washington, DC: U.S. Government Printing Office.

National Council on Disability. (1995). *Improving the implementation of the Individuals with Disabilities Education Act: Making schools work for all of America's children.* Washington, DC: Author.

National Institute on Alcohol Abuse and Addiction. (1990). Seventh special report to the U.S. Congress. Washington, DC: U.S. Government Printing Office.

National Institute on Drug Abuse. (1996). *National pregnancy and health survey.* Rockville, MD: Author.

The National PTA. (1998). *National standards for parent/family involvement programs.* Chicago, IL: Author.

The National PTA. (1999, October 25). *Learning to walk in anothers' shoes.* [Online] Available http://www.pta.org/programs/education/walk.htm.

The National PTA. (1999, October 27). *National PTA advocates for children award winner.* [Online] Available http://www.pta.org/programs/dvks.htm.

The National PTA. (1999, October 27). *The national PTA, disability document.* [Online] Available http://www.pta.org/monsterboard/index.htm.

National Research Council. (1993). *Understanding child abuse and neglect.* Washington, DC: National Academy Press.

National Resource Center for Family Support Programs. (1993). Family support programs and incarcerated parents [Fact sheet]. Chicago: Family Resource Coalition.

National Society for Autistic Children, Board of Directors and Professional Advisory Board. (1977). *A short definition of autism.* Albany, NY: Author.

National Symposium on Abuse and Neglect of Children with Disabilities. (1995). *Abuse and neglect of children with disabilities: Report and recommendations.* Lawrence: University of Kansas, Beach Center on Families and Disability/Erikson Institute of Chicago.

Neal, L. (1996). The case against transracial adoption. *Focal Point, 10*(1), 18–20.

Nelson, J. R., Smith, D. J., & Dodd, J. M. (1992). Understanding the cultural characteristics of American Indian families: Effective partnerships under the individualized family service plan (IFSP). *Rural Special Education Quarterly, 11*(2), 33–36.

Nerney, T. (1998). The poverty of human services: An introduction. In T.

Nerney & D. Shumway (Eds.), *The importance of income* (pp. 2–14). Concord, NH: The Robert Wood Johnson Foundation.

Newcomer, J. R., & Zirkel, P. A. (1999). An analysis of judicial outcomes of special education cases. *Exceptional Children, 65*(4), 469–480.

Nicholson, J., Nason, M. W., Calabresi, A. O., & Yando, R. (1998). Fathers with severe mental illness: Characteristics and comparisons. *American Journal of Orthopsychiatry, 69*(1), 134–141.

Nicholson, J., Sweeney, E. M., & Geller, J. L. (1998a). Mothers with mental illness: I. The competing demands of parenting and living with mental illness. *Psychiatric Services, 49*(5), 635–642.

Nicholson, J., Sweeney, E. M., & Geller, J. L. (1998b). Mothers with mental illness: II. Family relationships and the context of parenting. *Journal on Psychiatric Services, 49*(5), 643–649.

Nielsen, N. C., Jr., Hein, N., Reynolds, F. E., Miller, A. L., Karff, S. E., Cowan, A. C., McLean, P., Burford, G. G., Fenton, J. Y., Grillo, L., Leeper, E., & Forman, R. K. C. (1993). *Religions of the world* (3rd ed.). New York: St. Martin's Press.

North, S. (1997, July/August). The abcs of IEPs. *Volta Voices,* 22–25.

Nosek, M. A., Howland, C. A., & Young, M. E. (1997). Abuse of young women with disabilities: Policy implications. *Journal of Disability Policy Studies, 8*(1–2), 157–175.

Nuckolls, C. W. (1993). An introduction to the cross-cultural study of sibling relations. In C. W. Nuckolls (Ed.), *Siblings in South Asia: Brothers and sisters in cultural place* (pp. 19–44). New York: The Guilford Press.

Oberti v. Board of Education, 789 F. Supp. 1322 (D. N. J., 1992).

Obiakor, F. E. (1999). Teacher expectations of minority exceptional learners: Impact on "accuracy" of self-concepts. *Exceptional Children, 66*(1), 39–53.

O'Brien, J. (1997). *Implementing self-determination initiatives: Some notes on complex change.* Litho-

nia, GA: Responsive Systems Associates.

O'Brien, J., & Lyle-O'Brien, C. (1996). *Members of each other.* Toronto, Ontario: Inclusion Press.

O'Brien, J., & Lyle-O'Brien, C. (Eds.). (1998). *A little book about person centered planning.* Toronto, Ontario: Inclusion Press.

O'Brien, M. (1999). *Inclusive child care for infants and toddlers meeting individual and special needs.* Baltimore: Brookes.

O'Connell-Higgins, G. (1994). *Resilient adults overcoming a cruel past.* San Francisco: Jossey-Bass.

O'Connor, S. (1995). We're all one family: The positive construction of people with disabilities by family members. In S. J. Taylor, R. Bogdon, & Z. M. Lutfiyya (Eds.), *The variety of community experience: Qualitative studies of family and community life* (pp. 67–78). Baltimore: Brookes.

O'Halloran, J. M. (1995). *The celebration process* [Fact sheet]. In Parent articles 2 (pp. 195–96). Phoenix, AZ: Communication Skill Builders/The Psychological Corporation.

Oliver, J. M., Cole, N. H., & Hollingsworth, H. (1991). Learning disabilities as functions of familial learning problems and developmental problems. *Exceptional Children, 57*(5), 427–440.

Olson, D. H. (1988). Family types, family stress, and family satisfaction: A family development perspective. In C. J. Falicov (Ed.), *Family transitions: Continuity and change over the life cycle* (pp. 55–79). New York: The Guilford Press.

Olson, D. H., McCubbin, H. I., Barnes, H., Larsen, A., Muxen, M., & Wilson, M. (1983). *Families: What makes them work.* Beverly Hills, CA: Sage.

Olson, D. H., Russell, C. S., & Sprenkle, D. H. (1980). Circumplex model of marital and family systems II: Empirical studies and clinical intervention. *Advances in Family Intervention Assessment and Theory, 1,* 129–179.

Olson, D. H., Sprenkle, D. H., & Russell, C. S. (1979). Circumplex model of

marital and family systems I: Cohesion and adaptability dimensions, family types, and clinical applications. *Family Process, 18,* 3–28.

Olson, H., & Burgess, D. M. (1997). Early intervention for children prenatally exposed to alcohol and other drugs. In M. J. Guralnick (Ed.), *The effectiveness of early intervention* (pp. 109–145). Baltimore: Brookes.

O'Neill, A. M. (1985). Normal and bright children of mentally retarded parents: The Huck Finn syndrome. *Child Psychiatry and Human Development, 15,* 255–268.

Orsillo, S. M., McCaffrey, R. J., & Fisher, J. M. (1993). Siblings of head-injured individuals: A population at risk. *Journal of Head Trauma Rehabilitation, 8*(1), 102–115.

Orton, S. T. (1930). Familial occurrence of disorders in the acquisition of language. *Eugenics, 3,* 140–147.

Osmond, M. W., & Thorne, B. (1993). Feminist theories. In P. G. Boss, W. J. Doherty, R. LaRossa, W. R. Schumm, & S. K. Steinmetz (Eds.), *Sourcebook of family theories and methods: A contextual approach* (pp. 591–623). New York: Plenum Press.

Oswald, D. P., Coutinho, M. J., Best, A. M., & Singh, N. N. (1999). Ethnic representation in special education. *The Journal of Special Education, 32*(4), 194–206.

O'Toole, C. J. (1996). Disabled lesbians: Challenging monocultural constructs. *Sexuality and Disability, 14*(3), 221–236.

Otterbourg, S. D. (1994). *Parent involvement handbook.* Boston: The Educational Publishing Group.

Oyserman, D., Mowbray, C. T., & Zemencuk, J. K. (1994). Resources and supports for mothers with severe mental illness. *Health and Social Work, 19*(2), 132–142.

Ozer, E., & Bandura, A. (1990). Mechanisms governing empowerment effects: A self-efficacy analysis. *Journal of Personality and Social Psychology, 58*(3), 472–486.

Palmer, D. S., Borthwick-Duffy, S. A., Widaman, K., & Best, A. (1998a). Parent perceptions of inclusive practices for their children with significant cognitive disabilities. *Exceptional Children, 64*(2), 271–282.

Palmer, D. S., Borthwick-Duffy, S. A., Widaman, K., & Best, S. J. (1998b). Influences on parent perceptions of inclusive practices for their children with mental retardation. *American Journal on Mental Retardation, 103*(3), 272–287.

Palmer, S. (1998). *What parents and professionals should know about developmental skills leading to later self-determination: What? Why? When?* Paper presented at the Early Childhood Conference, Arlington, TX.

Parasnis, I. (Ed.). (1996). *Cultural and language diversity and the deaf experience.* Cambridge, MA: Cambridge University Press.

Parette, H. P., & Angelo, D. H. (1996). Augmentative and alternative communication impact on families: Trends and future directions. *Journal of Special Education, 30*(1), 77–98.

Park, J. (1998). *Qualitative study of the Korean families' perceptions and experiences: Special education and cultural diversity.* Unpublished master's thesis, University of Kansas, Lawrence.

Park, J., & Turnbull, A. P. (1999). *Cultural competency and special education.* Lawrence: The University of Kansas.

Parker, D. (with Moore, C.). (1991). *Achieving inclusion through the IEP process: A handbook for parents.* Hanover, MD: Maryland Coalition for Integrated Education.

Patrikakou, E. N. (1996). Investigating the academic achievement of adolescents with learning disabilities: A structural modeling approach. *Journal of Educational Psychology, 88*(3), 435–450.

Patterson, C. J. (1992). Children of lesbian and gay parents. *Child Development, 63,* 1,025–1,042.

Patterson, G. R., Reid, J. B., & Dishion, T. J. (1992). *Antisocial boys.* Eugene, OR: Castalia.

Patterson, J. M. (1991). A family systems perspective for working with youth with disability. *Pediatrician, 18,* 129–141.

Peirce, J. W., & Wardle, J. (1996). Body size, parental appraisal, and self-esteem in blind children. *Journal of Child Psychology and Psychiatry and Allied Disciplines, 37*(2), 205–212.

Pennsylvania Association for Retarded Citizens (PARC) v. Commonwealth of Pennsylvania, 334 F. Supp. 1257, 343 F. Supp. 279 (E. D. Pa. 1971, 1972).

Perez, L. (1986). Immigrant economic adjustment and family organization: The Cuban success story reexamined. *International Migration Review, 20,* 4–20.

Perl, J. (1995, Fall). Improving relationship skills for parent conferences. *Teaching Exceptional Children,* pp. 29–31.

Peterson, S. L., Robinson, E. A., & Littman, I. (1983). Parent-child interaction training for parents with a history of mental retardation. *Applied Research in Mental Retardation, 4,* 329–342.

Petr, C. G. (1994, April). Crises that threaten out-of-home placement of children with emotional and behavioral disorders. *Families in Society: The Journal of Contemporary Human Services, 75*(4), 195–203.

Petr, C. G. (1998). *Social work with children and their families: Pragmatic foundations.* New York: Oxford University Press.

Pewewardy, C. (1998). Will the real Indians please stand up? *Multicultural Review, 7*(2), 36–42.

Pfouts, J. H. (1980). Birth order, age spacing, I.Q. differences, and family relations. *Journal of Marriage and the Family, 42,* 517–521.

Phelps, L., & Grabowski, J. (1992). Fetal alcohol syndrome: Diagnostic features and psychoeducational risk factors. *School Psychology Quarterly, 7*(2), 112–128.

Pianta, R. C., & Lothman, D. J. (1994). Predicting behavior problems in children with epilepsy: Child factors, disease factors, family stress, and child-mother interactions. *Child Development, 65,* 1,415–1,428.

Pierce, J. W., & Wardle, J. (1996). Body size, parental appraisal, and self-esteem in blind children. *Journal of Child Psychology and Psychiatry and Allied Disciplines, 37*(2), 205–212.

Pinderhughes, E. (1994). Empowerment as an intervention goal: Early ideas. In L. Gutiérrez & P. Nurius (Eds.), *Education and research for empowerment practice* (pp. 17–30). Seattle, WA: University of Washington, School of Social Work, Center for Policy and Practice Research.

Pizzo, P. (1983). *Parent to parent.* Boston: Beacon.

Polloway, E. A., Bursuck, W. D., Jayanthi, M., Epstein, M. H., & Nelson, J. S. (1996). Treatment acceptability: Determining appropriate interventions within inclusive classrooms. *Interventions in School and Clinic, 31*(3), 133–144.

Polloway, E. A., Epstein, M. H., Bursuck, W. D., Roderique, T. W., McConeghy, J. L., & Jayanthi, M. (1994). Classroom grading: A national survey of policies. *Remedial and Special Education, 15*(3), 162–170.

Polloway, E. A., Epstein, M. H., & Foley, R. (1992). A comparison of the homework problems of students with learning disabilities and non-handicapped students. *Learning Disabilities, 7,* 203–209.

Popenoe, D. (1988). *Disturbing the nest.* New York: Aldine de Gruyter.

Poulsen, M. K. (1994). The development of policy recommendations to address individual and family needs of infants and young children affected by family substance abuse. *Topics in Early Childhood Special Education, 14*(2), 275–291.

Powell, D. S., Batsche, C. J., Ferro, J., Fox, L., & Dunlap, G. (1997). A strength-based approach in support of multi-risk families: Principles and issues. *Topics in Early Childhood Education, 17*(1), 1–26.

Powell, T. H., & Gallagher, P. A. (1993). *Brothers and sisters: A special part of exceptional families* (2nd ed.). Baltimore: Brookes.

Powers, L. E. (1996). Family and consumer activism in disability policy. In G. H. S. Singer, L. E. Powers, & A. L. Olson (Eds.), *Redefining* family support: Innovations in public-private partnerships* (pp. 413–434). Baltimore: Brookes.

Powers, L. E., Singer, G. H. S., & Sowers, J. A. (Eds.). (1996). *On the road to autonomy: Promoting self-competence among children and youth with disabilities.* Baltimore: Brookes.

Powers, L. E., Sowers, J. A., Turner, A., Nesbitt, M., Knowles, E., & Ellison, R. (1996). Take charge: A model for promoting self-determination among adolescents with challenges. In L. E. Powers, G. H. S. Singer, & J. A. Sowers (Eds.), *On the road to autonomy* (pp. 291–322). Baltimore: Brookes.

Pruett, K. D. (1997). How men and children affect each other's development. *Zero to Three, 18*(1), 3–11.

Pruett, K. D., & Litzenberger, B. (1992). Latency development in children of primary nurturing fathers: Eight-year follow-up. *Psychoanalytic Study of the Child, 47,* 85–101.

Pugach, M. C. (1995). On the failure of imagination in inclusive schools. *Journal of Special Education, 29,* 212–223.

Pugach, M., & Lilly, S. M. (1984). Reconceptualizing support services for classroom teachers: Implications for teacher education. *Journal of Teacher Education, 35,* 48–55.

Pugach, M. C., & Warger, C. L. (1996). *Curriculum trends, special education, and reform: Refocusing the conversation.* New York: Teachers College Press.

Pugach, M. C., & Wesson, C. L. (1995). Teachers' and students' views of team teaching general education and learning-disabled students in two fifth-grade classes. *Elementary School Journal, 95*(3), 279–295.

Pugliese, J., & Edwards, G. (1995). *Use of children's Supplemental Security Income (SSI) by families who have children with cerebral palsy or spina bifida.* Birmingham, AL: United Cerebral Palsy Association of Greater Birmingham.

Pyecha, J. N., Cox, J. L., Dewitt, D., Drummond, D., Jaffe, J., Kalt, M., Lane, C., & Pelosi, J. (1980). A national survey of Individualized Education Programs (IEPs) for handi-capped children (5 vols.). Durham, NC: Research Triangle Institute. (ERIC Document Reproduction Service Nos. ED 199 970–974).

Quinn, M. M., Gable, R. A., Rutherford, R. B., Nelson, C. M., & Howell, K. W. (1998). *Addressing student problem behavior: An IEP team's introduction to functional behavioral assessment and behavior intervention plans.* Washington, DC: The Center for Effective Collaboration and Practice.

Racino, J. A., Walker, P., O'Connor, S., & Taylor, S. J. (Eds.). (1993). *Housing, support, and community: Choices and strategies for adults with disabilities.* Baltimore: Brookes.

Raghavan, C., Weisner, T. S., & Patel, D. (1999). The adaptive project of parenting: South Asian families with children with developmental delays. *Education and Training in Mental Retardation and Developmental Disabilities, 34*(3), 281–292.

Raham, H. (1998). Full-service schools. *School and Business Affairs, 64*(6), 24–28.

Rainforth, B., & York-Barr, J. (1998). *Collaborative teams for students with severe disabilities: Integrating therapy and educational services* (2nd ed.). Baltimore: Brookes.

Rainforth, B., York, J., & Macdonald, C. (Eds.). (1992). *Collaborative teams for students with severe disabilities.* Baltimore: Brookes.

Ramirez, O. (1989). Mexican American children and adolescents. In J. T. Gibbs, L. Nahme Huang, & Associates (Eds.), *Children of color* (pp. 24–25). San Francisco: Jossey-Bass.

Ramirez, S. Z., Nguyen, T., & Kratochwill, T. R. (1998). Self-reported fears in Hispanic youth with mental retardation: A preliminary study. *Mental Retardation, 36*(2), 145–156.

Rappaport, J. (1981). In praise of paradox: A social policy of empowerment over prevention. *American Journal of Community Psychology, 9*(1), 1–25.

Ray, N. K., Rubenstein, H., & Russo, N. J. (1994). Understanding the par-ents who are mentally retarded: Guidelines for family preservation programs. *Child Welfare League of America, 123*(6), 725–743.

Raymond, C. L., & Benbow, C. P. (1989). Educational encouragement by parents: Its relationship to precocity and gender. *Gifted Child Quarterly, 33*(4), 144–151.

Raymond, E. B. (1997). It's all in the family. *Reaching Today's Youth, 1*(3), 32–36.

Redshaw, M., Wilgosh, L., & Bibby, M. A. (1990). The parental experiences of mothers of adolescents with hearing impairments. *American Annals of the Deaf, 135*(4), 293–298.

Reed, H., Thomas, E., Sprague, J. R., & Horner, R. H. (1997). Student guided functional assessment interview: An analysis of student and teacher agreement. *Journal of Behavioral Education, 7,* 33–49.

Regulatory flexibility in schools: What happens when schools are allowed to change the rules? (Letter Report, GAO/HEHS-94-102, 04/29/94).

Reibschleger, J. L. (1991). Families of chronically mentally ill people: Siblings speak to social workers. *Health and Social Work, 16*(2), 94–102.

Reichard, A., & Turnbull, A. P. (in press). Migrant education: A tale of two cultures. *Journal for Exceptional Children.*

Reichart, D. C., Lynch, E. C., Anderson, B. C., Svobodny, L. A., DiCola, J. M., & Mercury, M. G. (1989). Parental perspectives on integrated preschool opportunities for children with handicaps and children without handicaps. *Journal of Early Intervention, 13*(1), 6–13.

Reid, W. J. (1985). *Family problem solving.* New York: Columbia University Press.

Reiff, H. B., Gerber, P. J., & Ginsberg, R. (1997). *Exceeding expectations.* Austin, TX: Pro-ed.

Reiff, H., Gerber, P., & Ginsberg, R. (1998). Exceeding expectations: Successful adults with learning disabilities. *Remedial and Special Education, 19*(1), 59–60.

Renwick, R., Brown, I., & Raphael, D. (1998). *The family quality of life project* (Final Report). Toronto: University of Toronto.

Renzulli, J. S., & McGreevey, A. M. (1986). Twins included and not included in special programs for the gifted. *Roeper Review, 9,* 120–127.

Reppucci, J. C., & Haugaard, J. J. (1989). Prevention of child sexual abuse. *American Psychologist, 44,* 1,266–1,275.

Rhein, L. M., Ginsburg, K. R., Schwarz, D. F., Pinto-Martin, J. A., Zhao, H., Morgan, A. P., & Slap, G. B. (1997). Teen father participation in child rearing: Family perspectives. *Journal of Adolescent Health, 21*(4), 244–252.

Rhodes, R. L. (1996). Beyond our borders: Spanish-dominant migrant parents and the IEP process. *Rural Special Education Quarterly, 15*(2), 19–22.

Rich, D. (1993). Building the bridge to reach minority parents: Education infrastructure supporting success for all children. In N. F. Chavkin (Ed.), *Families and schools in a pluralistic society* (pp. 235–244). Albany: State University of New York Press.

Riley, B. J., Fryar, N., & Thornton, N. (1998). Homeless on the range: Meeting the needs of homeless families with young children in the rural west. *Zero to Three, 19*(1), 31–35.

Riley, R. W. (1995). Reflections on goals 2000. *Teachers College Record, 96*(3), 380–388.

Rimm, S., & Lowe, B. (1988). Family environments of underachieving gifted students. *Gifted Child Quarterly, 32*(4), 353–359.

Risley, T. (1996). Get a life! Positive behavioral intervention for challenging behavior through life arrangement and life coaching. In L. K. Koegal, R. L. Koegel, & G. Dunlap (Eds.), *Positive behavioral support: Including people with difficult behavior in the community* (pp. 425–438). Baltimore: Brookes.

Roach, M. A., Orsmond, G. I., & Barratt, M. S. (1999). Mothers and fathers of children with Down syndrome: Parental stress and involvement in childcare. *American Journal on Mental Retardation, 104*(5), 422–434.

Robbins, C., & Clayton, R. R. (1989). Gender-related differences in psychoactive drug use among older adults. *Journal of Drug Issues, 19*(2), 207–219.

Robbins, F. R., Dunlap, G., & Plienis, A. J. (1991). Family characteristics, family training, and the progress of young children with autism. *Journal of Early Intervention, 15*(2), 173–184.

Roberts, R. N., Rule, S., & Innocenti, M. S. (1998). *Strengthening the family-professional partnership in services for young children.* Baltimore: Paul H. Brookes.

Robinson, C., & Stalker, K. (Eds.). (1998). *Growing up with disability.* Philadelphia: Jessica Kingsley Publishers.

Robinson, E. G., & Rathbone, G. N. (1999). Impact of race, poverty, and ethnicity on services for persons with mental disabilities: Call for cultural competence. *American Journal on Mental Retardation,* 333–338.

Robinson, N. M., Weinberg, R. A., Redden, D., Ramey, S. L., & Ramey, C. T. (1998). Family factors associated with high academic competence among former head start children. *Gifted Children Quarterly, 42*(3), 148–155.

Robinson-Zañartu, C., & Majel-Dixon, J. (1996). Parent voices: American Indian relationships with schools. *Journal of American Indian Education, 36*(1), 33–54.

Rockowitz, R. J., & Davidson, P. W. (1979). Discussing diagnostic findings with parents. *Journal of Learning Disabilities, 12*(1), 11–16.

Rodger, S. (1995). Individual education plans revisited: A review of the literature. *International Journal of Disability, 42*(3), 221–239.

Rodgers, R. H., & White, J. M. (1993). Family development theory. In P. J. Boss, W. J. Doherty, R. LaRossa, W. R. Schumm, & S. K. Steinmetz (Eds.), *Sources of family theories and methods: A contextual approach* (pp. 225–254). New York: Plenum.

Rodgers-Arthur, C., & Gerken, K. C. (1998). Prenatal exposure and public policy: Implications for pregnant and parenting women and their families. *Infants and Young Children, 10*(4), 23–35.

Rodriguez, J. C. (1995). *Southeast Asians' conceptions of disabilities and special education intervention in American schools* (Research Report 143). Lowell, MA: Massachusetts University, College of Education.

Rodriguez, J. R., Geffkin, G. R., & Morgan, S. B. (1993). Perceived competence and behavioral adjustment of siblings of children with autism. *Journal of Autism and Developmental Disorders, 23*(4), 665–674.

Roedell, W. C. (1988). "I just want my child to be happy": Social development and young gifted children. *Understanding Our Gifted, 1*(1), 1, 7, 10–11.

Rogers, J. J. (1994). Is special education free? *Remedial and Special Education, 15*(3), 171–176.

Rogers-Dulan, J. (1998, April). Religious connectedness among urban African American families who have a child with disabilities. *Mental Retardation, 36*(2), 91–103.

Romer, E. F., & Umbreit, J. (1998). The effects of family-centered service coordination: A social validity study. *Journal of Early Intervention, 21*(2), 95–110.

Romski, M. A., & Sevick, R. A. (2000). Communication, assistive technology, and mental retardation. In M. L. Wehmeyer & J. R. Patton (Eds.), *Mental retardation in the 21st century* (pp. 299–314). Austin, TX: Pro-ed.

Roncker v. Walters, 700 F. 2d 1058 (6th Cir. 1983), cert. den. 464 U.S. 864, 104 S. Ct. 196, 78 L. Ed. 2d 171 (1983).

Rose, H. W. (1998). *Something's wrong with my child: A valuable resource in helping parents and professionals to better understand themselves in dealing with the emotionally* charged subject of children with disabilities (2nd ed.). Springfield, IL: Charles C. Thomas.

Rose, L. C., & Gallup, A. M. (1998). The 30th annual Phi Delta Kappa Gallup Poll of the public attitudes toward the public schools. *Phi Delta Kappan, 80*(1), 41–55.

Rosenfeld, L. (1994). *Your child and health care.* Baltimore: Brookes.

Rosenkoetter, S. E., Hains, A. H., & Fowler, S. A. (1994). *Bridging early services for children with special needs and their families: A practical guide for transition planning.* Baltimore: Brookes.

Rosenthal, J. A., Groze, V., & Aguilar, G. D. (1991). Adoption outcomes for children with handicaps. *Child Welfare, 70*(6), 623–636.

Roth, J., Hendrickson, J., Schilling, M., & Stowell, D. W. (1998). The risk of teen mothers having low birth weight babies: Implications of recent medical research for school health personnel. *Journal of School Health, 68*(7), 271–275.

Rousso, H. (1984). Fostering healthy self-esteem. *Exceptional Parent, 8*(14), 9–14.

Rueda, R. S. (1992). Characteristics of teacher-student discourses in computer-based dialogue journals: A descriptive study. *Learning Disability Quarterly, 15,* 187–206.

Rueda, R., & Martinez, I. (1992). Fiesta Educativa: One community's approach to parent training in developmental disabilities for Latino families. *Journal of the Association for Persons with Severe Handicaps, 17*(2), 95–103.

Ruef, M. (1995). *Informational priorities of parents regarding the challenging behaviors of their sons and daughters: Results of a national survey.* Unpublished manuscript, Beach Center on Families and Disability, University of Kansas.

Ruef, M. B., Turnbull, A. P., Turnbull, H. R., & Poston, D. (1999). Perspectives of five stakeholder groups: Challenging behavior of individuals with mental retardation and/or autism. *Journal of Positive Behavior Interventions, 1*(1), 43–58.

Ruiz, R. A., & Padilla, A. M. (1977). Counseling Latinos. *Personnel and Guidance Journal, 55,* 401–408.

Rumbaut, R. G. (1998, March). *Transformations: The post-immigrant generation in an age of diversity.* Paper presented at the "American Diversity: Past, Present, and Future" annual meeting of the Eastern Sociological Society, Philadelphia.

Rutstein, R. M., Conlon, C. J., & Batshaw, M. L. (1997). HIV and AIDS. In M. L. Batshaw (Ed.), *Children with disabilities* (4th ed., pp. 163–182). Baltimore: Brookes.

Ryan, L. B., & Rucker, C. N. (1986). Computerized vs. noncomputerized Individualized Education Programs: Teachers' attitudes, time, and cost. *Journal of Special Education Technology, 8*(1), 5–12.

Ryndak, D. L., Downing, J. E., Jacqueline, L. R., & Morrison, A. P. (1995). Parents' perceptions after inclusion of their children with moderate or severe disabilities. *Journal of the Association for Persons with Severe Handicaps, 20*(2), 147–157.

Ryndak, D. L., Downing, J. E., Morrison, A. P., & Williams, L. J. (1996). Parents' perceptions of educational settings and services for children with moderate or severe disabilities. *Remedial and Special Education, 17,* 106–118.

Safran, S. P., & Safran, J. S. (1996). Intervention assistance programs and prereferral teams: Direction for the twenty-first century. *Remedial and Special Education, 17,* 363–369.

Sager, C. J., Brown, H. S., Crohn, H., Engel, T., Rodstein, E., & Walker, L. (1983). *Treating the remarried family.* New York: Brunner/Mazel.

Sailor, W. (1991). Special education in the restructured school. *Remedial and Special Education, 12*(6), 8–22.

Sailor, W. (1996). School-linked services. In National Council on Disability, *Improving the implementation of the Individuals with Disabilities Education Act: Making schools work for all of America's children.* Supplement (pp. 661–684). Washington, DC: National Council on Disability.

Sailor, W. (Ed.). (in press-a). *Inclusive education and school/community partnerships.* New York: Teachers College Press.

Sailor, W. (in press-b). Devolution, school/community/family partnerships, and inclusive education. In W. Sailor (Ed.), *Inclusive education and school/community partnerships.* New York: Teachers College Press.

Sailor, W., Kleinhammer-Tramill, J., Skrtic, T., & Oas, B. K. (1996). Family participation in new community schools. In G. H. S. Singer, L. E. Powers, & A. L. Olson (Eds.), *Redefining family support* (pp. 313–332). Baltimore: Brookes.

Saleebey, D. (1996). The strengths perspective in social work practice: Extensions and cautions. *Social Work, 41,* 296–305.

Salembier, G., & Furney, K. S. (1994). Promoting self-advocacy and family participation in IEP and transition planning. *Journal for Vocational Special Needs Education, 17* (I), 12–17.

Salend, S. J. (1995, Spring). Using videocassette recorder technology in special education classrooms. *The Council for Exceptional Children,* 4–9.

Salend, S. J. (1998). Using portfolios to assess student performance. *Teaching Exceptional Children, 31*(2), 36–43.

Salend, S. J., & Schiff, J. (1989). An examination of the homework practices of teachers of students with learning disabilities. *Journal of Learning Disabilities, 22,* 621–623.

Salend, S. J., & Taylor, L. (1993). Working with families: A cross-cultural perspective. *Remedial and Special Education, 14*(5), 25–32, 39.

Sampson, P. D., Streissguth, A. P., Barr, H. M., & Bookstein, F. L. (1989). Neurobehavioral effects of prenatal alcohol. Part 2: Partial least squares analysis. *Neurotoxicology and Teratology, 11,* 477–491.

Sandel, A., McCallister, C., & Nash, W. R. (1993). Child search and screening activities for preschool gifted children. *Roeper Review, 16*(2), 98–102.

Sanders, M. G. (1999). Schools' programs and progress in the national network of partnership schools. *The Journal of Educational Research, 92*(4), 220–229.

Sanders, M. G., & Epstein, J. L. (1998a). School-family-community partnerships and educational change. *International Handbook of Educational Change, 482*–502.

Sanders, M. G., & Epstein, J. L. (1998b). *School-family-community partnerships in middle and high schools* (22). Baltimore: Johns Hopkins University & Howard University, Center for Research on the Education of Students Placed at Risk.

Sandler, A. (1997). *Living with spina bifida.* Chapel Hill: The University of North Carolina Press.

Sandler, A. G. (1998). Grandparents of children with disabilities: A closer look. *Education and Training in Mental Retardation and Developmental Disabilities, 33*(4), 350–356.

Sandler, A. G., & Mistretta, L. A. (1998). Positive adaption in parents of adults with disabilities. *Education and Training in Mental Retardation and Developmental Disabilities, 33*(2), 123–130.

Sandler, A. G., Warren, S. H., & Raver, S. A. (1995). Grandparents as a source of support for parents of children with disabilities: A brief report. *Mental Retardation, 33*(4), 248–250.

Sands, D. J., Spencer, K. C., Gliner, J., & Swaim, R. (1999). Structural equation modeling of student involvement in transition related actions: The path of least resistance. *Focus on Autism and Other Developmental Disabilities, 14*(1), 17–27.

Sands, D., & Wehmeyer, M. (Eds.). (1996). *Self-determination across the life span: Theory and practice.* Baltimore: Brookes.

Santelli, B. (1999). *Developing/expanding a statewide parent to parent program.* Lawrence, KS: Beach Center on Families and Disability.

Santelli, B., Singer, G. H. S., DiVenere, N., Ginsberg, C., & Powers, L. (1998). Participatory action research: Reflections on critical incidents in a PAR project. *Journal of the Association for Persons with Severe Handicaps, 23*(3), 211–222.

Santelli, B., Turnbull, A. P., Lerner, E., & Marquis, J. G. (1993). Parent to parent programs: A unique form of mutual support for families of persons with disabilities. In G. H. S. Singer & L. E. Powers (Eds.), *Families, disability, and empowerment* (pp. 27–66). Baltimore: Brookes.

Santelli, B., Turnbull, A. P., Marquis, J. G., & Lerner, E. (1993). Parent-to-parent programs: Ongoing support for parents of young adults with special needs. *Journal of Vocational Rehabilitation, 3*(2), 25–37.

Santelli, B., Turnbull, A. P., Marquis, J. G., & Lerner, E. P. (1995). Parent to parent programs: A unique form of mutual support. *Infants and Young Children, 8*(2), 48–57.

Santelli, B., Turnbull, A., Marquis, J., & Lerner, E. (1997). Parent to Parent programs: A resource for parents and professionals. *Journal of Early Intervention, 21*(1), 73–83.

Santelli, B., Turnbull, A., Sergeant, J., Lerner, E., & Marquis, J. (1996). Parent to parent programs: Parent preferences for support. *Infants and Young Children, 9*(1), 53–62.

Sarason, B. R., Sarason, I. G., & Pierce, G. R. (Eds.). (1990). *Social support.* New York: Wiley-Interscience Publication.

Satir, V. (1972). *Peoplemaking.* Palo Alto, CA: Science and Behavior Books.

Sattler, J. M. (1988). *Assessment of children.* San Diego: Author.

Sawyer, V., Nelson, J. S., Jayanthi, M., Bursuck, W. D., & Epstein, M. H. (1996, Spring). Views of students with learning disabilities of their homework in general education classes: Student interviews. *Learning Disability Quarterly, 19,* 70–84.

Schaffner, C. B., & Buswell, B. E. (1992). *Connecting students: A guide to thoughtful friendship facilitation for educators and families.* Colorado Springs: PEAK Parent Center.

Scheerenberger, R. C. (1983). A history of mental retardation. Baltimore: Brookes.

Schilling, R. F., Schinke, S. P., Blythe, B. J., & Barth, R. P. (1982). Child maltreatment and mentally retarded parents: Is there a relationship? *Mental Retardation, 20*(5), 201–209.

Schinke, S. P., Schilling, R. F., Kirkham, M. A., Gilchrist, L. D., Barth, R. P., & Blythe, B. (1986). Stress management skills for parents. *Journal of Child and Adolescent Psychotherapy, 3*(4), 293–298.

Schleien, S. J., Green, F. P., & Heyne, L. A. (1993). Integrated community recreation. In M. E. Snell (Ed.), *Instruction of students with severe disabilities* (4th ed., pp. 526–555). Englewood Cliffs, NJ: Merrill/Prentice-Hall.

Schleien, S. J., & Heyne, L. (1998, March/April). Can I play too? Choosing a community recreation program. *Tuesday's Child Magazine,* 10–11.

Schlosser, G. A., & Yewchuk, C. R. (1998). Growing up feeling special: Retrospective reflections of eminent Canadian women. *Roeper Review, 21*(2), 125–132.

Schoenwald, S. K., Borduin, C. M., & Henggeler, S. W. (1998). Multisystematic therapy: Changing the natural and service ecologies of adolescents and families. In M. H. Epstein, K. Kutash, & A. Duchnowski (Eds.), *Outcomes for children and youth with emotional and behavioral disorders and their families* (pp. 485–511). Austin, TX: Pro-ed.

Schofield, R. (1998). Empowerment education for individuals with serious mental illness. *Journal of Psychosocial Nursing, 36*(11), 35–40.

Schorr, L. B. (1997). *Common purpose.* New York: Anchor Books Doubleday.

Schorr, L. B., & Schorr, D. (1988). *Within our reach: Breaking the cycle of disadvantage.* New York: Doubleday.

Schradle, S. B., & Dougher, M. J. (1985). Social support as a mediator of stress: Theoretical and empirical issues. *Clinical Psychology Review, 5,* 641–661.

Schumaker, J. B., & Deshler, D. D. (1987). Implementing the regular education initiative in secondary schools. *Journal of Learning Disabilities, 21*(1), 36–42.

Schweitzer, R. D., Hier, S. J., & Terry, D. (1994). Parental bonding, family systems, and environmental predictors of adolescent homelessness. *Journal of Emotional and Behavioral Disorders, 2*(1), 39–45.

Scorgie, K., Wilgosh, L., & McDonald, L. (1996). A quantitative study of managing life when a child has a disability. *Developmental Disabilities Bulletin, 24*(2), 68–90.

Scorgie, K., Wilgosh, L., & McDonald, L. (1998). Stress and coping in families of children with disabilities: An examination of recent literature. *Developmental Disabilities Bulletin, 26*(1), 22–42.

Scorgie, K., Wilgosh, L., & McDonald, L. (1999). Transforming partnerships: Parent life management issues when a child has mental retardation. *Education and training in mental retardation and developmental disabilities, 34*(4), 395–405.

Scott, B. S., Atkinson, L., Minton, H. L., & Bowman, T. (1997). Psychological distress of parents of infants with Down syndrome. *American Journal on Mental Retardation, 102*(2), 161–171.

Scotti, J. R., Nangle, D. W., Masia, C. L., Ellis, J. T., Ujcich, K. J., Giacoletti, A. M., Vittimberga, G. L., & Carr, R. (1997). Providing an AIDS education and skills training program to persons with mild developmental disabilities. *Education and Training in Mental Retardation and Developmental Disabilities, 32*(2), 113–128.

Scotti, J. R., Speaks, L. V., Masia, C. L., Boggess, J. T., & Drabman, R. (1996). The educational effects of providing AIDS-risk information to persons with developmental disabilities: An exploratory study. *Education and Training in Mental Retardation and Developmental Disabilities, 31,* 115–122.

Scott-Jones, N. (1993). Families as educators in a pluralistic society. In N. F. Chavkin (Ed.), *Families and schools in a pluralistic society* (pp. 245–254). Albany: State University of New York Press.

Schwartz, D. B. (1997). *Who cares?* Boulder, CO: Westview Press.

Seagull, E. A., & Scheurer, S. L. (1986). Neglected and abused children of mentally retarded parents. *Child Abuse and Neglect, 10,* 493–500.

Searcy, S., Lee-Lawson, C., Trombino, B. (1995). Mentoring new leadership roles for parents of children with disabilities. *Remedial and Special Education, 16*(5), 307–314.

Sedlak, A. J., & Broadhurst, D. D. (1996). *The third national incidence study of child abuse and neglect.* Washington, DC: U.S. Department of Health and Human Services, Administration for Children, Youth, and Families.

Seligman, J. (1992, December 14). It's not like Mr. Mom. *Newsweek, 120*(24), 70–73.

Seligman, M. (1985). Handicapped children and their families. *Journal of Counseling and Development, 64,* 274–277.

Seligman, M. E. P. (1990). *Learned optimism: How to change your mind and your life.* New York: Pocket Books.

Seligman, M., & Darling, R. B. (1997). *Ordinary families, special children* (2nd ed.). New York: The Guilford Press.

Seligman, M., Goodwin, G., Paschal, K., Applegate, A., & Lehman, L. (1997). Grandparents of children with disabilities: Perceived levels of support. *Education and Training in Mental Retardation and Developmental Disabilities,* 293–303.

Seltzer, M. M., Greenberg, J. S., Krauss, M., Gordon, R. M., & Judge, K. (1997). Siblings of adults with mental retardation or mental illness: Effects on lifestyle and psychological well-being. *Family Relations, 46*(4), 395–405.

Seltzer, M. M., & Krauss, M. W. (1989). Aging parents with adult mentally retarded children: Family risk factors and sources of support. *American Journal of Mental Retardation, 94*(3), 303–312.

Seltzer, M. M., Krauss, M. W., & Janicki, M. P. (Eds.). (1994). *Life course perspectives on adulthood and old age.* Washington, DC: American Association on Mental Retardation.

Senge, P. M. (1990). *The fifth discipline: The art and practice of the learning organization.* New York: Doubleday.

Sen. Rep. 103-85, 103rd Cong., 1st Sess.

Sexton, D., Miller, J. H., & Rotatori, A. F. (1985). Determinants of professional-parental agreement for the development status of young handicapped children. *Journal of Psychoeducational Assessment, 3,* 377–390.

Sexton, D., Snyder, P., Rheams, T., Barron-Sharp, B., & Perez, J. (1991). Considerations in using written surveys to identify family strengths and needs during the IFSP process. *Topics in Early Childhood Special Education, 11*(3), 81–91.

Sexton, D., Thompson, B., Perez, J., & Rheams, T. (1990). Maternal versus professional estimates of developmental status of young children with handicaps: An ecological approach. *Topics in Early Childhood Special Education, 10*(3), 80–95.

Shafer, M. S., & Rangasamy, R. (1995). Transition and Native American youth: A follow-up study of school leavers on the Fort Apache Indian reservation. *Journal of Rehabilitation,* 60–65.

Shank, M. S., & Turnbull, A. P. (1993). Cooperative family problem solving: An intervention for single-parent families of children with disabilities. In G. H. S. Singer & L. E. Powers (Eds.), *Families, disability, and empowerment: Active coping skills and strategies for family interventions* (pp. 231–254). Baltimore: Brookes.

Shapiro, J., Blacher, J., & Lopez, S. R. (1998). Maternal reactions to children with mental retardation. In J. A. Burack, R. M. Hodapp, & E. Zigler (Eds.), *Handbook of mental retardation and development* (pp. 606–636). Cambridge, MA: Cambridge University Press.

Shapiro, J., & Simonsen, D. (1994). Educational/support group for Latino families of children with Down syndrome. *Mental Retardation, 32*(6), 403–415.

Sharifzadeh, V. S. (1992). Families with Middle Eastern roots. In E. W. Lynch & M. J. Hanson (Eds.), *Developing cross-cultural competence: A guide for working with young children and their families* (pp. 319–354). Baltimore: Brookes.

Shaw, J., Hammer, D., & Leland, H. (1991). Adaptive behavior of preschool children with developmental delays: Parent versus teacher ratings. *Mental Retardation, 29,* 49–53.

Shaw, L. (1998). Children's experiences of school. In C. Robinson & K. Stalker (Eds.), *Growing up with disability*. Philadelphia: Jessica Kingsley Publishers.

Shea, V. (1984). Explaining mental retardation and autism to parents. In E. Schopler & G. Mesibov (Eds.), *The effects of autism on the family* (pp. 265–288). New York: Plenum.

Shearer, M. S., & Shearer, D. E. (1977). Parent involvement. In J. B. Jordan, A. H. Hayden, M. B. Karnes, & M. M. Wood (Eds.), *Early childhood education for exceptional children* (pp. 208–235). Reston, VA: Council for Exceptional Children.

Sheffield, B. E. (1994). Watts/Jordan school-based health clinic: Promoting health and preventing violence in Los Angeles. *Family Resource Coalition Report, 13*(1 & 2), 12.

Shellady, S., Hendrickson, J., Reisen, Y., Samson, D., & Vance, P. (1994). *Stakeholder perceptions of the IEP process in Iowa—Study 2.* Des Moines: Iowa Department of Education, Bureau of Special Education and Mountain Plains Regional Resource Center.

Shelton, T. L., Jeppson, E. S., & Johnson, B. H. (1989). *Family-centered care for children with special health care needs.* Washington, DC: Association for the Care of Children's Health.

Shepheard, J. (1998). Learning disability: Empowerment. *Nursing Standard, 14*(12), 49–55.

Sherman, A. (1997). *Poverty matters.* Washington, DC: Children's Defense Fund.

Sherman, A., Amey, C., Duffield, B., Ebb, N., & Weinstein, D. (1998). *Early findings on family hardship and well-being.* Washington, DC: Children's Defense Fund.

Sherwood, S. K. (1990). A circle of friends in a 1st grade classroom. *Educational Leadership, 48*(3), 41.

Short, R. J., & Talley, R. C. (1996). Effects of teacher assistance teams on special education referrals in elementary schools. *Psychological Reports, 79,* 1,431–1,438.

Shriver, M. D., & Piersel, W. (1994). The long-term effects of intrauterine drug exposure: Review of recent research and implications for early childhood special education. *Topics in Early Childhood Special Education, 14*(2), 161–183.

Shumway, D. L. (1999). Freedom, support, authority, and responsibility: The Robert Wood Johnson Foundation national program on self-determination. *Focus on Autism and other Developmental Disabilities, 14*(1), 28–35.

Sidel, R. (1996). *Keeping women and children last.* New York: Penguin Books.

Sikora, D. M., & Plapinger, D. S. (1997). The role of informal parent and teacher assessment in diagnosing learning disabilities. *The Volta Review, 99*(1), 19–29.

Sileo, T., & Prater, M. A. (1998, November–December). Creating classroom environments that assess the linguistic and cultural backgrounds of students with disabilities: An Asian-Pacific-American experience. *Remedial and Special Education, 19*(6), 323–327.

Silver, J. A., Amster, B. J., & Haecker, T. (Eds.). (1999). *Young children and foster care.* Baltimore: Paul H. Brookes.

Simon, J. P. (1996). Lebanese families. In M. McGoldrick, J. Giordano, & J. K. Pearce (Eds.), *Ethnicity and family therapy* (2nd ed., pp. 364–375). New York: The Guilford Press.

Simpson, R. L., & Myles, B. S. (1989). Parents' mainstreaming modification preferences for children with educable mental handicaps, be-

havior disorders, and learning disabilities. *Psychology in the Schools, 26,* 292–301.

Sindelar, P. T., Griffin, C. C., Smith, S. W., & Watanabe, A. K. (1992). Prereferral intervention: Encouraging notes on preliminary findings. *Elementary School Journal, 92*(3), 245–259.

Singer, G. H. S., Glang, A., & Williams, J. (Eds.). (1996). *Children with acquired brain injury: Educating and supporting families.* Baltimore: Brookes.

Singer, G. H. S., Marquis, J., Powers, L., Blanchard, L., DiVenere, N., Santelli, B., & Sharp, M. (1999). A multi-site evaluation of Parent to Parent programs for parents of children with disabilities. *Journal of Early Intervention, 22*(3), 217–219.

Singer, G. H. S., & Nixon, C. (1996). A report on the concerns of parents of children with acquired brain injury. In G. H. S. Singer, A. Glang, & J. Williams (Eds.), *Children with acquired brain injury: Educating and supporting families* (pp. 23–52). Baltimore: Brookes.

Singer, G. H. S., Powers, L. E., & Olson, A. (1996). *Redefining family support: Innovations in public/private partnerships.* Baltimore: Brookes.

Singh, N. N., Curtis, W. J., Ellis, C. R., Wechsler, H. A., Best, A. M., & Cohen, R. (1997). Empowerment status of families whose children have serious emotional disturbance and attention-deficit/hyperactivity disorder. *Journal of Emotional and Behavioral Disorders, 5*(4), 223–229.

Sipes, D. S. B. (1993). Cultural values and American Indian families. In N. F. Chavkin (Ed.), *Families and schools in a pluralistic society* (pp. 157–174). Albany: State University of New York Press.

Sisco, C. B., & Pearson, C. L. (1994). Prevalence of alcoholism and drug abuse among female AFDC recipients. *Health and Social Work, 19*(1), 75–77.

Sitlington, P., & Frank, A. (1990). Are adolescents with learning disabilities successfully crossing the bridge to adult life? *Learning Disability Quarterly, 13,* 97–111.

Skrtic, T. M. (1991). *Behind special education: A critical analysis of professional culture and school organization.* Denver, CO: Love.

Skrtic, T. M. (Ed.). (1995). *Disability and democracy.* New York: Teachers College Press.

Skrtic, T. M., & Sailor, W. (1996). School-linked services integration. *Remedial and Special Education, 17*(5), 271–283.

Smith, G., Prouty, R., & Lakin, K. C. (1996). The HCB waiver program: The fading of Medicaid's "institutional bias." *Mental Retardation, 34,* 262–263.

Smith, M. J., & Ryan, A. S. (1987). Chinese-American families of children with developmental disabilities: An exploratory study of reactions to service providers. *Mental Retardation, 25*(6), 345–350.

Smith, M. S., & Scoll, B. W. (1995). The Clinton human capital agenda. *Teachers College Record, 96*(3), 389–404.

Smith, P. M. (1993). Opening many, many doors: Parent-to-parent support. In P. J. Beckman & G. B. Boyes (Eds.), *Deciphering the system: A guide for families of young children with disabilities* (pp. 129–142). Cambridge, MA: Brookline.

Smith, S. W. (1990, September). Individualized Education Programs (IEPs) in special education—From intent to acquiescence. *Exceptional Children, 57*(1), 6–14.

Smith, S. W., & Brownell, M. T. (1995). Individualized education program: Considering the broad context of reform. *Focus on Exceptional Children, 28*(1), 1–12.

Smith, S. W., & Simpson, R. L. (1989). An analysis of Individualized Education Programs (IEPs) of students with behavioral disorders. *Behavioral Disorders, 14,* 107–116.

Smith-Horn, B., & Singer, G. H. S. (1996). Self-esteem and learning disabilities: An exploration of theories of the self. In L. E. Powers, G. H. S. Singer, & J. A. Sowers (Eds.), *On the road to autonomy: Promoting self-competence in children and youth with disabilities* (pp. 135–154). Baltimore: Brookes.

Smrekar, C. E. (1993). Rethinking family-school interactions: A prologue to linking schools and social services. *Education and Urban Society, 25*(2), 175–186.

Smull, M. W., & Harrison, S. B. (1992). *Supporting people with severe retardation in the community.* Alexandria, VA: National Association of State Mental Retardation Program Directors.

Snell, M., & Janney, R. (1999). *Collaborative teaming.* Baltimore: Brookes.

Snowden, P. L., & Christian, L. G. (1999, February/March). Parenting the young gifted child: Supportive behaviors. *Roeper Review,* 215–221.

Snyder, C. R. (1994). *The psychology of hope: You can get there from here.* New York: Free Press/Macmillan.

Snyder, E. P., & Shapiro, E. S. (1997). Teaching students with emotional/behavioral disorders the skills to participate in the development of their own IEPs. *Behavioral Disorders, 22*(4), 246–259.

Snyder, P., Thompson, B., & Sexton, D. (1993). *Congruence in maternal and professional early intervention assessments of young children with disabilities.* Distinguished paper presented at the annual meeting of the American Educational Research Association, Atlanta, GA.

Sobsey, D. (1994). *Violence and abuse in the lives of people with disabilities.* Baltimore: Brookes.

Sobsey, D., Randall, W., & Parrila, R. K. (1997). Gender differences in abused children with and without disabilities. *Child Abuse and Neglect, 21*(8), 707–720.

Soderlund, J., Bursuck, B., Polloway, E. A., & Foley, R. (1995). A comparison of the homework problems of secondary school students with behavior disorders and nondisabled peers. *Journal of Emotional and Behavioral Disorders, 3*(3), 150–155.

Solis, M. L., & Abidin, R. R. (1991). The Spanish version parenting stress index: A psychometric study. *Journal of Clinical Child Psychology, 20*(4), 372–378.

Sontag, J. C., & Schacht, R. (1994). An ethnic comparison of parent participation and information needs in early intervention. *Exceptional Children, 60*(5), 422–433.

Southern, W. T., & Jones, E. (1991). *The academic acceleration of gifted children.* New York: Teachers College Press.

Spaulding, B. R., & Morgan, S. B. (1986). Spina bifida children and their parents: A population prone to family dysfunction? *Journal of Pediatric Psychology, 11,* 359–374.

Spinelli, C. G. (1999). Home-school collaboration at the early childhood level: Making it work. *Young Exceptional Children, 2,* 20–26.

Spradley, T. S., & Spradley, J. P. (1978). *Deaf like me.* New York: Random House.

Stainton, T., & Besser, H. (1998). The positive impact of children with an intellectual disability on the family. *Journal of Intellectual and Developmental Disability, 23*(1), 57–70.

Stallings, G., & Cook, S. (1997). *Another season* (1st ed.). Boston: Little, Brown Company.

Stanford Research Institute (SRI) International. (1990). *National longitudinal transition study of special education students.* Menlo Park, CA: Author.

Staton, J., Shuy, R. W., Peyton, J. K., & Reed, L. (1988). *Dialogue journal communication: Classroom, linguistic, social, and cognitive views.* Norwood, NJ: Ablex.

Stayton, V. D., & Karnes, M. B. (1994). Model programs for infants and toddlers with disabilities and their families. In L. J. Johnson, R. J. Gallagher, M. J. LaMontagne, J. B. Jordan, J. J. Gallagher, P. L. Hutinger, & M. B. Karnes (Eds.), *Meeting early intervention challenges: Issues from birth to three* (pp. 33–58). Baltimore: Brookes.

Steno, S. M. (1990). The elusive continuum of child welfare services: Implication for minority children and youths. *Child Welfare, 69,* 551–562.

Stephens, T. M., & Wolf, J. S. (1980). *Effective skills in parent/teacher conferencing.* Columbus: Ohio State University, National Center for Educational Materials and Media for the Handicapped.

Stephenson, J. (1992). The perspectives of mothers whose children are in special day classes for learning disabilities. *Journal of Learning Disabilities, 25*(8), 539–543.

Stevens-Simon, C., & Beach, R. K. (1992). School-based prenatal and postpartum care: Strategies for meeting the medical and educational needs of pregnant and parenting students. *Journal of School Health, 62,* 304–309.

Stoddard, K., Valcante, G., Roemer, F., & O'Shea, D. J. (1994). Preparing teachers for family support roles. *Learning Disabilities Forum, 19*(2), 33–35.

Stokes-Szanton, E. (1991). Services for children with special needs: Partnerships from the beginning between parents and practitioners. In D. G. Unger & D. R. Powell (Eds.), *Families as nurturing systems: Support across the life span* (pp. 87–97). New York: The Haworth Press.

Stoller, E. P. (1994). Teaching about gender: The experiences of family care of frail elderly relatives. *Educational Gerontology, 20,* 679–697.

Stoneman, Z. (1998). Research on siblings of children with mental retardation: Contributions of developmental theory and etiology. In J. A. Burack, R. M. Hodapp, & E. Zigler (Eds.), *Handbook of mental retardation and development* (pp. 669–692). Cambridge: Cambridge University Press.

Stoneman, Z., Brophy, G. H., Davis, C. H., & Crapps, J. M. (1987). Mentally retarded children and their older same-sex siblings: Naturalistic in-home observations. *American Journal on Mental Retardation, 92,* 290–298.

Stoneman, Z., & Waldman-Berman, P. (Eds.). (1993). *The effects of mental retardation, disability, and illness.* Baltimore: Paul H. Brookes.

Stonestreet, R. H., Johnston, R. G., & Acton, S. J. (1991). Guidelines for real partnerships with parents. *Infant-Toddler Intervention, 1*(1), 37–46.

Stormont-Spurgin, M. (1997). I lost my homework: Strategies for improving organization in students with ADHD. *Intervention in School and Clinic, 32*(5), 270–274.

Streissguth, A. P. (1994). Fetal alcohol syndrome: Understanding the problem; understanding the solution; what Indian communities can do. *American Indian Culture and Research Journal, 18*(3), 45–83.

Strickland, B. R. (1995). Research on sexual orientation and human development: A commentary. *Developmental Psychology, 31,* 137–140.

Stronge, J. H., & Tenhouse, C. (1990). *Educating homeless children: Issues and answers.* Bloomington, IN: Phi Delta Kappa Educational Foundation.

Stroul, B., & Friedman, R. (1986). *A system of care for children and youth with severe emotional disturbances* (Rev. ed.). Washington, DC: Georgetown University Child Development Center, National Technical Assistance Center for Children's Mental Health.

Subotnik, R. F. (1999). Talent developed: Conversations with masters in the arts and sciences. *Journal for the Education of the Gifted, 22*(3), 298–311.

Sue, D. W., & Sue, D. (1990). *Counseling the culturally different: Theory and practice* (2nd ed.). New York: John Wiley & Sons.

Sue, D. W., & Sue, D. (1996). *Counseling the culturally different: Theory and practice* (2nd ed). New York: John Wiley & Sons.

Sugai, G., Horner, R. H., Dunlap, G., Hieneman, M., Lewis, T. J., Nelson, C. M., Scott, T., Liaupsin, C., Sailor, W., Turnbull, A. P., Turnbull, H. R., Wickham, D., Ruef, M., & Wilcox, B. (1999). *Applying positive behavioral support and functional behavioral assessment in schools.* Washington, DC: U.S. Department of Education.

Sullivan, T. (1995). *Special parent. Special child.* New York: G. P. Putnam's Sons.

Summers, J. A. (1987a). *Defining successful family life in families with and without children with disabilities: A qualitative study.* Unpublished doctoral dissertation, University of Kansas, Lawrence.

Summers, J. A. (1987b). Family adjustment: Issues in research on families with developmentally disabled children. In V. B. Van Hasselt, P. S. Strain, & M. Hersen (Eds.), *Handbook of developmental disabilities* (pp. 79–90). New York: Pergamon.

Summers, J. A., Behr, S. K., & Turnbull, A. P. (1988). Positive adaptation and coping strengths of families who have children with disabilities. In G. H. S. Singer & L. K. Irvin (Eds.), *Support for caregiving families: Enabling positive adaptation to disability* (pp. 27–40). Baltimore: Brookes.

Summers, J. A., Dell'Oliver, C., Turnbull, A. P., Benson, H. A., Santelli, E., Campbell, M., & Siegel-Causey, E. (1990). Examining the Individualized Family Service Plan process: What are family and practitioner preferences? *Topics in Early Childhood Special Education, 10*(1), 78–99.

Summers, J. A., McMann, O. T., Kitchen, A., & Peck, L. (1995). *A qualitative study to identify best practices in serving families with multiple challenges: Using direct line staff as researchers.* Unpublished manuscript.

Summers, J. A., Templeton-McMann, O., & Fuger, K. L. (1997). Critical thinking: A method to guide staff in serving families with multiple challenges. In J. J. Carta (Ed.), *Topics in early childhood education* (pp. 27–52). Austin, TX: Pro-ed.

Suris, J. C., Resnick, M. D., Cassuto, N., & Blum, R. W. M. (1996). Sexual behavior of adolescents with chronic disease and disability. *Journal of Adolescent Health, 19*(2), 124–131.

Swenson-Pierce, A., Kohl, F. L., & Egel, A. L. (1987). Siblings as home trainers: A strategy for teaching domestic skills to children. *Journal of the Association for Persons with Severe Handicaps, 12*(1), 53–60.

Swick, K. (1988 Fall). Parental efficacy and involvement: Influences on Children. *Childhood Education, 65*(1) 37–42.

Swift, C., & G. Levin. (1987). Empowerment: An emerging mental health technology. *Journal of Primary Prevention, 8*(1 & 2), 71–94.

Switzer, L. S. (1985). Accepting the diagnosis: An educational intervention for parents of children with learning disabilities. *Journal of Learning Disabilities, 18*(3), 151–153.

Taanila, A., Järvelin, M. R., & Kokkonen, J. (1999). Cohesion and parents' social relations in families with a child with disability or chronic illness. *International Journal of Rehabilitation Research, 22*(2), 101–109.

Tabors, P. O. (1997). *One child, two languages.* Baltimore: Brookes.

Taner-Leff, P., & Walizer, E. H. (1992). *Building the healing partnership.* Cambridge, MA: Brookline Books.

Tang, C., Lee, A., & Cheung, F. (in press). Violence against women in Hong Kong. In F. M. Cheung (Ed.), *Violence against women in Asia.* Hong Kong: Equal Opportunities Commission.

Tanksley, C. K. (1993). Interactions between mothers and normal-hearing or hearing-impaired children. *Volta Review, 95,* 33–47.

Tannenbaum, A. J. (1986). The enrichment matrix model. In J. S. Renzulli (Ed.), *Systems and models for developing programs for the gifted and talented* (pp. 391–428). Mansfield Center, CT: Creative Learning.

Tartara, T. (1993). *Characteristics of children in substitute and adoptive care, Fiscal Year 1989.* Washington, DC: American Public Welfare Association.

Tavormina, J. B., Boll, T. J., Dunn, N. J., Luscomb, R. L., & Taylor, J. R. (1981). Psychosocial effects on parents of raising a physically handicapped child. *Journal of Abnormal Child Psychology, 9,* 121–131.

Taylor, R. J. (1988). Aging and supportive relationships among Black Americans. In J. Jackson (Ed.), *The Black American elderly: Research on physical and psychosocial health* (pp. 259–281). New York: Springer-Verlag.

Taylor, R. L., Richards, S. B., Goldstein, P. A., & Schilit, J. (1997). Teacher perspectives of inclusive settings. *The Council for Exceptional Children, 50*–54.

Taylor, S. E. (1989). *Positive illusions: Creative self-deception and the healthy mind.* New York: Basic Books.

Taylor, S. J., Knoll, J. A., Lehr, S., & Walker, P. M. (1989). Families for all children: Value-based services for children with disabilities and their families. In G. H. S. Singer & L. K. Irvin (Eds.), *Support for caregiving families: Enabling positive adaptation to disability* (pp. 27–40). Baltimore: Brookes.

Taylor-Greene, S. Brown, D., Nelson, L., Longton, J., Gassman, T., Cohen, J., Swartz, J., Horner, R. H., Sugai, G., & Hall, S. (1997). School-wide behavioral support: Starting the year off right. *Journal of Behavioral Education, 7,* 99–112.

Teglasi, H. (1985). Best practices in interpreting psychological assessment data to parents. In A. Thomas & J. Grimes (Eds.), *Best practices in school psychology* (pp. 415–430). Kent, OH: National Association of School Psychologists.

Terkelson, K. G. (1980). Toward a theory of family life cycle. In E. Carter & M. McGoldrick (Eds.), *The family life cycle: A framework of family therapy* (pp. 21–52). New York: Gardner.

Terman, L. (1916). *The measurement of intelligence.* Cambridge, MA: Riverside.

Tew, B. J., Payne, E. H., & Lawrence, K. M. (1974). Must a family with a handicapped child be a handicapped family? *Developmental Medicine and Child Neurology, 18* (Suppl. 32), 95–98.

Thomas, C. J. (1905). Congenital "word-blindness" and its treatment. *Ophthalmoscope, 3,* 380–385.

Thompson, L., Lobb, C., Elling, R., Herman, S., Jurkiewicz, T., & Hulleza, C. (1997). Pathways to family empowerment: Effects of family-centered delivery of early intervention services. *Exceptional Children, 64*(1), 99–113.

Thousand, J. S., Villa, R. A., & Nevin, A. I. (1994). *Creativity and collaborative learning: A practical guide to empowering students and teachers.* Baltimore: Brookes.

Thurlow, M. L., Ysseldyke, J. E., & Reid, C. L. (1997). High school graduation requirements for students with disabilities. *Journal of Learning Disabilities, 30*(6), 608–616.

Thurston, L. P. (1996). Support systems for rural families: Rationale, strategies, and examples. *Human Services in the Rural Environment, 20*(1), 19–26.

Tilley, C. M. (1996). Sexuality in women with physical disabilities: A social justice. *Sexuality and Disability, 14*(2), 139–151.

Timm, M. A. (1993). The regional intervention program: Family treatment by family members. *Behavioral Disorders, 19*(1), 34–43.

Timmons, J. C., & Whitney-Thomas, J. (1998). The most important member: Facilitating the focus person's participation in person centered planning. *Institute for Community Inclusion: Research to Practice, 4*(1), 1–4.

Todd, A. W., Horner, R. H., Sugai, G., & Sprague, J. R. (1999). Effective behavior support: Strengthening school-wide systems through a team based approach. *Effective School Practices, 17*(4), 23–37.

Todis, B., & Singer, G. (1991). Stress and stress management in families with adopted children who have severe disabilities. *Journal of the Association for Persons with Severe Handicaps, 16*(1), 3–13.

Todis, B., Irvin, L. K., Singer, G. H. S., & Yovanoff, P. (1993). The self-esteem parent program: Quantitative and qualitative evaluation of a cognitive-behavioral intervention. In G. H. S. Singer & L. K. Irvin (Eds.), *Support for caregiving families: Enabling positive adaptation to disability* (pp. 203–229). Baltimore: Brookes.

Traustadottir, R. (1991). Mothers who care: Gender, disability, and family life. *Journal of Family Issues, 12*(2), 211–228.

Traustadottir, R. (1995). A mother's work is never done: Constructing a "normal" life. In S. J. Taylor, R. Bogdan, & Z. M. Lutfiyya (Eds.), *The variety of community experience: Qualitative studies of family and community life* (pp. 47–65). Baltimore: Brookes.

Travers, K. D. (1997). Reducing inequalities through participatory research and community empowerment. *Health Education and Behavior, 24*(3), 344–356.

Trute, B., & Hauch, C. (1988). Building on family strength: A study of families with positive adjustment to the birth of a developmentally disabled child. *Journal of Marital and Family Therapy, 14*(2), 185–193.

Tucker, B. P. (1997). The dad and deaf culture: Contrasting precepts, conflicting results. *Annals of the American Academy of Political and Social Science, 549*, 24–36.

Tuma, J. M. (1989). Mental health services for children: The state of the art. *American Psychologist, 44*(2), 188–199.

Turbiville, V. P. (1994). *Fathers, their children, and disability.* Unpublished doctoral dissertation, University of Kansas, Lawrence.

Turbiville, V. P. (1995). *Parent handbook for individualized family service plans.* Lawrence: University of Kansas, Beach Center on Families and Disability.

Turbiville, V. P., Lee, I. M., Turnbull, A. P., & Murphy, D. L. (1993). *Handbook for the development of a family-friendly IFSP* (2nd ed.). Lawrence: University of Kansas, Beach Center on Families and Disability.

Turbiville, V. P., Turnbull, A. P., Garland, C. W., & Lee, I. M. (1996). Development and implementation of IFSPs and IEPs: Opportunities for empowerment. In S. L. Odom & M. E. McLean (Eds.), *Early intervention/early childhood special education: Recommended practices* (pp. 77–100). Austin, TX: Pro-Ed.

Turbiville, V. P., Turnbull, A. P., & Turnbull, H. R. (1995). Fathers and family-centered early intervention. *Infants & Young Children, 7*(4), 12–19.

Turbiville, V., Umbarger, G., & Guthrie, A. (1998). *Participation by fathers of children with and without disabilities in early childhood programs.* Unpublished manuscript, The University of Kansas at

Lawrence, Beach Center on Families and Disability.

Turnbull, A. P. (1988, December). The challenge of providing comprehensive support to families. *Education and Training in Mental Retardation, 23*(4), 261–272.

Turnbull, A. P. (1993). *My Best Teacher.*

Turnbull, A. P. (1993, December). *Belonging: A dimension of human development.* Paper presented at Zero to Three Eighth Biennial National Training Institute, Washington, DC.

Turnbull, A. P. (1994). [Unpublished raw data.] Lawrence: University of Kansas, Beach Center on Families and Disability.

Turnbull, A. P., Blue-Banning, M. J., Anderson, E. L., Turnbull, H. R., Seaton, K. A., & Dinas, P. A. (1996). Enhancing self-determination through Group Action Planning: A holistic emphasis. In D. Sands & M. Wehmeyer (Eds.), *Self-determination across the life span: Theory and practice* (pp. 237–256). Baltimore: Brookes.

Turnbull, A. P., Blue-Banning, M. J., Behr, S. K., & Kearns, G. (1986). Family research and intervention: A value and ethical examination. In P. R. Dobecki & R. M. Zaner (Eds.), *Ethics of dealing with persons with severe handicaps: Toward a research agenda* (pp. 119–140). Baltimore: Brookes.

Turnbull, A. P., Blue-Banning, M. J., Turbiville, V., & Park, J. (1999). From parent education to partnership education: A call for a transformed focus. *Topics in Early Childhood Special Education, 19*(2), 164–171.

Turnbull, A. P., Brotherson, M. J., & Summers, J. A. (1985). The impact of deinstitutionalization on families: A family systems approach. In R. H. Bruininks (Ed.), *Living and learning in the least restrictive environment* (pp. 115–152). Baltimore: Brookes.

Turnbull, A. P., & Bronicki, G. J. (1986). Changing second graders' attitudes toward people with mental retardation: Using kid power. *Mental Retardation, 24*(1), 44–45.

Turnbull, A. P., Friesen, B. J., & Ramirez, C. (1998). Participatory action research as a model for conducting family research. *Association for Persons with Severe Handicaps, 23*(3), 178–188.

Turnbull, A. P., Guess, D., Turnbull, H. R. (1988). Implications of biobehavioral states for the education and treatment of students with the most profoundly handicapping conditions. *Journal of the Association for Persons with Severe Handicaps, 13*(3), 163–174.

Turnbull, A. P., Patterson, J. M., Behr, S. K., Murphy, D. L., Marquis, J. G., & Blue-Banning, M. J. (Eds.). (1993). *Cognitive, coping, families, and disability.* Baltimore: Brookes.

Turnbull, A. P., Patterson, J. M., Behr, S. K., Murphy, D. L., Marquis, J. G., & Blue-Banning, M. J. (1993). *Cognitive coping, families, and disability.* Baltimore: Brookes.

Turnbull, A. P., Pereira, L., & Blue-Banning, M. (1999 Summer). Teachers as friendship facilitators. *Teaching Exceptional Children, 24*(2), 85–99.

Turnbull, A. P., Pereira, L., & Blue-Banning, M. (1999). Parents' facilitation of friendships between their children with a disability and friends without a disability. *Journal of the Association for Persons with Severe Handicaps, 24*(2), 85–99.

Turnbull, A. P., & Ruef, M. (1996). Family perspectives on problem behavior. *Mental Retardation, 34*(5), 280–293.

Turnbull, A. P., & Ruef, M. (1997). Family perspectives on inclusive lifestyle issues for people with problem behavior. *Exceptional Children, 63*(2), 211–227.

Turnbull, A. P., & Ruef, M. (in press-a). Family perspectives on problem behavior. *Mental Retardation.*

Turnbull, A. P., & Ruef, M. (in press-b). Family perspectives on inclusive lifestyle issues for individuals with problem behavior. *Exceptional Children.*

Turnbull, A. P., Ruef, M., & Reeves, C. (1995). *Family perspectives on inclusive lifestyle issues for individuals with problem behavior.*

Lawrence: University of Kansas, Beach Center on Families and Disability/The Family Connection.

Turnbull, A. P., Strickland, B., & Hammer, S. E. (1978). The Individualized Education Program. Part 1: Procedural guidelines. *Journal of Learning Disabilities, 11,* 40–46.

Turnbull, A. P., & Summers, J. A. (1987). From parent involvement to family support: Evolution to revolution. In S. M. Pueschel, C. Tingey, J. W. Rynders, A. C. Crocker, & D. M. Crutcher (Eds.), *New perspectives on Down syndrome* (pp. 289–306). Baltimore: Brookes.

Turnbull, A. P., Summers, J. A., & Brotherson, M. J. (1984). *Working with families with disabled members: A family systems approach.* Lawrence: University of Kansas, Kansas University Affiliated Facility.

Turnbull, A. P., Summers, J. A., & Brotherson, M. J. (1986). Family life cycle: Theoretical and empirical implications and future directions for families with mentally retarded members. In J. J. Gallagher & P. M. Vietze (Eds.), *Families of handicapped persons: Research, programs, and policy issues* (pp. 25–44). Baltimore: Brookes.

Turnbull, A. P., & Turbiville, V. P. (1995). Why must inclusion be such a challenge? *Journal of Early Intervention, 19*(3), 200–202.

Turnbull, A. P., Turbiville, V., Schaffer, R., & Schaffer, V. (1996, June/July). "Getting a shot at life" through group action planning. *Zero to Three,* 33–40.

Turnbull, A. P., Turbiville, V., & Turnbull, H. R. (in press). Evolution of family-professional partnership models: Collective empowerment as the model for the early 21st century. In J. P. Shonkoff & S. L. Meisels (Eds.), *The handbook of early childhood intervention* (2nd ed.). New York: Cambridge University Press.

Turnbull, A. P., Turbiville, V., Turnbull, H. R., & Gabbard, G. (1993, September). *Fathers' roles in intervention programs for children at special risks: Disabled, chronically ill, and children living in poverty.* Paper presented at the National Research Council, National Academy of Sciences, Washington, DC.

Turnbull, A. P., & Turnbull, H. R. (in press). Comprehensive lifestyle support for adults with challenging behavior: From rhetoric to rality. In J. Lucyshyn, G. Dunlap, & R. Albin, (Eds.) *Families and positive behavioral support: Addressing the challenge of problem behaviors in family contexts.* Baltimore, MD: Brookes.

Turnbull, A. P., & Turnbull, H. R. (1982). Assumptions concerning parent involvement: A legislative history. *Educational Evaluation and Policy Analysis, 4*(3), 281–291.

Turnbull, A. P., & Turnbull, H. R. (1985a). Developing independence. *Journal of Adolescent Health Care, 6*(2), 108–119.

Turnbull, A. P., & Turnbull, H. R. (1986). Stepping back from early intervention: An ethical perspective. *Journal of the Division for Early Childhood, 10,* 106–117.

Turnbull, A. P., & Turnbull, H. R. (1988). Toward great expectations for vocational opportunities: Family-professional partnerships. *Mental Retardation, 26*(6), 337–342.

Turnbull, A. P., & Turnbull, H. R. (1993). Enhancing beneficial linkages across the life span. *Disabilities Studies Quarterly, 13*(4), 34–36.

Turnbull, A. P., & Turnbull, H. R. (1996a). Group action planning as a strategy for providing comprehensive family support. In L. K. Koegel, R. L. Koegel, & G. Dunlap (Eds.), *Community, school, family, and social inclusion through positive behavioral support* (pp. 99–114). Baltimore: Brookes.

Turnbull, A. P., & Turnbull, H. R. (1996b). Self-determination within a culturally responsive family systems perspective. In L. E. Powers, G. H. S. Singer, & J. Powers (Eds.), *On the road to autonomy: Promoting self-competence among children and youth with disabilities* (pp. 195–220). Baltimore: Brookes.

Turnbull, A. P., & Turnbull, H. R. (1996c). The synchrony of stakeholders. In S. L. Kagan & N. E. Cohen (Eds.), *Reinventing early care and education* (pp. 290–305). San Francisco: Jossey-Bass.

Turnbull, A. P., & Turnbull, H. R. (1999, October). *Self-determination: Focus on the role of families in supporting individuals with significant cognitive disabilities.* Paper presented at the National Leadership Summit on Self-Determination, Bethesda, MD.

Turnbull, A. P., & Turnbull, H. R. (in press). Comprehensive lifestyle support: From rhetoric to reality. In J. Lucyshyn, G. Dunlap, & R. Albin (Eds.), *Families and positive behavioral support: Addressing the challenges of problem behaviors in family contexts.* Baltimore: Brookes.

Turnbull, A. P., Turnbull, H. R., & Blue-Banning, M. J. (1994). Enhancing inclusion of infants and toddlers with disabilities and their families: A theoretical and programmatic analysis. *Infants and Young Children, 72*(2), 1–14.

Turnbull, A. P., Turnbull, H. R., Shank, M., & Leal, D. (1995). *Exceptional lives: Special education in today's schools.* Englewood Cliffs, NJ: Merrill/Prentice-Hall.

Turnbull, A. P., Turnbull, H. R., Shank, M., & Leal, D. (1999). *Exceptional lives: Special education in today's schools* (2nd ed.). Englewood Cliffs, NJ: Merrill/Prentice-Hall.

Turnbull, H. R., Buchele-Ash, A., & Mitchell, L. (1994). *Abuse and neglect of children with disabilities: A policy analysis prepared for the National Symposium on Abuse and Neglect of Children with Disabilities.* Lawrence: University of Kansas, Beach Center on Families and Disability.

Turnbull, H. R., Garlow, J. A., & Barber, P. A. (1991). A policy analysis of family support for families with members with disabilities. *Kansas Law Review, 39*(3), 739–782.

Turnbull, H. R., Guess, D., & Turnbull, A. P. (1988). Vox populi and Baby Doe. *Mental Retardation, 26*(3), 127–132.

Turnbull, H. R., & Turnbull, A. P. (1985b). *Parents speak out: Then and now* (2nd ed.). Englewood

Cliffs, NJ: Merrill/Prentice-Hall.

Turnbull, H. R., & Turnbull, A. P. (2000). *Free appropriate public education: The law and children with disabilities* (6th ed.). Denver: Love.

Turnbull, H. R., Turnbull, A. P., & Wheat, M. (1982). Assumptions about parental participation: A legislative history. *Exceptional Education Quarterly, 3*(2), 1–8.

Turnbull, A. P., Winton, P. J., Blacher, J. B., & Salkind, N. (1983). Mainstreaming in the kindergarten classroom: Perspectives of parents of handicapped and nonhandicapped children. *Journal of the Division of Early Childhood, 6,* 14–20.

Turnbull, A. P., & Winton, P. J. (1984). Parent involvement policy and practice: Current research and implications for families of young severely handicapped children. In J. Blacher (Ed.), *Severely handicapped children and their families: Research in review* (pp. 377–397). New York: Academic Press.

Turner, L. (1995). Grandparent-caregivers: Their challenges and how to help. *Family Resource Coalition Report, 14*(1 & 2), 6–7.

Tuttle, D. H., & Cornell, D. G. (1993). Maternal labeling of gifted children: Effects on the sibling relationship. *Exceptional Children, 59*(5), 402–410.

Tymchuk, A. J. (1990). Parents with mental retardation: A national strategy. *Journal of Disability Policy Studies, 1*(4), 43–55.

Tymchuk, A. J. (1992). Predicting adequacy of parenting by people with mental retardation. *Child Abuse and Neglect, 16,* 165–178.

Tymchuk, A. J., Andron, L., & Rahbar, B. (1988). Effective decision-making/problem-solving training with mothers who have mental retardation. *American Journal on Mental Retardation, 92*(6), 510–516.

Tymchuk, A. J., Andron, L., & Unger, O. (1987). Parents with mental handicaps and adequate child care—A review. *Mental Handicaps, 15,* 49–54.

Uphoff, J. K. (1999). Religious diversity and education. In J. A. Banks & C. A. McGee-Banks (Eds.), *Multi-cultural education: Issues and perspectives* (3rd ed., pp. 108–128). New York: John Wiley & Sons.

Urwin, C. A. (1988). AIDS in children: A family concern. *Family Relations, 37,* 154–159.

U.S. Department of Education. (1981). *Assistance to states for education of handicapped children: Interpretation of the Individualized Education Program (IEP).* Washington, DC: U.S. Government Printing Office.

U.S. Department of Education. (1990, January 9). Reading and writing proficiency remains low. *Daily Education News,* pp. 1–7.

U.S. Department of Education. (1991). *The condition of bilingual education in the nation: A report to Congress and the president.* Washington, DC: Author.

U.S. Department of Education. (1992a). *Goals 2000. Educate America Act.* Washington, D.C.: U.S. Government Printing Office.

U.S. Department of Education. (1992b). *To assure the free appropriate public education of all children with disabilities: Fourteenth annual report to Congress on the implementation of the Individuals with Disabilities Education Act.* Washington, DC: Author.

U.S. Department of Education. (1993). *To assure the free appropriate public education of all children with disabilities: Fifteenth annual report to Congress on the implementation of the Individuals with Disabilities Education Act.* Washington, DC: Author.

U.S. Department of Education. (1994). *The condition of education in rural schools.* Washington, DC: Author.

U.S. Department of Education. (1995a). *The community action toolkit.* Washington, DC: Author.

U.S. Department of Education. (1995b). *To assure the free appropriate public education of all children with disabilities: Seventeenth annual report to Congress on the implementation of the Individuals with Disabilities Education Act.* Washington, DC: Author.

U.S. Department of Education. (1996). *To assure the free appropriate public education of all children with disabilities: Individuals with Disabilities Education Act, Section 618.* Washington, DC: Author.

U.S. Department of Education. (1997). *School-based and school-linked programs for pregnant and parenting teens and their children.* Paper presented at the synthesis of conference proceedings, Washington, DC.

U.S. Department of Education. (1998). *To assure the free appropriate public education of all children with disabilities.* Washington, DC: Twentieth annual report to Congress on the implementation of the Individuals with Disabilities Education Act.

U.S. Department of Education. (1999). *To assure the free appropriate public education of all children with disabilities.* Washington, DC: Twentieth annual report to Congress on the implementation of the Individuals with Disabilities Education U.S.C., Secs. 1400–1485 (Supp. 1996).

U.S. Department of Education & American Educational Research Association. (1995). *School-linked comprehensive services for children and families: What we know and what we need to know.* Washington, DC: Authors.

U.S. General Accounting Office. (1994). *Foster care: Parental drug abuse has alarming impact on young children.* Washington, DC: U.S. Government Printing Office.

Vacc, N. A., Vallecorsa, A. L., Parker, A., Bonner, S., Lester, C., Richardson, S., & Yates, C. (1985). Parents' and educators' participation in IEP conferences. *Education and Treatment of Children, 8*(2), 153–162.

Vadasy, P. F. (1986). Single mothers: A social phenomenon and population in need. In R. R. Fewell & P. F. Vadasy (Eds.), *Families of handicapped children: Needs and supports across the life span* (pp. 221–249). Austin, TX: Pro-ed.

Vadasy, P. F., Fewell, R. R., & Meyer, D. J. (1986). Grandparents of children with special needs: Insights into their experiences and concerns. *Journal of the Division for Early Childhood, 10*(1), 36–44.

Vadasy, P. F., Fewell, R. R., Meyer, D. J., & Greenberg, M. T. (1985). Supporting fathers of handicapped young children: Preliminary findings of program effects. *Analysis and Intervention in Developmental Disabilities, 5,*125–137.

Valentine, F. (1998). Empowerment: Family-centered care. *Journal of Pediatric Nursing, 10*(1), 24–27.

Van Reusen, A. K. (1998). Self-advocacy strategy instruction: Enhancing student motivation, self-determination, and responsibility in the learning process. In M. L. Wehmeyer & D. J. Sands (Eds.), *Making it happen.* Baltimore: Brookes.

Van Reusen, A. K., & Bos, C. S. (1990). I PLAN: Helping students communicate in planning conferences. *Teaching Exceptional Children, 22*(4), 30–32.

Van Reusen, A. K., & Bos, C. S. (1994). Facilitating student participation in Individualized Education Programs through motivation strategy instruction. *Exceptional Children, 60*(5), 466–475.

Van Reusen, A. K., Bos, C. S., Schumaker, J. B., & Deshler, D. D. (1987). *The education planning strategy.* Lawrence, KS: Edge Enterprises.

Van Reusen, A. K., Bos, C. S., Schumaker, J. B., & Deshler, D. D. (1994). *The self-advocacy strategy for education and transition planning: Preparing students to advocate at education and transition conferences.* Lawrence, KS: Edge Enterprises.

Van Reusen, A. K., Deshler, D. D., & Schumaker, J. B. (1989). Effects of a student participation strategy in facilitating the involvement of adolescents with learning disabilities in the Individualized Educational Program planning process. *Learning Disabilities, 1*(2), 23–34.

VanDenBerg, J. E., & Grealish, E. M. (1996). Individualized services and supports through the wraparound process: Philosophy and procedures. *Journal of Child and Family Studies, 5,* 7–22.

VanDenBerg, J., & Grealish, E. M. (1998). *The wraparound process.* Pittsburgh, PA: The Community Partnerships Group.

Vanderwood, M., McGrew, K. S., & Ysseldyke, J. E. (1998). Why we can't say much about students with disabilities during education reform. *Exceptional Children, 64*(3), 359–370.

Vatterott, C. (1994, February). A change in climate: Involving parents in school improvement. *Schools in the Middle, 3*(3), pp. 12–16.

Vaughn, S., Bos, C., Harrell, J., & Lasky, B. (1988). Parent participation in the initial placement/IEP conference ten years after mandated involvement. *Journal of Learning Disabilities, 21*(2), 82–89.

Vig, S. (1996). Young children's exposure to community violence. *Journal of Early Intervention, 20*(4), 319–328.

Villa, R. A., Thousand, J. S., Meyers, H., & Nevin, A. I. (1996). Teacher and administration perceptions of heterogeneous education. *Exceptional Children, 63,* 29–45.

Vining, E. P. G. (1989). Educational, social, and life-long effects of epilepsy. *Pediatric Clinics of North America, 36,* 449–461.

Voelker, S., Shore, D., Hakim-Larson, J., & Bruner, D. (1997). Discrepancies in parent and teacher ratings of adaptive behavior of children with multiple disabilities. *Mental Retardation, 35*(1), 10–17.

Vogel, S. A., Leonard, F., Scales, W., Hayeslip, P., Hermansen, J., & Donnells, L. (1998). The national learning disabilities postsecondary data bank: An overview. *Journal of Learning Disabilities, 31*(3), 234–247.

Vohs, J. (1993). On belonging: A place to stand, a gift to give. In A. P. Turnbull, J. M. Patterson, S. K. Behr, D. L. Murphy, J. G. Marquis, & M. J. Blue-Banning (Eds.), *Cognitive coping, families, and disability* (pp. 51–66). Baltimore: Brookes.

Vohs, J. R. (1997). Assistant secretary Judith E. Heumann. *Coalition Quarterly, 14*(1).

Vyas, P. (1983). Getting on with it. In T. Dougan, L. Isbell, & P. Vyas (Eds.), *We have been there* (pp. 17–19). Nashville, TN: Abingdon.

Wade, S. L., Taylor, H. G., Drotar, D., Stancin, T., & Yeates, K. O. (1996). Childhood traumatic brain injury: Initial impact on the family. *Journal of Learning Disabilities, 29*(6), 652–661.

Wade, S. M. (1994). *Focus group survey of parents of children with disabilities who are members of school improvement teams* [Report]. Tampa: University of South Florida, Florida Diagnostic and Learning Resources System.

Wagner, M., Newman, L., D'Amico, R., Jay, E. D., Butler-Nalin, P., Marder, C., & Cox, R. (1991). *Youth with disabilities: How are they doing? The first comprehensive report from the national study of special education students.* Menlo, CA: SRI International.

Wahlberg, H. J., Paschal, R. A., & Weinstein, T. (1985). Homework's powerful effects on learning. *Educational Leadership, 42*(7), 76–79.

Walcott, D. D. (1997 July–August). Education in human sexuality for young people with moderate and severe mental retardation. *The Council for Exceptional Children, 29*(6), 72–74.

Wald, J. L. (1996). *Culturally and linguistically diverse professionals in special education: A demographic analysis.* Reston, VA: National Clearinghouse for Professionals in Special Education, Council for Exceptional Children.

Walker, B., & Singer, G. H. S. (1993). Improving collaborative communication between professionals and parents. In G. H. S. Singer & L. E. Powers (Eds.), *Families, disability, and empowerment: Active coping skills and strategies for family interventions* (pp. 285–316). Baltimore: Brookes.

Walker, J. L. (1988). Young American Indian children. *Teaching Exceptional Children, 20*(4), 50–51.

Wallace-Rose, H. (1998). *Something's wrong with my child!* (2nd ed.). Springfield, IL: Charles C. Thomas.

Wallander, J. L., Pitt, L. C., & Mellins, C. A. (1990). Child functional independence and maternal psychosocial stress as risk factors threatening adaptation in mothers of physically or sensorially handicapped children. *Journal of Consulting and Clinical Psychology, 58*(6), 818–824.

Walther-Thomas, C., Hazel, J. S., Schumaker, J. B., Vernon, S., & Deshler, D. D. (1991). A program for families with children with learning disabilities. In M. J. Fine (Ed.), *Collaborative involvement with parents of exceptional children* (pp. 239–256). Brandon, VT: Clinical Psychology Publishing.

Wang, M. C., Reynolds, M. C., & Wahlberg, H. J. (1986). Rethinking special education. *Educational Leadership, 44*(1), 26–31.

Ward, S. (1996). My family: Formed by adoption. *Focal Point, 10*(1), 30–32.

Ware, L. P. (1994). Contextual barriers to collaboration. *Journal of Educational and Psychological Consultation, 5*(4), 339–357.

Warfield, M. E., & Hauser-Cram, P. (1996). Child care needs, arrangements, and satisfaction of mothers of children with developmental disabilities. *Mental Retardation, 34*, 294–302.

Warfield, M. J., Krauss, M. W., Hauser-Cram, P., Upshur, C., & Shonkoff, J. P. (1999, February). Adaptation during early childhood among mothers of children with disabilities. *Developmental and Behavioral Pediatrics, 20*(1), 9–16.

Warren, F. (1985). A society that is going to kill your children. In H. R. Turnbull & A. P. Turnbull (Eds.), *Parents speak out: Then and now* (2nd ed., pp. 201–232). Englewood Cliffs, NJ: Merrill/Prentice-Hall.

Warren, S. B. (1992). Lower threshold for referral for psychiatric treatment for adopted adolescents. *Journal of the American Academy of Child and Adolescent Psychiatry, 31*, 512–517.

Wasserman, R. C., Inui, T. S., Barriatua, R. D., Carter, W. B., & Lippincott, P. (1984). Pediatric clinicians' support for parents makes a difference: An outcome-based analysis of clinician-parent interaction. *Pediatrics, 74*(6), 1,047–1,053.

Wehman, P., Bricout, J., & Kregel, J. (2000). Supported employment in 2000: Changing the locus of control from agency to consumer. In M. Wehmeyer & J. R. Patton (Eds.), *Mental retardation in the year 2000*. Austin, TX: Pro-ed.

Wehman, P., Revell, G., & Kregel, J. (1998). Supported employment: A decade of rapid growth and impact. *American Rehabilitation,* 31–43.

Wehman, T. (1998). Family-centered early intervention services: Factors contributing to increased parent involvement and participation. *Focus on Autism and Other Developmental Disabilities, 13*(2), 80–86.

Wehmeyer, M. L. (1999). A functional model of self-determination: Describing development and implementing instruction. *Focus on Autism and Other Developmental Disabilities, 14*, 53–61.

Wehmeyer, M. L. (in press). Self-determination and mental retardation. *International Review of Research in Mental Retardation.*

Wehmeyer, M. L., & Agran, M. (in press). A national survey of teachers' promotion of self-determination and student-directed learning. *Journal of Special Education.*

Wehmeyer, M. L., Agran, M., & Hughes, C. (1998). *Teaching self-determination to students with disabilities: Basic skills for successful transition.* Baltimore: Brookes.

Wehmeyer, M. L., Bersani, H., & Gagne, R. (2000). Riding the third wave: Self-determination and self-advocacy in the 21st century. In M. L. Wehmeyer & J. R. Patton (Eds.), *Mental retardation in the 21st century.* Austin, TX: Pro-ed.

Wehmeyer, M. L., & Metzler, C. A. (1995). How self-determined are people with mental retardation? The national consumer survey. *Mental Retardation, 33*(2), 111–119.

Wehmeyer, M. L., Morningstar, M., & Husted, D. (1999). *Family involvement in transition planning and implementation.* Austin, TX: Pro-ed.

Wehmeyer, M. L., & Patton, J. R. (Eds.). (2000). *Mental retardation in the 21st century.* Austin, TX: Pro-ed.

Wehmeyer, M. L., & Sands, D. J. (1998). *Making it happen: Student involvement in education planning, decision-making, and instruction.* Baltimore: Paul H. Brookes.

Wehmeyer, M. L., Sands, D. J., Doll, B., & Palmer, S. (1997). The development of self-determination and implications for educational interventions with students with disabilities. *International Journal of Disability, Development and Education, 44*(4), 305–328.

Wehmeyer, M. L., & Schwartz, M. (1998). The relationship between self-determination, quality of life, and life satisfaction for adults with mental retardation. *Education and Training in Mental Retardation and Developmental Disabilities, 33*(3), 3–12.

Weicker, L. (1985). Sonny and public policy. In H. R. Turnbull & A. P. Turnbull (Eds.), Parents speak out: Then and now (2nd ed.) (pp. 281–287). Englewood Cliffs, NJ: Merrill/Prentice Hall.

Weigle, K. L. (1997). Positive behavior support as a model for promoting educational inclusion. *Journal of the Association for Persons with Severe Handicaps, 22*(1), 36–48.

Weisner, T. S., Beizer, L., & Stolze, L. (1991). Religion and families of children with developmental disabilities. *American Journal on Mental Retardation, 95*, 647–662.

Weiss, H. (1989). New state initiatives for family support and education programs: Challenges and opportunities. *Family Resource Coalition Report, 1,* 18–19.

Werner, E. E., & Smith, R. S. (1992). *Overcoming the odds: High risk children from birth to adulthood.* Ithaca, NY: Cornell University Press.

Wesson, C. L., & King, R. P. (1996 Winter). Portfolio assessment and special education students. *Teaching Exceptional Children, 28*(2), 44–48.

West, J. S. (1990). Educational collaboration in the restructuring of schools. *Journal of Educational and Psychological Consultation, 1*(1), 23–40.

West, M., Revell, G., Kregel, J., & Bricout, J. (1999). The Medicaid home and community-based waiver and supported employment. *American Journal on Mental Retardation, 104*(1), 78–87.

Weyhing, M. C. (1983). Parental reactions to handicapped children and familial adjustments to routines of care. In J. A. Mulick & S. M. Pueschel (Eds.), *Parent-professional partnerships in developmental disabilities* (pp. 125–138). Cambridge, MA: Ware.

Whitechurch, G. G., & Constantine, L. L. (1993). Systems theory. In P. G. Boss, W. J. Doherty, R. LaRossa, W. R. Schumm, & S. K. Steinmetz (Eds.), *Sourcebook of family theories and methods: A contextual approach* (pp. 325–352). New York: Plenum.

Whitehead, B. (1994). The failure of sex education. *American Educator, 18,* 22–29, 44–52.

Whitelaw-Downs, S., & Walker, D. (1996). Family support while you wait: Lessons from the Detroit family project. *Zero to Three, 16*(6), 25–33.

Whitman, B. Y., & Accardo, P. J. (Eds.). (1990). *When a parent is mentally retarded.* Baltimore: Brookes.

Whitman, B. Y., Graves, B., & Accardo, P. (1987). Mentally retarded parents in the community: Identification method and needs assessment survey. *American Journal of Mental Deficiency, 91*(6), 636–638.

Wholstetter, P., & Odden, A. (1992, November). Rethinking school-based management policy and research. *Educational Administration Quarterly, 28*(4), 529–549.

Wickham-Searl, P. (1992). Mothers with a mission. In P. M. Ferguson, D. L. Ferguson, & S. J. Taylor (Eds.), *Interpreting disability: A qualitative reader* (pp. 251–274). New York: Teachers College Press.

Williams, V. I., & Cartledge, G. (1997, Sept/Oct). Passing notes—to parents. *The Council for Exceptional Children—Family Involvement in Learning,* 30–34.

Willis, W. (1992). Families with African American roots. In E. W. Lynch & M. J. Hanson (Eds.), *Developing cross-cultural competence: A guide*

for working with young children and their families (pp. 121–150). Baltimore: Brookes.

Willoughby, J., & Glidden, L. (1995). Fathers helping out: Shared child care and marital satisfaction of parents of children with disabilities. *American Journal on Mental Retardation, 99,* 399–406.

Wilson, J., Blacher, J., & Baker, B. L. (1989). Siblings of children with severe handicaps. *Mental Retardation, 27,* 167–173.

Wilson, M. R. (1985, November). *Long-term inpatient psychiatric treatment of adolescent adopted children, a population at risk.* Paper presented at the seminar of the San Diego Society of Adolescent Psychiatry, San Diego, CA.

Winters, W. G. (1993). *African American mothers and urban schools.* New York: Lexington Books.

Winton, P. J. (1992). Family-centered intervention: Words can make a difference. *Focus, 1*(2), 1–5.

Winton, P. J., & DiVenere, N. (1995). Family-professional partnerships in early intervention personnel preparation guidelines and strategies. *Topics in Early Childhood Special Education, 15*(3), 295–312.

Witt, J. C., Miller, C. D., McIntyre, R. M., & Smith, D. (1984). Effects of variables on parental perceptions of staffings. *Exceptional Children, 51*(1), 27–32.

Wodrich, D. L. (1999). *Attention-deficit/hyperactivity disorder* (2nd ed.). Baltimore: Brookes.

Wolfensberger, W. (1972). *The principle of normalization in human services.* Toronto: National Institute on Mental Retardation.

Wolff-Heller, K., Gallagher, P. A., & Fredrick, L. D. (1999). Parents' perceptions of siblings' interactions with their brothers and sisters who are deaf-blind. *JASH, 24*(1), 33–43.

Woodroffe, T., Gorenflo, D. W., Meador, H. E., & Zazove, P. (1998). Knowledge and attitudes about AIDS among deaf and hard of hearing persons. *AIDS-Care, 10*(3), 377–386.

Worley, G., Rosenfeld, L. R., & Lipscomb, J. (1991). Financial coun-

seling for families of children with chronic disabilities. *Developmental Medicine and Child Neurology, 33,* 679–689.

Worrell, F. C., Gabelko, N. H., Roth, D. A., & Samuels, L. K. (1999). Parents' reports on homework amount and problems in academically talented elementary students. *Gifted Child Quarterly, 43*(2), 86–94.

Wright, B. A. (1991). Labeling: The need for greater person-environment individuation. In C. R. Snyder & D. Forsyth (Eds.), *The handbook of social and clinical psychology: The health perspective* (pp. 469–487). New York: Pergamon Press.

Wright, L., & Boyland, J. H. (1993). Using early childhood developmental portfolios in the identification and education of young, economically disadvantaged, potentially gifted students. *Roeper Review, 15*(4), 205–210.

Wright, R., Saleeby, D., Watts, T. D., & Lecca, P. J. (1983). *Transcultural perspectives in the human services: Organizational issues and trends.* Springfield, IL: Thomas.

Wurtele, S. K., & Miller-Perrin, C. L. (1986). An evaluation of side effects associated with participation in a child sexual abuse prevention program. *Journal of School Health, 57*(6), 228–231.

Yasutake, D. (1996). The effects of combining peer tutoring and attribution training on students' perceived self-competence. *Remedial and Special Education, 17*(2), 83–91.

Yates, A. (1987). Current status and future directions of research on the American Indian child. *American Journal of Psychiatry, 144*(9), 1,135–1,142.

Yocom, D. J., & Staebler, B. (1996). The impact of collaborative consultation on special education referral accuracy. *Journal of Educational and Psychological Consultation, 7*(2), 179–192.

Yoe, J. T., Santarcangelo, S., Atkins, M., & Burchard, J. D. (1996). Wrap-around care in Vermont program development implementation and evaluation of a statewide system of individualized services. *Journal of Child and Family Studies, 5,* 23–38.

York, J., & Tundidor, M. (1995). Issues raised in the name of inclusion: Perspectives of educators, parents, and students. *Journal of the Association for Persons with Severe Handicaps, 20*(1), 31–44.

Young, D. M., & Roopnarine, J. L. (1994). Fathers' childcare involvement with children with and without disabilities. *Topics in Early Childhood Special Education, 14*(4), 488–502.

Ysseldyke, J. E., Algozzine, B., & Mitchell, J. (1982). Special education team decision making: An analysis of current practice. *Personnel and Guidance Journal, 60*(5), 308–313.

Ysseldyke, J., & Olsen, K. (1999). Putting alternate assessments into practice: What to measure and possible sources of data. *Exceptional Children, 65*(2), 175–186.

Ysseldyke, J. E., Vanderwood, M. L., & Shriner, J. (1997). Changes over the past decade in special education referral to placement probability: An incredibly reliable practice. *Diagnostique, 23*(1), 193–201.

Yuan, S., Baker-McCue, T., & Witkin, K. (1996). Coalitions for family support and the creation of two flexible funding programs. In G. H. S. Singer, L. E. Powers, & A. L. Olson (Eds.), *Redefining family support: Innovations in public-private partnerships* (pp. 357–388). Baltimore: Brookes.

Zigler, E., & Muenchow, S. (1992). *Head Start: The inside story of America's most successful educational experiment.* New York: Basic Books.

Zimmerman, M. (1995). Psychological empowerment: Issues and illustrations. *American Journal of Community Psychology, 23*(5), 581–599.

Zimmerman, M. A., & Rappaport, J. (1988). Citizen participation, perceived control, and psychological empowerment. *American Journal of Community Psychology, 16*(5), 725–731.

Zimmerman, M. A. (1990). Toward a theory of learned hopefulness: A structural model analysis of participation and empowerment. *Journal of Research in Personality, 24,* 71–86.

Zipperlen, H., & O'Brien, J. (1994). *Cultivating thinking hearts: Letters from the Lifesharing Safeguards Project.* Kimberton, PA: Camphill Village, Kimberton Hills.

Zirpoli, T. J., Wieck, C., Hancox, D., & Skarnulis, E. R. (1994). Partners in policymaking: The first five years. *Mental Retardation, 32*(6), 422–425.

Ziskin, L. (1985). The story of Jennie. In H. R. Turnbull & A. P. Turnbull (Eds.), *Parents speak out: Then and now* (2nd ed.) (pp. 65–74). Englewood Cliffs, NJ: Merrill/Prentice-Hall.

Zukow, P. G. (Ed.). (1990). *Sibling interaction across culture.* New York: Springer-Verlag.

Zuniga, M. E. (1992). Families with Latino roots. In E. W. Lynch & M. J. Hanson (Eds.), *Developing cross-cultural competence: A guide for working with young children and their families* (pp. 151–180). Baltimore: Brookes.

Zuniga, M. E. (1998). Families with Latino roots. In E. W. Lynch & M. J. Hanson (Eds.), *Developing cross-cultural competence* (pp. 209–250). Baltimore: Brookes.

Index